# Complete Guide to Pain Relief

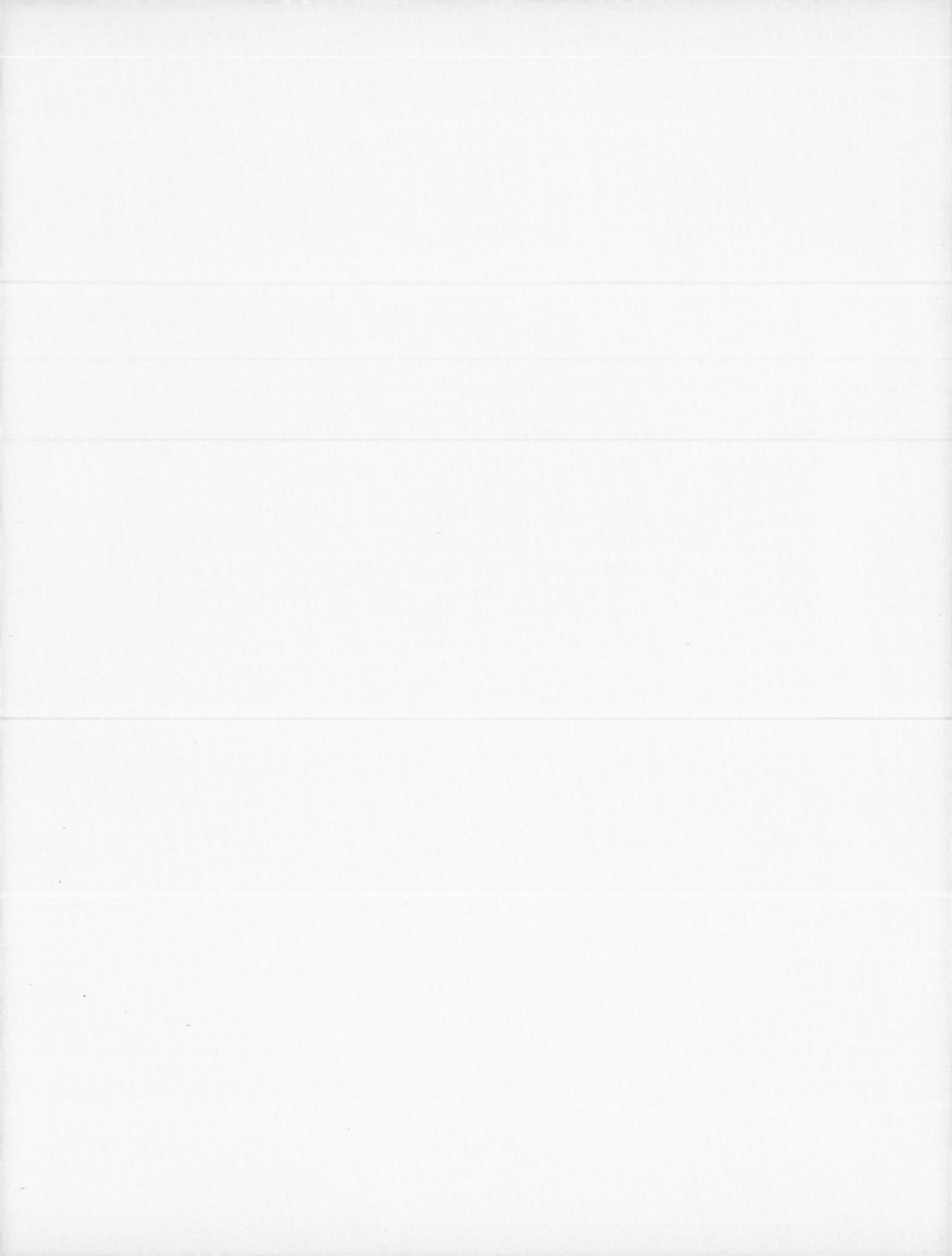

# COMPLETE GUIDE TO Pain Relief

The Reader's Digest Association (Canada) Ltd., Montreal

## CANADIAN STAFF

*Project Editors*
Andrew Jones
Anita Winterberg

*Designer*
Andrée Payette

*Copy Editor*
Gilles Humbert

*Production Manager*
Holger Lorenzen

*Production Coordinator*
Susan Wong

*Administrator*
Elizabeth Eastman

*Indexer*
Patricia Buchanan

---

## BOOKS AND HOME ENTERTAINMENT

*Vice President*
Deirdre Gilbert

*Managing Editor*
Philomena Rutherford

*Art Director*
John McGuffie

---

## U.S. STAFF

*Editorial Director*
Wayne Kalyn

*Design Director*
Barbara Rietschel

*Production Technology Manager*
Douglas A. Croll

*Editorial Manager*
Christine R. Guido

*Art Production Coordinator*
Jennifer R. Tokarski

## PRODUCED BY G.S. SHARPE COMMUNICATIONS, INC.

*President and Editorial Director*
Genell J. Subak-Sharpe, M.S.

*Medical Editor*
Morton D. Bogdonoff, M.D., *Internal Medicine*

*Canadian Medical Consultants*
Mark Berner, M.D., *Family Medicine*
Anne Gamsa, Ph.D., *Pain Specialist*
Gerald Rotenberg, B.Sc.Phm., *Pharmaceutical Consultant*

*U.S. Medical Consultants*
Marie Mulligan, M.D., *Pain Specialist*
Miyoko Munakata, P.T., *Physical Therapy*
Arthur J. Roberts, M.D., *Cardiovascular Surgery*
George D. Roston, D.D.S., *General Dentistry*
Elizabeth Saenger, Ph.D., *Mental Health*
Sarah E. Subak-Sharpe, M.D., *Internal Medicine*

*Writers*
Philip Bashe, Diana Benzaia, Elizabeth Saenger, Ph.D.
Julia Schulhoff, Susan A. Schwartz,
Genell J. Subak-Sharpe, M.S.

*Copy Editors*
Mary Lyn Maiscott, Karen Richardson

*Researchers*
Debra Rabinowitz, Sarah E. Subak-Sharpe, M.D.

*Desktop Publishing/Technical Support*
Karl Li, Debra Rabinowitz

**Canadian Cataloguing in Publication Data**

Main entry under title:

Reader's digest complete guide to pain relief

Includes index.
ISBN 0-88850-696-1
1. Analgesia—Popular works. 2. Pain—Popular works.
I. Title. II. Title: Complete guide to pain relief.

RB127.R392 2000    616'.0472    C00-900789-X



Printed in Canada    00 01 02 03 / 5 4 3 2 1

Address any comments about Complete Guide to Pain Relief to: Editor, Books and Home Entertainment, c/o Customer Service, Reader's Digest, 1125 Stanley Street, Montreal, Quebec H3B 5H5.

For information on this and other Reader's Digest products, or to request a catalogue, please call our 24-hour Customer Service hotline at 1-800-465-0780.

You can also visit us on the World Wide Web at **www.readersdigest.ca**

NOTE TO READERS
The information in this book should not be substituted for, or used to alter, medical therapy without your doctor's advice. For a specific health problem, consult your physician for guidance.

# Preface

By Anne Gamsa, Ph.D.

Unlike other diseases, pain is invisible to everyone but the person who suffers. We have very sophisticated machines to detect and diagnose disease, yet there is no test to show the doctor how much pain a person is feeling. This can be very frustrating. The reactions of family and friends can sometimes be even more upsetting. They may believe the person is shirking responsibility and complaining for nothing, especially if he or she looks well and seems healthy. When that happens, pain can be a very lonely and baffling experience.

For some pain, such as the acute pain of a toothache or pain from an injury or operation, relief is readily available. Chronic pain, on the other hand, is more difficult to treat and affects over 4 million Canadians a year. Yet, with the right treatment, chronic pain can be reduced significantly and sometimes completely relieved. The Reader's Digest *Complete Guide to Pain Relief* brings you up-to-date information on a wide array of pain 1treatments based on both the latest medical findings and ancient healing practices. You will find valuable facts on many health and pain problems, including pain from damaged nerves, migraines, chest pain, joint pain, back pain, abdominal pain, systemic pain, and emotional pain.

It was a decade ago that Dr. Ronald Melzack of McGill University published his landmark study, "The Tragedy of Needless Pain," in *Scientific American*. Yet, despite our growing knowledge of how pain works, many patients and doctors alike are still unaware of the full range of treatments available. This book offers comprehensive information about many different types of medical and complementary therapies for pain. While it is not meant to replace a visit to the doctor—it is always important to get medical advice before embarking on any treatment—it will arm you with the information you need to become an informed participant in your own care.

*(Dr. Gamsa is a pain specialist and Director of Psychological Services at the McGill-Montreal General Hospital Pain Centre.)*

# How to use this book

In today's world of health care cutbacks, patients must be prepared to press for their own health care and participate in important decisions. Nowhere is this more obvious than in the area of pain control. The old advice of "take two aspirin and see me if you still hurt" has given way to myriad choices incorporating the latest medical advances and ancient healing systems. The *Complete Guide to Pain Relief* provides the information you need to make informed decisions.

The first two chapters address the nature of pain and the basics of pain relief: drug vs. nondrug treatments; the roles of emotion and lifestyle in pain; an overview of alternative therapies; when to see a pain specialist; and pain control in the hospital.

The bulk of the book, however, is a comprehensive head-to-toe guide to hundreds of common pain syndromes. Each entry follows the same format, listing symptoms of the disorder, who is at risk, how it develops, what you can do, how it is treated, how it is prevented, and alternative therapies. Also included are important warnings and recent breakthroughs.

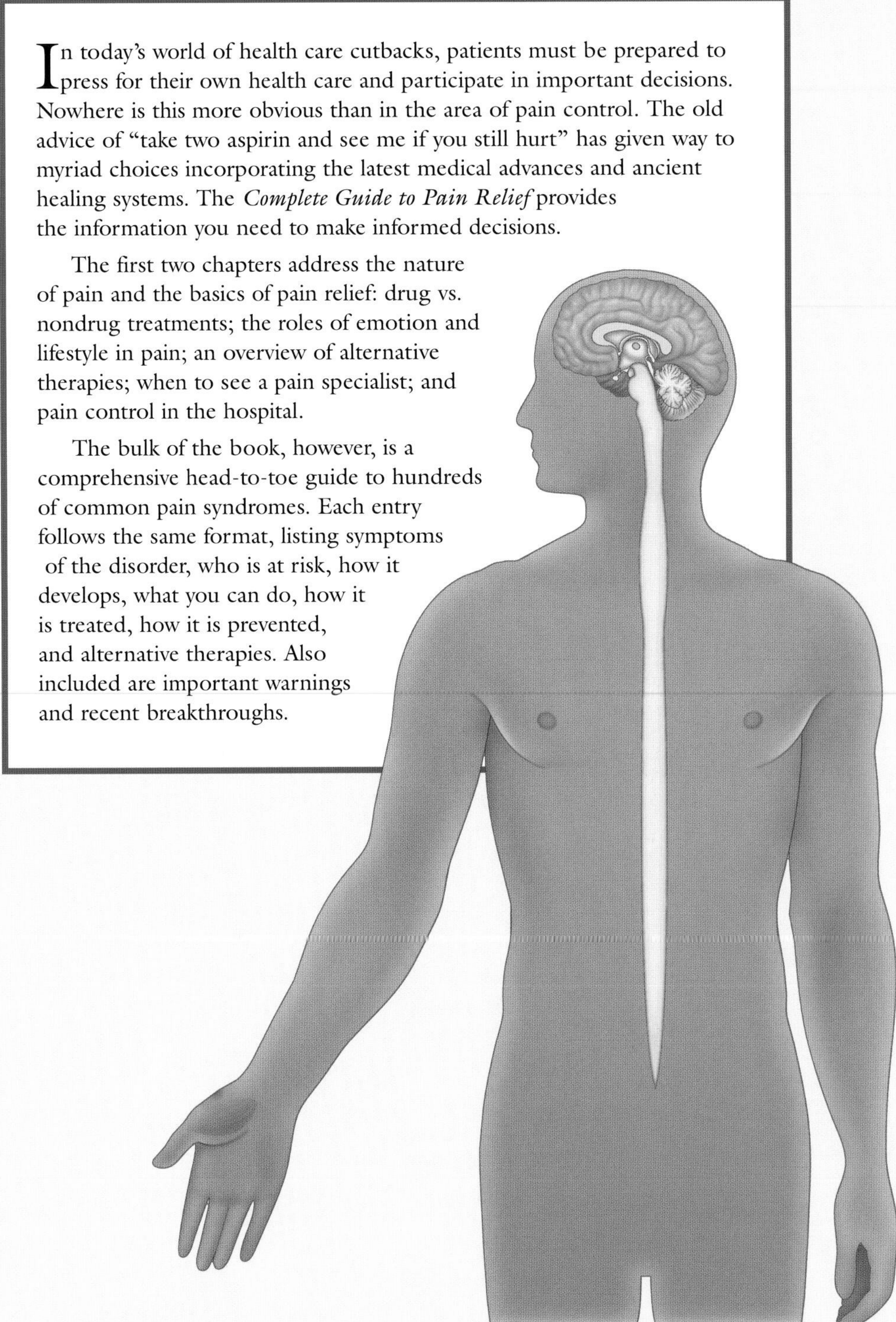

## About the Recommendations

A team of medical writers and editors working with medical specialists have made every effort to ensure that the information in this book is up-to-date and accurate. Still, the information should not be used to substitute for, replace, or alter medical therapy without your doctor's advice.

The *Alternative Therapies* sections give typical dosages for various herbal and nutraceutical products. These dosages may need to be adjusted for the individual. It should be noted, however, that herbal remedies and nutraceuticals are not risk-free. Check with your doctor or pharmacist before using them, especially if you take conventional medications or have a chronic disease; follow label instructions; and seek immediate medical help if you develop signs of a serious allergic reaction.

The following groups of people should not take herbal or nutraceutical products without their doctor's specific recommendations:

- **Pregnant and breast-feeding women** should avoid coenzyme $Q_{10}$, horehound, licorice, and red clover and juniper berry teas. Women should stop taking vitamin A three months before becoming pregnant. Certain supplements are needed during pregnancy and while breast-feeding; the amount must be determined by a doctor.
- **People taking aspirin and anticoagulants** should check with their doctor first before taking vitamin E, ginger, garlic, ginkgo biloba, hawthorn, and black currant, borage, or evening primrose oils. Check with your doctor before using hawthorn if you are taking digoxin.
- **People who have kidney stones,** kidney disease, or hemochromatosis should not take more than 500 mg of vitamin C daily. People with kidney or thyroid disease should also check with their doctor first before taking calcium.
- **Children under age 18.** Some of these products may interfere with a child's growth and development. Talk to your doctor before giving a child any medication, herbal or nutritional supplement.

Certain supplements also may interact with other medications or conditions, and should be taken with caution:

- **Goldenseal** should not be taken by people with heart disease, high blood pressure, diabetes, or glaucoma.
- **Echinacea** may worsen symptoms of certain autoimmune disorders such as multiple sclerosis. It may also be counterproductive in progressive infections such as tuberculosis.
- **Licorice** should be avoided if you have heart, kidney, or liver disease, have high blood pressure, or are taking diuretics or digoxin.
- **Ginkgo biloba** should not be taken if you are hypersensitive to poison ivy, cashews, or mangoes.
- **St. John's wort** should not be taken with AIDS drugs, antidepressants, antiepilepsy drugs, oral contraceptives, immunosuppressants, or anticoagulants.

# Table of Contents

## Understanding Pain



## The Basics Of Relief



## The Head



## The Chest



## The Digestive Organs



## The Reproductive And Urinary Organs



## The Skeleton And Muscles



## The Skin

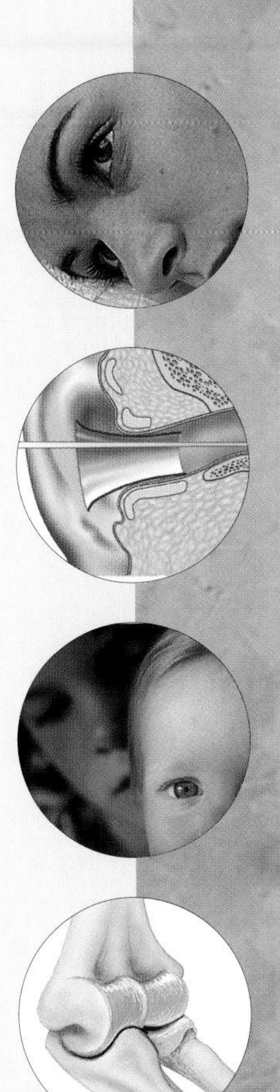

## Systemic Pain



## Emotional Pain

# UNDERSTANDING PAIN

# The Nature of Pain

*Pain is very personal—only the person who hurts can feel it. But pain can make life utterly miserable for both the sufferers and their loved ones. Happily, science is helping us find new and better ways to overcome it.*

## THE MANY FACES OF PAIN

In simple terms, pain is a symptom of some underlying condition or injury. It is purely subjective; thus, only the person experiencing it can describe what it feels like, and its intensity often bears little relationship to the underlying cause. For example, a person with very extensive, deep (third-degree) burns is usually in less pain than someone with relatively minor first- or second-degree burns. What may be perceived as only a minor annoyance to one person may be excruciating to someone else, even though the causes may be virtually identical.

Although pain is not a disease in and of itself, it often seems to "take over," persisting long after the precipitating cause clears up. Even though there may be no obvious cause of the pain, it can dominate your life, preventing you from carrying out normal day-to-day activities and interfering with sleep.

### A universal scourge

Pain is often called the great equalizer, afflicting young and old, rich and poor, and people of all ethnic and cultural backgrounds. Many Canadians suffer pain severe enough to curtail their normal activity a few days each month. According to some estimates, 5 to 15 percent of Canadians suffer a lifetime of chronic pain, including migraines, low-back pain, and others. Pain of one kind or another is a leading reason why Canadians see doctors. The cost for lost work time, insurance benefits, and medical attention is about $8 billion a year.

### Acute vs. chronic pain

Pain falls into two broad categories: acute and chronic. From time to time, virtually everyone experiences acute pain—for example, the sudden, sharp pain of a cut, burn, sprained ankle, or broken bone; the pounding or throbbing of a headache; the relentless pain of a toothache; the allover achiness that heralds a bout of flu. These and other types of acute pain are warning signs of something amiss that needs our attention. In this respect, acute pain signals a need to protect the body from further harm and seek new treatment.

### Not as long as it seems

Acute pain tends to be short-lived, but sufferers often overstate its duration. For example, persons who suffer from cluster headaches—one of the most severe types of head pain—typically tell their doctors that the pain goes on for hours, and then recurs after only a few minutes' respite. In reality, the opposite is

## How to Tell the Difference Between Acute and Chronic Pain

| CHARACTERISTICS | ACUTE PAIN | CHRONIC PAIN |
|---|---|---|
| Cause | Clearly defined, such as an injury. | Ill-defined or undetectable; may also be related to chronic disease, but severity of pain may be unrelated to severity of the disease. |
| Duration | Lessens and disappears as underlying cause is resolved; may also come and go or vary in intensity if pain is due to chronic disease. | Persists and worsens even if cause is identified and cured. |
| Physical responses | Increased blood pressure, rapid pulse, sweating, change in breathing rate. | Adaptation of autonomic nervous system; muscle spasms, stiffness, and atrophy due to inactivity. |
| Psychological and behavioral changes | Anxiety, agitation; takes action to seek relief. | Depression, trouble sleeping, loss of appetite, lowered libido, anger, irritability, withdrawal from normal activities, increasing dependence on medication and/or alcohol. |
| Relationship changes: with family | Desire for comforting and assurance. | Apathy or feelings of anger and rejection. |
| Relationship changes: with caregivers | Confidence in their ability to help. | Frustration, feelings of being ignored or disbelieved. |

more often the case: the headache is usually very intense and brief, lasting for only a few minutes and, although it may come back soon, there is usually a few hours or longer periods between attacks. Of course, such misperceptions do not alter the degree of suffering. But treatment quickly banishes most acute pain.

### Pain without a purpose

Chronic pain is much different. It is defined as any pain that occurs daily for six or more months and does not respond to treatment. Unlike acute pain, it generally has no protective function, even when it stems from a chronic disease, such as arthritis. In fact, the response to arthritis pain—inactivity—is often counterproductive. Spending long periods sitting around or lying in bed may actually worsen the condition, causing the joints to stiffen even more.

Chronic pain sometimes begins with an acute injury or illness, such as a wrenched back or herniated disk. But instead of going away as the original disorder heals, the pain lingers. In many cases, however, there is no obvious cause—the pain simply comes on without any apparent provocation and then takes on a life of its own, forcing sufferers to curtail their lifestyles to accommodate it. This is the pain that prompts the sufferer to try a variety of painkillers and to seek medical help, often seeing doctor after doctor and a variety of alternative practitioners in a futile effort to find relief. Chronic pain can strain relationships and ruin careers; it can transform an optimistic and outgoing person into an irritable and depressed recluse. But it doesn't have to be this way: The vast majority of people who suffer from chronic pain can be helped.

## HOW DOCTORS DEFINE PAIN

When doctors talk about pain, they generally classify it as superficial or deep. Superficial or "fast" pain occurs when pain nerve fibers in the skin and the outer linings of certain organs are stimulated. The intestines, the urinary tract, the cornea of the eye, the bile ducts, and the nose are especially rich in these fast-pain nerve fibers. When they are stimulated, they send an almost instantaneous message to the brain. If you touch a hot stove, for example, the pain message travels along the fast-pain pathway, reaching the brain in a split second. The brain responds just as fast, sending back a message to the nerves and muscles in the hand to jerk it away from the stove. All this happens in less than the blink of an eye, and without conscious effort.

Superficial pain, which is sometimes called somatic pain, is perceived as an intense burning pain. It may be steady or it may come and go, and the degree of intensity varies according to the underlying cause. For example, the passage of a kidney stone causes an intense burning pain that comes in colicky waves. A stomach ulcer or a backup (reflux) of stomach acid into the esophagus also produces waves of burning pain. A minor cut or superficial burn may be perceived as stinging or burning.

In contrast, deep pain, sometimes referred to as "slow" or visceral pain, originates from nerve fibers in the muscles, bones, or tissues of internal organs, such as the heart, liver, or kidneys. These pain messages take somewhat longer to reach the brain, and the resulting pain is deep and aching or throbbing, like an abdominal or muscle cramp. Often the two types of pain overlap, especially when they are due to an injury.

## Common Pain Syndromes And How They Differ

| CAUSE | DISTINGUISHING FEATURES | SOURCES OF RELIEF |
|---|---|---|
| Inflammation (arthritis, rheumatism, tumors, infection, abscesses) | • Cause is clearly defined, such as an injury.<br>• Area is red, warm, and tender to the touch.<br>• Localized swelling.<br>• Oozing of pus or clear liquid. | • Application of cold compresses, sometimes alternating with heat.<br>• Aspirin or other anti-inflammatory medications.<br>• Lancing and draining (of abscesses). |
| Physical injury (cuts, broken bones, strains and sprains) | • Intense burning pain at site of injury.<br>• Deep aching pain in case of broken bone. | • Rest of injured part.<br>• Treatment of underlying injury. |
| Widened, inflamed blood vessels (migraine headache, arteritis) | • Intense throbbing or pulsating pain.<br>• Pain localized to area of inflamed blood vessel. | • Resting in quiet, darkened room.<br>• Application of cold compresses.<br>• Medication to treat cause. |
| Insufficient blood flow (angina, leg pains) | • Pain provoked by exercise. | • Rest.<br>• Exercise conditioning.<br>• Medication to increase blood flow.<br>• Surgery to open or bypass clogged arteries.<br>• Dietary changes to lower high cholesterol. |
| Nerve pain (shingles, diabetic neuropathy, sciatica) | • Tingling or burning pain.<br>• Pain may radiate along nerve pathway. | • Treatment of cause.<br>• Acupuncture and other alternative therapies. |

# Messengers of Pain

*The journey of pain messages from the site of injury to the brain is complex, and still not fully understood. Some pain messages travel on a fast track; others take a more circuitous route where they can be modified by the body's natural painkillers.*

## A COMPLEX JOURNEY

Although pain messages reach the brain in a nanosecond, their journey from the site of injury is a complex one in which they travel along a series of nerves and pass through "gates," or relay stations. Along the way, the messages are interpreted and modified. The actual transmission of pain messages to the brain is called *nociception*, a term derived from the Latin word (*noxius*) for harmful or dangerous. Nerves that carry pain and other unpleasant messages to the brain are referred to as nociceptors.

### It starts with the nerves...

The first nociceptors are nerve endings in the skin and other tissues. They are unmyelinated, or without the fatty (myelin) covering of other nerves, and their endings react to specific body chemicals that make them sensitive to pain.

### Then on to the back

When the nociceptors are stimulated, they respond by carrying a pain message to the spinal cord. The message is transported across the midline of the spinal cord to a reflex center, which may order an instant action, such as jerking your hand away from a hot object. (This reflex action can be reinforced or overruled by the conscious brain, however. If you must cling to the hot object to avoid falling, for example, you can will the brain to overrule the natural reflex.)

### And finally to the brain

From the relay station in the spinal cord, the message is transmitted to another, larger pain fiber that carries it upward to the brain stem, which puts the body on alert, and then to the thalamus, which serves as a relay station for all of the body's sensory information.

In the thalamus, the pain message and other sensory information, such as visual images, are gathered together, and passed on to the cerebral cortex, the conscious part of the brain where the message is interpreted. The brain determines the specific area that is sending the message, and what action, if any, is necessary. This responsive message travels along another nerve pathway to the site of the injury.

## THE GATE THEORY

In 1965, Ronald Melzack, a Canadian researcher, and Patrick Wall, a British physician, published their gate theory of pain, shedding new light on why different people respond in such different ways to similar painful events. They theorized that the degree of pain is determined by how much substance P actually reaches the brain.

The initial pain message travels along a direct, fast route so the brain can take whatever immediate action is necessary to protect the body from danger. When you cut yourself, for example, you will drop the knife and clutch the wound to stem bleeding before feeling any pain, which may take a few seconds to develop. This is where the gate theory comes into play. Pain messages carried by substance P take longer to reach the brain because they must pass through a special metaphorical pain "gate" in the spinal cord.

At the same time that the pain signal directs the nerves to release substance P, another message is sounded calling for the brain to release endorphins, the body's natural chemical painkillers. Endorphins pass through the same pain gate as substance P, and wind up competing with substance P for neuron receptors. Thus, if large amounts of endorphins make it through the pain gate, there will be fewer receptor sites for substance P, resulting in lowered pain perception.

As the pain-provoking injury heals, the gate in the spinal cord gradually closes and pain disappears. In chronic pain, however, the pain messages continue to pass through. It's not known why this happens, but some researchers think that in some way the pain becomes a learned response. In effect, the pain messages continue to flow without needing a precipitating cause. At this stage, the pain no longer serves a useful purpose.

## "P" IS FOR PAIN

Various chemical messengers, called neurotransmitters, carry pain messages along the nerve pathways. One of these is substance P, a peptide found in nerve cells throughout the body. Scientists do not fully understand exactly how substance P works, but it is thought to be instrumental in mediating pain, touch, and temperature. The prevailing theory holds that substance P attaches to receptors on nerve cells (neurons) in the brain. The more neurons that substance P locks on to, the more intense the pain.

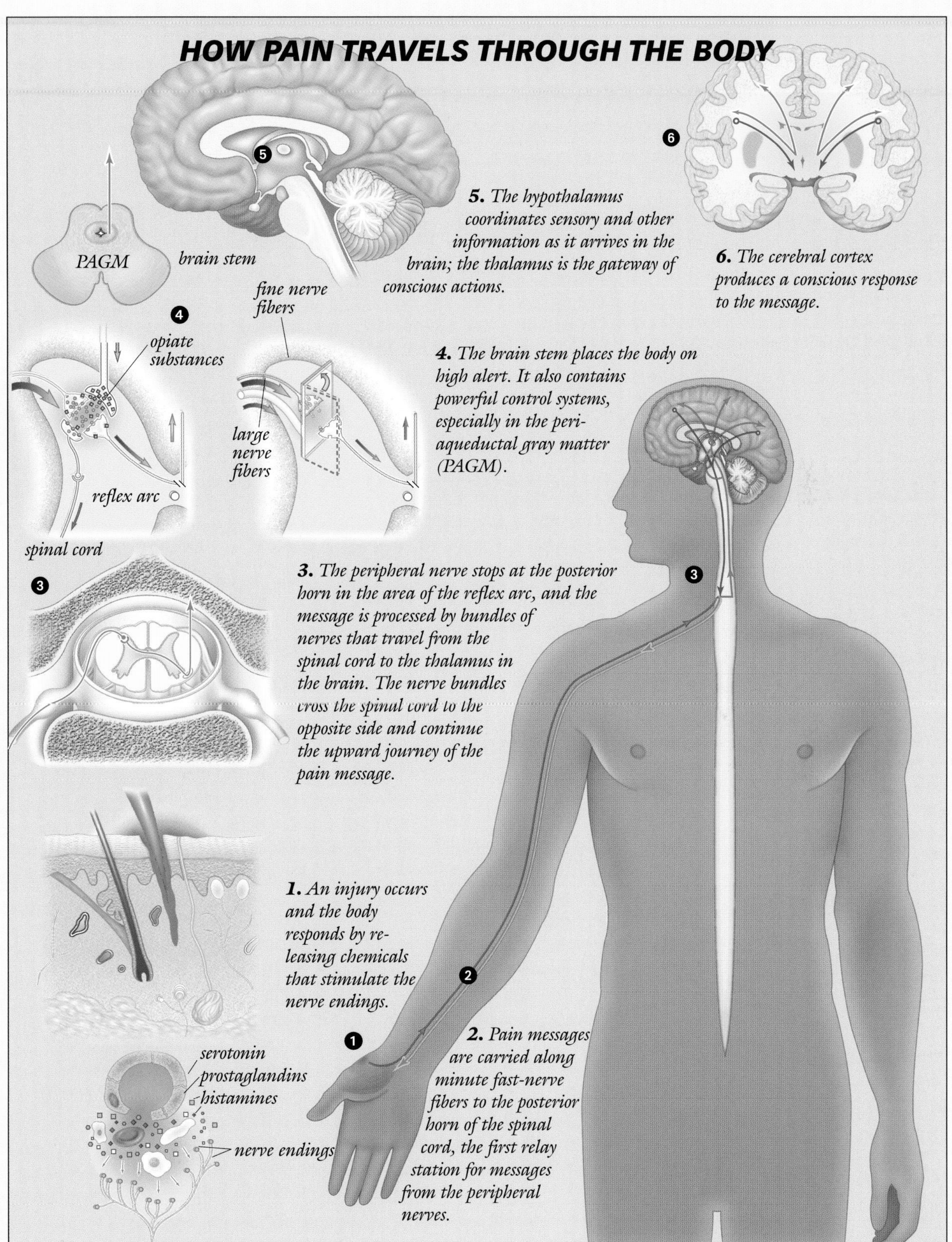
HOW PAIN TRAVELS THROUGH THE BODY
5
6
PAGM
brain stem
5. The hypothalamus coordinates sensory and other information as it arrives in the brain; the thalamus is the gateway of conscious actions.
6. The cerebral cortex produces a conscious response to the message.
fine nerve fibers
4
opiate substances
large nerve fibers
reflex arc
spinal cord
4. The brain stem places the body on high alert. It also contains powerful control systems, especially in the peri-aqueductal gray matter (PAGM).
3
3. The peripheral nerve stops at the posterior horn in the area of the reflex arc, and the message is processed by bundles of nerves that travel from the spinal cord to the thalamus in the brain. The nerve bundles cross the spinal cord to the opposite side and continue the upward journey of the pain message.
3
1. An injury occurs and the body responds by re-leasing chemicals that stimulate the nerve endings.
2
1
serotonin
prostaglandins
histamines
nerve endings
2. Pain messages are carried along minute fast-nerve fibers to the posterior horn of the spinal cord, the first relay station for messages from the peripheral nerves.

# Perceptions of Pain

*Pain is sometimes referred to as our seventh sense, but in reality, our responses to pain are closer to emotional reactions than sensory perceptions. They are also extremely variable from one person to another and even from time to time.*

## TO EACH HIS OWN PAIN TOLERANCE

A pain threshold is defined as the point at which a person exposed to a pain-provoking substance or circumstance will feel discomfort. Until recently, we assumed that some people had a low pain threshold, while others had a higher one. Recent studies tend to debunk this assumption. In one experiment, for example, participants were asked to hold metal rods that were then heated or chilled, and to indicate when they began to experience pain. Invariably, the rods caused pain when they were heated to 41°C (105°F) or chilled to –6°C (22°F). In other words, everyone in the experiment had pretty much the same pain threshold.

But the same did not hold for pain tolerance—the point at which the participants could no longer hold on to the rod. What's more, the ability to tolerate pain varied greatly according to the circumstances. In this regard, the power of suggestion proved powerful indeed. When participants were warned that the rods would be heated or frozen to the point where the metal could quickly cause serious burns or frozen tissue, within seconds, many started to grimace, cry out in pain, and drop the rods. The researchers had not, in fact, changed the temperatures at all—it was the anticipation of pain that produced the results.

### The power of distraction

When the rods were actually chilled or heated, the participants could tolerate more pain when they were distracted by music or other sensory input. They also showed a greater tolerance for pain if friends or colleagues were watching because they didn't want to look like sissies. Virtually everyone has experienced similar increased pain tolerance in everyday situations. Minor aches and pains lessen or seem to disappear when we become involved in something more engrossing than the pain. Very often, however, the pain returns when the distraction disappears.

The environment at the moment is also a factor in how much pain a person can tolerate. Studies have found that soldiers wounded during combat need less pain medication than civilians with more minor injuries. The soldiers often had not expected to survive, so simply being alive made their pain seem less significant. In contrast, civilians had not anticipated the personal consequences of war.

*In a test of mind over pain, a fire walker treads on embers, seemingly oblivious to any discomfort.*

### Emotional responses to pain

Pain usually evokes a strong emotional response—anger, shock, fear, despair, among others. The emotional responses to pain arise in the brain. After pain messages reach the cerebral cortex—the "thinking" center of the brain where they are inter-

## IF YOU EXPECT IT TO HURT...

Do these vignettes strike a familiar chord?

- You take your toddler to the doctor for a routine checkup and booster shots. As the nurse approaches with hypodermic needle in hand, the child clutches his arm and begins to wail: "No! No! You're hurting me!"
- At one time, Sally was an avid horseback rider. Then one day her horse slipped and fell, and Sally broke her leg. The leg has long since healed, but even the smell of a horse provokes a deep aching sensation at the site of the break.
- Martin, a successful attorney, suffered extensive burns in an apartment house fire several years ago. Just the sound of a fire engine brings feelings of panic and searing pain in his burn scars.

These all are examples of anticipatory pain, in which the distress is very real, even though there is no physical basis for the pain. Anticipatory pain illustrates the powerful role of the brain in remembering—and reliving—pain.

preted—they are relayed to the brain's limbic center, which produces emotional responses. Some of these responses are almost automatic reflexes; when you bang your thumb with a hammer, you may experience a quick burst of anger, and even utter a few uncharacteristic curses as you inspect the damage. Other responses are learned ones, based on past experience and expectations. Still others are conditioned according to what's going on at the moment, such as your level of stress, fatigue, or the sudden feelings of fear that arise when you suffer a fall or burn.

Emotions can intensify and diminish perception of pain. When you are tense and anxious, even a minor stimulus can produce intense pain. This often happens in the dentist's chair. If you feel anxious and certain that the procedure is going to hurt, even a gentle touch from a dental probe can be perceived as a sharp pain. In contrast, if you are relaxed, confident that the procedure will be painless, and concentrating on a pleasant pastime, chances are you will barely feel what would ordinarily be a painful process.

## Other factors affecting pain tolerance

Researchers have identified dozens of factors and circumstances that alter pain tolerance. They include:

- **Competing sensory input.** People who suffer from arthritis or another chronic, painful disorder often report that they hurt less when watching an engrossing movie or TV program or when having a stimulating conversation. It's no coincidence that you hurt more when lying quietly in a still, dimly lit room than when you are in a bright, cheerful, and engaging environment. In the dark, quiet room, the pain messages have little competition, so the brain concentrates on them and the discomfort seems more intense. But when there is other sensory input, fewer pain messages get through to the brain, and the person hurts less, even though the underlying condition may be unchanged.
- **Age.** In general, tolerance for pain decreases with advancing age. Not only do older people suffer more from arthritis and other painful conditions, but they also have less competing sensory input as hearing fades, vision dims, and other senses dull.
- **Expectations.** The anticipation of pain can be self-fulfilling—if you expect that an activity will be intolerably painful, chances are it will be. In contrast, if you are confident that it won't hurt, you are less likely to find the pain intolerable. (See *If You Expect It to Hurt*, p 16.)
- **Past experience.** Pain can be a learned experience. So if something hurt very badly in the past, you are likely to experience severe pain again in future encounters with a similar circumstance.
- **General health, depression, and fatigue.** People who are in poor health, tired, depressed, or otherwise out-of-sorts are also more likely to have a low tolerance for pain.
- **Prospects of a reward.** Virtually everyone can will themselves to endure pain in order to achieve a goal or reward. Take, for example, the runner who is so intent on winning a race that he's unaware of a painful muscle injury, or the new mother who quickly forgets the pain of childbirth as she snuggles her baby. Pavlov, the Russian scientist, demonstrated the value of a reward in overcoming pain in his many dog experiments. He subjected one of his dogs to a painful electrical shock, and then rewarded it with food. Before long, the shocks failed to provoke any pain behavior from the dog; instead, the animal wagged his tail and appeared excited and happy. The negative aspect of pain had been replaced by the positive prospect of food.

## PSYCHOLOGICAL PAIN

There is another important type of pain that is even harder to define than physical or organic pain; namely, psychological or emotional pain. Although this type of pain is not rooted in a physical injury or organic disease, it is just as real as any other type of pain, and often much harder to treat. Psychological pain ranges from the hurt feelings experienced at a perceived snub to the incapacitating grief or heartache many people experience with the loss of a loved one. It seems to have a language all its own: sick at heart, heartbroken, grief stricken, bereaved, among others. As with organic pain, psychological pain can disturb sleep and lead to withdrawal and medical depression. What's more, there is mounting evidence that prolonged psychological pain can weaken immune defenses and increase susceptibility to a host of diseases.

## THE CULTURE OF PAIN

In some cultures, the ability to endure severe pain is a rite of passage or a badge of honor. In many cultures, for example, male circumcision is celebrated as a rite of passage during adolescence. The honor and celebration seem to erase the discomfort of what would otherwise be a very painful experience. More extreme examples include the self-mutilation practiced as a tribal rite of passage in many societies. Depending upon the culture, youths will make burns or deep cuts on the face, chest, or other parts of the body. Their scars testify that they can endure enough pain to become warriors or members of adult society.

Religion has played an important role in shaping attitudes toward pain. Many religions teach that pain is something that human beings must endure as a consequence of original sin or transgressions in an earlier life. Under such views, suffering becomes a test of faith, and perhaps a means to a better life.

# The Mysteries of Pain

*Why is the pain of a heart attack often more intense in the back, jaw, or arm than in the chest? Why does an amputee still feel intense pain in the missing limb? Nerve pathways, as well as the brain, memory, and conditioning, are responsible.*

## PAIN THAT MOVES TO AND FRO

Acute pain is usually easy to pinpoint, but referred pain is a notable exception. This is pain that is felt in addition to, or perhaps elsewhere than, its site of origin. The most familiar example is the pain of a heart attack; it may travel down an arm or to the back, stomach, or jaw, and be even more intense in these areas than in the chest itself. Another common type of referred pain involves the gallbladder, in which passage of a gallstone may cause intense pain in the back or upper chest. Appendicitis pain is often more intense in the center of the abdomen, rather than in the immediate area of the appendix on the lower right side.

Referred pain occurs because the pain nerve fibers from a number of organs all enter the spinal cord at about the same place and travel along the same pathways. As a result, the pain messages from one site, such as the heart, stimulate the fibers from another area, such as the arm, jaw, back, or stomach, resulting in pain in parts of the body that are perfectly healthy.

Referred pain often misleads both doctors and patients. Many women having a heart attack complain of a vague back- or stomachache rather than the intense chest pains that typically occur in male heart attack victims. Consequently, many women delay seeking medical help during heart attacks, and those who do often are not diagnosed promptly because (1) their symptoms are not typical of those experienced by men, and (2) many doctors still regard heart attack as a male disease.

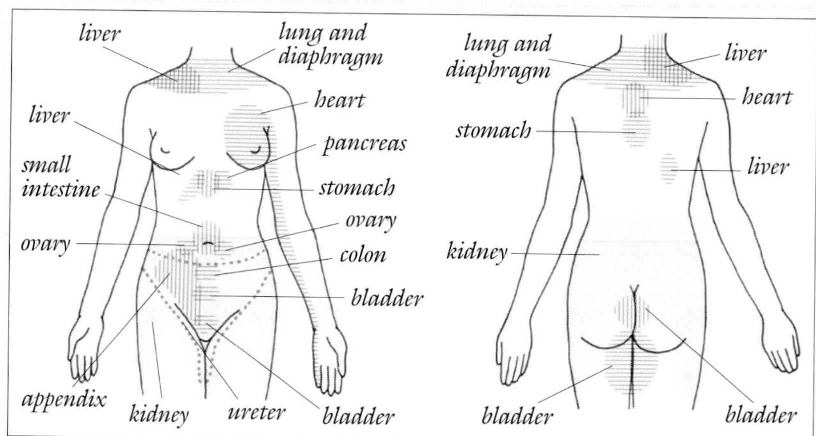


*Areas where referred pain is felt and the actual origin of it are often far removed from each other, as illustrated here.*

### When other organs are involved

Pain may also radiate from its original source if nearby organs are also involved. For example, diverticulitis—inflammation of small pouches in the colon wall—may cause intense abdominal pain that seems to travel upward if the inflammation obstructs other parts of the intestines.

Sometimes, if a nerve is injured, pain may travel along all or part of its length. Sciatica—the pain that travels from the back to the buttocks and down a leg—is one of the most common examples.

## THE BODY'S OWN PAINKILLERS

Almost at the same instant that pain messages begin their journey from the site of an injury to the brain, the body begins to marshal its own painkillers to dull the sensation. Here's what happens: Imagine that you drop a heavy object on your foot. Without thinking, you jerk your foot away, perhaps cursing and hopping about. This action is prompted by fast-track pain messages that are sent immediately to the reflex arc in the spinal cord, which controls the reflexive action.

At the same time, pain messages are rushing to the brain, which interprets them and sends response messages down the descending pain pathways. These pathways pass through the same pain gates in the brain and spinal cord as the nerves carrying the ascending messages to the brain. The response messages order the release of brain chemicals called endorphins. These are internal (*endo*) morphinelike substances that are potent painkillers. They work by helping block the transmission of pain messages. Endorphins use the same gates as pain messages; the more endorphins that flood the gates, the fewer the number of pain messages that get through. They also compete with pain messages for brain receptor sites.

### The fight-or-flight response

Studies show that some people make more endorphins than others, and these lucky souls have a greater tolerance for pain. Endorphins are released when the body is under stress. Whenever the body perceives that it is in danger, whether real or imagined, a host of automatic responses occur: the heart beats faster, blood pressure rises, muscles tense, and epinephrine, or adrenaline, floods the body. The extra endorphins are needed to block or dull pain and enable the body to concentrate on overcoming the danger. A person does not have to be in actual physical danger, however, to release endorphins. During exercise or prolonged physical activity, for example, endorphin levels rise. This is why conditioned runners are often able to keep going even when they have a painful condition like shin splints or a hairline fracture.

Some researchers think that endorphins may explain at least part of the anesthetic effect of acupuncture; inserting the acupuncture needles may prompt the brain to release endorphins. With practice and the use of biofeedback training, meditation, and other mental exercises, some people can actually learn how to control the release of endorphins, and thus help control pain.

## COMMON MYTHS ABOUT PAIN

When it comes to pain, the myths are often hard to sort out from the facts, in large part because it is complex and its nature varies from one person to another. Numerous studies show that people who understand the true nature of their pain and its underlying cause cope better than those whose perception is clouded with half-truths and misconceptions. Here are few of the more common myths about pain.

**Myth:** Cancer is always very painful.
**Fact:** Although it's certainly true that cancer can cause pain, it is by no means inevitable. In fact, most early, localized cancers are painless. Even after cancer has spread (metastasized), it may cause little or no pain. According to palliative care experts, 50 to 90 percent of advanced cancers produce varying degrees of pain. Palliative care experts at the McGill University Health Centre estimate between 90 and 95 percent of pains related to cancer can be effectively controlled using all available treatments, eliminating or tempering them down to a level where they do not interfere with daily life.

**Myth:** Most prescription painkillers are addictive.
**Fact:** Only a handful of the pain drugs that doctors prescribe are habit-forming, or addictive. Most of these are medications derived from morphine or morphine-like substances. Addiction is a problem when these drugs are abused. When properly used for a few weeks to treat intense pain, such as that resulting from surgery, these drugs are highly effective and will not lead to addiction. Unfortunately, the fear of addiction, rather than the problem itself, results in many people being denied the most effective pain relief.

**Myth:** Aspirin and similar OTC painkillers have no side effects.
**Fact:** There's no such thing as an absolutely safe medication, and this applies to aspirin as well as related nonsteroidal anti-inflammatory drugs (NSAIDs), such as ibuprofen and naproxen. Most NSAIDs hinder blood clotting and their use can result in severe intestinal bleeding. They can also cause or worsen ulcers and other intestinal problems. In addition, heavy use of aspirin can cause ringing in the ears and even hearing loss. The risk can be reduced by using the drugs only as needed, and always taking them with food and never with alcohol.

**Myth:** A worsening of chronic pain usually signifies a worsening of the underlying disease.
**Fact:** This is sometimes true, but more often, chronic pain persists and may even worsen long after the underlying condition has healed.

## THE AGONY OF PHANTOM PAIN

One of the most agonizing—and puzzling—forms of pain is that endured by people who have undergone an amputation. Referred to as phantom limb pain, it is usually an intense burning, itching, or tingling sensation that appears to come from the missing body part.

Here's how one patient described it:

"I lost my left leg just below the knee in a farm accident. At first, I had very little feeling at the site of the amputation. But as the stump healed, I'd have spells of itching and burning pain that seemed to come from my missing foot. Over time, the spells became less frequent and intense, but even now, years later, I sometimes feel twinges from my missing left foot."

Phantom limb pain is very common among accident victims who have lost a limb, or even fingers or toes. Pain is among the many different kinds of memories stored in the brain. As might be expected, extreme or prolonged pain makes more of an impression on the brain than mild or transient pain. In phantom limb pain, even minor stimulation of the nerves near the amputation site can send pain messages to the brain that activate memories of earlier pain. In effect, the pain message center of the brain reacts as if the limb were still there, sending out intense pain messages from its memory bank.

# Heeding Pain's Signals

*We often hear "No pain, no gain." Although there are times when you might benefit by "working through the pain," more often than not, ignoring pain's warning signs can be a big mistake, especially when it is due to an injury or an acute illness.*

## WHEN PAIN SERVES A USEFUL PURPOSE

Acute pain is a critical component of the body's early warning system. It occurs when damaged tissue releases chemicals that stimulate nearby nerve endings. When pain develops, our natural response is to do whatever we can to stop it. This entails getting away from the pain's source, if possible, or treating the underlying cause to ease the hurt. Much of the time, the cause is readily apparent—an infection, cut, burn, broken bone, foreign object in an eye, or another injury. But what about when the cause is not so obvious, or when the pain is accompanied by other symptoms? In general, the sudden onset of severe pain, with no known cause and unlike any you have experienced before, is a warning to see a doctor.

## WHEN PAIN SIGNALS AN EMERGENCY

Pain is a common symptom of many diseases, and most often, it lessens and disappears as the disorder clears up. In some instances, however, it points to a medical emergency. The following are common examples of pain requiring immediate action.

### Head pain

**Brain hemorrhage or stroke:** Sudden development of an unusual, intense headache, often accompanied by changes in vision, speech, consciousness, and partial paralysis, usually on one side of the body.

**Brain infection (e.g., meningitis):** A worsening headache accompanied by fever, vomiting, confusion, drowsiness, and a stiff neck.

**Brain tumor or abscess:** Severe headache that may worsen when lying down and may be accompanied by nausea, vomiting, confusion, memory loss, muscle weakness, double vision, speech disturbances, balance problems, seizures, drowsiness, and altered consciousness.

**Hemorrhage following head trauma:** Persistent dull headache that may be accompanied by any or all of the following: drowsiness, nausea and vomiting, vision or hearing changes, dizziness, altered consciousness, and partial paralysis.

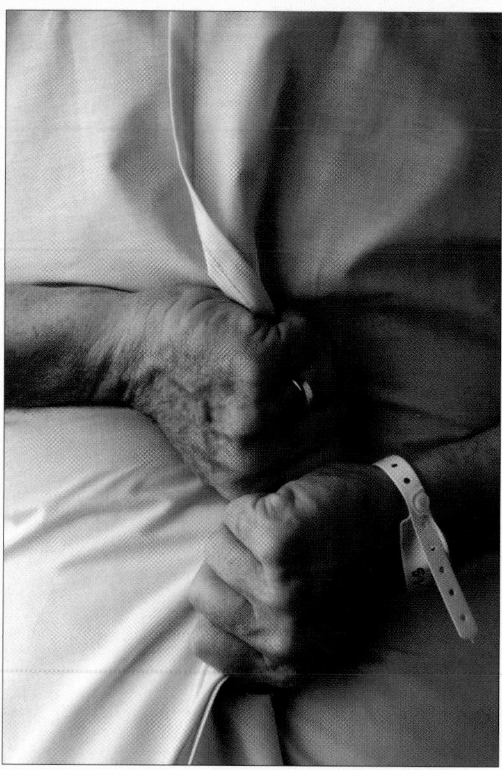

*Hospital patients often experience sudden intense pain as a result of surgery or other treatments.*

### Chest pain

**Heart attack:** Sudden chest pain of unknown cause that lasts for more than 15 minutes and is not relieved by rest; it may be intense and centered in the chest, or take the form of heavy pressure in the chest. Pain may spread to the shoulder, arm(s), back, neck, jaw, and teeth, and be accompanied by nausea, vomiting, sweating, shortness of breath, and anxiety.

**Pulmonary embolism:** Sudden, sharp chest pain that worsens when coughing or taking a deep breath; it may be accompanied by shortness of breath, rapid heartbeat, sweating, cough, and bloody sputum.

**Expanding or dissecting aortic aneurysm:** Worsening chest pain that may radiate to the back or abdomen (it may also take the form of severe backache); may be accompanied by difficulty swallowing, hoarseness, dizziness, fainting.

### Eye pain

**Corneal ulcer or infection:** Severe eye pain, blurred vision, tearing, increased sensitivity to light, reddening of the eye, visible ulcer or sore on the eye's surface.

**Detached retina:** Sudden onset of eye pain, blurred vision, seeing bright flashes of light, blind spots in part of field of vision.

### Abdominal pain

**Acute appendicitis:** Pain near the navel that spreads to lower right side, low-grade fever, nausea and vomiting, constipation (or, less commonly, diarrhea).

**Intestinal obstruction:** Abdominal pain, cramps, and bloating; nausea and vomiting; worsening constipation or inability to pass stools or gas.

**Kidney stones:** Spasms of severe colicky pain in flank and back, radiating through lower abdomen; nausea and vomiting; blood in urine; difficulty passing urine.

**Pancreatitis:** Sudden, severe abdominal pain, nausea and vomiting; weakness; fever; bloating; clammy skin.

## Back pain

**Ruptured (herniated) disk:** Severe lower back (or neck) pain that gets worse when you lift, cough, or strain; it may be accompanied by pain, numbness, or tingling in buttocks and leg (or arm); loss of bowel and/or bladder control.

**Spinal tumor:** Persistent and worsening back pain; may be accompanied by worsening tingling, numbness, and muscle weakness and loss of bowel and bladder control.

## Pelvic pain in women

**Ectopic (tubal) pregnancy:** Increasing pelvic pain, vaginal spotting; severe internal bleeding and fainting if the tube ruptures.

**Pelvic inflammatory disease (PID):** Increasingly severe lower pelvic pain, fever and chills, vaginal discharge.

**Ruptured ovarian cyst:** Sudden, severe abdominal pain, swelling, fainting (from internal bleeding).

## Pain in limbs

**Blockage due to blood clot:** Sudden, severe pain in arm or leg, accompanied by coldness and paleness or bluish tinge to the skin; local tenderness; swelling and fever.

**Acute Lyme disease or other infectious arthritis:** Sudden development of a swollen, painful, inflamed joint (often one or both knees), fever and chills, and possible rash.

## Getting Serious: Pains That Tell You to Seek Medical Help

*The following are some of the more common types of acute pain that warrant prompt medical attention.*

| TYPE OF PAIN | IMMEDIATE FIRST AID | POSSIBLE CAUSE/GETTING MEDICAL HELP |
|---|---|---|
| Sudden, severe headache unlike any you have had before; headache accompanied by stiff neck or following a head injury. | Stop what you are doing; rest quietly until help arrives. | Suspect a stroke, brain abscess, tumor, meningitis, or concussion. Call 911 or Emergency Medical Service (EMS) or have someone take you to nearest emergency room or hospital. |
| Chest pain that lasts more than a few minutes, or is accompanied by pain radiating to arm, back, jaw, or throat; possible nausea, vomiting, profuse sweating, anxiety. | Stop what you're doing; chew an aspirin; try to stay calm until help arrives. | Suspect a heart attack; call 911 or EMS. If EMS is not available, have someone drive you to the nearest emergency room or hospital with a cardiac care unit. |
| Chest pain that worsens when taking a deep breath, accompanied by prolonged, painful coughing or coughing up blood or green phlegm. | Assume sitting or semi-sitting position; loosen any tight clothing; try to breathe slowly. | Suspect pneumonia, acute bronchitis, lung tumor or abscess. Call your doctor for instructions; if breathing becomes more difficult, call 911 or EMS, or have someone take you to the nearest hospital or emergency room. |
| Severe abdominal pain; may be boring or colicky and accompanied by vomiting blood and local or diffuse abdominal tenderness. | DO NOT try to eat or drink anything; lie on left side (unless that worsens pain) with head turned to side in case of vomiting. | Suspect gallstones, kidney stones, appendicitis, perforated ulcer or ruptured esophagus, or pancreatitis. Call your doctor for instructions, which may include going to emergency room. |
| Eye injury or sudden onset of acute eye pain, perhaps accompanied by seeing flashing lights or change in vision. | Rinse eye with water if injury is due to chemical splash or foreign object; cover injured eye with clean gauze bandage or cloth. | If cause is not obvious, suspect detached retina or acute glaucoma. Call doctor for instructions or go to emergency room. |
| Joint swelling and pain following an injury; sudden swelling and joint inflammation, perhaps accompanied by fever, chills, as well as rash. | Start RICE, by resting joint, applying ice pack, compressing with an elastic bandage, and elevating injured joint to minimize swelling. | Suspect strain or sprain; if fever and chills develop, suspect acute infectious arthritis or Lyme disease. See a doctor if pain and swelling of strain or sprain persist for more than two days; call doctor immediately if fever, chills, or rash develops. |
| Sudden and severe back pain, perhaps accompanied by pain radiating down leg, numbness, or loss of bowel or bladder control. | Lie flat on your back on floor or firm bed; place a pillow under knees. | Suspect herniated spinal disk, muscle spasm in back. Call doctor if pain persists for more than two days; call immediately if there is leg numbness or loss of bowel or bladder control. |

# Yardsticks of Pain

*There's no universal test to assess pain; in fact, its subjective nature makes it impossible to measure pain in an objective way. So doctors ask many different questions and look for subtle clues to judge just how much it hurts and to find the most appropriate treatments.*

## WHEN YOU SEE YOUR DOCTOR

Each year, millions of Canadians visit their doctors because of chronic pain. A lucky few get the relief they seek, but most end up on a merry-go-round of doctors' appointments without any relief in sight. A 1999 article by *Maclean's* quotes pain experts who estimate "as many as 70 percent of Canadians who suffer pain do so without adequate treatment." Many of us complain that our doctors do not take our pain seriously or do not know enough about pain treatment. The fact is, however, that almost all pain patients can be helped, and there are many things that you, the patient, can do to make sure you get relief.

### Sample Pain Scale

| DEGREE | EXAMPLE |
|---|---|
| Very mild | Pinprick |
| Mild | Minor cut |
| Mild + | Small to moderate burn/blistering |
| Mild to moderate | Sprained ankle |
| Moderate | Burning pain of bronchitis |
| Moderate + | Bad migraine headache |
| Moderate to severe | Post-shingles neuropathy |
| Severe | Incision after abdominal surgery |
| Severe + | Herniated disk when straining, bad toothache |
| Extreme/worst ever | Broken bone, facial nerve pain, cluster headache |

### Don't delay

Many people put off seeing a doctor for months or even years. By that time, the body has been conditioned to respond to pain messages, even though the original injury or illness has cleared up (see *Why Pain Doesn't Go Away*, p 23). Pain specialists agree that the best way to deal with chronic pain is to prevent it from ever developing. This is why it is so important to see a doctor early, before the pain—and adapting to it—becomes a habit.

### Be prepared

The better the information you give your doctor, the more likely you are to get the most appropriate treatment. All too often, patients find it difficult to describe their pain. But it's very important to give as complete a description of the pain in order to help your doctor arrive at a proper diagnosis. As a start, keep a pain diary for a week or so. Copy the form on page 24, and take it with you when you see your doctor. This will help the two of you pinpoint the distinguishing characteristics of your particular pain.

In addition, be prepared to answer a number of questions. Some doctors use a pain questionnaire; others prefer to use an interview format. In either instance, here are some key questions that you should be prepared to answer. Review the list, and jot down the answers before seeing the doctor. Otherwise, you may overlook or forget important facts that your doctor should know.

*An accurate description of pain helps a doctor find the most effective treatment.*

**1.** Where exactly does it hurt the most? Does the pain stay in one place or move around?
**2.** How bad is the pain? How would you rate it on a scale of one to ten, with ten being the worst pain you have ever had (or can imagine), and one being very mild, brief, and quite tolerable?
**3.** When did the pain start? Under what circumstances? Do you know what caused it?
**4.** Have you ever had this pain before? If so, how long did it last? In what way is this pain the same? How is it different?
**5.** Have any members of your family, colleagues, or others close to you had a similar problem? If so, what were the circumstances?
**6.** What words best describe it? (See *The Language of Pain*, right, for a list of possibilities.)

7. What happened in the early stages of the pain? For example, did it get worse? Did it get better? Stay the same? Spread?
8. What makes the pain worse? What makes it better?
9. How is the pain affecting your life? For example: Are you able to work? Do you find it difficult to sleep? Is the pain affecting your appetite? Your relationship with others?

### Signs doctors look for

In addition to how patients describe their pain, doctors look for key signs of distress. Autonomic changes that develop when a person is in severe pain include an increased pulse rate, a rise in blood pressure, and pale skin color. Breathing also changes; a wave of pain is usually reflected with a sharp intake of breath, followed by shallow, rapid breathing as the pain subsides for a while. Other signs of extreme pain include:

- **Degree of restlessness.** Is the patient unable to find a comfortable position? Is he doubled over? Writhing? Twitching or trembling? Taut and tense?
- **Facial expression.** Is the jaw clenched? Is the patient grimacing?
- **Ability to focus.** Is it hard to distract the patient's attention from his or her pain?

## WHY PAIN DOESN'T GO AWAY

All too often, acute pain becomes chronic, lingering far beyond the time of normal healing. Unfortunately, this often happens when acute pain is not brought under early control. The peripheral pain receptors become increasingly sensitive, causing the pain gates to remain open. This leads to a downward spiral of conditioned responses—even though there is no tissue damage, the nerves keep sending pain messages. In time, the nerve cells along the spinal cord pain pathways become more sensitive to the messages. As the pain persists, feelings of frustration, anger, helplessness, depression, and anxiety are likely to get worse.

Sometimes the pain is due to a chronic disease, such as arthritis or diabetes, but more often, there is no obvious cause, or the pain is out of proportion to the underlying condition. This is the type of pain that has the greatest adverse effect on a persons day-to-day life, and also is the most difficult and frustrating to treat.

Doctors now recognize that chronic pain often can be prevented by treating acute pain as aggressively as possible. This is why it is important to seek medical attention for any pain that lasts longer than you think it should, especially after an injury or surgery. In the past, doctors in hospitals tended to give pain medications according to "need," meaning the patient had to wait until severe pain developed before getting an injection of morphine or another powerful painkiller. In effect, the pain was undertreated, and the medication was always lagging behind the pain. Now, a more enlightened approach calls for administering pain medication as a preventive measure, giving it at the first twinge of discomfort, or even before it occurs (for more details, see p 59). This approach short-circuits the pain messages, and allows healing to take place in relative comfort. More important, it prevents the acute pain from becoming chronic.

## The Language of Pain

| WHAT THE PAIN FEELS LIKE | HOW THE PAIN ACTS | EMOTIONAL AND PHYSICAL RESPONSES |
|---|---|---|
| aching | agonizing | anger |
| blinding | annoying | crying |
| boring | beating | depression |
| burning | cruel | dread |
| cold | exhausting | fatigue |
| cramping | frightful | fear |
| crushing | grueling | frustration |
| cutting | hurting | nausea |
| drawing | killing | sleeplessness |
| drilling | persistent | terror |
| dull | punishing | weakness |
| flashing | relentless | weeping |
| flickering | sickening | |
| gnawing | suffocating | |
| heavy | vicious | |
| hot | wretched | |
| intense | | |
| itching | | |
| jumping | | |
| nagging | | |
| numbing | | |
| penetrating | | |
| piercing | | |
| pounding | | |
| prickling | | |
| pulling | | |
| quivering | | |
| radiating | | |
| rasping | | |
| scalding | | |
| searing | | |
| sharp | | |
| shooting | | |
| smarting | | |
| splitting | | |
| spreading | | |
| squeezing | | |
| stinging | | |
| taut | | |
| tender | | |
| throbbing | | |
| tingling | | |
| tugging | | |
| twitching | | |
| wrenching | | |

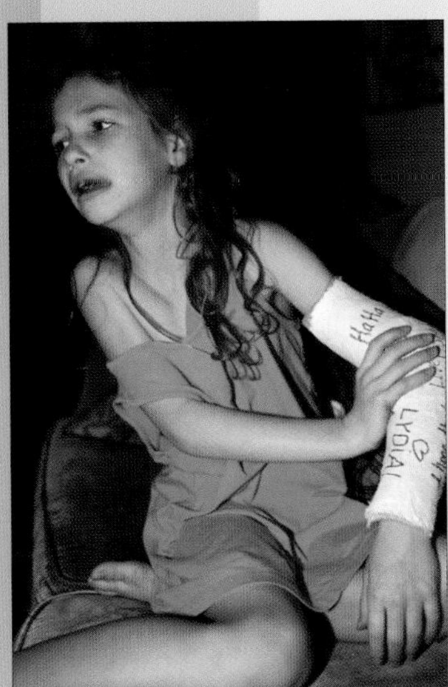

## Pain Diary

*Keeping a daily pain diary can help you remember when you experience the pain, its nature at any particular time, and what, if anything, brought relief. Here is a sample diary page for one day.*

| Time | Severity from 1 (very mild) to 10 (never worse) | Words that best describe it | What you were doing when it began | Name and amount of medication taken | Other actions (meditation, exercise, ice, heat) | Degree of relief (none, some, complete) |
|---|---|---|---|---|---|---|
| Midnight | | | | | | |
| 1 a.m. | | | | | | |
| 2 a.m. | | | | | | |
| 3 a.m. | | | | | | |
| 4 a.m. | | | | | | |
| 5 a.m. | | | | | | |
| 6 a.m. | | | | | | |
| 7 a.m. | | | | | | |
| 8 a.m. | | | | | | |
| 9 a.m. | | | | | | |
| 10 a.m. | | | | | | |
| 11 a.m. | | | | | | |
| Noon | | | | | | |
| 1 p.m. | | | | | | |
| 2 p.m. | | | | | | |
| 3 p.m. | | | | | | |
| 4 p.m. | | | | | | |
| 5 p.m. | | | | | | |
| 6 p.m. | | | | | | |
| 7 p.m. | | | | | | |
| 8 p.m. | | | | | | |
| 9 p.m. | | | | | | |
| 10 p.m. | | | | | | |
| 11 p.m. | | | | | | |

# Pain from Infancy to Old Age

*At each stage of life, we encounter different pains and experience them in different ways. Babies cannot tell you what hurts, but their cries make it clear that something does. Elderly people whose health is deteriorating may tend to focus on aches and pains.*

## WHEN BABIES FEEL PAIN

Even before birth, a baby responds to painful stimuli, but it is unknown whether this is an automatic reaction or if the developing fetus actually perceives pain. A newborn certainly feels pain, but not in the same way a more developed child does. If you prick a newborn's foot, for example, the infant will grimace, cry out in pain, and try to draw in all four limbs and roll into a fetal position. The baby obviously knows that something hurts, but the brain has not yet developed the pathways to determine the precise source of the pain. By pulling all the limbs inward and assuming a fetal position, the infant is instinctively trying to ward off further pain.

By the baby's first birthday, the brain has developed enough to recognize what hurts. So if the same foot is pricked, the baby will now try to pull it away while crying out in pain. Parents quickly learn to distinguish a baby's cries caused by pain from those signaling hunger, a soiled diaper, fatigue, or boredom. But until a child can talk, parents and doctors need to look for other clues to determine what hurts and how much. A baby with an earache, for example, may cry incessantly and rub or tug at the painful ear. Other clues can be drawn from the baby's facial expression, restlessness, loss of appetite, and changes in behavior, as well as from physical symptoms, such as a fever.

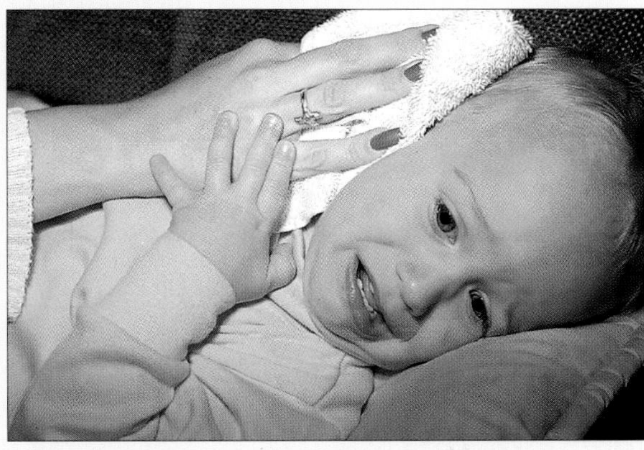

*Earaches are one of the most common causes of pain in young children.*

### How much does it hurt?

Pediatricians rely on various scales, including a coding of different facial expressions, to rate pain levels among newborns and young babies. By the age of four, most children can tell exactly where something hurts and describe the intensity of their pain by using visual aids. A child may be asked to rate his or her pain using the poker chip, or "pieces of hurt," method: one poker chip is a little hurt, two is a bit more, three is a lot of hurt, and four is the most hurt you can have. Somewhat older children may be shown a poster of faces, ranging from a happy smile to a grimace of great distress, and asked to pick the one that best reflects their degree of hurt.

## WE KNOW IT HURTS, BUT...

Contrary to popular belief, there is good evidence that even newborn babies are as capable of feeling pain as adults. In one study, most of the 374 caregivers in premature and neonatal nurseries surveyed said that they believed infants felt the same amount or even more pain than adults. They also ranked the amounts of pain produced by 12 common procedures. Circumcision and insertion of a chest tube were rated among the most painful, with airway suctioning and insertion of a feeding tube as less painful. But regardless of the degree of pain produced, painkillers were rarely used, and even time-honored methods of comforting, such as swaddling, holding, and rocking, were underused. The researchers concluded that there's considerable room for improvement in easing the pain of these youngest patients.

## COMMON CHILDHOOD PAINS

Injuries—ranging from minor cuts and scrapes to serious falls, burns, and wounds—are the most common sources of childhood pains. Ear infections are also very common, as are occasional headaches, stomach upsets, colds, flu, and other illnesses. Immunizations and other routine medical procedures can be intensely painful, but only for a brief period. More prolonged and severe pain is associated with surgery or chronic diseases such as juvenile rheumatoid arthritis, cancer, and AIDS.

## ADOLESCENCE

During adolescence, the frequent skinned knees and scrapes of early childhood are often supplanted by athletic injuries, such as muscle strains and sprains, shin splints and other overuse injuries, and broken bones. Adolescent girls may experience breast tenderness and, with menarche, menstrual cramps. Headaches, including migraines, are also relatively common.

### Growing pains

Many youngsters also experience vague leg pains, especially at night. Commonly referred to as "growing pains," doctors do not fully understand why these occur, and they eventually disappear. A medical checkup is warranted, however, to rule out a possible medical cause for the pains. Also, a doctor should be seen if the pains worsen, cause the child to limp, or are accompanied by other symptoms, such as a low-grade fever or deep bone pain.

### Emotional pain

The emotional turbulence that is a normal part of adolescence can also be a source of deep psychological pain. Parents, teachers, and others who are close to these young people should be on the alert for warning signs of depression, withdrawal, substance abuse, and deep-seated anger, and be prepared to help overcome problems while they are still in an early, manageable stage.

*Adolescence is often a time of great emotional pain.*

*Exercise is a critical key to health in the middle years.*

## THE MIDDLE YEARS

No time of life is pain-free, but for most young, healthy adults, it's usually an occasional thing with an identifiable cause—an injury, a stress-related headache, a bout of the flu or some other illness. When vague chronic pain of undetermined origin develops, it often signals a constellation of emotional and physical problems and requires a multifaceted approach to overcome.

For women, pregnancy, childbirth, and other aspects of reproductive function can produce pain. For some women, it's a source of recurring misery, but for most, the discomfort can be controlled enough so that it does not interfere with normal day-to-day activities.

### The onset of chronic problems

Some pain-producing chronic diseases—such as lupus, fibromyalgia, and rheumatoid arthritis—typically appear during early adulthood or middle age. Of course, cancer can occur at any age, but the risk rises steadily throughout adulthood.

Job-related pain problems, such as carpal tunnel syndrome and other repetitive stress injuries, are also relatively common. Keeping the pain under control is the big challenge in dealing with these chronic problems.

## THE LATER YEARS

There is nothing inherently painful about the aging process, nor is there any scientific evidence that we become more sensitive to pain as we age. But there is no doubt that older people suffer more aches and pains than their younger counterparts. There are a number of reasons for this. With advancing age comes a reduction in competing sensory input—vision dims, hearing becomes

### PAIN LINKED TO SEX AND REPRODUCTION

While sex is one of our most gratifying sources of pleasure, it can also have its painful side. Among women, recurring pain is often related to their reproductive functions and cycles. Common examples include the breast tenderness and bloating that many women experience as part of premenstrual syndrome (PMS), menstrual cramps, and the discomfort and pain associated with childbirth. Sexually transmitted diseases, such as genital herpes, genital warts, pelvic inflammatory disease in women, and urethritis in both men and women, are another common cause of reproductive-tract pain, especially among young adults.

less acute, and the senses of taste and smell are reduced. There is also an increased vulnerability to arthritis, osteoporosis, and other painful chronic diseases affecting the musculoskeletal system. The risk of cancer also rises with age. Shingles, a painful reactivation of the virus that caused chickenpox at an earlier age, afflicts many older people, and may cause nerve pain that lingers for months or even years. Type 2 (adult-onset or noninsulin-dependent) diabetes can also cause severe nerve pain, especially in the feet and legs.

## The value of distractions

Some older people become preoccupied with their various aches and pains, even though they are surprisingly healthy and free of ordinarily painful disorders. In contrast, there are those older people who have severe arthritis or other painful conditions who pay little or no attention to their discomfort. The difference often lies in the degree of pleasant distractions in their lives. Studies show that elderly people who are alone or housebound with little to occupy their thoughts complain more of pain than those who are out and about, and who are engaged in a variety of interesting activities.

A person's physical surroundings can have a profound effect on mood and his preoccupation with aches and pains. This is especially apparent in older people who move from a sunny, spacious apartment or house to a room in a nursing home or assisted-living facility. Away from a familiar setting and the mementoes gathered over a lifetime, many of these people seem to wither overnight, even though their physical health may be unchanged. They suddenly become more dependent, quiet, and withdrawn. They may be uncomplaining and stoic about their suffering, but inwardly, they focus more and more on their pain and disability. In such a situation, any pleasant distraction can help—the companionship of a gentle cat, dog, or another pet; something to nurture, if only a houseplant; favorite music to bring back memories of happy times. Lighting is also very important; a sunny, brightly lit room with an interesting view obviously provides more distractions than a dimly lit interior space.

*Interacting with a beloved pet can ease both emotional and physical pain.*

*Hobbies provide an important distraction from painful conditions, such as arthritis, that afflict many older people.*

## Pain treatment in the later years

Many older people with cancer and other chronic disorders suffer needlessly because their pain is not adequately treated. The most powerful narcotic painkillers are often denied them because their doctors or caregivers fear addiction, even though numerous studies discount this as a major problem. Others are undertreated because they cannot tolerate the side effects of some painkillers or their budgets cannot afford some of the newer, more expensive medications. In such situations, help usually can be found. Most large medical centers in Canada have specialists in geriatric pain who can prescribe a safe and effective regimen; most provinces provide financial help for seniors to buy essential medications through drug plans.

## A MATTER OF ATTITUDE

Feeling in control is an important first step in overcoming pain. Doctors repeatedly note that patients who maintain a calm, cheerful, and optimistic outlook weather pain better than those who feel helpless and pessimistic. Indeed, Dr. Bernie S. Siegel, author of *Love, Medicine & Miracles* and many other books on self-healing, maintains that healing begins with a positive attitude.

Knowledge is also important—the better you understand the source and meaning of pain, the more likely you are to learn how to control it. Studies of patients undergoing surgery show that those who experience the least pain are invariably the ones who ask questions, gather information, and understand what they can do to minimize any discomfort.

# THE BASICS OF RELIEF

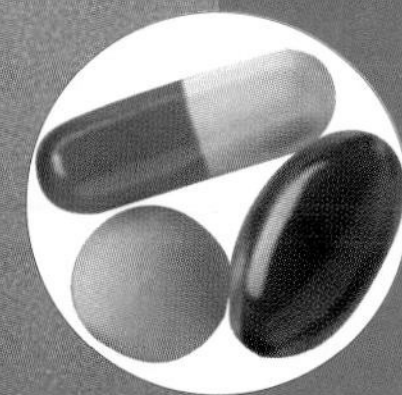
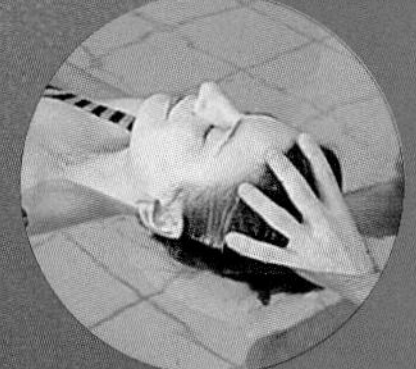
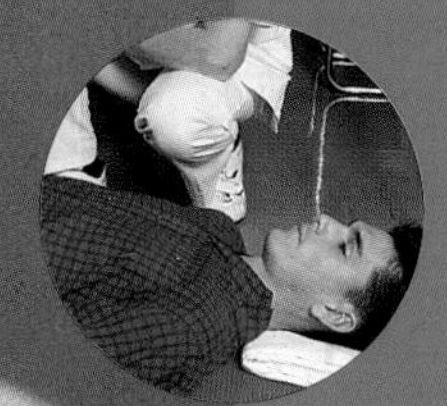



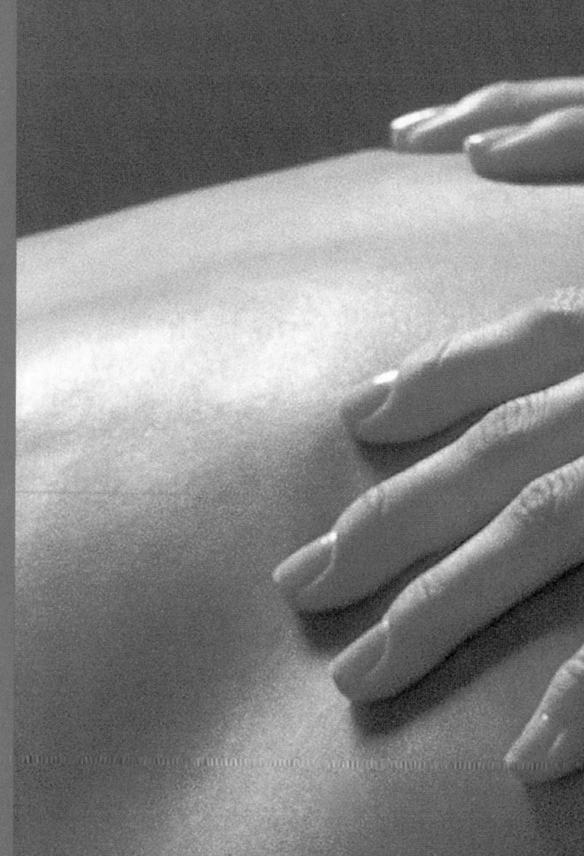

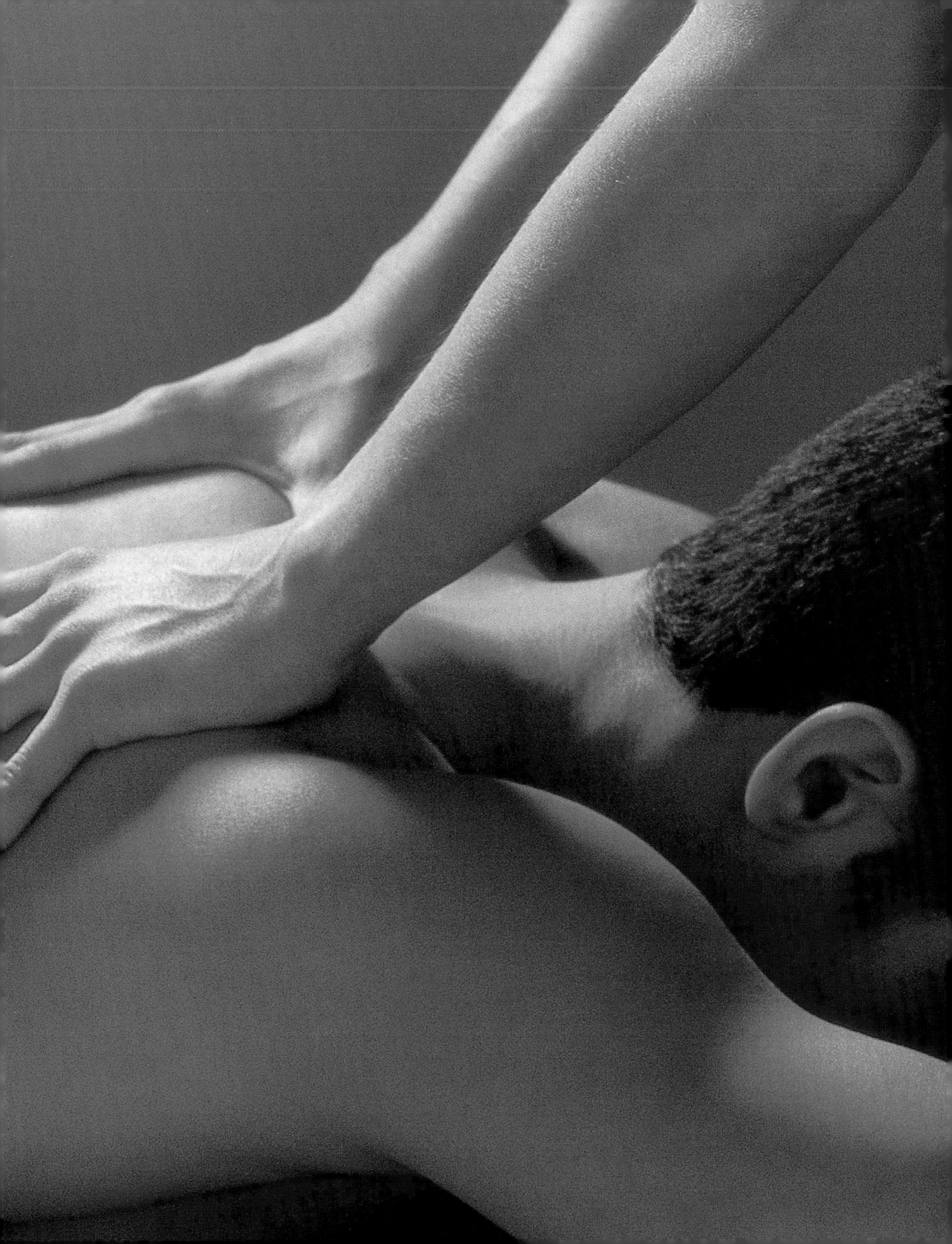

# Pain Medications

*Today we are blessed with a vast array of painkillers. No matter what the illness or the severity of the pain, doctors can almost always find a medication that delivers relief. But often a number of different medications or combinations must be tried to find what works best.*

## THE RATIONAL USE OF PAINKILLERS

When something hurts, it's only natural to want relief—and fast! For many, this means taking an analgesic medication, or in simpler terms, a painkiller—by far the most used medications in Canada. If you doubt this, simply peruse the shelves of pain medications at any pharmacy. You'll find row upon row of over-the-counter preparations and, behind the pharmacist's counter, scores of prescription products. Worldwide, more than 50 billion aspirin tablets are consumed each year. In North America, the total bill for painkillers—both prescription and OTC—comes to more than $4 billion a year.

With so many choices, picking a painkiller for even a minor problem can be daunting—a task that is further complicated by the fact that when it comes to pain control, there are no firm guidelines and goals. In contrast, when doctors prescribe drugs for high blood pressure, for example, there are specific numbers they use to measure success. But with pain, the degree of acceptable relief varies from one patient to another, and what works well for one person may barely faze the agony of another, even though the problems seem to be identical. In short, picking a painkiller is often a matter of trial-and-error until the desired level of relief is achieved with minimum adverse side effects.

As a general rule, doctors advise starting with the safest approach that is likely to do the job, and if this does not work, then moving up to the next level. Take common headaches, for example. A soothing bath or shower, massage, meditation, or another relaxation technique may be all that's needed to get rid of a muscle-tension or stress-related headache. If the headache persists, a nonprescription painkiller such as aspirin, acetaminophen, or low-dose ibuprofen is the likely next step. Stronger prescription drugs may be in order to treat the throbbing pain of a migraine. And an unusual, very severe headache that nothing seems to help and comes on suddenly, or is accompanied by other symptoms, such as a fever and stiff neck, causes you to awaken in the middle of the night, recurs in the same place, such as above or in an eye, may be a medical emergency, such as meningitis or a stroke.

## THE HUNT FOR BETTER PAINKILLERS

Researchers are constantly scouring the world, especially the rain forests and oceans, for more effective painkillers. Possibilities include:

- **Ziconotide,** which is extracted from the venom of a sea snail. It blocks pain signals from entering the spinal cord; the manufacturer is currently conducting human studies.
- **ABT-594** is the working name of a drug developed from a toxin in the skin of a tiny frog that lives in South American rain forests. It blocks the spinal cord and brain from processing pain messages. Human trials are under way, but approval is still several years off.
- **MorphiDex,** a combination of morphine and dextromethorphan, works by blocking secondary pain sensors. Studies indicate that it doubles the effectiveness of morphine without increasing the narcotic drug's side effects. The drug has been tested in humans. A new drug application was filed; however, the U.S. Food and Drug Administration (FDA) deemed MorphiDex not approvable in August 1999. More clinical analysis may be done, and the manufacturer is revising its application.

## TYPES OF PAINKILLERS

Pain medications fall into two broad categories: non-narcotic, which includes acetaminophen, ibuprofen, and many other over-the-counter and prescription drugs; and narcotic, which includes morphine and other opium-based drugs that can cause physical dependence. Because of its association with illegal drugs, the term "narcotic" is being used less and less in Canada by pain specialists, who prefer the term "opioid." Within these two broad categories are many subcategories. Some medications are targeted at specific disorders, others are systemic medications, such as the general anesthetics that are used during surgery. Of course, long-term pain relief depends upon the successful treatment of its underlying cause. Thus, analgesics may be given to relieve the obvious symptom of pain, while other totally unrelated medications or treatments are administered to cure the problem.

## NON-NARCOTIC PAIN MEDICATIONS

### Aspirin

Medically known as acetylsalicylic acid, aspirin is the oldest and most widely used pain medication. Hippocrates, in the fifth century BC, recommended treating pain with a relative of aspirin, a bitter powder made from willow bark. Even centuries before that, folk healers had relied on variations of the same remedy. It is now known that willows, as well as a number of other plants used as botanical painkillers, produce salicylic acid as part of their defense against infection (yes, plants get infections, too). The use of salicylic acid is limited, however, because it is very irritating to the stomach. So in the 1890s, Felix Hoffman, a German chemist, set about synthesizing a gentler compound. In 1897, the resulting acetylsalicylic acid (ASA) was introduced to the world as aspirin by Bayer & Co., which is still one of its leading makers.

Today, many pain relief products list aspirin or ASA as their main ingredient. Some of these products contain caffeine, which boosts the effectiveness of aspirin. (Taking aspirin with a cup of coffee produces the same result at a lower cost.) Aspirin works, at least in part, by suppressing the production of prostaglandins, hormonelike substances that are made throughout the body and carry out many functions, including stimulating the nerve endings that send pain messages to the brain. They also play an important role in the inflammatory process, blood clotting, temperature regulation, uterine contractions, and blood-vessel constriction. Thus, by blocking prostaglandins, aspirin goes beyond simply relieving pain. Reducing inflammation, for example, helps prevent arthritis damage to the joints. By hindering blood clotting, aspirin lowers the risk of a heart attack and stroke. By lowering a dangerously high fever, aspirin not only eases discomfort, but it also reduces the risk of brain damage.

There is also a negative side; aspirin's antiprostaglandin action sets the stage for some of its most serious side effects. Reducing the blood's ability to clot can lead to serious bleeding problems. In the stomach, prostaglandins stimulate production of the mucus that protects its lining from digestive acids. By inhibiting these prostaglandins, aspirin can cause or worsen peptic ulcers. In addition, aspirin itself is irritating to the delicate tissues that line the intestinal tract. This can be offset

**Common Forms of Pain Medication**

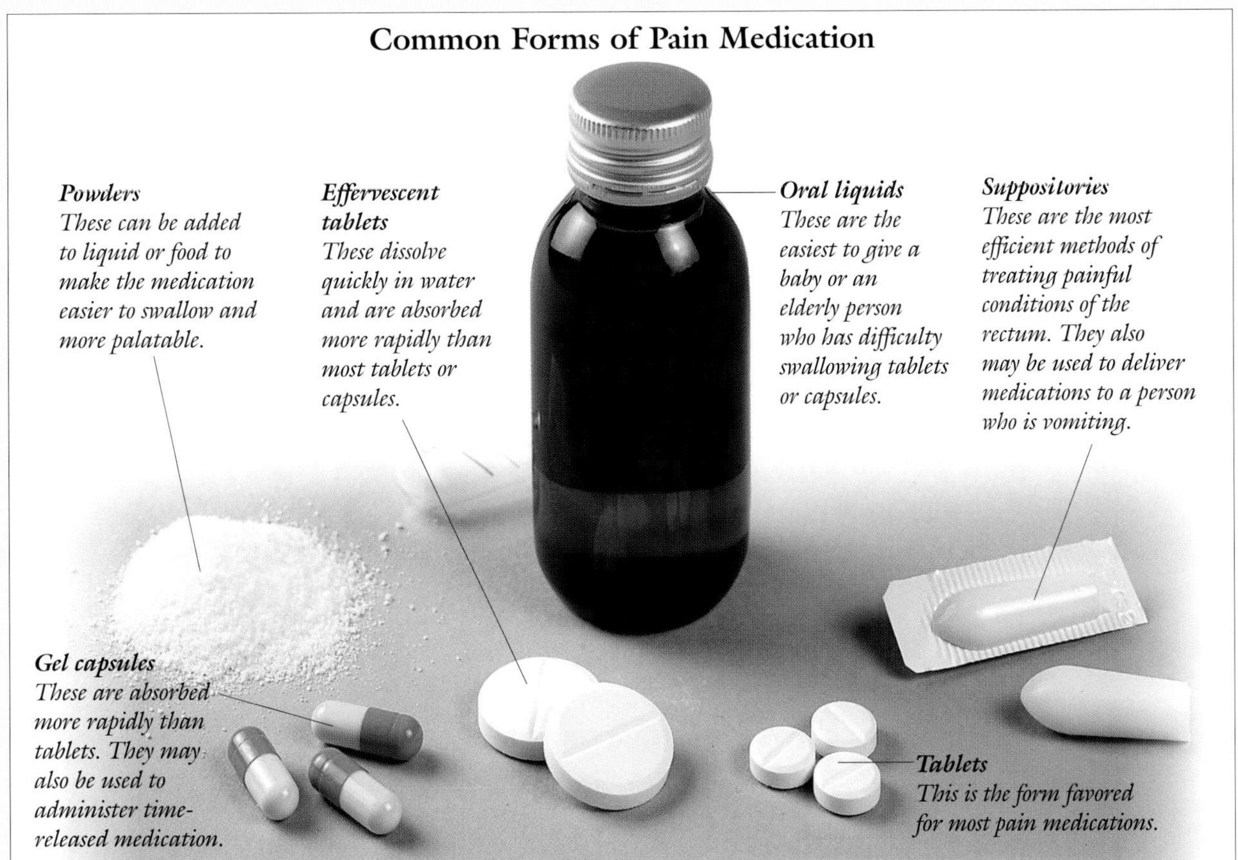
*Powders*
*These can be added to liquid or food to make the medication easier to swallow and more palatable.*
*Effervescent tablets*
*These dissolve quickly in water and are absorbed more rapidly than most tablets or capsules.*
*Oral liquids*
*These are the easiest to give a baby or an elderly person who has difficulty swallowing tablets or capsules.*
*Suppositories*
*These are the most efficient methods of treating painful conditions of the rectum. They also may be used to deliver medications to a person who is vomiting.*
*Gel capsules*
*These are absorbed more rapidly than tablets. They may also be used to administer time-released medication.*
*Tablets*
*This is the form favored for most pain medications.*

somewhat by taking aspirin with milk or other foods; coated or time-release aspirin—which is not dissolved until it reaches the small intestine—is gentler on the esophagus and stomach, but it takes longer to work than regular aspirin.

Regular-strength aspirin contains 325 mg of acetylsalicylic acid. The maximum adult dosage in a 24-hour period is 3 g. The usual adult dosage is one or two 325-mg tablets every four hours. Much higher doses may be prescribed for fever or rheumatoid arthritis, but prolonged high-dose use can lead to ringing in the ears (tinnitis) and hearing loss, as well as an increased risk of bleeding problems and stomach irritation. Aspirin should not be given to children under the age of 18 because of an increased risk of Reye's syndrome, a rare disease affecting the brain and liver. Health Canada also cautions prescribing ASA-like medications to children with influenza or chicken pox.

## NSAIDs—nonsteroidal anti-inflammatory drugs

Often promoted as stronger yet gentler alternatives to aspirin, NSAIDs are also prostaglandin inhibitors and work in much the same way as aspirin. While they carry many of the same risks as aspirin, most people can tolerate them better, often because they are taken in lower doses and, in some cases, work longer than aspirin. They are also more effective against bone and dental pain. These drugs include ibuprofen (Advil, Motrin, and others), naproxen (Naprosyn), and ketoprofen, (Orudis), which are sold in both OTC and prescription forms, and a number of prescription NSAIDs (see list of *Common NSAIDs,* right).

While NSAIDs all share certain characteristics and actions—for example, all fight inflammation and lower fever—they have subtle differences, and individual responses to them vary greatly. Thus, several may be tried before finding one that works well with minimal side effects. Dosages also vary; some are taken every four hours, others once or twice a day. So it's important to check the package insert and labels for specific dosage information. All should be taken with food to reduce the risk of stomach upset.

## Acetaminophen

Acetaminophen was introduced in the late 1970s as a nonprescription alternative to aspirin and other NSAIDs. Sold under the names of Tylenol, Atasol, Tempra, among others, acetaminophen comes in dosages of 325 and 500 mg. The usual adult dosage is 650 to 1000 mg every four hours, with a maximum of 4000 mg in a 24-hour period. No one knows exactly how it works, but many researchers theorize that acetaminophen somehow acts on the nerve endings to suppress the transmission of pain messages to the brain. It is effective against many types of pain and fever, but it does not reduce inflammation or pain from muscle contractions. Thus, acetaminophen is not as effective as aspirin and other NSAIDs in con-

### DON'T TAKE ASPIRIN IF…

Current Health Canada labeling requirements warn "consult a physician before taking aspirin during the last three months of pregnancy or when nursing." Aspirin is also contraindicated by people who:

- Have more than two alcoholic drinks a day, because of an increased risk of serious intestinal bleeding.
- Have a peptic ulcer, because it can worsen symptoms and increase the risk of intestinal perforation.
- Have asthma, because it can trigger an attack in people sensitive to salicylates.
- Have bleeding disorders or are taking a blood-thinning (anticoagulant) medication, because it increases the risk of bleeding.
- Have liver or kidney disease, because it can further damage these organs.

Talk to your doctor before taking aspirin if you are taking other medications.

### Common NSAIDs

| GENERIC NAME | BRAND NAME(S) |
|---|---|
| Diclofenac | Rx: Arthrotec, Voltaren |
| Diflunisal | Rx: Dolobid |
| Etodolac | Rx: Ultradol |
| Fenoprofen | Rx: Nalfon |
| Flurbiprofen | Rx: Ansaid, Froben |
| Ibuprofen | Rx and OTC: Advil, Motrin, Motrin IB, Novo-Profen |
| Indomethacin | Rx: Indocid |
| Ketoprofen | Rx: Orudis, Oruvail, Rhovail |
| Ketorolac | Rx: Toradol |
| Mefenamic acid | Rx: Ponstan |
| Nabumetone | Rx: Relafen |
| Naproxen | Rx: Anaprox, Naprosyn |
| Oxaprozin | Rx: Daypro |
| Piroxicam | Rx: Feldene |
| Sulindac | Rx: Apo-sulin, Clinoril, Nu-Sulindac |
| Tenoxicam | Rx: Mobiflex |
| Tolmetin | Rx: Tolectin |

trolling arthritis pain when the joints are inflamed; it may, however, be useful to relieve noninflammatory osteoarthritis, particularly in elderly patients. It does not increase the risk of Reye's syndrome, so it can be given to children.

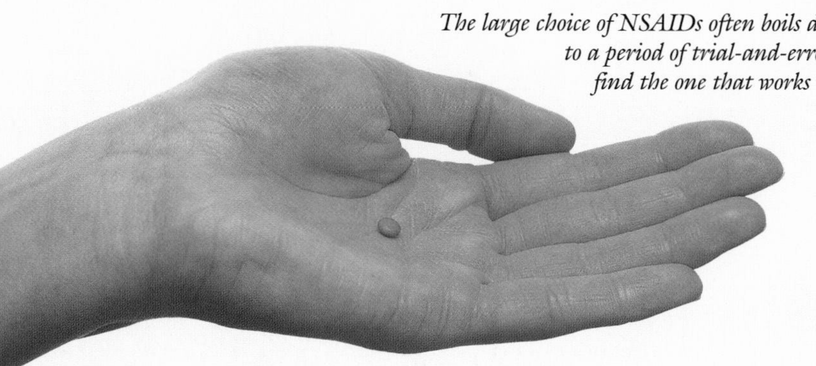

*The large choice of NSAIDs often boils down to a period of trial-and-error to find the one that works best.*

Because acetaminophen does not cause stomach upset and bleeding problems, it is often given to surgery patients who are at a high risk of developing ulcers and bleeding. Still, like all medications, it can cause serious side effects. Overdoses and prolonged usage, for example, can seriously damage the liver. Never take acetaminophen with alcohol; the combination can cause liver damage.

Acetaminophen is included in many combination pain products: Tylenol with codeine, Percocet. Acetaminophen may also be combined with antihistamines and/or decongestants as a remedy for colds and flu; some products combine acetaminophen and a muscle relaxant for relief of pain associated with muscle spasms. Check the labels of cold and flu remedies to see if they contain acetaminophen. An acetaminophen overdose can result in severe liver damage.

### $COX_2$ inhibitors

The newest class of non-narcotic painkillers, these drugs treat inflammation. Marketed under the brand names of Celebrex and Vioxx (with more drugs in the pipeline), they work by blocking an enzyme called cyclooxygenase-2, or $COX_2$ for short. This enzyme produces the prostaglandins that cause inflammation. Thus, $COX_2$ inhibitors work in much the same way as aspirin and other NSAIDs, but with a big difference: the earlier drugs indiscriminately work against other COX enzymes, which accounts for their diverse side effects. By selectively concentrating on the $COX_2$ enzymes, the new drugs counter inflammation just as well as NSAIDs, but are less likely to cause bleeding problems and stomach upset. Although some people taking Celebrex and Vioxx do experience intestinal upset, their numbers appear to be far fewer than the 30 percent who have problems taking other NSAIDs. However, they are much more expensive than NSAIDs, so if the older drugs are well tolerated, doctors generally do not recommend switching.

## NARCOTIC PAINKILLERS

These are the strongest—and most controversial—drugs used to control moderate to severe pain. Their controversy stems from the fact that their long-term use can cause physical dependence, in which withdrawal symptoms develop when the drugs are stopped. In the public mind, as well as legal circles, physical dependence is often equated with psychological dependence, or addiction, meaning that the person craves the drugs for reasons other than pain relief, such as getting "high." While the potential for abuse exists, studies show very few patients who take narcotic or opioid painkillers to ease severe, otherwise uncontrollable pain become addicted to them. An exception might be patients who have a history of substance abuse. Still, it is this fear of possible abuse that makes some doctors reluctant to prescribe these drugs.

Thus narcotics have been rarely considered the drugs of choice in

### GENERAL GUIDELINES THAT DOCTORS USE WHEN PRESCRIBING PAINKILLERS

1. **Determine cause and severity of pain.** This includes medical tests and careful evaluation and questioning of the patient.
2. **Try alternatives first.** Start with non-narcotic medications, and if they work without causing intolerable side effects, there's no need for a narcotic.
3. **Establish goals and a treatment plan.** This may include using a narcotic agent to control acute pain, and then tapering off the drug and substituting other painkillers as healing takes place.
4. **Have the patient agree to the plan.** It's important that the doctor and patient work as a team to use narcotic medications appropriately, not just "as required."
5. **Be realistic.** Even with the most potent narcotics, total pain relief may be impossible. In such cases, even moderate relief may make the difference between being incapacitated and being able to function.

## FIGHTING FIRE WITH FIRE

Capsaicin (Zostrix) is a modern version of an ancient folk remedy. The active ingredient in this topical cream is capsaicin, an oil extracted from hot chili peppers. It fights localized pain in two ways: It is a powerful counterirritant, and, when absorbed through the skin, it depletes the peripheral nerves of substance P, the chemical that carries pain messages along the nerves.

Capsaicin cream works best against pain originating near the body's surface, such as:

- Arthritic knees, fingers, and elbows.
- Nerve pain following an attack of shingles.
- Diabetic nerve pain in the legs.
- Pain from healed surgical wounds.

It should not be applied to broken or irritated skin. Always wash your hands immediately after applying to avoid getting it in your eyes and mouth, where it can damage delicate tissues. It can be applied several times a day and used long-term. At first, it can cause intense stinging, but this lessens with time. If capsaicin cream causes a rash or excessive skin irritation, stop using it. Store capsaicin cream away from light and extreme heat or cold, and keep it out of reach of children.

treating severe chronic pain, even when other medications or treatments do not work. This is an area where some pain specialists feel that the medications are often needlessly denied to patients who could benefit greatly from them, such as persons suffering from terminal cancer. This attitude may be changing in Canada, as a growing number of experts press for their wider use and new formulations reduce the risk of dependence. The Canadian Pain Society's Dr. Roman Jovey, and Dr. Brian Goldman, a pain expert from the University of Toronto, have campaigned for the responsible use of narcotic medications through numerous lectures and workshops.

In addition, the prescribing and dispensing of potent analgesics in Canada is subject to stringent federal laws. Improper use of these drugs can result in review by health care regulatory committees and disciplinary measures, if required. Although potent narcotic, or opioid, painkillers are primarily used in hospitals to relieve post-surgical pain, it is possible for cancer patients suffering from severe pain to benefit from supervised use of these products on an outpatient basis while at home.

### The opiates

These are drugs derived from opium, such as morphine and codeine. They are classified as narcotic agonist drugs, meaning that they work by binding to the opiate receptors in the brain and thereby blocking entry of pain messages. These drugs may be given by injection or as tablets. Morphine is also available in a liquid form and sustained-release capsules or tablets. Under some circumstances, such as following surgery or in easing the pain of terminal cancer, patients may be given a morphine pump to control their own dosages.

Codeine is classified as a "weak narcotic," and it is the first-choice drug when non-narcotic painkillers are not strong enough. It is often used in combination with acetaminophen or another non-narcotic painkiller, for example, to treat mild to moderate post-surgical pain.

### The opioids

These are synthetic narcotics; some are agonists and work in much the same way as morphine and other opium-derived drugs. They include oxycodone (Oxycontin), methadone, oxymorphone (Numorphan), meperidine (Demerol), hydromorphone (Dilaudid), and proproxyphene napsylate (Darvon-N). Other opioids, such as pentazocine (Talwin), are classified as antagonist narcotics because they block the effects of morphine at its receptor sites. These drugs will produce withdrawal symptoms if they are given to a narcotics addict. Like codeine, some of these opioids are combined with non-narcotic painkillers (see table of combinations on p 35).

### Side effects

In addition to their potential for dependency, narcotic medications have a number of possible side effects that limit their use. These include drowsiness, constipation, nausea and vomiting, dry mouth, mood changes, and possible seizures. In high doses, they depress breathing. Narcotic medications should

## THE PLACEBO EFFECT

The word "placebo" comes from the Latin term for "I will please." In medicine, placebos are sugar pills or other dummy medications or procedures. Any improvement that occurs when a person takes a placebo is attributed to psychological factors; the person is so convinced that the pill—or other therapies—will work, that, inexplicably, it does.

New drugs and procedures are usually tested against a placebo, in which neither the volunteers nor the researchers know who is getting the placebo and who is getting the real medication until the experiment ends. Invariably, 30 percent or more of those taking the placebo do, indeed, experience the desired effects. No one knows why placebos help so many people, but researchers increasingly believe the fact that they do confirms the brain's power to heal.

## Combinations of Narcotic and Non-narcotic Painkillers

| COMBINATION | BRAND NAME(S) |
|---|---|
| Codeine and acetaminophen | Atasol, Exdol, Tylenol with Codeine No. 1, 2, 3, and 4, Empracet |
| Codeine and ASA | 222, 282, 292 Tablets |
| Orphenadrine and ASA | Norgesic |
| Oxycodone and acetaminophen | Endocet, Oxycocet, Percocet, Percocet-Demi |
| Oxycodone and ASA | Endodan, Oxycodan, Percodan-Demi, Percodan |

never be taken with alcohol because both the alcohol and the drugs depress respiration, and they have a cumulative effect when taken together.

## OTHER PAINKILLERS

In addition to, or in place of, traditional analgesics, the arsenal of weapons against pain includes dozens of other medications. Some of these are used for a single disorder, such as drugs for migraine headaches. Others, such as antidepressants and anticonvulsants, may sometimes be used to relieve pain in addition to their primary purpose. Some painkillers are based on ancient herbal or folk remedies, while others are new medications developed with high-tech cloning or computer modeling techniques. Some of the more common examples follow.

### Topical medications

There are a number of topical creams, ointments, and gels that can ease arthritis and other localized pain. Some of these preparations contain ASA-like compounds, which are absorbed through the skin and work locally.

Topical medications produce a mild burning or stinging sensation, which lessens the perception of pain from injured tissue by sending out competing pain messages. Liniment and mustard oils are time-tested examples of such counterirritants. Newer ones are gentler to the skin and have become popular remedies to ease athletes' muscle soreness. One made from hot chili peppers is also a common arthritis remedy (see *Fighting Fire with Fire,* p 34).

### Corticosteroids

These are powerful anti-inflammatory medications; common generic examples include betamethasone, cortisone, hydrocortisone, and prednisone. They usually are not prescribed as painkillers, but they do relieve pain due to inflammation and swelling. They come in many forms: a corticosteroid is sometimes injected directly into a painful joint to relieve tendinitis, bursitis, or arthritis. Hydrocortisone cream is used to treat certain painful or inflammatory skin disorders; steroid suppositories may be prescribed for inflamed hemorrhoids and other painful rectal conditions. Systemic steroids are used to treat many conditions, but their use is limited by their long list of side effects: increased vulnerability to infections, bone loss, cataracts, high blood pressure, weight gain, easy bruising and skin thinning, among others.

### Antidepressants

To help ease chronic pain, even in the absence of depression, some doctors may prescribe antidepressant drugs such as amitriptyline (Elavil) or imipramine (Tofranil), perhaps with other painkillers, as an alternative to narcotic drugs. Unlike narcotic drugs, these drugs do not carry a risk of dependency; however, they can cause drowsiness, dizziness, nausea, dry mouth, blurred vision, and weakness.

### Muscle relaxants

These drugs are used mostly to relieve pain and spasms associated with muscle rigidity, such as those that occur in certain back problems and other neuromuscular disorders. These medications, which include chlorzoxazone (Parafon Forte, Extra Strength Tylenol Aches and Strains), cyclobenzapurine (Flexeril), methocarbamol (Robaxin), and orphenadrine (Norflex), should never be taken with alcohol or medications that depress the central nervous system. In rare cases, chlorzoxazone may cause liver damage.

### Anticonvulsants

These drugs, which are used to treat epilepsy, can also relieve chronic nerve pain, but how they work is unknown. Examples include phenytoin (Dilantin) and carbamazepine (Tegretol). Their side effects include drowsiness and mental confusion. Gabapentin (Neurontin), a newer anticonvulsant, tends to have fewer of these side effects.

### Stimulants

Certain stimulants, such as amphetamines, are sometimes prescribed along with narcotic painkillers to treat post-surgical and other severe pain. They do not act directly on the pain; instead, they ease related problems such as anxiety and the drowsiness that occurs with narcotic drugs. They are not indicated for long-term use because they, too, can be habit-forming. Caffeine, a milder stimulant, is added to a number of non-narcotic medications.

# Nondrug Approaches to Relief

*Electrical stimulation, whirlpool baths, hot and cold packs, massage, spinal manipulation, and posture correction—these are just a few of the drug-free pain therapies offered by doctors and alternative practitioners. And, if all else fails, surgery may be tried.*

## ELECTRICAL NERVE STIMULATION

### What is involved

This technique sends painless pulses of high-frequency, low-voltage electricity through the skin to disrupt the body's pain messages. The most common method is TENS (for transcutaneous electrical nerve stimulation), which uses a small, portable device and works through the peripheral nerves. Other, more advanced systems work directly on the spinal cord or the large nerves that arise from it.

Researchers do not fully understand why electrical stimulation eases pain, but there are at least two possible explanations. One is based on the gate theory, which holds that pain messages are transmitted to the brain along small, fast-acting C nerve fibers, which signal the pain gates to open and allow the stimuli to reach the brain. Larger A fibers, which are slower acting, signal the gates to close, blocking transmission of the pain messages. Some researchers believe that electrical stimulation activates the A fibers, thereby closing the pain gates. Another theory holds that electrical stimulation increases the release of endorphins, the body's natural painkillers.

### A little history

Ancient healers may not have understood electric nerve stimulation, but they nonetheless applied the basic principles. As early as 2000 BC, Egyptian physicians discovered that they could relieve pain by placing a live Nile electric fish, which has electric stingers similar to those of a catfish, over a patient's pain site.

### How it is used

In TENS, pairs of electrodes—similar to the ones of an ECG machine—are attached to the skin, either with a gel or as part of an adhesive pad. The electrodes are usually placed directly over or near where it hurts, although sometimes they may be attached on the opposite side of the body, or along the nerve pathway between the site of pain and the spinal cord. The electrodes are connected to wires on the TENS unit, a miniature generator about the size of a small camera or tape recorder that can be carried in a pocket or attached to a belt or another article of clothing. Controls on the generator allow the user to adjust the intensity and frequency of the electrical pulses.

A more complex system, known as Advanced Pain Therapies (APT) Neurostimulation, uses surgically implanted devices and works through the spinal cord rather than the peripheral nerves. There are two types of APT devices. The most commonly used one is about the size of a heart pacemaker and has a battery-operated pulse generator that is totally implanted under the skin, usually on the abdomen. One or more small wires, called leads, run from the generator to the desired place(s) along the spinal cord. The system can be adjusted and the intensity of the electrical impulses changed with an external computerized programming device. The other system has an implanted receiver and leads and an external battery-operated transmitter, which can be worn on a belt or carried in a pocket. An external antenna is taped to the skin over the implanted receiver. The user can change the settings, or turn the internal device off, by adjusting the external transmitter.

### When it is used

TENS and APT neurostimulation are used to treat both acute and chronic pain. Most often, they are employed by persons who suffer from chronic conditions that are not relieved by medications or by persons who cannot tolerate the painkilling drugs. Some users require almost continuous electrical stimulation; others wear a TENS device at night to help them sleep, and still others give themselves 30- or 45-minute treatments two or three times a day, or whenever pain develops.

### HEALING SOUND WAVES

Ultrasound is a technique that uses high-frequency sound waves to produce images of internal organs. It is not a specific pain therapy, but under some circumstances, it can provide relief. Also known as high-frequency heat therapy, ultrasound is employed by physical therapists to treat a variety of tendon and muscle injuries. Ultrasound machines have two modes: one sends out the sound waves in pulses and the other emits a continuous, or constant, flow of waves. The pulsing sound waves are used to treat acute injuries, such as a sprain, while the continuous mode is more useful in chronic conditions, such as arthritis. The constant flow of sound waves increases circulation and reduces inflammation.

*A warm whirlpool bath not only relieves back and muscle pain but also eases stress.*

Common conditions relieved by electrical stimulation include: chronic back pain, post-shingles nerve pain, circulatory problems such as Raynaud's syndrome, carpal tunnel syndrome and other repetitive stress injuries, cancer, fractures, phantom limb pain, and diabetic neuropathy. TENS is also used as an alternative (or in addition) to narcotic medications for post-surgical pain.

### Cautions and concerns

Persons who have heart pacemakers cannot use electrical nerve stimulation because the devices may interfere with each other. It also should not be used by patients with certain cardiac arrhythmias because it may alter the heartbeat. In addition, a TENS device should not be placed:

- Over the outer part of the neck because it can trigger muscle spasms of the larynx or pharynx.
- Directly on an incision or other unhealed wound.
- Atop areas with poor nerve function or numbness, which can result in skin burns because the user cannot tell if the intensity is set too high.
- Over the uterus of a pregnant woman unless it is being used to control pain during labor.

In general, electrical nerve stimulation is safe, but some people are allergic to the electrode gel or pad adhesives. Skin irritation sometimes develops; this can be prevented by frequent and proper cleaning of the electrode pads. As with any pain therapy, the relief may wear off as the body builds up a tolerance to the electrical stimulation.

## HYDROTHERAPY

### What is involved

Hydrotherapy uses water to relieve pain and treat disease—everything from muscle aches and arthritis to certain mental illnesses and stroke rehabilitation. Depending upon the type of hydrotherapy, the water may be hot or cold, fresh or mineral, still or pulsating, as in a shower massage.

### A little history

Hydrotherapy is older than recorded history; there is little doubt that our prehistoric ancestors recognized the soothing and cleansing properties of water. Archeologists have unearthed baths and water spas in ancient Greek and Roman ruins. Galen, the second-century Greek physician, incorporated elaborate forms of hydrotherapy into his hospital in Pergamum (now a part of Turkey). In more modern times, natural hot springs, or thermal spas, worldwide continue to draw millions of visitors a year who swear by the curative powers of these waters. Saunas, whirlpool baths, or hot tubs are now common home fixtures.

### How it works

Hydrotherapy works in many ways, depending upon its form and the condition being treated. In some forms, all or part of the body is immersed in a tub of hot or cold water. Others forms pour water over the body in a pulsating shower or gentle stream. Some call for boiling the water and exposing the person to the steam. In still others, a part of the body is wrapped in wet hot or cold compresses. Regardless of the form it takes, the goal of hydrotherapy is to harness the healing power of water. Immersion in warm water or sitting in a steam bath, for example, increases blood flow to the surface of the skin. Conversely, cold water or application of an ice pack reduces blood flow to the area, and

### WHAT'S YOUR PLEASURE—HOT OR COLD?

In general, hot water increases surface circulation. So to relieve the hand pain of Raynaud's syndrome, for example, try wrapping the hands in a wet hot towel or plunge them into a basin of warm water. Be careful that the water is not so hot that it causes tissue damage. Avoid handling ice cubes, a glass of cold water, or other cold objects.

Localized swelling, inflammation, and bruising are best treated with cold water or an ice pack, which helps divert blood flow from the injured area. In some conditions, such as inflammatory arthritis, alternating hot and cold works best. Don't be afraid to experiment to see what provides the best relief.

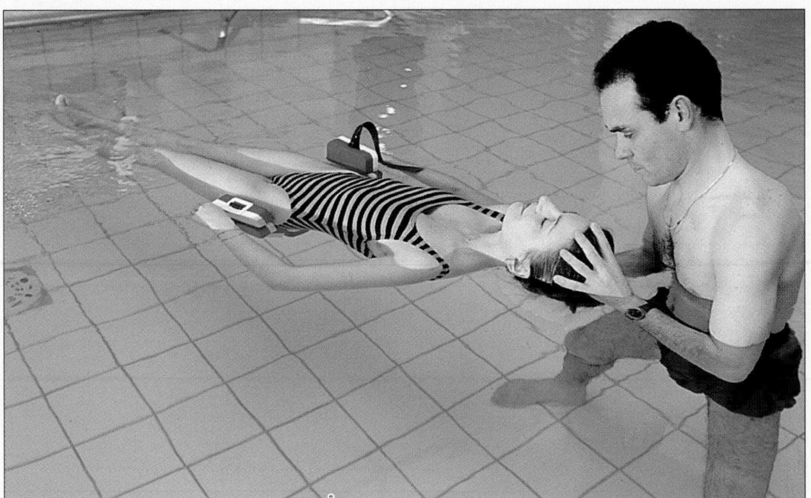

*Many physical and rehabilitation therapists use water exercise to improve muscle tone and coordination and to restore movement.*

can help reduce the swelling, inflammation, and pain that usually develop after a muscle injury.

It is easier to exercise when the body is immersed in water than on land because the water helps support body weight. As a result, people who are obese or have arthritis or other orthopedic disorders usually can work out when they are submerged in water without encountering the problems of exercising on land.

### When it is used

Specialists who employ hydrotherapy include physical therapists, athletic trainers, rehabilitation specialists, and mental health professionals. It is commonly used in the following situations:

- **To ease joint and muscle pain**—alternating hot and cold showers, thermal baths, whirlpool baths, shower massage, hot or cold packs or compresses.
- **To ease and prevent muscle cramps**—warm baths or showers to improve circulation; alternating hot and cold showers.
- **To increase joint mobility and improve muscle tone and strength**—exercising in water.
- **To relieve pain of hemorrhoids, anal fissures, and vaginal infections**—warm sitz baths.
- **To ease tension and calm anxiety**—warm baths, often combined with aromatherapy.
- **To relieve foot pain**—alternating hot and cold foot baths.
- **To relieve nasal and sinus congestion**—hot shower, steam bath, warm compresses on face, or simply inhaling steamy vapors.

### Cautions and concerns

People with high blood pressure, heart disease, diabetes, and severe varicose veins should not use saunas, hot tubs, and steam baths, which can raise blood pressure. Similarly, pregnant women should avoid these forms of hydrotherapy, as well as hot baths, because they can harm the fetus by raising the mother's core body temperature. However, swimming and exercising in cool water is fine during pregnancy.

Improperly maintained hot tubs can be a breeding ground for yeast and other microorganisms; change the water frequently, and use the proper disinfectants to kill mold.

## MASSAGE

### What is involved

Therapeutic massage uses systematic touch—stroking, kneading, pressing, thumping—to relieve pain, counter stress and muscle tension, and provide an enhanced sense of well-being.

In addition to various types of massage therapies, it is incorporated into treatments administered by physical therapists, athletic trainers and sports medicine specialists, rehabilitation physicians, osteopaths, chiropractors, aromatherapists, naturopaths, nurses, and other health professionals. Massage also can be self-administered or used to give physical pleasure or comfort to someone close to you.

### A little history

Massage is undoubtedly the oldest form of therapy; indeed, it is something that both humans and animals do almost instinctively to give comfort and ease pain. Every culture practices some sort of therapeutic massage; many of the techniques widely used today are described in the oldest medical texts. A Chinese text dating from 2700 BC advocates self-massage each morning to "protect against colds, keep the organs supple, and prevent minor ailments." Ayurveda, India's traditional system of medicine that dates to 1800 BC, uses therapeutic massage to apply healing aromatic oils and herbs to the skin. In more modern times, Swedish massage, a system developed in the 1830s by Per Henrik Ling, is widely practiced throughout the industrialized world.

### When it is used

Therapeutic massage is used for everything from relieving joint stiffness and muscle soreness to alleviating stress and treating specific medical disorders, such as lower back pain, migraine and muscle-tension headaches, and muscle cramps and spasms. The specific massage technique may vary according to the underlying problem and therapeutic goals. Some of the more popular forms of massage therapy, and conditions for which they may be used, include the following:

## A WORD OF WARNING

Almost anyone can learn simple massage techniques, but massage therapists need special training, so check out the credentials of any prospective therapist. The Canadian Massage Therapist Alliance (CMTA) is an alliance of professional associations of massage therapy in Canada. If you live in a province where massage therapists are unregulated, contact a professional association to obtain referrals or to discuss a therapist's credentials.

- **European or Swedish massage**, which employs various stroking movements, is used to treat back pain, muscle soreness, insomnia, and stress-related conditions.
- **Neuromuscular massage**, a type of deep massage in which the fingers are used to press upon individual muscles and pain trigger points, is used to break cycles of muscle spasms and to treat referred pain.
- **Pressure-point massage**, or acupressure, is used to alleviate pain and treat numerous ailments by pressing upon specific acupuncture points. A North American variation, called zone therapy or reflexology, concentrates on pressing or massaging specific points, usually on the hands and feet, to treat disorders in corresponding organs. For example, a sinus headache may be treated by pressing on the sinus pressure point located at the tip of the big toe.
- **Deep massage**, such as Rolfing, involves pummeling to manipulate deep connective tissue (fascia). It is used to improve movement by releasing knotted muscles and to relieve stress.
- **Shiatsu**, a Japanese technique that combines the philosophy of acupuncture with massage, involves pressing upon specific pressure points (tsubos) to restore the natural flow of vital energy (qi). It is used to treat numerous disorders, especially muscle-tension headaches.
- **Lymph drainage massage** uses rhythmic strokes to improve the flow of lymph and reduce swelling.
- **Water massage**, which combines hydrotherapy (see p 37) as well as massage, is used to treat various muscle aches and joint pain, such as that of osteoarthritis.

### Cautions and concerns

For the most part, massage is a safe and relaxing therapy. There are, however, times when it should not be used. For example, persons with osteoporosis or other disorders that weaken the bones should avoid Rolfing and other vigorous deep massage techniques that can cause fractures of fragile bones. Massage can be harmful in the following situations:

- Massaging an inflamed leg during a bout of phlebitis can dislodge a part of the clot and lead to a heart attack or pulmonary embolism if it reaches the heart or lungs.
- A massage during a fever can raise the temperature even more by increasing circulation.
- Massaging directly over a wound, incision, inflamed or infected area, bruise, or burn can slow healing and even worsen the underlying problem. Instead, gently massage the area adjacent to the injury to ease discomfort. Lastly, your shiatsu practitioner should know if you are taking medications, you are pregnant, or you have a long-term condition such as cancer, AIDS, or high blood pressure.

## MOVEMENT THERAPIES

### What is involved

Movement therapies use a combination of structured exercises and meditation or focused concentration to ease muscle tension, relieve pain, improve balance, increase strength, and promote emotional well-being. They range from the gentle, concentrated regimens of t'ai chi and yoga to the more difficult martial arts of karate and judo. While the movements of each are quite different, all incorporate meditation, deep breathing techniques, and some sort of spiritualism into their regimens.

### A little history

Most movement therapies originated in ancient Asian practices and philosophy. Yoga, for example, is thought to be about 5,000 years old, and it is described in the earliest Sanskrit medical texts of more than 2,000 years ago. The word "yoga" comes from the Sanskrit term for "yoke," or "to

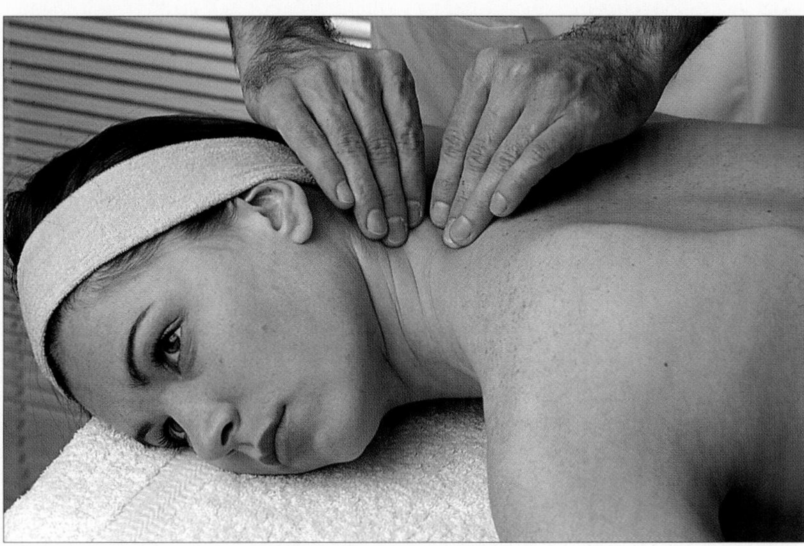

*Vigorous deep-massage techniques can be harmful to people with osteoporosis.*

join together," referring to its joining the human and universal spirits.

The roots of t'ai chi are thought to be almost as old as yoga, but are not as well documented. One legend credits its development to a Chinese monk who based it on the swift, subtle movements of a snake under attack by a bird. T'ai chi is closely related to the martial arts, but without the elaborate self-defense maneuvers and weapons. Today, judo, karate, and other martial arts are practiced mostly as a sport and means of self-defense, but in the past, they were important "weapons" of war and other conflicts.

*T'ai chi is practiced daily throughout China, especially by older city dwellers.*

### When they are used

Movement therapies have many applications. The meditation and focused concentration inherent in these disciplines are ideal for easing stress and relieving muscle tension. By improving muscle tone and posture, they can ease back pain. T'ai chi is often taught to stroke patients and the infirm elderly to improve balance and movement and to increase strength. Its gentle range-of-motion exercises are ideal for persons with arthritis, osteoporosis, and other painful joint or musculoskeletal problems. Many people who undertake t'ai chi and yoga become more physically active, which helps them lose excess weight and ease stress on aching arthritic joints.

Persons suffering from chronic pain may turn to yoga for help. The Yoga Association of Alberta offers workshops in using yoga to not only control pain, but also to attain a sense of serenity. People confined to bed or wheelchairs can learn certain karate and judo movements to improve muscle tone and circulation. Children who suffer from shyness often gain self-esteem by learning judo or karate.

### Cautions and concerns

Although yoga looks easy, some of the movements are actually very difficult, and require expert instruction, time, and much practice to master. There are also many types of yoga. Start by taking yoga classes from a qualified instructor (yogi) and gradually work up to the more complicated movements. Stop if a particular movement or position produces sharp pain or worsens existing pain.

Learning one of the martial arts also requires the help of an experienced teacher and much practice. When done improperly, karate or judo throws, falls, and other movements can cause injury.

## DON'T MOVE: HOW IMMOBILIZATION HELPS

While movement therapies might be just what the doctor ordered for some painful conditions, in others, immobilization prevails.

- **A neck brace** is often prescribed after a whiplash or another neck injury to avoid further injury and allow healing.
- **Casts** are used to allow broken bones to heal and to relieve pain.
- **Immobilization with an elastic bandage** eases pain and helps reduce swelling of a sprain or partially torn tendon.
- **Wrist braces** can alleviate carpal tunnel syndrome.
- **A knee brace** is worn while torn or surgically repaired tendons heal.

Whenever using immobilization, however, it's important to follow a doctor's instructions. Prolonged immobilization can lead to weakness and loss of muscle tone; premature removal of the immobilizing device can allow further injury.

## NEUROSURGERY FOR PAIN

### What is involved

If pain is due to a compressed nerve, as might be the case with a herniated spinal disk, surgery can often help the underlying problem. However, when other pain therapies fail to be effective, neurosurgical procedures, such as implants of neurostimulator devices or medication pumps, may provide better analgesia.

Other, more drastic neurosurgical procedures call for interrupting the pain nerve pathway by destroying (ablating) a key nerve. This is usually the treatment of last resort, used only when medications and other therapies fail. The most common ablative operation is called a cordotomy, in which a lesion is created either in the tract of the spinal cord that leads to the thalamus or at the spinal root of a sensory nerve. This prevents pain messages from entering the spinal cord and moving on to the brain.

### A little history

Ambroise Paré, a sixteenth-century French surgeon, discovered that, by severing certain nerves, he could eliminate chronic hand and arm pain. But the possible side effects of paralysis and referred pain were often worse than the original problem. Although these problems still limit the use of nerve ablation, new approaches have made the operation safer and more effective. One uses a technique called percutaneous stereotactic radiofrequency thermal rhizotomy—a procedure that applies heat very precisely to a nerve root to destroy it. This approach prevents the transmission of nerve messages without (in most cases) causing permanent paralysis, although there may be some uncomfortable numbness and altered sensation.

### When it is used

In general, neurosurgery is used only after other pain treatments prove inadequate. An exception might be when the pain is due to a compressed nerve. For example, the severe facial pain known as trigeminal neuralgia is sometimes caused by compression of the nerve root by a blood vessel. In such cases, surgery to reposition the blood vessel can cure the problem. Otherwise, stereotactic thermal surgery may be tried.

A cordotomy may be done to relieve severe, localized cancer pain. Less often, it is used to alleviate incapacitating pain from other causes.

Localized nerve ablation is not done very often, but some recent studies have identified areas in which it may prove useful. For example, a group of Taiwanese researchers reported encouraging results for a procedure designed to help women who suffer from severe menstrual pain that is not relieved by medications. The operation—laparoscopic presacral neurectomy—helped 80 percent of the 34 women who underwent it. A small incision is made near the navel, and a viewing tube (laparoscope) is inserted. The surgeon then manipulates tiny instruments through the laparoscope to ablate the nerve.

### Cautions and concerns

Numbness and paralysis are two common complications of nerve ablation, although their incidence and severity have been reduced by newer, more precise techniques. Following stereotactic surgery to relieve trigeminal neuralgia, for example, there may be numbness in the area of the pain, but paralysis rarely occurs.

Unfortunately, pain neurosurgery doesn't always work or the relief is only temporary. Following a cordotomy procedure, about 90 percent of patients experience immediate relief, but after six months, the figure drops to 50 percent and falls to 40 percent after a year. In addition, about 7 to 10 percent of patients develop mirror pain on the opposite side of the body, and 2 percent experience a persistent burning pain that is often worse than the original problem.

#### BLOCK THAT NERVE

Intractable pain often can be controlled by nerve blocks—the injection of a local anesthetic or a drug such as alcohol or phenol, which destroys the offending nerve. As with other types of nerve ablation, these are considered treatments of last resort, and are most commonly used to ease intractable pain in patients suffering from terminal cancer.

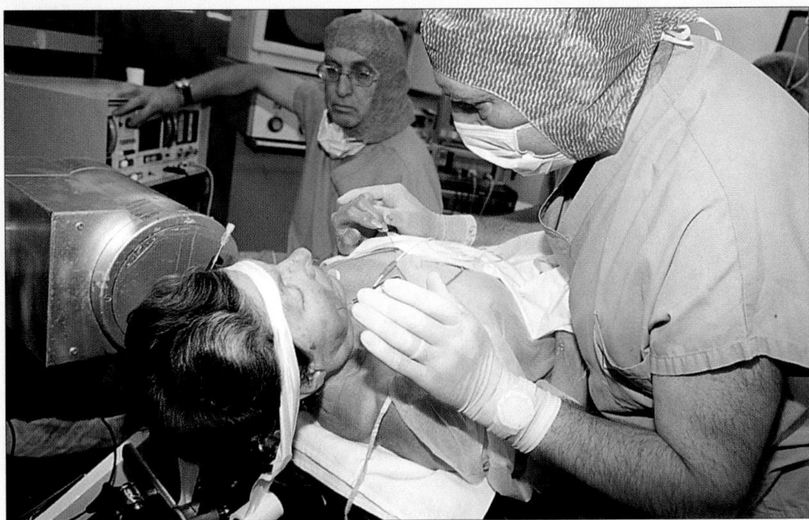

*Unrelenting facial nerve pain may be eliminated by thermal neurosurgery.*

## PHYSICAL THERAPY

### What is involved

Physical therapy covers all aspects of movement and pain control—everything from working with stroke patients and accident victims to regain mobility to helping patients with back pain or athletes overcome chronic tendinitis. Most physical therapists work with doctors, chiropractors, osteo-paths, or rehabilitation specialists, although a growing number are establishing free-standing practices. They employ many techniques—massage, hot and cold packs, hydrotherapy, weight training, exercise—tailored to meet individual needs.

## A little history

Physical therapy grew out of rehabilitation medicine and, until the fitness boom of the 1970s and '80s, most of their work was devoted to helping patients who had suffered a stroke or serious accident, or who had a crippling disease, such as polio or arthritis. As more health professionals have come to recognize the importance of exercise in health and longevity, physical therapy has expanded into preventive medicine. And as our population ages, the demand for physical therapy is growing.

## When it is used

In general, physical therapy is divided into three broad categories:

- **Rehabilitative medicine**, in which physical therapists work with patients to overcome a long-term painful or debilitating condition, such as a stroke, spinal cord injury, or chronic back pain. In this role, the therapists may see patients almost daily for an extended period. Increasingly, physical therapy is an important part of arthritis treatment, in which the therapist works with patients to increase mobility, overcome pain, and perform daily tasks.
- **Short-term treatment programs**, in which the therapy is aimed at treating a specific problem, such as acute back pain, tendinitis, rotator-cuff shoulder problems, and numerous other musculoskeletal problems. Therapists may also work with patients recovering from joint-replacement surgery, coronary bypass surgery, fractures, or other problems that entail short-term disability.
- **Preventive medicine**, in which the therapy is aimed at improving overall health and preventing future problems. Many organized weight-loss programs employ physical therapists to help sedentary obese patients embark on an exercise program. Other areas in which physical therapists are being used include preventive cardiology, weight-training programs to prevent osteoporosis, and diabetes treatment centers.

## Cautions and concerns

Almost anyone with a musculoskeletal problem can benefit from physical therapy. The only precaution needed is to make sure the physical therapist has been trained to treat the particular problem at hand. Just as medicine has become increasingly specialized, so too has physical therapy. Thus, a therapist trained to work with athletes and other basically healthy people may lack the expertise to work with a stroke patient or a paraplegic.

# POSTURE CORRECTION THERAPIES

## What is involved

Faulty posture is at the root of many pain syndromes, especially of the neck and back. Anyone who has spent hours hunched over a computer keyboard, cradling a telephone against a shoulder, or bending over to tend a garden knows that it doesn't take long to develop stiffness and tingling or shooting pains in the neck and back. If one's job involves prolonged and repeated abnormal postures, the resulting muscle tension, neuromuscular imbalances, and pain can become chronic. Posture correction therapies, which include the Alexander Technique, the Feldenkrais Method, Hellerwork, and the Munakata Technique, all concentrate on teaching persons to identify and correct posture-related problems.

## A little history

The Alexander Technique, one of the oldest and most widely practiced posture therapies, was developed in the late 1800s by F. Mathias Alexander, an Australian actor who was losing his voice. While practicing in front of a triple mirror, he noticed that he often assumed tense and abnormal postures of his head, neck, and torso. When he corrected these postures, his voice returned to normal, and in 1908, he published a pamphlet on posture correction. He soon attracted a following, and the Alexander Technique is now taught worldwide.

A number of new posture therapies have emerged since the 1970s. The Feldenkrais Method, developed by a Russian-born Israeli educator, Moshe Feldenkrais, is based on two principles: awareness through movement, which involves pleasurable exercises, and functional integration, in which the therapist uses touch and passive movement to improve function. Hellerwork, developed by Joseph Heller, a former Rolfing therapist, is based on an 11-session course that stresses movement re-education to perform everyday tasks, such as sitting and walking.

The Munakata Technique, developed by a Japanese/American physical therapist, Miyoka Munakata, teaches back exercises to correct neuromuscular imbalances that lead to faulty posture and other exercises to strengthen supporting muscles.

### CRANIOSACRAL THERAPY

This technique, founded in 1977 by an osteopath, Dr. John Upledger, and Ernest Retzlaff, Ph.D., concentrates on soft tissue and body fluids rather than correcting bone alignments. The practitioner uses touch (palpation) to locate and treat dysfunctions of the craniosacral system, which includes the head, spinal column, and sacrum. Problems are diagnosed by feeling for "pulses" of the circulating cerebrospinal fluid, and then corrected by applying slight pressure (about the weight of a nickel) to various areas to re-establish a normal flow of fluid and energy through the craniosacral system. Dr. Upledger claims great success in treating chronic pain, migraine headaches, Ménière's disease, learning disorders, and many other conditions in which there is no identifiable structural problem. Many doctors, however, attribute any success of craniosacral therapy to the placebo effect (see p 34).

### When it is used

Posture correction therapies are most useful in helping persons overcome chronic back and neck problems, stiffness, and muscle soreness that stem from stooping and other abnormal postures. Some, such as the Alexander and Munakata Techniques, are also used to treat specific musculoskeletal problems, such as mild scoliosis and spinal arthritis. There is also growing interest in the preventive value of posture correction. For example, people who are vulnerable to repetitive stress injuries, such as computer operators and pianists, are often helped by a few sessions with an Alexander Technique instructor. Groups of musicians, including the New York Philharmonic Orchestra, also employ Alexander Technique instructors to prevent back and neck problems commonly encountered by violinists and other performers.

These various posture-correction techniques are taught by certified instructors. Before enrolling in a program, ask the instructor about his or her training and credentials.

### Cautions and concerns

At first, posture correction exercises may produce stiffness and soreness as under- or misused muscles are retrained. But this soon passes, and when properly taught, there should be no complications from posture correction therapy. An exception might be if a person has a ruptured spinal disk, which may be worsened by some movements.

## SPINAL MANIPULATION

### What is involved

Spinal manipulation involves energetic hands-on therapy aimed at correcting malalignments of the spinal vertebrae. It is practiced mainly by chiropractors and osteopaths, although some physical and massage therapists also employ some of the techniques. The objective of the manipulation is to improve the flow of nerve impulses.

### A little history

Ancient healers manipulated the back to relieve pain in various parts of the body. But it wasn't until the late 1890s that spinal manipulation emerged as a distinct and systematic medical discipline. In 1895, a self-taught, Ontario-born healer named Daniel David Palmer was credited with curing a patient's deafness by manipulating a displaced vertebra. Over the next few years, Palmer refined his spinal treatments, and established the Palmer Infirmary and Chiropractic Institute in Davenport, Iowa, to teach the technique and offer treatments. Despite past opposition from mainstream physician groups, chiropractic is now licensed in 10 provinces. Some provincial health plans partially cover treatments. Indeed, chiropractic is now a standard treatment for back and neck pain, as well as certain other pain syndromes. In addition, chiropractors may use electrical nerve stimulation, provide nutrition counseling, and practice acupuncture and other alternative therapies.

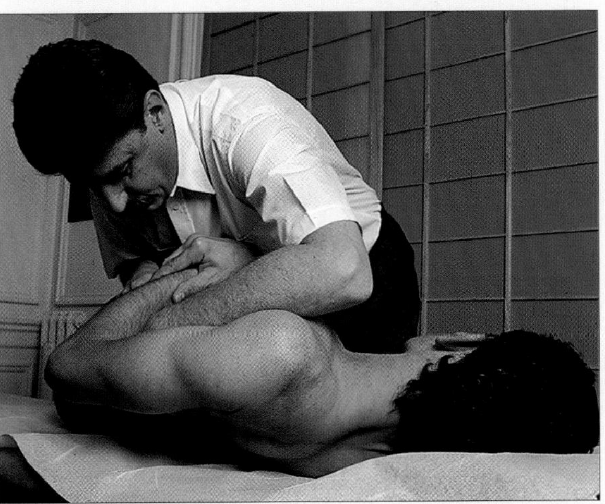

*Chiropractors and osteopaths use forceful manipulation to correct spinal malalignment.*

Osteopathy also employs spinal and joint manipulation to treat pain. It was developed in the late 1800s by a country doctor, Andrew Taylor Still, to overcome what he felt were shortcomings of conventional medicine. In 1892, he founded the American School of Osteopathy in the U.S. In Canada, diplomas in osteopathy are offered in Montreal and Toronto. There are only a handful of practicing doctors of osteopathy (DO) in Canada. The overriding philosophy is that all of the body's organ systems form an interrelated whole, and a problem in one organ affects the whole body.

### When it is used

Most people who seek spinal manipulation do so because of acute or chronic pain, especially of the lower back. Chiropractors and osteopaths treat a variety of other problems, including stress-related headaches, sports and overuse joint and muscle injuries, carpal tunnel syndrome, and persistent vague syndromes, such as chronic fatigue. Studies show that manipulation can relieve such conditions, but the benefits are often temporary.

### Cautions and concerns

While spinal manipulation has its place in medical practice, it is not the cure-all that many of its practitioners claim. Be wary of a chiropractor who makes extravagant claims for curing cancer, diabetes, and other serious organic diseases. Also, chiropractic treatments are safe for most people, but there are exceptions; persons who have osteoporosis and other disorders characterized by weak or easily fractured bones should not undergo vigorous spinal manipulation.

# Mind/Body Therapies

*A growing body of research indicates that the brain is instrumental in and closely linked to how well the immune system functions. And since the brain processes all pain messages, it makes sense that enlisting this organ should be a first step in fighting chronic pain.*

## BIOFEEDBACK TRAINING

### How it works

Biofeedback training teaches a person to at least partially control bodily functions that are ordinarily involuntary, such as the pulse rate, blood pressure, skin temperature, and brain-wave patterns. During a typical training session, a person goes into a quiet, dimly lit room where there are no other distractions. Electrical sensors are attached to certain parts of the body; these transmit specific bodily responses to a monitor, which then gives off visual or audio responses. For example, a person who suffers from painful muscle spasms will be instructed to concentrate on relaxing the tensed muscles. As the muscles relax, the monitor gives off one type of signal. If the muscles tense, however, the monitor sends out a different signal.

The patient learns how to control pain by trying to elicit the desired signals from the monitor. Eventually, the person is able to alter the bodily response without the aid of an electronic monitor. So at the first sign of a tense muscle the person can call upon the biofeedback technique to prevent painful spasms.

### A little history

The first biofeedback studies were conducted in the 1950s by researchers studying the pattern of brain waves during sleep. They discovered that by using an electroencephalograph (EEG), a machine that records brain waves, volunteers could learn to control certain brain waves and achieve a state of relaxed alertness. Soon after, researchers at the Menninger Foundation in Kansas taught patients how to self-treat migraine headaches by redirecting some blood flow from the constricted vessels in the scalp to their hands.

### When it is used

Biofeedback training has a growing number of medical applications. It is widely used to treat chronic pain, especially back pain, headaches, and fibromyalgia. It may also help patients with cancer, arthritis, and painful nerve disorders reduce their dosages of pain medications. In some instances, biofeedback training is combined with other mind/body therapies, such as self-hypnosis and guided imagery.

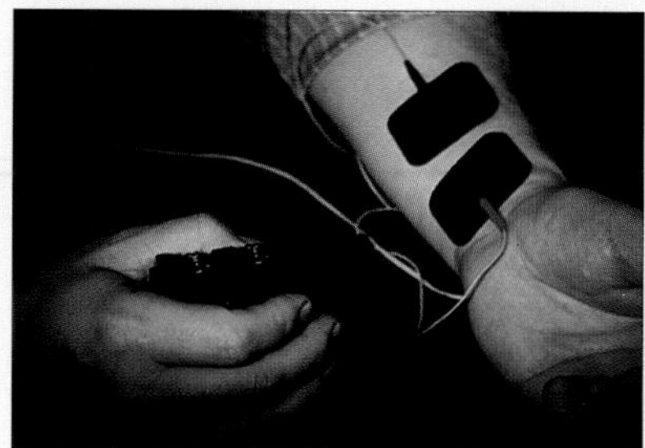

*Biofeedback training allows persons to monitor and alter certain automatic bodily functions to reduce pain.*

Although the principles are the same, the form of biofeedback varies according to the underlying problem. The most common types are summarized below.

- **EMG** (for electromyograph) biofeedback uses sensors that measure the electrical activity of the muscles underlying the skin. It is especially helpful in treating persons with painful muscle spasms, such as wryneck, chronic neck and lower back pain, facial and jaw pain from temporomandibular joint (TMJ) dysfunction, and headaches.
- **Temperature** biofeedback monitors minute changes in skin temperature. This type of treatment is used to treat painful circulatory problems, such as Raynaud's disease, a condition marked by reduced blood flow to the hands when they are exposed to cold. It is also used to treat migraine headaches and to help control stress.
- **EEG** biofeedback measures changes in brain waves (see *A little history,* above). It is used to treat

## BIOFEEDBACK: CHANGING FOR THE BETTER

Behavior modification, an important component of many mind/body therapies, is often difficult to accomplish through willpower alone. This is one area in which biofeedback is proving to be a highly useful tool. Researchers have demonstrated that biofeedback can help alter some of the harmful aspects of Type A behavior, especially feelings of anger and hostility. As part of a heart attack prevention program, researchers have used biofeedback to help high-risk Type A personality types alter their behavior. Similarly, researchers at pain clinics have found that biofeedback training can help patients overcome behavioral responses, such as tooth grinding and jaw clenching in persons with TMJ dysfunction, that contribute to chronic pain.

anxiety, insomnia, and seizure disorders; researchers are investigating its potential in treating Parkinson's disease and other neurological problems.

- **Galvanic skin response** (GSR) biofeedback measures the activity of the skin's sweat glands. Also called electrodermal response biofeedback, it is used to treat anxiety and stress-related disorders.
- **Vital function** biofeedback monitors changes in the heartbeat, blood pressure, and respiration. It is used to teach patients how to lower high blood pressure and perhaps short-circuit cardiac arrhythmias.

### Cautions and concerns

Biofeedback training itself is safe. Caution is needed, however, when buying biofeedback monitors for home use. To find a therapist, ask your doctor. Learn biofeedback techniques from a qualified instructor, who can also advise you on where to find reliable equipment.

## GUIDED IMAGERY

### How it works

Guided imagery is based on the premise that mental pictures, or visualization, can be used to overcome pain and heal the body. The idea is to create a strong mental image of one's disease or symptom, and then to manipulate the image to gain control over it. For example, a patient with chronic back pain may be instructed to visualize his pain as a bright red light. Then he can reduce the pain by either learning how to make it dimmer or transform it into a soothing blue light. A number of studies have found that guided imagery can strengthen the body's immune defenses and have an impact on healing. While guided imagery cannot cure cancer, AIDS, and other serious diseases, it may help bolster the effectiveness of other treatments and lessen pain and other symptoms.

### A little history

The principles of guided imagery are age-old; shamans and other native healers have long called upon mental visions in healing ceremonies. But as a structured medical therapy, guided imagery is relatively new, bolstered by recent research confirming the mind/body connection in illness and healing. In his book *Love, Medicine and Miracles* and other writings on the mind and healing, Dr. Bernie S. Siegel has emphasized the power of guided imagery in activating the body's immune system to fight AIDS, cancer, and other diseases.

*A number of studies have shown that guided imagery—focusing, for example, on a mental image of a favorite place or landscape—can strengthen the immune system.*

### When it is used

Many cancer and AIDS centers now teach guided imagery to their patients as a device to help control pain and as a complementary therapy to other conventional treatments. It is also taught in pain clinics, and many doctors and psychiatrists also use it to empower patients to help heal themselves. It can also be self-taught by using instructions available in books or on videotapes.

Many healthy people, especially athletes, actors, and ballet dancers, use guided imagery to improve performance. For example, a number of Olympic skaters have described how they "practice" a certain maneuver over and over in their minds until they can actually execute it flawlessly during competition by calling upon their mental images.

### Cautions and concerns

There are no hazards from guided imagery itself. The only danger would be if it were used as a substitute for, rather than an adjunct to, necessary medical treatment.

## HYPNOSIS

### How it works

Hypnosis is an altered state of consciousness in which a person's entire attention is focused on a single thought or image. Contrary to popular belief, persons under hypnosis are not asleep; they are fully awake, but largely unaware of what is going on around them. Therapeutic hypnosis is usually induced by a trained hypnotist who uses the power of suggestion to help the patient relax and set aside all other thoughts except the goal of the therapy, such as diminishing and eliminating pain. Hypnosis cannot be used to make persons engage in behavior they would otherwise avoid, nor can it enable a person to demonstrate abilities he does not possess.

## HOW TO HYPNOTIZE YOURSELF

People who are capable of entering a hypnotic state usually can learn to hypnotize themselves. One method, called autogenic training (AT), uses a series of mental exercises designed to make the limbs feel heavy and warm—a common technique used by hypnotherapists. Other systems use counting backward, focusing on a specific object that is just above the line of sight, or mental imagery to induce a hypnotic state.

Regardless of the device used, all require that you be comfortably seated and taking deep, even breaths. At first, you may need to consciously tense and then relax each muscle group, starting with the hands and arms, then the face and neck, moving down the body. By the time you reach your toes, you should feel calm and fully relaxed. To confirm that you are under hypnosis, tell yourself that when you pinch your hand, you will not feel any pain. If you are in a hypnotic state, you should feel a slight pressure but no pain. You are now ready to begin your hypnotic suggestions—for example, "The pain in my back is moving down, down, down. It is now leaving my feet and I am no longer in pain." To come out of the hypnosis, tell yourself to count from one to five. "With each number, I am feeling more alert." Finally, at the count of five, the hypnosis is lifted, and you should feel calm, rested, and fully aware of your surroundings.

With practice, most people can learn to induce hypnosis by simply repeating a specific word or visualizing a certain image.

Hypnosis can, however, induce hallucinations, such as seeing submerged images from the past or hearing nonexistent music.

### A little history

Ancient healers recognized that some patients could be put into a trancelike state. The term "mesmerizing" derives from an eighteenth-century Vienna physician, Franz Mesmer, who practiced a form of hypnotism that he called "animal magnetism." He credited his "miracle cures" to magnetic forces that he could realign with metal rods and soothing words while his patients were hypnotized.

Until the 1950s, doctors regarded hypnosis as more of a nightclub act than a legitimate medical therapy. Then psychiatrists demonstrated that it had a legitimate place in treating patients suffering from anxiety, phobias, traumatic amnesia, multiple personalities, and various other mental illnesses. Soon thereafter, pain clinics adopted hypnotherapy as another treatment for chronic pain. Today, it is widely used for a variety of ailments.

### When it is used

Hypnosis may be used alone or in conjunction with guided imagery, biofeedback, and relaxation techniques in controlling chronic pain. Under hypnosis, patients are made acutely aware of various bodily sensations, including pain, and ways to diminish or eliminate them. At first, the hypnosis is induced by a trained hypnotherapist. The patients are then taught self-hypnosis. Dr. David Segal and fellow researchers at Stanford University have found that women with advanced breast cancer who practice self-hypnosis not only need less pain medication, but they also survive longer than their counterparts who don't use the technique.

A number of dentists employ hypnosis for patients who cannot tolerate anesthesia or who suffer from dental phobia. It can also be used to safely reduce the pain of childbirth or following surgery. Psychiatrists, law-enforcement officers, and others often use hypnosis to uncover hidden memories or to treat amnesia victims. Hypnosis is also a useful tool in behavior modification; for example, it is used to help people stop smoking or overcome eating disorders.

### Cautions and concerns

Because the mechanisms of hypnosis are poorly understood, there is no way of predicting whether or not it will work. Not everyone is capable of being hypnotized, and even among those who can be, not all will respond to hypnotic suggestions.

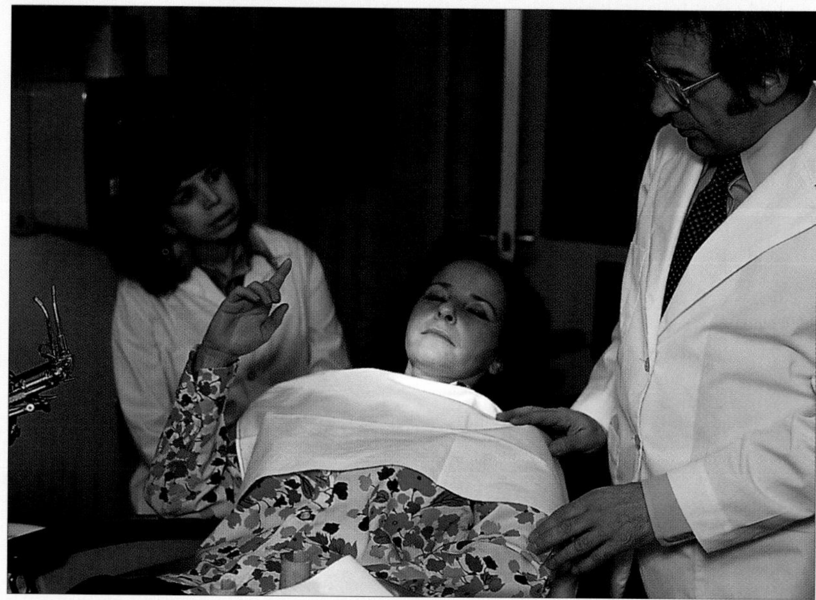

*Dentists often use hypnosis for patients who cannot tolerate chemical anesthetics.*

## RELAXATION THERAPIES

### How they work

Relaxation therapies are designed to help us cope with the many stressors that we encounter each day. In our evolutionary past, we developed a protective fight-or-flight response—an automatic reaction that causes stress hormones from the adrenal glands to flood the body and put us on full-alert. Blood pressure rises, the heart speeds up, and muscles tense, preparing us to flee from what the body perceives as danger. While we no longer confront the dangers of our cave-dwelling ancestors, our bodies continue to react as if we do. Instead of man-eating tigers, we become stressed out over everything from money worries and job pressures to traffic jams and other minor annoyances. Consequently, every day all of us are subjected to many different stressors, both external and internal, physical and emotional, that trigger a fight-or-flight response.

All this stress has a profound effect on our physical and mental states, resulting in fatigue, muscle strain, headaches, back and neck pain, digestive disorders, and an increased vulnerability to serious illnesses, including heart disease and cancer. While it's impossible to remove all stress from our lives, it is possible to develop better coping strategies.

### TAKE A DEEP BREATH AND...

Various breathing exercises can be highly effective relaxation techniques, and concentrating on breathing is a diversionary tactic to alleviate both acute and chronic pain. The type of breathing exercise varies according to the type of pain.

- **During childbirth.** Between contractions, take slow, deep breaths, inhaling through the nose and slowly exhaling by breathing out through slightly pursed lips. At the first twinge of a contraction, change to rapid, shallow panting. As the contraction subsides, switch back to the slow, deep breathing.
- **Acute colicky pain or muscle spasms.** The waves of intense pain that characterize kidney stones, gallbladder attacks, appendicitis, pancreatitis, and other acute illnesses can be somewhat alleviated by practicing deep breathing. Just the tense anxiety of anticipating the next wave of pain makes it even more intense. Deep breathing fosters relaxation and quells anxiety. Concentrating on breathing rather than anticipating the next wave of pain helps lessen its impact when it finally hits.
- **Chronic pain.** To help control low back pain and other chronic pain, try combining deep breathing exercises and meditation. The deep breathing promotes relaxation and helps crowd out distracting thoughts, thereby increasing the effectiveness of meditation in controlling the pain.

*Deep breathing may be combined with yoga or meditation to increase its effectiveness in overcoming pain.*

### A little history

Some relaxation therapies, such as meditation, have been used for centuries, mostly by Eastern healers or medical systems, such as Ayurveda, India's 5,000-year-old medical tradition. Western doctors have only recently come to recognize the role of stress in health. In the 1960s, two researchers, Drs. Thomas H. Holmes and Richard H. Rahe, devised a scale that ranks the health impact of 100 different stressors. They demonstrated that the more stressful the events, the greater the likelihood of developing a serious illness.

In the mid-1970s, Dr. Herbert Benson, a Harvard cardiologist, coined the term "relaxation response" to describe the health benefits of relaxation achieved through meditation. Today, relaxation therapies are an integral part of treatment for numerous stress-related disorders, including high blood pressure, headaches, and chronic pain syndromes.

### When they are used

Meditation and other relaxation therapies are widely used in stress management programs, pain clinics, and cardiac rehabilitation programs. In pain management, relaxation is often combined with other therapies, such as hydrotherapy, biofeedback, and hypnosis. In addition to pain management, relaxation therapies are employed as a complementary add-on in the treatment of such conditions as anxiety, asthma, high blood pressure, and angina. They are also useful in easing withdrawal symptoms when quitting smoking or treating drug addiction.

### Cautions and concerns

Although meditation and other relaxation therapies have their place in the treatment of many medical disorders, they should be used as an adjunct to, not a substitute for, medication to lower blood pressure or to stop an asthma attack. Always check with your doctor before altering any prescribed medication regimen.

# Alternative Therapies

*Although medications—prescription and over-the-counter—remain the No. 1 weapon against pain, there are major drawbacks: They don't always work and they can cause serious side effects. No wonder there's mounting interest in alternative approaches to controlling pain.*

## INTEGRATIVE MEDICINE COMES INTO ITS OWN

Until recently, most practitioners of Western, science-based medicine dismissed alternative medicine as a collection of unproved remedies with little or no value beyond the placebo effect. But this attitude is changing as a growing number of physicians and patients alike use a combination of alternative and conventional, or orthodox, therapies. Indeed, the preferred term for alternative therapies is now complementary or integrative medicine.

Much of this integrative approach has been pioneered in pain clinics, where doctors and other health-care professionals have a long tradition of fighting intractable chronic pain with unorthodox approaches. In addition to the nondrug and mind/body approaches discussed earlier, many pain clinics offer acupuncture, music therapy, nutritional and herbal remedies, therapeutic magnets, and even healing touch.

Of course, the rise of integrative medicine has been spearheaded by the patients themselves, who are often more willing than their doctors to try unproved remedies. According to a 1997 CTV/Angus Reid poll, more than 4 out of 10 Canadians (42 percent) reported using alternative medicines and practices. A 1999 national survey estimated that more than 3 million Canadian have tried acupuncture at least once. And in Quebec, nearly a quarter of the population have visited an alternative health practitioner (excluding acupuncturists and chiropractors), compared to the national average of 18 percent. Overall in Canada there has been an 81 percent increase in the usage of alternative medicine between 1992 and 1997. The big unanswered question is: Are we getting our money's worth? A growing number of Canadians seem to be answering with a resounding "yes," as sales of everything from herbal remedies and nutritional supplements to therapeutic magnets continue to skyrocket. And a growing number of doctors are taking courses in complementary therapies, especially botanical (herbal) medicine, acupuncture, and homeopathy, so that they can offer patients a broader range of services and compete with alternative practitioners. Others form partnerships with alternative practitioners to provide an integrative approach to patient care.

## ACUPUNCTURE AND ACUPRESSURE

### How they work

Acupuncture is a foundation of Chinese medicine, which holds that good health depends upon keeping the opposing life forces of yin and yang in their proper balance. Central to this concept is the belief that all body organs are connected by channels, or meridians, that carry vital energy, or qi (pronounced *chee*). Illness occurs when a meridian becomes blocked, or an imbalance of yin and yang energy occurs. Acupuncture—the insertion of fine needles into acupoints along the blocked channel—can restore health by opening the channel and allowing qi, as well as blood and other body fluids, to flow freely once again. The process is enhanced when the acupuncturist twirls the needles, thereby imparting some of his or her qi to the patient. In a common variation, the needles are stimulated electrically. For added effectiveness, an herb called moxa may be attached to the needles and burned as they are twirled to produce a penetrating heat that increases blood flow.

In acupressure, a needleless variation of acupuncture, therapists (or the persons themselves) stimulate one or more acupoints by pressing firmly on them with a thumb or finger. Sometimes special bracelets or other devices are worn to apply steady pressure to an acupoint. For example, bracelets designed to prevent motion sickness stimulate a nausea acupoint in the wrist.

How acupuncture works remains a mystery. The placebo effect (see p 34) may play a role, but most ex-

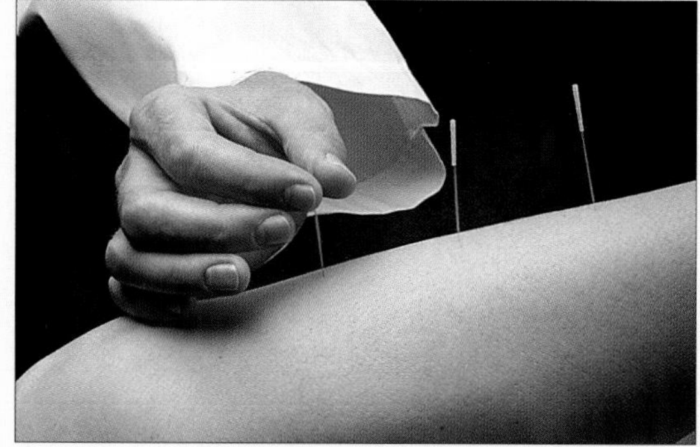

*In a typical acupuncture pain treatment, several needles are placed into acupoints along a meridian, one of the channels that carry the vital energy, or qi, through the body.*

perts agree that acupuncture evokes other systemic effects. Patients undergoing it typically experience warmth and tingling sensations in parts of the body distant from where the needles are inserted, leading some researchers to theorize that acupuncture somehow stimulates the autonomic nervous system. A typical pain treatment takes 20 to 30 minutes, and is repeated up to three times a week for 6 to 10 weeks. Generally if no improvement is noted after six treatments, it is doubtful that further sessions will be of much help.

### A little history

Acupuncture, an outgrowth of Taoist religious philosophy, is more than 3,000 years old. It was not until the eighteenth century, however, that the West was introduced to acupuncture when Christian missionaries expelled from China brought it back to Europe. During the nineteenth century, Chinese railroad workers emigrating to the United States and Canada brought with them their traditional medical practices, including acupuncture. In recent decades, Western adoption of acupuncture has been spurred by its use in pain clinics and the growing interest in all forms of alternative medicine.

### When it is used

In traditional Chinese medicine, acupuncture is used to treat almost every illness, often in combination with herbal medicine and other therapies. In Western medicine, it is employed mostly for pain relief, although some studies have found that it may also help in circulatory disorders, such as Raynaud's syndrome; tinnitis; digestive problems, especially nausea and irritable bowel syndrome; asthma and allergies; and substance abuse.

Acupuncture is sometimes used to provide anesthesia for patients who cannot tolerate conventional anesthetics. This is especially useful for dental procedures and minor operations that require only light anesthesia. Acupuncture also provides a safe and effective method of pain relief during childbirth. Other pain problems that appear to be especially amenable to treatments include the following:

- **Back pain,** such as chronic low back and neck pain.
- **Arthritis,** both rheumatoid and osteoarthritis.
- **Nerve pain,** such as diabetic shin gles and post-shingles neuropathy and facial pain from trigeminal neuralgia.
- **Chronic tendinitis and/or bursitis,** such as tennis elbow.
- **Cancer pain.** Acupuncture and acupressure are also useful in minimizing side effects of chemotherapy and radiation treatment. Acupuncture can also help strengthen the immune system.

### Cautions and concerns

It takes training and considerable practice to become a skilled acupuncturist. In Canada, practitioners are licensed in Quebec and British Columbia, and may be registered in Alberta. Most provinces allow physicians with acupuncture training to perform the procedure. Before undergoing treatment, ask the acupuncturist about his training and certification. Also, serious infections, including HIV and hepatitis, can be spread by contaminated acupuncture needles. Insist that disposable needles be used.

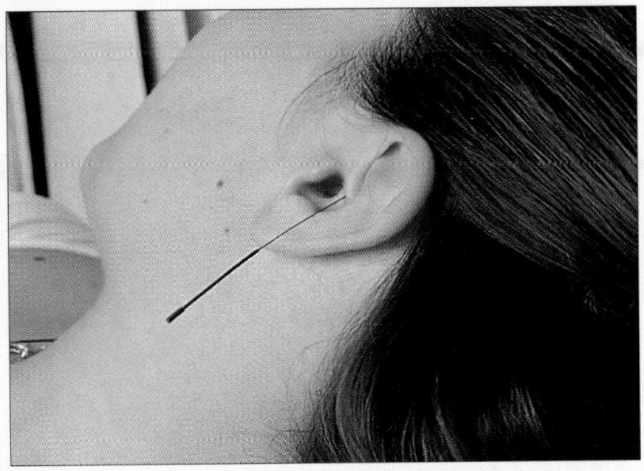

*The ear has acupuncture points commonly used to help patients stop smoking and overcome other addiction problems.*

#### REFLEX ACTIONS

Reflexology, or zone therapy, follows some of the same principles as acupuncture and acupressure. Brought to the West by Dr. William Fitzgerald, it involves massaging or pressing certain pressure points, mostly in the feet and hands, that correspond to specific internal organs. Because the foot contains pressure points that correspond to almost all internal organs, foot massage is an important component of reflexology.

## AROMATHERAPY

### How it works

Aromatherapy uses the essential oils of herbs and other aromatic plants to treat pain and many other conditions. It is often combined with massage and hydrotherapy; the aromatic oils also may be inhaled in steamy vapor or used as a compress.

### A little history

Aromatic oils have been used for at least 5,000 years to cleanse and heal both the mind and body. Ancient Egyptians used cedar and frankincense oils for embalming, and early Ayurvedic medical texts from India describe therapies using aromatic oils. During the Middle Ages, aromatic oils were credited with protecting many perfumers and others from plague and cholera. By the end of the nineteenth century, scientific studies began to identify antibiotic properties of certain plants.

Modern aromatherapy dates to the 1920s when Dr. René-Maurice Gattefosse, a French perfume chemist, severely burned a hand and then plunged it into a container of lavender oil. The burn healed very quickly with little scarring, prompting Dr. Gattefosse to coin the term "aromatherapie" and to seek out other healing aromatic oils. More recently, Dr. Marguerite Maury, a French biochemist, introduced the use of essential oils as a beauty treatment to rejuvenate the skin.

### When it is used

Aromatherapists treat everything from acne and depression to muscle aches and menstrual cramps. The oils, which are diluted in a carrier or lotion, such as wheat germ, safflower, and olive oil, may be used alone or in combination. They are applied directly to the skin, vaporized and inhaled, added to bathwater or a compress, or used as a mouthwash. (See *Aromatherapy for Pain*, right, for an overview of common conditions and aromatic oils recommended for their treatment.)

### Cautions and concerns

Aromatic oils should never be taken internally. Even so, some oils used in aromatherapy are toxic if used at full strength or applied over a long period. To avoid problems, it's a good idea to consult a trained aromatherapist before using essential aromatic oils. Some oils can produce allergic reactions, so before using an oil, test it first on a small area of skin. Also, some oils may cause problems during pregnancy or for people with high blood pressure or who suffer from epilepsy, migraine headaches, and certain nerve disorders.

Some oils—especially angelica, bergamot, bitter orange, lemon, lime, mandarin, and sweet orange—increase the skin's sensitivity to sunlight. Wait at least four hours after using them before exposing the skin to the sun.

### BACH FLOWER REMEDIES

In the early 1900s, a British homeopath and bacteriologist, Dr. Edward Bach, developed a set of flower remedies that he believed were more effective than conventional medications in treating emotional illnesses. Now known as Bach flower remedies, these are made by placing flowers in water and then exposing the mixture to heat or sunlight. Specific combinations and formulas are used for various illnesses; for example, a drop or two of agrimony is claimed to calm anxiety, and impatiens is recommended to reduce irritability. As with aromatherapy, caution is advised to avoid absorbing toxic substances.

## HERBAL MEDICINE

### How it works

Herbal, or botanical, medicines are substances derived from plants that have therapeutic or pharmacologic properties. In botany, an herb is defined as "a seed-producing plant that does not develop persistent woody tissue." Herbalists, however, broaden the definition to also include shrubs, trees, mosses, lichens, algae, seaweed, and mushrooms (fungi). In some traditions, such as Chinese medicine, herbalists also incorporate animal parts, insects, shells, rocks, minerals, and even gemstones into their herbal medicines. Increasingly, nutraceuticals—nutrients that have a pharmacological effect when they are taken in amounts greater than those found in an ordinary diet—are included in herbal medicine.

Depending upon the plant, medicines can be derived from the leaves, stems, bark, flowers, essential oils, sap or resins, roots, fruits, or seeds. The form in which the herb is consumed also varies widely—some are brewed into teas or boiled and then simmered to make a decoction. Some are applied as a compress or poultice, others are consumed as food, and still others are taken in pill, capsule, or lozenge form.

### Aromatherapy for Pain

| CONDITION | POSSIBLE AROMATHERAPY REMEDIES |
|---|---|
| Arthritis/ rheumatism | Black pepper, chamomile, clary sage, ginger, juniper berry, eucalyptus, lavender, lemon, marjoram, rosemary |
| Cold sores/herpes | Eucalyptus, geranium, lavender, lemon |
| Headaches | Chamomile, eucalyptus, lavender, marjoram, melissa, peppermint, rosemary |
| Hemorrhoids | Cypress, lemon, juniper berry, peppermint, rosemary, sandalwood |
| Menstrual cramps | Chamomile, clary sage, cypress, juniper berry, marjoram, melissa, rose otto |
| Mouth ulcers/ canker sores | Geranium, lavender, lemon, myrrh, tea tree |
| Muscle cramps | Chamomile, marjoram, mandarin |
| Sinusitis | Eucalyptus, lavender, peppermint |
| Sore throat | Cedarwood, clary sage, eucalyptus, geranium, lavender, lemon, peppermint, sandalwood, tea tree |
| Sprains | Lavender, marjoram, rosemary |
| Varicose veins | Cypress, peppermint, sandalwood |

### A little history

Every culture has evolved a formal tradition of herbal medicine. The oldest medical texts of China, India, Egypt, Persia, and ancient Greece all contain healing herbal formulas. Galen, the second-century Greek physician, codified herbal medicine into more than a dozen texts that were followed until modern times. In North America, doctors and pharmacists relied heavily on botanical medicines until the 1930s, when pharmaceutical companies began to synthesize drugs from chemical compounds. Even today, about half of all standardized medications contain ingredients that originated in plants, most of which can now be synthesized in the laboratory.

The 1990s witnessed a renewed interest in herbal medicine among both consumers and physicians as part of the trend toward integrating alternative and conventional therapies. The number of Canadians using herbal remedies grew by 58 percent between 1996 and 1997 with market sales of between $340 million and $375 million. The market is led by such products as St. John's wort to relieve mild depression and anxiety, echinacea to bolster immunity, and valerian to promote sleep and ease anxiety.

### When it is used

Herbal medicine is emerging as a cornerstone of self-treatment. There is an herbal or nutraceutical counterpart for a large array of pharmaceutical products. As a result, herbal medicines and nutraceuticals are being taken to prevent and treat disease, relieve pain, promote healing, and foster a sense of well-being. Common examples of herbals and nutraceuticals to relieve pain include:

- **Aloe vera:** topical application to treat minor burns and skin wounds.
- **Arnica:** used topically only to treat sprains, bruises, inflammation, and muscle aches.
- **Capsaicin:** used topically only to treat joint pain and inflammation of arthritis as well as nerve pain.
- **Chamomile:** taken orally to treat bowel inflammation, heartburn, and digestive upset.
- **Comfrey:** used topically only to heal wounds, treat inflammation.
- **Echinacea:** taken orally to treat achiness of colds and flu; applied topically to heal skin sores.
- **Evening primrose:** taken orally to ease rheumatoid arthritis, menstrual cramps, and inflammatory disorders.
- **Feverfew:** taken orally to prevent and treat migraine headaches.
- **Ginkgo biloba:** taken orally to ease pain from poor circulation.
- **Licorice:** taken orally to relieve intestinal irritation and sore throats.
- **Peppermint:** taken orally to reduce intestinal spasms and pain of irritable bowel syndrome.
- **Saw palmetto:** taken orally to relieve benign prostate disorders and inflammation.
- **Uva-ursi:** taken orally to relieve urinary tract infections.

*Many of the herbs used in herbal medicine are consumed as teas, made either by steeping (standard infusion) or simmering (decoction).*

### Cautions and concerns

Many people mistakenly think that because herbal medicines are "natural" they are safe. The fact is that some herbs are toxic, even deadly, and many interact with each other and with pharmaceutical products. St. John's wort, for example, interacts with fluoxetine (Prozac) and other antidepressants. Some are dangerous if taken during pregnancy and breast-feeding; others are harmful if they are taken by persons with liver or kidney problems. Before taking any herbal or nutraceutical product, check with your doctor or pharmacist to make sure it is safe and will not interact with your medications.

## DON'T BE GREEN WHEN BUYING HERBS

Currently herbal products fall under the Food and Drugs Act in Canada. Explicit claims about a product's ability to alleviate symptoms or treat a recognized medical condition can only be made after a thorough approval process by Health Canada. When a product meets Health Canada's requirements, it is granted a drug identification number, or DIN, which always appears on the label. If there is no DIN:

- Check to see if the product is standardized to provide a specific percentage of an active ingredient. For example, ginkgo biloba should be a standardized 50:1 extract, with 24 percent ginkgo flavone glycosides.
- Look for trusted brand names.
- Buy from a known, reputable outlet, such as a pharmacy, health-food store, or nutrition center. Be wary of cut-rate Internet sellers.
- Enlist the advice of a trained herbalist, physician, pharmacist, or nutritionist who is knowledgeable about herbal medicine and alternative therapies.

## HOMEOPATHY

### How it works

Homeopathy is a healing method based on the concept of "like cures like"; namely, that the cause of a disease is very similar to its cure. Thus, homeopaths treat a disorder by giving a greatly diluted dose of a substance that, if taken in a larger quantity, would produce symptoms similar to the disease.

### A little history

Homeopathy was developed by a German physician and chemist, Samuel Hahnemann, who conducted a series of experiments from 1790 to 1810 showing that therapeutic substances themselves cause symptoms, and that what worked best against a particular illness was the remedy that caused similar symptoms. He interpreted these findings to mean that symptoms were a sign that the body was trying to heal itself, and giving a minute dosage of a substance producing similar symptoms reinforced this natural healing process.

Today, homeopaths draw upon more than 2,000 remedies that are classified according to the symptoms they are thought to relieve. Most of these remedies are derived from plants, many of which are poisonous. The substances are repeatedly diluted until only an infinitesimal, usually undetectable amount remains. Critics of homeopathy argue that it makes no sense that something that cannot be detected by standard methods of chemical analysis could cure, and any benefit must come from a placebo effect (see p 34). Supporters of homeopathy counter that self-healing is the basis of all treatments, and homeopathic remedies simply prod the body to heal itself.

### When it is used

Homeopathy has long been accepted as a standard medical practice in Germany and many other European countries, and it is gaining popularity in the United States and Canada. In addition to being offered by practitioners specializing in homeopathy, it is also practiced by naturopathic doctors (NDs) and some chiropractors. It is rarely practiced by medical doctors in Canada. In general, homeopathy seems to work best against illnesses that produce pain and other symptoms without causing tissue damage, such as chronic fatigue and fibromyalgia. It is also used as an adjunct to conventional therapies to treat arthritis and other diseases.

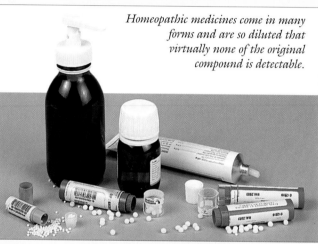

*Homeopathic medicines come in many forms and are so diluted that virtually none of the original compound is detectable.*

Studies comparing homeopathy to other therapies have produced mixed results. For example, some have shown that homeopathy may help against rheumatoid arthritis, and others have found no effect.

### Cautions and concerns

Homeopathy is not advisable for traumatic injuries or chronic diseases that entail extensive tissue damage, such as advanced liver disease. It also should not be viewed as a substitute for needed medications, such as antibiotics to treat infection or insulin to control diabetes.

## MAGNET THERAPY

### How it works

Magnet therapy is based on the theory that magnets have a natural effect on charged electrical particles in the blood. Tiny amounts of electricity constantly flow through the body, making it possible for the muscles (including the heart) to contract and nerve messages to reach their destinations. Blood is the body's natural conductor of electricity, and electrolytes (sodium, potassium, calcium, and magnesium, which are electrically charged particles) carry these electrical currents. When these electrolytes pass a magnetic field, their positive and negative charges separate. This releases tiny bits of heat and increases blood flow. Supporters of magnet therapy believe that this increased circulation in areas exposed to static magnets—the type that you use to post notes on the refrigerator door—helps speed healing. Another theory holds that the electrical effects of the magnets disrupt the flow of pain messages to the brain. These theories are unproved, but this has not dissuaded thousands of Canadians from trying magnets.

### A little history

For hundreds of years, folk healers have used magnets to relieve arthritis and other musculoskeletal pain, promote bone healing, and even reduce dandruff with magnetic combs. It is only in the last few years, however, that medical science has paid any attention to magnet therapy. In 1999, Dr. Michael Weintraub, a neurologist at New York Medical College, reported a double-blind study in which magnets appeared to ease the burning foot pain suffered by a group of diabetic patients. This has prompted other researchers to take a more serious look at magnet therapy.

### When it is used

Conditions that magnet therapy reportedly benefits include:

- Sprains, muscle tears, tennis elbow, rotator-cuff injuries, and numerous other musculoskeletal problems suffered by athletes and others who engage in exercise.

- Wrist pain caused by carpal tunnel syndrome and other types of repetitive stress injuries.
- Joint pain and inflammation due to arthritis.
- Bone pain resulting from fractures or bruising.
- Nerve pain, such as diabetic and post-shingles neuropathy.
- Chronic back pain.

### Cautions and concerns

Magnets should not be applied immediately after a sprain or other injury has occurred. The increased blood flow to the area can actually worsen the condition by increasing swelling and inflammation. This is why ice packs are the preferred initial treatment. As soon as the swelling is under control, magnets are generally safe to use.

Magnets do not work for every pain condition, and their effectiveness varies from one person to another. Consumers should be aware that although home-use static magnets have been granted a license, this does not mean Health Canada has evaluated or endorses the claims made.

*Music therapists treat everything from chronic pain to developmental and emotional disorders.*

## MUSIC THERAPY

### How it works

Not only does music soothe a troubled mind and elevate one's mood, but it also appears to ease nagging pain for many sufferers. The healing effects of music on the mind and body are well documented, but medical science has not been able to explain how it works. For some, music has a calming, sedative effect; for others, it is invigorating. Of course, the type of music being played influences what effects it has, but even so, the individual response to a given piece of music varies greatly from one person to another.

Some pain researchers theorize that music provides a distraction that reduces the perception of pain. Recent research indicates that music prompts the brain to increase its production of endorphins, body chemicals that act as natural painkillers. Because music counters stress and promotes relaxation, this may explain its benefits in controlling pain related to muscle tension.

### A little history

Music is truly a universal language, and one that is important to healers in almost every culture in all parts of the world. In the second century, the Greek physician Galen used music therapy in his hospital in Pergamum (now a part of Turkey). In the U.S., music therapy was introduced in the 1940s, when the Veterans Administration incorporated it into its rehabilitation programs for disabled soldiers returning from World War II. The National Association for Music Therapy was established in 1950. In Canada, the Canadian Association for Music Therapy (CAMT) was founded in 1974.

### When it is used

Music therapy is widely used in rehabilitation centers, pain clinics, hospitals, general and psychiatric hospitals, nursing homes, senior centers, and hospice programs, among others. Music therapists also work with disabled and developmentally impaired children as well as in prisons and

## THE HEALING POWER OF THE CREATIVE ARTS

Expressing your inner feelings is often a critical aspect in controlling chronic pain, yet many people find this next to impossible to do. Creative arts therapies are designed to give people a nonverbal form of self-expression. These therapies are especially useful for patients whose pain is related to stress or has a strong emotional component; for example, headaches and digestive problems. In addition to music therapy (see above), creative arts therapies employed by some pain clinics and specialists include the following:

- **Art therapy**, which uses painting, clay modeling, or sculpting as a means of self-expression or, in some instances, guided imagery (see p 45). Pain patients may be asked to draw a picture of their pain and how it affects them. The therapist can then use the art to help the patients gain control over their pain.
- **Dance therapy**, which is usually done as a part of group therapy. Under the guidance of a dance therapist, patients learn to express their feelings by moving to music. For example, a pain patient may be instructed to devise a dance that squelches a chronic pain that has no organic cause.
- **Drama therapy**, which is also done in a group setting. By pretending to be someone or somewhere else, a person can gain new insight into the real problems underlying his or her pain and come up with solutions.

schools. Dentists and surgeons have long employed music as a substitute for or an adjunct to anesthesia. As early as 1914, a researcher using a wind-up phonograph showed the benefits of music in calming surgery patients before administering an anesthetic. Since then, a number of studies have found that, when music is played in the operating and recovery rooms, patients need less anesthesia and post-surgical medication.

### Cautions and concerns

In general, music therapy has no harmful side effects. There is, however, a big difference between simply listening to one's favorite music and undergoing formal music therapy to treat a specific problem. The latter should be directed by a music therapist certified by the Canadian Association of Music Therapy.

## NATUROPATHY

### How it works

Naturopathy is based on the belief that the body can heal itself. It embraces the entire realm of natural and complementary healing practices, with special emphasis on patient education and responsibility and disease prevention. Many NDs (for doctor of naturopathic medicine) function much as conventional family physicians, with one major exception—they rely on standardized botanical medicines to treat ailments and pain instead of synthetic pharmaceutical products. Others confine themselves to a stricter form of natural therapies, focusing on diet, lifestyle modification, hydrotherapy, and periodic fasting and "detoxification" to cleanse the body. Pain therapies used by naturopaths include manipulation, massage, and acupuncture.

### A little history

Naturopathy traces its philosophical roots to Hippocrates and the school of medicine he founded in about 400 BC. Hippocrates rejected the prevailing notion that illness was punishment rendered by the gods, and that healing could be accomplished through divine intervention and magic. Instead, he taught that diet and lifestyle were the keys to good health, and healing was best achieved by natural means, which remains the basic philosophy of naturopathy. As a distinct medical discipline, however, it dates from 1902, when a German-born osteopath and chiropractor, Benedict Lust, founded the American School of Naturopathy in New York. Lust maintained that pain-free good health rested with the proper diet, clean living (with no alcohol, tea, coffee, or cocoa), exercise, breathing exercises, water treatments, and periodic fasting. By 1920, naturopathic practice was well established in Canada. Lust's teachings were followed until the mid-1930s.

But by 1938, the appeal of naturopathy began to wane amid widespread charges of quackery. By the late 1960s, naturopathy had all but disappeared from North American medicine. Then came the back-to-nature movement of the 1970s, and renewed interest in naturopathy and other forms of alternative medicine.

### When it is used

Naturopathy is more a way of life than a distinct set of medical practices, so many of its tenets are incorporated into various forms of alternative and conventional medicine. An individual interested in trying herbal medicine or diet therapy, for example, may seek the services of a naturopathic physician.

### Cautions and concerns

Naturopathy alone is not an effective treatment for serious diseases, such as insulin-dependent (juvenile) diabetes, acute infections, and cancer. In such instances, it should be consid-

### THE POWER OF FAITH

Touch therapy is often equated with faith, or spiritual, healing. Although there are some similarities, faith healing is based more on religion or a strong belief in a supernatural power. Many cultures and religions have healing ceremonies. Some Native American shamans, for example, practice a type of spiritual healing using chants, meditation, and perhaps peyote, a hallucinogenic plant. Each year, tens of thousands of believers flock to Lourdes in France to pray for a miracle cure. The curandero healers of Mexico, Cuba, Puerto Rico, and Hispanic communities in North America believe that pain and many illnesses are spells, or hexes, cast by evil spirits, and can be cured by enlisting supernatural forces. Regardless of the form of faith healing, many conventional physicians note that some sort of spiritual belief often helps patients face pain and illness with unusual strength and calmness.

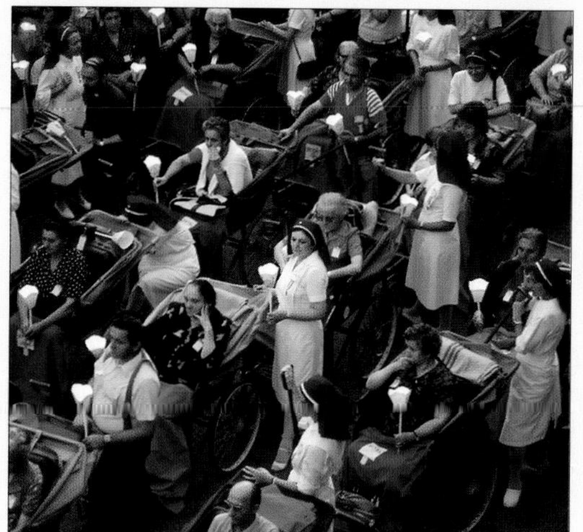

*Every year, thousands of ill people from throughout the world journey to Lourdes in France in search of miracle cures.*

ered an adjunct to, not a substitute for, conventional medicine. Also, check the credentials of your ND to see that he or she has graduated from an accredited school (see *Directory of Resources*, p 366).

## THERAPEUTIC TOUCH

### How it works

Therapeutic, or healing, touch is based on a belief in universal healing energy, and the concept that the healing vital energy of one person can be transmitted to another. Sometimes referred to as "laying on of hands," in practice, it is not necessary for the therapist to actually touch the patient in order to transfer healing energy. Although healing techniques vary among therapists, most are performed inches or even feet away from the patient's body.

In a typical session, the practitioner moves his or her hands above the patient to examine the surrounding space, feeling for variations in the stream of energy flowing from the person. In a healthy person, energy flows in a smooth, gliding stream. But pain, illness, anger, or other physical or emotional problems interfere with the flow of energy, which the therapist can feel as congestion, holes, patches of heaviness, vibrations, or hot or cold spots in the air. The goal of therapy is to normalize the flow of energy. This may be accomplished through meditation, touch, or simply talking with the patient about the underlying problem.

Touch therapists are usually nurses, but it is also practiced by massage therapists, naturopaths, medical hypnotists, and other healers who are trained to develop a sensitivity to the subtle differences in energy in and around a patient.

### A little history

The concept of universal energy—"qi" in China and Japan, "parna" in India, "mana" in Hawaii, "animal magnetism" in nineteenth-century Europe—has been a part of healing traditions for at least 5,000 years. Healing by laying on of hands is described in the Bible and ancient medical texts. But until recently, Western, scientific-based medicine dismissed touch therapy as little more than quackery. This began to change in the 1970s, thanks to the efforts of Dolores Krieger, a professor of nursing at New York University, and Dora Kunz, her teacher of healing. Together, they developed a technique of therapeutic touch, and began teaching it in nursing classes and workshops. By the 1990s, therapeutic touch was being taught and practiced nationwide.

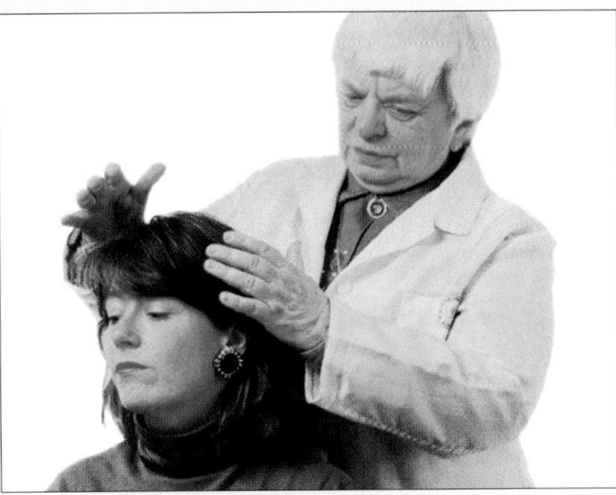

*Some studies suggest that touch therapy can bring about changes in pulse rate, hormone levels, and blood pressure.*

### When it is used

Touch therapy is practiced in many settings—hospitals, operating rooms, newborn nurseries and neonatal intensive care units, pain clinics, labor and delivery rooms, and psychiatric units, to name but a few. Does it work? The lay press and medical journals alike have published accounts of amazing, almost unbelievable cures attributed to touch therapy—the spontaneous disappearance of tumors, the sudden lifting of migraine headaches, normalization of dangerous heart arrhythmias, the abrupt disappearance of a raging fever, the calming of panic attacks or psychotic episodes. Most of these are anecdotal accounts, and as such, they are not considered scientific proof that therapeutic touch actually works. Controlled studies have produced mixed results. Some studies have found that touch therapy can bring about measurable changes in the pulse rate, skin temperature, hormone levels, blood pressure, and other physical parameters. Others have found little or no change in the body functions and attribute any improvement in pain and other symptoms to a placebo effect.

Still, advocates of touch therapy contend that some study results far exceed the 30 percent improvement that is standard for a placebo. In one dramatic study, 44 healthy male volunteers underwent identical skin biopsies. Half were given therapeutic touch and half were not. The wounds were then observed to see if there was any difference in the rate of healing. By the sixteenth day, the wounds of 12 of the 22 who had received touch therapy had completely healed, compared to none in the control group. Similar dramatic differences have been reported in healing time among patients undergoing open-heart surgery at New York Presbyterian Hospitals. Therapeutic touch has also been approved by the Victorian Order of Nurses (VON).

### Cautions and concerns

At this stage, therapeutic touch is considered an alternative to conventional treatments for conditions that have no identifiable cause—for example, recurrent headaches, chronic back pain unrelated to a physical abnormality, chronic fatigue, and emotional disorders. It may be a useful adjunct to medical treatment, but it is not considered appropriate primary treatment for conditions such as diabetes, cancer, and heart disease.

# When to See a Pain Specialist

*All doctors are trained to treat varying degrees of pain, so the search for relief should usually start with your primary-care physician. But if your doctor says "nothing more can be done" and you still hurt, it's time to seek out a pain specialist or clinic.*

## WHO ARE THE PAIN SPECIALISTS?

While pain management is not yet formally recognized as a distinct medical specialty in Canada, we have many pain specialists who are trained to deal with chronic or intractable pain. The Canadian Pain Society, consisting of more than 500 members, is very active in all aspects of pain treatment, research, and making policy recommendations. It publishes its own journal, *Pain Research & Management.* Most pain specialists come from other fields of medicine, most notably anesthesiology, neurology, and rehabilitation medicine. In addition to direct patient care, a pain specialist may provide any of the following:

- Prescribing medication and rehabilitation services.
- Performing pain surgery or other pain-relieving procedures, such as nerve block.
- Counseling patients with chronic pain and their families.
- Directing a multidisciplinary team and coordinating care with other health care providers.
- Providing consultative services to public and private agencies.

Pain management's parameters are often hard to define, especially when compared to such disciplines as rheumatology, ophthalmology, or hematology. Pain specialists also work in a variety of settings—hospitals and rehabilitation centers, nursing homes and hospices, private and group practices, broad-spectrum pain clinics, and clinics that specialize in treating a single painful disorder, such as cancer, headaches, arthritis, and back problems.

Some pain specialists concentrate on specific types of pain, such as headaches, cancer, or burns. Others treat a variety of painful conditions, but focus on a specific approach such as one of the following:

- **Medical strategies**, which center on using medication, injections, or surgical interventions.
- **Rehabilitation**, which uses exercise, physical therapy, and other conditioning techniques.
- **Behavioral or cognitive techniques**, such as biofeedback training, relaxation, and learning ways to manage pain and improve the quality of life.

Although many pain specialists offer a combination of these approaches, one generally predominates. Regardless of their medical background, overall approach, and the setting in which they practice, pain specialists may be more receptive to trying innovative approaches—including the alternative therapies described earlier in this chapter—than other physicians.

Pain specialists also help patients set realistic goals. It is rarely possible to totally eliminate 100 percent of the pain, especially if it is chronic and related to an incurable disease such as arthritis. Instead, the objective is to control the pain enough to allow the patient to carry out normal day-to-day activities in reasonable comfort.

## WHY PAIN GOES UNTREATED

With so many choices in pain management, it's hard to understand why millions of Canadians continue to suffer from chronic pain. But suffer they do. In a commentary in the winter 1998 issue of *Pain Research & Management*, Dr. Neil Hagen found that 17 percent of adult Canadians suffer from chronic pain, while 2.5 percent suffer severe chronic pain. Dr. John Clark, President of the Canadian Pain Society, puts the figure

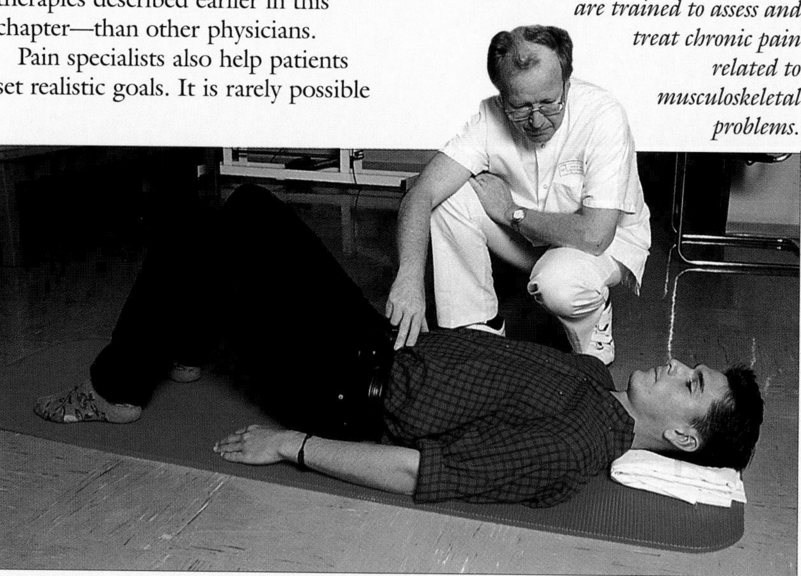

*Physical therapists are trained to assess and treat chronic pain related to musculoskeletal problems.*

a little lower: between 10 and 15 percent of Canadians suffer from chronic pain, with many of them not getting adequate treatment for their pain. Why is this?

A consensus among pain specialists says the blame is shared by three groups:

**1. The patients themselves**, who often believe that pain is inevitable and something that they must endure without complaining. Many also shun taking adequate pain medications in the mistaken fear that they will become addicted to the drugs, especially narcotics.

**2. Medical professionals**, who may lack the necessary training in pain management, and who may also be reluctant to prescribe adequate pain medication because of misinformation. Some physicians also hesitate to try alternative therapies because their benefits have not been proved.

**3. Provincial Insurance and Workers' Compensation Insurance Boards**, who may refuse to acknowledge liability for pain in the absence of obvious physical findings. This can be very distressing for patients and pain specialists who know that pain and physical findings do not necessarily correlate.

Experts generally agree that the latter roadblock to pain control is especially self-defeating. Early and adequate pain treatment is less of a strain on the health care system than waiting until patients are so disabled that they cannot work or carry out other normal activities. In rare cases, they may require surgery and other treatments far more costly than what was denied earlier.

Many pain specialists are cast in the role of patient advocates for aggressive pain management after competent and qualified physicians have determined there is nothing further to be done for the pain. Doctors at the McGill-Montreal General Hospital Pain Centre often have to convince reluctant primary care physicians to prescribe medications such as opioids to help relieve pain. Fortunately, this has been much less of a concern in recent years, and now doctors are more likely to consult a multidisciplinary pain center for advice on prescribing for a particular patient.

## Types of Pain Treatment Facilities

| TYPE | OVERVIEW OF SERVICES |
|---|---|
| Rehabilitation/Physical Medicine | Patients may be treated on either in- or outpatient basis; emphasis is on conditioning, exercise, and other modalities needed to live as normally as possible. Most also offer a variety of alternative therapies, self-help techniques, and support groups. |
| Hospital-based (outpatient) | Offers many of same services as rehabilitation centers, but with more emphasis on medical or surgical intervention. Some are multidisciplinary. |
| Office-based | Many feature a treatment team of a physician, physical therapist, and an acupuncturist or other alternative practitioners. Practice often focuses on a specific disease or modality; patients are seen at regular intervals; cognitive and behavioral approaches may be offered. |
| Disease-oriented | Clinic, center, or practice focuses on a specific disease. The most common examples are headaches, cancer, arthritis, back pain, and chronic nerve and muscle disorders. |

## SOURCES OF HELP

Finding the most appropriate pain specialist for a particular problem is often a frustrating round of going from one specialist to another until the patient gives up in despair. Many others fall into the hands of unscrupulous or incompetent practitioners. Such mistakes can be avoided by learning in advance the type of specialist who is most likely to provide the kind of relief you're seeking. Start by talking frankly to your primary care doctor, who may be unaware of your suffering. Keep a pain diary (see p 24) and use the Sample Pain Scale (see p 22) to detail the nature of the problem. Show these to your doctor and ask how you can work together to achieve better control of your pain.

If your informs you doctor that there's nothing more that he or she can do, ask for a referral to a pain clinic or specialist. At the same time, do some research yourself. The Internet has a number of excellent sites devoted to providing information about pain centers and specialists. (Be cautious, however, because many are also devoted to selling products of dubious benefit.) If you don't have a computer, most public libraries offer help in conducting Internet searches.

There are also numerous helpful pain organizations and support groups in Canada. The North American Chronic Pain Association of Canada (NACPAC) (www.chronicpaincanada.org) provides a directory of pain clinics and specialists throughout Canada. The Canadian Pain Society (www.medicine.dal.ca/gorgs/cps) provides information to both consumers and medical professionals. The Canadian Injured Workers Alliance (www.ciwa.ca) provides information and help to people suffering from work-related pain. (For additional resources, see *Useful Phone Numbers* on p 58 and *Directory of Resources* on p 366.)

# Specialized Pain Centers

*Scattered across the country are hundreds of clinics and other facilities dedicated to the treatment of specific pain disorders—everything from such common problems as headaches and back problems to life-threatening burns and severe sports injuries.*

## WHO NEEDS SPECIAL PAIN CLINICS?

Most of the estimated 10 to 15 percent of Canadians who suffer from chronic pain are treated on an outpatient basis. But each year, several million check into special treatment centers seeking relief from specific pain conditions. Some, such as burn victims and patients with cancer or AIDS, require intensive medical treatment in addition to pain relief. Others, such as people who suffer from recurring headaches and chronic back pain, may not have a serious medical disorder, but their pain interferes with a normal lifestyle. Still others, such as the terminally ill, are not seeking treatment of their underlying disease, but instead, a comfortable death.

### Back-pain clinics

Depending upon the underlying cause, patients may be treated in either an in- or an outpatient program. Types of problems commonly treated at back clinics include chronic low back pain, disk problems, spinal arthritis and stenosis (stiffening of the spine), and back injuries and rehabilitation. Patients who continue to suffer back pain after surgery, drug treatment, chiropractic and osteopathic manipulation, or other standard treatments are often taught new ways to overcome their pain using exercise, biofeedback training, and relaxation techniques.

### Burn units

Each year, thousands of Canadians suffering severe burns are admitted to special burn trauma units. These units, which are usually associated with major medical centers, have more than doubled the survival rate for victims in the last 50 years.

Most burn units use a team approach that requires the services of many medical specialists: general and plastic surgeons, critical-care physicians and nurses, internists, pulmonologists, infectious disease experts, psychiatrists, nutritionists, social workers, and physical and occupational therapists. As healing takes place, pain may require morphine and other powerful painkillers. Rehabilitation typically includes extensive physical and occupational therapy.

### Headache clinics

Most headache clinics provide treatment on an outpatient basis, and most use a team approach that includes both conventional and alternative therapies. In fact, many are simply extensions of a medical practice that also offers acupuncture, herbal medicine, and other complementary therapies. Before enrolling in a headache treatment program, the Migraine Association of Canada urges consumers to check the qualifications of its proprietors.

### Hospices/Palliative care

Hospice or palliative care is designed specifically to ease pain and suffering for terminally ill patients. About 90 percent of hospice care is provided in the patient's home; the remaining 10 percent is given in hospice or palliative care centers. However, more and more, palliative care units in most large Canadian hospitals treat patients with chronic pain who are not terminally ill, because they have the expertise to do so. Hospices also offer personal care, nutritional support, and grief counseling.

## Useful Phone Numbers

*The following organizations provide information and area referrals; for a more complete list, see the Directory of Resources.*

| TYPE OF PAIN | FOR INFORMATION, CONTACT |
|---|---|
| Arthritis | Arthritis Foundation 1-800-321-1433 |
| Back pain | Back Association of Canada (416) 967-4670 |
| Cancer pain | Canadian Cancer Society 1-888-939-3333<br>Canadian Breast Cancer Network 1-800-685-8820 |
| Chronic pain | North American Chronic Pain Association of Canada 1-800-616-PAIN<br>Canadian Pain Society (613) 234-0812 |
| Headaches | Migraine Association of Canada 1-800-663-3557 |
| Hospice and palliative care | Canadian Palliative Care Association 1-800-668-2785<br>Hospice Association of Ontario 1-800-349-3111 |
| Nerve pain | Canadian Neuropathic Association (416) 233-1043 |

# Pain Control in the Hospital

*Most of the conditions that require hospitalization are painful, and providing adequate pain relief should be an integral part of treatment. Unfortunately, this does not always happen unless you, the patient, demand it.*

## REMOVING THE HURT FROM HOSPITALS

Most hospital patients require varying degrees of pain relief. Some come to the hospital because they are in intense pain, either from a disease or an injury. Others develop pain from an operation or another hospital procedure.

Regardless of the source of the pain, relieving it not only makes the patient more comfortable but also helps speed recovery. While this seems obvious, until recently, adequate pain control was an often neglected aspect of hospital care for several reasons: Many hospital patients expected to encounter pain and, rather than complain or demand relief, they elected to endure it stoically. Doctors and nurses tended to undertreat pain by administering opioids and other strong painkillers according to a strict schedule, regardless of the degree of pain. So instead of giving the drugs before the pain had a chance to "take hold" and thereby keeping it under control, the schedule approach often meant that the medication was always "chasing the pain."

Fortunately, this outmoded approach is being abandoned in favor of more aggressive pain control that often entails giving the patient control over administering his or her medication as it is needed. The doctors are still in charge of ordering pain medications, which are then dispensed by nurses or aides. But new devices, especially computer-operated morphine pumps, allow patients to take a medication when they feel the need, rather than wait for a nurse to give it to them. Here's how it works: A reservoir of morphine is attached to an intravenous line and the patient is given a pump device that allows a measured dose of morphine to enter the IV line. When the patient feels the need for pain medication, he or she simply presses a button on the morphine pump, which releases the dose. Studies have found that patients using a morphine pump not only achieve better pain control, but also use less of the drug than those who are treated on a traditional medication schedule.

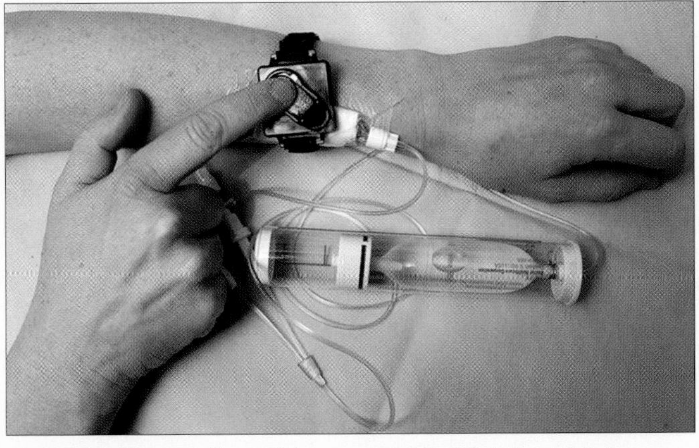

*A morphine pump allows patients to control the timing of their pain medication.*

Morphine pumps can also be used on an outpatient basis by cancer patients and others who suffer from intensely painful conditions. Fears that these patients will become addicted to the drug have been unfounded; numerous studies show that addiction is rarely a problem when narcotic drugs are used for pain control by people who do not have a history of substance abuse.

### In the emergency room

In the past, pain management was not a major concern of emergency room doctors. In fact, many ER doctors were reluctant to eliminate the pain for fear that this might make diagnosis more difficult. This is no longer the case. Although the emphasis is still on stabilizing vital functions (blood pressure, heartbeat, and respiration), early pain treatment is also an emergency room priority. Doctors now know that giving a shot of morphine to ease the chest pain of a suspected heart attack, for example, will not interfere with any of the diagnostic tests or alter the prognosis. But it will ease anxiety and certainly make the patient more comfortable.

The choice of pain medication varies according to the circumstances. Meperidine (Demerol) is usually the first choice for very severe pain (a broken bone, heart attack, acute abdominal distress). Demerol is not recommended for long-term use. A sedative may also be given to calm anxiety.

Less severe pain can usually be treated with codeine or another weak narcotic; acetaminophen or aspirin and other nonsteroidal anti-inflammatory drugs (NSAIDs) may be adequate to relieve musculoskeletal pain or the discomfort of an infection. A local anesthetic, such as procaine

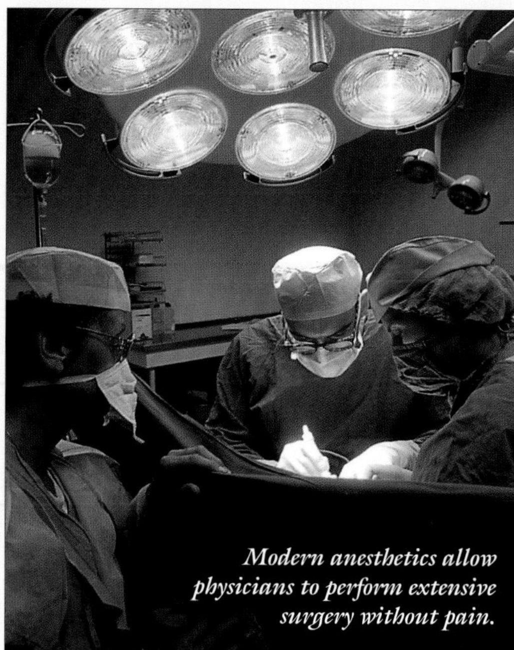

*Modern anesthetics allow physicians to perform extensive surgery without pain.*

hydrochloride (Novocain), is used for minor emergency room procedures, such as stitching a wound or when doing a lumbar puncture and other painful tests.

## In the operating room

Anesthesiologists are the medical specialists in charge of pain control in the operating room and, very often, in the immediate post-surgical period.

General anesthetics, which are used in most major operations, induce a deep state of paralytic sleep that prevents movement, prevents the brain from processing pain messages, and blocks any memory of the procedure. Before the patient goes to the operating room, an IV line is inserted and a sedative drug (often Valium or a related medication) is given to quell anxiety and induce drowsiness.

There are three methods of inducing general anesthesia:

- **Rapid-sequence induction**, in which a short-acting barbiturate is given to bring about an immediate loss of consciousness, followed by an injection of a strong muscle relaxant to allow quick insertion of a breathing tube. All of this requires only 60 to 90 seconds.
- **Inhalation induction**, which takes three to five minutes, entails inhaling nitrous oxide and an anesthetic, such as halothane, to produce anesthesia.
- **Combined intravenous-inhalation induction,** which involves giving a short-acting IV anesthetic before inhaling the more potent and longer-lasting drug.

Unconsciousness and paralysis are maintained during the operation through the continued administration of the anesthetic; a muscle relaxant and narcotic painkiller may also be given. Throughout the procedure, the anesthesiologist monitors the heart rate, blood pressure, and blood gases (levels of oxygen and carbon dioxide).

When the surgeon is finished with the operation, the anesthesia is stopped, and a drug may be administered to help the patient regain consciousness. Nausea and vomiting are common complications of general anesthesia, which is why it's important not to eat or drink anything for at least 10 to 12 hours before undergoing an operation.

Local or regional anesthetics block pain sensations and prevent movement of a specific area of the body. One of the most familiar is Novocain and similar local anesthetics that dentists use. Surgeons use stronger local anesthetics for operations in which a limb or other limited part of the body needs to be deadened. For example, an epidural anesthetic is injected into the lumbar (lower) spine to deaden pain sensations below the site. This type of anesthesia is often used for gynecologic or orthopedic surgery, for example, cesarean deliveries and arthroscopic repair of knee ligaments. In some instances, the patient is fully conscious and alert; in others, a sedative is given. The patient can breathe normally and does not need to be put on a ventilator.

Blood loss from some operations is reduced, there is also a lower risk of blood clots, and recovery is faster than with general anesthesia. Headache is the most common anesthesia-related complication; there may also be nausea and vomiting and a marked drop in blood pressure.

## In the recovery room

Most surgery patients spend at least a few hours in the recovery room immediately following an operation. Blood pressure, heart rate, and respiration are carefully monitored as the patient regains consciousness. As the anesthesia wears off, morphine may be given to control immediate post-operative pain. In some cases, regional anesthesia may also be used. For example, after abdominal surgery, a nerve block will anesthetize the area for 12 to 24 hours.

## In the patient's room

After the patient regains consciousness and is stable, he or she will be moved to a patient ward. Depending upon the operation and patient's condition, he may first go to an intensive care unit or step-down unit before being moved to a regular hospital room. Pain control is continued in all of these units. If pain is severe, morphine or another narcotic drug will be continued—perhaps with a patient-controlled pump. But as pain subsides, the patient will be weaned off the morphine and switched to milder painkillers.

## Going home

Typically, the patient will be given a prescription for continued pain relief and perhaps a day's supply of the medication. It's a good idea to talk to your surgeon about post-operative pain control before undergoing the operation, and if a prescription drug will be needed, to have it on hand before going home.

# Lifestyle and Pain

*The search for pain relief all too often means trying different painkillers and going from doctor to doctor. Very often, however, a few simple lifestyle changes are more effective and not only help overcome pain but also improve overall health.*

## THE ROLE OF EXERCISE

Study after study confirms that regular exercise is crucial to virtually every aspect of good health. Not only do people who exercise tend to live longer than their sedentary peers, but they also enjoy an enhanced sense of well-being and have fewer aches and pains. Indeed, regular exercise is a potent natural painkiller, and often the only "treatment" needed for many of our most common sources of pain. For example:

- Exercise improves muscle tone and increases strength, and strong and flexible muscles are less likely to develop painful cramps or feel stiff and sore when called upon for extra work.
- It keeps joints strong and flexible, and a combination of regular exercise and rest reduces pain and helps control arthritis.
- It keeps bones strong and reduces the risk of osteoporosis, the bone loss that occurs with aging. Walking, strength training, and other weight-bearing exercises exert a certain amount of stress on the bones, which helps them retain calcium and other minerals.
- It improves circulation, especially in the legs and feet. Walking, cycling, and other aerobic exercises are especially important for people with varicose veins, diabetes, hardening of the arteries (atherosclerosis), and other conditions affecting circulation to the lower limbs.
- It benefits the heart and lungs. Exercise conditioning is a mainstay of cardiac rehabilitation after a heart attack or open-heart surgery. It also plays a major role in controlling asthma and emphysema.
- It improves mood and helps overcome mild to moderate clinical depression. Studies have found that regular aerobic exercise can help patients reduce or even eliminate their need for antidepressants.
- It counters stress and relaxes tensed muscles—common causes of headaches, neck and back pain, digestive problems, and many other painful conditions.

### How exercise works

Exercise naturally causes a certain amount of pain as it exerts extra pressure on muscles, tendons, ligaments, and other body structures. This prompts the brain to step up production of endorphins, body chemicals that block pain messages in much the same manner as morphine. In fact, endorphins attach themselves to the same brain receptors as morphine. Not only do endorphins block out the pain messages that are being sent to the brain from peripheral nerves, but they also elevate mood. This accounts for the "high" that many long-distance runners experience when they are competing in a marathon.

Athletes and other people who exercise regularly also experience an emotional and physical "low" when they are laid up for a few days. While endorphins are not as addictive as morphine, a sudden drop in their levels can produce feelings of nervousness, mild depression, and other withdrawal symptoms.

### Getting started

All too often, people in pain become sedentary because they fear that exercise will increase their suffering and cause further damage to whatever is hurting them. While this is true in the case of acute pain from, for example, a sprain or fracture, it does not necessarily hold for many of the disorders that cause chronic pain, such as arthritis, muscle-tension headaches, or back problems. In fact, inactivity can actually worsen chronic pain by causing stiff, weak muscles and promoting weight gain, which puts extra stress on painful joints. Still, caution is needed when embarking on an exercise program after prolonged inactivity. Check

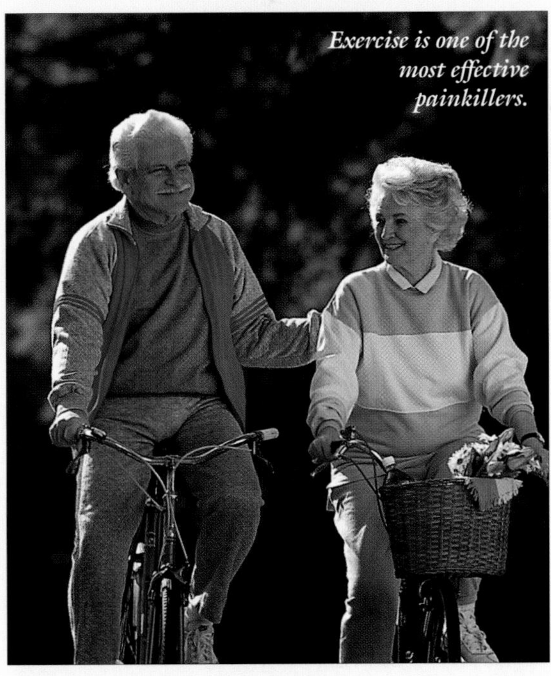

*Exercise is one of the most effective painkillers.*

with your doctor first, especially if you smoke or have a history of heart disease, high blood pressure, diabetes, or other conditions that increase the risk of a heart attack. You may need an exercise tolerance test to determine a safe level of exercise.

In some instances, specific exercises are part of the treatment regimen; these are usually developed by a physical therapist, rehabilitation physician, or other medical professional. More often, however, a program that combines aerobic and strength-building exercises will suffice. In planning such an exercise program, find activities that you enjoy and are likely to stick with. Walking is something that almost anyone can do and all you need are a pair of comfortable shoes and a safe place to walk. If arthritis or a severe weight problem makes walking difficult, a stationary bicycle or exercising in water may be more appropriate.

Whatever activity you decide to do, start slowly and gradually build up your tolerance and strength. In the beginning, you may only be able to walk for a block or two or work out for just three or four minutes. But if you increase your exercise a bit every few days, you'll soon work up to the level that most doctors recommend—20 to 30 minutes of aerobic exercise vigorous enough to raise your pulse rate at least three or four times a week.

Remember, too, that you need strong muscles in order to exercise effectively. Strength training is the best way to tone and strengthen weak, underused muscles. It's a good idea to have a physical therapist or a personal trainer experienced in exercise physiology show you strength-building exercises that are safe and appropriate for you.

It's not necessary to invest in fancy exercise equipment or join a health club; you can develop a suitable routine using handheld free weights or therapeutic elastic bands. The important thing is to work all the muscle groups by lifting weights or doing resistance exercises for 30 to 40 minutes two or three times a week. Start each session with 5 to 10 minutes of warm-up stretching exercises. Again, a physical therapist or personal trainer can help you develop a stretching routine; sample exercises are described in the accompanying box, *Stretch Away Your Pain*.

## Stretch Away Your Pain

*Start by repeating each of the following twice, and gradually work up to 10 repetitions per session.*

| PART OF BODY STRETCHED | WHAT TO DO |
|---|---|
| Back | Sit on a mat or firm mattress with your legs extended straight out. Slowly lean forward and reach your fingers toward your toes. Use a fluid motion; never jerk or bounce. |
| Neck | Sit in a comfortable position and slowly bend your head forward until your chin touches your neck. Without moving your shoulders, rotate your head slowly and try to touch your right shoulder with your chin. Go back to the middle, and repeat rotation toward your left shoulder. |
| Shoulders and arms | Reach one hand over the head and as far down your back as you can. You can use the opposite hand to push the elbow toward your back. Repeat with the opposite hand. |
| Pelvis | Lie on your back with your knees bent. Squeeze your buttocks and tip your pelvis forward. Hold for a count of five and repeat 5 to 10 times. |
| Legs | Lie flat on your back with both legs fully extended. Bend one knee and grasp the leg just above the knee with both hands and slowly bring the knee toward your chest. Repeat with the other leg, and then do both knees together. |
| Calf muscles | Stand facing a wall with your feet about four inches apart and 10 to 12 inches away from the wall. Keeping your back straight, lean forward and press your shoulders against the wall until you feel a pulling or stretching of the calf muscles. Hold for 30 seconds and repeat three times. |
| Whole body | Lie flat on your back with your legs extended. Raise your arms above your head and reach as far as you can while pointing your toes and stretching your legs. Hold for a count of five and repeat three times. |

## THE ROLE OF DIET

Diet plays a dual role in fighting pain: achieving and maintaining ideal weight reduces stress on arthritic joints, and specific foods and nutrients are natural painkillers. By the same token, some foods can also provoke pain.

### Weight control

Obesity is our most common chronic health problem, second only to tobacco use as a cause of premature death. According to a 1997 Canadian Heart Health survey, nearly half of adult Canadians are overweight, and one in six is obese, defined as having

*Brightly colored fruits and vegetables are high in beta carotene and bioflavonoids—natural anti-inflammatories.*

a body mass index (BMI) over 30. Being overweight increases the risk of some of our most serious diseases including: heart attacks, high blood pressure, stroke, diabetes, and a number of cancers. It also exacerbates osteoarthritis, chronic back and foot problems, varicose veins and other circulatory disorders, constipation, and gallbladder disease.

Obesity is a complex medical problem that doctors do not fully understand, and losing excess weight is notoriously difficult. Every year, millions of Canadians go on some sort of weight-loss diet, and while most succeed in losing at least some weight, more than 90 percent of these dieters regain whatever they lost within five years. Still, a commonsense approach that combines increased exercise with a reduced intake of calories can achieve a gradual loss of one or two pounds a week. Over the course of a year, this adds up to 50 or more pounds—enough to bring the BMIs of a large number of overweight people into a healthful range. Similarly, the combination of weight loss and increased exercise can help ease arthritis pain, chronic backaches, and other common pain syndromes.

## Food as painkillers

Science-based medicine is at long last beginning to accept the age-old wisdom of folk healers in regard to the many different aspects of diet and health. Long before aspirin and other modern painkillers were developed, folk healers knew that certain foods, herbs, and teas could stop a headache, ease aching joints, calm an upset stomach, soothe menstrual cramps, and treat myriad other types of pain. Similarly, they also recognized that certain foods could exacerbate specific types of pain and other medical problems. Identifying the offending foods is often difficult because symptoms may not develop for hours or even days after eating. Keeping a food-and-symptoms diary can help spot patterns; you can then eliminate the suspected food for 10 to 14 days, and see if reintroducing it into your diet provokes a recurrence of symptoms. Following are some of the more common conditions in which foods can help or provoke pain; more detailed discussions can be found in entries dealing with the specific conditions.

### Arthritis

**Foods that help:** Two types of fatty acids act as natural anti-inflammatory agents: omega-3 fatty acids, which are found in salmon, sardines, and other cold-water fish, and gamma linolenic acid (GLA), such as evening primrose, borage, black currant, and hemp seed oils. Citrus fruits and brightly colored fruits and vegetables are high in beta carotene, vitamin C, and bioflavonoids, which also have an anti-inflammatory effect. Herbs that are natural anti-inflammatories include ginger, green tea, and turmeric, among others.

**Foods that hurt:** Fatty beef and pork and vegetable oils may provoke inflammation and worsen arthritis. A high-fat diet also promotes excessive weight gain, which further stresses and damages knees, hips, and other weight-bearing joints.

### Circulatory problems

**Foods that help:** Salmon, sardines, and other oily fish; fresh fruits and vegetables that are high in vitamin C; seeds, nuts, wheat germ, eggs, fortified breads and cereals and other foods high in vitamin E.

**Foods that hurt:** Fatty meat, whole-fat milk and cheese, baked goods made with palm or coconut oils, more than two alcoholic beverages a day.

### Digestive problems

**Foods that help:** High-fiber fruits and vegetables, whole-grain cereals and breads, at least 8 to 10 glasses of nonalcoholic fluids a day.

**Foods that hurt:** Fatty meats and other high-fat foods; beans, onions, cabbage, and other foods that produce excessive intestinal gas; milk and other dairy products in people who are lactose intolerant.

## MISCELLANEOUS OTHER FACTORS

In addition to exercise and diet, other lifestyle factors that have an impact on pain and its treatment include the following:

- **Adequate sleep**. Needs vary from one person to another, but most people need seven or more hours of sleep a night in order to feel their best.
- **Good stress-coping techniques**. Stress is a normal part of day-to-day life; it's how well you cope with excessive stress that determines whether it impairs health. Persons who suffer from frequent muscle-tension headaches, unexplained neck and back pain, and stomach upsets may benefit from learning yoga or other stress-reduction techniques.

# THE HEAD

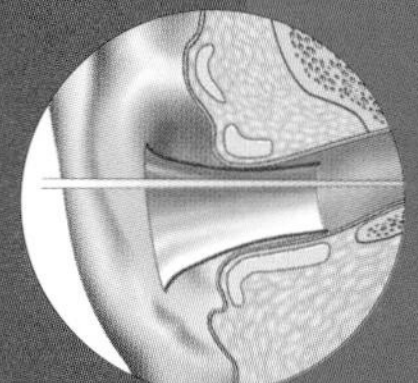

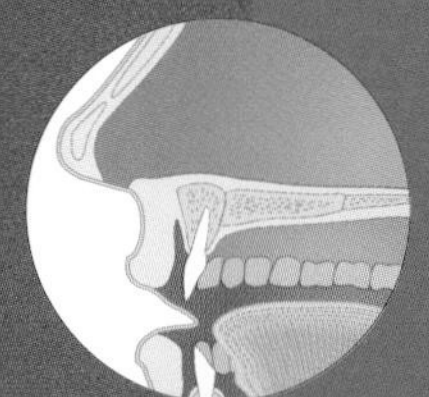

# The Head

*Although the brain receives and decodes all pain messages, it has no pain nerves of its own. As a result, headaches usually do not reflect a problem in the brain itself, but instead originate in the head's blood vessels or muscles.*

## Headaches, Cluster

### SYMPTOMS

- *Excruciating head pain on one side of the head, usually centered around an eye, that comes on and ends abruptly and recurs frequently over a period of days or weeks.*
- *Eye on affected side may be red and teary, with a drooping eyelid.*
- *Possible stuffy or runny nose and flushed face.*

### WHO IS AT RISK

*Cluster headaches affect over 300,000 Canadians, mostly men, who make up 85 percent of all cluster headache sufferers. The precise cause is unknown, although recent studies by a group of British neurologists indicate that a subtle structural abnormality in the brain may be a factor (see* Breakthroughs!*). Some people who have migraine headaches also develop cluster headaches, but this is the exception rather than the rule.*

*Sometimes the headaches are secondary to sinusitis if a swollen sinus presses on the nerves around an eye. Other contributing factors may include an abnormality in or inflammation of the head's blood vessels.*

*Personality may also play a role; some studies have found that hard-driving, time-conscious Type A individuals are more likely to have cluster headaches than less-aggressive Type Bs. People who suffer from cluster headaches usually can identify one or more triggers: common ones include alcohol, tobacco smoke, and certain foods, most often chocolate, eggs, and dairy products. Some people find the headaches recur at about the same time each year, so seasonal or weather factors may play a role. Other possible triggers include allergies, exposure to heat or cold, and a history of a head injury severe enough to cause unconsciousness. During a cluster, headaches can be provoked by taking nitroglycerin, but the reason for this is unknown.*

### HOW IT DEVELOPS

As their name implies, the headaches come in clusters, often after several hours of sleep. The intense, nonfluctuating pain comes on suddenly without warning, reaching a crescendo within minutes, and typically lasting for 30 minutes to 2 hours (the average is 45 minutes), and then disappearing as abruptly as it started. After a respite of a few minutes up to a few hours, the headache returns. This pattern continues, with some people experiencing three or four headaches during the course of a day. The headaches typically recur at the same time each day for a week up to a month or so, and then they disappear for months or even years. Most people with these headaches experience one or two clusters a year. In a few people, however, they become chronic, with an attack persisting for four or five years or longer; in fact, there have been reports of bouts lasting 25 years. Eventually, the clusters taper off and disappear altogether.

### WHAT YOU CAN DO

Keep a diary to help identify specific triggers, and then avoid them as much as possible. If there appears to be a seasonal pattern, talk to your doctor about preventive medications (see *How to Treat It* on the next page). During an attack, inhaling pure oxygen for 10 to 15 minutes stops the pain in about 80 percent of patients. Thus, people who suffer from cluster headaches are often advised to have a portable oxygen inhaler on hand, especially during a cluster.

Using your fingers to massage or press gently on the temporal artery on the affected side—the large blood vessel that you can feel pulsating in the temple area—can provide temporary relief in about 40 percent of patients. Some sufferers find that vigorous exercise, such as jogging or running up and down stairs, at the earliest sign of an attack can stop it.

### BREAKTHROUGHS!

**A 1999 report from researchers at London's Institute of Neurology challenges some long-held assumptions about possible causes of cluster headaches, and perhaps migraines as well. Until now, it has been assumed that cluster headaches were due to some unidentified abnormal function within a structurally normal brain. But using advanced brain imaging techniques, the British researchers discovered that cluster headache sufferers have extra gray matter in the brain's hypothalamus, the area of the brain associated with circadian rhythms, the body's internal clock. If further studies confirm these preliminary findings, it would explain why the headaches tend to strike with clocklike regularity.**

## HOW TO TREAT IT

There are two approaches to treating cluster headaches: abortive, which stops a headache in progress, and preventive, which requires taking medication daily.

**Abortive medications.** Most oral medications are not effective in stopping a headache in progress because they take too long to work. However, an injection or nasal spray of sumatriptan (Imitrex)—a drug used to treat migraine headaches—may stop a headache, but it is not effective in preventing a recurrence a few hours later. Aerosol ergotamine preparations are effective in stopping an attack about 80 percent of the time and are generally safer than oral forms of these drugs (see *Warning!*). Lidocaine—a short-acting anesthetic—dripped into a nostril will abort a headache in 60 percent of patients, but another headache may come on in a few hours.

**WARNING!**

***If you take an ergotamine preparation to treat cluster headaches, be careful not to exceed the recommended dosage. Taking these drugs repeatedly for frequently recurring headaches can lead to ergot toxicity. Symptoms include weakness, loss of muscle coordination, tremors, convulsions, and—in extreme cases—severely reduced circulation to the hands and feet, causing tissue death.***

**Preventive medications.** A number of drugs can help prevent cluster headaches; among the most effective are calcium channel blockers, such as verapamil (Isoptin). These drugs, which are also used to treat high blood pressure, work by preventing a narrowing (constriction) of blood vessels. Other possible preventive medications include: corticosteroids, which reduce swelling and inflammation; cyproheptadine (Periactin), an antihistamine that also prevents inflammation and swelling; and lithium, a drug more often used to treat manic depressive disorder. During a cluster, oral antimigraine ergotamine drugs may be used as preventive medications.

## HOW TO PREVENT IT

In addition to taking one of the preventive medications listed above, avoid common triggers, especially alcohol and exposure to tobacco smoke.

### ALTERNATIVE THERAPIES

**Acupressure**

Use of the following technique at the beginning of a headache may shorten its course: Place a fingertip on the pressure point located between the eyebrows and above the bridge of the nose. Press gently for about two minutes; repeat three to five times. To prevent a recurrence, do it every few hours.

# Headaches, Migraine

*Visual distortions are common preludes of classic migraines.*

### SYMPTOMS

***Common Migraine** (without aura)*

- *Warning phase (prodrome) marked by fatigue, anxiety, mood swings, and other vague symptoms.*
- *Intense throbbing or pounding head pain.*
- *Nausea and perhaps vomiting.*
- *Increased sensitivity to light and sound.*

***Classic Migraine***

*Headache is preceded by an aura and marked by:*

- *Distorted vision, such as seeing flashing lights.*
- *Feelings of disorientation and dizziness.*
- *Possible one-sided facial numbness or tingling.*
- *Speech problems, such as garbled words.*

### WHO IS AT RISK

*Migraine headaches afflict about 3.2 million adults in Canada, with women outnumbering men about two to one. They are most common among people 20 to 45 years of age, although they can occur from childhood into old age. Heredity appears to play an important role; if both parents have migraines, there is a 75 percent chance that any offspring will also have the headaches. The risk drops to 50 percent if one parent has migraines.*

## HOW IT DEVELOPS

Eighty to 90 percent of migraines are classified as the common type, which has a warning phase of vague symptoms lasting anywhere from a few hours to three or four days. The remaining 10 to 20 percent are classic migraines, which are preceded by visual disturbances, speech problems, and other typical aura symptoms.

Both migraine types involve a complex biochemical process that researchers are only beginning to understand. It is believed to start with a triggering factor (see *Common Migraine Triggers,* p 69) that sets off an inflammatory response in the trigeminal nerve—the large, branching facial nerve. The response causes a clumping of platelets, the blood cells instrumental in inflammation and clot formation. Chemical messengers from the trigeminal nerve signal the brain to release serotonin, a substance that dulls pain perception and also narrows, or constricts, blood vessels. Researchers have discovered that migraine sufferers experience unexplained periodic drops in serotonin levels, causing the constricted blood vessels—typically on one side of the head—to open up. At the same time, there is not enough serotonin to deflect pain coming from these distended arteries, resulting in the throbbing or pulsating head pain.

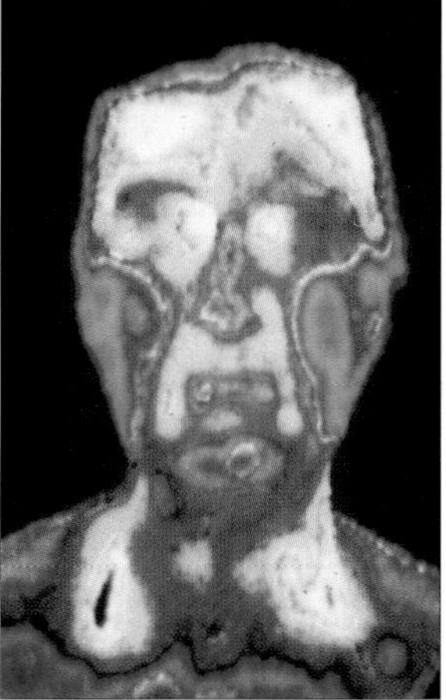
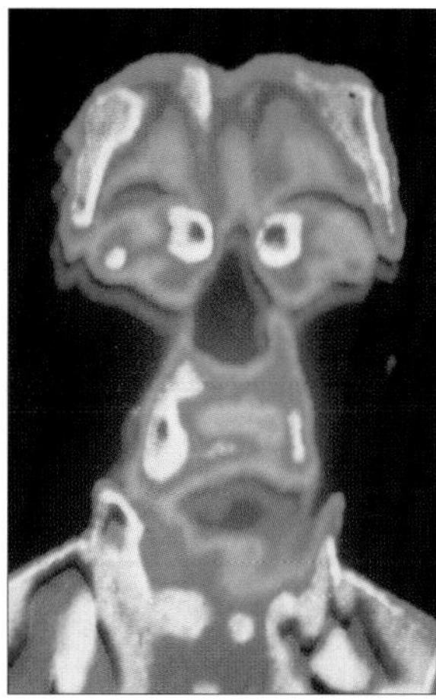

*These thermographic scans show the changes in blood flow in a migraine. The scan at the left shows the increased blood flow through dilated vessels, while the scan at the right shows reduced flow through constricted vessels.*

## WHAT YOU CAN DO

Migraines can often be aborted by taking action at the first hint of an impending headache. When you sense a headache coming on, stop what you are doing, take aspirin, ibuprofen, or a similar nonprescription painkiller with a cup of strong coffee or cola, and lie down in a quiet, darkened room with a cool compress on your forehead. The aspirin or ibuprofen helps block the pain-causing prostaglandins that are released by expanded and inflamed blood vessels; caffeine speeds the action of the painkiller; and the cool compress prevents the rush of blood to the underlying arteries. If this doesn't work, or if you get migraines on a regular basis, see a doctor.

## HOW TO TREAT IT

Conventional migraine treatment entails taking medications to either stop (abort) or prevent the headaches. Abortive medications are most effective when taken early in the course of a migraine; preventive drugs are taken daily and are usually prescribed for people who suffer one or more headaches a month. Medications include:

- **Nonprescription painkillers,** which range from acetaminophen and aspirin and other nonsteroidal anti-inflammatory drugs (NSAIDs) or combination products such as aspirin or acetaminophen with codeine and/or butalbital (a barbiturate).
- **Ergotamine preparations,** such as Cafergot, Wigraine, Ergomar, and DHE, which work by constricting the distended arteries in the head. These drugs must be used with caution—high dosages can cause toxicity, and even at low doses, possible side effects include serious circulatory problems, high blood pressure, an irregular heartbeat, nausea and vomiting, and numbness and weakness. Some people also experience a recurrence of headaches when they stop taking ergotamine.
- **Selective vasoconstrictors,** drugs that include sumatriptan (Imitrex), zolmitriptan (Zomig), and rizatriptan (Maxalt), work by constricting the small arteries of the head. They can be taken orally, or in the case of Imitrex, by injection or nasal spray. They are generally safer than ergotamine, but must be used cautiously because they can cause chest pain, shortness of breath, and high blood pressure and should not be used by anyone with heart disease or uncontrolled high blood pressure.
- **Opioids,** such as codeine or combinations of codeine and acetaminophen or aspirin, work by blocking pain messages in the brain.
- **Preventive medications** work in a variety of ways. The most common are calcium channel blockers and beta blockers, drugs more commonly used to treat high blood pressure, which help prevent migraines by acting directly on the blood vessels. Another drug that may be tried is valproic acid (Depakene), an anticonvulsant; although

### BREAKTHROUGHS!

**A novel approach to treating migraines was reported at a 1999 Boston gathering of headache specialists. W. J. Binder of the University of California at Los Angeles described results of a study using Botox, the botulism toxin that, when injected in tiny amounts, relaxes tensed muscles. It is used to treat wryneck and painful muscle spasms, as well as to reduce frown lines and other facial wrinkles. According to Dr. Binder, a Botox injection can abort a migraine in about an hour, and in one study, the injections eliminated recurring headaches in more than half of patients, and halved the number of headaches for another 35 percent. A single treatment gives three to four months of relief, and no adverse effects have been reported.**

scientists don't know how it works, studies show it can prevent migraines.

## HOW TO PREVENT IT

Start by trying to identify any migraine triggers. Keep a diary of foods, weather patterns, menstrual cycle, and other possible factors to see whether there is a pattern of triggers you can avoid to prevent migraines.

Strive for a moderate lifestyle: Get enough sleep, but avoid sleeping in—too little and too much sleep can trigger migraines. Use alcohol in moderation, if at all, and limit your intake of caffeinated drinks to two or three a day. Stress is a factor in many migraines; try to reduce unnecessary stressors, and consider taking up meditation, yoga, or another relaxation technique to improve your stress-coping abilities. Regular aerobic exercise, such as brisk walking, not only counters stress, but also improves circulation and increases levels of endorphins, the body's natural painkillers. If these strategies don't work, talk to your doctor about preventive medications.

### ALTERNATIVE THERAPIES

**Acupuncture**

Improvement should be noted in six or fewer treatments; if not, further treatments probably won't help.

**Biofeedback training**

This technique involves learning how to divert some blood flow from the scalp to other parts of the body.

**Herbal medicine**

Feverfew, an ancient herbal migraine remedy, can help prevent migraines in up to 50 to 60 percent of patients. The recommended daily dosage is 250 mg of dried feverfew leaves or an extract standardized to provide at least 0.4 percent of parthenolide, its active ingredient. Recent French studies show that ginkgo biloba extract—a product that increases blood flow, prevents platelet clumping, and has an anti-inflammatory action—may prevent migraines. The daily dosage is 120 to 240 mg. Check with your doctor before using either if you are taking anticoagulant drugs. Use only standardized extracts of ginkgo, and avoid if you are hypersensitive to poison ivy, cashews, or mangoes.

**Nutritional supplements**

Magnesium and omega-3 fatty acids show promise in preventing migraines. Studies show that patients who take 200 to 350 mg of magnesium a day have significantly fewer migraines, and when headaches do occur, they tend to be shorter and more mild. Omega-3 fatty acids, which are found in flaxseed oils and salmon and other fatty cold-water fish, have an anti-inflammatory effect and also prevent platelet clumping.

### COMMON MIGRAINE TRIGGERS

- **Caffeine.** More than three or four cups of coffee, tea, and cola drinks trigger migraines in some people.
- **Foods.** The most common offenders are foods high in tyramine, a substance found in aged cheeses, organ meats, cured meats, and red wine, among others. Other possibilities include: monosodium glutamate (MSG), soy sauce, and ginger; dried fruits and nuts; yeasty breads; citrus fruits; pickles; and dried peas and beans.
- **Hormonal changes.** About two-thirds of migraines in women are related to their menstrual cycles.
- **Medications.** Drugs used to treat ulcers, high blood pressure, heart disease, and circulatory disorders trigger migraines in some people.
- **Weather changes.** An abrupt drop in barometric pressure can trigger migraines in susceptible people, and a sudden clearing of stormy weather can cause a migraine to go away.

# Headaches, Muscle-Tension

### SYMPTOMS

- *Persistent or recurring head pain that is steady (nonpulsating), moderately severe, and may feel like a band tightening around the head.*
- *Pain tends to be on both sides of head (bilateral) and headaches last anywhere from a few hours to days.*
- *More frequent headaches during periods of stress.*

### WHO IS AT RISK

*Virtually everyone suffers a muscle-tension headache at one time or another. They are especially common among people whose jobs entail holding their head in one position for a long time, such as computer operators.*

## HOW IT DEVELOPS

Tensed muscles cause head pain by their prolonged contraction. It is analogous to having a cramp, in which the tightened muscles go into a spasm. The pain often develops over the eyes or back of the head, and may spread to neck and shoulders. People who suffer from migraines often develop mixed headaches, in which muscle tension contributes to the migraine.

## WHAT YOU CAN DO

Try massaging the temples and back of your neck. If the headache comes on while you are hunched over a desk or driving, take a break. Stretch, rotate your neck and head, and then just sit quietly for a few minutes with your eyes closed and your thoughts focused on a relaxing image. If the headache persists, lie down in a quiet, dimly lit room with a cool compress on your forehead. If you suffer frequently recurring headaches, and your doctor cannot find a medical cause for them, examine the sources of stress in your life and see what you can change.

## HOW TO TREAT IT

Nonprescription painkillers—acetaminophen, aspirin, or low-dose ibuprofen—and other prescribed nonsteroidal anti-inflammatory drugs (NSAIDs) will relieve most simple muscle-tension headaches. If these and the self-help measures described above don't help, try some of the alternative approaches below. If the headaches still persist, consult a doctor.

## HOW TO PREVENT IT

The best way to prevent muscle-tension headaches is to identify and eliminate the contributing causes. Most muscle-tension headaches are related to stress, which causes the muscles to contract and stimulates nerves to send pain messages to the brain. Other contributing factors include eye strain, faulty posture, anxiety and other mood disorders, excessive alcohol intake, and fatigue.

### ALTERNATIVE THERAPIES

**Acupressure and reflexology**

Place one index finger at a point midway between the eyebrows and the other directly in the middle on the top of the head. Apply moderate pressure simultaneously with both fingertips, hold for 5 seconds, relax for 30 seconds, and repeat. Three sets should help ease the pain. Alternatively, grasp the center of the soft pad of tissue between the thumb and the first finger with the thumb and index finger of the other hand, and apply pressure with the thumb for 5 seconds, relax for 30 seconds, and repeat. Reflexologists recommend massaging the big toe as a substitute for a neck and back massage.

**Aromatherapy**

Essential oils recommended for headaches include lavender, chamomile, peppermint, wintergreen, and juniper berry. The diluted oils can be massaged into the skin or added to steamy bathwater, or the vapors can be inhaled from a few drops sprinkled on a handkerchief.

### WARNING!

***See a doctor as soon as possible for:***

- *A headache accompanied by a fever and stiff neck—signs of meningitis.*
- *A headache after a head injury.*
- *A headache accompanied by neurological changes, such as confusion or paralysis.*
- *Recurring headaches in the same place or with increasing frequency.*
- *Headaches that wake you up.*

## The Many Types of Headaches and How They Differ

| TYPE | DISTINGUISHING FEATURES |
|---|---|
| Brain abscess, tumor, subdural hematoma, and other growths in skull | Pain came on recently and is unlike other headaches; often present upon awakening; may come and go, but tends to worsen with time. Other symptoms may include nausea, mood changes, altered consciousness, partial paralysis, and numbness. |
| Cluster | Brief (often less than an hour), very severe one-sided headaches that often recur one after another for several days or weeks followed by a period without headaches. |
| Eye problems | Pain is over the eyes or in the front of the head; often worsens after reading or using eyes; person may also become sensitive to light and eyes may appear red (iritis). |
| Hypertension | Spasms of throbbing pain felt at the top of the head; usually due to periodic, very sharp rises in blood pressure, sometimes due to a tumor of the adrenal gland. |
| Migraine | Throbbing, one-sided headache, usually preceded by warning symptoms (prodrome or aura); may be accompanied by nausea, vomiting, and sensitivity to light and sound. |
| Muscle tension | Frequent headaches marked by steady dull or intense pain on the front or back of head and often a sensation of a tightening band around the head. Pain may spread to the neck and shoulders. |
| Secondary | Headache is accompanied by fever, chills, rash, nausea, vomiting, stiff neck, or other symptoms suggesting that it is due to another illness. |
| Sinus | Pain is usually steady, centered on the front of the head, and most intense in the morning. Moving the head can ease or worsen pain; aspirin and other painkillers have little effect. |

**Massage**

Massaging the neck, shoulders, back, and temples is a time-honored treatment to relax tensed muscles and relieve headaches. Deep, pressure-point massage techniques, such as Shiatsu, usually produce longer-lasting results than gentle, more superficial massage.

**Meditation**

Meditation promotes relaxation and also helps block the transmission of pain messages.

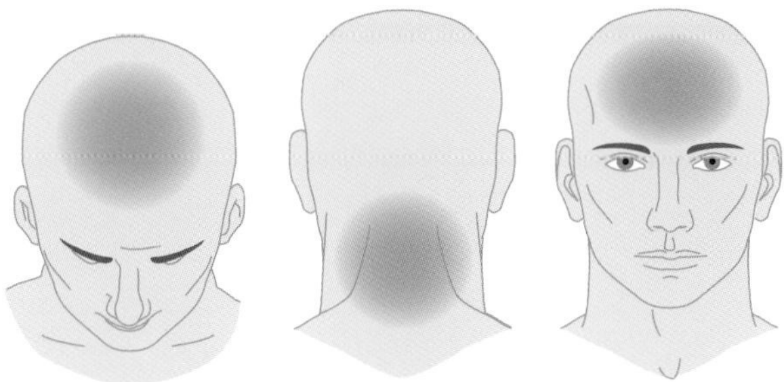
*Hot buttons: common sites of muscle-tension headaches*

**Posture-correction exercises**

Faulty posture can cause headaches, especially if the head and neck are held in awkward or unnatural positions. The Alexander Technique, in which a person learns to correct faulty posture, may help.

**Spinal manipulation**

Chronic muscle-tension headaches may be relieved by chiropractic or osteopathic treatments to correct misaligned vertebrae and relax tensed muscles. For cautions concerning chiropractic treatments, see p 246.

# Trauma

## SYMPTOMS

- *Persistent dull headache, often lasting months after the initial injury has healed (postconcussion syndrome).*
- *Dizziness, difficulty concentrating, confusion, memory problems, and behavior or mood changes.*
- *Loss of consciousness; abnormal nerve reflexes.*
- *Asymmetry of facial movements, such as squinting or drooping of one side of the mouth.*
- *Nausea and vomiting; difficulty walking.*
- *Ringing in the ears and/or vision changes.*
- *Possible seizures and partial paralysis.*
- *In severe head trauma, deformed skull, dilated or unequal pupils, bruising of both eyes (raccoon's sign) or behind the ears, and bleeding from nose or ears.*

## WHO IS AT RISK

*Anyone can suffer a head injury, but it is most common among people involved in automobile accidents. Also at risk are athletes who participate in contact sports (or activities with a high risk of falls, such as cycling, horseback riding, rock climbing, or gymnastics). Shaken-baby syndrome—severe head trauma inflicted when an infant is shaken—is a distressingly common form of child abuse.*

## HOW IT DEVELOPS

Head trauma is often a double-edged sword—first the injury itself and then the later consequences. The extent of brain damage inflicted by the trauma itself varies greatly. Even a seemingly minor bump can cause bruising and bleeding as the brain is shaken around within the skull. If the skull is badly fractured, additional damage may result from bits of bone penetrating the brain. An initial loss of consciousness is common.

If the injury is relatively minor, the person may quickly regain consciousness and appear relatively normal. But hours later, second-impact syndrome (SIS) may set in, and if it is not properly treated, the consequence can be more devastating than the original trauma. SIS is marked by brain swelling due to an accumulation of fluid or pressure from an expanding blood mass (hematoma) inside the skull. If untreated, the swelling can lead to permanent brain damage and even death.

Postconcussion syndrome is poorly understood and often develops weeks after healing takes place. A persistent dull headache develops, which sometimes evolves into a migraine; in fact, some migraine sufferers trace the beginning of their headaches to a head injury. Other symptoms include chronic fatigue, irritability and mood swings, difficulty concentrating, and memory problems. Symptoms may last for months, and then gradually disappear.

## WHAT YOU CAN DO

Call the Emergency Medical Service (EMS) or dial 911. A head injury severe enough to cause even temporary loss of consciousness warrants an immediate trip to the emergency room for a neurological exam, X rays, and perhaps a CT scan or an MRI to assess a possible brain injury and bleeding.

Even if the injury appears minor, a medical examination is in order if brain-injury symptoms—drowsiness, confusion, nausea, ringing in the ears, blurred vision, among others—develop.

## HOW TO TREAT IT

The EMS team or doctor will quickly assess vital signs (blood pressure, heartbeat, breathing, level of consciousness) and then order a CT scan or an MRI to look for a possible brain injury. Treatment depends upon the type and severity of the injury.

### Medications

In the immediate post-trauma period, drugs may be given to relieve pain, calm agitation, and minimize brain swelling. If needed, extra oxygen may also be administered. Postconcussion syndrome, which may develop days or weeks later, may be treated with aspirin, ibuprofen, or other prescribed nonsteroidal anti-inflammatory drugs (NSAIDs) and muscle relaxants. If migraine-like headaches develop, preventive medications such as beta blockers or calcium channel blockers—drugs that work directly on the blood vessels—may be prescribed.

## Hypothermia

This is a relatively new approach that involves lowering the body temperature to 31.6° to 32.2°C/89° to 90°F, which in turn slows metabolism and the cascade of chemical changes that occur following a head injury. Within hours after a head injury, levels of glutamate, a brain chemical, can rise a thousandfold, setting off a chemical chain reaction that causes the death of brain cells. Studies show that hypothermia for up to 48 hours often prevents the rise in glutamate and helps preserve brain cells. The body temperature is lowered gradually to a point where metabolism slows down, but not enough to cause an irregular heartbeat and other potentially fatal complications. After 24 to 48 hours, the body is slowly rewarmed to its normal temperature. Several studies have found that hypothermia is superior to drugs and oxygen in preserving brain tissue.

**WARNING!**

***Do not move an accident victim if there is any chance of a neck or back injury. Instead, call the emergency medical service (in most areas, reached by dialing 911), and keep the person warm and as quiet and still as possible until medical help arrives.***

## Surgery

Emergency surgery may be necessary to repair a badly fractured skull and relieve pressure inside the skull due to brain swelling. An expanding blood clot (a hematoma) can be surgically removed.

# HOW TO PREVENT IT

Experts agree that half or more of all head trauma can be prevented by following basic safety rules:

- Always wear protective head gear when riding on a motorcycle or engaging in any sport that carries a risk of head injury. Make sure that children wear a properly fitted helmet when bicycling, in-line skating, skiing, and skate boarding.

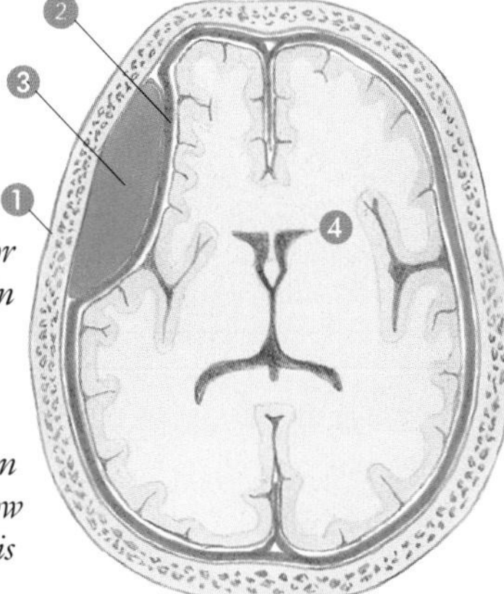


*Bleeding from an injury to the skull (1) or the covering of the brain (2) can result in a hematoma (3), which compresses the interior of the brain (4) and can cause swelling as the flow of spinal cerebral fluid is disrupted.*

**BREAKTHROUGHS!**

**Israeli researchers have discovered that cannabinoid, a synthetic form of the active ingredient in marijuana, lowers pressure inside the skull after head trauma more effectively than medications now in use. It also protects the brain by reducing inflammation and, as a powerful antioxidant, prevents cell damage from unstable molecules released when the body burns oxygen. This synthetic compound does not have any of the psychological effects of natural forms of marijuana.**

**In a study carried out at six Israeli trauma centers, the cannabinoid drug, called dexanabinol (HU-211), was given to 30 unconscious head-trauma patients, while 37 others who had similar severe injuries received a placebo. Mortality was cut by 26 percent among those who received dexanabinol, and recovery was faster and more complete in these patients.**

**Clinical trials in the U.S. began in 1999, and if the initial results are confirmed, dexanabinol represents a promising alternative for victims of head trauma.**

- When riding in a car, always wear seat belts and make sure that babies and young children ride in the backseat in properly installed safety seats.
- Never shake a baby; if you feel yourself losing control, call for help—a parenting hotline, or your pediatrician, neighbor, family member, or someone else who can care for the child while you take a break.

### ALTERNATIVE THERAPIES

These are more effective during rehabilitation or to ease symptoms of postconcussion syndrome rather than as a component of the primary treatment.

**Acupuncture**

Treatments are aimed at relieving the chronic headaches that are a hallmark of postconcussion syndrome.

**Aromatherapy**

The essential oils recommended for migraines (lavender, chamomile, peppermint, wintergreen, and juniper berry) may relieve postconcussion headaches. These oils, diluted in a neutral oil such as olive oil, may be massaged into the skin or added to bathwater and inhaled as steamy vapors.

**Exercise and movement therapies**

A daily walk, along with t'ai chi or another movement therapy, can help counter chronic fatigue, increase energy levels, and enhance a sense of well-being for persons suffering from postconcussion syndrome.

**Physical therapy**

A specially tailored regimen of physical treatments and exercises can help victims of head trauma improve balance and gait as well as regain varying degrees of nerve and muscle function. Exercising in water (hydrotherapy) may help persons who have difficulty walking.

# Tumors/Abscesses

## SYMPTOMS

- *Headache of recent origin; it may come and go and is usually worse in the morning.*
- *Nausea and vomiting.*
- *Mental and personality changes; speech problems.*
- *Possible seizures, progressive weakness, and paralysis.*
- *Impaired senses (vision, hearing, taste).*
- *Movement disorders; gait changes.*

## WHO IS AT RISK

*About 10,000 Canadians are diagnosed with brain tumors each year. They can occur at any age, but are most prevalent in childhood and after age 50. The cause of most brain cancer is unknown, but possible risk factors include exposure to X rays, vinyl chloride, and industrial chemicals. Media reports linking the use of cellular phones to an increased risk of brain cancer are unproved.*

*Brain abscesses can occur at any age and are most common among people with compromised immune systems, such as AIDS patients or head trauma victims.*

## HOW IT DEVELOPS

Some brain tumors grow slowly and exist for many years without causing symptoms; others develop suddenly and progress rapidly. Any expanding mass that is in the skull is always serious because it takes up space normally occupied by the brain. As the brain becomes more compressed, symptoms worsen and, if the pressure is not relieved, permanent brain damage—and even death—are possible consequences.

### BREAKTHROUGHS!

**Stereotactic, or gamma knife, radiosurgery is an exciting new alternative to neurosurgery for the treatment of many types of brain tumors and abnormal blood vessels, such as aneurysms or tangles of small arteries. Before the procedure, the patient's head is placed in a special stereotactic head frame, and a CT scan or an MRI is done to locate the tumor precisely. The doctors then map out a treatment plan, and program the gamma knife computer. The patient is given a mild sedative and then placed on a special table that moves the head into the proper position inside the gamma hemisphere. The machine emits some 200 finely focused beams of gamma radiation that are programmed to intersect the precise location of the tumor. A typical treatment takes only a few minutes and there is no incision, bleeding, or pain. Most patients stay in the hospital overnight, and over the next few days or weeks, depending upon the type of tumor, symptoms abate as the mass shrinks and, in many cases, disappears.**

## WHAT YOU CAN DO

There is no effective self-treatment for a brain tumor. Your best approach is to see a neurologist as soon as possible. Imaging studies, especially CT scans and an MRI, can usually pinpoint the problem. A biopsy is needed to diagnose cancer.

## HOW TO TREAT IT

Recent years have witnessed great advances in the treatment of various types of brain tumors; now, virtually all can be treated and many are curable.

### WARNING!

***Early diagnosis is critical in assuring the best possible outcome of treatment for a brain tumor or abscess. Any unusual headache and other symptoms suggesting a possible brain tumor warrant prompt investigation by a neurologist.***

### Chemotherapy

Brain abscesses and some types of brain cancer respond well to drug treatment. In the past, a major difficulty has involved getting adequate amounts of drugs past the blood-brain barrier, the body's mechanism to protect the brain from harmful chemicals. This problem has been overcome, at least in part, by new implanted devices that deliver drugs directly to the brain.

### Neurosurgery

New microsurgery techniques enable neurosurgeons to remove many tumors that were once considered inoperable. Conventional surgery is still used to remove hematomas, certain types of cysts, and localized tumors.

### Radiation therapy

Radiation is often used as an adjunct to neurosurgery to kill any remaining malignant cells. It is also used to treat inoperable brain tumors, as well as metastatic cancers that have spread to the brain from elsewhere in the body. The radiation may be delivered by external beams or internally through brachytherapy, a procedure in which radioactive substances are delivered directly into the tumor through a small catheter.

## HOW TO PREVENT IT

There are no sure means of preventing brain tumors aside from minimizing exposure to industrial chemicals and X rays. If your job entails working with chemicals, always wear protective masks and clothing.

### ALTERNATIVE THERAPIES

Physical therapy can be very helpful in regaining motor skills during the recovery period. In any instance, no alternative therapy should be used without first checking with the primary doctor.

# The Face

*Because the face is richly endowed with both large and small nerves, it is exquisitely sensitive to pain and other sensations. The facial area is also home to four of the body's major sensory organs—the eyes, nose, ears, and mouth—all common sources of pain.*

## Facial Shingles

### SYMPTOMS

- *Tingling, itching, and pain on one side of the face.*
- *Possible paralysis on one side of the face and partial loss of sense of taste.*
- *Two to four days after onset of pain, development of a red rash, with clusters of painful, itchy blisters.*

### WHO IS AT RISK

*Shingles can develop in anyone who once had chickenpox, a childhood disease caused by the same herpes zoster virus. It most commonly occurs in older people, especially those whose immune systems have been weakened by other diseases, such as AIDS, or unusual stress.*

### HOW IT DEVELOPS

As chickenpox clears up, the herpes zoster virus goes into hiding in a group of nerve cell bodies (ganglia) of a spinal nerve or the fifth (cranial or trigeminal) nerve. The dormant virus may never flare up again, but in a large number of mostly older people, it inexplicably comes to life and causes an outbreak of shingles.

The pain that heralds the rash occurs along a nerve path on one side of the body, most often on the torso. But if the virus has been dormant in the ganglia of a cranial nerve, the face will be involved. Facial shingles is more serious than when it occurs on the torso because it can spread to the eye, ear, brain, and other areas served by branches of the cranial nerve. Half to three-fourths of patients who develop a shingles rash on the forehead or around the nose will have the infection spread to the eye and threaten vision.

The blisters continue to form for several days, and then gradually disappear, but the pain, itchiness, and malaise may linger for weeks. Shingles is most severe in people with lowered immunity; the rash is often more extensive, and the infection may spread to internal organs. Most people recover in a few weeks, but about 10 percent go on to develop postherpetic neuralgia—nerve pain that may persist for years.

**BREAKTHROUGHS!**

**In the coming years, the incidence of shingles is expected to decline sharply thanks to the recent development and growing use of a childhood vaccine against chickenpox. Preventing this disease means that the virus that causes shingles will not enter the body.**

### WHAT YOU CAN DO

Make every effort to avoid scratching the blisters, which can increase the risk of a secondary bacterial infection. Bathe the area frequently with a mild antibacterial soap, rinse thoroughly, and pat dry. Cool compresses applied to the skin rash can ease pain and itching. Calamine lotion may also ease itching; swabbing the area with 20 percent rubbing alcohol helps dry the blisters. Be careful, however, when applying any substance to the skin near the eyes. To promote healing and prevent scarring, apply vitamin E oil and the gel from an aloe vera plant to the blisters every two or three hours.

**WARNING!**

***See an eye specialist (an ophthalmologist) as soon as possible if facial shingles develops. Prompt treatment can help prevent the virus from spreading to the eye and brain.***

Nonprescription painkillers are usually adequate to ease the pain. But if these are not strong enough, talk to your doctor about a prescription for codeine, especially if the pain keeps you awake at night.

Shingles can be very debilitating, especially if it has been triggered by an underlying disease. Get extra rest, and make sure your diet includes at least five daily servings of fruits and vegetables to provide the vitamin C you need to help heal the skin lesions and also fight off the infection (see also *Alternative Therapies,* p 75).

### HOW TO TREAT IT

An antiviral drug, such as acyclovir (Zovirax), famciclovir (Famvir), or valacyclovir (Valtrex), started in the early stages of shingles and continued for seven days may hasten healing, reduce the risk of eye complications, and help prevent postherpetic neuralgia. If the eye is involved, an eye ointment containing dexamethasone, a corticosteroid, is prescribed, along with medication to dilate the pupils. Frequent visits to an ophthalmologist are necessary to monitor for glaucoma.

## HOW TO PREVENT IT

There is no known means of preventing shingles among people who have had chickenpox. However, immunizing against chickenpox not only prevents this common childhood disease, but it also protects against adult outbreaks of shingles (see *Breakthroughs!*, p 74).

### ALTERNATIVE THERAPIES

**Acupuncture**

Treatments can reduce the nerve pain associated with active shingles as well as postherpetic neuralgia.

**Capsaicin**

If nerve pain persists after the blisters are healed, applications of a cream such as Zostrix, which contains capsaicin—the substance that gives hot peppers their "bite"—may relieve it. Be sure to wait until the blisters are fully healed; never apply capsaicin to broken skin or mucous membranes, and never use it anywhere near the eyes.

**Herbal medicine**

Compresses soaked in green tea or a tea made of peppermint or lemon balm can soothe the itchy, painful blisters caused by shingles.

**Nutraceuticals**

Some studies have found that high doses of vitamin E (1200 to 1600 IU a day) for one to two weeks may shorten the course of shingles and help prevent postherpetic neuralgia. Be sure to check with your doctor first, however, especially if you are taking aspirin or another blood-thinning medication or have high blood pressure.

# Sinusitis

### SYMPTOMS

- *Tenderness and swelling over affected sinuses.*
- *Uncomfortable feeling of fullness, pressure, or heaviness in the face and behind the eyes.*
- *Nasal obstruction or runny nose and postnasal drip.*
- *Possible foul-smelling green or yellow nasal discharge.*
- *Headache, general malaise, and possible fever.*
- *Bad breath and possible pain in the upper teeth.*

### WHO IS AT RISK

*Sinusitis is a very common condition, afflicting millions of Canadians each year. At some point, about one out of three people will suffer a bout of it. It is especially common among people who get frequent colds or suffer from asthma, hay fever, and other nasal allergies (allergic rhinitis). Other possible risk factors include nasal polyps (small, benign growths in the nose), enlarged adenoids, chronic tonsillitis, a crooked (deviated) septum, poorly controlled diabetes, and immune deficiency disorders.*

## HOW IT DEVELOPS

The sinuses are air-filled cavities in the facial bones. They are lined with mucous membranes and millions of tiny hairlike structures, called cilia, that beat in waves to move mucus toward tiny drainage tubes. Acute sinusitis develops when the membranes become inflamed and swollen, usually during a bout of the flu or a cold. The cilia are destroyed, allowing a buildup of mucus. The congested sinus cavities become an ideal breeding ground for bacteria, most commonly *Hemophilus influenzae*, or a streptococcal or staphylococcal organism. In rare instances, a fungal infection may develop. Sinusitis usually starts in one pair of sinuses, and often spreads to other pairs. The spreading infection produces further inflammation and congestion. If untreated, the sinusitis may become chronic, especially in people with allergies or diabetes.

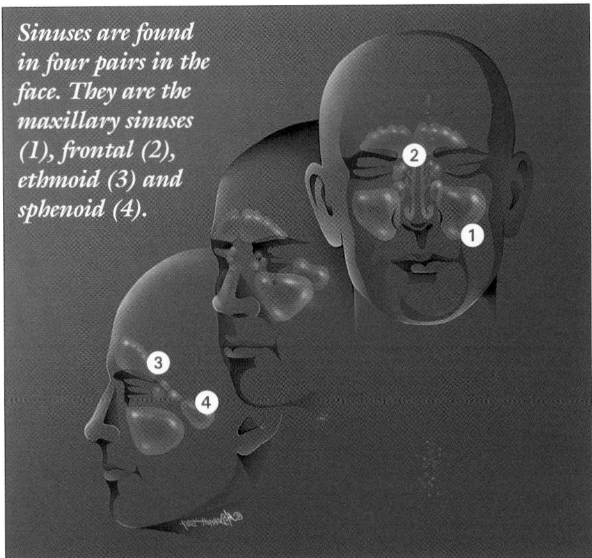


*Sinuses are found in four pairs in the face. They are the maxillary sinuses (1), frontal (2), ethmoid (3) and sphenoid (4).*

## WHAT YOU CAN DO

Drink ample fluids—at least eight or more glasses of water a day. Hot steamy broth is especially helpful in thinning mucus and promoting drainage of the clogged sinuses. Hot, spicy foods such chilies, horseradish, and garlic also help clear sinuses. For temporary relief, place a warm wet compress over the forehead or take a steamy shower. Avoid alcohol, which has a dehydrating effect that thickens mucus. Do not smoke and avoid secondhand smoke and other irritating fumes; cigarette smoke paralyzes the sinuses' cilia, and irritating fumes worsen sinus inflammation and swelling.

Some doctors recommend nasal washes for people with nasal allergies or sinusitis. Fill a nasal syringe with warm, salty water, draw it into one nostril, tilt the head back to fill the sinus cavities, and then bend forward to let the fluid flow out. Repeat with the other nostril.

## HOW TO TREAT IT

### Medications

Antibiotics are the mainstay of acute bacterial sinusitis treatment. It's important to complete the full course, usually 7 to 14 days, of antibiotic treatment. Management of chronic sinusitis involves looking for and treating the underlying cause—for example, using a nasal corticosteroid if the cause is an allergy. A short course (a week or less) of a nasal spray containing oxymetazoline (Dristan Spray) or an oral medication containing pseudoephedrine (Sudafed) may be prescribed to reduce swelling.

**WARNING!**

***People with diabetes or weakened immune systems are susceptible to a life-threatening form of sinusitis caused by a fungal infection. Clumps of dead tissue collect in the sinus cavities; large nasal polyps also may develop. Symptoms include headaches, blindness, and other neurologic problems. Prompt treatment with an antifungal drug, such as amphotericin B, is necessary to prevent permanent brain damage and even death.***

### Surgery

If medications fail to clear up chronic or severe sinusitis, surgery may be needed to open the blocked sinuses, remove dead tissue and other debris, and improve drainage. One procedure entails using a special instrument to create a small opening in the bottom of the frontal sinuses in the forehead. Another, called endoscopic sinus surgery, involves inserting a small viewing tube through the nose and into the sinuses; this enables the surgeon to inspect the inside of the cavities, open clogged drainage passages, and remove debris.

## HOW TO PREVENT IT

When you have a cold or flu, blow your nose gently to prevent forcing nasal discharges into the sinus cavities. When you feel a cold coming on, try taking echinacea to shorten the duration of the cold and prevent complications like sinusitis. Use a misting vaporizer, especially in the winter, to moisten overly dry air.

### ALTERNATIVE THERAPIES

**Acupressure**

To help ease the swelling and pain of congested sinuses, try this acupressure treatment: Place the tips of each index finger on the acupressure points on both sides of the lower nose, just below the cheekbones. While breathing deeply, apply gentle pressure by pressing upward toward the cheekbone for about one minute.

**Aromatherapy**

Inhalation of eucalyptus, peppermint, basil, or lavender oil helps clear clogged sinuses. Add a few drops of an oil to a bowl or pan of hot water and inhale the vapors.

**Herbal medicine**

In addition to echinacea (200 mg, four times daily), some herbalists recommend goldenseal to help clear up sinusitis due to an infection. Irrigate the sinuses with 1 1/2 teaspoons of goldenseal extract to one cup of saline solution twice daily for five days. For cautions concerning echinacea and goldenseal, see *About the Recommendations*, p 7. Garlic, preferably the herb itself rather than an extract or pill, is a natural antibiotic. The recommended daily dosage is a half clove of raw or barely cooked garlic. Cayenne and horseradish also help clear clogged sinuses.

**Homeopathy**

The numerous homeopathic remedies used to treat sinusitis include Euphrasia, Kali bichromicum, Mercuris vivus, Natrum muriaticum, and Nux vomica. The remedy should be tailored to the specific symptoms, such as the type of nasal discharge and the site of the pain.

# Temporal Arteritis

### SYMPTOMS

- *Severe, throbbing headache that comes on suddenly and is mainly in the temples and back of the head.*
- *Pain when chewing or moving the jaw.*
- *Joint and muscle pain, especially in the morning.*
- *Eye pain, double vision, and blindness—usually temporary but sometimes permanent—in one or both eyes.*
- *Possible fever, weight loss, and general malaise, especially in the elderly.*

### WHO IS AT RISK

*Temporal arteritis is relatively uncommon—the overall chances of developing it after age 50 are about one in a thousand. Women are afflicted somewhat more often than men. The disorder is rare in people under age 50 and in those of African descent.*

## HOW IT DEVELOPS

Temporal arteritis involves chronic inflammation of one or more arteries, most often the large temporal arteries in the head. The cause is unknown, but possible contributing factors include a genetic predisposition, a virus or another infectious agent, or a defect in the immune system. It may be related to, or be a variation of, polymyalgia rheumatica—a condition marked by aching joints—because the two often occur together.

Symptoms may come on suddenly or develop slowly over time. Sometimes it affects only a small segment of a temporal artery and its branches; in other instances, it is widespread, involving the aorta (the body's largest artery, which is attached to the heart), the coronary arteries, the carotid artery in the neck, and smaller peripheral blood vessels. The pain is caused mostly by inflammation of the arteries, but as the affected vessels become stiff and thickened, the reduced blood flow and lack of oxygen (ischemia) also produce pain.

Sometimes the disease disappears on its own; more often, however, it progresses and can lead to blindness if the blood supply to the optic nerve is cut off.

## WHAT YOU CAN DO

Cool compresses over the forehead may help ease the throbbing headache. Avoid vigorous hair brushing or other activities that provoke head pain.

## HOW TO TREAT IT

A corticosteroid drug, usually prednisone, is the mainstay of treatment. Doctors start with 40 to 60 mg of prednisone a day, divided into two to four divided doses. After the symptoms abate—usually in a few weeks—the prednisone can be taken in a single morning pill. If the condition remains stabilized, the dosage may be gradually reduced; the goal is to eventually wean the patient off the prednisone without producing a flare-up of symptoms. This usually takes one to two years, although some people need to be treated much longer.

Unfortunately, prednisone and other corticosteroids have many adverse side effects, including thinning of bones, indigestion, diabetes, acne, cataracts, and glaucoma.

## HOW TO PREVENT IT

There are no known means of preventing the condition.

### ALTERNATIVE THERAPIES

Although there are no alternative therapies that are a substitute for corticosteroid treatment, some can minimize side effects of the drugs and also relieve symptoms.

**WARNING!**

***Unexplained eye pain and any abrupt change in vision should be checked as soon as possible by an ophthalmologist. If you have been diagnosed with temporal arteritis, be especially alert to any eye symptoms—double or blurred vision, blind spots, temporary loss of sight—and call your doctor immediately if they develop. A delay in treatment can result in permanent blindness.***

**Exercise**

Weight-bearing aerobic exercise, such as brisk walking, along with strength training, can help strengthen bones and prevent the accelerated osteoporosis that occurs when taking prednisone.

**Nutraceuticals**

To help counter the side effects of prednisone, doctors generally recommend taking 1000 to 1500 mg of calcium a day, combined with 400 to 800 IU of vitamin D, to help prevent bone loss; 1000 mg of vitamin C to strengthen capillary walls and help prevent bruising; and 800 or more IU of vitamin E to fight inflammation and increase blood flow. Nutraceuticals that are effective against inflammation include gamma-linolenic acid (GLA), which is found in fish, borage, and evening primrose oils. Ginkgo biloba extract (GBE) increases blood flow to the head and through peripheral arteries, and may improve circulation in temporal arteritis. However, check with a doctor before taking supplements or herbal preparations; some interact with medications or each other.

# Trigeminal Neuralgia

### SYMPTOMS

- *Repeated brief episodes of intense shooting pains—similar to an electric shock—on one side of the face.*
- *Over time, a continuous dull ache or burning sensation in the affected area between the intense attacks.*

### WHO IS AT RISK

*Trigeminal neuralgia can occur at any age, but it usually strikes after age 40 and becomes increasingly common with advancing age. Women are affected more often than men; the reason for this is unknown but hormones may play a role. People with multiple sclerosis also have a high risk of developing trigeminal neuralgia.*

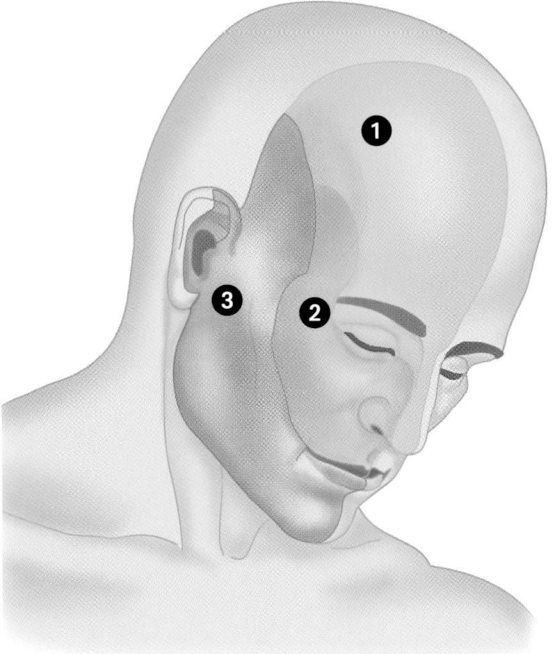


*The trigeminal nerve has three major branches: The ophthalmic (1), the maxillary (2), and the mandibular (3).*

## HOW IT DEVELOPS

Trigeminal neuralgia, or tic douloureux as it is also known, arises in the large, branching trigeminal (fifth cranial) nerve of the face. Sometimes trigeminal neuralgia is secondary to another condition, such as a tumor or aneurysm (a bulging blood vessel) pressing on the nerve. More often, however, the cause is unknown. Some researchers theorize that irritation from a nearby blood vessel may be responsible, and in some cases the attacks can be stopped by surgically moving a misplaced artery.

Regardless of the cause, victims of trigeminal neuralgia invariably describe the pain as the worst they have ever experienced. During an attack, a bolt of intense pain comes on suddenly and lasts for only a few seconds, or a minute at the most. Because the pain is so intense, however, an attack may seem much longer. The pain disappears as suddenly as it hits, only to return with equal intensity a few moments later. Some victims suffer 100 or more episodes a day, and this can go on for weeks or even months during which the person is usually incapacitated by the pain. Many lose weight because they are reluctant to chew or even swallow for fear of triggering the pain. Then, for no apparent reason, the attack ends. Weeks, months, or even years may elapse between attacks, but they invariably return.

**WARNING!**

***The drugs used to treat trigeminal neuralgia often cause drowsiness; patients taking them should not drive or operate dangerous machinery. Regular blood tests are needed to monitor for other possible side effects, including aplastic anemia, a serious blood disease.***

Many ordinarily benign events can set off an attack. These vary from one person to another, but common triggers include a light touch to a specific spot on the face, exposure to cold, a cool breeze blowing across the face, and everyday events like shaving or eating.

## WHAT YOU CAN DO

Try to identify any environmental triggers, and avoid them as much as possible. Many sufferers are very sensitive to the cold; stay indoors if possible, and wear a hat and warm scarf to protect the face when going outdoors. If eating causes pain, try sipping a high-nutrition liquid supplement. Some patients benefit from capsaicin ointment; others find it worsens the attacks. If you try it, be very careful not to get it near the eyes.

## HOW TO TREAT IT

### Medications

Antiseizure medications can bring at least temporary relief, but finding a drug that works is often a matter of trial and error. The usual first choice is carbamazepine (Tegretol), which controls attacks in up to 80 percent of patients. As the disease progresses, however, the drug loses its effectiveness. Giving it along with baclofen (Lioresal) or another medication may work for a while, and doctors often try various combinations and regimens to find one that provides relief.

**BREAKTHROUGHS!**

**Gamma-knife radiation therapy shows promise in treating some patients with trigeminal neuralgia. This involves using precisely beamed gamma radiation to destroy part of the nerve and thereby prevent the transmission of pain messages. Because it does not require general anesthesia or an incision, it is less risky than conventional surgery and it usually can be done on an outpatient basis.**

### Surgery

If medications cannot provide adequate relief, one of several operations may be considered. One of the most successful is microvascular decompression, which involves making a small opening in the skull, just behind the ear, on the affected side. The neurosurgeon then locates where the trigeminal nerve comes out of the brain stem, and looks for any blood vessel that is touching the nerve. The blood vessel is moved slightly, and a small piece of Teflon padding is inserted between it and the nerve to prevent future contact.

Another approach calls for blocking a certain amount of the trigeminal nerve's function. This is done by passing a probe through the face and into the gasserian ganglion, the point where the trigeminal nerve divides into its three main branches. The ganglion is then damaged by an electrical current, compression with a balloon device, or an injection. The goal is to interfere with the nerve's ability to conduct pain messages. Unfortunately, relief is often temporary and symptoms eventually return. But for many sufferers, even a few months of relief are welcome, and when symptoms return, another tactic can be tried.

Another procedure—radiofrequency rhizotomy—uses heat to destroy a portion of the trigeminal nerve and thereby interrupt the transmission of pain messages to the brain. The procedure causes some facial numbness, but it does not cause facial paralysis.

## HOW TO PREVENT IT

Aside from trying to avoid triggering factors, there is no known way of preventing trigeminal neuralgia.

### ALTERNATIVE THERAPIES

**Acupuncture**

The ancient Chinese technique relieves many types of nerve pain, and is worth a try against trigeminal neuralgia. However, if there is no improvement after 6 to 10 treatments, it is unlikely that any more will produce results.

# The Eyes

*Vision is the most specialized of the five senses. The eyes are blessed with a complex network of nerves that makes sight possible and the eyes themselves exquisitely sensitive to pain—so much so that even a speck of dust can feel like a boulder.*

## Blepharitis

**SYMPTOMS**

- *Itchy, stinging, swollen, and reddened eyelids.*
- *Sensation of something gritty in the eye.*
- *Scaling skin and small ulcers at lid margins.*
- *Watery, light-sensitive eyes.*
- *Eye discharge that causes crusting of lashes and lids during sleep.*

**WHO IS AT RISK**

*Dandruff, cradle cap, and other forms of seborrheic dermatitis—an inflammatory skin condition—increase the risk of developing inflammation of the eyelid margins, known as blepharitis. Other risk factors include recurrent sties (infected eyelash follicles), chalazia (blocked oil glands in the eyelid), and eczema and skin allergies.*

### HOW IT DEVELOPS

Blepharitis is usually caused by a staphylococcal infection of the edges of the eyelids, where the lashes grow. It usually starts with an itching or burning sensation and swelling of the eyelids. The conjunctiva—the membranes covering the eye and lining the lids—may be irritated. Greasy scales, similar to those of cradle cap, line the lid margins and, in severe cases, small, painful ulcers form. Lashes break off, and occasionally an oil gland becomes clogged, resulting in a hard swelling. The eyes often feel like they have sand or grit in them, especially after a night's sleep. Blepharitis is uncomfortable and often unsightly, but it rarely harms the eye.

**WARNING!**

***See a doctor as soon as possible if the entire eyelid becomes swollen, red, and painful. These are signs of possible eyelid cellulitis, a serious infection that requires intensive antibiotic treatment. Even more serious is orbital cellulitis, which invades the area behind the eye and requires hospitalization and intravenous antibiotics.***

### WHAT YOU CAN DO

Use a diluted solution of baby shampoo—a few drops in a half cup of warm water—to bathe the eyelids morning and night. Dip a cotton swab or corner of a clean washcloth in the shampoo solution and carefully wash the lids, paying special attention to the margins and lashes. Don't worry if the shampoo gets into the eyes; it is specially formulated so it won't "sting."

Warm compresses can ease discomfort and also help soften the waxy plugs that sometimes develop in oil-secreting glands. Soaking the compresses in a solution of one tablespoon of baking soda to one cup of water is more soothing than plain water. Leave the compresses on for 15 minutes three or four times a day. Avoid using eye makeup while the lids are inflamed. Don't use eyelash curlers, which can cause further breakage of lashes.

**Anatomy of the Eye**

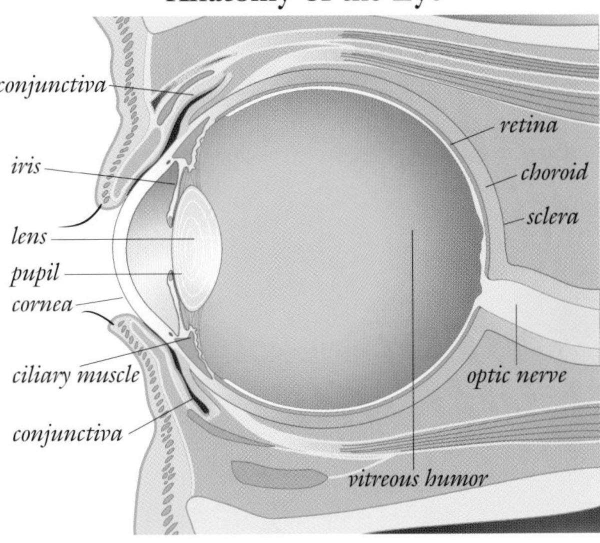


### HOW TO TREAT IT

Ulcerative blepharitis is treated with an eye ointment containing antibiotics, such as gentamicin or bacitracin and polymycin B. A 7- to 10-day course of treatment usually clears up the ulcers that form along the lid margins.

Chronic blepharitis can be very resistant to self-treatment. If the condition persists for more than two or three months, see a doctor about a prescription for an antibiotic eye ointment, which may need to be used for three months or longer.

## HOW TO PREVENT IT

If you have dandruff, wash your hair frequently using an antidandruff shampoo. If you have oily skin, wash your face twice daily to reduce the surface oil, which the staph bacteria feed on. Be careful not to apply moisturizers and oily makeup in the eye area. Use only your own eye makeup and replace it every three months. Finally, wash your hands frequently, and avoid rubbing or touching the eyelids, which can spread the infection.

### ALTERNATIVE THERAPIES

**Herbal medicine**

Herbalists often recommend eyebright compresses to treat blepharitis and other eye irritations. However, doctors warn against exposing the eyes to eyebright, or any other herbal remedy, because the herbs often harbor microorganisms that can cause a serious eye infection.

# Conjunctivitis

### SYMPTOMS

- *Painful burning and itching of one or both eyes.*
- *Uncomfortable sensation of sand or a foreign substance in the eye.*
- *White part of the eye is pink or red.*
- *Tearing and possible sticky clear or yellowish discharge.*

### WHO IS AT RISK

*Anyone can develop conjunctivitis, but the highly contagious viral forms are especially common among schoolchildren. Hay fever sufferers often develop allergic conjunctivitis. Infants born to women who have a genital chlamydia infection have a high risk of inclusion conjunctivitis, an eye disorder similar to trachoma. Environmental factors, such as exposure of the eyes to bright lights, wind, smoke, and air pollution, can contribute to conjunctivitis.*

## HOW IT DEVELOPS

**Viral conjunctivitis** develops 5 to 12 days after exposure. Typically, the person first notices extra tearing, and then may wake up with the lids of one or both eyes stuck together. The whites of the affected eye will be red or pink. Viral conjunctivitis usually clears up on its own in a week or so; until then, it is highly contagious. In **bacterial conjunctivitis,** the eye discharge contains pus. Without treatment, bacterial conjunctivitis usually clears up in three weeks, and in one or two days with treatment.

**Neonatal inclusion conjunctivitis,** which is contracted during birth from chlamydia harbored in an infected mother's vagina, usually develops in 5 to 15 days after birth. Older children and adults sometimes contract inclusion conjunctivitis from swimming pools or, more commonly, by spreading genital secretions to the eyes.

**Allergic conjunctivitis** is usually a reaction to pollen and other airborne allergens. It may also be an adverse reaction to eye makeup.

## WHAT YOU CAN DO

See a doctor for a proper diagnosis. Although most conjunctivitis will heal itself, the course can be shortened with treatment. If the lashes are encrusted with a sticky discharge, carefully bathe the lids with diluted baby shampoo, which will not "sting" if you get some in the eyes. To ease eye irritation, wash eyes with warm salt water or an antiseptic eye wash; however, do not use eyedrops until you have seen an eye doctor, and then use only what he or she advises.

## HOW TO TREAT IT

Viral conjunctivitis doesn't require special treatment unless a secondary bacterial infection or another complication develops, which is unusual. A 7- to 10-day course of antibiotic eyedrops or ointments are prescribed for bacterial conjunctivitis. Infants with chlamydial conjunctivitis need oral antibiotics, both to clear up the eye problem and to treat or prevent chlamydial pneumonia, which develops in half of these babies. Adults with this type of conjunctivitis are also given oral antibiotics, but usually for only one week. Allergic conjunctivitis can be treated with eyedrops or ointments containing antihistamines and perhaps a corticosteroid.

## HOW TO PREVENT IT

The best preventive measure is to wash your hands frequently and avoid touching your eyes, especially when you have a cold or flu. Schoolchildren with viral conjunctivitis should be kept home to avoid spreading it.

If you are susceptible to hay fever along with seasonal allergic conjunctivitis, consider undergoing desensitiza-

### THE CONJUNCTIVITIS THAT BLINDS

Most types of conjunctivitis are relatively harmless, but there is a major exception—an eye infection due to *Neisseria gonorrhoeae*, the organism that causes the sexually transmitted disease gonorrhea. Gonococcal conjunctivitis, although rare, can cause corneal ulcers, perforation of the eyeball, and blindness. Babies born to women with gonorrhea are at the highest risk, but adults can also develop gonococcal conjunctivitis if the organism is carried to the eyes on unwashed hands or other objects. Antibiotics can cure the underlying gonorrhea and prevent blindness and other serious eye complications.

tion (allergy shots). These are given over a three- to five-year period, and when the course is completed, they can prevent future allergic reactions. Use sterile water to bathe the eyes, and if you use eyedrops, make sure the applicator does not touch the eye itself. Even so, wash it after each use, and replace the drops frequently. If you have other allergies, look for hypoallergenic brands of eye makeup, which are less likely to provoke a reaction. Makeup is also a very common source of eye infections; replace it at least every three months. Never borrow or lend eye makeup and never use saliva to moisten it or applicators. Similarly, use a sterile solution to clean contact lenses, and never moisten them in your mouth. Finally, protect your eyes from dust, sun, and other environmental irritants.

### ALTERNATIVE THERAPIES

**Herbal medicine**

Because herbs can be contaminated with bacteria and other organisms, doctors advise against putting any herbal product in or on the eyes. Herbalists recommend compresses soaked in a solution containing eyebright to treat conjunctivitis, and this remedy is still described in many older texts of herbal medicine. However, it is much safer—and probably just as effective—to drink eyebright tea rather than put it in the eyes.

**Homeopathy**

Argentum nitricum, Mercuris sol, and Hepar sulfuris are among the remedies that homeopaths use to treat conjunctivitis. However, these should be used only as complementary therapies if antibiotics are prescribed.

# Corneal Ulcers

### SYMPTOMS

- *Initially, dull aching and a sensation of something foreign in the affected eye; as ulcer forms, more intense pain.*
- *Eye becomes swollen, and sensitive to light.*
- *Excessive tearing and blurred vision.*
- *Appearance of a small superficial opaque area and then an ulcer with an open center.*

### WHO IS AT RISK

*People who wear contact lenses, especially for extended periods or while sleeping, may develop a corneal ulcer. Indeed, the marked rise in corneal ulcers in recent years has been attributed to widespread use of extended-wear soft contact lenses. Long-term use of steroid eyedrops or ointments also increases the risk.*

*Corneal ulcers may also be a complication of an eye infection, such as herpes simplex, ocular shingles, and various fungal and bacterial infections. Chemical and other burns can result in a corneal ulcer, as can even a minor injury—for example, a foreign body in the eye or accidentally scratching it with a fingernail. So too can disorders that prevent the eyelid from closing, such as Bell's palsy, or an eyelash that turns inward and invades the cornea. Nutritional deficiencies, especially of protein and vitamin A, increase the risk of corneal ulcers; these are rare in the Western world, but common in developing nations. People with diabetes, multiple sclerosis, or those who have sustained a chemical burn of the eye are susceptible to neurotrophic corneal ulcers, which are due to damaged nerves in the cornea.*

## HOW IT DEVELOPS

The first symptoms are usually a dull aching sensation, reddening and watering of the eye, and sensitivity to light. The ulcer begins as a dull, grayish spot on the cornea, the eye's transparent outer covering. As the ulcerated tissue dies, it is shed as a puslike discharge, and a hole forms in the center of the ulcer. The eyeball appears swollen, and vision is impaired. As healing occurs, scar tissue may form and cloud vision. Without treatment, the entire eye may be destroyed.

## WHAT YOU CAN DO

See an eye specialist immediately; don't wait for the ulcer symptoms if you suffer any type of eye injury or burn, have a foreign object in the eye that doesn't wash out, or you develop conjunctivitis or another eye infection. While awaiting treatment, a warm compress over the eye can ease discomfort.

While the ulcer heals, rest the eyes often. Protect them from bright lights and limit television watching to brief periods. Nonprescription painkillers are usually all that is needed to ease pain.

## HOW TO TREAT IT

An uncomplicated corneal ulcer usually heals in a few weeks; however, deep ulcers or those due to a fungal infection may take much longer.

### BREAKTHROUGHS!

**A group of Italian researchers have discovered a promising treatment for neurotrophic corneal ulcers. Normally, these ulcers require surgical treatment, and even then, they usually cause impaired vision. In a landmark study, ophthalmologists at the University of Rome treated 14 neurotrophic ulcers with a newly discovered natural body substance called nerve growth factor. Within six weeks, all the ulcers had healed, and vision improved in 13 of the 14 treated eyes. Follow-up examinations 3 to 15 months after treatment found no evidence of relapse.**

## Medications

Drug therapy varies according to the underlying cause. Antibiotic or antifungal drops or an ointment may be prescribed; some are administered hourly.

## Surgery

In severe cases, eye surgery, either conventional or using a laser (an intense beam of light), may be necessary to repair the cornea. Surgery is also used to treat neurotrophic ulcers. If the cornea is severely scarred, normal vision may be restored by replacing the damaged cornea with a donor graft.

## HOW TO PREVENT IT

If you wear contact lenses, use them for only the recommended periods, and avoid sleeping with them in the eyes. Use a sterile solution to clean them, and never put a lens in the mouth.

Always wear protective eye goggles when working with chemicals or operating machinery that can cause an object to fly into the eye. Also protect your eyes from the sun and bright ultraviolet lights. If you notice an eyelash growing inward, see a doctor to have it removed.

# Foreign Object in the Eye

### SYMPTOMS

- *Eye pain, often disproportionately severe in relationship to the object.*
- *Nagging sensation of something in the eye; may be intermittent if the object is in a corner.*
- *Redness, tearing, blinking, and increased sensitivity to light of affected eye.*
- *Blurred vision, swelling, and bleeding if object penetrates the eyeball.*
- *Searing pain if a caustic chemical gets into the eye.*

### WHO IS AT RISK

*Everyone gets a foreign object in an eye from time to time. People who are at special risk are construction workers, wood crafters, welders, and machine operators, all of whom may be exposed to flying fragments.*

## HOW IT DEVELOPS

The initial symptoms vary according to the object and situation. If the foreign matter is small, such as a tiny insect or grain of sand, the person is immediately aware that something has invaded the eye. Depending upon the location and size of the object, the pain can range from intermittent and annoying to excruciating. If the object is not removed, it can cause inflammation, tearing, and perhaps blurred vision.

If the object scratches the eye's surface or penetrates the eye itself, it can cause a corneal ulcer, which is marked by extreme pain, blurred vision, and the appearance of an opaque sore on the eye's surface. A caustic chemical, such as lye, that is splashed into an eye can cause extensive tissue damage and even blindness if it is not washed out immediately.

## WHAT YOU CAN DO

Small flying insects, specks of dust or sand, and other such objects often can be removed simply by flushing the eye with clean water. If you can see the object on the white part of the eye, you may be able to remove it with a cotton swab or corner of sterile gauze, a clean tissue, or a handkerchief.

If the object is under an eyelid, gently pull the lid forward, roll the eyeball in a direction to make the object more visible, and use a cotton swab, clean handkerchief corner, or similar object to gently remove it from the exposed inner part of the lid. If you have difficulty removing the object, or if the eye appears to be injured in any way, go to the emergency room or see a doctor right away.

> **WARNING!**
>
> ***Never rub an eye that may have a foreign object in it. This can scratch the cornea and drive the object deeper into the eye. If a foreign object becomes lodged in a child's eye—or you are called upon to help someone with an eye injury—wrap a gauze bandage or clean cloth around the head to firmly cover both eyes. This prevents eye rubbing, and eases pain. Proceed to hospital.***

If a chemical has splashed into the eye, start to wash it out immediately. Position the head under an open faucet, and let cool water irrigate the eye. If a faucet is not available, pour water over the eye by hand. The water should be clean, but don't waste time looking for bottled or sterile water—use whatever is handy. Pour the water from the inside corner, across the eyeball, and to the outside corner, positioning the head so that the water does not run into the other eye (see illustration). Be sure to remove any contact lens first; otherwise, some of the chemical may be trapped under it. Try to roll the

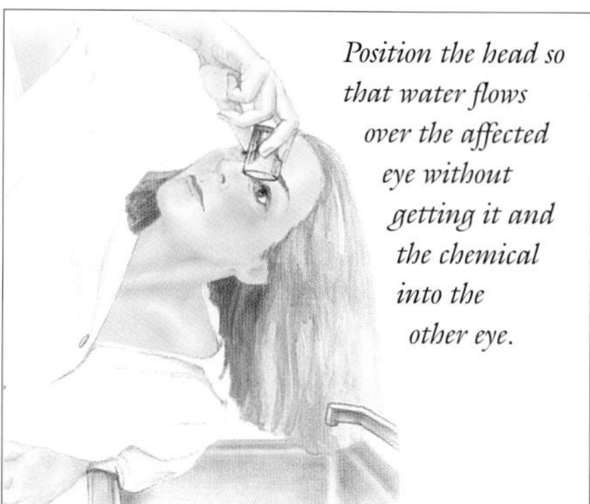

*Position the head so that water flows over the affected eye without getting it and the chemical into the other eye.*

eyeball while irrigating the eye to remove the chemical from under the lids. Irrigate the eye for at least 15 to 30 minutes, and then go to an emergency room.

## HOW TO TREAT IT

Any object that is difficult to remove, is embedded in the eye tissue, or has penetrated the eyeball is a medical emergency. A doctor can usually remove an object embedded in the cornea or lodged under an eyelid by using tweezerlike instruments. Antibiotic eyedrops will be prescribed to speed healing and prevent infection and a corneal ulcer. An eye patch may be worn for a few days to protect the eye and also ease pain. If OTC painkillers are not strong enough, codeine may be prescribed.

An object embedded in the eye itself requires surgical removal and probably a hospital stay.

## HOW TO PREVENT IT

Almost half of all eye injuries occur at home, compared to less than 20 percent in the workplace. Always wear protective eye goggles when mowing the lawn or doing household chores that pose a risk to the eyes, just as you would when working with chemicals, a welding iron, or other machinery or materials that might send a foreign object flying into the eyes. Goggles also should be worn when riding a motorcycle, an all-terrain vehicle, or engaging in other sports that might cause an eye injury.

# Glaucoma, Acute

### SYMPTOMS

- *Very severe, throbbing pain in the entire eye.*
- *Sensitivity to light.*
- *Excessive tearing and redness, especially around the iris, the colored circle surrounding the pupil.*
- *The pupil of the affected eye is dilated (opened), and remains so even when exposed to bright light.*
- *The cornea (the clear covering of the eye) becomes cloudy, the person may see colored halos, and vision in that eye quickly deteriorates.*

### WHO IS AT RISK

*Acute glaucoma generally occurs among the elderly, and women are afflicted more often than men. A family history of the more common open-angle glaucoma increases the vulnerability to acute glaucoma. Racial characteristics affecting the shape of the eye are also a factor, which is why acute glaucoma is most common among Asians and the Inuit. Acute glaucoma may also be secondary to other eye disorders, especially those that block the pupil and pull the iris out of its normal placement, such as diabetes and inflammatory disorders.*

## HOW IT DEVELOPS

All types of glaucoma involve a buildup of pressure inside the eyeball. The eye's chambers are filled with a thin fluid called *aqueous humor*, which is produced in the back (posterior) chamber and passes through the pupil into the front (anterior) chamber, where it drains out of the eye through small outflow channels located at the edge of the iris. With glaucoma, the flow of fluid is blocked and fluid accumulates in the chambers. In the most common type, open-angle glaucoma, the outflow channels remain open. This condition comes on silently and does not cause symptoms until it reaches an advanced stage; by then, vision may be damaged.

In about 10 percent of cases, the channels are blocked by the iris, resulting in angle-closure glaucoma, which causes attacks of acute glaucoma. An attack comes on suddenly and usually affects one eye. The space between the iris and the cornea, where the outflow channels are located, becomes abnormally narrow. When the pupil dilates, such as when going into a dimly lit room or having eyedrops during an eye examination, it encroaches on the iris and blocks the drainage channels. If the pupil remains dilated, pressure quickly builds up in the eye's chambers and leads to an acute, very painful attack. Without immediate treatment, sight quickly deteriorates and permanent blindness results. Symptoms abate with prompt treatment, but the attacks may recur, with each one causing further vision loss.

## WHAT YOU CAN DO

There is no self-treatment for acute glaucoma; see a doctor or go to the emergency room immediately.

## HOW TO TREAT IT

### Medications

The immediate goal is to reduce eye pressure by increasing the outflow of aqueous humor and also decreasing its production. Pilocarpine or carbachol eyedrops may be administered to constrict the pupil and increase fluid out-

### HOW TO USE EYEDROPS AND EYE OINTMENTS

First, wash your hands thoroughly. If you are applying the drops or ointment yourself, lean the head back and look upward. (If someone else is applying them, it is best done with you lying down.) Use a forefinger to pull the lower lid downward, creating a small pocket between the lid and the eyeball. Then place the drops or a thin strip of the ointment in the pocket, and blink to distribute the medication over the eye itself. To prevent contamination, don't let the applicator touch the eye tissue.

flow. Drugs called carbonic anhydrase inhibitors are also given to decrease aqueous production; these drugs may be taken in pill form or as eyedrops. Beta blocker eyedrops are also used to reduce aqueous production. Less frequent and reduced dosages of these or other eyedrops are continued even after symptoms abate to help prevent a recurrence. In severe cases, osmotic diuretics are also used to, in effect, draw fluid from the eye. Examples include mannitol, which is given intravenously, or a glycerin drink.

**WARNING!**

***Acute glaucoma can cause permanent blindness if it goes untreated for even a few days. Any onset of severe eye pain should be considered a medical emergency; go to the emergency room if your eye doctor is not available to see you right away.***

### Surgery

Eye surgery is almost always recommended to prevent recurring attacks; the operation of choice is called laser peripheral iridotomy. If the cornea is clear, the operation can be done immediately; otherwise, the surgeon waits until any inflammation clears up. The procedure involves using very concentrated, computer-controlled light beams to make a small hole in the iris, thereby allowing the aqueous fluid to flow freely from the posterior to the anterior chamber. The eye's outflow channels may also be enlarged during the operation. If laser surgery does not cure the problem, a conventional operation using a scalpel will be performed.

## HOW TO PREVENT IT

Surgery to widen the outflow channels will prevent future attacks. If the outflow channels are narrowed in the other eye, it, too, may be operated on to prevent acute glaucoma from developing. If you are over age 40, you should have a yearly eye exam that includes testing for glaucoma. This is especially important if you have a family history of glaucoma or are of Asian or Inuit descent. Even more frequent eye exams may be recommended for people with diabetes or eye disorders that predispose them to acute glaucoma.

# Keratitis

**SYMPTOMS**

- *Eye pain, ranging from mild to very severe.*
- *Sensation of a foreign body in the eyes.*
- *Painful red eyes.*
- *Swollen lids and cornea.*
- *Light sensitivity; possible hazy vision.*
- *Possible corneal ulceration and scarring.*
- *Impaired vision from recurrent infections.*

**WHO IS AT RISK**

*Keratitis strikes people of all ages and males and females alike, but depending upon the causes, some groups are especially vulnerable. People with frequent herpes fever blisters, or cold sores, have a higher risk of herpes keratitis. Children aged 6 months to 5 years are especially vulnerable. Bacterial keratitis is common among people who wear contact lenses or use eye makeup that may become contaminated by bacteria. Skiers, lifeguards, and others who spend a lot of time in the bright sunshine, as well as welders, are vulnerable to solar keratitis.*

## HOW IT DEVELOPS

The term "keratitis" covers a variety of corneal infections, irritations, and inflammation. One of the most common types is **herpes simplex keratitis,** which is caused by the virus responsible for cold sores. The first signs are usually red, irritated, somewhat painful and watery eyes. At this stage, the infection resembles conjunctivitis, and may

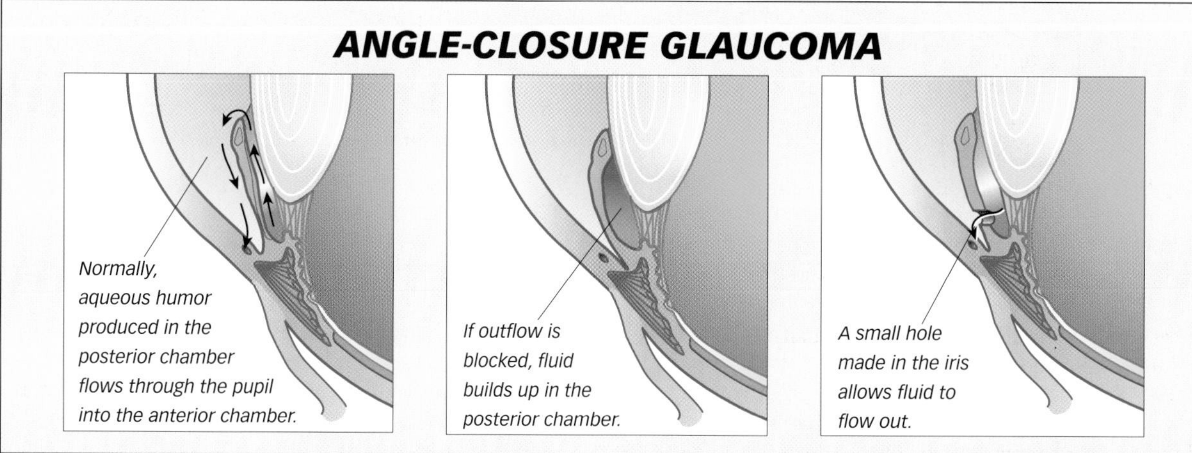

ANGLE-CLOSURE GLAUCOMA
Normally, aqueous humor produced in the posterior chamber flows through the pupil into the anterior chamber.
If outflow is blocked, fluid builds up in the posterior chamber.
A small hole made in the iris allows fluid to flow out.

## BREAKTHROUGHS!

**Long-term preventive treatment with acyclovir (Zovirax) can reduce recurrence of herpes keratitis by more than 40 percent, according to a study carried out at 74 university and community eye clinics. Until now, the drug has been used mostly to treat genital herpes and shingles. Now the researchers who conducted the study, which involved 703 patients who had suffered herpes keratitis in the preceding year, report that it can help prevent the vision loss that often occurs with recurring herpes eye infections. The drug is taken daily as a pill. As an added benefit, patients receiving acyclovir also develop fewer herpes cold sores.**

clear up on its own. But it often recurs, and each recurrence causes increasing damage to the cornea, including ulceration, scarring, and impaired vision.

**Bacterial keratitis** is usually due to *Staphylococcus aureus,* but among people who wear contact lenses or use eye cosmetics, *Pseudomonas aeruginosa* is the more common cause. Bacterial keratitis is much more painful than herpes keratitis, the cornea is inflamed and swollen, and there is a thick, yellowish discharge in addition to profuse tearing, blurred vision, and light sensitivity. The infection can quickly lead to a corneal ulcer.

**Solar,** or ultraviolet (UV), **keratitis** results from overexposure to bright UV light, such as from welding arcs, tanning booths, or the reflection of sunlight from the snow or water. Symptoms—intense eye pain, redness, tearing, light sensitivity, blurring and decreased visual acuity, and eyelid spasms—start 6 to 12 hours after exposure. Without treatment, the cornea may be permanently damaged and vision impaired.

## WHAT YOU CAN DO

See an eye specialist as soon as possible. In the meantime, rinsing the eye with tepid saline washes may ease irritation. Until healing occurs, dim lights and wear dark glasses to reduce light sensitivity. Rest the eyes as much as possible; avoid watching TV or working at a computer monitor. Cool compresses can help ease pain, and during the early stages of healing, doctors usually advise wearing an eye patch as much as possible; patches restrict eye movement and help speed healing.

## HOW TO TREAT IT

### Medications

Keratitis is treated with the frequent application of prescription eyedrops, which must be tailored to the underlying cause. Herpes simplex keratitis is usually treated with topical antiviral drugs such as idoxuridine (Herplex-D). At first the medication is applied every one to two hours; as the eye lesion begins to regress, the frequency is reduced to every three or four hours. The eye usually heals in 7 to 10 days, but the medication may be continued for another week.

Antibiotic drops or ointments are used to treat bacterial keratitis. The doctor usually starts with a broad-spectrum antibiotic, such as ciprofloxacin (Ciloxan), with two drops given every 15 minutes for 6 hours, and then every 30 minutes for 18 hours, and further tapered as healing progresses. Other eye medications, such as cyclopentolate (Cyclogyl) or atropine (Atropisol), will be given to relax muscles and reduce eye spasms. After the infection is cleared up, steroid eyedrops are prescribed to reduce swelling and inflammation. Until healing is complete, daily doctor visits are advised.

In ultraviolet keratitis, the eyes are flushed for several minutes with water or a saline solution. Drops of cyclopentolate or a similar drug can ease pain and relax spasms. Antibiotic drops or eye ointment are put into the eyes, which are then covered with a patch or bandage to reduce movement. Painkillers are also prescribed, and daily doctor visits to monitor the keratitis may be necessary until healing is complete.

## WARNING!

***Don't try to treat inflamed eyes yourself. Above all, do not use nonprescription eyedrops containing corticosteroids. These may worsen keratitis, and even cause perforation of the eyeball and blindness.***

### Debridement and surgery

In some cases, doctors must remove (debride) the dead tissue from the cornea. In severe cases, in which there is extensive corneal ulceration and scarring, the cornea may have to be removed surgically and replaced with a graft (see also *Corneal Ulcers,* p 81).

## HOW TO PREVENT IT

Wash your hands frequently, and avoid touching near the eyes, especially if you have a cold sore or fever blister. Never look directly into the sun, and wear protective dark glasses that filter out UV light when outdoors on a sunny day. These are always needed when you are skiing or are out on the water, because snow and water reflect UV rays even when it's cloudy. Also wear light-protective glasses if you work with an arc welder, strobe photography lights, or other strong sources of UV radiation.

### ALTERNATIVE THERAPIES

**Acupuncture**

This ancient Chinese technique can help ease pain and thereby reduce the need for powerful painkillers. Improvement should be noted after five or six treatments.

**Meditation**

Practicing meditation or another relaxation technique can have a calming effect if you feel anxious when wearing an eye patch or bandage.

# Sty and Chalazion

## SYMPTOMS

- ***Sty (or stye):*** *A painful, red, pimplelike bump on the edge of an eyelid.*
- ***Chalazion:*** *A well-defined, painful lump inside the eyelid's layers of tissue.*
- ***Both:*** *Excessive tearing and uncomfortable sensation of something in the eye.*

## WHO IS AT RISK

*Anyone can develop a sty or chalazion, but they are especially common in children. Chronic inflammation of an eyelid (blepharitis) increases the risk of sties and chalazia.*

## HOW IT DEVELOPS

A sty, or hordeolum as it is known medically, develops when the staphylococcal bacteria that normally live on the skin invade one or more of the oil (sebaceous) glands at the root (follicle) of an eyelash. It often starts as a tingling or irritation just under an eyelid. Within a day or so, a painful, red swelling that looks like a pus-filled pimple appears. The entire lid may become swollen and very painful. After a few days, the sty ruptures and disappears. Most sties are not a threat to overall eye health and vision, but they are unsightly and can cause considerable discomfort.

Most sties are external, but sometimes one will develop on the inside of the eyelid; this is known as an internal hordeolum. They are more painful and cause more swelling than external sties, and they may not rupture; instead, they tend to gradually subside. Both types of sties tend to recur, but the likelihood of recurrence is greater with the internal ones.

A chalazion is similar to a sty except that it develops in a blocked oil gland within the eyelid plate. It is not as painful as sties, but it can cause more eyelid swelling.

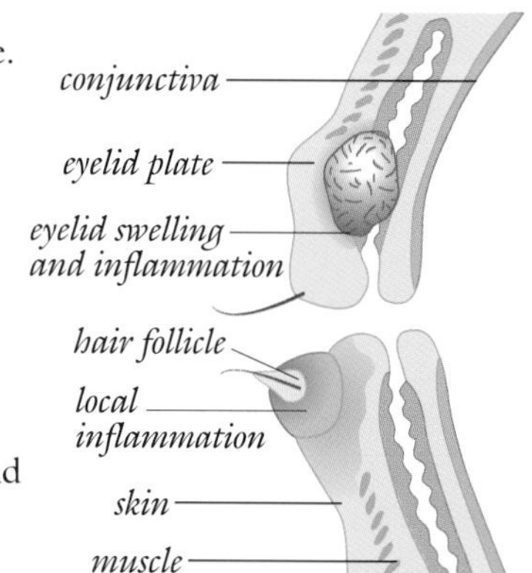

*A chalazion (top) develops in the eyelid; a sty (lower) forms in a hair follicle.*

## WHAT YOU CAN DO

Warm compresses are the mainstay of treatment for both sties and chalazia. Soak a clean cloth in comfortably hot (not scalding) water and place it directly over the affected eye. Do this every hour or so; in most cases, the sty will come to a head, rupture, and disappear in a day or two. If the sty is due to an ingrown eyelash, gently removing the lash will cure the problem.

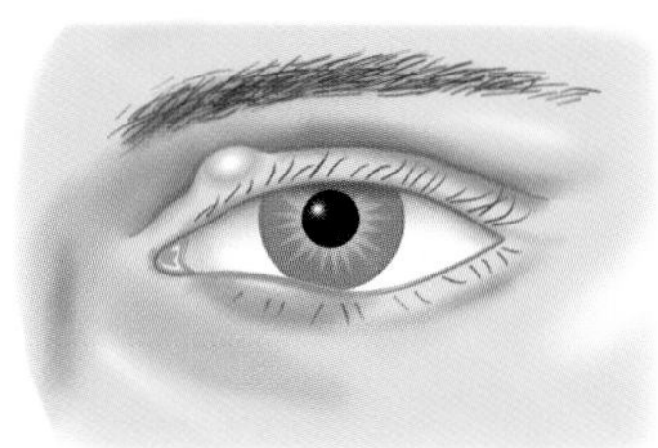
*Sties (bottom) cause painful eyelid swelling whereas a chalazion (top) develops as a lump in the eyelid plate.*

Chalazia usually take longer to clear up, and sometimes they become chronic. If the lump does not disappear within six weeks, consult a doctor.

## HOW TO TREAT IT

### Medications

Sometimes a doctor will prescribe an antibiotic ointment to be applied directly to the sty. However, nonprescription topical antibiotics usually are not effective against sties; it is better to use a stronger prescription product.

If a chalazion does not disappear within six weeks, a doctor may inject it with a corticosteroid. This usually reduces the inflammation and clears up the lump.

### Surgery

Very large and painful sties sometimes require surgical drainage. This is a simple office procedure in which a doctor lances the abscess and presses gently on it to squeeze out pus and other debris. Surgical drainage is followed by a few days of topical antibiotics.

A chronic chalazion that lingers even after a steroid injection can be removed surgically. Again, this is an office or hospital outpatient procedure that is done under local anesthesia. Afterward, the eye is covered with a pressure bandage and an eye patch for a few hours to help control swelling.

> **WARNING!**
>
> ***See a doctor as soon as possible if a chalazion is large enough to press upon the eye, temporarily changing the eye's shape and resulting in an astigmatism (a disorder in which images entering the eye fail to focus normally on the retina). Sometimes a chalazion develops into a fleshy growth called a granuloma, which should be removed, especially if it presses on the eye.***

## HOW TO PREVENT IT

There are no sure-fire means of prevention, but paying attention to good hygiene may help. If you have oily hair and skin, shampoo your hair frequently and wash your face with a mild soap twice a day. This reduces the oil secretions that feed staph bacteria. To help prevent recurrent sties, doctors often recommend washing the eyelids daily with a baby shampoo (see also *Blepharitis,* p 79).

ALTERNATIVE THERAPIES

**Herbal medicine**

Herbalists often recommend eyebright eyedrops or compresses to treat sties and other painful eye conditions. Doctors warn against putting eyebright, or any other herbal or home remedy, into the eyes because this increases the risk of a serious eye infection.

# Uveitis/Iritis

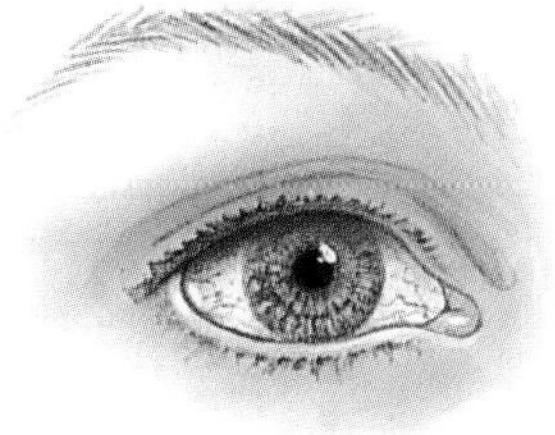

*In iritis, the straight lines that radiate through the normal iris (top) are obscured (bottom) and the iris appears swollen.*

**SYMPTOMS**

*These vary according to the site of inflammation. Anterior uveitis, or iritis, is the type that causes the most symptoms, which include:*

- *Severe eye pain, often accompanied by a headache.*
- *Redness, tearing, sensitivity to light, and hazy vision.*
- *Swollen and dull iris (the eye's colored circle) with an obscuring of its lines.*
- *Small, irregularly shaped pupil.*

**WHO IS AT RISK**

*In most cases, uveitis has no local identifiable cause, and it occurs at any age and equally in males and females. However, the presence of another inflammatory disorder—in particular spinal arthritis (ankylosing spondylitis), lupus, rheumatoid arthritis, and inflammatory bowel disease—increases the risk of uveitis, especially iritis. Children with juvenile rheumatoid arthritis often develop iritis or other forms of uveitis.*

## HOW IT DEVELOPS

**Uveitis** is defined as inflammation anywhere in the uveal tract, which consists of the iris, the ciliary body (the muscles on either side of the iris that control the lens), and the choroid (the inner lining of the eye that extends from the ciliary body to the optic nerve). **Diffuse uveitis** involves the entire tract; more often, only a portion becomes inflamed. **Iritis,** inflammation of the iris itself, is one of the more common types, and the one most likely to produce severe pain. In the other types, the early symptoms are subtle and easily overlooked or misinterpreted as eye strain or conjunctivitis. "Floaters"—objects that appear to swim about in the field of vision—are common in **intermediate** and **posterior uveitis,** which affect the ciliary body and choroid, respectively. These are due to clumps of cells in the vitreous humor.

Regardless of the site of inflammation and severity of the symptoms, untreated uveitis can result in permanent loss of vision. It can also cause cataracts, glaucoma, detached retina, and damage to the retina, optic nerve, iris, and other parts of the eye.

## WHAT YOU CAN DO

See an eye specialist as soon as possible. There is no effective self-treatment for iritis and other forms of uveitis. While undergoing medical treatment, symptoms can be eased by wearing dark glasses to protect the eyes from bright lights. Rest the eyes often, and avoid or minimize watching TV. Cool compresses applied over the eyes can help relieve pain.

Patients who have iritis are advised to undergo a thorough physical exam to look for hidden systemic diseases, such as lupus, that often accompany it.

**WARNING!**

***In addition to seeing an eye specialist, anyone with uveitis should also undergo a complete physical examination to look for an undiagnosed related disorder, such as lupus. In some cases, uveitis is the first obvious symptom of a related disease.***

## HOW TO TREAT IT

Treatment consists of corticosteroid eyedrops to counter the inflammation. Other drops, such as atropine (Atropisol), may be given to dilate the pupil. In some cases, oral steroids are also prescribed. During treatment, frequent eye checkups are necessary to make sure the uveitis is improving, and that the steroids are not causing a cataract and other adverse side effects.

## HOW TO PREVENT IT

There are no known means of prevention. However, children with juvenile rheumatoid arthritis should have frequent eye examinations—at least every six months, and sometimes more often. The same is true of people with spinal arthritis and other forms of inflammatory arthritis. Treating uveitis early helps prevent vision loss.

# The Nose

*The human nose, which can distinguish more than 10,000 odors, is made up of bone and cartilage, with rich networks of blood vessels and nerves. Nose pain is seldom serious, but it can be annoying enough to interfere with daily activities.*

## Foreign Object in the Nose

**SYMPTOMS**

- *Pain and stuffiness, usually in one nostril.*
- *Thick, pus-filled, and malodorous discharge, also from one nostril.*

**WHO IS AT RISK**

*In most cases, foreign objects are found in the noses of children between the ages of two and six years.*

### HOW IT DEVELOPS

The most common scenario is that a young child shoves a pea, bead, or similar object up a nostril and it gets stuck there, causing pain, inflammation, and swelling. As the object becomes more firmly imbedded, an infection may develop, resulting in a thick, yellowish discharge with an unpleasant odor. Bits of meat or other food stuffed up the nose can also cause a foul odor as it begins to rot.

### WHAT YOU CAN DO

If the object has just been put in the nose and it isn't embedded in the nasal membranes, you might try removing it with a pair of tweezers. In most cases, however, it is best to leave this to a doctor or nurse rather than risk shoving it further into the nostril.

### HOW TO TREAT IT

A doctor may be able to remove the object using special forceps or tweezers. General anesthesia is often necessary, especially if the object has been in the nose for some time and is firmly embedded in the mucous membrane. This can be done on an outpatient basis using a short-acting anesthetic. Afterward, the nostril will be flushed with a saline solution and an antibiotic may be prescribed.

**WARNING!**

***A malodorous discharge from one nostril often indicates that there's a foreign object in the nose, and that it has been there for some time. Take a child to a doctor as soon as possible; otherwise, it can cause an infection that spreads to the nearby sinuses.***

*The upper part of the nasal passages contains the nerves instrumental in the sense of smell. Foreign objects often become embedded in the nose's soft tissue, especially among young children.*

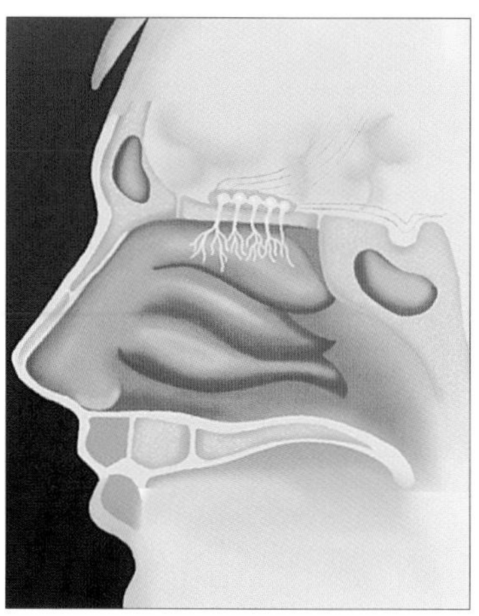

### HOW TO PREVENT IT

Young children take great delight in exploring their bodies and putting small objects into various openings. Remove beads and other small objects from the reach of young children, and at a very early age, teach a child never to put an object into the nose, an ear, the rectum, or other body openings.

## Nasal Infections

**SYMPTOMS**

- ***Viral infection:*** *Intermittent stinging or burning sensation in the nose, sneezing, nasal stuffiness, runny nose, loss of sense of taste.*
- ***Bacterial infection:*** *Increasing pain, inflammation and nasal swelling that may spread to other parts of the face; nosebleeds; and thick, yellow-green, malodorous nasal secretions.*
- ***Nasal folliculitis:*** *Pain and inflammation arising from the root (follicle) of a nasal hair.*

**WHO IS AT RISK**

*Most people have two or three colds a year, one of the most common infections affecting the nose. Chronic rhinitis—inflammation of the nasal passages—is usually due to allergies or a more serious bacterial or fungal infection of the nasal passages.*

*Teach a child to blow his nose gently, one nostril at a time.*

*Nasal folliculitis can occur at any age, but is somewhat more common among older people, especially if they pluck out their nasal hairs for cosmetic reasons. Children who pick their nose a lot also have an increased risk of developing folliculitis.*

## HOW IT DEVELOPS

The nasal passages are lined with mucous membranes that provide an ideal environment for infection. When viruses, fungi, and other organisms are inhaled, they are trapped by tiny hairs and mucus in the nose. Most are expelled from the body in nasal secretions, but even a few left behind can proliferate and cause an infection. Indeed, most colds start in the nose, and are heralded by sneezing, a runny nose, and sometimes nasal discomfort. These viral infections seldom last more than 7 to 10 days.

**Nasal folliculitis,** which is usually caused by a staphylococcus bacterium, starts as a painful swelling and sore around a nasal hair. Crusts form over the sore, and the area bleeds when they are picked off. Sometimes the infected hair root develops into a boil, or furuncle, which can be very painful. In rare instances, the boil evolves into spreading cellulitis, a serious infection of the skin and underlying tissue. The tip of the nose may become inflamed and very painful, and the infection sometimes spreads to other parts of the face.

Even more serious nasal infections, such as those caused by fungi or due to tuberculosis, leprosy, and other serious diseases, can destroy soft tissue, cartilage, and even bone. These infections can produce severe pain, worsening nasal obstruction, bleeding, and a thick, malodorous discharge; fortunately, they are now quite rare, at least in industrialized countries.

### WARNING!

***Many over-the counter cold medications claim to relieve a dozen or more cold symptoms. However, you rarely if ever need to treat so many symptoms. Look for a product whose ingredients are aimed at your specific symptoms. For example, antihistamines and pseudoephedrine are ingredients that reduce nasal stuffiness and swelling. In any event, these drugs should be used with caution if you have high blood pressure, glaucoma, or are taking other medications.***

## WHAT YOU CAN DO

See a doctor if nasal congestion lingers for more than two weeks; go sooner if there is severe nasal pain or a thick, malodorous discharge. For a cold or other viral infections, drink plenty of fluids to help thin the nasal secretions. Use a cool-mist humidifier, especially in the bedroom, to moisten the air.

Don't pick the nose, which can cause bleeding and a possible infection, such as folliculitis. Blow the nose gently, one nostril at a time, and avoid sniffing so hard that the mucus is forced into the sinus cavities. A saline nasal wash of two to three teaspoons of noniodized salt in one quart of warm water can ease discomfort. Fill a nasal syringe with warm salt water and draw it into a nostril, tilt the head back for a few seconds, and then bend the head forward to let the fluid flow out. Repeat with the other nostril. Over-the-counter painkillers and cold medications can ease symptoms, but must be used with caution to avoid side effects (see *Warning!*).

Warm compresses can ease the discomfort of folliculitis and nasal furuncles, but antibiotics are needed to cure the underlying infection.

## HOW TO TREAT IT

If a doctor suspects a bacterial or fungal nasal infection, a culture will be done to identify the organism, and then an antibiotic or antifungal medication will be prescribed. Other medications may be prescribed to ease nasal stuffiness. Folliculitis is usually treated with a two-week course of an antibiotic ointment containing bacitracin, gramicidin, polymyxin, and/or neomycin. Systemic antibiotics are needed to treat furuncles and nasal cellulitis. Hot soaks encourage drainage of the infectious material.

### THOSE PESKY NASAL POLYPS

Nasal allergies and other chronic irritations of the nose often lead to the formation of nasal polyps, an overgrowth of the mucous membranes. The polyps, which look like tiny grapes, are harmless, but they can obstruct breathing, interfere with the senses of taste and smell, and cause frequent nosebleeds. Headaches may develop if polyps block the drainage opening to the nasal passage.

Surgical removal of the polyps solves the problem, but they often recur if the underlying irritation continues. If you are prone to developing nasal polyps, try to get any allergies under control and avoid taking aspirin and nonprescription nose drops and nasal sprays. These products prompt the development of even more polyps.

## HOW TO PREVENT IT

Wash your hands frequently, and discard used tissues immediately rather than carry them around in a pocket or purse. Avoid picking the nose, and teach young children not to put foreign objects in the nose.

### ALTERNATIVE THERAPIES

**Aromatherapy**

The essential oil of eucalyptus, peppermint, basil, or lavender may help clear a stuffy nose. Add a few drops of an oil to a bowl or pan of very hot water and inhale the steamy vapors, or sprinkle a few drops on a handkerchief and hold it over the nose for a few minutes.

**Herbal medicine**

A combination of echinacea and goldenseal may help shorten the duration of a cold. Take 125 mg of goldenseal in combination with 200 mg of echinacea five times daily for five days. Goldenseal should not be taken by people with heart disease, high blood pressure, diabetes, or glaucoma; for cautions concerning echinacea, see *About the Recommendations* on p 7. Using small amounts of raw garlic, cayenne or hot chilies, and horseradish to flavor foods helps clear clogged nasal passages. **Note:** Some herbal texts recommend inhaling cayenne pepper to clear clogged passages. Doctors strongly advise against the practice because the cayenne can burn delicate nasal tissues.

# Nose Trauma

**SYMPTOMS**

- *Sharp pain following a blow to the nose.*
- *Nosebleed and progressive swelling; nose is usually misshapen or appears askew.*

**WHO IS AT RISK**

*Most broken noses are sustained in automobile accidents or falls in which the nose is hit. A broken nose is also a very common injury among boxers, football players, and other athletes who engage in contact sports.*

## HOW IT DEVELOPS

A broken nose is almost immediately apparent; the initial pain is intense, but it lessens after an hour or two. There may be profuse bleeding from one or both nostrils, and swelling develops rapidly. The nose itself is usually deformed. If bones have been broken into fragments, the nose will probably look flattened.

## WHAT YOU CAN DO

Pinch the nostrils above the break to stop the bleeding. Lean forward so that the blood can drain out of the nose (see *Stopping a Nosebleed,* below). Place an ice pack on the forehead and nose; this will help quell the bleeding and also slow the swelling. Get to an emergency room or doctor as soon as possible.

## HOW TO TREAT IT

An X ray may be ordered to assess the extent of the fracture; otherwise, the doctor may gently feel the nose to determine where it is broken. He or she will also check to see whether a septal hematoma (a collection of clotted blood) has developed in the nasal passage; if so, it is drained to prevent infection. The fractured bones will then be manipulated into place. An adult usually needs only local anesthesia; a child, however, is usually given a short-acting general anesthetic.

**WARNING!**

***A septal hematoma needs prompt drainage by a doctor; otherwise, it can cause a serious infection that may destroy the septal cartilage.***

After the broken bones have been set, internal packing and an external splint are used to hold them in place. The pain usually subsides after the bones are reset; in the meantime, a nonprescription painkiller such as aspirin or acetaminophen can be taken.

A broken septum—the strip of cartilage that separates the two nostrils—is difficult to stabilize, and may have to be repaired surgically after it heals. A badly broken nose may also require later plastic surgery.

## HOW TO PREVENT IT

Always wear a seatbelt when riding in a car, including in the backseat. Athletes who engage in contact sports should wear a protective face mask.

### ALTERNATIVE THERAPIES

There are no specific alternative therapies for a broken nose, but acupuncture or self-hypnosis may be a useful technique in relieving pain.

### STOPPING A NOSEBLEED

Most nosebleeds stop after a few minutes of applying pressure to the bridge of the nose. If not, follow these steps.

1. Sit with the upper body leaning forward to allow the blood to drain out of the nose into a cup or bowl, rather than leaning back, which allows the blood to run down the throat and may cause choking.
2. Gently squeeze both nostrils near the bridge of the nose. To reduce blood flow, apply ice or a cold compress to the upper back of the neck and forehead.
3. If bleeding persists, pack the nostril with gauze and seek medical attention. Don't pack the nose with tissue or cotton balls, which will stick and may cause rebleeding.

# The Ears

*As the organs of hearing and balance, the ears play a role in virtually every activity. The ear's complex network of nerves and its close proximity to nasal and throat passages make these organs very sensitive to pain and vulnerable to infection.*

## Ear Infections

### SYMPTOMS

- ***Outer ear (otitis external)***: *Earache, ranging from mild and chronic to severe and intermittent; itching; foul-smelling or bloody discharge; possible hearing loss, which is usually temporary.*
- ***Middle ear (otitis media)***: *Persistent, severe earache; fever; possible sore throat, nausea, vomiting, and diarrhea, especially in babies; decreased hearing acuity.*
- ***Inner ear (labyrinthitis)***: *Severe dizziness, nausea and vomiting, hearing loss (often permanent), ringing in the ears (tinnitus), possible facial paralysis.*

### WHO IS AT RISK

*Babies and young children, aged three months to three years, are especially vulnerable to middle-ear infections, the most common childhood ear problem. Allergies and exposure to secondhand smoke predispose a child to even more ear infections; bottle-fed babies also have more of these infections than those who are breast-fed. Outer-ear infections are more prevalent in older children and adults; they are especially common among swimmers—so much so that they are often called "swimmer's ear." Other predisposing factors include allergies, psoriasis, and eczema. Inner-ear infections are relatively rare, and usually occur in adults. But they sometimes develop in children who have frequent middle-ear infections; they also may be a complication of facial shingles.*

**WARNING!**

***If antibiotics are prescribed, be sure to give the full course of treatment. Symptoms may improve in a day or so, but stopping too soon increases the risk of a recurrence with an antibiotic-resistant organism that is much more difficult to treat.***

### HOW IT DEVELOPS

**Outer-ear infections** start with itching and pain, often quite severe, arising from the visible ear and its canal. The skin lining the canal will be red and swollen; it may also harbor small boils (furuncles), and there is usually a copious, malodorous ear discharge. Swollen membranes may cause a temporary loss of hearing.

**Structures of the Ear**

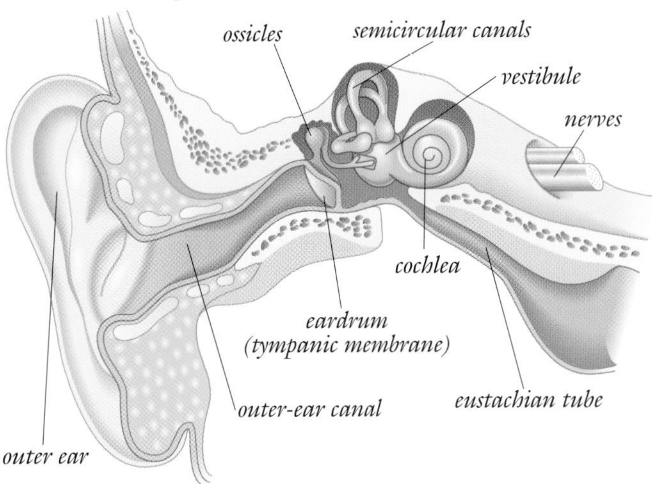


**Middle-ear infections** often develop on the heels of a cold or some other upper-respiratory infection, and can be caused by either viruses or bacteria. At the onset, a baby will be unusually fussy, and will tug or rub at an ear; there is often a low-grade fever as well as nausea, vomiting, and other intestinal symptoms. An older child will complain of an earache. As the infection worsens, the eardrum and other middle-ear structures become swollen and inflamed. Fluid and pus accumulate in the eardrum, creating pressure and added pain. If the eardrum ruptures, the pus drains out and the pain abates. However, the infection may become chronic, and eventually result in a loss of hearing. In rare cases, it can spread to the mastoid, the bone behind the ear, resulting in a serious infection called mastoiditis.

**Inner-ear infections** are usually secondary to other bacterial infections. Referred to as purulent labyrinthitis, these infections occur when bacteria invade the semicircular canals and other inner-ear structures. They are very serious and can result in permanent hearing loss, as well as meningitis and mastoiditis. Viruses can also cause labyrinthitis; this form is less serious than the bacterial infections. Both types cause severe dizziness (vertigo), nausea, vomiting, and, often, facial paralysis.

### WHAT YOU CAN DO

Consult a doctor as soon as possible for any persistent ear pain, especially if it is accompanied by a fever, dizziness,

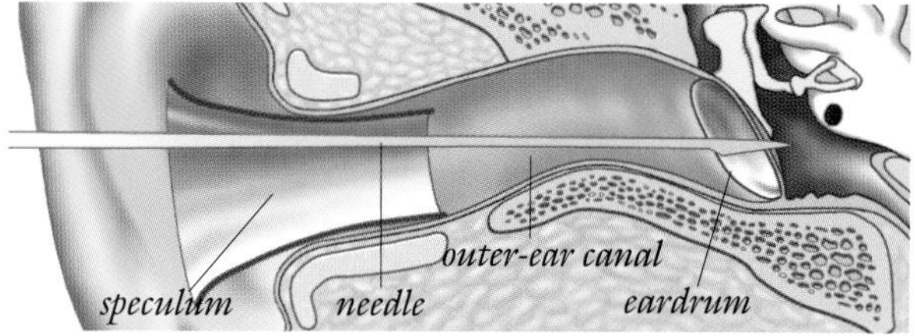


*To prevent spontaneous rupture of a swollen eardrum, a doctor may do a myringotomy. A speculum is inserted into the ear canal, and a thin, sharp needle is used to puncture the eardrum and allow pus to drain out. The puncture heals in a few days with no damage to hearing.*

and other symptoms. In the meantime, aspirin (for adults only) or acetaminophen can ease pain and lower a fever. Dry heat also helps; hold a hot towel or heating pad over the affected ear for five minutes, and repeat several times a day. Some people find that alternating hot and cold works even better. Apply heat for two to five minutes, and then switch to an ice pack wrapped in a towel for the same amount of time. If there is also a sore throat, gargle with warm salt water. Doctors warn against putting warm drops of oil in the ear; this is now considered dangerous, especially if the eardrum has ruptured.

To self-treat swimmer's ear, try placing a cotton ball soaked in Buro-Sol or rubbing alcohol into the ear overnight. In the morning, rinse the ear with a tablespoon of 3 percent hydrogen peroxide and $1/4$ cup of warm water. Alternatively, use equal parts of rubbing alcohol and white vinegar. **Note:** These remedies should be cleared with your doctor first, and should not be used if the eardrum has been perforated or if drainage tubes have been inserted in the middle ear.

Bed rest is usually essential until labyrinthitis passes because any movement can provoke attacks of vertigo and nausea. Lie as still as possible, resting the head on the side of the affected ear. If both ears are affected, lying on the back may be preferable.

## HOW TO TREAT IT

### Medications

Antibiotics are the mainstay of treating bacterial ear infections, although there is some controversy over using them to treat recurrent middle-ear infections in children.

Intravenous antibiotics will be given for severe purulent labyrinthitis. An inner-ear infection due to shingles will be treated with prednisone or another corticosteroid, as well as an antiviral drug such as acyclovir (Zovirax). Codeine or another narcotic painkiller may be prescribed if severe pain develops.

If swimmer's ear does not clear up with self-care, antibiotic/corticosteroid ear drops are prescribed. Treatment is usually continued for a week. An oral antibiotic is sometimes needed to cure the infection.

### Surgery

An in-office or outpatient procedure called myringotomy, in which the eardrum is punctured, may be used to drain fluid and pus from the middle ear (see illustration, left).

If the eustachian tubes are blocked due to swelling, a small tube may be inserted to keep them open; this is known as tympanocentesis (see below). This procedure, which requires general anesthesia, is not as popular today as it was a few years ago because doctors have found that it may lead to infection and other complications.

In some children, chronic middle-ear infections are exacerbated by enlarged adenoids and infected tonsils; their removal can help cure the problem.

In severe cases of labyrinthitis, surgical drainage of the inner ear may be necessary.

## HOW TO PREVENT IT

Babies and young children are vulnerable to middle-ear infections because they have very short and narrow eustachian tubes, the passages that link the middle ear and the top of the throat. This structure allows organisms in the throat and nose to invade the middle ear. Nasal washes (see p 89) at the first sign of a cold may help prevent an ear infection. A baby's feeding position is also important to prevent foreign matter from entering the tubes. Make sure that the baby is held in a semi-upright position, and that the nose is not blocked.

Many middle-ear infections can be prevented by treating contributing disorders, especially allergies and sinusitis. If your child suffers from allergies, talk to your doctor about antihistamine and decongestant medications.

Keeping the outer-ear canal dry is the key to preventing swimmer's ear and other outer-ear infections. Wear a bathing cap and protective ear plugs while swimming, and swim only in water that you know is clean. After showering or washing your hair, tilt the head to each side to drain water out of the ears. To dry the canal, use a hair dryer set on low to blow warm air into the ear.

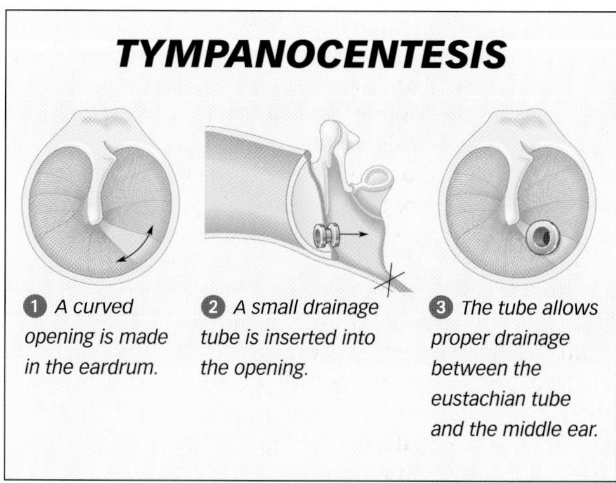

TYMPANOCENTESIS
1 A curved opening is made in the eardrum.
2 A small drainage tube is inserted into the opening.
3 The tube allows proper drainage between the eustachian tube and the middle ear.

ALTERNATIVE THERAPIES

**Aromatherapy**

Diluted oils of eucalyptus and lavender may ease discomfort and hasten healing of outer-ear infections. The oils can be diluted in olive oil and massaged into the ear lobe and the area around the outer ear. Be careful, however, not to let the oil run into the ear itself.

**Herbal medicine**

To treat swimmer's ear, herbalists recommend placing drops containing mullein, an herb with anti-inflammatory properties, on the skin of the outer ear. Echinacea may be taken by adults to help overcome an infection, but it should not be given to children. For further cautions concerning echinacea, see *About the Recommendations*, p 7.

**Reflexology**

Pressing on the acupressure points located at the base of the ring finger and the middle portion of the little finger may help ease ear pain. Hold the points between the thumb and index finger and apply gentle pressure for three minutes until the pain eases. Repeat on the other hand and do this hourly. Then press or massage the points every four hours for the next few days.

# Foreign Body in the Ear

**SYMPTOMS**

- *Pain in one ear. The discomfort can range from sharp and intermittent pain to itching, burning, or a steady, dull ache.*
- *Uncomfortable feeling of something in the ear.*
- *A young child may fuss with and tug at the ear as if he has an earache.*
- *Possible buzzing or ringing noise and diminished hearing in the affected ear.*

**WHO IS AT RISK**

*Young children are apt to put almost any small object into an ear; favored items include beads, peas, dried beans, and pencil erasers. Insects, such as earwigs, spiders, and cockroaches, can also crawl into an ear, causing a very unpleasant sensation, pain, or buzzing.*

## HOW IT DEVELOPS

The ear canal contains many nerve endings, so even a slight touch or pressure from a foreign object can be very painful. As the foreign object moves further into the ear canal, it not only causes increasing pain, but it can also damage the eardrum and other middle- and inner-ear structures. Inflammation, swelling, and pain worsen the longer the object stays in the ear.

## WHAT YOU CAN DO

If a child has put an object into the ear, take him or her to a doctor as soon as possible to have it removed. If the foreign object is an insect, try going into a dark room and shining a bright light into the ear. Sometimes this prompts the insect to crawl out on its own. If this doesn't work, you can kill the insect by flooding the ear with mineral oil or rubbing alcohol. This will provide relief until you can get to a doctor to have the object removed.

## HOW TO TREAT IT

A glass bead can sometimes be flushed out with mineral oil or warm water, but only a doctor should do this. Otherwise, depending upon the object, a doctor will try to remove it by either snaring it and pulling it out, or using a tiny rake-like instrument to scoop it out. A young child usually needs general anesthesia during the procedure. After the object is out, drops may be put in the ear to reduce swelling and relieve pain. Antibiotics are prescribed if an infection has developed.

**WARNING!**

***NEVER try to remove a foreign object from a child's ear yourself. Entering the ear canal with tweezers, a swab, or a blunt object is likely to push the object farther into the ear, where it can cause serious damage.***

## HOW TO PREVENT IT

Teach a young child never to put any object into the ear—or the nose, rectum, and other body openings. Use window screens to keep insects from invading your home; if you are camping, inspect sleeping bags and blankets for insects before going to bed, and use mosquito netting to prevent them from crawling into the bed while you sleep. To avoid damaging the ear, never insert hairpins, cotton swabs, and similar objects into it.

### HOW TO ADMINISTER EAR DROPS

1. Start by measuring the exact amount of medication into the applicator; have a clean cotton ball nearby.
2. Lie down with the affected ear up and the hair moved away so that the ear is exposed.
3. Use one hand to cup the ear and pull it slightly upward. Insert the dropper into the opening of the ear canal, and squeeze out the medication so that it runs inward along the side of the ear canal to allow air to escape.
4. Before rising, gently insert the cotton ball into the opening of the canal to keep the medication in.
5. If a child's ear canal is too swollen to allow the medicine to flow into it, a doctor will insert a wick—a strip of cotton or spongy material—and saturate it with the drops.

# Noise Damage

## *SYMPTOM*

*Acoustic trauma results from exposure to a sudden blast of very loud noise, such as an explosion or a gunshot. Symptoms include:*

- *Sudden, sharp pain in the ears followed by persistent ringing (tinnitus).*
- *Hearing loss, which is often permanent.*

## *WHO IS AT RISK*

*We live in an increasingly noisy world—noise pollution is a growing environmental concern—and doctors are seeing more noise-related hearing loss among ever-younger people. Chronic exposure to noise above 85 decibels—for example, amplified rock music, a snowmobile, a jackhammer, or chain saw—can also cause temporary ear pain, tinnitus, and hearing loss. Those at special risk include rock musicians and devotees who listen to very loud music, especially those who use headsets, and construction workers, loggers, and others who operate noisy machinery.*

*Acoustic trauma is common among road crews and other workers exposed to dynamite blasts, as well as hunters and people who frequent shooting galleries without wearing protective earmuffs.*

## HOW IT DEVELOPS

Exposure to noise loud enough to cause acoustic trauma destroys the delicate hair cells of the inner ear, resulting in almost immediate hearing loss. The noise itself causes extreme pain, and may also rupture the eardrum. In most instances, some, but not all, hearing returns as the ears recover from the acoustic trauma. In other cases, the deafness is permanent. The hearing loss associated with chronic noise exposure comes on more gradually and is permanent. Any exposure to noise that causes ear pain and ringing in the ears is destroying hair cells and damaging hearing, even though the effects may take years to become apparent. Noise-related tinnitus is unpredictable—sometimes it comes and goes, disappears completely, or becomes a permanent annoyance.

*Protective earmuffs can prevent job-related noise damage.*

**WARNING!**

***About one of every 5,000 North Americans a year suffers sudden deafness. When this happens in an older person, the culprit usually involves reduced blood flow to the acoustic nerve because of a stroke. But most victims are young children and young or middle-aged adults; in these people, the cause is usually an infection, such as flu, chicken pox, or mononucleosis. Hearing often returns in 10 to 14 days, but a prompt visit to a doctor is in order in case treatment is needed.***

## WHAT YOU CAN DO

Do whatever you can to protect your ears from sudden loud noises (see *How to Prevent It*, below). For example, if you are unexpectedly exposed to fire engine or police sirens, press your hands over your ears until the source of the noise passes.

Ringing in the ears can be very annoying and interfere with sleep. A white-noise machine, a device that plays a pleasant albeit monotonous sound, such as breaking waves or falling rain, can mask the ringing in the ears and make it easier for a person to fall asleep.

## HOW TO TREAT IT

If acoustic trauma results in permanent hearing loss, a hearing aid may help.

## HOW TO PREVENT IT

Take stock of daily activities that may be damaging your ears. Even a hair dryer held close to the ears produces enough noise to be damaging. Many other household appliances, such as blenders and vacuum cleaners, produce excessive noise, as do lawn mowers and leaf blowers.

If you listen to a headset, keep the volume low. Wear special noise-protective earplugs whenever you know you are going to be exposed to loud noise. (Cotton balls or toilet paper are not adequate substitutes.) Many rock musicians wear these. Anyone whose job exposes him or her to very loud noise should wear ear-protective earmuffs, such as those filled with glycerin, to absorb noise.

### ALTERNATIVE THERAPIES

**Meditation and self-hypnosis**

These techniques may be helpful in coping with persistent ringing in the ears.

**Reflexology**

Reflexologists use the acupressure points at the tips of the middle and ring fingers to help restore at least some of the temporary hearing loss suffered from mild acoustic trauma. Try pressing these points between the thumb and index finger of the opposite hand for two or three minutes every four hours to speed up return of hearing.

# Ruptured Eardrum

## SYMPTOMS

- *Sudden severe ear pain followed by bleeding from the ear and hearing loss.*
- *Dizziness (vertigo) and ringing in the ear (tinnitus).*

## WHO IS AT RISK

*Children with severe middle-ear infections frequently suffer a ruptured eardrum (tympanic membrane). Ruptures also occur due to a sudden change of pressure inside the ear; likely causes include an explosion, a hard slap, a sharp plane descent, or a diving accident. Boxers, skydivers, and deep-sea divers all have an increased risk of ruptured eardrums. Finally, any sharp or pointed object—pencils, matchsticks, hairpins, even cotton swabs—thrust into an ear can rupture the eardrum.*

## HOW IT DEVELOPS

The eardrum is a thin membrane stretched across the opening of the middle ear, separating it from the outer-ear canal. When sound waves entering the ear canal hit the eardrum, they set off vibrations that are passed on to the ossicles, three tiny bones at the top of the middle ear, and then to the inner ear, where they are transformed into electrical impulses and eventually sent to the brain for decoding. The eustachian tube—a long, narrow channel—links the middle ear to the top of the throat, and admits air to the middle ear, thereby equalizing pressure on both sides of the eardrum.

A drastic or sudden change of pressure between the middle and outer ear can rupture the eardrum. When a child has a severe middle-ear infection, for example, the eustachian tube can swell shut, and mounting pressure from fluid and pus collecting in the middle ear may cause the eardrum to burst. There will be a sharp pain, and as the pus and fluid drain out of the ear, the pressure eases and the pain subsides.

In contrast, a sharp increase in ambient, or atmospheric, pressure—for example, a sudden plane descent or a deep-sea dive—requires a rapid movement of air through the eustachian tube to equalize the pressure on the other side of the eardrum. This is what causes your ears to "pop" and perhaps hurt during a plane's takeoff and landing. If the tube is blocked, as might happen if you have a cold, a condition called barotitis media can develop, marked by pain, temporary hearing loss, tinnitus, and—in extreme cases—a ruptured eardrum.

A hard blow to the ear, such as those often suffered by boxers, can also damage the ossicular bones and inner-ear structures. Bleeding from the ears, severe vertigo, hearing loss, and ringing in the ears immediately follow the injury, and may last for hours or even days, depending on the extent of the damage.

### WARNING!

***NEVER put drops or other fluids in an ear with a ruptured eardrum unless your doctor specifically tells you to do so. The drops can seep through the torn tympanic membrane and damage the inner-ear structures.***

### EARWAX BUILDUP

The earwax (cerumen) that normally lines and protects the ear canal can often build up and cause itching, pain, ringing in the ear (tinnitus), and temporary hearing loss. Older people are especially prone to a buildup of earwax; they often mistakenly assume that their diminished hearing is due to aging. However, a doctor can quickly detect the buildup by simply looking into the ear canal with an otoscope. The wax is easily removed by rolling it out with a small spoonlike instrument, called a curet, or by suctioning it out with a device attached to a vacuum.

You can also remove the wax yourself using a commercial kit available in most pharmacies. But NEVER try to remove the wax with a paper clip, hairpin, swab, fingernail, or other such objects.

## WHAT YOU CAN DO

Keep the ear dry, especially if the eardrum ruptures. See a doctor if ringing in the ears and hearing loss persist for more than a few days. Go sooner if there is severe pain, a bloody discharge, or sudden deafness.

## HOW TO TREAT IT

Antibiotics are prescribed if there is an infection. Most eardrum ruptures heal on their own within a week or two; if not, the eardrum may need surgical repair. In cases of persisting vertigo and hearing loss, the inner ear may also be damaged and require surgical repair.

## HOW TO PREVENT IT

Make sure that middle-ear infections are treated early and adequately (see *Ear Infections*, p 91). Avoid flying when you have a cold or hay fever. If you must fly despite a stuffy nose, use a decongestant nasal spray 30 to 60 minutes before takeoff and, if the flight lasts more than a few hours, again before landing.

# The Mouth

*The mouth plays an important role in multiple functions, including digestion, speech, and breathing. It also speaks volumes about your emotions—everything from happy smiles to expressions of surprise, anger, and pain.*

## Canker Sores

### SYMPTOMS

- *Localized pain and tingling in the mouth or inner lip, especially when a sore is touched or exposed to spicy or acidic foods.*
- *One or more white or yellow ulcers with red margins.*
- *Possible swollen lymph nodes in the neck, fever, and general malaise.*

### WHO IS AT RISK

*Canker sores occur most often in teenagers and young adults, and women are afflicted more than men. They often develop during times of high stress. Hormones may play a role, because many women get them just before menstruation. Nutritional deficiencies—especially of iron, folic acid, and vitamin $B_{12}$—increase the risk of canker sores or other mouth ulcers. Some people find that ingredients in some toothpastes or mouthwashes and certain foods—especially nuts and acidic foods—trigger the sores; other risk factors include allergies, irritation from dentures or orthodontic appliances, and a tendency to bite one's lip or cheek. Smoking and chewing tobacco also exacerbate canker sores.*

### HOW IT DEVELOPS

A canker sore, known medically as *aphthous stomatitis*, starts with localized tingling and sometimes numbness. Within a day, a small ulcer forms, usually on the inside of the lip or cheek, but sometimes on the tongue or roof of the mouth. The most common type, *minor aphthae*, are less than a fifth of an inch across. Although they are not a threat to health and a sore heals without a scar in 10 days or less, they can be exquisitely painful and make it difficult to eat and speak. In contrast, *major aphthae* are one-fourth of an inch across or larger, they can last for weeks, and often leave scars. Both types of canker sores tend to recur two or three times a year.

**WARNING!**

***See a doctor if a canker sore or other mouth lesion persists for more than two weeks; it may be due to an infection or more serious cause. Some mouth cancers look like canker sores at first, but they are generally painless.***

### WHAT YOU CAN DO

Until the sore heals, forgo spicy and acidic foods, such as tomatoes and orange juice. Hold an ice cube against the sore to dull the pain temporarily. Before eating, try coating the sore with a protective paste, such as Orabase, to ease pain and prevent exposing it to irritating foods and fluids. Various herbal mouthwashes may also help (see *Alternative Therapies* on the facing page).

*Foods—especially those shown here—are common canker sore triggers.*

### HOW TO TREAT IT

#### Medications

A doctor or dentist may prescribe lidocaine (Xylocaine) to be applied to the sore or used as a mouth rinse. It temporarily relieves the pain, and makes eating easier, although it also dulls the sense of taste. Large or frequently recurring sores can be treated with a mouthwash containing the antibiotic tetracycline. The pain of large, slow-healing sores can be eased by a doctor applying silver nitrate, which destroys the nerve endings under the sore.

#### Surgery

In severe cases, laser surgery may be recommended to destroy the sore and reduce the risk of recurrences. Laser surgery uses powerful concentrated light beams to vaporize unwanted tissue.

### HOW TO PREVENT IT

Do not smoke and avoid foods that trigger an outbreak; common offenders include citrus fruits, cheese, hot chili peppers and other spicy foods, and walnuts. Some studies show that mild deficiencies of the B vitamins increase susceptibility to canker sores; a daily vitamin pill that meets the daily requirements for the B-complex group may reduce recurrences. Other studies have found that using a tetracycline mouthwash during the tingling stage may prevent a full-blown sore.

If canker sores tend to recur in the same place, have a dentist check for a jagged tooth, ill-fitting denture or dental appliance, or other source of irritation. Also pay attention to possible nervous habits, such as sucking or chewing on the inside of a lip or the cheek.

### ALTERNATIVE THERAPIES

**Herbal medicine**

Herbalists often treat canker sores with mouthwashes containing goldenseal, chamomile, or myrrh. Mix one teaspoon of powdered goldenseal in eight ounces of water, and use it three or four times a day. Or brew a strong chamomile tea (two heaping teaspoons of dried chamomile per eight ounces of water), let it cool, and use it as a mouth rinse. Hold either of these rinses in the mouth for two or three minutes; they can then be swallowed or spit out. A myrrh rinse is made by adding 5 to 10 drops of tincture to eight ounces of water; use it to rinse the mouth before meals. Some people apply a drop of the undiluted tincture directly to the sore; this is said to hasten healing while relieving the pain. But it can also cause intense stinging; if so, use the diluted rinse.

**Relaxation techniques**

Stress-related canker sores may be prevented by practicing meditation, progressive relaxation exercises, and other stress-reduction techniques.

# Cold Sores

### SYMPTOMS

- *A very painful blister on the lips, gums, or palate, and, less commonly, on the fingers.*
- *Possible fever, swollen lymph nodes, and a feeling of general malaise.*

### WHO IS AT RISK

*Almost everyone has had at least a few cold sores or fever blisters, which are caused by the herpes simplex virus. They are highly contagious and easily passed from person to person by direct skin contact. In the past, dentists and dental hygienists often developed a variation of cold sores on their fingers; this is now less common with dentists and other health professionals routinely wearing protective latex gloves.*

## HOW IT DEVELOPS

Oral herpes infections start with a primary outbreak, which is the initial incidence. After that, recurrences are usually reactivations of the original infection. The primary infection typically occurs early in life when an adult with a cold sore unwittingly passes the virus to a child. The primary infection is usually the most severe and is centered in the mouth—the gums are inflamed and painful, and there may be a fever and swollen lymph nodes. After two or three days, small blisters form, and as they rupture, the mouth becomes even more raw and painful. These symptoms, which are often mistaken for teething, usually last for about a week.

Although the blisters heal completely, the virus remains dormant by taking refuge in nerve endings around the mouth. Future flare-ups take the form of cold sores, which can be triggered by many factors—colds, a fever, sunburn, dental work, mouth injury, allergies, even stress. A person can often tell when a cold sore is about to erupt because the area—usually on a lip or under the nose—itches or tingles for a day or two. The blisters ooze and crust over; they can be very painful and unsightly. Most cold sores heal in a week, but some people, especially those with lowered immunity, are plagued with frequently recurring sores (see *Warning!*, above).

**WARNING!**

***Large, persistent cold sores can be life-threatening for people with severely compromised immune systems, such as AIDS patients and persons undergoing cancer chemotherapy or a bone marrow transplant. In these people, there is a danger that the herpes virus can spread to the brain, which can be fatal. Prompt intravenous treatment with an antiviral drug such as Zovirax can be life-saving.***

## WHAT YOU CAN DO

Use cold to fight a cold sore. When you first feel the characteristic tingling, hold an ice cube or cold compress over the area—this sometimes keeps the blister from erupting. If a blister does develop, cold compresses or a cotton ball dipped in cold milk soothes the pain and speeds healing. Avoid hot foods and drinks, especially if blisters develop in the mouth. Instead, eat foods that are cold or at room temperature and drink iced liquids or suck on frozen juice bars. Coating the blister with a petroleum salve, vitamin E oil, or over-the-counter anesthetic ointment can ease pain and soften the scabs that form as the blister heals. A mouthwash made by dissolving one tablespoon of baking soda in one-fourth cup of cold water soothes blisters that form in the mouth.

## HOW TO TREAT IT

A doctor may prescribe an antiviral ointment, such as acyclovir (Zovirax), or an antiviral solution (Herplex-D), which are most effective if applied at the first warning sign of a flare-up. An antibiotic ointment is sometimes needed to treat a secondary bacterial infection. When blisters develop in the mouth, an anesthetic mouthwash containing lidocaine (Xylocaine) can dull pain.

## HOW TO PREVENT IT

Try to identify any triggers, and avoid them. Use zinc oxide or another sunblock to protect the lips and skin around the mouth from sunburns. Take care not to pass the virus to others, especially young children; avoid kissing and other skin contact, and do not share drinking glasses, towels, washcloths, and other personal items. Remember, too, that you can spread the herpes virus to other parts of your body. Wash your hands frequently when you have a cold sore; never touch a cold sore and then rub your eyes, which can cause ocular herpes. Similarly, be careful not to spread the virus to the genital area, either through touch or oral sex.

### ALTERNATIVE THERAPIES

**Herbal medicine**

Echinacea, taken as tablets, tea, or tincture, helps fight off viral infections. To treat a flare-up, take 200 mg four times a day. For cautions concerning echinacea, see *About the Recommendations*, p 7. Witch hazel, available at most pharmacies, is an astringent herb that can help dry up the oozing blisters.

**Homeopathy**

Homeopathic remedies for cold sores include: Natrum muriaticum (especially for sores triggered by exposure to the sun), Rhus toxicodendron, and Apis mellifica. They are taken three or four times a day.

**Nutraceuticals**

Taking 1000 to 2000 mg of vitamin C during the tingling stage may hasten healing of a cold sore.

# Mouth Cancer

### SYMPTOMS

- *Raised white or red patches in the mouth.*
- *Mouth ulcers (canker sores) or sores on the lips that fail to heal; persistent tongue soreness or pain.*

### WHO IS AT RISK

*Mouth cancer usually strikes after age 40 and men are twice as likely as women to develop it. It is relatively rare except among people who smoke or chew tobacco; the risk is even higher among those who use both alcohol and tobacco. Other risk factors include exposure to radiation and industrial chemicals, such as those used in plastic manufacturing, and chronic iron deficiency. Lip cancers are most common among pipe smokers or people who spend a lot of time in the sun.*

## HOW IT DEVELOPS

About 90 percent of all oral cancers start in the squamous cells that make up the surface layer of mouth tissue. Initially, they appear as precancerous patches (plaques) of white (leukoplakia) or red (erythroplasia) tissue. At this stage, the cancer is painless and is often detected during a routine dental examination. As the cancer develops, the plaques form small bumps and take on the appearance of a raspberry. Some form a small ulcer that looks like a canker sore. As the cancer invades the underlying tissue, it becomes painful and, depending upon its site, may interfere with speech and eating.

## WHAT YOU CAN DO

See a doctor as soon as possible if you notice red or white patches that don't go away, or if you develop a mouth ulcer that doesn't heal. Mouth cancer often interferes with eating, but it's important to maintain good nutrition. A puréed or liquid diet that includes enriched nutritional drinks and supplements of vitamins and minerals may be necessary.

## HOW TO TREAT IT

Precancerous plaques and small oral cancers on the floor of the mouth or tip of the tongue usually can be removed surgically, either with a scalpel or destroyed by a laser (intense beam of light), an electric needle, or freezing (cryotherapy). Lip cancer is treated with surgery or radiation. If the cancer shows evidence that it has spread—for example, the nearby lymph nodes are enlarged—treatment usually entails surgical removal of the tumor plus a radical neck dissection, in which the lymph nodes are also removed. This is followed by radiation treatments and, in some instances, chemotherapy. Reconstructive plastic surgery may be needed, especially if parts of the jawbone and other facial structures are removed.

**WARNING!**

***Mouth cancer often is not detected in an early stage because the precancerous plaques are usually on the floor of the mouth, inside the cheeks, or around the gums of the back teeth. Have your dentist carefully check your mouth for any precancerous plaques at each dental checkup, especially if you have a history of tobacco use.***

## HOW TO PREVENT IT

If you smoke or chew tobacco, make every effort to stop. Use alcohol only in moderation, if at all, especially if you have a history of tobacco use. Apply a special lip sunblock to protect your lips from cancer-causing ultraviolet (UV) rays when you go outdoors.

### ALTERNATIVE THERAPIES

There are no alternative therapies for the cancer itself, but some help minimize the effects of treatment and are useful during rehabilitation.

**Herbal medicine**

Rinsing the mouth frequently with strong green tea (one to two teaspoons of tea per cup of water) promotes the healing of radiation- or chemotherapy-induced mouth sores. An aloe vera mouth rinse has similar benefits.

**Physical and speech therapy**

These may be needed to regain the ability to eat and speak following radical mouth and/or neck surgery.

# Salivary Gland Blockage

## SYMPTOMS

- *Painful swelling under lower jaw that comes and goes, but is most pronounced at mealtime.*
- *Possible dry mouth.*

## WHO IS AT RISK

*The risk of salivary stones increases with age; otherwise, anyone can develop a blocked salivary gland. Possible causes include infection, an injury, or a tumor.*

## HOW IT DEVELOPS

There are three pairs of salivary glands: the *parotids*, which are in front of the ears; the *submandibulars*, which are under the jaw; and the *sublinguals*, which are under the tongue. A blockage of the ducts between the glands and the mouth can cause a backup of saliva, resulting in swelling, inflammation, pain, and a possible dry mouth. When a calcium stone lodges in a duct, swelling increases at mealtime because eating stimulates saliva flow; the swelling may disappear completely between meals.

**WARNING!**

***Antihistamines and many other medications reduce saliva production and cause a dry mouth. If you notice this side effect, ask your dentist about ways to prevent tooth decay.***

A dry mouth makes chewing and swallowing food difficult and can increase the risk of choking. Saliva also helps stem the growth of oral bacteria; thus, a chronic dry mouth increases the risk of dental caries and also fosters bad breath.

## WHAT YOU CAN DO

This self-test can determine whether the blockage is due to a stone in a salivary duct: Place something sour in your mouth—for example, a little pickle or lemon juice—to stimulate the flow of saliva. Increased swelling and pain indicate the presence of a stone. Sometimes massaging the swelling can dislodge the stone, but it's better to leave that to a doctor or dentist.

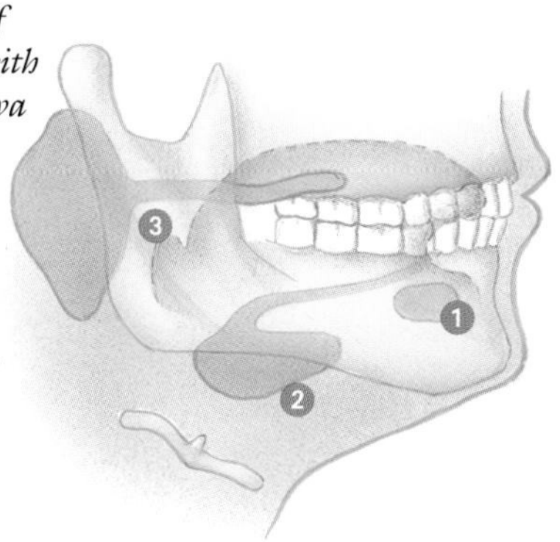


*There are three pairs of salivary glands, each with a duct that carries saliva to the mouth. The sublinguals (1) are under the tongue; the submandibulars (2) are on the floor of the mouth under the lower jaw; and the parotids (3), the largest of the salivary glands, are in front of the ears.*

Aspirin, ibuprofen, and other nonprescription anti-inflammatory medications can relieve pain and inflammation of a swollen salivary gland. To make eating easier, mash or puree foods, and take frequent sips of water during a meal. There are also nonprescription saliva substitutes that are available as mouth sprays or gels. These help moisten mouth tissues and reduce the risk of dental caries due to a lack of saliva. An antiseptic mouthwash also reduces oral bacteria and helps prevent tooth decay and bad breath.

## HOW TO TREAT IT

To confirm that the problem is due to a calcium stone, a CT scan or an MRI may be ordered; these tests can also determine whether a tumor is present. A dentist may be able to dislodge a small stone by pressing on the duct. If this doesn't work, it can be removed by snaring it with a special instrument or by dental surgery performed under local anesthesia. Antibiotics are prescribed to treat salivary blockages due to a bacterial infection; a tumor will likely require surgical removal.

## HOW TO PREVENT IT

Drinking at least eight glasses of fluid a day may help prevent formation of stones; otherwise, there are no specific preventive measures.

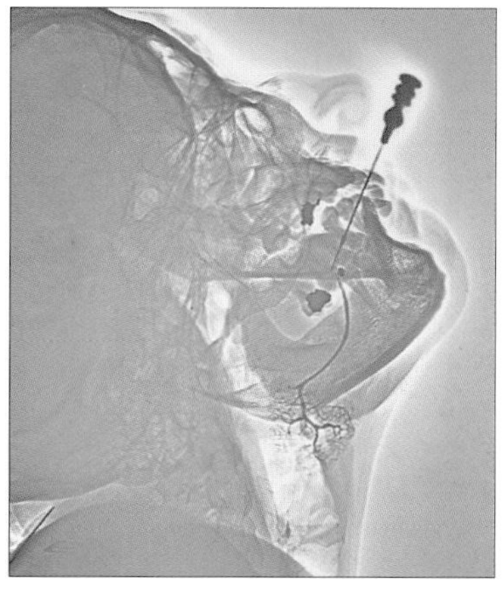

*Salivary stones can be detected by special X rays taken after injection of a fluid that is used to make the glands visible on X-ray film.*

### ALTERNATIVE THERAPIES

**Herbal medicine**

Sour or bitter herbs, such as Chinese green tea or teas made from lemon balm, ginger, or chamomile, help stimulate the flow of saliva.

> **BREAKTHROUGHS!**
>
> **Surgical removal of a large calcium stone may be avoided by lithotripsy, a relatively new procedure in which shock waves directed into the clogged duct are used to break up the stone into tiny bits. The small particles can then flow out of the gland in the saliva.**

# Sore Tongue

### SYMPTOMS

- *Painful swelling, inflammation, or burning sensation affecting the tongue.*
- *Ulcers or cracks (fissures), most commonly along the sides of the tongue.*
- *Tongue may appear smooth and discolored or "furry."*
- *Curdlike patches and bleeding.*

### WHO IS AT RISK

*A sore red tongue is a common sign of pernicious anemia, or vitamin $B_{12}$ deficiency. Iron deficiency anemia makes the tongue smooth and pale. Tongue swelling and inflammation are usually due to an infection, most commonly from the herpes simplex virus that causes cold sores or a bacterial infection. Oral thrush, a fungal infection, can cause curdlike patches that bleed easily on the sides of the tongue. Ulcers or cracks are often due to accidental bites or irritation from a broken tooth, ill-fitting dentures, or orthodontic appliances. Unconscious habits, such as tongue thrusting, biting, or chewing, can also cause soreness. Other common causes of tongue sores include allergies, highly spiced foods, alcohol, and tobacco use (both smoking and chewing it).*

## HOW IT DEVELOPS

The tongue is made up of muscle tissue covered by a mucous membrane that contains the taste buds. It has millions of nerve endings that make it very sensitive to heat, cold, touch, and pain. The tip and the sides, where most bites and ulcers occur, are especially sensitive to pain. The tongue tends to heal quickly, but until it does, even a minor injury can be very painful.

A sore or discolored tongue due to anemia usually develops gradually, and may not be noticed until the anemia is severe enough to produce other symptoms, such as shortness of breath.

## WHAT YOU CAN DO

See a doctor promptly if symptoms point to possible anemia, or if a sore does not heal in a week or so. Avoid eating spicy or highly acidic foods and abstain from alcohol until the tongue heals. If you smoke or chew tobacco, now is a good time to stop.

To soothe soreness and burning, try rinsing the mouth with one tablespoon of baking soda mixed with one-fourth cup of water. To clean the teeth, use a soft toothbrush and baking soda until the tongue heals.

## HOW TO TREAT IT

Anemia is treated by correcting the underlying nutritional deficiency. Pernicious anemia is treated with vitamin $B_{12}$ injections or pills; iron supplements are prescribed for the more common iron-deficiency anemia.

Depending upon the organism involved, infections are treated with antibiotics or antifungal medications. These can usually be taken as oral medications; in very severe infections they are given intravenously.

## HOW TO PREVENT IT

Using an antiseptic mouthwash can help keep oral bacteria in check and prevent oral infections. A dentist should be consulted if the problem is due to a broken tooth or irritation from dentures or a dental appliance; correcting the problem will allow the tongue to heal. If cancer is present, early treatment increases the chance of a cure.

Avoid foods and drinks that provoke allergic reactions or irritate delicate oral tissues, including the tongue. If you habitually bite your tongue, especially while sleeping, talk to your dentist about wearing a night appliance that prevents biting and tooth grinding. Above all, do not chew tobacco or smoke; tobacco contains a number of irritating compounds, and chewing it is a leading cause of oral cancer (see *Warning!*).

> **WARNING!**
>
> ***Most oral cancers start on the sides of the tongue or the area just under it. Any persistent sore or lump on one side of the tongue, as well as unexplained red or white patches that last more than two weeks, should be examined by a doctor as soon as possible.***

### ALTERNATIVE THERAPIES

**Herbal medicine**

Herbalists recommend various healing mouthwashes and teas. Chinese green tea has mild antiseptic and healing properties. Sage tea is also healing; steep two teaspoons of the dried herb in a cup of hot water for five to eight minutes, strain, and drink. A calendula mouth rinse is also soothing or healing. Use a diluted tincture or make a strong tea using one tablespoon of dried leaves per cup of water; strain and use as a mouthwash.

# The Teeth, Gums, and Jaw

*All too often, we take our teeth for granted until a toothache strikes—one of our most painful maladies. Fortunately, most toothaches and other dental problems can be prevented by practicing good oral hygiene and getting regular checkups.*

## Caries/Cavities

### SYMPTOMS

*As dental decay advances, pain and other symptoms become increasingly severe.*

- ***Mild decay:** Momentary twinges when tooth is exposed to heat, cold, or something sweet.*
- ***Moderate decay:** Increasing and more persistent pain with less provocation, such as eating or touching the tooth with the tongue.*
- ***Severe decay:** Intense, persistent toothache that may be accompanied by swollen gums and jaw, difficulty opening the mouth, bad breath, and a pus-filled abscess.*

### WHO IS AT RISK

*Many people have at least a few dental caries, or cavities, by the time they reach adulthood. The risk is especially high among people who eat a lot of sweets and neglect regular brushing and flossing; smoking or chewing tobacco also promotes dental disease. Anything that interferes with the production and flow of saliva increases the risk of cavities. Babies and toddlers who are allowed to fall asleep sucking a bottle of milk or juice can suffer extensive decay of their baby (primary) teeth, which also affects the health of the underlying permanent teeth.*

**WARNING!**

**Don't be misled by the abrupt disappearance of a toothache. This often indicates that the tooth's pulp and its pain-causing nerves have died. But the infection most likely is continuing to spread and, unless stopped, it can invade the underlying bone and surrounding soft tissue.**

### HOW IT DEVELOPS

Tooth decay is caused by acid-producing bacteria in the mouth, most commonly *Streptococcus mutans*. The cavities themselves develop differently, depending upon their location. **Pit and fissure decay,** which usually starts in late childhood, develops in the grooves on the chewing surfaces. The back teeth are the most vulnerable, and this type of decay advances rapidly. In contrast, **smooth-surface cavities,** which are most common during young adulthood, grow slowly, starting as a white spot where

**Anatomy of a Tooth**

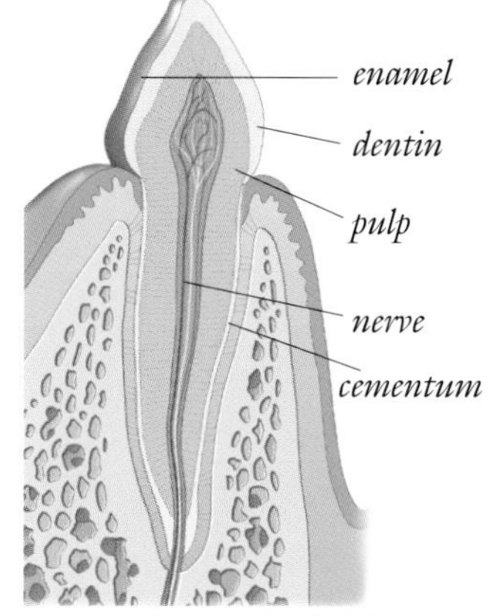


*A normal tooth fits tightly into underlying bone tissue, with the gums fitting firmly around the root line.*

the bacteria are dissolving calcium in the surface enamel, often between the teeth. **Root decay,** which is most common after age 50, starts in the cementum, the hard tissue that covers the root surfaces and is increasingly exposed by receding gums.

Pain typically starts when the decay reaches the dentin, the layer under the tooth's harder enamel surface. Pain is intermittent, occurring when you eat or drink something hot, cold, or sugary. At this stage, the tooth can usually be saved. But if the decay invades the inner pulp chamber, the pain is more severe and persistent, and damage to the tooth is irreversible. The ache temporarily subsides when the pulp dies, but a throbbing pain soon develops as the infection spreads and an abscess forms. The abscess may push the tooth out of its socket; pushing it back into place produces intense pain. The spreading infection causes swelling of the jaw and cheek, and pus drains into the mouth or perhaps through an opening in the skin.

### WHAT YOU CAN DO

See a dentist promptly if a tooth is unusually sensitive to hot or cold. If a toothache develops, aspirin or acetaminophen can provide temporary relief. However, don't try the old home remedy of holding an aspirin (for adults only) against the aching tooth; this can damage the enamel and gum tissue, and may also cause a canker sore. A warm compress or heating pad held against the jaw provides temporary relief. But don't use heat for throbbing pain, which indicates an infection. Instead, apply an ice pack for 5 to 10 minutes every hour; this will reduce swelling and ease pain until you can get to your dentist.

### HOW TO TREAT IT

A dentist will take X rays to determine the extent of the cavity; he or she will also tap the tooth and expose it to a

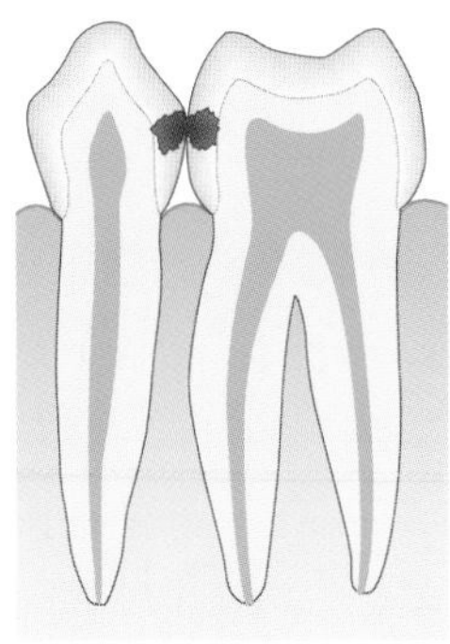
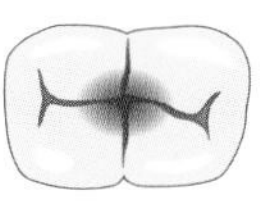
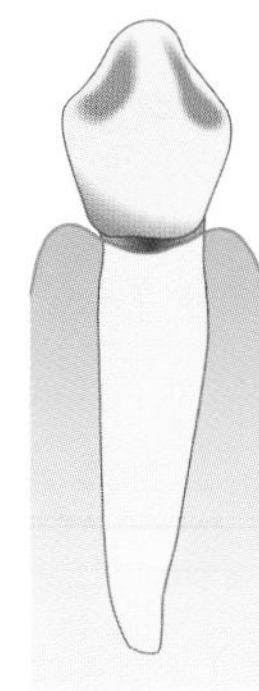

*Dental caries most often start where two teeth meet (left), on the chewing surface (center), or along the gum line (right).*

jet of cold water or air to determine whether the pulp is still alive. If it is, the dentist can drill out the decayed enamel and dentin and fill the cavity. If the cavity is very deep, the dentist may insert a calcium solution into it to stimulate dentin growth and then add a temporary filling over it. This will be removed and replaced with a permanent one in a few weeks.

A small hole is drilled in an abscessed tooth to allow the pus to drain out. Antibiotics are prescribed to treat the underlying infection. The tooth may be extracted, but if it can be salvaged, root canal (endodontic) treatment will be needed to eliminate pain. This involves removing the tooth's diseased pulp and, if necessary, deadening the underlying nerve. The tooth can then be filled and sealed; a crown or cap may be placed over it to protect the chewing surface and improve its appearance.

## HOW TO PREVENT IT

Most cavities can be prevented by practicing good dental hygiene: brushing and flossing at least once every 24 hours, rinsing after meals and snacks (especially sweet and sticky foods), and seeing a dentist or dental hygienist every six months. Fluoride strengthens the tooth enamel; use a toothpaste that contains fluoride, and if your drinking water is not fluoridated, talk to your dentist about fluoride treatments. A protective fluoride coating can be applied directly to the tooth surface.

Dental sealants—a long-lasting plastic coating that is applied to the chewing surfaces—may be recommended for people who are especially prone to develop cavities. For people who suffer from a dry mouth, an artificial saliva solution (Moi-Stir) can help prevent tooth decay. An antibacterial mouthwash may also be prescribed to control mouth bacteria that are normally kept in check by saliva.

### BREAKTHROUGHS!

**New composite resins and porcelain fillings are increasingly replacing the more conspicuous silver fillings. To treat gum-line and root decay, a tooth-colored filling made of a glass ionomer can be formulated to release fluoride.**

A diet that provides approximately 800 to 1100 mg of calcium a day helps maintain tooth enamel. Many women experience a sudden surge in tooth decay following menopause; recent studies indicate that this can be prevented by post-menopausal estrogen replacement therapy (ERT) plus calcium supplements.

### ALTERNATIVE THERAPIES

**Acupressure**

The acupressure point to ease tooth pain is located in the fleshy web between the thumb and index finger on the affected side. Use the thumb and first finger of the other hand to squeeze this area for 30 to 60 seconds. Repeat hourly until the pain eases, and see a dentist promptly.

**Herbal medicine**

Fresh aloe vera gel, squeezed from a cut leaf and then applied around the tooth, can temporarily ease pain. Aloe vera also has antibiotic properties, so it may slow the decay process. **Note:** Some older herbal medicine texts recommend applying full-strength oil of cloves or cinnamon to an aching tooth. Dentists, however, discourage this practice because these oils can damage delicate oral tissue as well as the dental pulp.

# Gum Disorders

### SYMPTOMS

***Gingivitis***

- *Red, painful gums that bleed easily.*
- *Swelling and inflammation of gums.*

***Periodontitis***

- *More severe pain and bleeding from the gums.*
- *Bad breath and an unpleasant taste in the mouth.*
- *Increasing sensitivity of the teeth to heat and cold.*
- *Loosening and eventual loss of teeth as gums and supporting bone tissue recede.*
- *Formation of pockets between the teeth and gums that harbor bacteria.*

### WHO IS AT RISK

*Gum disease, the leading cause of tooth loss among Canadians, is very common. Poor dental hygiene is by far the major cause; contributing factors include smoking, poor nutrition, and a number of medical conditions, especially diabetes, leukemia, and AIDS. The hormonal changes during pregnancy and after menopause appear to predispose women to gingivitis and periodontal disease. Certain drugs—for example, birth control pills, calcium channel blockers used to treat high blood pressure, and anticonvulsant drugs like phenytoin—can cause an overgrowth of gum tissue and aggravate gingivitis.*

## HOW IT DEVELOPS

Gum disease usually starts during adolescence, but the real culprit is poor dental hygiene. Inadequate brushing and flossing allow a buildup of plaque—a sticky film that harbors bacteria and is made up of food debris, dead cells, and mucin, a component of mucus. Plaque irritates the gums and, if it is not removed daily, it hardens into tartar. As plaque and tartar accumulate around the gumline, the soft gum tissue becomes red, swollen, and flabby. The gums bleed easily, and are often moderately painful—hallmarks of gingivitis. Unless gingivitis is treated, it advances to periodontitis. The gums become increasingly inflamed and they pull away from the tooth, creating pockets that fill with plaque. The pockets deepen, and as the plaque moves down to the tooth's root, it destroys the supporting bone tissue, causing the tooth to loosen and eventually fall out.

## WHAT YOU CAN DO

If you have tender, bleeding gums, see a dentist or dental hygienist—only a professional can remove tartar. After the tartar is removed, you can restore gum health by carefully brushing your teeth twice and flossing once a day. If you find it difficult to manipulate dental floss to clean between your teeth, you may want to try one of the new flossing devices. Your dentist or dental hygienist can show you how to use it. To promote healing, use an antiseptic mouthwash, or rinse the mouth with equal parts of 3 percent hydrogen peroxide and water. Massaging the gums also helps firm the tissue; you can use the rubber tip on a toothbrush, a gum stimulating device such as an interproximal brush or an interdental stimulator, or a water gum irrigator.

**WARNING!**

***Acute leukemia patients and others who bleed easily usually cannot brush and floss because this can provoke serious bleeding. Instead, they are instructed to gently wipe the teeth with a gauze pad, and then use a chlorhexidine mouth rinse.***

## HOW TO TREAT IT

A dentist or dental hygienist will use scaling and root planing devices to carefully remove tartar from the teeth and pockets below the gumline. Antibiotics may be prescribed, especially if abscesses have formed in the pockets. Small filament disks that contain antibiotics are sometimes inserted into the pockets to hasten healing. The gums are then covered with a special dressing material for a few days to allow them to heal. Until the gums heal, patients use a prescription mouth rinse in lieu of brushing. When brushing resumes, a soft-bristle brush is used, and an antiseptic mouthwash is often recommended. Flossing should resume when gums are fully healed.

### Surgery

Pockets deeper than one-fourth of an inch may require local anesthesia and surgery to remove the tartar. The procedure is done by a dental surgeon or a periodontist, who may also remove part of the loose gum tissue, allowing the remaining gum to reattach tightly to the teeth.

More extensive surgery is needed if the underlying bone has eroded. The gums are drawn back to expose the bone tissue, which is recontoured. In very severe cases, small grafts of bone tissue may be used to replace the lost bone. The gum flaps are then replaced and sutured in place, and a dressing is applied to allow healing.

## HOW TO PREVENT IT

Meticulous daily tooth brushing and flossing will prevent most gingivitis and periodontal disease. Use a soft-bristle brush to carefully clean all of the tooth surfaces and the gums. Floss between each tooth, making sure that you work the floss under the gumline. (Have a dentist or dental hygienist show you proper brushing and flossing techniques.) You can use a tartar-control toothpaste, or a paste made of hydrogen peroxide and baking soda. After brushing and flossing, rinse the mouth with an antiseptic mouthwash or a salt or hydrogen peroxide solution. Rinsing after meals rids the mouth of food debris.

Have a dentist or dental hygienist examine your gums at least every six months, and more often if you have diabetes or another condition that contributes to gum disease. You may also need to use special prescription mouthwashes, such as chlorhexidine.

### ALTERNATIVE THERAPIES

**Note:** Any alternative therapy should be an adjunct to professional dental treatment.

**Herbal medicine**

For mild gingivitis, herbalists recommend a mouthwash of diluted tincture of myrrh to heal bleeding gums. Massaging the gums with fresh aloe vera gel hastens healing and helps control oral bacteria. Green tea also has mild antibiotic properties; two cups a day can help prevent gingivitis.

**Homeopathy**

Homeopathic remedies for gingivitis include Arnica, Gelsemium, and Mercurius sol.

**Nutraceuticals**

Vitamin C supplements of 1000 mg a day may help restore gum health. People who have kidney stones, kidney disease or hemochromatosis should not take more than 500 mg of vitamin C. Other daily supplements may include 4 mg of folic acid, 15 mg of niacin, 15 mg of zinc, and 1000 to 1200 mg of calcium. People who have thyroid or kidney disease should check with their doctor before taking calcium. Massaging the gums with vitamin E oil also promotes healing.

# Impacted Teeth

**SYMPTOMS**

- *Mild to moderate jaw pain, usually lasting 7 to 10 days.*
- *Swelling, inflammation, and infection of gum tissue over the impacted tooth.*
- *Possible fever, swollen lymph nodes in the neck, and difficulty chewing and swallowing.*

**WHO IS AT RISK**

*People with small mouths and jaws are the most likely to develop one or more impacted teeth. The molars—often referred to as wisdom teeth because they normally erupt in early adulthood—are the most likely to be impacted. If the molars have not fully erupted by age 20, they are probably impacted. Less frequently, the canine teeth are impacted; this occurs between the ages of 9 and 12.*

## HOW IT DEVELOPS

Both the primary and permanent teeth develop in the jaws, below the gums, and gradually push their way to the surface. A tooth becomes impacted when it is unable to fully erupt. The rising incidence of impacted teeth is attributed to the increasingly refined diet of the past millennium. Unlike our prehistoric ancestors, humans no longer need to tear off and chew chunks of tough meat or crunch hard grains. Consequently, our mouths and jaws have grown smaller. For large numbers of people, this means that there simply is not room for all of their teeth. Because the molars are the last teeth to erupt, they are most commonly affected. Less commonly, the canine teeth are crowded out of the upper jaw; they may erupt only partially, or come in at an odd angle. Bits of food are easily trapped at the site of an impacted tooth, setting the stage for gum disease and decay of the adjacent teeth. The tissue overlying the obstructed tooth—usually a third molar—often becomes inflamed and infected, a condition called pericoronitis. The pain usually subsides after a week or 10 days, but cysts may form around the impacted teeth. In their early stages, the cysts do not produce symptoms; instead, they silently destroy the underlying bone. These cysts are usually diagnosed during a dental checkup that includes a full set of mouth X rays.

**WARNING!**

***Impacted molars should be removed as soon as possible after they are diagnosed. A delay can result in infection, bone loss, and damage to the adjacent teeth.***

## WHAT YOU CAN DO

Consult a dentist if a child's teeth are overly crowded or if the full set of molars has not erupted by age 20. Pay special attention to brushing and flossing the back teeth to prevent food debris from becoming trapped around the base of the teeth that have erupted.

Gum inflammation (pericoronitis) usually can be controlled with frequent saltwater soaks. Add one tablespoon of salt to a glass of hot water (it should be about the same temperature as your coffee or tea), hold a mouthful on the affected side until the water cools; spit it out and repeat until the glass is empty. Repeat the treatment three or four times a day, and see a dentist as soon as possible. The saltwater soaks usually bring the inflammation under control in two or three days; if not, or if dental treatment is delayed, an antibiotic is given.

## HOW TO TREAT IT

Removal is the only treatment for impacted molars. A dental surgeon will remove all the impacted teeth at the

### EASING TEETHING PAIN

A baby's first tooth is just one of the many milestones that parents look for during a child's first year. It typically happens when the baby is three or four months old, and is heralded by drooling and fussiness. The baby will "chew" on his hand, your finger, the edge of a blanket or toy, or anything else he can get into his mouth. Many of the other symptoms that parents attribute to teething—fever, a runny nose, upset stomach, diarrhea, diaper and other skin rashes, loss of appetite, among others—are more likely due to an upper-respiratory infection, primary herpes, or another disorder that is totally unrelated to getting a tooth.

Gently massaging the baby's gums can ease the discomfort of an erupting tooth. So, too, can letting the baby "chew" on something hard, such as a teething ring (NOT the kind that can be frozen—the extreme cold can damage gum tissue), a hard pretzel, an unsweetened teething biscuit, or even a corner of a clean washcloth. Be careful, however, not to give the baby anything on which he can choke. If the baby seems very uncomfortable, ask your pediatrician about acetaminophen drops.

If a fever or other symptoms develop, don't attribute them to teething; instead, call your pediatrician. Teething may cause a slight rise in temperature, but a higher fever points to an infection.

same time; the procedure may be done under local or general anesthesia. The extraction site will be covered with gauze and you will be instructed to bite down on it for an hour or so to control bleeding. The mouth and jaw will be swollen and painful for a few days; if a nonprescription painkiller is not strong enough, codeine may be prescribed. Saltwater soaks and rinses promote healing and help reduce inflammation. An antibiotic may also be prescribed to prevent infection.

Unlike the situation with the molars, dentists will make every effort to save impacted canines. To encourage them to grow in normally, a dentist may remove the primary molars to make room for the permanent teeth. When the canines grow in sideways or above the other teeth, a dentist will wait until all of the primary teeth have fallen out, and then undertake orthodontic treatment to move the teeth into their proper alignment.

## HOW TO PREVENT IT

Aside from the early removal of some of the primary teeth, there is no way to prevent impacted teeth. However, infection and bone loss can be prevented by removing impacted molars.

### ALTERNATIVE THERAPIES

**Herbal medicine**

Green tea can help control post-extraction bleeding, reduce the risk of infection, and hasten healing. Momentarily soak a green tea bag in warm water (either plain or salted), and place the bag over the extraction site. Bite down gently to hold it in place for 30 minutes. Repeat three or four times a day until the wound heals. Aloe vera gel, squeezed from a freshly cut leaf, has a similar effect. Place the gel on a gauze pad and hold it against the extraction site for 30 minutes. Don't worry if you swallow some of the gel; small amounts of aloe are not harmful, although too much can cause diarrhea. Mouth rinses of sage or green tea promote healing and soothe pain.

## How Long Will It Hurt?

| PROCEDURE | HEALING TIME | REMEDIES TO EASE THE PAIN |
|---|---|---|
| Root canal work | 2–3 days | Don't chew on affected side; take OTC painkillers; rinse mouth with warm salt water. |
| Periodontal treatment | 12–24 hours | Gently massage gums with aloe gel; take OTC painkillers; rinse with warm salt water or green tea. |
| Periodontal flap surgery | 1–3 days | Use antiseptic mouthwash as instructed by dentist; take OTC or prescription painkillers; apply ice packs (15 minutes every 2 or 3 hours) to reduce swelling and numb pain. |
| Extraction | 4–7 days | Apply ice packs (as above) to jaw to reduce swelling and numb pain; take OTC painkillers; apply a wet green tea bag to extraction site (see *Impacted Teeth*). |
| Removal of cyst | 8–10 days or until stitches are removed | Apply ice packs to jaw; rinse mouth often with warm salt water or green tea; take OTC or prescription painkiller; use very soft (surgical) toothbrush. |

# Temporomandibular Disorders

### SYMPTOMS

*Temporomandibular joint (TMJ) dysfunction is a general term covering a broad range of painful disorders originating in the jaw's joints; symptoms may include one or more of the following:*

- *Sharp, localized pain centered in front of the ear.*
- *Tenderness or feeling of tightness of chewing muscles.*
- *Clicking or locking of the jaw, especially when chewing.*
- *Difficulty eating and opening the mouth wide.*
- *Recurring headaches, earaches, or neck and upper-back pain that don't respond to the usual treatments.*

### WHO IS AT RISK

*People who unconsciously clench their jaw, grind their teeth, or thrust the tongue against the teeth often develop muscle spasms and tightness, leading to TMJ dysfunction. Teeth that don't meet properly (malocclusion) or poorly fitted dentures can also affect the jaw joints. Arthritis is also a relatively common cause of TMJ pain and dysfunction. Sometimes TMJ problems stem from a jaw injury or dental work. Other contributing factors include stress, poor posture, and psychological problems.*

## HOW IT DEVELOPS

The temporomandibular joint is situated just in front of the ear where the temporal bone of the face and the jaw (mandible) bone meet. Area muscles are involved in

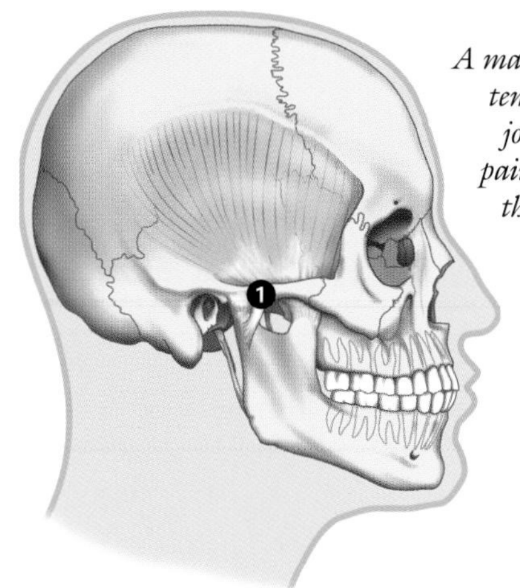


*A malalignment of the temporomandibular joint (1) can cause pain that radiates to the ears, scalp, and other parts of the head and neck.*

chewing, swallowing, talking, and movement of the head and neck. TMJ disorders manifest themselves in many ways, and sufferers often see many doctors or dentists in search of a correct diagnosis. Quite often, the problem begins with recurring ear pain or headaches, while others may experience neck pain. Pain and difficulty in chewing and swallowing are more obvious, but many people with TMJ disorders do not experience these symptoms. About 80 percent of TMJ disorders improve without treatment within six months. The ones most likely to worsen or require treatment are those caused by arthritis, an injury, or abnormality of the joint.

## WHAT YOU CAN DO

Take stock of habits that may be contributing to the problem. Are you under a lot of stress? If so, do you respond by clenching your jaw? Have you been told that you grind your teeth while sleeping? Are you a person who suppresses anger and other negative emotions? Do you tend to thrust your tongue against your teeth? Often, simply being aware of habits that can irritate the TMJ can prompt a conscious effort to change them.

To relieve pain, apply a heating pad or hot compresses to the jaw area several times a day. Don't chew gum, smoke a pipe, or chew on pencils or similar objects. Switch to soft foods for a few weeks to allow the jaw muscles to heal.

Aspirin or ibuprofen can usually relieve pain and inflammation, but if self-care measures fail to bring improvement, see a dentist or doctor who specializes in TMJ disorders.

**WARNING!**

***Be sure to get a second and even a third opinion from a dentist or surgeon with special training in TMJ disorders before undergoing any surgical treatment. Some patients who undergo extensive surgery end up worse off than they were originally, and the operation usually cannot be reversed.***

## HOW TO TREAT IT

### Medications

A muscle relaxant, such as diazepam (Valium), may be prescribed to ease painful muscle spasms. Nonsteroidal anti-inflammatory drugs (NSAIDs) are prescribed if arthritis and inflammation are contributing to the problem. A steroid injected into the joint can also reduce inflammation and swelling. Antidepressant drugs may help overcome psychological problems.

### Splints and devices

Occlusal splints—plastic appliances that change the way that teeth come together—are used if malocclusion is the problem. Mock splints are designed to make a person aware of tongue thrusting or jaw clenching and help him overcome the habitual movements.

### Dental work

Sometimes orthodontic work is needed to correct a faulty bite. In other instances, equilibration—the building up and grinding down of uneven biting surfaces—is needed.

### Surgery

Surgery may be done to repair an arthritic joint or one damaged by a jaw injury. The operation may be done through a conventional open incision or by microsurgery, in which a viewing tube is inserted through a small incision and the operation is performed by manipulating very small instruments through another tube. In rare instances, such as correcting a birth defect, full-mouth reconstruction is recommended. This involves surgery to reposition the jaw and perhaps orthodontic work to realign the teeth.

## HOW TO PREVENT IT

The best prevention involves paying attention to unconscious habits like tooth grinding and jaw clenching.

### ALTERNATIVE THERAPIES

**Biofeedback training**

This technique, in which a person is taught to control normally involuntary actions, is useful in relaxing chronically tensed muscles and muscle spasms.

**Physical therapy**

There is a subspecialty of physical therapy devoted to TMJ disorders. These therapists use a combination of therapies: exercises, ultrasound treatments, diathermy (the use of electrical current to stimulate deep-muscle heat), TENS (transcutaneous electrical nerve stimulation to interrupt transmission of pain messages), and posture correction.

**Psychological counseling**

Suppressed anger and other psychological factors often underlie TMJ disorders. In such cases, a short course of counseling or group therapy can be beneficial.

# The Throat

*Because the throat is the point of entry for both the digestive and respiratory systems, it is exposed to a variety of germs, allergens, and irritants that make it especially vulnerable to infection and pain. It also houses the larynx, another source of problems.*

## Colds and Flu

### SYMPTOMS

- ***Common cold:*** *Sore throat, sneezing, nasal congestion, and runny nose.*
- ***Flu (Influenza):*** *Abrupt onset of cold symptoms plus muscle aches, headache, and possible fever.*

### WHO IS AT RISK

*Everyone is susceptible to colds and flu, especially the very young and the aged. On average, adults have two to four colds a year; children can have 10 or more. People with diabetes, emphysema, and other chronic diseases, as well as those taking drugs that weaken the immune system, are especially vulnerable to flu. A bout of flu confers immunity against that particular strain of the influenza virus. But because new strains of flu viruses constantly evolve, many people come down with flu every year or two.*

### HOW IT DEVELOPS

The **common cold** typically starts with a sore or scratchy throat, runny nose, and sneezing. A few days later, a cough may develop. Although a cold makes a person feel miserable, most healthy adults are able to go about their regular routines, especially after the first two or three days. Healthy persons usually recover in 7 to 10 days. However, people who have asthma, emphysema, or other chronic respiratory disorders are susceptible to complications, such as bronchitis or pneumonia.

Early **flu** symptoms are similar to those of a cold, but they come on faster and are more severe. They are usually accompanied by muscle achiness, a fever, and general malaise; most people are so sick that they need to stay home for a few days or even a week or more. In the very young, the elderly, or persons with lowered immunity, flu can be quite serious. In fact, flu accounts for about 75,000 hospitalizations and nearly 7,000 deaths a year in Canada. And every now and then, a killer flu develops and causes a global epidemic, such as the 1918–19 epidemic of Spanish flu that killed 20 million people.

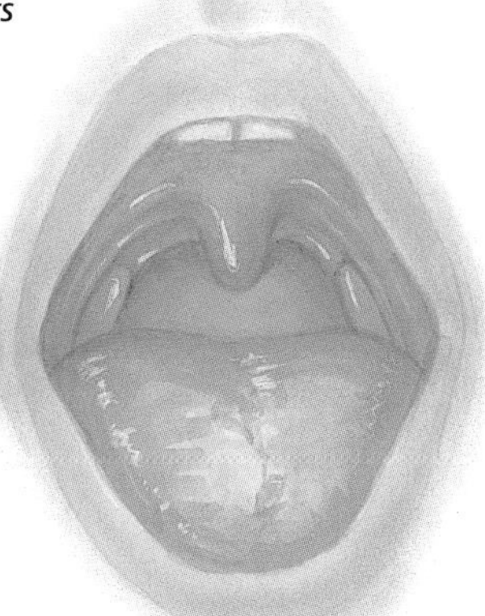

*The throat is the entry point for bacteria and viruses, making it a common site of infection.*

### WHAT YOU CAN DO

Extra rest helps speed recovery from both a cold or flu. Have chicken soup or steamy broth and drink plenty of other nonalcoholic fluids to thin mucus and help prevent dehydration, especially if there is a fever. A cool-mist humidifier moistens air and helps ease nasal congestion. Try gargling with warm salt water or double-strength green tea first thing in the morning, when a sore throat is usually most intense. Do not smoke and avoid second-hand smoke, which worsens and prolongs symptoms; also abstain from alcohol, which lowers immunity, until symptoms disappear.

If you have the flu, try to stay in bed for a few days; the extra rest helps your body fight off the flu virus, and by staying home, you minimize the risk of passing it to others. Call your doctor if you fall into a high-risk group for complications—for example, if you have asthma, diabetes, or another chronic disease. See a doctor if symptoms persist for more than 8 to 10 days, or sooner if you have a high fever or difficulty breathing.

### HOW TO TREAT IT

Aspirin (for adults only), acetaminophen, or ibuprofen will lower a fever and help ease muscle aches and the headache that often accompany flu. In addition, there are dozens of nonprescription cold and flu remedies that can ease other symptoms. However, look for formulations that treat only your symptoms; taking medications with numerous ingredients to fight a dozen or more symptoms increases the risk of adverse drug reactions.

Because colds and flu are viral diseases, antibiotics are of no value in treating them. However, an antibiotic may be prescribed to prevent a secondary bacterial infection in people who have asthma or another lung disorder.

### HOW TO PREVENT IT

Wash your hands frequently and, during the winter months, avoid crowded indoor events. To keep from spreading the virus, cover your nose and mouth with a tissue when sneezing and coughing, and dispose of used tissues. Avoid sharing drinking glasses and similar personal items with others.

Health Canada recommends annual flu shots that protect against influenza A—the most common type that occurs in yearly outbreaks—for everyone aged 65 and over, and for people of any age who live in a nursing home or chronic care facility. Amantadine (Symmetrel), an antiviral drug, is prescribed for the prevention and treatment of respiratory infections caused by the influenza A virus.

**WARNING!**

***Although zinc is essential for proper immune function, high doses (more than 300 mg a day) actually lower immunity. Long-term zinc supplements should not exceed 15 mg a day.***

### ALTERNATIVE THERAPIES

**Herbal medicine**

Echinacea, taken at the onset of symptoms, can shorten the duration and lessen the severity of symptoms. For cautions concerning echinacea, see *About the Recommendations*, p 7. Gargling with fenugreek tea or sucking slippery elm lozenges soothes a sore throat. Cayenne tea, hot chilies, and fresh garlic help clear nasal and sinus congestion; goldenseal tea soothes a sore throat.

**Homeopathy**

Homeopathic remedies for cold-related sore throats include Aconite and Kali bichromicum.

**Nutraceuticals**

Some studies have found that extra vitamin C (1000 to 3000 mg a day for 7 to 10 days) can cut the duration and severity of a cold. People who have kidney stones, kidney disease or hemochromatosis should not take more than 500 mg of vitamin C. Lozenges containing 15 to 25 mg of zinc soothe a sore throat; zinc also boosts immunity and may hasten recovery. However, do not exceed 150 mg a day.

**BREAKTHROUGHS!**

**Zanamivir (Relenza), an inhaled, neuramindase-inhibiting drug, represents a new approach to flu treatment in people over age 12. At the onset of symptoms, Relenza is inhaled twice a day through a handheld device similar to an asthma puffer. When the medication encounters the flu virus in the airways and lungs, it prevents it from entering the cells where it would normally replicate itself. Clinical studies show that Relenza shortens the duration of flu symptoms by two to three days, and in many patients, they never progress beyond a day or so of sneezing and mild achiness. Another new drug in this class, oseltamivir (Tamiflu), is available orally to treat acute flu in patients over age 18. Both drugs are effective against influenza A and B.**

# Laryngitis

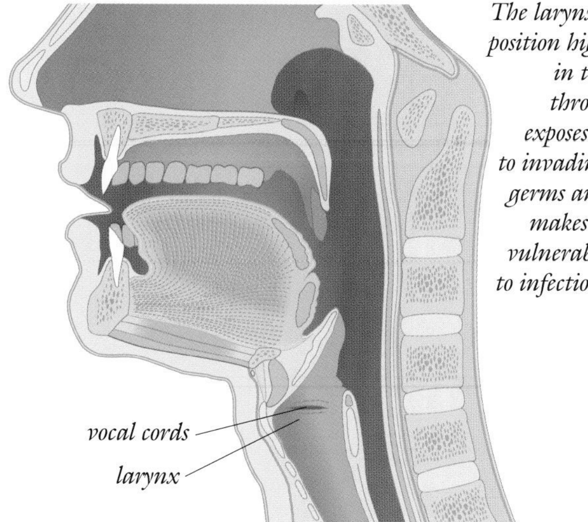


*The larynx's position high in the throat exposes it to invading germs and makes it vulnerable to infection.*

### SYMPTOMS

- *Sore throat, dry cough, and increasing hoarseness.*
- *In severe cases, total loss of voice and possible difficulty swallowing and breathing.*

### WHO IS AT RISK

*Almost anyone who catches a cold can develop laryngitis; it is also a possible complication of bronchitis, pneumonia, and allergies. Cigarette smoking or exposure to environmental irritants can cause chronic laryngitis; excessive yelling or screaming can also result in irritation of the larynx and hoarseness.*

## HOW IT DEVELOPS

Laryngitis usually starts with a cold that moves down the respiratory tract to infect the larynx, which is located at the top of the windpipe (trachea). The vocal cords and surrounding tissue become inflamed and swollen and are unable to vibrate freely to produce speech.

Chronic laryngitis is sometimes due to polyps or other benign growths on the vocal cords—a common consequence of excessive shouting or abuse of the voice.

## WHAT YOU CAN DO

Give the vocal cords a chance to heal by refraining from speaking and especially whispering, which is even harder on the vocal cords than talking. Drink ample fluids—at least eight glasses a day—and try sucking on sour lemon drops or chewing sugarless gum to stimulate the flow of saliva, which moistens the vocal cords. Refrain from smoking and alcohol, which irritate the vocal cords and exacerbate laryngitis.

## HOW TO TREAT IT

Viral laryngitis heals itself, but a doctor will prescribe antibiotics if the cause is a bacterial infection. Vocal cord polyps are removed surgically, often with a laser—a concentrated beam of light that vaporizes the growths.

Spraying a few drops of epinephrine directly on the swollen vocal cords temporarily reduces swelling and allows normal speech. This is occasionally done to allow an actor with laryngitis to perform.

**WARNING!**

***A vocal cord infection sometimes spreads to the epiglottis, the leaf-shaped flap of cartilage that closes during swallowing to prevent food and fluids from entering the larynx and trachea. A swollen epiglottis can block the airways and result in suffocation. Any difficulty breathing during a bout of laryngitis demands immediate treatment.***

## HOW TO PREVENT IT

Chronic laryngitis often can be prevented by not smoking, using alcohol only in moderation, and refraining from excessive shouting. When you have a cold, don't take cold pills that contain antihistamines, which have a drying effect and worsen hoarseness.

### ALTERNATIVE THERAPIES

**Herbal medicine**

Gargling several times a day with sage tea helps reduce inflammation of the vocal cords and surrounding tissue. Slippery elm and eucalyptus lozenges also soothe inflammation and promote healing.

# Pharyngitis/ Sore Throat

**SYMPTOMS**

- *Pain, inflammation, and swelling of the pharynx, the part of the throat that extends from the back of the mouth to the esophagus.*
- *Possible fever, swollen lymph nodes in the neck, and discharge (sometimes profuse) of pus-filled sputum.*

**WHO IS AT RISK**

*From time to time, everyone suffers a bout of pharyngitis. It is a common component of colds and flu (see also p 107), and children with enlarged tonsils are especially vulnerable.*

*Steamy vapors can soothe a sore throat.*

## HOW IT DEVELOPS

Pharyngitis may be due to either a viral or bacterial infection, which causes increasing discomfort when swallowing. Bacterial pharyngitis, such as strep throat, produces more severe symptoms than a viral infection; there is often a pus-filled discharge, severe throat pain, mild to moderate fever, and swollen lymph nodes. If untreated, the infection can spread to other organs.

## WHAT YOU CAN DO

Gargling with warm salt water and drinking hot, steamy broth and other nonalcoholic beverages are time-honored remedies to soothe a sore throat. Honey and herbal lozenges are also soothing. To avoid further irritation to the inflamed pharynx, don't smoke and avoid secondhand smoke and other environmental irritants. Switch to soups, juices, and pureed foods until the throat heals. See a doctor promptly if the sore throat persists or is accompanied by a fever, swollen lymph nodes, and a discharge of thick yellow or greenish sputum.

**WARNING!**

***If strep or another type of bacterial pharyngitis is diagnosed, be sure to take the full course—usually 10 days—of the prescribed antibiotic. Stopping the drug early can result in a recurrence with bacteria that are resistant to the original antibiotic. A different, more potent antibiotic will be needed. Also, a smoldering infection can result in rheumatic fever.***

## HOW TO TREAT IT

A doctor will order a throat culture, but if strep is suspected, he or she will start antibiotic therapy, even before getting the culture results, with a drug that works against a broad spectrum of organisms. The choice of antibiotic may be changed later after the organism is identified.

Aspirin (for adults), acetaminophen, or ibuprofen can lower a fever and ease discomfort.

## HOW TO PREVENT IT

Both viral and bacterial pharyngitis are highly contagious. Wash your hands frequently, and avoid sharing drinking glasses, eating utensils, and other personal items. Discard used tissues promptly. Also, abstain from kissing while you or your partner has a sore throat.

### ALTERNATIVE THERAPIES

**Aromatherapy**

Steamy vapors containing oils of eucalyptus, geranium, lavender, and sage are soothing. Add a few drops of diluted oil to a warm bath or inhale them from a bowl of hot water.

**Herbal medicine**

Echinacea can help hasten healing. For cautions concerning echinacea, see *About the Recommendations*, p 7. A gargle made from one cup of sage tea and a teaspoon each of honey and cider vinegar soothes inflamed tissue and promotes healing. Lozenges that contain eucalyptus or slippery elm are soothing, as is green tea, which also hastens healing of inflamed tissue. Double-strength green tea is good for gargling.

# Throat Cancer

## SYMPTOMS

*Throat cancer most often develops in the voice box (larynx), the upper throat (nasopharynx), or the tonsils. Predominant symptoms include:*

- ***Larynx cancer:*** *Persistent and worsening hoarseness, pain and difficulty swallowing, spitting up blood, and a lump or swelling at the front of the neck.*
- ***Cancer of the nasopharynx:*** *Nasal blockage, ear pain, nasal discharge of bloody pus, unexplained nosebleeds, swollen lymph nodes.*
- ***Tonsil cancer:*** *Persistent sore throat on one side, with pain radiating to the ear; neck lump or swelling.*

## WHO IS AT RISK

*Larynx cancer, the most prevalent tumor of the head and neck, usually occurs after age 50 and is most common among men who smoke. Alcohol use increases the risk even more. Nasopharynx cancer, which is linked to the Epstein-Barr virus (the organism that causes mononucleosis), usually develops during childhood. It is relatively rare in Canada, but is one of the most common cancers in Asia. Tonsil cancer, like larynx cancer, occurs mostly in men who smoke and also use alcohol.*

## HOW IT DEVELOPS

**Larynx cancer** usually starts on one of the vocal cords, so hoarseness is an early symptom. As the cancer grows, it causes throat pain that may extend to an ear; other symptoms include difficulty swallowing and a chronic cough that produces bloody sputum.

**Nasopharynx cancer** often begins as a chronic earache because the tumor usually blocks a nasal passage and the eustachian tube, the passage that links the middle ear and the upper throat. The blockage causes a buildup of fluid in the middle ear, resulting in pain and a bloody discharge from the nose. If the tumor presses on the facial nerve, part of the face may become paralyzed.

**Tonsil cancer** starts as a sore throat that radiates to the ear on the affected side. As the tumor grows, it causes difficulty swallowing and bleeding from the mouth.

### WARNING!

***Smokers often develop a chronic cough and hoarseness, which they tend to dismiss as harmless. In reality, these are early warning signs of throat cancer. Anyone who smokes should undergo yearly examinations of the mouth and throat, and see a doctor promptly if hoarseness persists for more than two weeks.***

## WHAT YOU CAN DO

See a doctor as soon as possible if symptoms suggest throat cancer. If you smoke and/or use alcohol, make every effort to stop. While awaiting treatment for larynx cancer, avoid shouting and taxing your voice. A liquid diet may be needed to reduce the risk of choking.

## HOW TO TREAT IT

Early **larynx cancer** may be treated with radiation therapy to kill the cancer cells and shrink the tumor while preserving normal speech. A small tumor on the vocal cord can be removed by laser surgery. More advanced cancer often requires removal of the entire larynx (a laryngectomy). Chemotherapy may also be needed, especially if the cancer has spread to the lymph nodes.

**Nasopharynx cancer** is usually treated with radiation therapy. Surgery is needed, however, if the cancer is large. Reconstructive plastic surgery helps minimize disfigurement. **Tonsil cancer** is treated with a combination of radiation therapy and surgery, which may be followed by chemotherapy.

## HOW TO PREVENT IT

Don't smoke and use alcohol only in moderation.

### ALTERNATIVE THERAPIES

**Herbal medicine**

Several studies in China have found that green tea, which is rich in polyphenols and other antioxidants, inhibits the growth of precancerous lesions in the mouth and throat. More studies are needed on tea's anticancer benefits; in the meantime, drinking two or three cups of green tea a day certainly can't harm, and may help protect against throat and other cancers.

**Nutrition therapy**

Intravenous feeding may be necessary during treatment for throat cancer because swallowing may be impossible. Even after treatment, many patients require a liquid diet to reduce the risk of choking. A dietitian can help devise a diet that provides proper nutrition.

**Speech therapy**

After a laryngectomy, a speech therapist can teach a patient alternative ways of talking. Some patients use a mechanical device or an artificial larynx; others learn how to form sounds using air trapped in the upper esophagus.

# Tonsillitis

**SYMPTOMS**

- *A sore throat that comes on suddenly, is most intense when swallowing, and may radiate to the ear.*
- *Fever, possible headache and vomiting.*
- *Swollen lymph nodes in the neck.*

**WHO IS AT RISK**

*Tonsillitis occurs mostly during childhood. It is usually caused by a streptococcal bacterium, but may also be due to other bacteria and viruses.*

## HOW IT DEVELOPS

The tonsils are actually a pair of lymph nodes nestled in the soft tissue at the juncture of the mouth and throat. Their job is to filter out harmful bacteria and viruses that enter the body through the mouth and nose. When the tonsils themselves are infected, tonsillitis results. The initial symptom is an intense sore throat that makes swallowing difficult and very painful. There is often a fever and swollen lymph nodes in the neck. Viral tonsillitis usually clears up without treatment in a week or so; bacterial tonsillitis is a more serious disease, and requires treatment to prevent it from spreading to other organs of the body.



*Red, swollen, and very painful tonsils are the hallmarks of tonsillitis.*

## WHAT YOU CAN DO

See a doctor as soon as possible to prevent serious complications for untreated bacterial tonsillitis. In the meantime, gargling with warm salt water (one teaspoon stirred into a half cup of water) or green tea can soothe the sore throat.

## HOW TO TREAT IT

### Medication

After examining the swollen and inflamed tonsils, a doctor will use a swab to collect a sample of secretions to be examined under a microscope and perhaps cultured to identify the organism. Strep tonsillitis is usually treated with a 10-day course of penicillin or another antibiotic. Acetaminophen can be given to reduce a fever and ease pain; children should not take aspirin because it increases the risk of Reye's syndrome, a rare childhood disease affecting the brain and liver.

### Surgery

Removal of the tonsils may be recommended if a child suffers repeated bouts of tonsillitis, or if the tonsils are chronically swollen and inflamed.

## HOW TO PREVENT IT

As with strep throat, tonsillitis is contagious, and some people harbor the infecting organisms in their throats without developing symptoms. Siblings and other family members should have throat cultures done and undergo antibiotic therapy if they are found to carry the strep organism. Good hygiene—keeping pencils and similar objects out of your mouth, always washing your hands before eating, not sharing drinking glasses—can reduce the risk of spreading tonsillitis.

**WARNING!**

***Untreated strep tonsillitis can spread to the kidneys, causing acute glomerulonephritis. This is a very serious infection that can lead to chronic renal failure.***

### ALTERNATIVE THERAPIES

**Note:** Any alternative remedy should be an adjunct to, not a substitute for, antibiotics in treating bacterial tonsillitis.

**Herbal medicine**

Echinacea can hasten healing of both viral and bacterial infections; add goldenseal to the regimen for increased effectiveness. For cautions concerning these herbs, see *About the Recommendations*, p 7. Gargling with warm sage tea also eases throat pain. Slippery elm teas are also soothing. A hot onion/garlic soup with ginger and horseradish may help fight infection.

**Nutraceuticals**

Drink extra fruit and berry juices to increase intake of vitamin C and bioflavonoids. Lozenges with 15 to 25 mg of zinc are soothing. Do not exceed 150 mg a day.

### QUINSY AND ABSCESSES

Quinsy develops when strep or another bacterium infects the tissue between a tonsil and the pharyngeal muscle at the back of the throat. The infected area is red, swollen, and very painful. Without prompt antibiotic treatment, a pus-filled abscess forms and, as it swells, can block the airway and lead to suffocation. To prevent this, a doctor will puncture the abscess and allow the pus to drain out. The patient may be hospitalized to receive intravenous antibiotics for a day or two, and then discharged to continue oral antibiotics.

# THE CHEST

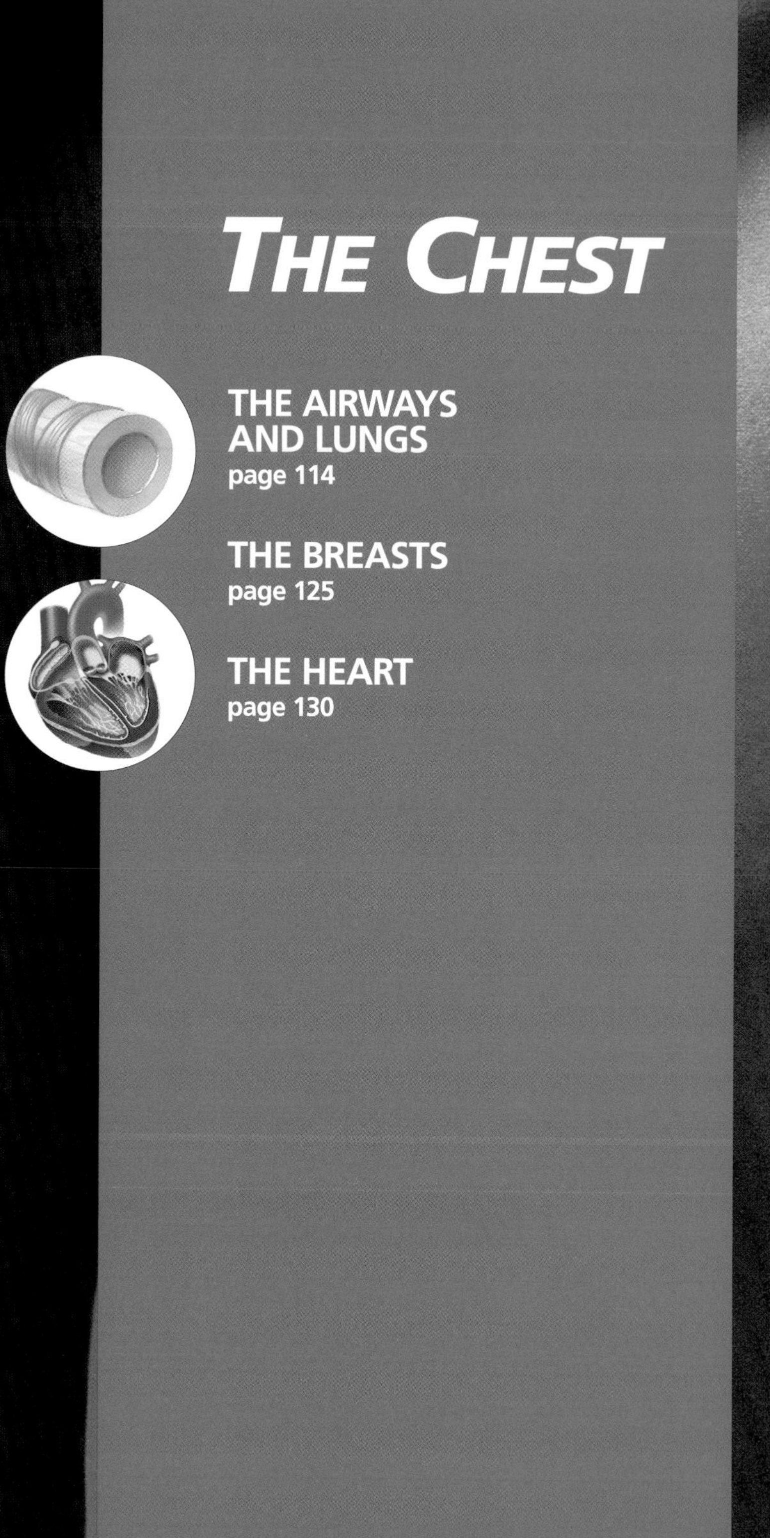

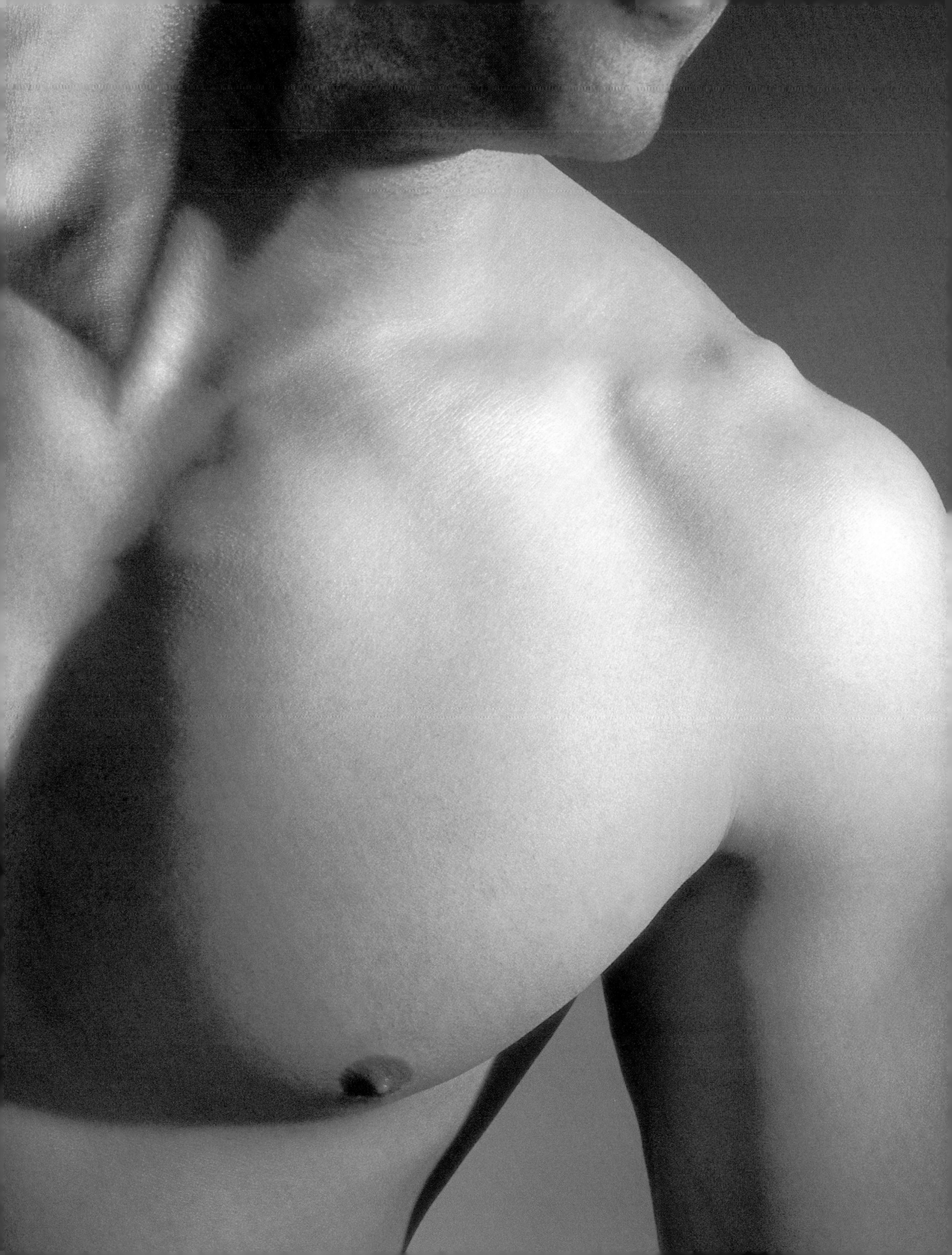

# The Airways and Lungs

*Breathing is an automatic process that most of us take for granted until something goes awry and leaves a person gasping for breath. In addition, many of the disorders that interfere with breathing can also produce chest pain.*

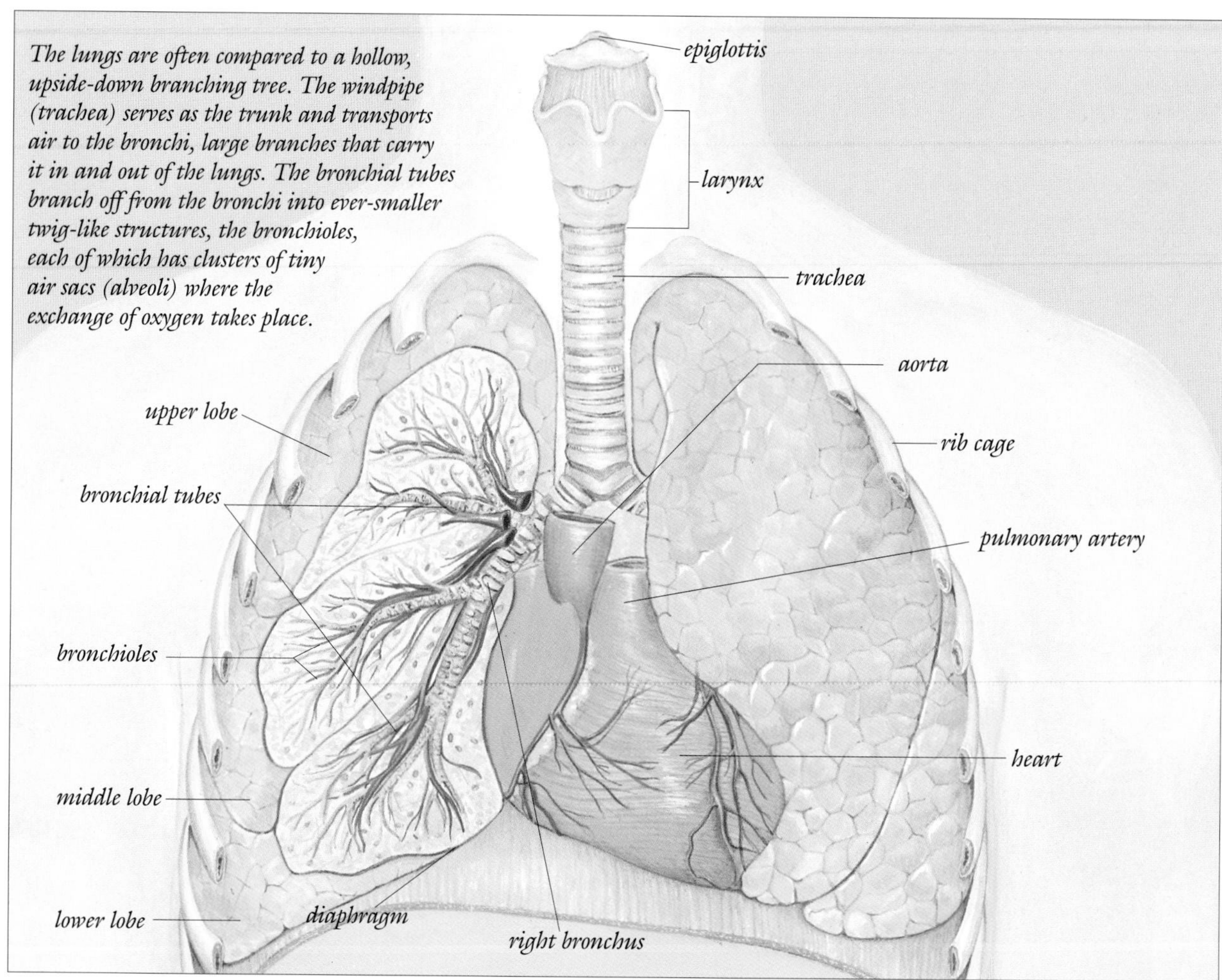
The lungs are often compared to a hollow, upside-down branching tree. The windpipe (trachea) serves as the trunk and transports air to the bronchi, large branches that carry it in and out of the lungs. The bronchial tubes branch off from the bronchi into ever-smaller twig-like structures, the bronchioles, each of which has clusters of tiny air sacs (alveoli) where the exchange of oxygen takes place.
epiglottis
larynx
trachea
aorta
upper lobe
rib cage
bronchial tubes
pulmonary artery
bronchioles
heart
middle lobe
lower lobe
diaphragm
right bronchus

# Asthma

**SYMPTOMS**

- *Uncomfortable feeling of chest tightness; periodic attacks of wheezing, coughing, and gasping for breath.*
- *In very severe cases, lips, fingers, and nailbeds turn blue, and breathing becomes increasingly difficult.*

**WHO IS AT RISK**

Five to 10 percent of adult Canadians and as many as 20 percent of children have asthma. Worldwide, the incidence of asthma and the mortality rate are increasing. Although theories abound, the reasons for the increase are unknown. The incidence worldwide is highest among inner-city children, but asthma strikes all racial groups and social and economic classes. A family history of allergies and asthma increases the risk.

## HOW IT DEVELOPS

Asthma usually becomes apparent in early childhood, although some people are not affected until adulthood or even old age. Asthmatic airways are chronically inflamed and "twitchy," or hypersensitive, causing them to react to ordinarily harmless substances, such as pollen, dust mites, and animal dander (see *Common Asthma Triggers*, p 116).

During an asthma attack, the smooth muscles that control the size of the airways constrict. The choked airways become increasingly inflamed, swollen, and clogged with mucus. Because fresh air cannot enter or stale air exit the alveoli, the body becomes increasingly starved for oxygen. This leads to extreme discomfort and a very frightening feeling of suffocation.

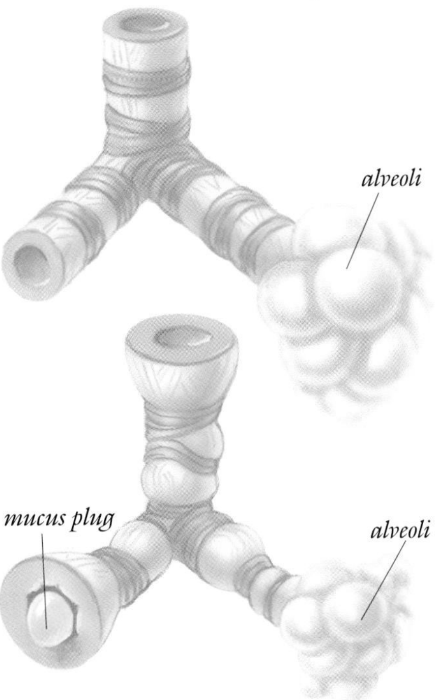


*When asthmatic lungs are exposed to an asthma trigger, the airways tighten, thereby preventing fresh air from entering the lungs.*

## WHAT YOU CAN DO

If you suspect you or your child has asthma, see a doctor for a proper diagnosis, and then follow the prescribed treatment regimen. Learn to recognize the warning signs of an impending attack. Blowing into a peak flow meter—a simple handheld device that measures the openness of airways—can often gauge the severity of an attack before breathing symptoms worsen. Take the proper medication to open the airways and try to stay calm; panic can worsen an attack. Drink some water, which helps thin mucus. Better still, drink tea, which is calming and also contains a compound (xanthine) that helps open the airways. Sit quietly, leaning slightly forward to ease breathing, and cough to help clear mucus from the airways.

## HOW TO TREAT IT

Asthma varies greatly from one person to another, so treatment must be individualized. The two major classes of asthma drugs are:

- **Anti-inflammatory agents,** which include corticosteroids, cromolyn sodium, and nedocromil sodium. These are usually inhaled so the medication acts directly on the airways. There are also two new medications—zafirlukast (Accolate) and montelukast sodium (Singulair)—which work by blocking the molecules that cause airway inflammation.
- **Bronchodilators** such as salbutamol and epinephrine are taken during an attack to relax the smooth muscles and open the airways. Long-acting bronchodilators such as salmeterol (Serevent) and formoterol (Ox-eze) are used in the daily treatment of asthma.

### BREAKTHROUGHS!

**A number of new drugs that promise to simplify asthma treatment are being tested. The goal is to develop a single medication that quells inflammation and also opens the airways. Among the more promising are:**

- **Ariflo, which blocks an enzyme that is instrumental in causing inflammation.**
- **Nuvance, which blocks interleukin-4, a substance made by the immune system that is high in people with asthma.**
- **E25, a compound that neutralizes a body chemical instrumental in asthma attacks.**

## HOW TO PREVENT IT

Most asthma can be controlled through careful self-care. Keep a diary to help identify asthma triggers. If possible, stay indoors when it's very cold or during pollution alerts; if you must go outdoors, use a face mask. Install air-conditioning or an air-filtering system and keep your house as free of dust and dust-catchers (i.e., carpets, drapes, Venetian blinds) as possible. Don't smoke and avoid secondhand smoke, which also irritates the lungs.

It's also important to work with a doctor to develop a treatment plan. Studies show that most asthma patients fail to take their medications properly, often because they don't understand the need to take drugs between asthma attacks when they are not having symptoms.

### ALTERNATIVE THERAPIES

**Note:** Alternative therapies should be used as an adjunct to, not a substitute for, asthma medications.

**Exercise**

Because exercise can provoke asthma symptoms, many asthmatics avoid it. This is a big mistake since regular physical activity improves lung function. Good exercise choices for asthmatics include swimming in a heated pool (the humidity eases breathing), walking, cycling, tennis, and ballroom dancing. Activities that probably should be avoided include long-distance running and other endurance sports, as well as those that are played outdoors in a dusty or pollen-laden environment.

## Common Asthma Triggers

| TYPE | SOURCES |
|---|---|
| Allergens | Pollen, animal dander (especially from cats), dust mites, cockroach and mouse droppings, kapock, feathers. |
| Environmental irritants | Cold air, wind, tobacco smoke, perfumes, air pollutants, dust, molds, heat and high humidity, aerosol sprays, room fresheners, pesticides, paint and other fumes. |
| Foods and additives | Food preservatives (especially sulfites), food dyes and additives, aspirin and aspirin-like drugs, eggs, cow's milk, shellfish, nuts, peanuts, wheat. |
| Miscellaneous | Stress, anxiety, hormonal changes, viruses. |

**Herbal medicine**

Ephedra (also called Ma huang) contains ephedrine, a bronchodilator. Herbalists often recommend it to treat mild asthma, but doctors warn against using the herbal preparations for several reasons: the dosages are hard to control and ephedrine can cause dangerously high blood pressure and cardiac arrhythmias. Safer herbs to calm twitchy and inflamed lungs include marshmallow root and mullein. They are best taken as teas.

**Homeopathy**

Homeopathic preparations, which are used mostly as preventive measures or to reduce drug side effects, include Arsenicum album and Aconite.

**Nutraceuticals**

A recent source suggests that extra vitamin A may help control asthma symptoms. Dosages up to 25,000 IU may be taken for short periods (one month), such as when recovering from a lung infection. For long-term use (more than three months), the maximum safe dosage for adults is up to 10,000 IU a day.

**Note:** High doses of vitamin A can cause serious birth defects; stop supplements at least three months before becoming pregnant. Children should not take vitamin A pills.

### WARNING!

***Each week in Canada 10 people die from asthma. Many of these deaths are due to delayed emergency treatment. If, after taking medication to stop an attack, symptoms persist for more than a few minutes or worsen, call 911 or get to the nearest emergency room.***

**Yoga and t'ai chi**

Yoga and other relaxation techniques can help counter stress, a common asthma trigger. T'ai chi is calming and also provides gentle exercise conditioning.

# Bronchitis

### SYMPTOMS

***Acute bronchitis:*** *Difficulty breathing; frequent spells of coughing that produce thick yellow or gray phlegm; pain in the upper chest that is worsened by coughing; possible fever, sore throat, and flulike symptoms.*

***Chronic bronchitis:*** *Mucus-producing cough lasting three or more months and recurring at least two years in a row; wheezing and shortness of breath; possible weight loss.*

### WHO IS AT RISK

*Anyone can develop acute bronchitis—an inflammation of the lungs' large air passages (bronchi)—on the heels of a common cold or bout of flu. Chronic bronchitis is most common among middle-aged or older smokers or people frequently exposed to air pollution. Chronic lung disorders also increase the risk. Dust, irritating fumes, and air pollution can also cause bronchitis.*

## HOW IT DEVELOPS

Acute bronchitis usually strikes during the winter cold-and-flu season. If a respiratory viral infection spreads downward to the lungs, it can set the stage for a secondary bacterial infection. The mucous membranes lining the bronchi become inflamed and step up their produc-

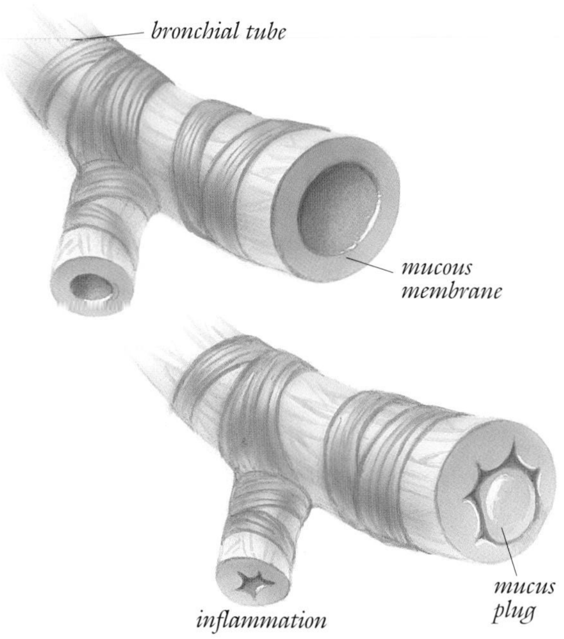


*A normal bronchial tube is lined with a thin mucous membrane (top), which becomes inflamed and clogged with mucus during an attack of bronchitis (bottom).*

tion of a thick, sticky mucus that clogs the airways. Coughing spells bring up large amounts of phlegm. This coughing often interferes with sleep; it may also provoke pain in the upper chest.

Bronchitis usually clears up in two or three weeks. But when it lingers for three or more months and recurs year after year, it is classified as chronic bronchitis. This form can lead to emphysema, a progressive form of chronic obstructive pulmonary disease (COPD).

## WHAT YOU CAN DO

Drink plenty of fluids to help thin the mucus. Keep warm and get plenty of rest. Use a misting vaporizer to humidify the air, especially in the bedroom. Inhaling warm, moist air can also calm a coughing attack. If coughing interferes with sleep, take a hot, steamy shower before going to bed. Using an extra pillow or elevating the head of your bed makes it easier to breathe. Postural drainage—coughing while lying facedown over the edge of a bed—also clears the lungs.

**WARNING!**

***If you have a history of chronic bronchitis, call your doctor at the first sign of a cold or flu. Although antibiotics do not work against cold or flu viruses, people with chronic bronchitis are often advised to take them to prevent a secondary bacterial infection.***

A nonprescription cough expectorant, which thins mucus, can help clear the airways. However, do not take a cough suppressant unless advised to do so by your doctor; coughing is necessary to clear the airways of mucus. Hugging a pillow to the chest helps relieve pain when coughing. Aspirin (for adults only) or acetaminophen can ease the chest pain of bronchitis and also lower a fever.

If you smoke, make every effort to stop and avoid secondhand smoke; tobacco smoke irritates the airways. Not smoking is especially critical for people with chronic bronchitis to reduce the risk of developing COPD.

## HOW TO TREAT IT

Antibiotics are usually prescribed. A doctor may do a sputum culture to identify the bacterium; otherwise, penicillin or another antibiotic that works against a wider range of organisms will be prescribed. Be sure to take the full course of the drug; symptoms usually ease in a few days, but stopping antibiotics too soon can result in a recurrence caused by an organism that is now resistant to the original medication.

## HOW TO PREVENT IT

There is no specific way to prevent bronchitis, but you can take commonsense protective measures: An annual flu shot is recommended if you are 65 or older, live in a nursing home or chronic care facility, or have a medical condition such as heart disease, emphysema, diabetes, or cancer. Try to minimize contact with people who have colds or flu and, to reduce your risk of infection, wash your hands frequently. Stay indoors during periods of high air pollution, and if you work with chemicals or other lung irritants, wear a protective face mask.

### ALTERNATIVE THERAPIES

**Herbal medicine**

Taking echinacea at the first sign of a cold or the flu may prevent bronchitis or at least shorten its course. Echinacea may worsen symptoms of autoimmune disorders. It may also be counterproductive in progressive infections such as TB. Expectorant herbs that help clear the lungs include mullein and eucalyptus; they can be taken as tea or lozenges. Slippery elm and marshmallow root teas are demulcents, which coat and soothe irritated and inflamed mucous membranes.

# Collapsed Lung

**SYMPTOMS**

- *Sudden, sharp pain in the lower chest.*
- *Difficulty breathing and a dry, hacking cough.*
- *In very severe cases: a feeling of suffocation and shock.*

**WHO IS AT RISK**

*A collapsed lung, known medically as a pneumothorax, can result from a severe chest injury. It also develops spontaneously in otherwise healthy young people, usually males, or shortly after birth in babies who have a congenital weakness in their lungs. It is also common in older persons whose lungs have been damaged by smoking, chronic bronchitis, asthma, or other disorders.*

## HOW IT DEVELOPS

A lung collapses when air leaks into the pleural space surrounding the lung. In an open pneumothorax, outside air enters the space through a chest wound. A closed pneumothorax occurs when air leaks from the lungs because of an injury or rupture of one or more air sacs (alveoli). The person experiences sudden, unexplained chest pain followed by shortness of breath. In very severe cases, the person may go into shock and suffer fatal circulatory collapse.

**WARNING!**

***Never ignore unexplained chest pain, especially if it is accompanied by shortness of breath. Even if normal breathing returns, a doctor should be consulted to rule out heart disease or other serious disorders with symptoms similar to a spontaneous pneumothorax.***

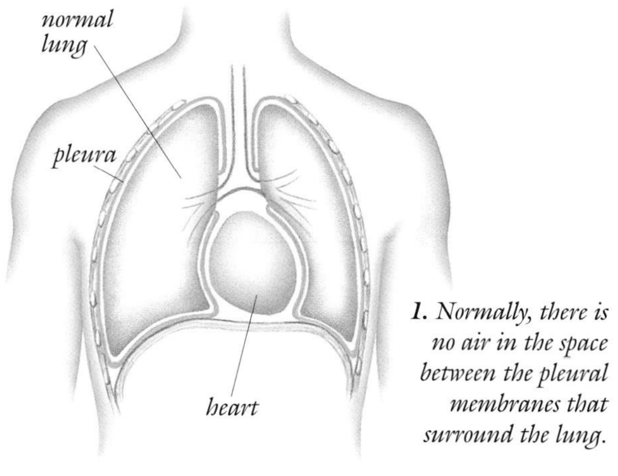

*1. Normally, there is no air in the space between the pleural membranes that surround the lung.*

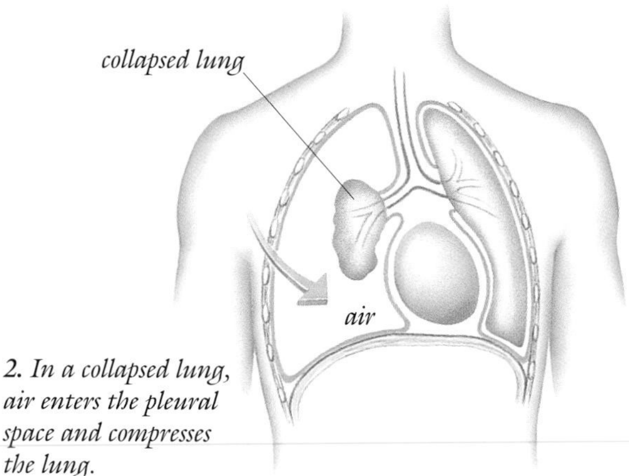

*2. In a collapsed lung, air enters the pleural space and compresses the lung.*

## WHAT YOU CAN DO

Seek immediate medical attention, either by calling 911 or having someone take you to the emergency room.

## HOW TO TREAT IT

A small spontaneous pneumothorax may require no treatment other than repeated X rays to make sure that it is not expanding and that the lung is returning to normal. The air in the chest cavity is gradually reabsorbed into the body. More extensive ruptures, however, may require insertion of a chest tube to suction the air from the pleural space. Sometimes surgical repair is needed if the pneumothorax continues to expand or it recurs.

## HOW TO PREVENT IT

There is no way to prevent a spontaneous pneumothorax. Always wearing a seat belt when riding in a car can help prevent a collapsed lung caused by a chest injury. Other general preventive measures include not smoking and making sure that bronchitis and other lung disorders are treated promptly.

# Emphysema

### SYMPTOMS

- *Chronic cough that brings up yellow or greenish sputum.*
- *Nagging chest discomfort and increasing shortness of breath.*
- *Weight loss, leg swelling, difficulty walking.*

### WHO IS AT RISK

*Emphysema, or chronic obstructive pulmonary disease (COPD), is the fifth leading cause of death in North America. Smokers are by far the most common victims of emphysema; most are over the age of 55 with men outnumbering women. However, this statistic is changing as women are starting to smoke more, and at an earlier age.*

## HOW IT DEVELOPS

The onset is insidious, typically beginning with a morning "smoker's cough" and increasing vulnerability to bronchitis, which eventually becomes chronic. Next comes wheezing and increasing difficulty breathing and fatigue. Normal daily activities can produce extreme fatigue; weight loss is common, as is the development of nagging chest discomfort. All of these symptoms are due to the progressive stiffening of the air sacs (alveoli), the tiny lung structures where oxygen exchange takes place. Stale air becomes trapped in the lungs, and the chest cavity expands to accommodate the distended lungs.

**WARNING!**

***Home use of oxygen requires special precautions. Most people are aware of the danger of smoking near an oxygen tank, but many are unaware of the hazards from other open flames, such as candles or a fireplace.***

## WHAT YOU CAN DO

First and foremost, do not smoke and avoid secondhand smoke and other inhaled irritants, which increase airway inflammation and clogging with mucus. Be extra careful to reduce exposure to colds and flu; get annual flu shots and avoid crowded areas during the cold season. Talk to your doctor about preventive antibiotics if you do de-

**BREAKTHROUGHS!**

**A rare type of COPD that develops in young people is caused by a deficiency in an essential protein, alpha$_1$-antitrypsin. Until recently, this form of emphysema usually led to an early death; it can now be treated with weekly intravenous injections of the missing alpha$_1$-antitrypsin protein.**

velop a cold. Drink at least eight glasses of nonalcoholic fluids a day to help thin lung secretions. Breathing exercises are also important (see illustration, below) to force as much stale air from the lungs as possible.

## HOW TO TREAT IT

### Medications

Doctors prescribe inhaled corticosteroids to reduce lung inflammation and bronchodilator drugs—the same ones used to treat asthma—to help open the airways.

### Oxygen

Oxygen therapy not only improves function but also prolongs life. Home oxygen concentrators, which take oxygen from the air and concentrate it in a tubing system, are more convenient and less costly than tanks of compressed oxygen. For trips outside the home, a person can use a portable tank of compressed oxygen. There are also small portable tanks that hold liquid oxygen.

### Surgery

A new approach involves reducing lung size by removing a portion of the diseased tissue. The remaining lung tissue then has more room in the chest cavity and can function better. In advanced cases, a lung transplant is life-saving, but this operation is usually reserved for persons under age 55.

## HOW TO PREVENT IT

Stop smoking or, better still, never start. COPD symptoms often start after only 5 to 10 years of smoking.

### ALTERNATIVE THERAPIES

**Physical therapy**

Regular exercise, although tiring, is necessary to retain as much lung function as possible. A physical therapist can help develop an exercise program that will not be overtaxing, yet vigorous enough to maintain strength and muscle tone. Walking, stationary cycling, and moderate stair climbing are good aerobic exercises; these are usually combined with weight-lifting to increase strength.

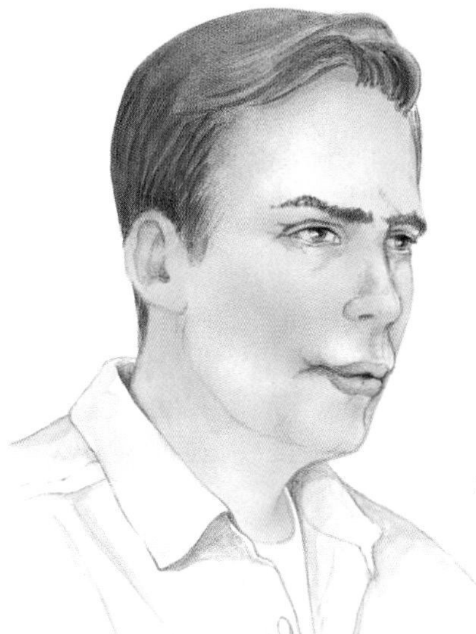

*A technique for helping to rid the lungs of stale air is to exhale slowly through lips pursed as if you were going to whistle.*

# Fractured Rib

**SYMPTOMS**

- *Severe, even excruciating chest pain following a direct blow to the ribs.*
- *Pain worsens with movement, coughing, laughing, and taking a deep breath.*

**WHO IS AT RISK**

*Most fractured ribs are sustained in car accidents or falls. Elderly people who fall often break a rib or other bones. Athletes who play football and other contact sports also have a high risk of broken ribs.*

## HOW IT DEVELOPS

Although a simple rib fracture can be very painful, it is unlikely to cause serious medical problems and most heal in a few weeks. However, a broken rib that punctures a lung or the heart can be life-threatening. Similarly, one that protrudes through the chest muscle and skin is also a medical emergency because of bleeding and the risk of serious infection.

## WHAT YOU CAN DO

Seek medical attention as soon as possible; call 911 or take the accident victim to the emergency room if he or she has difficulty breathing. To ease pain, apply an ice pack or cold compress while waiting for help to arrive.

## HOW TO TREAT IT

A doctor will X-ray the chest to determine the extent of the damage. A simple fracture heals on its own. The chest may be taped, but it is impossible to immobilize the rib cage because it must move during breathing. If there are multiple fractures, surgery is usually necessary to pin or staple the bones together to allow them to heal. If a nonprescription painkiller is not strong enough, a doctor may prescribe codeine or a prescription-strength nonsteroidal anti-inflammatory drug (NSAID).

**WARNING!**

***If you are called upon to give first aid to someone with a broken rib, make the person comfortable, but avoid any unnecessary movement. Above all, do not rub the area or try to reposition a broken bone that is protruding through the skin; this can increase the damage.***

## HOW TO PREVENT IT

Aside from always wearing a seat belt while riding in a car and avoiding situations that may result in falls, there's not much you can do to prevent this type of accident. To avoid a refracture, make sure that the rib is fully healed before lifting heavy objects or engaging in sports.

### ALTERNATIVE THERAPIES

**Nutraceuticals**

Extra calcium—1200 to 1800 mg a day from a combination of food and supplements—may help speed healing. To ensure maximum absorption, take no more than 600 mg at a time. People with thyroid or kidney disease should check with their doctor before taking calcium. Also take 400 IU of vitamin D and 300 mg of magnesium, and eat plenty of leafy greens rich in vitamin K, such as kale and turnip, as well as citrus fruits and other good sources of vitamin C.

# Lung Cancer

### SYMPTOMS

- *Persistent cough, often with bloody sputum, and increasing hoarseness.*
- *Increasing discomfort and pain in the chest, shoulder, arm, and, as the cancer spreads, the bones.*
- *Frequent bouts of pneumonia or bronchitis.*
- *Loss of appetite and weight and mounting fatigue.*
- *Swelling of the face and neck.*

### WHO IS AT RISK

*Smoking is by far the leading cause of lung cancer, increasing the risk 15-fold over that of nonsmokers. Health Canada figures estimate that over 300 nonsmokers die from lung cancer due to secondhand smoke yearly. Among smokers, women of all races appear to be the most vulnerable to developing lung cancer. Other risk factors include advancing age and exposure to secondhand smoke, asbestos, radon, and industrial chemicals and pollutants.*

## HOW IT DEVELOPS

Most lung cancers develop slowly, often taking 20 or more years for a tumor to form. But once a tumor is established, it tends to spread rapidly to the nearby lymph nodes and then throughout the body. Indeed, by the time most lung tumors are detected they already have caused secondary (metastatic) cancers, usually in the bones, bone marrow, liver, or brain.

### BREAKTHROUGHS!

**Photodynamic therapy is being studied as an alternative to surgery to treat early lung cancer. The patient is given a drug that is absorbed by cancer cells and is also very sensitive to light. A viewing tube (bronchoscope) is then inserted into the chest and a laser is used to beam strong light onto the tumor. This light activates the drug, which then destroys the cancer cells.**

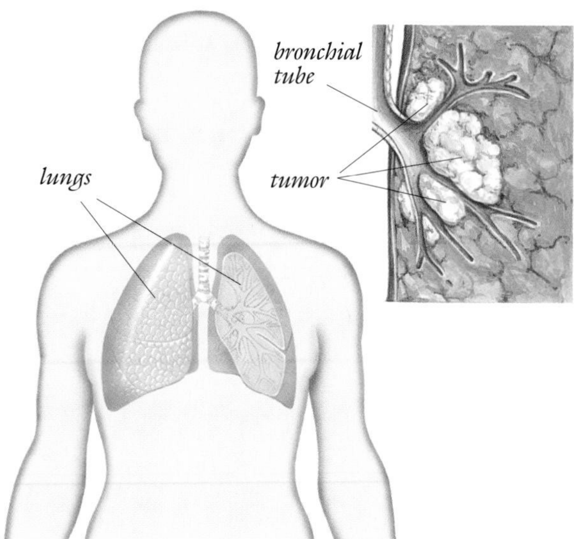


*Lung cancer often starts in one or more places near a bronchial tube, and quickly spreads to the nearby lymph nodes.*

## WHAT YOU CAN DO

See a doctor as soon as possible if you have any symptoms suggesting lung cancer. If you still smoke, it's imperative that you stop and also avoid exposure to secondhand smoke, air pollution, and industrial chemicals. This may slow the cancers growth.

While undergoing cancer treatment, strive to maintain a balance of rest and daily exercise, and eat a nutritious diet that includes ample fruits, vegetables, and grain products—foods that are high in the antioxidant vitamins and minerals that help fight cancer. The diet also should provide extra calories to prevent or slow any weight loss.

## HOW TO TREAT IT

About one-third of lung cancers are treated surgically by removing part or all of the affected lung. Surgery may be followed by radiation therapy and/or chemotherapy. If the cancer is inoperable, radiation may be administered to shrink the tumor, and chemotherapy is given to kill as many of the cancer cells as possible.

Lung cancer is difficult to cure and, as it advances, it can cause severe chest and bone pain. If non-narcotic painkillers are inadequate, a morphine pump that allows patients to administer small amounts of this drug as needed should be considered.

## HOW TO PREVENT IT

Not smoking is by far the best way to prevent lung cancer. Within weeks of stopping, precancerous lung lesions begin to heal, and in 5 to 10 years, the cancer risk of ex-smokers is only slightly higher than that of people who have never smoked. Other preventive measures include having your home checked for radon gas and sealing it off if high levels are found. Avoid secondhand smoke as much as possible and wear protective masks when working with industrial chemicals or materials that contain asbestos or other particles that can be inhaled.

### ALTERNATIVE THERAPIES

**Herbal medicine**

Green tea and garlic contain anticancer compounds; studies show that two or more cups of green tea a day can lower cancer risk. Garlic intensifies the effects of anticoagulants and aspirin; consult your doctor first.

**Nutraceuticals**

Recent studies found that high doses (1000 to 1500 IU a day) of vitamin E reduced the lung cancer risk among a group of smokers by more than 30 percent. Check with your doctor before taking vitamin E if you are also taking aspirin or other blood-thinning medication. Selenium in doses of 100 to 200 micrograms a day also appears to lower cancer risk. Earlier studies showed that antioxidant nutrients—especially beta carotene, which the body uses to make vitamin A, and sulforaphane, an anticancer compound found in broccoli and other members of the cabbage family—help lower lung cancer risk. Have one or two daily servings of brightly colored vegetables and fruits (foods high in beta carotene) and three or four servings of broccoli, Brussels sprouts, and other cruciferous vegetables a week.

**WARNING!**

***Lung cancer commonly recurs, even after surgical removal of a small, seemingly localized tumor. Patients should see their doctor every three months for blood tests and imaging studies (X rays or a CT scan or an MRI) for the first two years after treatment, and every six months for the next two years. More frequent visits are needed if symptoms develop.***

# Pleurisy

### SYMPTOMS

- *Sharp, fleeting chest pain that is worsened by taking a deep breath, coughing, sneezing, or any sudden movement of the upper body.*
- *Chest pain that is relieved by holding your breath.*
- *Depending upon the cause, possible fever and pus-filled or bloody sputum.*

### WHO IS AT RISK

*Pleurisy is usually a complication of another lung disorder or injury, such as pneumonia, cancer, pulmonary embolism (blood clot in the lung), a collapsed lung, or a fractured rib. Less commonly, it may develop in people who have lupus, rheumatoid arthritis, or other inflammatory disorders affecting connective tissues.*

## HOW IT DEVELOPS

The lungs are covered with a thin, double-layered membrane called the pleura. The layers are separated by the pleural space, which contains a small amount of fluid that allows the membranes to move as the lungs expand and contract during breathing. Pleurisy develops when one or both of the membranes becomes inflamed and roughened. Then any movement—breathing, coughing, sneezing—produces a sharp pain as the roughened membranes rub against each other. A doctor can hear a characteristic rubbing noise by listening to the chest sounds through a stethoscope. Tapping on the chest at the site of the rubbing sound may also produce a rattling vibration.

## WHAT YOU CAN DO

See a doctor as soon as possible; not only does pleurisy demand prompt treatment, but X rays and other tests also may be needed to detect the underlying cause. In the meantime, try to breathe deeply and cough periodically to clear the lungs. Hugging a pillow to your chest while

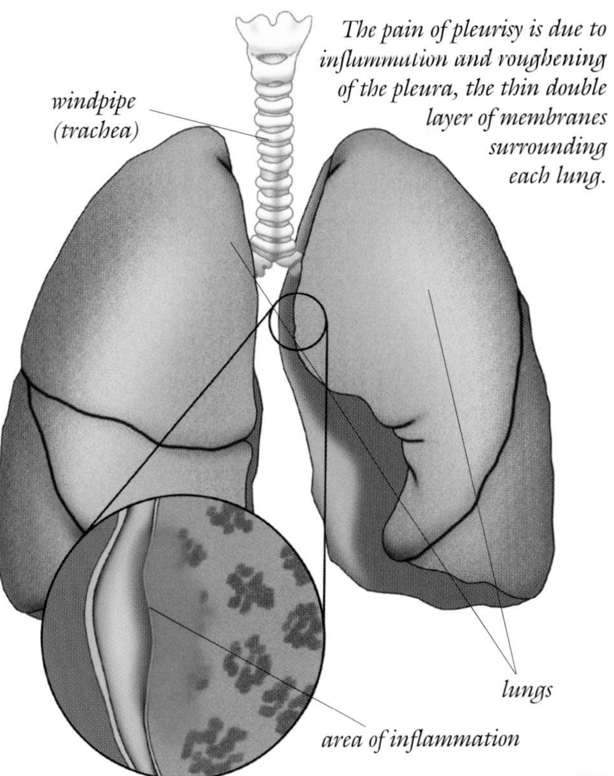


*The pain of pleurisy is due to inflammation and roughening of the pleura, the thin double layer of membranes surrounding each lung.*

**WARNING!**

*Pleurisy often develops into pleural effusion, a buildup of fluid between the membranes. The chest pain lessens, but breathing becomes more difficult as the fluid compresses the lungs. Pleural effusion requires prompt drainage of the excess fluid and treatment of the underlying cause, which can range from infection to cancer.*

coughing can make it less painful. Take aspirin (adults only) or acetaminophen to relieve pain and to lower fever. Rest as much as possible until the pleurisy clears up.

Tobacco smoke can worsen pleurisy; refrain from smoking and avoid exposure to secondhand smoke.

## HOW TO TREAT IT

Treatment varies according to the cause. Antibiotics are prescribed to treat bacterial pneumonia or other infections. A short course of corticosteroids may be given to quell the inflammation; alternatively, a nonsteroidal anti-inflammatory drug (NSAID) is taken. If a stronger painkiller is needed, codeine is usually the first choice. Hospitalization is necessary if the cause is a pulmonary embolism, cancer, or another life-threatening lung disorder.

## HOW TO PREVENT IT

Early diagnosis and treatment of chest injuries, pneumonia, and other lung disorders can help prevent pleurisy. Not smoking and minimizing exposure of the lungs to air pollution, industrial chemicals, asbestos, and other environmental hazards can help prevent the serious disorders that often lead to pleurisy.

### ALTERNATIVE THERAPIES

**Note:** Alternative therapies should not be a substitute for antibiotics and other pleurisy treatments that are prescribed by a doctor.

**Aromatherapy**

Two to three drops of camphor oil added to a steamy bath or a cool-mist vaporizer may relieve a cough and make breathing easier.

**Herbal medicine**

Teas made from marshmallow, mullein, and slippery elm are soothing to the lungs and can ease a productive cough; for a dry cough, try horehound tea or lozenges. Do not use horehound if you have heart disease or are pregnant.

**Homeopathy**

Homeopathic remedies are used to ease fever, a cough, and other symptoms, and should be taken as preventive measures early in the course of a cold or bout of flu. They include Aconite, Belladonna, Ferrum phosphoricum, and Nux vomica. Hepar sulfuris is used if a cough produces a large amount of sputum.

# Pneumonia

### SYMPTOMS

***Viral pneumonia:*** *Chest pain, muscle aches, sore throat, low-grade fever and chills, coughing, fatigue, and enlarged lymph nodes in the neck; symptoms generally come on rapidly.*

***Bacterial pneumonia:*** *Sharp chest pain that is aggravated by breathing deeply, high fever, night sweats, cough that produces thick yellow or greenish sputum, shortness of breath, and rapid, shallow breathing; symptoms develop over two or three days.*

***Aspiration pneumonia:*** *Fever, chest pain, cough that produces blood-tinged sputum, loss of appetite.*

### WHO IS AT RISK

*Viral and so-called walking pneumonia, a mild form that is often mistaken for a bad cold or the flu, is most common among children and young adults. Bacterial pneumonia often develops as a complication of a cold or flu, especially among the elderly or people who are debilitated by diabetes, AIDS, or another chronic disease, or who have chronic bronchitis, asthma, or emphysema. It is also common among hospital and nursing-home patients. Aspiration pneumonia usually occurs among surgery patients, alcoholics, or others who are likely to vomit when they are unconscious or sleeping soundly.*

## HOW IT DEVELOPS

Pneumonia, which is characterized by inflammation of the lungs, has many causes and its course varies according to its type. **Viral pneumonia** comes on rapidly and, in otherwise healthy people, it usually clears up in two weeks, although fatigue may linger for a month or more.

**Bacterial pneumonia** develops more slowly and its symptoms are more pronounced. If untreated, it can be fatal, especially among the very young, the elderly, and people who suffer from a chronic or debilitating disease

**BREAKTHROUGHS!**

**Antibiotic-resistant pneumonia is a growing problem in hospitals. One of the most worrisome is a strain of staphylococcus that is resistant to even vancomycin—up until now the only drug that could wipe out a deadly form of staph pneumonia that traditionally lurks in hospitals.**

**Synercid, an entirely new type of antibiotic, is now available to treat vancomycin-resistant staph pneumonia and life-threatening skin infections that develop mostly among hospital patients. The intravenous drug is made up of two molecules that work together to stop bacteria from synthesizing essential proteins.**

**Aspiration pneumonia** develops when bacteria and other material from the stomach and mouth are inhaled into the lungs. Symptoms usually appear a few days after undergoing surgery.

AIDS patients or others with compromised immunity are vulnerable to rare types of pneumonia caused by fungi or organisms that are usually harmless.

## WHAT YOU CAN DO

See a doctor as soon as possible if symptoms point to possible pneumonia. Viral pneumonia is usually treated with bed rest at home until the fever disappears. Normal activities can then be gradually resumed, but extra rest may be needed for six or more weeks.

Warm compresses or a heating pad placed on the chest can ease pain. However, do not fall asleep with a heating pad; this can result in a burn. Aspirin (for adults only) or acetaminophen can help lower a fever and ease muscle aches and other pain.

Drink at least 8 to 10 glasses of water, steamy broth, juice, tea, or other nonalcoholic beverages a day. Extra fluids, along with an expectorant cough remedy, help thin mucus and make it easier to cough up. However, do not take a cough suppressant unless your doctor specifically recommends one; it is important to clear the lungs of the mucus that builds up during pneumonia. Postural drainage also helps clear the lungs; lay face down across a bed with the upper part of the body hanging over the edge, and then cough up as much mucus as you can. Having someone gently tap your back also loosens the mucus and makes it easier to expel from the lungs.

## HOW TO TREAT IT

Bacterial pneumonia is treated with antibiotics; in many cases, hospitalization for intravenous antibiotics is necessary. Intravenous antibiotics are also given for aspiration and AIDS-related pneumonias.

*Postural drainage uses gravity to help clear the lungs.*

## HOW TO PREVENT IT

A vaccine is available to prevent the more common types of bacterial pneumonia; immunization is recommended for everyone over the age of 65 as well as for people with diabetes, emphysema and other chronic lung disorders, and AIDS and other diseases that lower immunity. Aspiration pneumonia can be prevented by refraining from all food and drink for 10 to 12 hours before undergoing surgery that requires general anesthesia.

**WARNING!**

***A rare form of pneumonia called psittacosis can be transmitted to humans by parrots, lovebirds, and parakeets. Bird owners who develop pneumonia symptoms should be tested for this disease.***

### ALTERNATIVE THERAPIES

**Note:** These should be used only as additions to, not substitutes for, conventional medical treatments.

**Herbal medicine**

Echinacea, either alone or with goldenseal, can be taken as a tea three times a day or in tincture or capsule forms. (For cautions concerning echinacea and goldenseal, see *About the Recommendations*, p 7.) Green tea boosts immunity; drink two or more cups a day. Teas made from marshmallow root, mullein, or slippery elm soothe lung inflammation.

**Homeopathy**

Remedies prescribed for pneumonia symptoms include Arsenicum album, Bryonia, Sulphur, and Phosphorus.

**Nutraceuticals**

Zinc supplements may bolster immunity; however, long-term dosages should not exceed 25 mg a day. Vitamin E, up to 800 IU a day, along with 10,000 to 25,000 IU of vitamin A (taken for no more than one month), helps repair lung tissue damaged by pneumonia. (For cautions concerning vitamins A and E, see *About the Recommendations*, p 7.)

# Pulmonary Embolism

### SYMPTOMS

- *Increasing chest pain, especially when taking a deep breath or coughing.*
- *Difficulty breathing.*
- *Bloody sputum, rapid heartbeat, anxiety, and sweating.*

### WHO IS AT RISK

*More than 500,000 North Americans are stricken with pulmonary emboli each year. Surgery patients have a high risk of a pulmonary embolism, especially if they are bedridden; other high-risk groups include women who smoke and take birth control pills (or estrogen replacement therapy), airline passengers who sit still for very long periods, and people who are obese and sedentary. Conditions that can lead to a pulmonary embolism include thrombophlebitis (inflammation of a vein in the leg), emphysema, a fractured hip or leg, and severe varicose veins.*

## HOW IT DEVELOPS

A pulmonary embolism develops when a clot forms elsewhere in the body—usually a deep vein in a leg or the pelvic area—and travels through the bloodstream to lodge in a lung. Less often the obstruction is due to a fat globule that enters the bloodstream following a hip or leg fracture. The first symptoms are usually sudden, unexplained shortness of breath accompanied by chest pain that is exacerbated by coughing or taking a deep breath.

The site of the lung obstruction determines the severity of the condition. A clot that blocks a small artery near the edge of a lung often causes little damage; in contrast, a blockage of a large artery near its entrance to the lung is life-threatening.

## WHAT YOU CAN DO

Any unexplained shortness of breath warrants prompt medical attention. Otherwise, there is no self-treatment for a pulmonary embolism.

## HOW TO TREAT IT

### Medications

Most pulmonary emboli are treated with clot-dissolving (thrombolytic) drugs, such as tissue plasminogen activator (TPA) or streptokinase. To prevent new clots, a blood-thinning drug, such as warfarin (Coumadin), is usually prescribed. In some cases, doses of 80 to 325 mg of aspirin a day will suffice.

If pain is severe, morphine or another strong painkiller will be given. Antibiotics will be prescribed if the embolism results in a lung or heart infection. Other possible complications, such as a disturbance in heart rhythm or pulmonary hypertension, are also treated with drugs. Supplemental oxygen can ease the labored breathing.

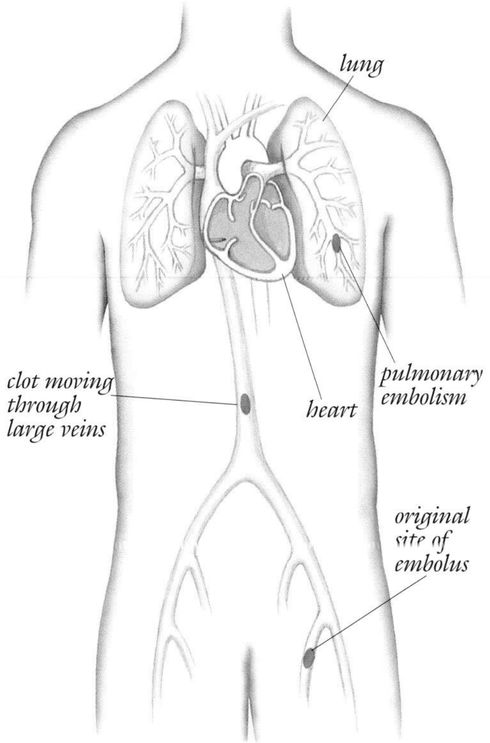

*A pulmonary embolism typically develops when a blood clot in the leg travels through the bloodstream and lodges in a lung.*

**WARNING!**

***Large numbers of pulmonary emboli can be prevented by early ambulation following surgery, childbirth, fractures, or a stroke. If you can't get out of bed, have a caregiver passively move the legs several times a day to keep blood from pooling in the veins and increasing the risk of blood clots.***

### Surgery

In severe cases, surgery may be necessary to remove the clot and perhaps a portion of the lung if tissue death and scarring develop.

## HOW TO PREVENT IT

As much as possible, avoid long periods of bed rest or other types of immobility. If you must be bedridden, ask your doctor about wearing pneumatic leg wraps, which inflate periodically to boost circulation, or surgical elastic stockings. Leg and foot exercises also promote circulation in the lower limbs. If you have varicose veins, avoid long periods of standing or sitting in one position, exercise regularly, rest periodically with your legs elevated, and consider wearing prescription elastic stockings to improve circulation.

When on a long airplane flight, get up and walk around at least once every hour or so. Women who take birth control pills (or estrogen replacement) should not smoke; those with a history of blood clotting disorders should consider alternative forms of birth control (and hormone therapy). Other preventive measures include exercising regularly and losing excess weight.

### ALTERNATIVE THERAPIES

**Note:** Any alternative therapy should be an adjunct to, not a substitute for, prompt medical treatment.

**Herbal medicine**

Ginkgo biloba thins blood and improves leg circulation; the usual dose is 120 to 240 mg a day. (For cautions concerning ginkgo, see *About the Recommendations*, p 7.)

**Nutraceuticals**

Vitamin E, in dosages of 400 to 800 IU a day, also improves circulation and reduces clotting. Check with a doctor before taking a vitamin E supplement if you are also taking aspirin or other blood-thinning medication.

# The Breasts

*Virtually every woman experiences some type of breast pain or tenderness at one time or another. The causes range from harmless cysts or monthly hormonal changes to abscesses, injuries, and the disease that many women dread most—breast cancer.*

## Abscesses/Mastitis

### SYMPTOMS

- *Soreness, inflammation, and swelling of a breast, usually near the nipple, and a pus-filled nipple discharge.*
- *Formation of a hard lump that is warm to the touch.*
- *Fever, fatigue, and general malaise.*

### WHO IS AT RISK

*Mastitis—defined as breast inflammation and infection—and breast abscesses are most common among breast-feeding women, especially during the first few weeks. Improper breast-feeding techniques or the use of a breast pump increases the risk. Less commonly the infection results from a breast injury or an open sore.*

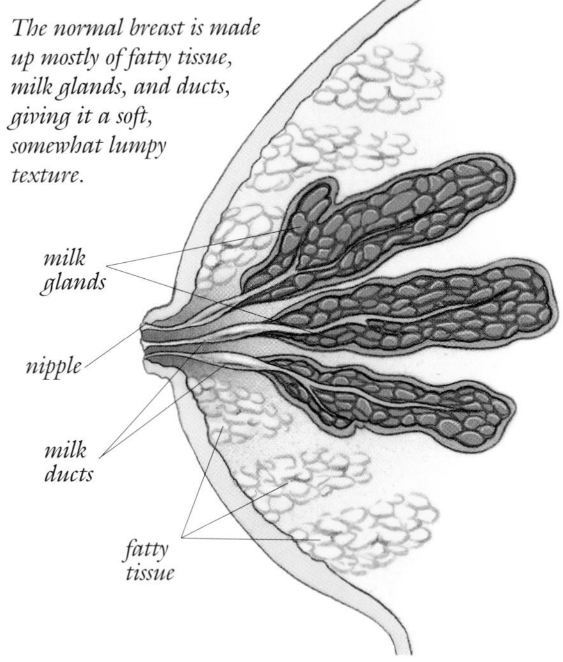

*The normal breast is made up mostly of fatty tissue, milk glands, and ducts, giving it a soft, somewhat lumpy texture.*

### HOW IT DEVELOPS

Mastitis occurs when bacteria invade the breast, usually through tiny cracks (fissures) in and around a nipple. Sore, cracked nipples are very common during the first few weeks of breast-feeding, which is when most mastitis occurs. The bacteria, usually the staphylococcal organisms that live harmlessly on the mother's or baby's skin, make their way into a milk duct or gland, where they find an ideal environment in which to multiply rapidly. At first, the woman may mistake mastitis for breast engorgement, which often occurs in the first few days of breast-feeding when milk production steps up. But fever and a pus-filled discharge point to mastitis.

The structure of the breast, with its discrete glands and abundant fatty tissue, helps localize the infection, rather than having it spread through the breast and to other parts of the body. White blood cells and other immune-system cells rush to the site and help wall off the bacteria, forming an abscess. At this stage, the breast can be very painful, swollen, and warm to the touch. Most women develop a fever, which may rise to 39.4°C/103°F, as well as muscle aches and other flu-like symptoms.

### WHAT YOU CAN DO

Mild mastitis usually clears up with self-care, but see your doctor if symptoms persist for more than three or four days or if you develop a high fever (38.9°C/102°F or higher), abscess, or profuse yellow or greenish nipple discharge. Continue breast-feeding unless your doctor advises you to stop. Apply warm compresses to the breast for 10 to 15 minutes every few hours and before nursing to ease discomfort and keep milk flowing. Gently massaging the breasts during a hot shower has the same effect.

Start each nursing session with the infected breast to empty it as much as possible. Sometimes a baby may seem to reject milk from the infected breast; this is because the infection may give it a salty flavor. However, it does not affect the milk's nutritious quality, and any bacteria that the baby ingests are killed by digestive juices.

Take acetaminophen to relieve pain and lower any fever. Rest as much as possible and take preventive measures to heal sore and cracked nipples (see *How to Prevent It*, p 126).

### HOW TO TREAT IT

#### Medications

If the mastitis is severe or persists for more than a few days, a doctor will prescribe an antibiotic. Small amounts of the drug may enter the breast milk, but it won't harm the baby, although it may cause mild diarrhea. If the mastitis persists or worsens, a culture should be done to identify the bacterium. A growing number of staphylococcus organisms, especially those acquired in a hospital, are antibiotic-resistant and can cause life-threatening infections unless they are treated with special antibiotics.

### Surgery

Breast abscesses usually require surgical drainage, which can be done in a doctor's office. It may be necessary to stop nursing from the infected breast until it heals; to prevent painful engorgement, however, the breast should be emptied of its milk several times a day.

## HOW TO PREVENT IT

Prevention starts with proper breast-feeding techniques and steps to avoid cracked nipples. Make sure the baby "latches on" properly, with the entire nipple in his or her mouth. Wash the breasts with warm water and dry them carefully before and after each feeding; to further prevent cracking, gently massage the nipples with cocoa butter or a cream recommended by your doctor. Expose the breasts to air as much as possible; using a heat lamp (a 100-watt bulb is sufficient) for 10 minutes after nursing also promotes healing. If the breasts become engorged, try to empty them as much as possible, even if this means expressing the milk yourself.

**WARNING!**

***Women who are not breast-feeding and develop mastitis-like symptoms should see a doctor as soon as possible. Any persistent breast inflammation, lump, or hardening requires tests to rule out possible breast cancer.***

### ALTERNATIVE THERAPIES

**Herbal medicine**

Gently massaging the nipples with fresh aloe gel (not to be confused with aloe latex) after nursing promotes healing and its anti-infective properties help prevent bacteria from invading the breast. Be sure to thoroughly wash any aloe residue from the breast before the next breast-feeding, since it can give the baby an upset stomach and diarrhea.

# Breast Cancer

**SYMPTOMS**

- *Breast lump or thickening; change in breast shape, size, or symmetry.*
- *Persistent breast pain or tenderness.*
- *Redness, pitting, dimpling, or inflammation of skin.*
- *Clear or bloody nipple discharge; retraction or indentation of nipple.*

**WHO IS AT RISK**

*About one of every nine Canadian women face a lifetime risk of developing breast cancer, which is by far the most common female malignancy with more than 18,000 new cases diagnosed each year. The risk increases with advancing age, with most cases developing after age 50. Other risk factors include:*

- *A strong family history of the disease.*
- *The presence of a mutated breast-cancer gene (see* Breakthroughs!, *p 128).*
- *Early (before age 12) onset of menstruation, a late (after age 30) first pregnancy, or menopause after age 55.*
- *Obesity.*
- *A history of a previous breast cancer or endometrial or ovarian cancer.*

*Some studies also suggest that risk is increased by:*

- *Long-term hormone replacement therapy following menopause.*
- *Smoking.*
- *Consuming more than two alcoholic drinks a day.*

*Cancer experts stress, however, that 80 percent of women who develop the disease do not fall into a high-risk group, and that all women should be diligent about early detection of the disease.*

## HOW IT DEVELOPS

This varies according to the type of breast cancer. About 90 percent of breast cancers arise in the glandular tissue, usually in a milk duct or a lobe. Paget's breast cancer is a rare form that begins in the nipple; inflammatory cancer is an even rarer type in which the skin becomes inflamed and pitted, resembling an orange peel.

Some breast cancers grow very slowly and remain localized for many years; others double in size every few days. On average, however, breast cancers double in size about every 100 days, and may go undetected for several years. As the cancer cells multiply, they may invade adjacent tissue and spread to the axillary lymph nodes in the armpit; less often, they spread to the nodes in the neck or near the collarbone. As the cancer advances, it most commonly spreads to the bones, lungs, and liver.

Most breast cancers are not painful at first, but as the tumors grow and spread, they cause persistent breast tenderness or pain. Severe pain results if the cancer spreads to the bones or other parts of the body.

## WHAT YOU CAN DO

See your doctor as soon as possible if you develop any warning sign of breast cancer; early detection and treatment are key to surviving this disease. Practice monthly breast self-examination (see *How to Examine Your Breasts*, p 127), and have your doctor examine your breasts at least once a year. The Cancer Society recommends mammography screening in combination with physical examination of the breasts by a health professional every two years for women between the ages of 50 and 69.

If you are diagnosed with breast cancer, learn all you can about your treatment options. Remember that almost 85 percent of women diagnosed with breast cancer are alive and free of the disease five years later. Still, fighting breast cancer is always emotionally trying, regardless of the prognosis; many women find that joining a support group of women in similar circumstances makes the ordeal easier. There are also support groups for loved ones.

During and after treatment there are many small steps you can take to minimize discomfort. For example, to prevent painful swelling following surgery, exercise the arm on the affected side as much as possible. Simply reaching above your head will help; ask your doctor about other arm exercises. Also be careful not to constrict the arm; switch any tight bracelets or wristwatch to the other side and use a shoulder bag or backpack instead of carrying a handbag or other weighty object on the arm.

## HOW TO TREAT IT

Breast cancer treatment is constantly evolving, and even the experts disagree as to what is the best approach. In all but the most advanced cancers, however, treatment begins with surgical removal of the cancer along with varying amounts of breast tissue, ranging from a lumpectomy to a mastectomy. Surgery is usually followed by one or more of the following additional therapies:

- **Radiation**, which usually follows a lumpectomy. Treatments are administered on an outpatient basis, typically five days a week for four to six weeks. Side effects include fatigue, tissue swelling, and a thickening of the skin exposed to the powerful X rays.
- **Chemotherapy**, which is usually administered if the tumor is very large or has spread to the lymph nodes or other parts of the body. Sometimes the anticancer drugs are given for several weeks before surgery to shrink a very large tumor and treat any metastases. But what drugs are used and when and how long they are administered vary according to the type of cancer.
- **Hormone therapy**, which is usually given if the tumor cells have receptors for estrogen, the major female sex hormone. The first-choice drug is tamoxifen (Nolvadex), which blocks estrogen receptors and prevents tumor growth. The duration of treatment depends on the patient's response. The drug is taken as long as there is a favorable response; side effects include hot flashes and other menopausal symptoms, especially among women who are still menstruating. Sometimes the

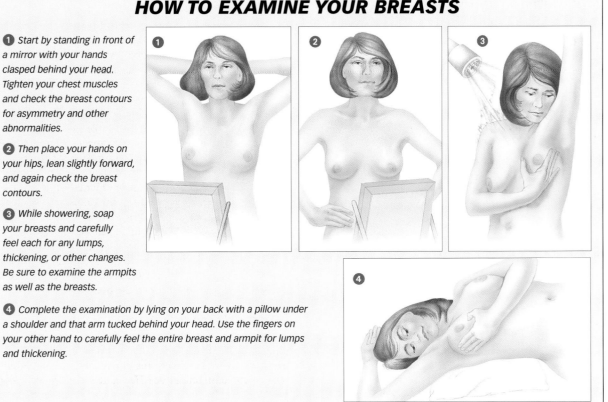

## HOW TO EXAMINE YOUR BREASTS

*❶ Start by standing in front of a mirror with your hands clasped behind your head. Tighten your chest muscles and check the breast contours for asymmetry and other abnormalities.*

*❷ Then place your hands on your hips, lean slightly forward, and again check the breast contours.*

*❸ While showering, soap your breasts and carefully feel each for any lumps, thickening, or other changes. Be sure to examine the armpits as well as the breasts.*

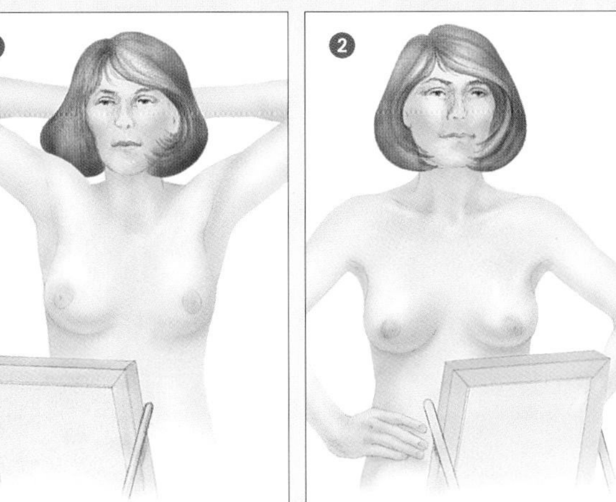

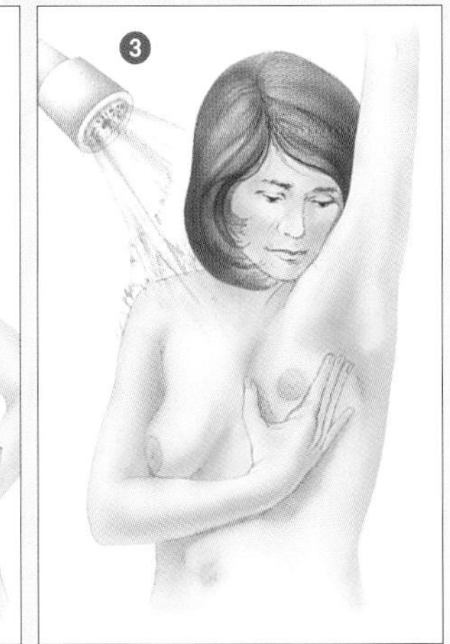

*❹ Complete the examination by lying on your back with a pillow under a shoulder and that arm tucked behind your head. Use the fingers on your other hand to carefully feel the entire breast and armpit for lumps and thickening.*

ovaries are removed to halt their hormone production.

- **Experimental treatments**, including immunotherapy with interferon or other agents classified as biologic response modifiers; these are designed to stimulate the body's natural defenses against cancer. Another experimental—and controversial—therapy involves a bone marrow transplant, in which the patient's bone marrow is destroyed and replaced with healthy marrow or immature blood cells from donor marrow. It has not been proved whether this actually prolongs life.

The need for pain control varies greatly from one woman to another. The discomfort of a lumpectomy can usually be controlled with a few days of codeine and then acetaminophen or another mild painkiller as healing takes place. More extensive surgery may require a short course of morphine, and then codeine and other painkillers. A morphine pump may be used for advanced breast cancer that has spread to the bones.

## HOW TO PREVENT IT

Because the cause of most breast cancer is unknown, there is no sure-fire means of prevention. Some women who have a very high breast-cancer risk (see *Breakthroughs!*, below) elect to undergo preventive mastectomies, in which one or both breasts are removed, usually followed by reconstructive breast surgery. But this is a drastic step that many women find unacceptable. Many experts feel the best approach is to concentrate on early detection while avoiding or minimizing risk factors that can be changed, namely:

- Achieving and maintaining ideal weight.
- Limiting alcohol intake to one drink a day.
- Talking to your doctor about alternatives to long-term estrogen replacement therapy.

### ALTERNATIVE THERAPIES

**Note:** Alternative therapies should be considered as adjuncts to conventional medical and surgical breast-cancer treatments.

### BREAKTHROUGHS!

**New genetic tests can identify women who carry hereditary mutated genes—BRCA1 and BRCA2—that are strongly linked to breast cancer. One of the genes—BRCA1—is linked to both breast and ovarian cancers; carriers of the other gene—BRCA2—have an 86 percent chance of developing breast cancer. Genetic testing may be advisable for women who have a strong history of first-degree relatives (mothers, grandmothers, sisters) who developed breast cancer before age 50. If they are found to carry either of the genes, they can take preventive measures, such as more frequent mammography or, for women who are especially fearful of breast cancer, preventive mastectomies.**

**Guided imagery and self-hypnosis**

These are among the self-help strategies that are taught at many cancer centers to help women cope with pain and other aspects of advanced breast cancer. Studies show that women who use these therapies have significantly longer survival rates compared to those who do not. Researchers theorize that these and other mind/body therapies may prod the immune system to put up a more aggressive fight against the cancer.

### WARNING!

***After a mastectomy, let all health-care providers know that they should not use the arm on the affected side to measure blood pressure. The tight cuff can compress the already compromised lymph circulation and increase arm swelling.***

**Herbal medicine**

To promote skin healing after radiation treatments, apply fresh aloe gel to the site. Ginger tea can help quell the nausea that may be a side effect of both chemotherapy and radiation treatments.

**Nutraceuticals**

Anticancer dietary supplements include: antioxidants such as vitamin C and related bioflavonoids; vitamin E, beta carotene and carotenoids, and selenium, which are also antioxidants; green tea or green tea extracts; coenzyme $Q_{10}$ (check with your doctor if you are pregnant or nursing); glutathione; and Beta Glucan. Soy protein and other soy products are high in isoflavones, plant estrogens that may reduce menopause symptoms and provide other benefits of estrogen replacement without the increased risk of breast cancer. Some studies suggest that soy isoflavones may help forestall breast cancer. To promote incision healing and reduce scar formation, massage vitamin E oil into the area. However, wait until all drains have been removed and your surgeon gives his or her approval for this aspect of self-care.

# Fibrocystic Breasts

### SYMPTOMS

- *Breast swelling, tenderness, and lumpiness, especially during the premenstrual phase of a woman's monthly menstrual cycle.*
- *Dull breast pain, especially near the armpit.*
- *Development of breast lumps, which are usually soft and easily moved under the skin.*

### WHO IS AT RISK

*Half or more of all premenopausal women have fibrocystic breasts, which are characterized by the development of fluid-filled sacs, or cysts.*

## HOW IT DEVELOPS

Fluctuating levels of estrogen and progesterone—the major female sex hormones—stimulate the breast changes during a woman's menstrual cycle. During the premen strual phase, breasts tend to become tender or even painful as they swell with extra fluid and blood; cysts of varying sizes may also develop. If conception does not occur, hormone levels fall, the breast swelling recedes, the tenderness goes away, and many of the cysts disappear. Cyst formation tends to increase as women enter their 40s and approach menopause; after menopause, however, they are quite rare.

Sometimes, one or more cysts remain and, in time, may fill with the solid, fibrous material characteristic of fibrocystic breasts. At one time, this was referred to as a disease and was considered a risk factor for breast cancer. Doctors now recognize that fibrocystic breasts are an exaggeration of normal changes and are unrelated to cancer.

Solid benign growths called fibroadenomas may also develop, especially in young adults. These are also harmless, but because they are difficult to tell from cancerous tumors, any new breast lump that persists through two or three menstrual cycles should be checked by a doctor.

## WHAT YOU CAN DO

Acetaminophen or ibuprofen can usually relieve mild discomfort. Try wearing a well-fitted bra that is one size larger than usual when the breasts are swollen during the premenstrual phase. Regular exercise may also help; one study found that women who run an average of 10 miles a week had an improvement in their breast symptoms.

## HOW TO TREAT IT

A mild diuretic (water pill) may be prescribed to reduce premenstrual swelling and fluid retention. In very severe cases, drugs that block estrogen—danazol (Cyclomen), tamoxifen (Nolvadex), or bromocriptine (Parlodel)—may be prescribed. However, the problem may return when the drugs are stopped.

Most breast cysts clear up on their own and disappear completely after menopause. A doctor may elect to drain very large or painful cysts. Some fibroadenomas grow large enough to distort the breast contour and require surgical removal. In addition, many doctors recommend routine removal of fibroadenomas, especially when they occur in middle-aged or older women. Although the growths themselves are benign, they can be difficult to distinguish from cancerous tumors. Removal allows a doctor to examine the tissue for any abnormal cells.

## HOW TO PREVENT IT

Cutting down on salt, especially in your premenstrual phase, may help limit breast swelling and cyst formation. Some studies have found that reducing or, better still, eliminating caffeine and methylxanthines—substances found in coffee, chocolate, tea, and colas—eases breast tenderness. Studies indicate that women who suffer from severe breast tenderness tend to be overly sensitive to caffeine and methylxanthines, and that eliminating them from the diet will provide relief for many. Adopting a low-fat diet and losing excess weight may also help by preventing the body from producing too much estrogen—a likely factor in fibrocystic breast tenderness.

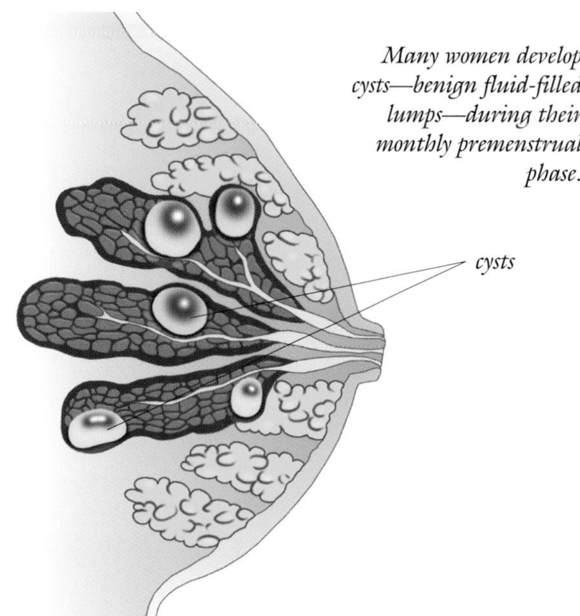


*Many women develop cysts—benign fluid-filled lumps—during their monthly premenstrual phase.*

### ALTERNATIVE THERAPIES

**Herbal medicine**

An extract of vitex fruit—also known as chaste tree or monk's pepper—is an ancient herbal remedy for cystic breasts and other premenstrual symptoms. It is available as concentrated liquid, powder, or tablets; it should be taken daily for at least four months. Raspberry leaf tea is another tonic that some women find eases breast symptoms. Some studies have found that evening primrose oil, in doses of 1000 mg three times a day, relieves breast pain. Do not use evening primrose oil if you are taking anticoagulants.

**Nutraceuticals**

There are numerous anecdotal reports that vitamin E, in doses of 400 to 800 IU a day, reduces symptoms related to fibrocystic breasts. Check with your doctor before taking vitamin E if you are also taking aspirin or other blood-thinning medication.

**WARNING!**

***Hormone manipulation should be considered a treatment of last resort for fibrocystic breast pain. The drugs used can cause menopausal symptoms and other side effects that may be worse than the breast discomfort.***

# The Heart

*Heartache usually refers to grief and other emotional pain, and has nothing to do with heart function itself. In contrast, angina—chest pain, uncomfortable feelings of pressure or tightness, and shortness of breath—often signals serious heart disease.*

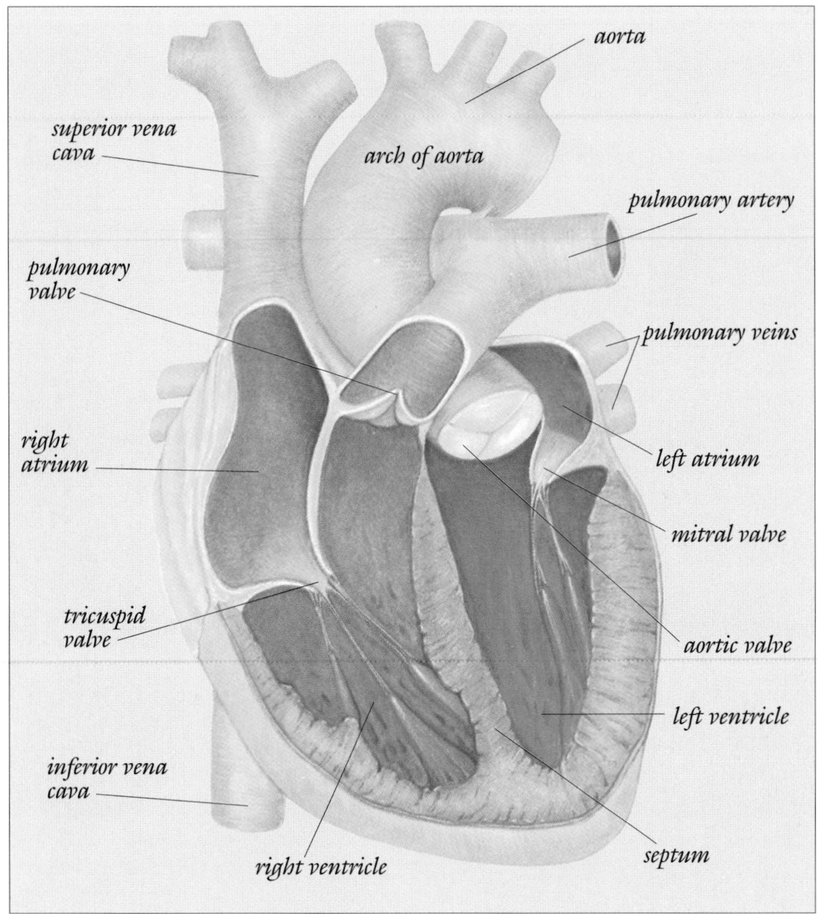


*The heart is a double pump, in which oxygen-depleted blood enters on the right side and is passed to the lungs for a fresh supply of oxygen. It then flows into the left side and is pumped into the aorta to begin a new trip through the body's circulatory system.*

**WHO IS AT RISK**

*Atherosclerosis, the buildup of fatty deposits (plaque) in the artery walls, is the major risk factor for angina pectoris, the medical term for chest pain. The exact cause of atherosclerosis is unknown, but contributing factors include high blood cholesterol, diabetes, and tobacco use. Recent studies also implicate high levels of homocysteine, a protein (amino acid) that can damage the artery walls; chlamydial respiratory infections; and chronic gingivitis, a gum disease.*

## HOW IT DEVELOPS

Angina is one of the most common manifestations of coronary artery disease (CAD), in which the blood vessels nourishing the heart itself cannot deliver enough blood to the cardiac muscle. Any extra demands on the heart—exercise, stress, exposure to cold, digesting a heavy meal—can lead to ischemia, a condition in which areas of muscle are starved for oxygen. Chest pain, tightness, or other discomfort is the most common symptom, but some people experience shortness of breath instead of (or in addition to) the classic pain.

**Stable angina** is usually very predictable; for example, symptoms invariably develop when a person reaches a specific level of exertion, such as climbing two flights of stairs or walking three blocks at a brisk pace. Symptoms usually subside after resting a few minutes or after taking nitroglycerin, a drug that increases blood flow in the coronary arteries and reduces the heart's workload.

Some people develop **atypical angina**, in which symptoms develop during rest but are not usually provoked by exercise. It is usually due to spasms of the smooth muscles that control the size of the coronary arteries. Spasms generally occur at the site of fatty deposits,

# Angina

**SYMPTOMS**

- *Pain, tightness, or other discomfort starting in the center of the chest and radiating (or occurring only) in the arm, neck, shoulder, jaw, or back, especially on the left side.*
- *Pain or other symptoms exacerbated by exercise, stress, exposure to cold and wind, or eating a heavy meal.*

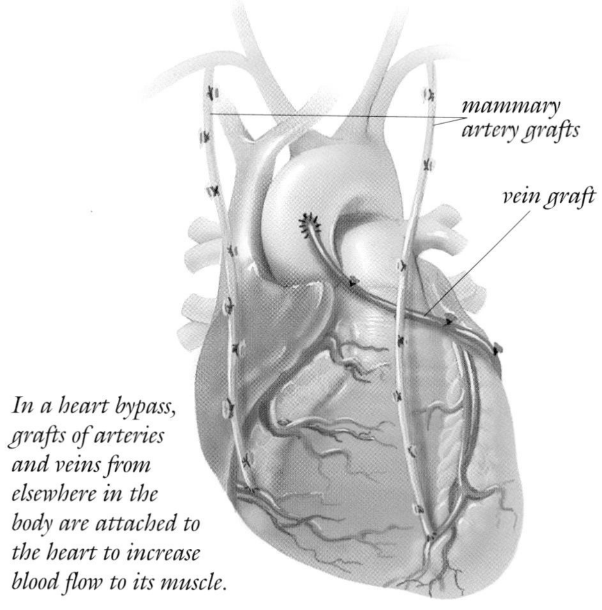


*In a heart bypass, grafts of arteries and veins from elsewhere in the body are attached to the heart to increase blood flow to its muscle.*

but sometimes people free of atherosclerosis develop atypical angina; the cause for this is unknown.

**Unstable angina**—another variant—is highly unpredictable; sometimes it occurs during rest, and at others during strenuous exercise. It often represents a worsening of CAD (see *Warning!*, p 132).

## WHAT YOU CAN DO

Stop whatever you are doing, rest quietly until symptoms subside, and see a doctor as soon as possible. If you have been diagnosed with CAD, follow your doctor's instructions for what to do when angina develops. If you smoke, it's imperative to stop. Similarly, work with your doctor to control disorders that contribute to cardiovascular risk, especially elevated blood cholesterol, high blood pressure, and diabetes, and strive to achieve and maintain ideal weight.

Regular exercise also helps lower cholesterol and high blood pressure, control diabetes, and improve heart function. But check with your doctor before undertaking an exercise program; an exercise stress test may be needed to determine a safe regimen. Other lifestyle changes that may improve angina include stress reduction and behavior modification to reduce feelings of hostility and anger.

## HOW TO TREAT IT

### Medications

Drugs used to treat or prevent angina include:

- **Nitroglycerin,** which may be placed under the tongue for fast relief during attack, and taken prophylactically in the form of long-acting tablets. Topical ointments and time-release medicated patches allow the drug to be absorbed through the skin for prophylaxis.
- **Beta blockers,** which block the receptors that transmit messages to the heart to beat faster and harder, thereby lowering the heart rate and the cardiac muscle's oxygen needs.
- **Calcium-channel blockers,** which prevent certain amounts of calcium from entering the smooth muscles that control the size of the coronary arteries. In effect, this allows the arteries to open wider, increasing blood flow to the heart muscle.

### Surgery

Angina that cannot be controlled by medication or is worsening may require surgical treatment. Procedures include:

- **Angioplasty,** which uses a thin tube (catheter) that has a deflated balloon attached to its tip. The catheter is inserted into a blood vessel in the groin or arm, and threaded through the arteries until it reaches the clogged coronary vessels. The balloon is then inflated to flatten the fatty plaque and widen the artery's channel. In some instances, a tiny rooter device may be used to shave the fatty plaque; a newer procedure uses a laser attached to the catheter to vaporize the deposits. More than 90 percent of patients undergoing angioplasty get relief from their angina, but it is often temporary; about 30 percent will experience a recurrence of chest pains in six months, and more than half will relapse within three or four years.
- **Coronary bypass surgery,** in which healthy segments of blood vessels from elsewhere in the body are attached to the coronary arteries to bypass the clogged areas. The operation is riskier and requires a longer hospital stay and recuperation than angioplasty, but the benefits also tend to last 10 years or even longer.

*Angioplasty increases blood flow by using an inflated balloon to flatten fatty deposits that are clogging a coronary artery.*

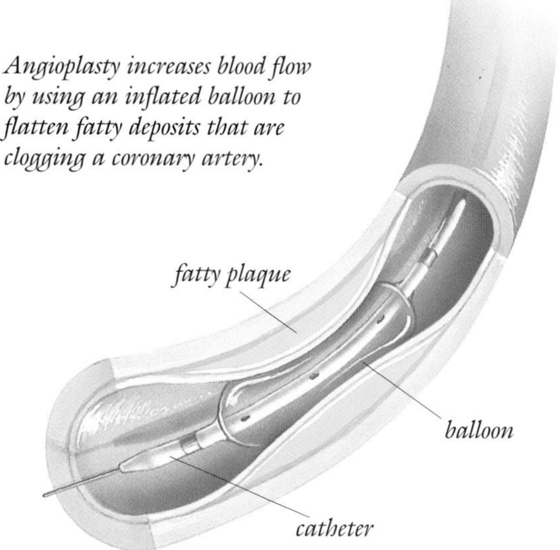

## HOW TO PREVENT IT

The beta-blocker or calcium-channel blocker drugs described on the previous page can usually prevent episodes of angina. If angina persists despite preventive medications, surgical treatment may be necessary to increase blood flow to the heart muscle. Of course, adopting a lifestyle that reduces or eliminates cardiovascular risk factors may help prevent the atherosclerosis and other underlying conditions that lead to CAD and angina.

### ALTERNATIVE THERAPIES

**Exercise conditioning**

Numerous studies show that exercise conditioning can improve cardiovascular function and reduce the episodes of angina. The regimen, which should be developed by a doctor or cardiac rehabilitation therapist following an exercise stress test, calls for a gradual buildup in the amount of exercise. Prophylactic medication may be taken before each session to increase the duration of exercise without provoking symptoms.

**Herbal medicine**

Extract of hawthorn is an ancient heart tonic. It is rich in flavonoids, potent antioxidants that may reduce the buildup of fatty plaque; its diuretic properties help lower high blood pressure; and it appears to strengthen the heartbeat. German studies have found that hawthorn pills, in daily dosages of 300 to 450 mg, can reduce the incidence of angina attacks. It is also available in tincture, powder, or tea forms. Check with your doctor before using hawthorn if you are taking digoxin or anticoagulants.

**Nutraceuticals**

Daily supplements of 400 to 800 micrograms of folic acid and 1000 micrograms of vitamin $B_{12}$ may lower risk by reducing elevated homocysteine levels. Vitamin C, in dosages of 1000 to 2000 mg a day, helps repair damaged blood vessels, which are more vulnerable to fatty plaque. (Don't take more than 500 mg a day if you have kidney stones, kidney disease, or hemochromatosis.) 400 to 800 IU of vitamin E helps prevent the formation of blood clots. (Check with your doctor if you are already taking aspirin or other blood-thinning medication.)

Other supplements that help reduce the risk of atherosclerosis include grape seed extract (100 to 200 mg a day); fish oils and other omega-3 fatty acids (3000 mg a day or three or four servings of salmon, sardines, and other fatty fish a week); calcium (1000 mg a day); and coenzyme $Q_{10}$ (100 mg a day). Pregnant and nursing women must check with their doctor before taking coenzyme $Q_{10}$.

**WARNING!**

***Any change or worsening of angina requires prompt medical evaluation. Unstable angina is highly unpredictable and may occur even when resting. It can often be a prelude to a heart attack.***

**BREAKTHROUGHS!**

**Researchers at several institutions are refining genetic engineering and other techniques to grow new coronary blood vessels or to keep bypass grafts from clogging. Experimental techniques include:**

- **Veins to be used as bypass grafts are bathed in a solution of altered genes that are designed to prevent the vessels from filling with plaque.**
- **Cells taken from the umbilical cords of newborns are injected into the heart to stimulate growth of new blood vessels.**
- **A laser is used to make tiny holes in the heart muscle, which then stimulates the heart to grow new blood vessels.**

**These techniques have been used successfully in laboratory animals, and human experiments are under way. Although more study is needed, researchers call the techniques among the most promising new developments in treating coronary artery disease.**

# Cardiac Arrhythmias

### SYMPTOMS

- *Palpitations or sensations of missed beats, thumping, fluttering, or racing of the heart.*
- *Chest pain and shortness of breath.*
- *Fatigue, unexplained light-headedness and dizziness, and possible fainting.*

### WHO IS AT RISK

*Everyone now and then experiences skipped or extra heartbeats; they usually are not a cause for concern. But every year, more than 300,000 North Americans die from a sudden cardiac arrest, usually due to a serious disturbance in the electrical system that controls the heart's rhythmic beating. Very often, the arrhythmia is caused by diseased coronary arteries or heart valves. Sometimes the problem lies in the heart muscle itself, and may be due to inflammation or scarring of the conducting tissue. The risk increases with age; other risk factors include untreated high blood pressure, a heart attack, and congenital abnormalities of the heart's electrical conduction system.*

## HOW IT DEVELOPS

Some arrhythmias are harmless; others develop slowly over a period of months or years and increase the risk of a stroke or heart attack; still others come on suddenly and can kill within minutes. One of the most familiar examples of the latter is ventricular fibrillation, an arrhythmia in which the heart's pumping chambers (the ventricles) quiver ineffectively and are unable to pump blood out of the heart to the rest of the body. Death occurs in three or four minutes unless the arrhythmia is stopped by a defibrillator—a device that sends an electrical shock into the heart to stop the quivering and restart its normal beating.

Chest pain similar to angina is a common symptom of cardiac arrhythmias. The pain occurs when the heart is unable to pump enough blood to nourish the heart muscle. Light-headedness, fatigue, and fainting are due to diminished blood flow to the brain.

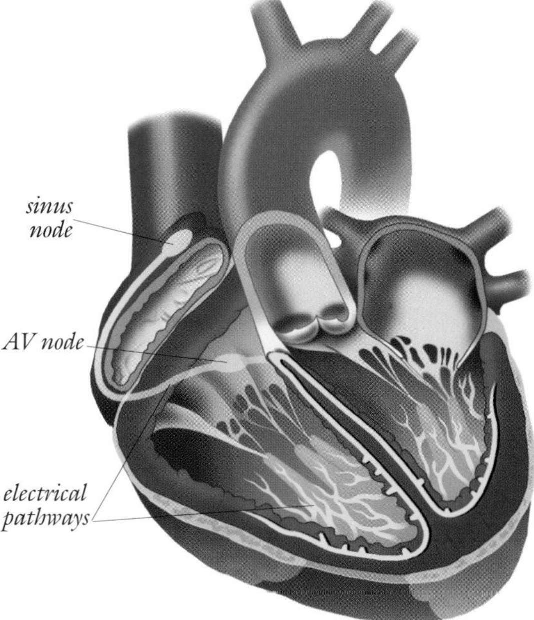


*The heartbeat is controlled by electrical impulses that originate in the sinus node, travel to the AV node, and then along pathways in the heart muscle. En route they stimulate the rhythmic contractions that pump blood first to the lungs and then out of the heart and to the rest of the body.*

## WHAT YOU CAN DO

See your doctor as soon as possible if you notice any change in your heart's usual rhythm or experience chest pain, light-headedness, and other symptoms. If you feel your heart racing, you may be able to slow its beating by holding your breath for a few moments, coughing, taking a slow drink of water, or bathing your face with cold water. If none of these work, try holding your nostrils closed and then forcing air into the closed nostrils. Don't worry if your eardrums seem to "pop" while doing this.

If you have been diagnosed with a cardiac arrhythmia, follow your doctor's instructions for controlling it, as well as the preventive measures outlined below. Call your doctor immediately if you note any change in its usual pattern or experience symptoms. Call 911 or the Emergency Medical Service (EMS) if you witness a person who collapses suddenly. Check for a heartbeat and respiration and, if they are absent, start CPR while waiting for the EMS crew to arrive.

## HOW TO TREAT IT

Treatment varies according to the type of arrhythmia and its severity.

### Medications

- **Beta blockers** slow a fast heartbeat by inhibiting the effects of certain hormones on the heart.
- **Calcium-channel blockers** slow the heartbeat by inhibiting the flow of calcium in and out of cells, thereby changing the heart's electrical properties.
- **Quinidine** (Quinidex) stabilizes irregular heartbeats by acting through the nerves that lead to the heart muscle. Procainamide (Procan SR) and disopyramide (Norpace) are synthetic compounds whose effects on the nerves are similar to quinidine's.
- **Tocainide** (Tonocard) and **mexiletine** (Mexitil) work by suppressing ventricular arrhythmias; they are often used along with other antiarrhythmic drugs.
- **Flecainide** (Tambocor) and **propafenone** (Rythmol) work by slowing the conduction of electrical impulses in the atrioventricular area.

**WARNING!**

***Atrial arrhythmias increase the risk of a stroke because blood tends to pool in the heart and form clots that then travel to the brain. The risk can be lowered by taking Coumadin or another anticoagulant medication.***

Amiodarone (Cordarone) is a very potent antiarrhythmic medication, yet has many serious side effects. It is reserved for only the most serious arrhythmias that cannot be controlled by other drugs.

### Pacemakers

If a slow heartbeat (bradycardia) is debilitating, an artificial pacemaker may help. These small, surgically

**BREAKTHROUGHS!**

**The development of a small implantable defibrillator is providing new hope for people who have a high risk of sudden death from ventricular fibrillation or ventricular tachycardia. The device, called an automatic implantable cardioverter-defibrillator, or AICD, does not prevent life-threatening arrhythmias; instead, it is programmed to detect and stop them within seconds by delivering a series of electrical shocks to the heart.**

## Types of Cardiac Arrhythmias

| SLOW HEARTBEATS (BRADYCARDIA) | |
|---|---|
| Sinus bradycardia | Heart rate that is consistently slower than 60 beats per minute. |
| Sick sinus syndrome | Failure of the sinus node to generate or conduct electrical impulses. |
| Heart block | Malfunction of the conduction of electrical impulses between the heart's upper (atria) and lower (ventricles) chambers. |
| **RAPID HEARTBEATS (TACHYCARDIA)** | |
| Supraventricular tachycardia | Rapid heartbeat arising in the atria or AV node. |
| Atrial flutter | Abnormal current that pushes atrial rate to 250 to 350 beats per minute. |
| Atrial fibrillation | Uncoordinated atrial beats that exceed 350 beats per minute and result in quivering. |
| Paroxysmal supraventricular tachycardia (PSVT) | Sudden increase in heart rate to 140 to 250 beats per minute. |
| Wolff-Parkinson-White syndrome | Recurrent tachycardias caused by abnormal conduction pathways. |
| Premature ventricular contractions | Early or extra beats, often occurring in normal hearts. |
| Ventricular tachycardia | Rapid heartbeat that arises in the ventricles; potentially life-threatening. |
| Ventricular fibrillation | Quivering of the ventricles, which cease to pump blood; can be fatal in minutes. |

implanted devices are about the size of a cigarette lighter and work in much the same way as the heart's natural pacemaker. Its batteries produce electrical impulses that travel through tiny wires attached to the heart and stimulate the muscle to contract. Each pacemaker is programmed according to individual needs; the devices must be checked periodically to make sure they are working properly. Every few years, the batteries are replaced in a surgical procedure usually done on an outpatient basis.

### Surgery

Some arrhythmias are due to the presence of an extra electrical pathway. These may be cured surgically by cutting out or destroying (ablating) the abnormal pathway. This approach is usually reserved for arrhythmias that cannot be controlled by drugs; they may also be considered for young patients who otherwise would have to take powerful drugs throughout life.

## HOW TO PREVENT IT

Do not smoke, and abstain from alcohol; both nicotine and alcohol can provoke arrhythmias. Also cut down on—or even eliminate—caffeine and other stimulants; decaffeinated coffee, tea, and soft drinks are generally harmless. Decongestant ingredients, such as phenylpropanolamine, in many cold and allergy preparations speed up the heartbeat and should be avoided. Finally, make every effort to avoid emotional turmoil and anxiety.

### ALTERNATIVE THERAPIES

**Biofeedback training**

This technique teaches patients how to slow a fast heartbeat, at least temporarily.

**Meditation**

This and other relaxation techniques can help persons with mild arrhythmias slow a fast heartbeat, especially during periods of stress.

# Endocarditis

**SYMPTOMS**

*Symptoms are often vague and vary according to the site and type of heart infection.*

***Acute bacterial endocarditis (ABE):*** *High fever, chest pain, difficulty breathing, rapidly worsening condition that may lead to shock and collapse.*

***Subacute bacterial endocarditis (SBE):*** *Low-grade fever, flulike symptoms including chills, joint pain, fatigue, and malaise; possible stroke, diffuse pain, and blood in the urine.*

***Prosthetic valvular endocarditis (PVE):*** *In addition to symptoms of ABE or SBE, symptoms may include cardiac arrhythmias and other heart abnormalities.*

***Right-sided endocarditis (RSE):*** *Fever, pleurisy-like chest pain that worsens when taking a deep breath or coughing; circulatory problems due to clots (emboli) in the bloodstream, and severe difficulty breathing.*

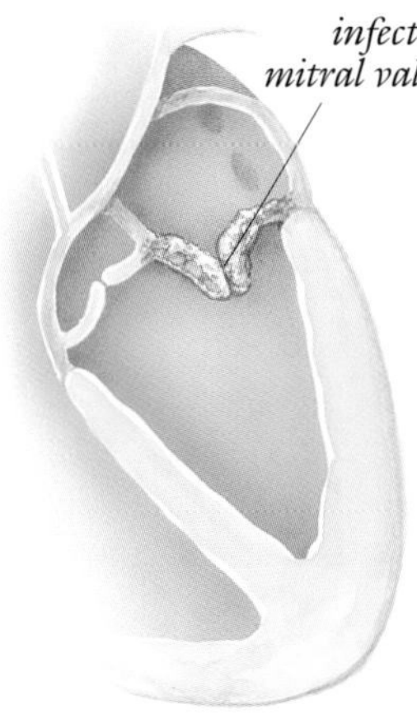


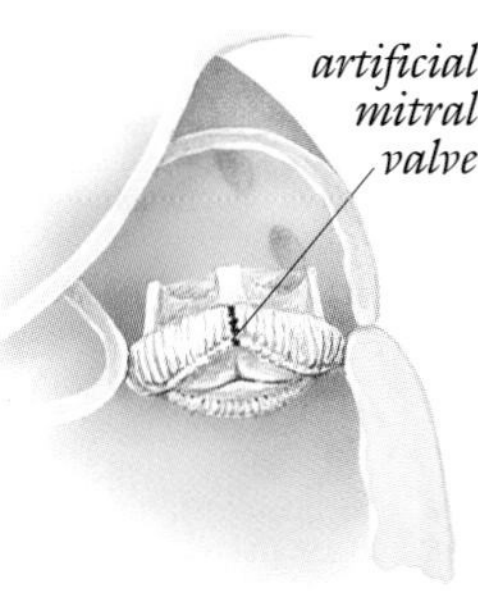


*The mitral valve is especially vulnerable to bacterial endocarditis, which often necessitates replacement with an artificial valve.*

**WHO IS AT RISK**

*Endocarditis, a serious infection and inflammation of the membrane lining the heart's four chambers, almost always develops among persons who have a damaged heart valve or other heart abnormalities. In the past, a history of rheumatic fever was the most common indirect cause of both ABE and SBE; today, the risk is greatest among persons born with a defective heart valve or who have an artificial valve. RSE, which affects the valves on the right side of the heart, develops mostly among intravenous drug users or persons who have an IV line for medical purposes.*

## HOW IT DEVELOPS

All types of endocarditis develop when bacteria (or, less commonly, fungi) infect the inner lining of a heart valve, and form small nodules or polyps that look like miniature cauliflowers. The disease often has an insidious start that mimics flu or other viral infections; early symptoms include fatigue, a low-grade fever, aching joints, and weakness. As the organism colonies grow, they can cause holes in the valve, distort its shape, and disrupt the normal flow of blood through the heart's chambers. A doctor will suspect endocarditis if flulike symptoms are accompanied by a strong heart murmur, an abnormal sound that occurs when blood passes through a diseased valve.

Small clots often form at the site of infection, enter the bloodstream, and then block small blood vessels in other organs. Depending upon the target organ, these clots can cause a stroke, blood in the urine, severe shortness of breath, and limb pain and numbness. If untreated, the infection can lead to numerous complications, including heart failure, blood poisoning (sepsis), meningitis, and death.

## WHAT YOU CAN DO

See a doctor as soon as possible if flulike symptoms persist and worsen, especially if you have an artificial heart valve, heart murmur, or another heart-valve disorder. Follow your doctor's instructions for taking preventive antibiotics (see *How to Prevent It,* below).

## HOW TO TREAT IT

### Medications

The person will be hospitalized and given high doses of intravenous antibiotics (or antifungal drugs if fungi are involved). Penicillin remains a first-choice drug for bacterial endocarditis because it works against a broad spectrum of organisms. If, however, the infecting organisms are penicillin-resistant or the patient is allergic to the drug, high-risk patients may be given powerful antibiotics such as vancomycin and gentamicin.

### Surgery

Valve surgery is sometimes necessary to remove the colonies of bacteria and replace the diseased valve with an artificial one. The operation is usually done after 24 to 72 hours of antibiotic therapy, but if the endocarditis is causing worsening heart failure, it will be done sooner.

## HOW TO PREVENT IT

Prevention is the best approach to endocarditis. If you have an artificial heart valve, a history of a heart murmur, or even a minor condition such as mitral valve prolapse, make sure that your dentist and all your doctors know you are at risk of developing endocarditis. You should always take prophylactic antibiotics before any procedure that can allow bacteria to enter the bloodstream. These include tooth extractions, periodontal treatments, or any other dental procedure that causes bleeding and any surgery or invasive tests involving the respiratory, intestinal, urinary, or reproductive systems. Also call your doctor if you develop a skin or lung infection; prophylactic antibiotics may be advisable to protect against bacterial endocarditis.

**WARNING!**

***Smoldering subacute endocarditis often goes undetected in persons with lowered immunity due to chemotherapy, an organ transplant, or a chronic disease such as AIDS. The disease has also become endemic and a major cause of death among IV drug users, especially those who share needles.***

#### ALTERNATIVE THERAPIES

**Nutraceuticals**

Mushroom and yeast extracts that contain Beta Glucan have been shown to enhance the immune system. A number of studies in Norway and Belgium have demonstrated that Beta 1,3/1,6 Glucan increases resistance against bacterial and viral infections. Studies indicate that an adult dosage of 750 mg a day produces the maximum benefit.

However, these high dosages can be quite expensive, and some manufacturers are offering lower-dose Beta Glucan products that also appear to enhance immunity.

# Heart Attack

## SYMPTOMS

- *Intense, prolonged (more than 15 minutes) chest pain or feeling of heavy pressure; alternatively, pain in the stomach area or back.*
- *Pain originating in the chest and radiating to the shoulder, arm, back, or jaw, usually on the left side.*
- *Shortness of breath and perhaps fainting.*
- *Nausea, vomiting, intense sweating, and anxiety.*

## WHO IS AT RISK

*Heart attack risk factors are divided into two groups: those that are beyond your control and those that can be eliminated or reduced by lifestyle changes. Risk factors over which you have no control include:*

- ***Advancing age.** More than half of all heart attacks and 80 percent of the fatal ones occur after age 65.*
- ***Heredity.** If you have one or more first-degree relatives (mother, father, sister, brother) who have had a heart attack or developed angina prior to age 60.*
- ***Gender.** Although heart attacks are the leading cause of death among both men and women, men are vulnerable at an earlier age. Following menopause, however, the incidence of heart attacks among women increases dramatically.*

*Reducible risk factors include:*

- ***High blood pressure,** which makes the heart work harder, causing it to enlarge and weaken over time.*
- ***High blood cholesterol,** generally defined as above 240 mg/dl (6.2 mmol/l).*
- ***Diabetes,** especially the Type 2 form that develops during adulthood.*
- ***Cigarette smoking,** which is thought to account for one-third of heart-attack deaths.*
- ***Obesity,** defined as a BMI (body mass index) of 30 or higher.*

*Other possible risk factors include a sedentary lifestyle, stress, high blood levels of the proteins homocysteine and fibrinogen, and certain aspects of Type A behavior, such as excessive hostility and anger. Recent studies also implicate chlamydial infections and gum disease (gingivitis), which may allow bacteria to enter the bloodstream and damage the coronary arteries, making them more vulnerable to atherosclerosis.*

### WARNING!

***Women heart-attack victims often experience symptoms different from those of men, such as a stomach- or backache instead of crushing chest pain. Women tend to delay seeking help longer than men, and when they do see a doctor, they are often misdiagnosed. Consequently, the heart-attack mortality rate is actually higher among women than men. All women should learn more about heart disease, which is their No. 1 killer, and not hesitate to seek immediate medical help if symptoms develop.***

## HOW IT DEVELOPS

A heart attack, or myocardial infarction (MI) as it is known medically, occurs when a blockage in a coronary artery results in the death of varying amounts of heart muscle tissue. An MI may also disrupt the heart's electrical system and set the stage for serious or fatal cardiac arrhythmias.

The prospects for recovery are good if the heart attack damages only a small amount of heart muscle, preferably on the back of the heart's right side, and does not disrupt its electrical system. The most serious heart attacks however, are those affecting the left ventricle, the heart's main pumping chamber, because they limit the heart's ability to supply blood to the body. In general, a heart attack that damages 40 percent or more of the heart muscle is likely to be disabling or even fatal.

## WHAT YOU CAN DO

The single most important thing you can do is call 911 or your local EMS and say you may be having a heart attack. Don't waste time calling your doctor; it's critical to get to the hospital as soon as possible. Each year about 24,000 Canadians die from heart attacks; almost half of these deaths occur before the victim reaches the hospital. Many take an antacid for indigestion or wait to see if the symptoms worsen; they don't want to be embarrassed if it's only indigestion or an anxiety attack. Even if they survive, the delay in treatment often results in permanent heart damage that could have been prevented with new drugs and emergency procedures.

While waiting for help to arrive, chew a regular uncoated aspirin and try to stay as quiet and calm as possible. If you have nitroglycerin, place a tablet under your tongue. The aspirin immediately goes to work to prevent new clots from forming; the nitroglycerin lessens the heart's workload and may ease the pain. However, don't try to eat or drink anything.

### BREAKTHROUGHS!

**Left ventricular hypertrophy—a weakening and overgrowth of the muscle forming the heart's main pumping chamber—is a common consequence of a heart attack. A promising new approach calls for removing a wedge of the overgrown heart muscle; the smaller chamber is then able to pump more efficiently, reducing the risk of heart failure and other complications.**

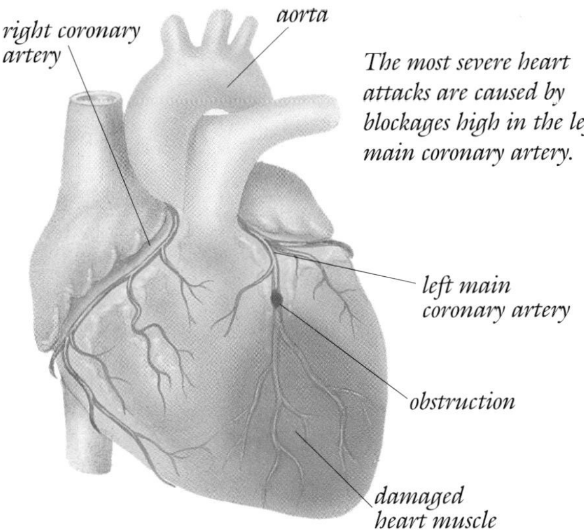


*The most severe heart attacks are caused by blockages high in the left main coronary artery.*

## HOW TO TREAT IT

The EMS crew will quickly evaluate vital signs (blood pressure, heart rate, respiration, and level of consciousness) and, while en route to the hospital, may start emergency treatment following telephone instructions from the emergency room doctors. At the hospital, doctors will do an immediate electrocardiogram (ECG), looking for changes characteristic of a heart attack. They will also order blood tests to look for a rise in enzymes that are released by damaged heart muscle. Other possible tests include echocardiography, the use of sound waves to study the heart's structures and function; and angiography, special X rays taken after injection of a dye into the coronary arteries during cardiac catheterization.

### Medications

Morphine, a tranquilizer, and perhaps nitroglycerin may be given to relieve pain and ease anxiety; supplemental oxygen is administered either through nasal prongs or a mask. Aspirin is given to lower the risk of further clot formation.

More than 90 percent of all heart attacks are due to a blood clot forming in a coronary artery clogged with fatty plaque. The introduction of thrombolytic therapy to dissolve these clots has reduced hospital heart-attack mortality by 30 to 50 percent; it can also prevent permanent tissue death (infarction) if given within the first six or seven hours of an MI. The most benefit, however, is achieved if the clot-dissolving drugs are given within the first three hours.

Other medications given within the first few hours include beta blockers and angiotensin converting enzyme (ACE) inhibitors, which reduce the heart's workload and lower the risk of death. In fact, a 1999 study found that one ACE inhibitor, ramipril (Altace), cut the risk of death from heart attacks and strokes by 20 to 25 percent.

### Surgery

Two procedures may limit the damage of a heart attack and even be life-saving in some circumstances:

- **Angioplasty,** a procedure in which a thin, balloon-tipped tube (catheter) is inserted into an incision in the groin or arm and threaded through the arteries until it reaches the site of the blocked coronary artery. The balloon is then inflated to reopen the artery and allow blood to flow through it. This procedure should only be done by highly skilled doctors at a hospital with a good success record.
- **Coronary bypass surgery,** in which segments of healthy blood vessels from elsewhere in the body are attached to the heart to increase circulation to the damaged heart muscle. This operation is usually done during the recovery period, or even before a heart attack in patients with worsening angina and other symptoms that are not controlled by medication. Sometimes, however, it is done on an emergency basis if a patient has suffered a massive heart attack and has very low blood pressure (hypotension) or shock.

### Recovery and rehabilitation

As soon as possible, patients are encouraged to get out of bed and move about. Many patients who suffer an uncomplicated heart attack—especially those who are successfully treated with clot-dissolving drugs—are discharged from the hospital in five days, and sometimes even sooner. If possible, they are enrolled in a cardiac rehabilitation program that includes supervised exercise, dietary education, group and family therapy, smoking cessation clinics, and other lifestyle changes to lower the risk of another heart attack.

## HOW TO PREVENT IT

Heart-attack mortality has been reduced dramatically in the last 30 years, thanks largely to a combination of risk-factor reduction and improved treatments. Proven preventive measures include:

- Reduction of elevated blood cholesterol and high blood pressure and control of diabetes.
- Low-dose aspirin therapy (80 to 135 mg of aspirin a day) for some people.
- Stopping smoking or, better still, not starting.
- Exercising for at least 20 to 30 minutes three or four times a week.

In addition, a number of studies show that a glass of wine—either red or white—a day lowers heart-attack risk. Caution is needed, however; excessive alcohol damages the heart and many other organs.

#### ALTERNATIVE THERAPIES

The alternative therapies recommended for angina also apply to heart attack; for details, see p 132.

# Heart Failure

## SYMPTOMS

- *Waking up at night with a sensation of choking or smothering.*
- *Rapid unexplained weight gain and swollen ankles and feet, especially at the end of the day.*
- *Chest discomfort, rapid heartbeat, wheezing and increasing shortness of breath, coughing and bloody sputum.*
- *Bluish tinge of the lips and nails.*
- *Persistent fatigue.*

## WHO IS AT RISK

*Between 200,000 and 300,000 Canadians suffer from chronic heart failure, which develops when the heart cannot pump enough blood to meet the body's needs for oxygen and other nutrients. It is a common consequence of a heart attack, heart-valve disease, congenital heart defects, clogged coronary arteries, untreated high blood pressure, and cardiomyopathy, a disease affecting the heart muscle.*

## HOW IT DEVELOPS

The typical first symptoms are swollen ankles and feet during the day and a sensation of choking or not being able to breathe after a few hours of sleep. These symptoms are signs of fluid building up in the limbs or lungs instead of circulating through the body.

Elevating the legs reduces the swelling, but lying down causes the lungs to become waterlogged, a condition called pulmonary edema. There may also be an uncomfortable feeling of pressure or tightness in the chest, and even modest exertion brings on debilitating fatigue. X rays, echocardiography, and other imaging studies will show an enlarged heart and fluid in the lungs. In time, the edema becomes more widespread, leading to an uncomfortable feeling of fullness and tenderness in the neck and abdomen.

## WHAT YOU CAN DO

To prevent ankle and foot swelling, avoid standing or sitting in one position for long periods. Rest in a semi-sitting position several times a day with your legs elevated. Elevate the head of your bed six inches or so, and if you still awaken with a feeling of being unable to breathe, use several firm pillows under your upper body so that you sleep in a semi-sitting position. Some people end up sleeping in a comfortable chair rather than in bed.

Eliminate as much salt from the diet as possible. Do not smoke and abstain from alcohol; both nicotine and alcohol increase the heart's workload and also damage the heart muscle. Exercise conditioning may improve endurance, but check with your doctor first.

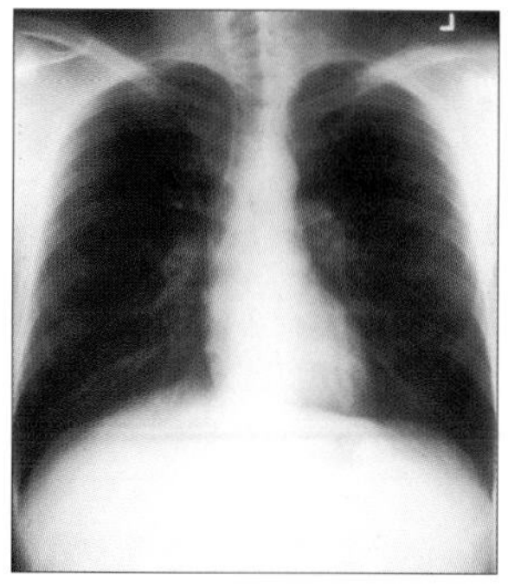

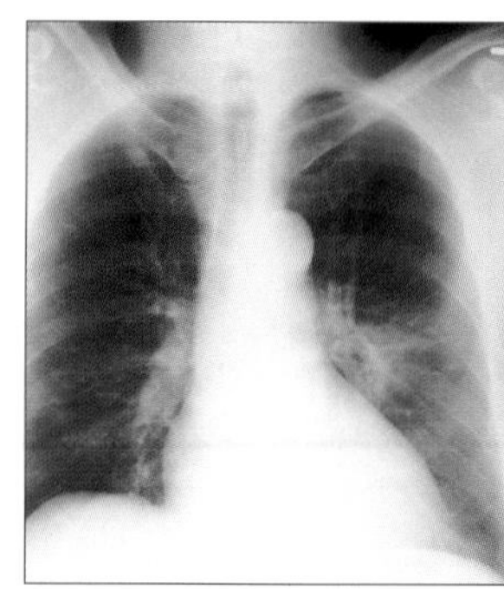

*X ray of a normal-sized heart (left). X ray showing an enlarged heart and fluid in the lungs (right).*

## HOW TO TREAT IT

### Medications

- **Diuretics** are prescribed to reduce swelling by ridding the body of excess fluids.
- **Digoxin,** one of the most common treatments for heart failure, works by strengthening the heartbeat.
- **Vasodilators** reduce the heart's workload by widening blood vessels; the first choice is usually an angiotensin converting enzyme (ACE) inhibitor, which may be prescribed along with a diuretic. (A 1999 study found that daily use of one ACE inhibitor, ramipril (Altace), cut the heart attack and stroke death rate by 20 to 25 percent.)
- **Beta blockers** decrease symptoms, improve quality of life, and decrease mortality in patients with moderate to severe heart failure.
- **Antiarrhythmic drugs** may be added to the regimen if an irregular heartbeat interferes with heart function.

### Surgery

Aside from a heart transplant—the treatment of last resort—there are no operations for heart failure itself. But surgery, such as a coronary bypass operation or heart-valve replacement, may be considered to correct contributing problems.

### BREAKTHROUGHS!

**Promising experimental treatments for heart failure include the following:**

- **Dynamic cardiomyoplasty, in which strips of muscle from elsewhere in the body are wrapped around the heart to boost its pumping action. Early studies show improvement in 80 percent of patients.**
- **Implantable pumping devices, which assist the left ventricle in forcing blood out of the heart, are being used experimentally to sustain patients awaiting a heart transplant. New ventricular-assist devices are also being developed that may eliminate the need for a transplant.**

## HOW TO PREVENT IT

Some types of heart failure, such as heart-muscle disease caused by a viral infection, cannot be prevented. In general, however, reducing cardiovascular risk factors can help; these include not smoking, using alcohol only in moderation, normalizing high blood pressure, exercising regularly, and maintaining ideal weight. In recent years, cocaine abuse has resulted in a rise in premature heart failure, especially among young people.

### ALTERNATIVE THERAPIES

**Note:** Alternative therapies should be used only as an adjunct to treatment prescribed by a doctor.

**WARNING!**

***Even small overdoses of digoxin can cause serious toxicity. Frequent doctor visits are necessary to adjust the dosage; symptoms to watch for include nausea, vomiting, loss of appetite, diarrhea, confusion, and impaired vision.***

**Herbal medicine**

Hawthorn extract taken in daily dosages of 300 to 450 mg may work against heart failure in several ways: it is a diuretic that helps lower high blood pressure and prevent a buildup of excess body fluid, and it also strengthens the heartbeat. People taking dixogin or anticoagulants must discuss hawthorn use with their doctor. Dandelion tea is also a diuretic that may reduce ankle and foot swelling.

# Heart-Valve Disorders

### SYMPTOMS

- *Chest pain and palpitations.*
- *Shortness of breath.*
- *Dizziness, fatigue, possible fainting.*
- *Heart murmurs, clicks, and other abnormal sounds.*
- *Increased vulnerability to migraine headaches.*
- *Possible uncomfortable fluttering in the chest and neck.*

### WHO IS AT RISK

*Congenital heart defects are among the most common causes of heart-valve disorders. In the past, rheumatic fever was a major cause, but this is now rare in developed countries thanks to the use of antibiotics to treat strep throat. A heart attack may damage the heart valves; other possible causes include untreated high blood pressure and endocarditis, a heart infection. Some inflammatory disorders, such as rheumatoid arthritis, spinal arthritis (ankylosing spondylitis), lupus, and ulcerative colitis, also increase the risk of some forms of valvular disease.*

## HOW IT DEVELOPS

There are two major types of valvular disease—**regurgitation**, in which the faulty valve does not close properly and allows a backflow of blood, and **stenosis,** in which the valve is stiff and does not open properly. The mitral and aortic valves, which are located on the left side of the heart, are the most common sites of valvular disease, which usually develops slowly and is often without symptoms or other problems. Sometimes, however, valvular disease is apparent shortly after birth and, depending upon the valve involved, it progresses rapidly.

As valvular disease worsens, normal blood flow is disrupted, resulting in chest pain, shortness of breath, fatigue, dizziness, and other symptoms. Severe valvular disease can lead to heart failure; another danger is an increased vulnerability to endocarditis, a serious infection of the membrane lining the heart's chambers.

Mitral valve prolapse (MVP), one of the most common—and benign—valvular disorders, affects 2 to 5 percent of women. The mitral valve has two tiny flaps, or leaflets, that open and close to regulate blood flow between the left atrium and left ventricle. In MVP, the leaflets fail to close properly, allowing blood to leak back into the atrium. Most people with MVP are unaware of the condition; others experience chest pain, palpitations, fatigue, shortness of breath, dizziness, and increased migraine headaches. In rare instances, the valve may rupture, a life-threatening medical emergency.

## WHAT YOU CAN DO

Do not smoke, and abstain from alcohol, or use it only in moderation. Mild exercise is usually tolerated, but avoid strenuous exertion. If you have been diagnosed with any

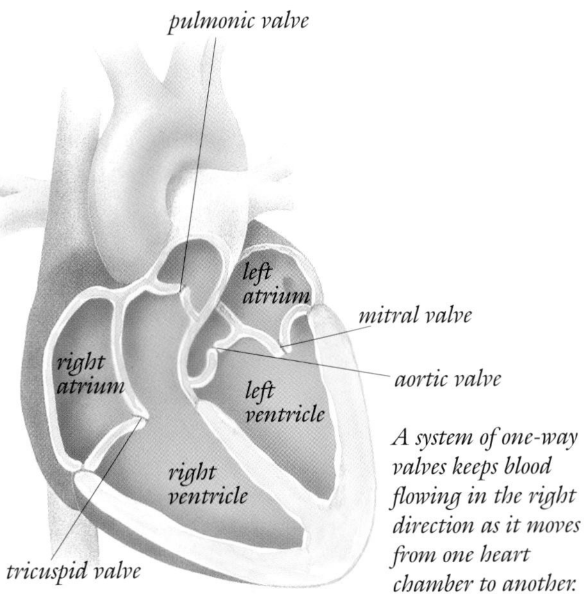


*A system of one-way valves keeps blood flowing in the right direction as it moves from one heart chamber to another.*

type of heart-valve disease, inform your dentist, doctors, and other health-care providers so they can prescribe preventive antibiotics before any procedure that increases the risk of endocarditis (see also *Endocarditis*, p 134).

## HOW TO TREAT IT

### Medications

Beta blockers or calcium-channel blockers may be prescribed to reduce the heart rate and control palpitations. A daily dose of aspirin or a stronger anticoagulant, such as warfarin (Coumadin), may be prescribed to reduce the risk of stroke and other complications from blood clots. Depending upon symptoms, other possible medications include: digoxin, which strengthens the heartbeat; vasodilators, which increase blood flow by widening the arteries; diuretics, which reduce blood volume; and antiarrhythmic drugs, which regulate an irregular heartbeat.

### Surgery

- **Balloon valvuloplasty,** in which a balloon-tipped catheter is inserted into a stiffened (stenosed) valve. The balloon is then inflated to widen the valve and allow normal blood flow. This procedure works best in children, but it may also be done in older patients with severe stenosis.
- **Surgical repair,** in which a surgeon stretches the opening of a stenosed valve, stitches tears, tightens loose leaflets, or removes colonies of bacteria or fungi.
- **Valve replacement,** in which the diseased heart valve is removed and replaced with a mechanical device made of plastic, metal alloys, and other materials, or a biological valve, which is made from human or animal tissue. Mechanical devices are more durable and last longer than biological ones, but clots tend to form in them; therefore, anticoagulant therapy, usually with warfarin (Coumadin), is necessary as a preventive measure.

**WARNING!**

***Even mild heart-valve disease can cause orthostatic hypotension, a sudden drop in blood pressure when abruptly changing position, such as arising from bed or a chair. To minimize dizziness and the risk of fainting, rise from a chair slowly and, when getting out of bed, sit at the side for a few moments before attempting to stand up.***

## HOW TO PREVENT IT

Although rheumatic fever is now rare, it can still occur if a child's strep throat is untreated or antibiotics are stopped too soon. Preventive antibiotics should also be taken before dental work, surgery, and other procedures that cause bleeding by anyone who has MVP or other types of heart murmurs.

**BREAKTHROUGHS!**

**Researchers at Children's Hospital in Boston have successfully grown new lamb heart valves in a test tube. The scientists use cells from a lamb's artery to grow a mass in a test tube. They then attach the mass of cells to biodegradable polymers that are arranged in the shape of a heart valve. Within two weeks, the cells completely envelop the polymer scaffold, which then decays. The new valve is then used to replace the corresponding one in the lamb's heart. The researchers estimate that by 2005 they will have perfected human valves grown in a test tube.**

### ALTERNATIVE THERAPIES

**Nutraceuticals**

Vitamin E, in dosages of 400 to 800 IU a day, helps prevent abnormal blood clotting; check with your doctor first if you are taking aspirin or other blood-thinning medication. Magnesium helps stabilize irregular heartbeats; 400 mg a day is the recommended dosage. People with kidney disease should talk to their doctor before taking magnesium. Other supplements that benefit heart function include folic acid (400 to 800 micrograms a day); vitamin $B_{12}$ (1000 micrograms a day), and 1000 to 2000 mg a day of vitamin C (no more than 500 mg a day if you have kidney stones, kidney disease, or hemochromatosis). Calcium, in doses of 1000 to 1500 mg a day, may also promote good heart function. People who have thyroid or kidney disease should check with their doctor before taking calcium. In addition, the diet should include at least five (and preferably nine or more) daily servings of fruits and vegetables.

# Pericarditis

### SYMPTOMS

***Acute pericarditis:*** *Sharp pain in the center of the chest that worsens when taking a deep breath, coughing, or moving the upper body; pain may mimic that of angina or a heart attack.*

***Chronic pericarditis:*** *Shortness of breath, swelling of the feet, ankles, and abdomen; other symptoms similar to those of heart failure.*

***Pericardial effusion:*** *Dizziness, light-headedness, drop in blood pressure, possible fainting.*

### WHO IS AT RISK

***Acute pericarditis****—an inflammation of the membrane surrounding the heart—is usually caused by an infection; it may also develop in association with rheumatoid arthritis, rheumatic fever, lupus, kidney failure, scleroderma, and certain tumors. Sometimes pericarditis is a complication of a heart attack, heart surgery, or a chest injury.*

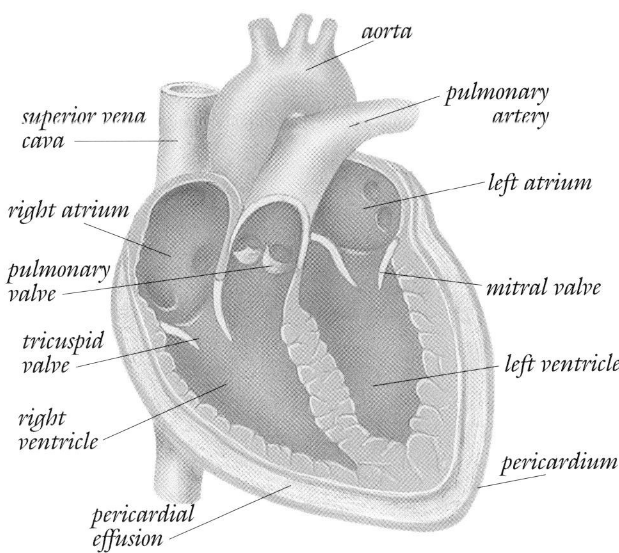


*The major danger of pericarditis is an accumulation of fluid in the space between the pericardium—the membrane covering the heart—and the heart itself.*

***Chronic pericarditis** develops slowly and is usually caused by a chronic infection, such as tuberculosis. It can lead to **constrictive pericarditis,** which squeezes the heart and interferes with its ability to receive and pump blood.*

***Pericardial effusion,** an accumulation of fluid under the pericardium, is a complication of acute pericarditis.*

## HOW IT DEVELOPS

**Acute pericarditis** comes on suddenly and its symptoms are often mistaken for a heart attack or angina. But unlike these heart disorders, pericarditis is exacerbated by movement, such as breathing deeply or coughing. Viral pericarditis usually clears up in a few weeks, but as with other forms, it can result in pericardial effusion.

**Chronic pericarditis** usually does not produce symptoms in its early stages, but long-term inflammation can cause the pericardium to thicken and shrink. This can result in **constrictive pericarditis**, which can prevent the heart from expanding enough to fill with blood. In effect, the tightening pericardium reduces the amount of blood that the heart can pump into the circulation, resulting in symptoms of heart failure—shortness of breath and swelling (edema) due to a buildup of fluid in the body.

## WHAT YOU CAN DO

See your doctor as soon as possible, especially if you develop shortness of breath, dizziness, or swelling. Most cases of pericarditis are uncomplicated and resolve themselves in a few weeks. In the meantime, aspirin, ibuprofen, or other nonsteroidal anti-inflammatory drugs (NSAIDs) can relieve pain and inflammation. To minimize discomfort, avoid abrupt movements and hug a pillow to your chest when coughing. Stay warm and rest as much as possible. A salt-restricted diet can help reduce edema from constrictive pericarditis.

## HOW TO TREAT IT

### Tests

A doctor can usually diagnose pericarditis by listening for a characteristic rubbing sound through a stethoscope; tests generally include a chest X ray, an electrocardiogram (ECG), and an echocardiogram, the use of sound waves to map the heart's structures. Blood tests and cultures, and perhaps obtaining a sample of pericardial fluid, may be needed to identify the cause.

### Medications

Pain is treated according to its severity; nonprescription painkillers are often sufficient, but some patients require morphine or other narcotic medications. A diuretic may be given to reduce edema and pleural effusion; corticosteroids may be prescribed to control the inflammation, especially if it is due to a heart attack. Bacterial infections are treated with antibiotics.

### Surgery

Needle aspiration may be necessary to remove the fluid of pericardial effusion. A surgeon will insert a hollow needle between two ribs and into the pericardium to drain off the fluid; the procedure is done using ultrasound as a guide to prevent damaging the heart.

Severe constrictive pericarditis may require surgical removal of the pericardium, especially if it is producing symptoms of heart failure. This is a major operation that requires opening the chest to expose the heart. Afterward, morphine or other strong painkillers may be necessary until the chest incision heals.

## HOW TO PREVENT IT

Most cases cannot be prevented, but prompt diagnosis can reduce the risk of complications.

### WARNING!

***Severe pericardial effusion can block the return of blood to the heart from the veins, leading to cardiac compression (tamponade) and falling blood pressure. Removal of the pericardial fluid is necessary to prevent shock from occurring.***

### ALTERNATIVE THERAPIES

**Herbal medicine**

The therapies recommended for heart failure also apply to heart attack; for details, see p 139.

**Nutraceuticals**

Calcium, in doses of 1000 to 1500 mg a day, may have a diuretic effect and promote overall heart function. People who have thyroid or kidney disease should check with their doctor first.

# THE DIGESTIVE ORGANS

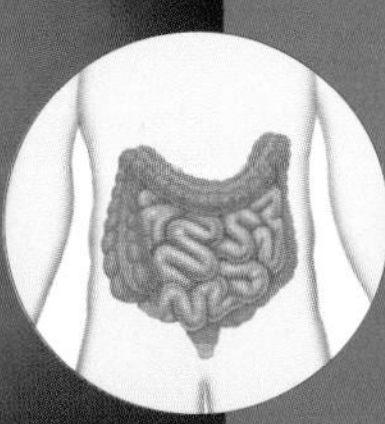

# The Esophagus

*Swallowing sets off an automatic process that propels food from the mouth, into the esophagus, and then on to the stomach. Pain and other problems arise when food gets stuck in the esophagus or when stomach contents flow back up into it.*

## Cancer of the Esophagus

### SYMPTOMS

- *Pain and difficulty swallowing (dysphagia).*
- *Persistent pain in the throat or upper back.*
- *Severe weight loss.*
- *Hoarseness, chronic cough; coughing up blood.*
- *Enlarged lymph nodes, especially over the collarbone.*

### WHO IS AT RISK

*Smoking and heavy alcohol consumption greatly increase the risk of esophageal cancer; nicotine and alcohol together seem to produce the condition. While fairly common in some parts of the world, esophageal cancer accounts for less than one percent of all cancers in North America. It affects men about twice as often as women, the overall incidence being highest among older (over age 60) men of African descent who both drink and smoke. Also at increased risk are women who have had radiation treatments for breast cancer and persons with a history of chronic reflux (a backup of stomach acids into the esophagus) and esophageal narrowing (stricture) due to inflammation, ulceration, or swallowing a caustic substance.*

### BREAKTHROUGHS!

**A number of experimental treatments holds new hope for patients with advanced esophageal cancer. Patients with esophageal cancer are urged to investigate clinical studies; possibilities include:**

- **Multimodality therapy, in which surgery, radiation, and chemotherapy are used in different sequences. For example, radiation and chemotherapy may be given before rather than after surgery, which is the more common approach**
- **Photodynamic therapy, in which a light-sensitive drug is injected into the body. Two days later, after the drug has been excreted by normal cells, a tube containing a tiny laser is inserted into the esophagus near the tumor site. The laser then pulses a bright light for 15 minutes; the light activates the drug, which destroys the cancer cells.**

## HOW IT DEVELOPS

Most esophageal cancer starts in the surface cells that line the esophagus; less often, the tumor arises in the mucous glands. As the tumor grows, it tends to encircle the esophagus and invade the underlying muscle tissue; as the esophagus becomes progressively narrowed, pain and difficulty swallowing develop. The nearby lymph nodes over the left collarbone may swell; if untreated, the cancer eventually spreads to nearby organs and also travels through the lymph system and circulation to other parts of the body.

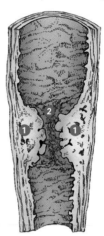

*A cancer growing into the esophagus (1) narrows the passageway (2) and makes swallowing painful and difficult.*

## WHAT YOU CAN DO

See a doctor as soon as possible if you develop a persistent sore throat and hoarseness, and are coughing up blood. Esophageal cancer usually is not detected until it is too advanced to cure; anyone with a long history of both drinking and smoking should undergo diagnostic tests if they develop any symptoms suggesting esophageal cancer (See *How to Treat It*, below).

While undergoing treatment, you may need to adopt a liquid diet or even have a feeding tube inserted directly into the stomach to supply nutritional needs. It is imperative that you abstain from smoking and alcohol, both of which exacerbate the cancer and also hinder treatment.

## HOW TO TREAT IT

### Tests

Diagnostic studies for esophageal cancer include one or more of the following:

- **CT or MRI scans,** which produce two-dimensional images of internal structures.
- **Contrast X-ray studies,** which are taken after swallowing barium, a chalky substance that coats the esophagus to make its structures more visible.
- **Exfoliative cytology,** in which cells taken from the esophagus lining are studied under a microscope.

- **Endoscopic ultrasound,** in which an ultrasound sensor is inserted into the esophagus through a viewing tube to study the depth of any growth.
- **Esophagoscopy,** examination of the esophagus using a lighted viewing tube (endoscope).

## Medications

At some point, most esophageal cancers are treated with anticancer drugs; they may be given alone in inoperable cancer or administered in combination with surgery and/or radiation. Mild pain may be controlled with nonprescription painkillers or codeine; as the cancer advances, morphine or other more powerful narcotic medications may be needed.

## Surgery

Early esophageal cancer that has not invaded the muscle tissue may be cured by removing the diseased portion and rejoining the two ends. This is more likely to be successful if the cancer is in the lower portion of the esophagus. Surgery may be followed by radiation and/or chemotherapy to kill any remaining cancer cells. Unfortunately, very few esophageal cancers are detected in this early, highly treatable stage.

Sometimes radiation treatments are administered before surgery to shrink a large tumor and make it easier to remove. If the entire esophagus must be removed, a new food passageway may be created by moving the stomach up or using a portion of the small intestine or colon to reconstruct a tube that links the throat and stomach.

**PATHWAY TO THE STOMACH**

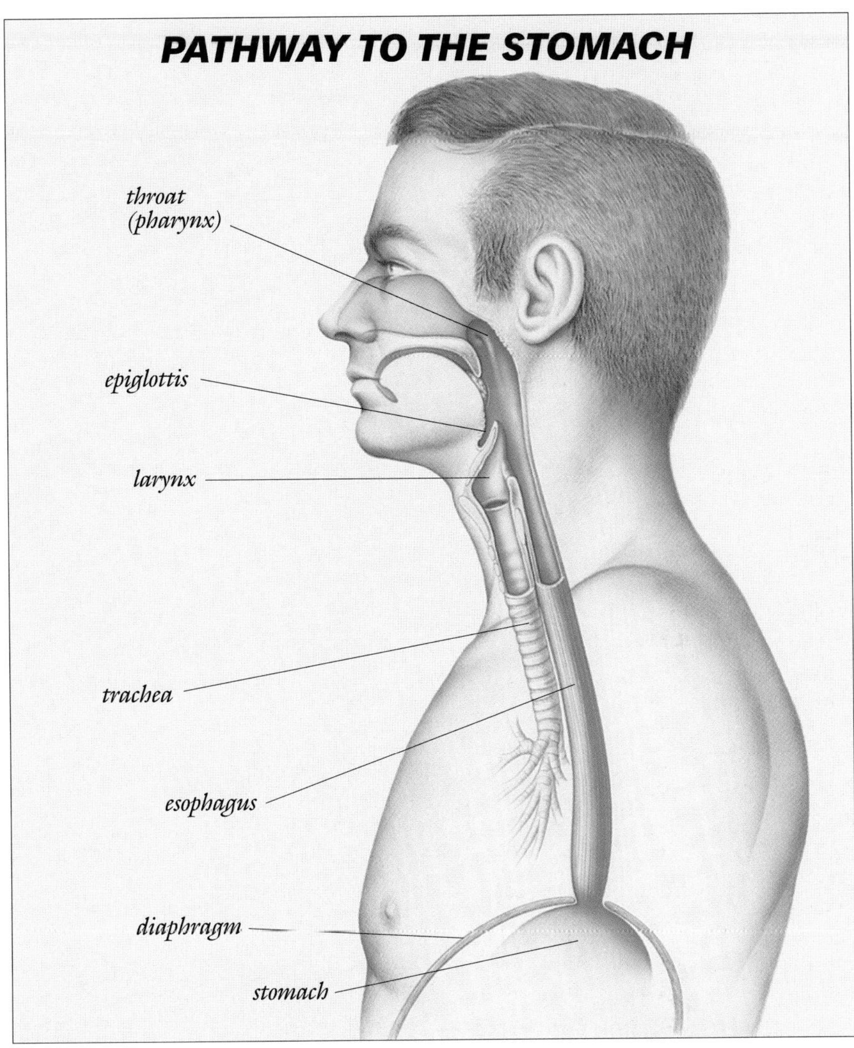


*The esophagus, a 10-inch muscular tube, lies just behind the windpipe (trachea). When swallowing, a tiny flap of cartilage called the epiglottis acts as a lid over the windpipe to prevent food from going down the wrong tube.*

## Palliative therapies

An inoperable tumor that is blocking the esophagus and preventing swallowing may be relieved temporarily by inserting a tube through the cancer from above to allow liquids to flow into the stomach.

A newer approach, developed by doctors at the University of Vienna, calls for implanting special expanding devices, called nitinol stents, in the esophagus to keep it open and allow patients to swallow normally. A laser—an intense light beam that vaporizes tissues—is sometimes used to create an opening through the cancer, allowing fluids and perhaps food to pass through it. These approaches do not treat the underlying cancer, but they ease symptoms and allow patients to eat and drink more normally. If they cannot be done, a feeding tube can be inserted directly into the stomach through a small abdominal incision. Nutritional supplements are then poured into the tube.

**WARNING!**

***A Philadelphia study found that 15 percent of patients who use nonprescription antacids to treat themselves for chronic heartburn are actually suffering from esophageal cancer. Frequently recurring heartburn should be checked by a doctor to rule out cancer.***

## HOW TO PREVENT IT

Abstaining from smoking and heavy alcohol use are the best approaches to preventing esophageal cancer. Other possible preventive measures include prompt treatment of esophageal narrowing, inflammation, and chronic heartburn from gastroesophageal reflux disease (GERD).

### ALTERNATIVE THERAPIES

**Note:** There is no alternative treatment for the cancer itself; the following may be helpful adjunct therapies.

**Herbal medicine**

Numerous studies in China indicate that green tea, which is high in anticancer compounds, lowers the risk of some cancers, especially those of the esophagus and other digestive organs. Slippery elm, ginger, or mullein teas soothe a sore throat, and may help ease discomfort of radiation or chemotherapy administered to the larynx and upper part of the esophagus. Do not take on an empty stomach.

**Meditation and guided imagery**

These self-help techniques are taught at many cancer treatment centers to help control pain. Other helpful techniques include self-hypnosis and biofeedback training.

# Esophageal Spasm/Achalasia

### SYMPTOMS

- *Pain centered in the upper chest, perhaps radiating to the neck, jaw, and arms.*
- *Pain and difficulty when swallowing.*
- *Uncomfortable sensation of food stuck in the throat.*
- *Chronic cough, especially at night.*

### WHO IS AT RISK

*Recurring esophageal spasms can develop at any age, but they typically begin between ages 20 and 40; men and women are affected equally. People who suffer from chronic heartburn or indigestion have an increased risk of spasms, which are often aggravated by stress and very hot or cold liquids.*

### BREAKTHROUGHS!

**A new treatment of refractory spasms or achalasia uses injections of botulinum toxin (Botox), the nerve toxin that causes botulism. Tiny amounts of the Botox are injected into the muscle controlling the lower esophageal sphincter, causing it to relax. This works in 70 to 80 percent of patients. However, the effects wear off in 6 to 12 months, at which time the injection can be repeated.**

## HOW IT DEVELOPS

The cause of primary esophageal spasm is unknown. Chest pain, which is often mistaken for a heart attack, develops when the muscles that normally contract in orderly waves, called *peristalsis*, suddenly go into a spasm. These spasms generally occur while eating or drinking, prompting the sphincter muscles, which allow food and fluids to pass into the stomach, to clamp shut. This results in difficulty swallowing and a sensation that something is stuck in the throat.

Over time, the spasms may evolve into achalasia, a disorder marked by faulty communication between the esophageal muscles and the nerves that control them. The esophagus bulges outward and then narrows just above the lower esophageal sphincter. In very severe cases, the esophagus may rupture due to excessive pressure caused by the distended esophagus and constricted sphincter.

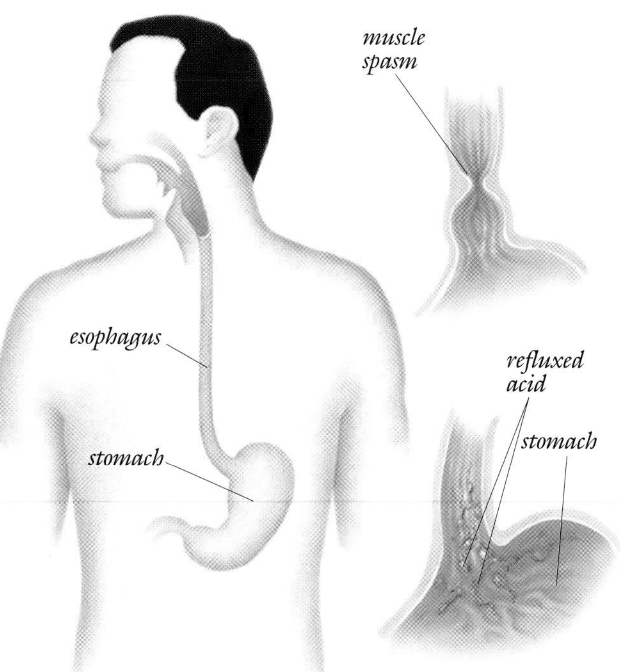


*A muscle spasm in the lower esophagus (upper right) can allow acid to flow from the stomach into the esophagus, resulting in inflammation and ulcers.*

## WHAT YOU CAN DO

If you are diagnosed with esophageal spasms or achalasia, eat slowly and chew your food thoroughly before swallowing. Switching to a liquid or soft-food diet may help. Antacids may also provide relief, especially if the spasms are related to gastroesophageal reflux disease (GERD) or indigestion. If food seems to be stuck in your throat, an exercise called a *Valsalva maneuver* may help pass it to the stomach. Take a deep breath, hold your nostrils closed, clamp your mouth shut, and then try to forcefully expel the air from your lungs. You may feel your ears pop, but this is harmless.

## HOW TO TREAT IT

### Tests

Diagnostic studies are done to rule out cancer and other possible causes of the symptoms, and to pinpoint the areas of spasm. These may include:

- **Upper GI series,** in which X rays are taken after swallowing barium, a chalky substance that coats the esophagus. In achalasia, the esophagus will appear dilated for some or all of its length and then narrowed just above the lower sphincter that separates it from the stomach.
- **Esophageal manometry,** a study that measures muscle contractions and sphincter pressure.
- **Esophagoscopy,** in which a viewing tube is passed into the esophagus to detect areas of spasm. It can also rule out other disorders, such as cancer or esophageal narrowing due to inflammation, ulceration, and polyps.

**WARNING!**

***Any unexplained chest pain needs to be checked by a doctor to rule out more serious disorders, such as heart disease and cancer.***

### Medications

Calcium-channel blockers, which inhibit smooth-muscle contractions, work in most cases of uncomplicated spasms. Other drugs that may be tried include nitroglycerin and anticholinergics. Severe pain may require codeine or stronger narcotic medications; however, these should be used for only short periods.

### Surgery

If the problem is due to obstruction or stiffening (stenosis) of the lower esophageal sphincter, treatment may entail forceful or pneumatic dilation. A special dilating instrument is passed through the esophagus and activated when it reaches the sphincter to force it open.

If dilation and other therapies fail to help, a procedure called a *Heller myotomy* may be performed. This operation involves cutting muscle fibers in the lower esophageal sphincter.

## HOW TO PREVENT IT

There are no specific preventive measures, although some people find that avoiding stressful situations helps reduce the incidence of spasms.

### ALTERNATIVE THERAPIES

**Relaxation therapies**

Meditation, self-hypnosis, and other relaxation therapies may help prevent stress-related esophageal spasms.

# Heartburn/Reflux

**SYMPTOMS**

- *Burning pain in the upper chest that may radiate to the throat and jaw; it usually develops after eating.*
- *Burning chest pain that awakens you at night.*
- *Less commonly, persistent mild abdominal pain.*
- *Belching, regurgitation, and a bitter taste in the mouth.*
- *Possible difficulty swallowing and vomiting.*

**WHO IS AT RISK**

*Almost half of all adults experience heartburn occasionally, but for some it is a daily ordeal. It occurs at all ages, but is most common among middle-aged adults. Possible contributing factors include obesity, smoking, alcohol use, consuming large amounts of coffee or other caffeinated drinks, a high-fat diet, and eating a large meal shortly before going to bed.*

## HOW IT DEVELOPS

Heartburn is most often precipitated by gastroesophageal reflux disease (GERD), in which gastric juices and other stomach contents flow backward into the esophagus. This is usually due to a weakening of the muscular ring (the lower esophageal sphincter) that opens to allow food and fluids to pass into the stomach, and then shuts to prevent a backflow. Reflux may also be due to a hiatal hernia, a condition in which the upper part of the stomach pushes through the opening in the diaphragm—the heavy muscle that separates the chest and abdominal cavities (see *How a Hiatal Hernia Hurts*, p 148).

Whatever the cause, the results are the same: the digestive acids irritate the esophagus and, in time, can result in ulceration, erosion, scarring, and narrowing. It also increases the risk of esophageal bleeding, rupture, and even cancer; chronic inflammation may spread to nearby lung tissue and cause breathing problems.

## WHAT YOU CAN DO

See a doctor if you suffer from recurring heartburn. In the meantime, a nonprescription antacid may bring relief. However, do not try to self-treat recurring heartburn; the symptoms may be due to a more serious disorder.

**BREAKTHROUGHS!**

**Powerful new drugs that inhibit gastric acid production have revolutionized the treatment of esophageal ulcers and erosion caused by chronic reflux. Four to eight weeks of daily treatment with omeprazole (Losec) or lansoprazole (Prevacid) heal the erosion in most patients.**

## HOW A HIATAL HERNIA HURTS

Normally, the stomach and esophagus are separated by the diaphragm, the wall of muscle between the chest and abdominal cavities. The lowermost part of the esophagus passes through a small opening in the diaphragm, called the hiatus (far left).

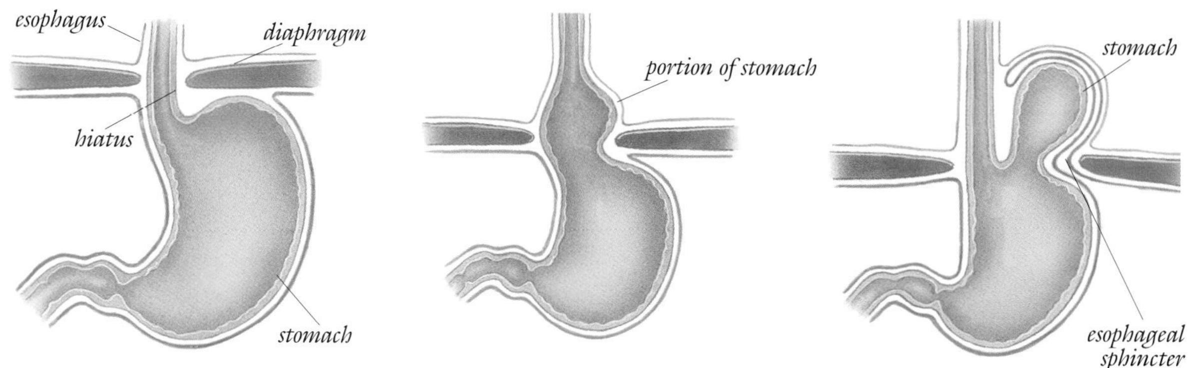


Stretching or weakening of the hiatus allows a portion of the stomach to bulge upward through the opening, permitting digestive juices and other stomach contents to flow into the esophagus, as shown in the center. Sometimes the hiatal opening is large enough to allow herniation of not only the uppermost part of the stomach but also the lower esophagus and its sphincter, as illustrated at the far right. This type of hernia is potentially serious because blood flow to the herniated portion may be cut off, raising the risk of strangulation or rupture.

## HOW TO TREAT IT

### Medications

Uncomplicated GERD and heartburn can usually be controlled by self-care and nonprescription antacids. If prescription medications are needed, doctors usually start with a histamine ($H_2$) blocker, such as cimetidine (Tagamet), ranitidine (Zantac), or famotidine (Pepcid), which may be given along with metoclopramide (Reglan) or other drugs that improve sphincter tone and hasten stomach emptying into the small intestine. Newer, more powerful medications are prescribed if GERD has caused esophageal inflammation and erosion; these include omeprazole (Losec) and lansoprazole (Prevacid).

### Surgery

Severe esophageal bleeding or a larger hiatal hernia may require surgical repair. Other complications of chronic GERD, such as esophageal narrowing (stricture) and ulceration, may also be treated surgically. Most of these operations can be performed using laparoscopic techniques, in which a flexible viewing tube with a tiny video camera is inserted into the esophagus. A surgeon can then manipulate tiny instruments through the laparoscope.

## HOW TO PREVENT IT

A nonprescription antacid taken before a meal may help prevent heartburn. Eat small, frequent meals, and avoid bending over or lying down for two hours after eating. Certain foods, especially chocolate and fats, may provoke heartburn and indigestion; the same is true of caffeine, alcohol, and nicotine. Do not smoke, and consume alcohol, caffeine, and chocolate in moderation, if at all.

Because obesity contributes to reflux, strive to maintain ideal weight. To prevent nighttime attacks, elevate the head of your bed six inches; this can be done by placing heavy books or bricks under the bed legs. Finally, avoid wearing tight belts and other constrictive clothing.

### ALTERNATIVE THERAPIES

**Herbal medicine**

Bitter herbs, which stimulate the flow of gastric juices, may relieve symptoms due to indigestion. Drink a tea made from gentian root, goldenseal, or dandelion root extract 15 to 30 minutes before eating. For cautions concerning goldenseal, see *About the Recommendations*, p 7.

**Homeopathy**

Remedies recommended for heartburn include Natrum phosphoricum; it can be taken every 30 minutes for up to two hours after eating.

**Naturopathy**

Naturopaths often treat heartburn and indigestion with various digestive enzymes, such as pancreatin, or papaya tablets, which contain natural digestive enzymes.

**WARNING!**

***Heartburn symptoms that last for more than 15 minutes and are not relieved by sitting or standing erect may be due to a heart attack. Call 911 or your local EMS at once; delaying may be fatal.***

# The Stomach and Duodenum

*Powerful acids, enzymes, and other digestive chemicals work in the stomach and duodenum to convert food into forms that can be used by body tissues. Ironically, these same chemicals can also cause painful ulcers, gastritis, and other digestive problems.*

## Gastritis

### SYMPTOMS

- *Upper abdominal pain and/or general discomfort.*
- *Heartburn, nausea, and vomiting.*
- *Bloating; loss of appetite.*
- *Possible erosion and bleeding, signified by dark, tarry stools.*

### WHO IS AT RISK

*Anyone can develop gastritis, which involves inflammation and perhaps bleeding and erosion of the stomach lining. People who take a lot of aspirin and similar drugs are especially vulnerable to developing gastritis; it is also common among alcoholics. In some people, very spicy foods irritate the lining and may cause mild gastritis.*

*Acute erosive gastritis is usually brought on by a severe illness, shock, infection, extensive burns, or other serious injuries; it may also develop as a complication of surgery. Chronic nonerosive gastritis is usually due to* Helicobacter pylori, *the only bacterium that can live in the stomach's normal acidic environment. This type of gastritis tends to cluster in families, nursing homes, and other areas where people live in close quarters; it can be transmitted by kissing and other direct contact with infected body fluids. Viruses and fungi can also cause gastritis in persons with lowered immunity. (See the table* Miscellaneous Types of Gastritis *on p 150 for an overview of less common forms of stomach inflammation.)*

### HOW IT DEVELOPS

The stomach is lined with mucous membranes that have many folds and glands. A thick layer of mucus coats the stomach and protects the underlying muscle tissue from the strong acids and digestive juices that would otherwise eat through it. Gastritis develops when there is not enough of this protective mucus.

**Acute stress gastritis** comes on quickly; the inflammation causes small surface sores that usually do not penetrate beyond the mucous membranes. Very often, the person is so ill that the initial stomach discomfort may go unnoticed. If the underlying illness or injury persists, however, small stomach erosions or sores may form. Bleeding from these ulcers causes dark, tarry stools, and chronic blood loss can lead to iron-deficiency anemia. Severe bleeding can be life-threatening.

**Chronic erosive gastritis** develops more slowly; early symptoms include upper abdominal pain and perhaps nausea and vomiting. In some people, the pain worsens when the stomach is empty. A doctor viewing the stomach through an endoscope will find numerous

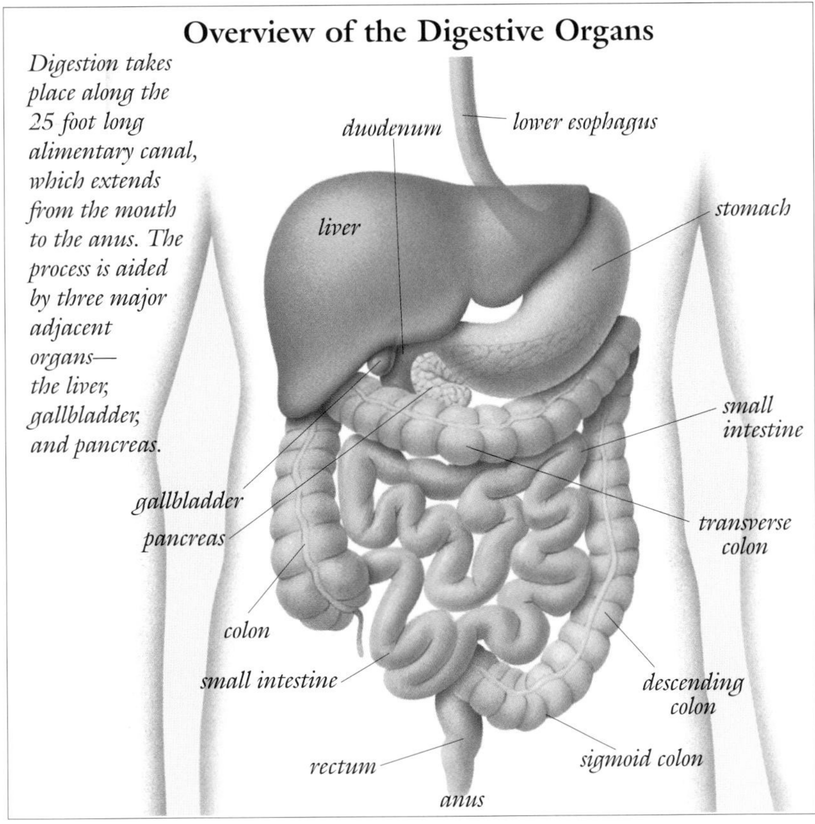

## Miscellaneous Types of Gastritis

| TYPE | CAUSES | CHARACTERISTICS |
|---|---|---|
| Atrophic gastritis | Antibodies attack the stomach lining. | Usually occurs in people who have had part of the stomach removed; lining becomes very thin; may cause pernicious anemia. |
| Eosinophilic gastritis | Often an allergic reaction to roundworms. | Stomach wall is inflamed due to accumulation of a type of white blood cell (eosinophils); may cause vomiting due to obstruction of stomach's outlet into the duodenum. |
| Hypertrophic gastritis (Ménétrier's disease) | Unknown | Stomach walls thicken, develop large folds, cysts, and enlarged mucous glands; reduces protein absorption; may lead to stomach cancer. |
| Plasma cell gastritis | Unknown | Plasma blood cells accumulate in stomach wall; may cause skin rash, vomiting, and diarrhea. |
| Radiation-induced gastritis | Side effect of radiation therapy | Causes pain, nausea, heartburn, and ulcers; ulcer may perforate stomach wall and lead to peritonitis, requiring surgery. Radiation may also damage stomach lining and result in very painful and serious bacterial infection. |

erosions that resemble canker sores. (Unlike ulcers, erosions normally do not penetrate into the muscle wall.)

**Nonerosive gastritis** usually produces mild symptoms, at least at first, but the smoldering infection can cause extensive damage to the stomach lining. It may also lead to ulcers and an increased risk of stomach cancer.

## WHAT YOU CAN DO

See a doctor if symptoms persist; go to the emergency room if there are signs of severe stomach bleeding, such as vomiting blood. Do not take aspirin and other nonsteroidal anti-inflammatory drugs (NSAIDs), such as ibuprofen. Abstain from alcohol, which worsens gastritis. Nonprescription antacids may relieve the discomfort, but they can also mask symptoms of a serious underlying disease or chronic infection.

## HOW TO TREAT IT

Pain and other symptoms are controlled by treating the underlying disease; approaches vary according to the type of gastritis. Acute stress gastritis usually heals itself in a few days as the underlying cause clears up.

**WARNING!**

***Vomiting blood is often a sign of severe stomach bleeding, which can be life-threatening. Call 911 or the EMS, or have someone take you to the nearest emergency room.***

### Medications

Antibiotics are prescribed to treat chronic gastritis due to an *H. pylori* infection. They are sometimes given along with bismuth (Pepto-Bismol and other brand names) to relieve the stomach pain and other symptoms.

Antacids or stronger drugs that block production of stomach acid are given to relieve gastritis pain; they are also administered to surgery patients, burn or trauma victims, and others who are at high risk of developing acute stress ulcers.

### Surgery

Emergency surgery may be necessary to stop severe bleeding. Sometimes, however, the bleeding can be stopped by chilling the area; a tube is passed into the stomach and ice water is flushed through it to constrict the blood vessels. Alternatively, an electric needle may be used to seal off (cauterize) the erosions.

If the bleeding persists or is life-threatening, all or part of the stomach may have to be removed. In fact, this is the only effective treatment for hypertrophic gastritis, also known as Ménétrier's disease.

## HOW TO PREVENT IT

Gastritis often can be prevented by using aspirin and other NSAIDs only occasionally and always taking such medications with food. If these anti-inflammatory drugs must be used more often to treat arthritis or another

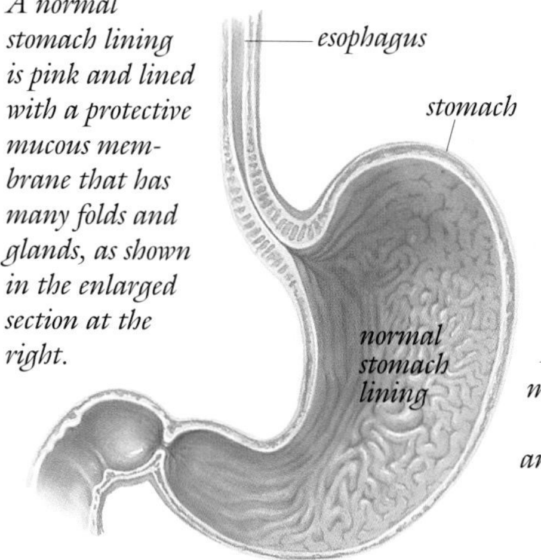


*A normal stomach lining is pink and lined with a protective mucous membrane that has many folds and glands, as shown in the enlarged section at the right.*

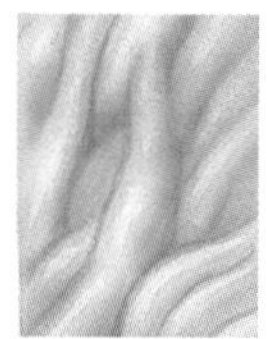

*In gastritis, the membrane is red and inflamed and small bruises or ulcers may develop.*

inflammatory disorder, taking enteric-coated pills, which pass through the stomach without dissolving, may prevent gastritis. Other preventive measures include using alcohol only in moderation and avoiding foods that provoke symptoms.

If gastritis due to *H. pylori* is diagnosed, other family members should be treated if they are also having symptoms. Practicing good hygiene can help prevent spreading the infection to others.

*Alcohol and hot spices can cause or further irritate gastritis. They should be avoided until healing is complete, and then used only in moderation.*

### ALTERNATIVE THERAPIES

**Herbal medicine**

Slippery elm, marshmallow root, and mullein are among the herbs that are high in mucilage; they ease the discomfort of gastritis by coating and soothing irritated intestinal linings. They are most effective when consumed as tea before meals.

**Nutraceuticals**

Chronic blood loss from gastric bleeding can cause serious anemia, which may require iron supplements (check with your doctor, however, before taking iron). Atrophic gastritis (see *Miscellaneous Types of Gastritis,* p 150) can cause pernicious anemia because it prevents absorption of vitamin $B_{12}$; in such cases, $B_{12}$ injections are needed.

# Indigestion

### SYMPTOMS

- *Gnawing or burning pain in the upper abdomen and chest.*
- *Bloating, belching, and stomach rumbling sounds.*
- *Possible loss of appetite, nausea, flatulence, and constipation or diarrhea.*

### WHO IS AT RISK

*Indigestion, known medically as dyspepsia, is a very common complaint that often has no identifiable cause, although stress, anxiety, and depression often play a role. It may be associated with other stomach disorders, such as ulcers, gastritis, gallbladder disease, and stomach cancer, but it is unclear as to whether these conditions can actually cause indigestion. Air swallowing (aerophagia)—an unconscious habit among people who sigh a lot, chew gum, or eat while talking or chew with their mouths open—may be a factor. Other possible factors include a high-fat diet, food allergies, smoking, and overindulging in caffeine or alcohol.*

## HOW IT DEVELOPS

A burning pain in the upper chest, similar to heartburn, is often the initial symptom. In some people, the discomfort is relieved by eating; in others, food makes it worse. In either case, the person may complain of feeling full and bloated after eating only a small amount of food. Nausea, flatulence, and loss of appetite are common.

## WHAT YOU CAN DO

If a doctor is unable to find a cause for your symptoms, examine what is going on in your life for possible clues. Are you under a lot of stress? Do you feel anxious or depressed? Do you unconsciously swallow a lot of air by gulping down your food or chewing with your mouth open? Do certain foods, especially fats and milk, provoke the symptoms? Do you smoke or drink a lot? Once you have identified possible contributing factors, work on changing them to see if the indigestion abates.

## HOW TO TREAT IT

Most cases of indigestion are classified as *functional dyspepsia*, meaning it has no identifiable cause and no specific treatment other than reassurance that it is not serious. This can be very frustrating for both physician and patient. In some people, antacids help ease the stomach discomfort. Alternatively, a course of omeprazole (Losec) therapy may be prescribed. In some patients, a histamine ($H_2$) blocker, such as cimetidine (Tagamet), ranitidine (Zantac), or famotidine (Pepcid), may be tried; these drugs can relieve symptoms by reducing stomach acid. A tranquilizer or antidepressant may also help, especially if stress and emotional problems are thought to be a factor.

## HOW TO PREVENT IT

Try to reduce stress or adopt better techniques for coping with it. Avoid fried and other fatty foods; keep a food diary to identify specific foods that provoke symptoms. If bloating and gas are your main symptoms, try eliminating onions, beans, cabbage, and other gas-producing foods from your diet. Eat small, frequent meals; chew slowly with your mouth closed to avoid swallowing air. If you smoke, make every effort to stop, and abstain from alcohol, especially before or just after meals; also cut back on coffee, colas, and other sources of caffeine, all of which can promote indigestion.

## ALTERNATIVE THERAPIES

**Aromatherapy**

Essential oils that may aid digestion include basil, black pepper, chamomile, and lavender. Try putting a few drops of diluted oil on one of your wrists and inhaling it 30 to 60 minutes before meals.

**Herbal medicine**

A cup of green tea before a meal can aid digestion. Teas made from bitter herbs, such as gentian root and dandelion root, stimulate the flow of stomach acids. Dandelion tea reduces bloating and relieves constipation; peppermint or fennel tea or extracts alleviate gas and flatulence. Drink a cup 15 to 30 minutes before eating.

**WARNING!**

***Indigestion symptoms that develop following travel to an undeveloped area may be due to a parasitic infection, such as amebiasis or giardiasis. Let your doctor know of any recent travel, including a camping trip or possible exposure to contaminated water.***

**Homeopathy**

Homeopaths prescribe Amonium crudum for indigestion accompanied by nausea, and Natrum phosphoricum for belching and gasiness.

**Naturopathy**

Naturopaths treat indigestion with various digestive enzymes, such as papain, which is derived from papayas and pancreatin. These are taken with meals.

# Peptic Ulcers

## SYMPTOMS

*Stomach pain is the primary symptom, but it varies according to the location of the ulcer.*

***Gastric (stomach) ulcer:*** *Gnawing or burning pain under the breastbone (sternum); possible bloating, nausea, and vomiting.*

***Duodenal ulcer:*** *Stomach pain that typically develops in the midmorning and is relieved by eating; pain may also awaken person at night.*

***Both types:*** *Bleeding and possible perforation of the stomach or intestinal wall.*

## WHO IS AT RISK

*Ulcers can occur at any age, but they are most common among middle-aged and older people. Persons who take a lot of aspirin, ibuprofen, and other nonsteroidal anti-inflammatory drugs (NSAIDs) have a high risk of developing peptic ulcers. Although stress does not cause ulcers, as was once thought, it can exacerbate symptoms. Other contributing factors include smoking and heavy consumption of alcohol and caffeine.*

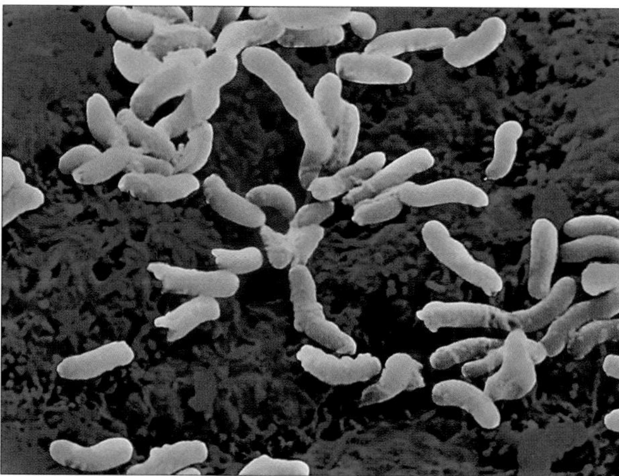

*The* H. pylori *bacterium can survive exposure to the stomach's powerful acids, which destroy other organisms. Doctors only recently discovered that most peptic ulcers are due to a chronic* H. pylori *infection.*

## HOW IT DEVELOPS

Normally, the mucous membranes that line the stomach and intestines provide protection from pepsin, an enzyme that breaks down proteins, and other powerful digestive juices. Ulcers develop in areas where the lining is thin or fails to secrete enough protective mucus. Aspirin and other NSAIDs set the stage for peptic ulcers by damaging the protective lining. Similarly, the *H. pylori* bacterium injures the protective mucous membrane and makes it more susceptible to acid damage.

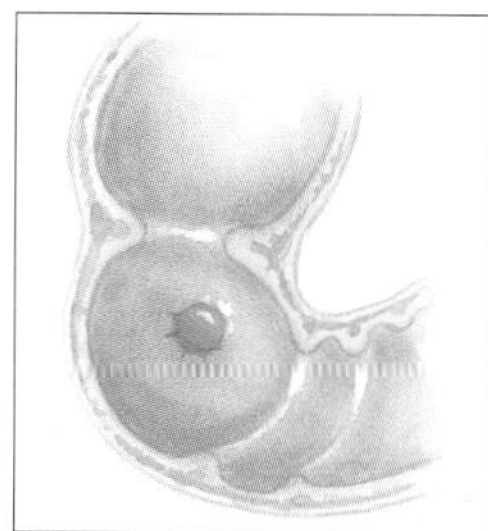

*Duodenal ulcers, which develop in the first few inches of the small intestine, form a crater that invades the underlying muscle tissue.*

Many ulcers heal themselves in 6 to 12 months, provided the mucosal lining is not subjected to further irritation from NSAIDs, smoking, alcohol, and other irritating substances. Ulcers often cause chronic bleeding, which can lead to anemia. Sometimes massive hemorrhaging develops, which can be life-threatening.

Perforation, in which the ulcer bores through the muscle wall and allows the stomach or intestinal contents to spill into the abdominal cavity, is another potentially fatal complication (see *Warning!* on next page).

**BREAKTHROUGHS!**

**The realization that a bacterium, *H. pylori*, and not stress, is the real culprit behind most peptic ulcers has revolutionized treatment for the disorder. Instead of prescribing a bland diet and antacids, doctors now turn to a combination of antibiotics, antacids, and drugs to suppress acid production. This approach not only relieves pain and other symptoms, but it usually cures most ulcers in 6 to 12 months.**

## WHAT YOU CAN DO

Consider discontinuing aspirin and other NSAIDs. If you suffer from arthritis or other inflammatory disorders requiring NSAID treatment, talk to your doctor about the new $COX_2$ inhibitors, a class of NSAIDs that fight inflammation and pain but are less likely to damage intestinal linings. Abstain from alcohol and smoking, and eliminate or at least limit coffee consumption to a cup a day. Simply switching to decaffeinated coffee is unlikely to help; both caffeinated and decaffeinated coffee exacerbate ulcers by increasing the flow of stomach acids. Avoid highly spiced foods if they provoke symptoms.

Although stress itself does not appear to cause ulcers, it can worsen symptoms. Set aside a few minutes two or three times each day to practice deep breathing exercises, meditation, or other relaxation techniques.

## HOW TO TREAT IT

### Medications

In order to provide permanent relief from the stomach pain and other symptoms, it is necessary to heal the ulcers. Doctors have a number of highly effective ulcer medications; more than one may be prescribed to speed the healing process. Even after the ulcers heal, which often takes 6 to 12 months, they have a tendency to recur.

Antacids remain the standard ulcer therapy because they not only relieve pain and other symptoms but they also aid in healing. The first choice is usually one of the histamine ($H_2$) blockers (see *How to Treat It*, p 151). These drugs, which are available in both nonprescription and prescription strengths, work by reducing stomach acid. If they do not provide adequate relief, omeprazole (Losec) or lansoprazole (Prevacid) may be prescribed; they work by blocking acid secretion. For peptic ulcers due to *H. pylori*, a combination of omeprazole (Losec) with the antibiotics clarithromycin (Biaxin) and either amoxicillin (Amoxil) or metronidazole (Flagyl) is used.

Another drug that eases pain and promotes healing is sucralfate (Sulcrate); this drug works by forming a protective coating over the ulcer to shield it from acid, pepsin, bile, and other irritating substances. Prostaglandin agents, such as misoprostol (Cytotec), protect the stomach lining from the damage caused by aspirin and other NSAIDs, such as ibuprofen.

### Surgery

A perforated ulcer usually requires emergency surgery to repair the damaged area; severe hemorrhaging may also require surgery to stop the bleeding.

## HOW TO PREVENT IT

Do not smoke, which can increase the risk of ulcers. Avoid overuse of aspirin and other NSAIDs, especially if they cause stomach pain. An enteric-coated product, which does not dissolve until it reaches the small intestine, may be tolerated better than tablets that dissolve in the stomach. But even these medications should not be used if the duodenum harbors a peptic ulcer, as is often the case.

#### ALTERNATIVE THERAPIES

**Herbal medicine**

Teas that herbalists use to treat gastritis—slippery elm and marshmallow root—may also relieve the discomfort of ulcers. They are high in mucilage, which helps coat the stomach and protect it from acids. In addition, some studies show that DGL licorice may inhibit growth of *H. pylori*. Be sure to use deglycyrrhizinated licorice (DGL) wafers, which don't raise blood pressure as regular licorice does.

**Meditation**

This and other relaxation therapies are helpful in overcoming stress, which can exacerbate ulcer symptoms.

**Naturopathy**

Some naturopaths recommend drinking a glass of raw cabbage juice with meals to help dilute stomach acids and relieve ulcer discomfort. Some studies have confirmed the benefits of cabbage juice. Milk—once a standby in ulcer therapy—is no longer recommended. Although milk may provide temporary relief, it has a rebound effect that can actually worsen ulcer symptoms because its protein stimulates increased acid production.

**Nutraceuticals**

Iron pills may be needed to treat anemia caused by bleeding ulcers; never take an iron supplement unless your doctor recommends it. The time-release forms do not cause as much stomach upset as the regular iron pills. Zinc, in dosages up to 25 mg a day, and up to 10,000 IU of vitamin A may speed ulcer healing. Caution is needed, however; excessive zinc suppresses the immune system and high doses of vitamin A can cause birth defects. See *About the Recommendations*, p 7.

**WARNING!**

***The sudden onset of severe abdominal pain points to a possible perforated ulcer and peritonitis. The pain may subside after a few hours, followed by a high fever and shock (fast pulse, cold clammy skin, and drop in blood pressure). This is a grave medical emergency that calls for immediate hospital treatment.***

# Liver/Gallbladder/Pancreas

*The liver and pancreas are essential to proper digestion and metabolism and, because of their multiple roles, are vulnerable to a variety of painful disorders. The gallbladder, while not as complex or essential, is an even more common source of often excruciating pain.*

## Gallstones

### SYMPTOMS

- *Intense pain in the upper right abdomen, often radiating upward toward the right collarbone.*
- *Pain intensifies when taking a deep breath, bending, or pressing on the upper right abdomen.*
- *Belching, abdominal bloating, sweating, possible nausea and vomiting, and low-grade fever.*

### WHO IS AT RISK

*About 15 percent of Canadians over the age of 40 have gallstones. The risk increases with age. Twenty percent of Canadian women and 10 percent of men have gallstones by the age of 60. Women between the ages of 20 and 60 are three times more likely to develop gallstones than men; researchers theorize that high levels of estrogen may contribute to stone formation. Other risk factors include obesity, smoking, a high-fat, low-fiber diet, chronic constipation, and a family history of gallbladder disease. Although it is not clear why, 70 to 80 percent of Canada's aboriginal peoples have gallstone problems.*

### HOW IT DEVELOPS

In many people, gallstones—known medically as *cholelithiasis*—are silent and never cause symptoms or other problems. The stones are usually made up of cholesterol, and small ones pass without problems from the gallbladder, through the bile duct, and into the duodenum, where they are broken up.

An acute gallbladder attack occurs when one or more stones block a duct, resulting in inflammation and pain. Most attacks develop after eating a heavy, high-fat meal. Temporary obstruction causes waves of intense abdominal pain until the stone passes through the duct. If the stone gets stuck, however, the pain is constant and gets progressively worse; nausea and vomiting are common. Most attacks subside gradually; those lasting for more than a few days point to serious complications.

### WHAT YOU CAN DO

See a doctor as soon as possible, especially if the pain persists for more than a day. Even if the attack subsides, tests are necessary to determine whether the gallbladder is harboring stones.

During an attack, refrain from eating and rest as much as possible. Nonprescription painkillers may help, but often stronger medications, such as codeine, are needed to bring relief.

### HOW TO TREAT IT

Doctors must first determine whether the pain is due to a gallbladder attack or from other abdominal disorders that cause similar pain, such as appendicitis or inflammation of the pancreas (pancreatitis). Ultrasound—the use of

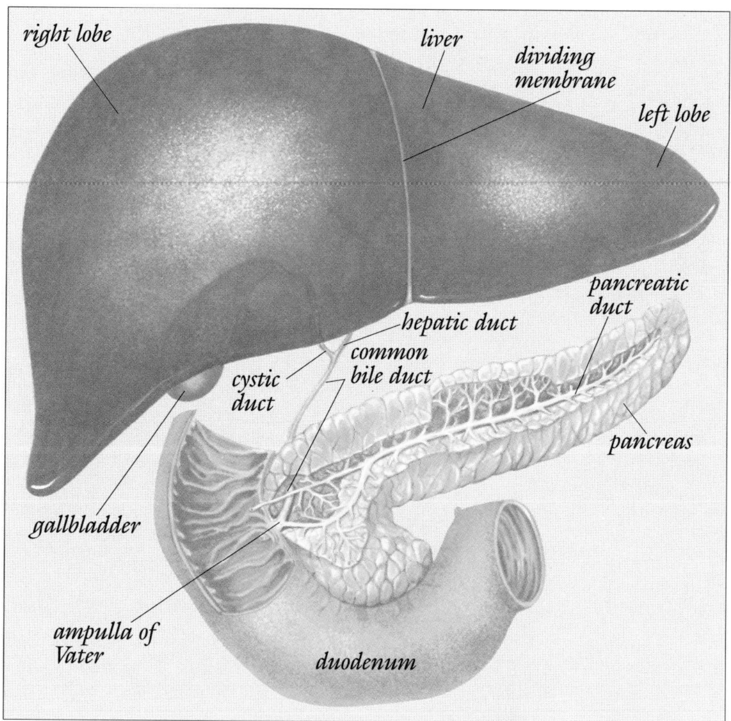


*The liver, the largest internal organ, serves as the body's chemical factory, manufacturing bile and cholesterol, processing and storing nutrients, and detoxifying alcohol and other harmful substances. The gallbladder concentrates the bile produced by the liver; the pancreas produces essential digestive enzymes as well as insulin, the hormone needed to metabolize blood sugar.*

**BREAKTHROUGHS!**

**Laparoscopic cholecystectomy has revolutionized gallbladder surgery. Here's what it entails:**

1. **Four small punctures are made in the abdomen so that a laparoscope—a tube with special viewing devices and a miniature television camera—can be inserted into the upper abdomen.**
2. **The surgeon passes miniature instruments through the laparoscope.**
3. **The surgeon, while viewing the site of the operation on a video monitor, manipulates the instruments and removes the gallbladder through the laparoscope.**

**The patient can usually leave the hospital in a day or two; there is little or no blood loss and, unlike in the past, no painful abdominal incision to heal.**

high-frequency sound waves to map internal structures in the body—can usually detect stones that are obstructing a duct. Another possible test, called *cholescintigraphy*, entails injecting a small amount of radioactive substance into the bloodstream and then using an isotope scanner to follow its travels through the liver, bile ducts, and the gallbladder itself.

## Medications

Ursodiol (Urso) can dissolve gallstones. However, it does not relieve an acute attack because it takes the drug months to dissolve the stones. Lithotripsy—the use of sound waves to pulverize the gallstones—may provide faster relief, followed by drug therapy to prevent new stones from forming. When the medication is stopped, however, new stones can develop. Consequently, drug therapy is prescribed mostly for patients who have only occasional mild attacks, are willing to take a medication for life, and are not good candidates for surgery.

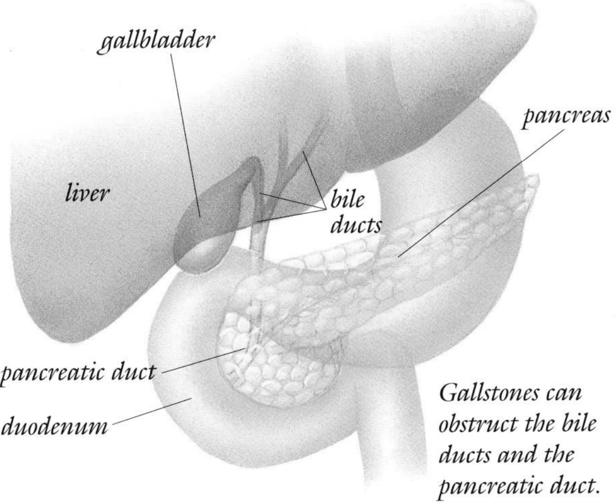


*Gallstones can obstruct the bile ducts and the pancreatic duct.*

## Surgery

Removal of the gallbladder is usually recommended for recurring gallbladder attacks. In recent years, the operation has been greatly simplified by using microsurgery techniques (see *Breakthroughs!*, left). In most sufferers, this solves the problem. Sometimes, however, the painful attacks recur, even though the gallbladder has been removed. The reasons for this are not always clear; sometimes the pain is traced to residual stones or to inflammation and blockage of other ducts and their openings (sphincters). Additional surgery may be needed to relieve or eliminate the pain.

# HOW TO PREVENT IT

Gallbladder disease is very unpredictable, and attacks cannot always be prevented. In some people, losing excess weight, adopting a low-fat, high-fiber (or even vegetarian) diet, and lowering high cholesterol help. Some doctors also recommend abstaining from alcohol or using it only in moderation, especially if drinking provokes a gallbladder attack. Women with a history of gallbladder disease are often advised against taking birth control pills or, after menopause, estrogen replacement therapy (ERT).

### ALTERNATIVE THERAPIES

**Note:** Alternative therapies are unlikely to relieve pain during an attack, but they may help prevent future attacks.

**Herbal medicine**

Milk thistle extract may reduce the amount of cholesterol in the bile and help prevent gallstones. Herbalists recommend taking 300 to 600 mg a day of an extract standardized to provide 70 to 80 percent of silymarin. In addition, dandelion root extract, taken either as capsules or tea, may also have a preventive effect by lowering bile cholesterol.

**Nutraceuticals**

Vitamin C, in dosages of 1000 to 2000 mg a day, may lower bile cholesterol and prevent gallstone formation. Do not take more than 500 mg if you have kidney stones, kidney disease, or hemochromatosis. If your diet does not provide at least 25 grams of fiber a day, take one tablespoon of psyllium powder (or its equivalent in capsule form) twice a day. Psyllium absorbs a lot of water in the intestines, so be sure to drink at least 8 to 10 glasses of water, juice, or other nonalcoholic beverages during the day. Other supplements that promote good gallbladder function include one tablespoon of flaxseed oil a day and 1200 mg of lecithin.

**WARNING!**

***A gallbladder attack lasting more than two days and accompanied by a high fever and jaundice is a medical emergency; possible complications include inflammation of the liver and/or pancreas, perforation of a duct or the gallbladder itself, and tissue death.***

# Hepatitis

## SYMPTOMS

- *Right-sided abdominal tenderness and possible swelling.*
- *Diffuse muscle and joint pain, loss of appetite, nausea and vomiting, fever, and other flulike symptoms.*
- *Jaundice (yellowing of the skin and whites of the eyes), severe itchiness, darkening of urine, and light, clay-colored stools.*

## WHO IS AT RISK

*Risk varies according to the type of hepatitis, a general term for inflammation of the liver. The most common causes are any of six viruses, excessive alcohol intake, and various drugs and toxins. Most cases of viral hepatitis are contracted through contaminated food and water, blood transfusions, the sharing of needles by IV drug users, and having an infected person as a sexual partner. Travel to areas where hepatitis is endemic, such as parts of Africa, Asia, and Mediterranean countries, carries a risk of exposure to the disease.*

## HOW IT DEVELOPS

Most acute viral hepatitis goes through three stages:

- **The prodromal phase,** marked by loss of appetite and flulike symptoms. This phase lasts 3 to 10 days.
- **The icteric phase,** in which the urine darkens and jaundice and severe itchiness develop. These symptoms, which are due to a buildup of bile in the blood, peak in one to two weeks.
- **The recovery phase,** in which the jaundice and other symptoms diminish. Most people recover in two to four weeks, although liver swelling and tenderness may persist for weeks or even months.

Most healthy people recover from viral hepatitis without complications, but the disease sometimes becomes chronic and causes severe liver damage. One type, caused by the hepatitis C virus, often causes only mild symptoms initially, but can then smolder for years and eventually lead to severe scarring of the liver (cirrhosis) or liver cancer. Chronic hepatitis B also increases the risk of liver scarring and cancer.

### BREAKTHROUGHS!

**While the outlook for patients with chronic hepatitis C is generally poor, people suffering from chronic hepatitis B can benefit from a new oral antiviral medication. Lamivudine (Heptovir) acts directly against the hepatitis B virus. Canada was one of the first countries to approve lamivudine, and recent Canadian clinical studies have shown that lamivudine may help control disease progression by suppressing viral reproduction in the liver in most treated patients. It leads to an inactive infection in a minority of patients. It is taken by mouth once a day and is generally tolerated.**

## WHAT YOU CAN DO

Bed rest usually is not necessary if the symptoms are mild, but you should stay at home and take frequent naps or rests. Abstain from alcohol and check with your doctor before taking any medication; in general, aspirin is usually safe to relieve achiness and fever, but acetaminophen should be avoided because it can cause further liver damage, especially if it is taken with alcohol. Women with hepatitis should not take birth control pills or estrogen replacement therapy (ERT).

### WARNING!

***Hepatitis is endemic in some Mediterranean countries, especially Greece, as well as many undeveloped nations of Africa and Asia. Before traveling to these areas, talk to your doctor about hepatitis immunization and other preventive measures.***

To temporarily ease the itchiness, which can be severe, try alternating hot and cold showers. Start with water as hot as you can tolerate. After three minutes, switch to very cold water for three minutes, then back to hot water. Many people find that this shower routine before going to bed eases the itching enough to let them get to sleep.

Pay special attention to personal hygiene to avoid spreading the virus to household members. Wash your hands frequently, do not handle food that is intended for others, and use a separate set of drinking glasses, dishes, and eating utensils.

## HOW TO TREAT IT

Aside from rest, there is no special treatment for most viral hepatitis. Treatment of the underlying disease is in order for other types, such as hepatitis due to bacterial, fungal, or parasitic infections.

## HOW TO PREVENT IT

Hepatitis A usually can be prevented by good hygiene and avoiding any possibly contaminated water or food, especially raw shellfish. Hepatitis B and C and other types that are spread by blood contact, sharing of contaminated needles, sexual contact, and exposure to other bodily fluids are prevented by screening all blood transfusions for the viruses and, of course, avoiding other contact with possibly infected blood.

There are now vaccines against hepatitis A and B; these are recommended for high-risk groups, such as health-care workers who come in contact with patients' blood, close family members and sexual partners of infected persons, and travelers to areas where these hepatitis strains are prevalent. Increasingly, vaccination is also being recommended for infants and adolescents.

Immune gamma globulin—a substance that contains high levels of antibodies against hepatitis—is sometimes given to persons who have been exposed to hepatitis A and B. It should be given along with the relevant hepatitis vaccine.

### ALTERNATIVE THERAPIES

**Herbal medicine**

Herbalists use milk thistle capsules as a general liver tonic. The recommended dose is up to 250 mg standardized to contain 70 to 80 percent silymarin. Dandelion root extract, which can be taken as tea or 500 mg capsules, also promotes liver health.

# Liver Cancer

### SYMPTOMS

- *Vague discomfort or nagging pain in the upper-right abdomen, with possible spread to the middle of the back and right shoulder.*
- *Loss of appetite, weight loss, nausea, and fatigue.*
- *Possible low-grade fever.*
- *A lump below the ribs on the right side.*
- *Jaundice (yellowing of the skin and whites of the eyes).*
- *Abdominal swelling (ascites) as cancer advances.*

### WHO IS AT RISK

*Primary liver cancer, which originates in the organ itself, is relatively rare in Canada, and is usually related to alcohol-induced cirrhosis. More often, the tumors start elsewhere, especially the breast, ovaries, and colon and other abdominal organs, and spread (metastasize) to the liver.*

*In other parts of the world, however, primary liver cancer is one of the most common types of cancer and causes more deaths than any other kind of cancer. The rates are highest in Asia and parts of Africa and are believed to be related to infection by the hepatitis B virus. In addition to alcohol abuse, risk factors include the use of anabolic steroids by athletes and bodybuilders, and exposure to pesticides, industrial chemicals, and aflatoxin, a mold found in nuts and grains.*

**WARNING!**

***Anyone who has chronic hepatitis, cirrhosis, or a history of exposure to cancer-causing chemicals should undergo periodic liver-function tests, which may help detect cancer in an early stage when a cure may be possible.***

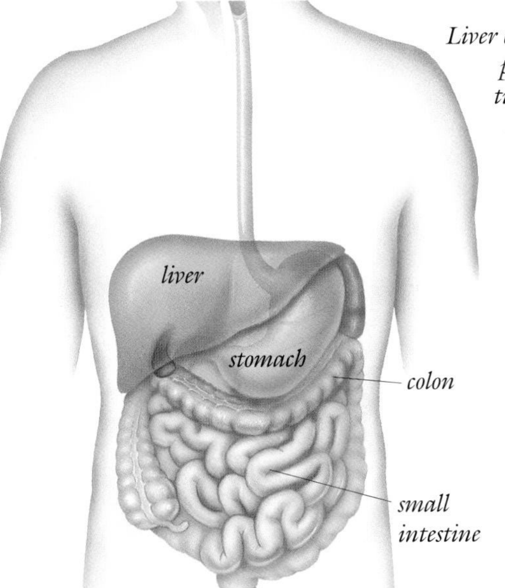

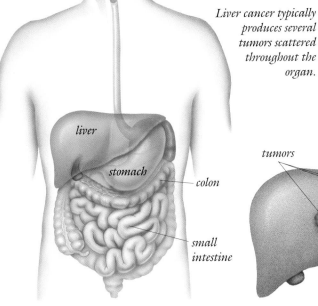

*Liver cancer typically produces several tumors scattered throughout the organ.*

## HOW IT DEVELOPS

Early liver cancer usually does not produce symptoms. As the disease advances, however, pain and other symptoms become more pronounced: intermittent abdominal discomfort becomes a nagging pain, and weight loss, jaundice, and bloating are more noticeable. In the advanced stages, pain may be severe and ascites—abdominal swelling due to fluid retention—adds to the discomfort. Nausea and digestive problems develop and there may be a low-grade fever.

## WHAT YOU CAN DO

If you have been diagnosed with liver cancer, reduce demands on the organ as much as possible. Eat small, frequent meals and limit fatty foods, which are hard to digest. A dietitian experienced in the nutritional needs of cancer patients can help you plan a diet that will not overtax the liver. Abstain from alcohol and take only those medications recommended by your doctor. Ask your doctor to recommend painkillers that are not harmful to the liver; in general, acetaminophen is not a good choice because it can increase liver damage. Aspirin or ibuprofen may be better choices, especially if fever is adding to the discomfort. Avoid salty foods, which increase fluid retention.

## HOW TO TREAT IT

### Surgery

The liver has an amazing capacity to regenerate itself. Removal of a localized tumor offers the best chance for a cure; techniques include freezing (cryosurgery) and destroying the tumor with radiologic techniques (see *Breakthroughs!*, p 158). Unfortunately, liver cancer is often scattered

## Breakthroughs!

Experimental therapies that show promise in treating liver cancer include:

- **Transcatheter arterial embolization (TAE),** in which a catheter or implantable pump is inserted into the hepatic artery, and anticancer drugs, along with substances that reduce the blood flow to the liver, are infused into the organ. This approach reduces the amount of oxygen available to the cancer cells, and also gives the drugs more time to work.
- **Radiofrequency ablation,** in which special substances are infused into the liver through the hepatic artery to make tumor cells more sensitive to radiation. High doses of radiation are then beamed into the tumor area to destroy as many cancer cells as possible.

throughout the organ and not all of it can be removed surgically. Also, the presence of liver cirrhosis reduces the prospects for surgical treatment. Even if surgery is unlikely to produce a cure, it may be worthwhile to relieve pain and other symptoms. In some unusual cases, a liver transplant may be considered.

### Medications

Morphine and other narcotic drugs may be administered to relieve severe pain. Diuretics may be prescribed to reduce abdominal swelling. Inoperable liver cancer, as well as cancer that has spread from other parts of the body, may be treated with anticancer drugs.

### Combination therapies

Sometimes liver cancer is treated with surgery to remove large tumors and then radiation and chemotherapy to reduce or destroy those that cannot be excised. This approach may not cure the cancer, but it can ease pain.

## HOW TO PREVENT IT

The best approach to preventing primary liver cancer is to abstain from alcohol or use it only in moderation. Immunization against hepatitis is also protective.

### ALTERNATIVE THERAPIES

**Note:** There are no alternative therapies to treat the cancer itself, but some may be helpful in relieving pain and other symptoms.

**Acupuncture**

Cancer centers may offer acupuncture as an alternative approach to controlling pain. It may be especially useful for patients suffering from liver cancer because they may not be able to take certain painkillers.

**Meditation**

The mind/body therapies helpful in controlling cancer pain include meditation, self-hypnosis, yoga, and guided imagery.

# Pancreatic Cancer

### SYMPTOMS

- *Increasingly intense pain that seems to bore through the abdomen and into the back.*
- *Pain worsens at night and is aggravated by lying flat on the back or stomach.*
- *Unexplained loss of appetite and weight.*
- *Nausea, vomiting, and digestive problems, especially after eating fatty foods.*
- *Gas, bloating, and alternating diarrhea and constipation.*
- *Possible onset or worsening of diabetes.*
- *Jaundice, itchiness, swollen legs, dark urine, and clay-colored stool.*
- *Worsening fatigue.*

### WHO IS AT RISK

*Pancreatic cancer is the fourth leading adult malignancy in Canada. Today the number of new cases is more than 2,800 a year. Its incidence increases with age, with most cases developing after 50. Other risk factors include smoking, exposure to solvents and petroleum compounds, and a family history of the disease.*

## HOW IT DEVELOPS

About 90 percent of pancreatic cancers develop in the exocrine part of the pancreas, which makes and secretes digestive enzymes. Most of the remaining cancers are called islet cell carcinomas because they develop in the cells that produce insulin and glucagon, the hormones that regulate blood sugar (glucose). The cancer often spreads to the liver and other abdominal organs.

The early symptoms are vague and often attributed to indigestion. As the cancer progresses, however, increasingly severe pain, weight loss, jaundice, and other symptoms prompt victims to seek medical attention.

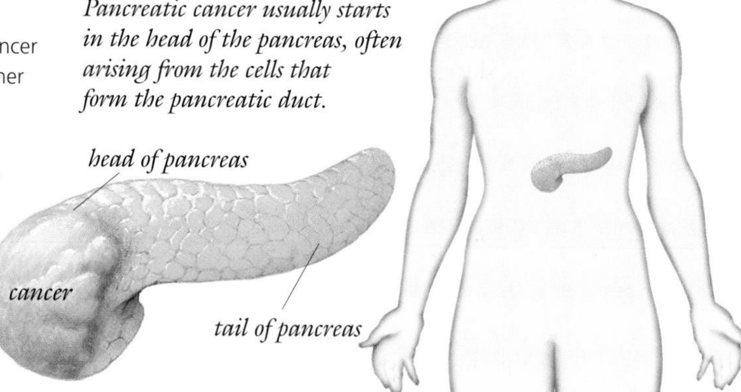


*Pancreatic cancer usually starts in the head of the pancreas, often arising from the cells that form the pancreatic duct.*

## WHAT YOU CAN DO

In the early stages, sleeping in a fetal position or sitting up and bending forward often eases the abdominal pain. As the cancer progresses, however, more severe pain may develop. At first, nonprescription painkillers may provide relief, but often codeine or stronger narcotic medications are needed. Eventually even these may not provide adequate relief, and a nerve block may be needed (see *Breakthroughs!,* right). Talk to your doctor about pain control, or seek a referral to a pain specialist.

Avoid fatty foods and ask your doctor about pancreatic enzyme pills to improve digestion. These pills are taken with meals or immediately after eating. Itching may be relieved by alternating hot and cold showers—three to five minutes of a very hot shower or bath, for example, followed by a very cold shower.

## HOW TO TREAT IT

### Surgery

Early pancreatic cancer that is confined to the head of the organ is sometimes cured by an extensive operation called a Whipple procedure; it entails removing the head of the pancreas, duodenum, the lowermost portion of the stomach, gallbladder, common bile duct, and nearby lymph nodes. In a modified Whipple procedure, the stomach is left intact, which helps maintain weight.

If the tumor cannot be removed, symptoms may be relieved by creating an intestinal bypass around obstructed areas so the person can digest food. A tube, or stent, may be inserted in a blocked duct to allow a normal flow of bile and other digestive juices.

**WARNING!**

***A type of pancreatic cancer called an insulinoma can cause dangerous drops in blood sugar (hypoglycemia). Symptoms include sluggishness, behavior changes, drowsiness, inability to think clearly, seizures, and coma.***

### Combination therapies

Surgery may be followed (or preceded) by chemotherapy and/or radiation. These approaches do not cure the cancer, but they can reduce symptoms and prolong life.

## HOW TO PREVENT IT

Not smoking may reduce the risk of pancreatic cancer, but since its cause is unknown, there are no clear-cut preventive strategies.

### ALTERNATIVE THERAPIES

**Note:** There are no alternative therapies to treat pancreatic cancer, but some may be helpful in relieving pain and other symptoms.

**BREAKTHROUGHS!**

**Researchers seeking better means of controlling the pain report promising results from an approach called percutaneous celiac axis nerve block. This involves injecting nerves in the area of the pancreas with alcohol to block pain messages from being sent to the brain.**

**Acupuncture**

Acupuncture may help control pain and reduce the need for painkillers.

**Biofeedback training**

Patients are taught to reduce pain by controlling certain involuntary bodily functions. Using this technique, for example, a patient may lessen pain by concentrating on redirecting nerve impulses.

**Meditation**

Many cancer centers teach various mind/body techniques to help patients learn how to control their pain. In addition to meditation, these may include self-hypnosis, yoga, and guided imagery.

# Pancreatitis

### SYMPTOMS

***Acute pancreatitis***

- *Abdominal pain, often severe and debilitating, centered below the breastbone (sternum) and often boring through to the back.*
- *Steady penetrating pain that starts suddenly, intensifies rapidly, and persists for days.*
- *Movement, coughing, or taking a deep breath worsens pain; bending forward may ease it.*
- *Nausea and vomiting; possible abdominal swelling.*
- *Fever and jaundice.*
- *Drop in blood pressure and dizziness or possible fainting when standing up.*

***Chronic pancreatitis***

- *Abdominal pain, ranging from mild and intermittent to severe and constant.*
- *Digestive problems, including malabsorption of fats.*
- *Unexplained weight loss.*
- *Onset or worsening of diabetes.*

### WHO IS AT RISK

*Gallstones and long-term alcohol abuse are the major causes of acute pancreatitis. Women outnumber men with gallstone-related pancreatitis, while alcohol-induced attacks predominate among men.*

*Alcohol abuse is also a major cause of chronic pancreatitis. In the unusual instances in which chronic pancreatitis develops in children, however, the disease is usually the result of a metabolic abnormality or cystic fibrosis or another inherited condition.*

## HOW IT DEVELOPS

Acute pancreatitis comes on suddenly when the duct that carries digestive enzymes from the pancreas to the duodenum becomes blocked, either by a gallstone or alcohol-induced clogging of the smaller ducts that drain into the main pancreatic duct. The blockage causes a backup of digestive enzymes, which begin to erode the pancreas itself, causing severe inflammation. An attack may last for several days, during which the person suffers intense abdominal pain.

Chronic pancreatitis develops more slowly, usually with less pain than the acute form. Loose, foul-smelling bowel movements and unexplained weight loss are common early symptoms.

## WHAT YOU CAN DO

See a doctor or go to the nearest emergency room. While awaiting help, try sitting with the knees drawn up to help ease pain. Above all, do not eat or drink anything; it's critical to rest the pancreas and give it a chance to heal.

For chronic pancreatitis, abstain from alcohol. Cutting back on fat is also critical; consult a clinical dietitian to plan a low-fat diet that is high in protein and carbohydrates. Nutritional supplements and digestive enzymes may be needed.

## HOW TO TREAT IT

Hospitalization in an intensive care unit is usually necessary to treat acute pancreatitis. Intravenous fluids are given, but all food is withheld to rest the pancreas. Morphine or another powerful painkiller will be given, but even these drugs often do not completely block the intense pain. If a gallstone is obstructing the pancreatic duct, it may be removed by endoscopy (see illustration, below). Sometimes surgery is needed to open ducts that are clogged.

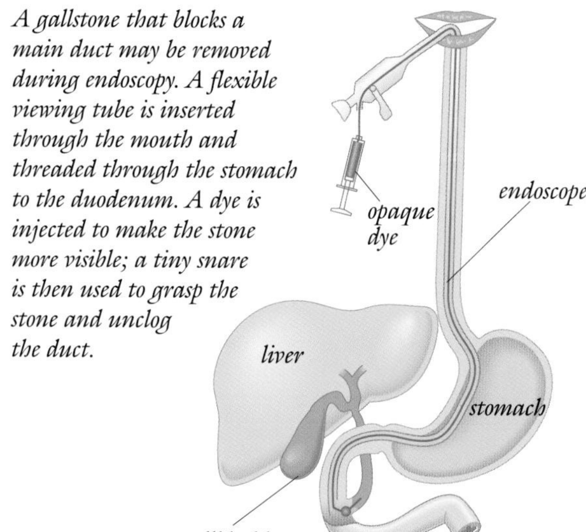


*A gallstone that blocks a main duct may be removed during endoscopy. A flexible viewing tube is inserted through the mouth and threaded through the stomach to the duodenum. A dye is injected to make the stone more visible; a tiny snare is then used to grasp the stone and unclog the duct.*

### BREAKTHROUGHS!

**Russian researchers have found that using low-intensity laser radiation and pulsed electric current, in addition to the standard treatments of acute pancreatitis, may speed recovery. Two sets of semiconductor lasers are applied to the front and back at the site of pain. The pulsed electric current is similar to that administered by a TENS (transcutaneous electrical nerve stimulation) unit. Researchers are conducting further studies on the technique to see if it might be adopted in North America.**

A flare-up of chronic pancreatitis may also require hospitalization and treatment similar to that of the acute disease. Fasting and IV fluids allow the pancreas to heal. In mild cases, however, symptoms can be controlled by simply eating small meals that are low in fat and protein and taking antacids or an $H_2$ blocker, such as cimetidine (Tagamet) or ranitidine (Zantac).

### WARNING!

***Vomiting blood during an attack of pancreatitis is usually a sign of severe hemorrhaging. This can be life-threatening; call 911 or the EMS to take you to the nearest emergency room.***

Chronic pancreatic pain may be relieved by high doses of pancreatic enzymes to help inhibit the pancreas from producing them. Under this regimen, as many as six pills of oral pancreatic enzymes (for example, pancrelipase) may be taken with each meal. This approach seems to work best against chronic pancreatitis whose cause is unknown; it is less successful in relieving the pain of chronic alcohol-induced pancreatitis. If pain still persists, surgery may be necessary.

## HOW TO PREVENT IT

Abstaining from alcohol or using it only in moderation is the best means of preventing alcohol-induced pancreatitis. Removal of the gallbladder can prevent pancreatitis due to recurrent gallstones. Other preventive strategies include adopting a low-fat diet and eating small, frequent meals to reduce the pancreas' workload.

### ALTERNATIVE THERAPIES

**Naturopathy**

Naturopaths often recommend pancreatin, a preparation made from pig pancreatic enzymes, or natural enzymes, such as bromelain from pineapples or papain from papayas. They are taken with or immediately after meals. Check with a doctor before using digestive enzymes, however; they may interact with the body's own digestive juices.

# Small Intestine/Colon

*The small intestine, which measures 18 to 23 feet in adults, lies looped within the abdominal cavity and surrounded by the six-foot-long colon. Although both intestines are common sources of pain, the colon poses the most problems.*

## Appendicitis

### SYMPTOMS

- *Severe pain that begins suddenly, usually in the area around the navel, and then spreads to the lower right side.*
- *Loss of appetite, nausea and vomiting, constipation or, more rarely, diarrhea.*
- *Low-grade fever (37.8° to 38.4°C/100° to 101°F), which can rise sharply if the appendix ruptures.*

### WHO IS AT RISK

*Appendicitis can develop at any age, but is most common between ages 10 and 30.*

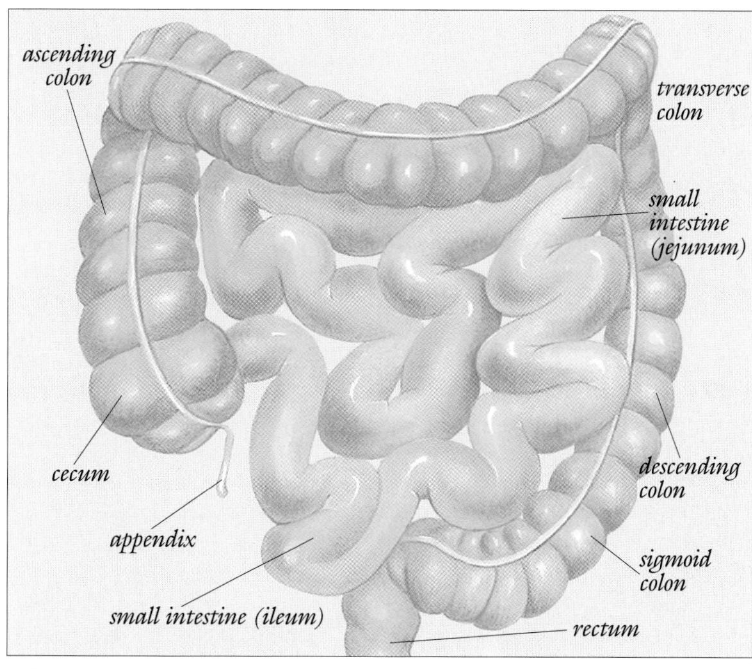


*Digestion is completed in the duodenum, the uppermost portion of the small intestine, and nutrients are then absorbed into the body from the jejunum and ileum sections. The residue—typically about 5 percent of the average diet—empties into the cecum and is slowly propelled along the colon until it exits the body in a bowel movement.*

### HOW IT DEVELOPS

The appendix may have had a useful purpose earlier in human evolution; today it has no known function, although some researchers theorize it may play a role in immunity. What causes appendicitis is unknown, but it may be that a blockage causes it to become infected and inflamed. Symptoms usually come on rapidly, starting with general malaise and mounting abdominal pain. If untreated, the inflamed appendix may rupture, allowing infectious material to spill into the abdomen. This can lead to a life-threatening infection called *peritonitis*. Sometimes an abscess forms; in women, this can infect the ovaries and fallopian tubes and lead to pelvic inflammatory disease (PID) and infertility.

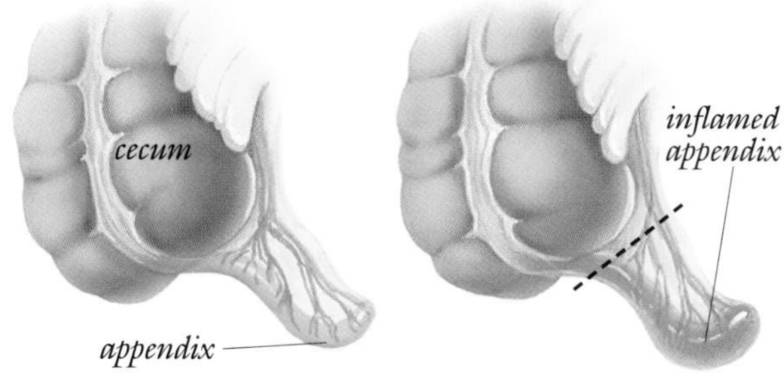


*The appendix is a three-inch-long pouch that extends from the cecum near its juncture with the small intestine. Appendicitis occurs when it becomes inflamed and swollen. The broken line shows where it is usually removed.*

### WHAT YOU CAN DO

See a doctor as soon as possible if symptoms suggest appendicitis. To ease pain while awaiting medical help, apply an ice pack to the abdomen and stay as quiet as possible. Constipation is common, but you should not take a laxative, which can cause the appendix to rupture.

When recovering from surgery, an ice pack applied to the abdomen helps numb pain around the incision. After the surgical staples or stitches are removed, rubbing vitamin E oil or cream into the incision speeds healing and reduces scarring. Avoid lifting heavy objects and straining, especially when having a bowel movement, until the incision is fully healed—usually about six weeks.

## HOW TO TREAT IT

Appendicitis calls for a prompt appendectomy—surgery to remove the infected appendix. Most people can leave the hospital in two or three days, and complete recovery takes another week or so.

> **WARNING!**
>
> ***An infected appendix can rupture within 24 hours. Do not delay seeing a doctor if symptoms suggest appendicitis.***

If the appendix has ruptured, intravenous antibiotics are given to prevent or treat peritonitis, inflammation of the membrane (the peritoneum) that covers the abdominal organs and walls of the abdomen. Additional surgery may be needed to remove infected tissue.

## HOW TO PREVENT IT

A high-fiber diet may help prevent appendicitis, although this has not been proved scientifically. However, population studies show that people who eat a diet low in meat and fat and high in grains, fruits, and vegetables have a reduced incidence of appendicitis.

### ALTERNATIVE THERAPIES

There are no alternative therapies for acute appendicitis. Meditation, self-hypnosis, and other relaxation therapies may help ease pain during recovery.

# Colon/Rectal Cancer

### SYMPTOMS

*Symptoms vary according to the site in which the cancer develops:*

***Ascending and transverse colon:*** *Increasing fatigue and weakness.*

***Descending colon:*** *Abdominal pain, ranging from crampy and intermittent to severe and constant; alternating constipation and frequent bowel movements; narrowing of the stool; abdominal bloating.*

***Rectum:*** *Pain and bleeding during bowel movements; straining and feeling of inadequate emptying of the rectum; diarrhea; possible pain when sitting.*

### WHO IS AT RISK

*Colon cancer is the second most common cancer in both men and women, exceeded only by lung cancer. An estimated 16,600 Canadians were diagnosed with colon cancer in 1999. People over the age of 50 are more likely to develop colon cancer; the risk is highest among persons with a family history of colon cancer or a type of inherited polyps (familial polyposis); other possible risk factors include having had ulcerative colitis, Crohn's disease, or breast or ovarian cancer.*

## HOW IT DEVELOPS

Most colon cancer starts as a small growth or polyp on the intestinal lining, often in several places at the same time. Tumors in the ascending colon (on the right side) often grow inward into the intestine. They can become quite large before causing symptoms, usually fatigue and weakness due to anemia from chronic bleeding. In contrast, tumors in the descending colon and rectum encircle the intestine, causing obstruction. They are more likely to cause pain, changes in bowel habits, and bloody stools. As the cancer invades the intestinal wall, it tends to spread to nearby lymph nodes and the liver.

## WHAT YOU CAN DO

See a doctor as soon as possible if you have symptoms suggesting possible colon cancer. Individuals with a family history of colon cancer should talk to their doctor about screening (see *What Will My Doctor Do?*, p 163).

Early colon cancer is unlikely to be painful, but advanced cancer can cause severe abdominal pain and also interfere with normal bowel function. If non-narcotic pain medication is inadequate, talk to your doctor about a morphine pump or other pain therapy.

## HOW TO TREAT IT

### Surgery

Early colon and rectal cancer can be cured by removing the tumor and the sections of the intestine on both sides of it. Nearby lymph nodes are removed to see if they harbor cancer cells. Polyps—small growths extending from the intestinal wall—can be removed during colonoscopy

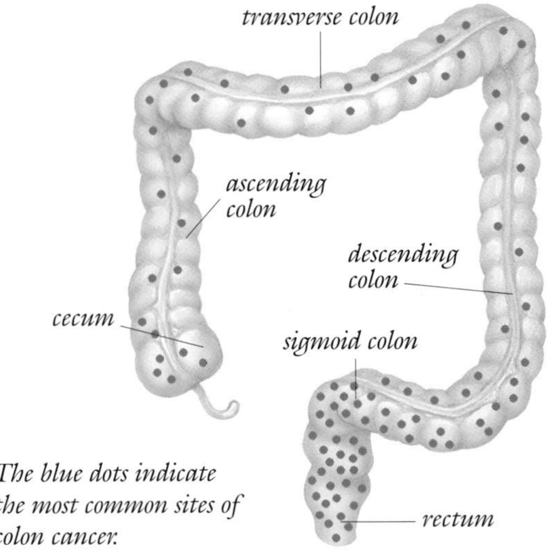


*The blue dots indicate the most common sites of colon cancer.*

## BREAKTHROUGHS!

**At one time, colon-cancer surgery usually entailed having a colostomy, an opening in the abdomen for the exit of body wastes. This is now rarely needed, thanks to new surgical techniques. Even after removal of the entire colon and/or rectum, a section of small intestine can be used to replace it and attached to the anal sphincter, thereby restoring reasonably normal bowel function.**

and then analyzed for cancer cells. Electrocoagulation—using an electric needle to seal off a tumor—may be an option for persons who are too weak or ill to undergo surgery. This is unlikely to cure the cancer, but it can ease pain, intestinal obstruction, and other symptoms.

### Combination therapies

Chemotherapy and/or radiation treatments are often administered following surgery. Numerous studies show that a combination of treatments reduces the risk of cancer recurrence, especially if the tumor has invaded the intestinal muscle wall or nearby lymph nodes.

## HOW TO PREVENT IT

Diet appears to play an important role in the development of colon cancer. A number of studies have found that people who eat a lot of animal fats have an increased risk of colon and rectal cancer. When fat is metabolized, intestinal bacteria release irritating substances that are thought to stimulate the growth of colon polyps—common precursors of cancer. Dietary fiber may be protective because it reduces the concentration of fats and speeds their transit through the colon (see *Nutraceuticals*).

Recent studies indicate that taking an aspirin or ibuprofen every other day may lower the risk of colon cancer. More study is needed, however, to prove this; in the meantime, many doctors advise patients to use low-dose aspirin or ibuprofen (see *Warning!*).

## WHAT WILL MY DOCTOR DO?

After hearing about your symptoms, your doctor will check them out with one or more of these tests:

- **Digital rectal exam.** The doctor will insert a lubricated, gloved finger into the rectum and feel for abnormal areas.
- **Fecal occult blood test.** A test to check for hidden (occult) blood in the stool.
- **Sigmoidoscopy.** The doctor will slowly and gently insert a hollow tube with a light at one end into your rectum and lower part of your colon, to see if there are any polyps or tumors.
- **Colonoscopy.** The doctor will gently insert a hollow, flexible tube into the rectum and large bowel. The tube is made of fibers that send light, making it possible for your doctor to see the entire length of the colon.

### ALTERNATIVE THERAPIES

**Herbal medicine**

Studies in China have found that green tea (at least two cups a day) may lower the risk of all types of intestinal cancer. Garlic, onions, and other herbs high in sulfur, which inhibits tumor development, may also protect against colon cancer; these are best eaten fresh or lightly cooked in small amounts daily.

**Nutraceuticals**

A high-fiber diet may protect against colon and rectal cancer; experts recommend 25 grams a day. Good sources are whole-grain breads and cereals and fresh fruits and vegetables. Studies also indicate that 1000 mg of calcium a day, taken with 400 mg of vitamin D, reduces the risk of colon cancer. People with thyroid or kidney disease should check with their doctor before taking calcium. Other daily supplements that may protect against colon cancer include 200 to 400 micrograms of selenium, 50 mg of coenzyme $Q_{10}$ (pregnant and nursing women must check with their doctor before taking coenzyme $Q_{10}$), 50 mg of beta carotene (consult your doctor first if you have kidney or liver disease, or a sluggish thyroid), 1000 mg of vitamin C along with 50 to 100 mg of bioflavonoids, substances that enhance the antioxidant activity of vitamin C.

## WARNING!

***Although there is some evidence that low-dose aspirin or ibuprofen may protect against colon cancer, these medications are not without risk. They should not be taken by anyone with a history of ulcers or inflammatory bowel disease. Persons taking these medications, even in low doses, should watch for symptoms of chronic bleeding—fatigue, weakness, easy bruising, and prolonged bleeding from minor cuts.***

# Constipation

### SYMPTOMS

- *Infrequent, hard stools that are difficult—and often painful—to pass.*
- *Straining, rectal pain and bleeding, possible abdominal cramps, uncomfortable bloating, and gassiness.*

### WHO IS AT RISK

*A tendency to be constipated increases with age and is most common among sedentary persons, especially the bedridden elderly. Some medications, (such as codeine) and nutritional supplements like calcium (e.g., 1000 to*

*1500 mg a day), can cause constipation; other risk factors include a low-fiber diet, an underactive thyroid (hypothyroidism), and neurologic disorders, such as Parkinson's disease, stroke, or a spinal cord injury. Overuse of laxatives can disrupt normal bowel function and result in constipation when stopped. Stress, inactivity, depression, obesity, and advancing pregnancy may also provoke constipation.*

## HOW IT DEVELOPS

Many people mistakenly think they are constipated if they fail to have a daily bowel movement. In reality, normal bowel function varies from one person to another; some people may have two or three bowel movements a day, while others have only one or two a week. True constipation is marked by a hard stool that is difficult—often painful—to pass. It is frequently a chronic condition among people who are obese; it is also common in sedentary or bedridden older people or those who overuse laxatives and enemas.

Most constipation is not medically serious; an exception is acute constipation, which comes on abruptly without apparent cause and lasts for more than a few days. In such cases, doctors look for an underlying cause, such as infection, a tumor, or bowel obstruction. Constipation alternating with diarrhea also points to an underlying disease, such as irritable bowel syndrome.

*A high-fiber diet that includes ample fruits and vegetables can help prevent constipation.*

## WHAT YOU CAN DO

As much as possible, avoid straining, which increases the risk of developing painful hemorrhoids and anal fissures. When going to the toilet, many people find that sitting with their feet drawn up a few inches and resting on a low stool is more comfortable than having them flat on the floor; leaning forward slightly also reduces the need to strain to have a bowel movement.

Poor bowel habits foster constipation, and a few simple changes often remedy the problem. Don't put off going to the toilet when you feel an urge to have a bowel movement; delay can result in further drying of the stool. Set aside a specific time each day when you can devote 10 or 15 minutes to an unhurried bowel movement. For many people, this is after having breakfast, a morning cup of coffee, or glass of warm water; eating or drinking stimulates peristalsis, the waves of muscular contractions that move the stool through the colon. Don't resort to over-the-counter laxatives without consulting a doctor (see *Warning!*); instead, try drinking a cup of prune juice or eating a few prunes in the evening. Prunes contain a gentle, natural laxative that does not interfere with normal bowel function.

### WARNING!

***Never take a laxative for acute constipation, especially if it is accompanied by severe abdominal pain, fever, and other symptoms. The cause may be appendicitis or another problem that is worsened by a laxative. Also avoid long-term use of mineral oil and fast-acting laxatives; they can interfere with absorption of important vitamins, minerals, and medications.***

## HOW TO TREAT IT

If the bowel is impacted, a doctor will try to clear it with enemas; if this does not work, the mass must be broken into smaller pieces and removed manually. This can be quite painful, therefore an ointment formulated with lidocaine or another local anesthetic is used; in rare cases, general anesthesia is necessary.

If a laxative is needed, doctors often recommend starting with a bulk laxative, such as psyllium powder (Metamucil), which makes the stool softer, larger, and easier to pass (for psyllium to work, drink at least 8 to 10 glasses of water a day). Other choices include magnesium hydroxide liquid (Milk of Magnesia); stimulant laxatives such as bisacodyl (Dulcolax); stool softeners such as docusate (Colace), mineral oil, and glycerin suppositories, which stimulate the rectum. Osmotic agents, such as sorbitol and magnesium, draw water into the colon to soften the stool and stimulate its passage; these are used mostly to clear the bowel for examination or surgery.

## HOW TO PREVENT IT

Most constipation is related to lifestyle—usually inadequate fiber and fluid intake combined with limited exercise. Ordinary constipation can often be overcome by drinking at least 8 to 10 glasses of water a day, exercising for at least 20 to 30 minutes four or five days a week, and increasing your intake of whole-grain products, fruits, and vegetables to provide the recommended daily intake of at least 6 to 10 grams of crude dietary fiber, especially legumes. Do this gradually; taking bran supplements or suddenly increasing your fiber intake can cause uncomfortable bloating and gas.

### ALTERNATIVE THERAPIES

**Herbal medicine**

Herbs that have a natural laxative effect include cascara sagrada (avoid if you are pregnant or nursing), chicory, dandelion, and elderberry. They can be taken in pill form or as tea, preferably before going to bed at night. Castor oil, an old herbal remedy for constipation, should be avoided; it can cause nausea and vomiting and also interferes with absorption of important nutrients.

**Homeopathy**

Homeopathic treatments for constipation include Nux vomica and Sepia; Sulfur may ease constipation that alternates with diarrhea.

# Diarrhea

### SYMPTOMS

- *Frequent, urgent passage of watery stools.*
- *Abdominal pain or cramps, gassiness; possible fever and blood in the stools.*

### WHO IS AT RISK

*Everyone now and then experiences episodes of diarrhea, often due to an underlying infection or food poisoning. Stress or eating certain foods can result in diarrhea; it may also be related to lactose intolerance and various intestinal disorders, such as diverticulosis or irritable bowel syndrome. Travelers are especially vulnerable to diarrhea, which may be due to contaminated food or water or simply consuming unfamiliar foods and encountering new strains of intestinal bacteria. Antibiotics often cause diarrhea because they disrupt the normal balance of intestinal bacteria and yeasts.*

*For most people, diarrhea is short-lived and is not dangerous; exceptions include babies and the elderly, who may become dehydrated from excessive fluid loss.*

## HOW IT DEVELOPS

Diarrhea usually comes on suddenly and resolves itself in 24 to 48 hours. Chronic or frequently recurring diarrhea is usually due to an underlying disease.

## WHAT YOU CAN DO

A nonprescription medication that contains bismuth (Pepto-Bismol), attapulgite (Kaopectate), or loperamide (Imodium) can usually quell mild diarrhea, stomach cramps, and other symptoms. An ice pack or heating pad may help ease abdominal pain and cramps. Call your doctor, however, if symptoms persist for more than a day or two or recur frequently. During a bout of diarrhea, do not eat solid foods, fruit juices, coffee, and milk products.

*The BRAT diet—bananas, rice, applesauce, and toast (unbuttered)—emphasizes binding foods that may help quell diarrhea.*

To prevent dehydration, take frequent sips of water, tea, or flat ginger ale or cola. Salty broth or clear soups help replace fluids and lost salts and other minerals; alternatively, you can use a sports drink or commercial rehydration fluid. You can make your own hydration fluid by adding 1/4 teaspoon of baking soda, a pinch of salt, and a teaspoon of honey or corn syrup to an eight-ounce glass of water.

As the diarrhea subsides, gradually resume solid foods, starting with bland, binding ones such as bananas, rice, chicken breast, soda crackers, mashed potatoes, and applesauce. Avoid raw fruits, fruit juices, milk, and fatty foods until bowel function is again fully normal.

## HOW TO TREAT IT

Diarrhea that is accompanied by waves of cramps and intestinal spasms may be treated with an opium-containing preparation such as Donnagel-PG, or a diphenoxylate atropine compound (Lomotil). These prescription drugs relieve the cramps and diarrhea by reducing intestinal motility, the waves of muscle contractions that move food and fluids through the digestive tract. Babies and others who are in serious danger of dehydration may be hospitalized and given intravenous fluids. Antibiotics or other drugs will be prescribed if the diarrhea is due to infection or intestinal parasites, such as Giardia.

## HOW TO PREVENT IT

Diarrhea caused by antibiotics may be prevented by taking acidophilus pills or eating yogurt made with live cultures of lactobacilli and bifidobacteria. These beneficial organisms normally live in the intestinal tract and are killed by antibiotics, resulting in diarrhea.

Food poisoning—one of the most common causes of diarrhea—can be prevented by thoroughly cooking all meats and eggs, scrupulously cleaning all food preparation surfaces and utensils, and discarding any foods or leftovers that smell or look "off." When traveling, especially in underdeveloped countries, avoid fresh salads, raw vegetables, and unpeeled fruits, and be extra careful about what you drink, sticking to reliable bottled water, carbonated beverages, or tea made with boiled water. In restaurants, make sure the bottled water is sealed; some establishments simply fill used bottles with tap water.

### ALTERNATIVE THERAPIES

**Herbal medicine**

Green tea or teas made from agrimony (do not use with anticoagulants), red raspberry leaf, or blackberry leaf are high in tannins that help the body absorb fluids from the intestinal tract. Drinking four or five cups of these teas during a bout of diarrhea also helps replenish lost body fluids. One to three tablespoons of powdered psyllium seeds dissolved in water once a day may also ease diarrhea by absorbing water from the intestinal tract and forming a more solid stool. Be sure to drink extra water throughout the day.

**Homeopathy**

Homeopathic remedies for diarrhea include Arsenicum album, Argentum nitricum, Pulsatilla, and Sulfur; the choice of remedy varies according to the cause.

**Nutraceuticals**

Acidophilus, two pills three times a day on an empty stomach, helps to restore levels of healthy bacteria to the intestine. Acidophilus may be used with OTC diarrheal aids, though not taken at the same time of the day.

**WARNING!**

***Diarrhea lasting more than 24 hours can cause life-threatening dehydration in babies under the age of two years, especially if the child also has a fever. Giving a nonprescription rehydration formula, such as Pedialyte, can prevent serious dehydration. Even so, check with your doctor if diarrhea persists for more than a day in a child under two and more than two days in older children.***

# Diverticulitis

### SYMPTOMS

- *Pain and areas of tenderness, usually in the lower left abdomen; pain may vary from mild and intermittent to intense and spasmodic.*
- *Possible fever, bloody stools, and general malaise.*

### WHO IS AT RISK

*Diverticula are small pockets, or outpouches, that develop in weakened segments of the colon, usually in the sigmoid portion on the lower left side. Their presence, a condition called diverticulosis, is rare before age 40. They become increasingly common with advancing age and, by age 80, almost everyone has at least a few.*

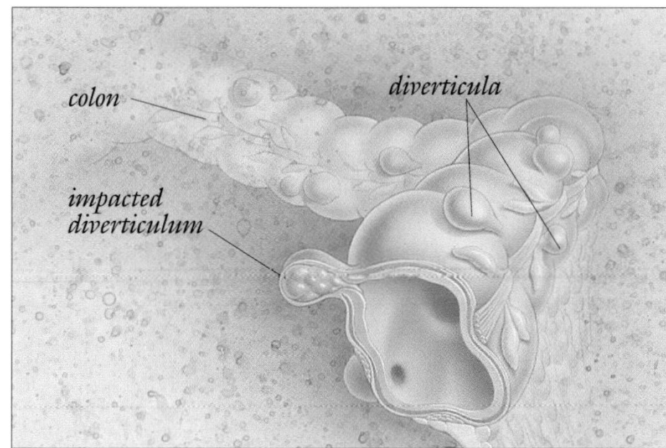


*Diverticulitis develops when small pockets bulge out along weakened segments of the intestinal wall, fill with fecal material, and become infected and inflamed.*

## HOW IT DEVELOPS

A low-fiber diet made up of highly processed foods, along with chronic constipation, is believed to cause diverticulosis. Most people with diverticula never experience symptoms. If the pouches fill with fecal material, however, they become infected and inflamed, which can lead to intense pain and fever. Sometimes an inflamed pouch ruptures and spills infective material into the abdominal cavity, causing intense pain, a high fever, and a life-threatening infection (peritonitis); severe bleeding is also a serious risk (see *Warning!*, p 167).

## WHAT YOU CAN DO

See a doctor as soon as possible if you develop abdominal pain, bloody stools, and other symptoms of diverticulitis. During a flare-up, applying an ice pack to the painful area may bring relief; however, do not use a heating pad, which can worsen inflammation and may even cause a diverticulum to rupture.

Mild diverticulitis can usually be treated at home with oral antibiotics and a liquid diet to give the colon a chance to heal. Symptoms usually abate in a few days; then a soft diet of bland, pureed foods can be started. Avoid raw fruits or vegetables, whole grains, berries with seeds, corn, hot spices, alcohol, and caffeine.

**BREAKTHROUGHS!**

**The development of laparoscopic surgical techniques now makes it possible to remove diseased segments of the colon without making a large incision. Several small punctures are made near the navel, and special viewing tubes and a tiny video camera are inserted into the abdominal cavity. Surgeons can then remove the infected diverticula through the tubes. Because there is no large incision to heal, postsurgical pain is minimal and recovery is speeded up.**

## HOW TO TREAT IT

Imaging studies, such as a CT scan or ultrasound, may be needed to rule out appendicitis, colon cancer, and other disorders that can cause similar symptoms. An attack marked by severe pain, high fever, and possible intestinal bleeding usually requires hospitalization. Morphine may be given to ease the pain, and intravenous antibiotics are administered to quell the infection. A ruptured diverticulum, severe bleeding, and fistulas (abnormal connections with other organs) may require surgery to remove the diseased segment of the colon. A liquid diet, or even IV nutrition, may be necessary until the colon heals.

**WARNING!**

***Sometimes impacted diverticula erode nearby blood vessels, which can cause severe bleeding. Chronic inflammation can also lead to the formation of abnormal links, called fistulas, with the bladder or other adjacent organs, allowing colon bacteria to invade the affected organ.***

## HOW TO PREVENT IT

Change your diet to prevent or at least reduce intestinal spasms, which can force fecal material into the diverticular pockets. Switch to a high-fiber diet that emphasizes whole-grain breads and cereals and lightly processed or raw fruits and vegetables. Many people also need to take a bulk laxative, such as powdered psyllium. Avoid foods that contain a lot of seeds (e.g., raspberries, tomatoes, corn); also important are regular exercise, maintaining ideal weight, abstaining from alcohol, and using caffeine and carbonated drinks in moderation, if at all.

### ALTERNATIVE THERAPIES

**Herbal medicine**

Chamomile tea, one cup three times a day, acts as an anti-inflammatory. Peppermint tea, one cup three times a day, relaxes digestive spasms. Aloe vera products that are formulated for internal use may also help prevent flare-ups of diverticulitis. Stop taking them, however, if the aloe causes diarrhea.

# Hernia

**SYMPTOMS**

- *Soft abdominal (or groin) swelling that is mildly to moderately painful.*

**WHO IS AT RISK**

*Hernias are most common in infants, especially those born prematurely, the elderly, and persons who are obese. They can also develop in people with chronic coughs, those whose jobs entail a lot of heavy lifting, and people who are chronically constipated. Some hernias, especially those in the groin area of young males, are due to a congenital weakness or malformation of the inguinal canal, the structure through which the testicles descend as they move into the scrotum.*

## HOW IT DEVELOPS

A hernia develops when a portion of the intestine or another organ pushes through a weakened segment of supporting muscle. They most commonly form in the inguinal area, the juncture of the lower abdomen and the upper thigh.

Hernias that bulge inward, while not visible, still cause pain and other symptoms; examples include a hiatal hernia in the muscle wall (the diaphragm) separating the chest and abdominal cavities or an inguinal hernia that extends into the male scrotum or female vagina. Symptoms vary according to the site of the hernia, and may include indigestion, heartburn, or urinary problems.

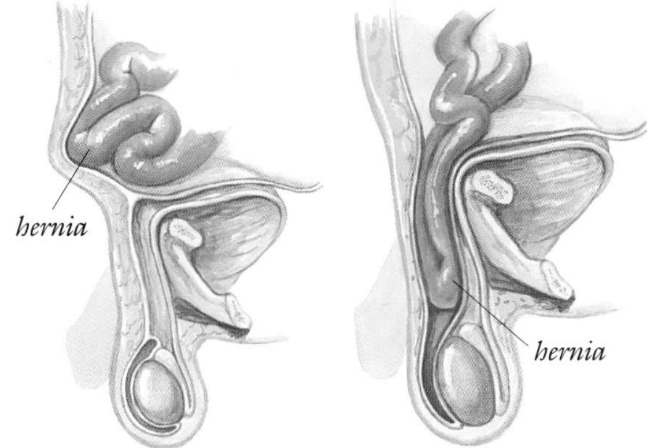


*In an abdominal hernia (left), a portion of intestine bulges through the abdominal muscles; whereas in an inguinal hernia (right), the intestine pushes into the groin. In men, it may enter the scrotum.*

Most hernias are not medically serious unless the herniated intestine becomes trapped (strangulated), resulting in a loss of blood supply and tissue death (gangrene). This can be life-threatening.

**BREAKTHROUGHS!**

**In the past, hernias often recurred following surgery, especially among overweight patients. This can now be prevented by new techniques to reinforce the weakened muscle wall with a patch of fine wire mesh or fascia, the strong connective tissue that covers muscle, taken from elsewhere in the body.**

## Types of Hernias

| TYPE | LOCATION OF BULGING |
|---|---|
| Abdominal | Abdominal muscle wall. |
| Diaphragmatic (also called hiatal hernia) | Hiatal opening in the diaphragm (the muscle separating the chest and abdominal cavities) allowing stomach or other abdominal organs to push upward into the chest area. |
| Incisional | Site of a surgical incision. |
| Inguinal or femoral | The groin; also the scrotum in men or vagina in women. |
| Umbilical | Near or within the navel; very common in babies. |

## WHAT YOU CAN DO

See your doctor if you develop a soft bulge in the abdominal wall or groin. In the meantime, you can ease the pain by lying down and gently pushing the bulging intestine back into its proper place in the abdomen. Avoid straining, lifting heavy objects, and making sudden, jerking movements. Try to suppress coughing or sneezing; if this is impossible, hug a pillow firmly to your abdomen until the coughing or sneezing stops.

## HOW TO TREAT IT

Most hernias call for surgical repair; the exceptions are umbilical hernias in babies, which usually disappear on their own by age four or five. During the operation, the surgeon makes an incision at the site of the hernia, moves the intestine back into its proper place, and sews the weakened muscle wall together.

**WARNING!**

***Do not try to self-treat a hernia by wearing a truss, a pad attached to a belt to exert pressure on the abdomen. A truss cannot cure a hernia, and it should not be used unless recommended by a doctor.***

## HOW TO PREVENT IT

Many hernias are due to congenital weakness and cannot be prevented. Maintaining ideal weight may help prevent those associated with obesity; adopting a high-fiber diet and increasing exercise reduce the risk of those associated with constipation and straining.

### ALTERNATIVE THERAPIES

**Physical therapy**

Following hernia surgery, exercises to strengthen abdominal muscles may help prevent a recurrence. However, any exercise program should be designed by a physical therapist who works with abdominal surgery patients.

# Inflammatory Bowel Disease

### SYMPTOMS

*Inflammatory bowel disease (IBD) is a general term referring to several disorders affecting the intestinal tract; symptoms vary according to the site and nature of the inflammation. Symptoms of the two most common types include the following:*

***Crohn's disease:*** *Chronic abdominal pain and diarrhea with flare-ups of more intense pain that may mimic appendicitis; loss of appetite and weight; tender, swollen lymph nodes; painful anal cracks (fissures) and development of fistulas (abnormal connections to other organs); fever and possible anemia; stunted growth in children; possible arthritis.*

***Ulcerative colitis:*** *Periodic attacks of lower-abdominal cramps and pain, diarrhea streaked with blood and mucus; possible fever, weight loss, anemia, and general malaise.*

### WHO IS AT RISK

*The worldwide incidence of IBD, which afflicts more than 250,000 Canadians, has increased markedly in recent decades; the reasons are unknown. What causes IBD is also unknown, although a genetic predisposition is thought to play a role. The onset may be triggered by an infection or another factor that prompts the immune system to, in effect, attack the intestines.*

***Crohn's disease*** *generally begins before age 30, and about one in six patients has a close relative who also has the disease or another IBD. Cigarette smoking appears to contribute to its development and progression.*

***Ulcerative colitis*** *most often starts between the ages of 15 and 30; less often, it may develop among persons 50 to 70 years old. It is less likely to run in families than Crohn's disease, and smoking does not seem to be a factor.*

## HOW IT DEVELOPS

**Crohn's disease**, which is also called *ileitis* or *regional enteritis*, can affect any part of the digestive tract, but it most commonly attacks the ileum, the lowermost segment of the small intestine, and the colon. It starts with patches of inflamed tissue and small ulcers along segments of the intestine. As the inflammation worsens and spreads, abscesses form and the intestinal walls become swollen and thickened and fistulas may form between the intestines and other abdominal organs. Other possible complications include arthritis, especially of the spine; kidney stones, urinary tract infections, and other urinary disorders; gallstones, malabsorption of nutrients, and other digestive problems; and abnormal blood clotting.

## BREAKTHROUGHS!

**After removal of the entire colon (colectomy), except for a small rectal stump, creation of an ileoanal connection (anastomosis) can restore normal bowel function. In this procedure, the ilium—the lowermost portion of the small intestine—is attached to the remaining muscles of the rectum. An internal pouch to collect fecal waste is fashioned from a segment of the small intestine. The operation is usually performed after the colectomy has healed.**

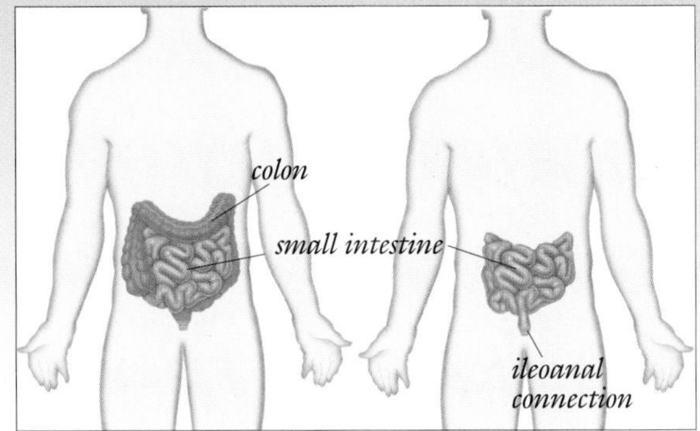


**Ulcerative colitis** typically begins with inflammation and ulcers in the rectum that spread upward and eventually involve the entire colon. Severe abdominal cramps and a rectal discharge of blood-streaked mucus, both with and between bowel movements, are common early signs. At first, constipation may be a problem, but as the inflammation spreads upward, stools become more blood-streaked, more frequent, and looser. The chronic blood loss can lead to fatigue and anemia; fever and loss of weight and appetite are common. There is also an increased risk of colon cancer.

## WHAT YOU CAN DO

Inflammatory bowel disorders tend to come and go, so see your doctor as soon as possible if symptoms flare up. An ice pack placed on the abdomen may ease cramping and dull pain, but do not use a heating pad, which can worsen inflammation. Rest as much as possible; reduced physical activity lowers bowel action (motility) and gives it a chance to heal.

If you have Crohn's disease and smoke, make every effort to stop. Because diet is instrumental in controlling IBD, be sure to follow the diet prescribed by your doctor or nutritionist. Eat small, frequent meals and avoid spicy or fatty dishes and other foods that aggravate symptoms (see *Nutraceuticals*, right). Increase your intake of fluids to lower the risk of dehydration, but avoid caffeine, alcohol, and carbonated drinks, which stimulate the intestines and can worsen symptoms. Stress also exacerbates IBD, so try to lower your stress level.

## HOW TO TREAT IT

### Medications

Codeine or another narcotic may be prescribed for pain and also to control diarrhea; specific antidiarrheal medications may also be needed. Drugs to counter inflammation include prednisone or other steroids as well as mesalamine (Pentasa) and sulfasalazine (Salazopyrin). Antibiotics and drugs to quell intestinal spasms, such as tincture of belladonna, may also be prescribed, especially for ulcerative colitis. Mild forms of IBD can usually be treated on an outpatient basis, but severe symptoms call for hospitalization for intravenous fluids and other medications, as well as blood transfusions if severe anemia has developed due to chronic bleeding.

### Surgery

Many patients with Crohn's disease and ulcerative colitis require surgery. Fistulas and the affected portions of the small intestine and colon often must be removed to prevent more serious complications in Crohn's disease. Surgical removal of the entire colon is a standard treatment for severe ulcerative colitis (see *Breakthroughs!*, left).

## HOW TO PREVENT IT

Because the cause of IBD is unknown, there is no way to prevent these disorders.

### ALTERNATIVE THERAPIES

**Diet therapy**

Patients with Crohn's disease are usually given a high-protein, low-fiber diet. Avoid raw vegetables and fruits, milk products, whole-grain and other high-fiber products, foods that cause gas, and highly spiced, fried, or fatty foods; also abstain from alcohol and avoid caffeinated and carbonated beverages, which increase intestinal activity. Similar dietary restrictions may be prescribed for persons with mild to moderate ulcerative colitis. To allow the colon to heal, patients with severe colitis may be given total parenteral feeding, in which all nutrition is administered intravenously.

**Nutraceuticals**

IBD often interferes with the absorption of nutrients, so a high-potency multiple vitamin is usually needed, often along with a high-nutrition supplement. Iron pills are prescribed to treat anemia; if regular pills cause an upset stomach, try a time-release product. PABA, one of the B-complex vitamins, and vitamin E both have anti-inflammatory effects; recommended daily dosages are 800 IU of vitamin E and 3000 mg of PABA divided into three doses during flare-ups and 1000 mg twice a day at other times. Do not take PABA with sulfa drugs. Recent studies indicate that vitamin A promotes healing of the IBD ulcerations; take 25,000 IU a day during flare-ups and reduce to 8000 to 10,000 at other times. **Note:** High doses of vitamin A can cause serious birth defects; stop supplements at least

**WARNING!**

***Chronic diarrhea and bleeding can cause serious dehydration, anemia, and an upset in body chemistry. Symptoms include dry mouth and skin, a dry or furrowed tongue, muscle weakness, a prickling or tingling sensation, a rapid heartbeat, and possible fever. Seek immediate medical attention if any of these develop.***

three months before becoming pregnant. Long-term use of sulfasalazine (Salazopyrin), a drug often used to help keep IBD in check, interferes with folic acid metabolism, which can be corrected by taking a 1000 to 2000 microgram supplement.

**Herbal medicine**

Herbs that soothe and help heal IBD include marshmallow root and slippery elm. They are best taken in three to five cups of tea a day; they are also available as capsules and tinctures. Deglycyrrhizinated licorice (DGL) has healing properties; chew two wafers (380 mg) three times a day between meals. The tannins in green tea are astringent and promote intestinal healing; its polyphenols may reduce the risk of colon cancer.

**Relaxation therapies**

Meditation, yoga, and self-hypnosis are among the therapies that counter stress, which exacerbates IBD.

# Irritable Bowel Syndrome

## SYMPTOMS

- *Abdominal discomfort, bloating, cramps, and gassiness.*
- *Alternating constipation and diarrhea.*
- *Possible nausea, backaches, fatigue, and malaise.*

## WHO IS AT RISK

*Irritable bowel syndrome (IBS) is one of the most common intestinal disorders, affecting more than 40 million North Americans. It typically starts during adolescence or early adulthood; women IBS sufferers outnumber men about two to one. There are no detectable physical abnormalities, but allergies and food sensitivities, infection, stress, emotional factors, diet, hormonal changes, and overuse of antibiotics and certain other medications are among the many factors that can start a flare-up or worsen symptoms.*

## HOW IT DEVELOPS

An attack usually starts with abdominal discomfort, cramps, bloating, and bouts of constipation alternating with diarrhea. The symptoms are due to abnormal peristalsis, the intestinal muscle contractions that move food and waste material through the digestive tract. The contractions are normally so gentle and well-coordinated that they go unnoticed until a person experiences an urge to have a bowel movement. In IBS, however, the intestinal muscles go into painful spasms and then relax, resulting in contractions that are either too forceful or too weak and causing cramps, constipation, diarrhea, and other symptoms. Why some people also experience backaches, fatigue, and other symptoms unrelated to digestion is unknown, but some experts theorize that allergies or emotional factors may play a role.

## WHAT YOU CAN DO

A heating pad or soaking in a hot bath may ease abdominal cramps. Do not smoke, and abstain from alcohol and caffeine, which stimulate peristalsis. A high-fiber diet may help, but avoid gas-producing foods, such as onions, cabbage, and dried peas and beans (legumes). Keep a food diary to help identify foods that trigger symptoms, and then avoid them. During a flare-up, eliminate spicy and fried and other fatty foods. Also avoid sweeteners that contain sorbitol and mannitol, which can cause gas.

## HOW TO TREAT IT

In treating the various symptoms associated with IBS, the following may be tried: psyllium (Metamucil), taken with 8 to 10 glasses of water, or Lactulose (Cephulac), for constipation; short-term use of loperamide (Imodium) or diphenoxylate (Lomotil), for diarrhea; simethicone (Phazyme) gives relief for excess gas causing bloating. Antispasmodic medications such as dicyclomine (Bentylol) may also be used to relieve painful abdominal cramps. These drugs are taken 30 to 60 minutes before eating. Low-dose tricyclic antidepressants often help relieve IBS symptoms, but how they work is not known.

## HOW TO PREVENT IT

Lifestyle changes, especially reducing stress or adopting better coping techniques, are critical in preventing IBS flare-ups. Regular exercise not only improves bowel function but also helps control stress. Getting at least seven hours of sleep a night is also important, as are increasing fiber intake and eating regular small meals low in fat.

### ALTERNATIVE THERAPIES

**Aromatherapy**

To counter stress, try adding a few drops of rose oil to warm bathwater. To relieve diarrhea, aromatherapists

**BREAKTHROUGHS!**

**Alosetron (Lotronex) is currently under priority review at Health Canada. This highly selective serotonin receptor antagonist is believed to work peripherally in the gastrointestinal tract to modify pain signals that travel to the brain, thereby inhibiting the sensation of pain and exaggerated motility experienced by IBS patients.**

recommend inhaling the vapors of rosemary or black pepper oils, and switching to marjoram oil if constipation develops.

**Herbal medicine**

Peppermint oil can ease abdominal cramps by relaxing the smooth muscles of the intestine and reducing gas production; it should be taken in the form of enteric-coated capsules, which are not dissolved until they reach the small intestine. Start with one 0.2 milliliter capsule about two hours before eating and, if necessary, increase the dosage to two capsules a day between meals. Other herbs that may produce similar benefits include chamomile and fennel seeds. Both can be brewed into teas and consumed before meals; chamomile can also be taken in capsule form containing two to three grams of the herb. To increase fiber intake, take one to three teaspoons of ground psyllium seeds a day. Be sure to drink at least 8 to 10 glasses of water a day when taking psyllium, which adds bulk to the stool and helps regulate intestinal contractions.

**Nutraceuticals**

Supplements that may help include acidophilus, which helps restore beneficial intestinal bacteria that may be lost during a bout of diarrhea. Women who experience a worsening of IBS during their premenstrual phase may benefit from taking evening primrose oil capsules that contain at least 350 mg of gamma linolenic acid (GLA). Evening primrose oil should not be used by people taking anticoagulants.

**WARNING!**

***See a doctor if the stool contains blood. Although bleeding sometimes occurs in IBS, other more serious causes, such as colon cancer or ulcerative colitis, must be ruled out.***

**Relaxation therapies**

Yoga, meditation, self-hypnosis, and massage therapy are among the many relaxation strategies that can reduce stress and improve IBS symptoms.

# Malabsorption

## SYMPTOMS

- *Abdominal cramps, bloating, gassiness, and other discomfort.*
- *Weight loss and possible diarrhea and nutritional deficiencies.*
- *Bulky, malodorous stools that contain undigested fat (steatorrhea).*

## WHO IS AT RISK

*There are many different malabsorption syndromes, all of which are characterized by an inability to digest and absorb specific nutrients. The more common types include:*

*Digestion is normally completed as food moves through the small intestine (right) and nutrients are absorbed into the body through the intestines' tiny hair-like projections, called villi (bottom left). Malabsorption occurs when the villi are widened or flat (bottom right).*

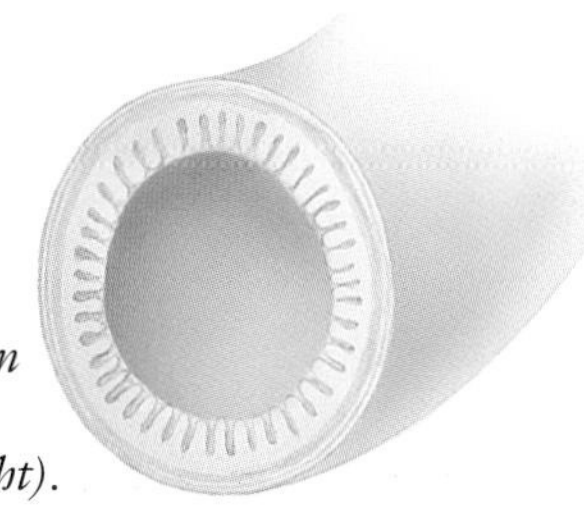

*normal small intestine*

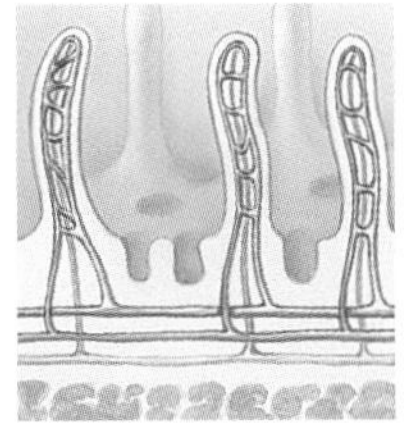

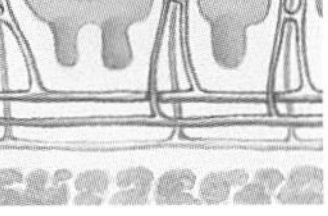

*normal villi*

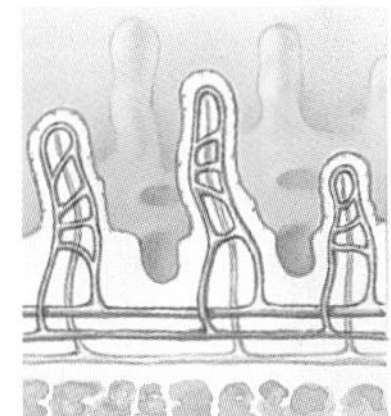

*abnormal villi*

- ***Lactose intolerance,*** *which is due to a deficiency of lactase, the enzyme needed to digest milk sugar (lactose). Although it affects all racial groups, it is especially common among persons of African or Asian heritage; the risk of developing it increases with age.*
- ***Celiac disease,*** *a hereditary disorder in which the person is unable to digest gluten, the protein in cereal grains, especially wheat and rye. The disease usually becomes apparent when a baby starts eating solid foods.*
- ***Tropical sprue,*** *which occurs mostly among natives of and visitors to the Caribbean, southern India, and Southeast Asia. The cause is unknown, although an infection or food poisoning may trigger it. Victims are unable to absorb many vitamins and minerals.*

*Malabsorption may also develop among people who have an abnormally short or deformed small intestine and various genetic diseases. Infection and worms (**see* Worms and Other Intestinal Parasites, *p 172)* *can cause malabsorption; so too can inflammatory bowel disorders, AIDS, cystic fibrosis, and various digestive disorders.*

## HOW IT DEVELOPS

**Lactose intolerance** starts with uncomfortable bloating and gassiness after consuming milk and other foods containing lactose. Symptoms usually worsen with age.

Painful abdominal bloating and the passage of bulky, pale, malodorous stools are common early signs of **celiac disease**; anemia and other nutritional deficiencies may develop if the condition is not treated. Early signs of **tropical sprue** include a sore tongue, diarrhea, and weight loss; these are usually followed by deficiency diseases, especially megaloblastic anemia due to an inability to absorb folic acid and vitamin $B_{12}$.

## WORMS AND OTHER INTESTINAL PARASITES

The human intestinal tract is home to numerous organisms, including millions of beneficial bacteria that aid in digestion and manufacture certain vitamins. Not so friendly are various parasitic worms that can cause painful abdominal bloating and possible intestinal obstruction, diarrhea or constipation, intense itching, and anemia and other nutritional deficiencies. Climate and sanitary conditions determine the type of intestinal parasites in a given area; following are the more common examples.

- **Pinworms,** which afflict about 5 to 15 percent of Canadians (mostly children) at any given time, mature in the colon. While the host sleeps, the adult female worm lays thousands of eggs around the anus, causing skin irritation and intense itching. During scratching, some of the tiny eggs attach to the fingers or get under the fingernails; they can also be picked up from clothing or inhaled if they become airborne. Eggs that are swallowed begin a new cycle of infestation.
- **Hookworms,** which infect about 25 percent of the world's population, are relatively uncommon in Canada. Eggs are discharged in the stool, hatch in the soil, and the larvae enter the body through the skin, usually on the soles of persons who go barefoot. They travel first to the lungs, are coughed up, and then swallowed. The adult worms live in the small intestine (see illustration), where they feed on blood. They can cause abdominal pain and iron-deficiency anemia.
- **Threadworms,** which have a life cycle similar to hookworms, can cause shortness of breath and pneumonia when lodged in the lungs, and abdominal pain and diarrhea when they are in the small intestine.
- **Roundworms,** which enter the body as eggs in contaminated water or food, normally live in the small intestine, where they can cause abdominal cramps, obstruction, and nutritional deficiencies. They sometimes migrate to the pancreas, liver, appendix, and other organs, where they can cause pain, inflammation, and obstruction.
- **Tapeworms,** which are common in developing countries but rare in Canada, enter the body in cysts found in undercooked meat or fish. They can grow up to 30 feet in length and can cause abdominal pain, diarrhea, and anemia.

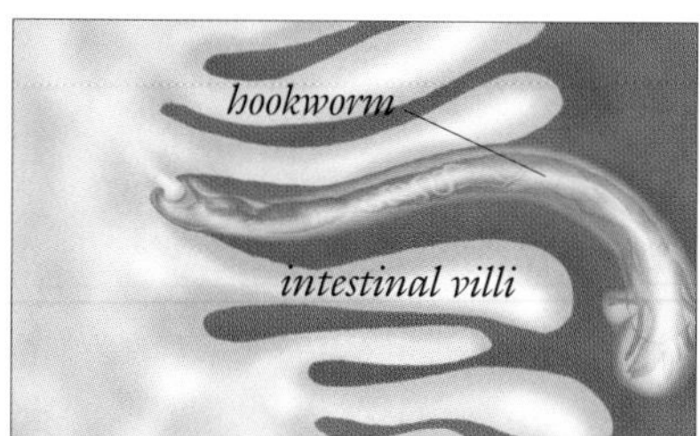


*Hookworms, which live on blood, attach themselves to the villi that line the small intestine.*

## WHAT YOU CAN DO

The bloating and discomfort of lactose intolerance and celiac disease are best controlled by eliminating the dietary substances that provoke symptoms. In lactose intolerance, this means eliminating milk and certain milk products; some people can tolerate yogurt and some cheeses because their lactose is already partially digested. Or you can take lactase tablets (see *Nutraceuticals*, right) or look for milk that is lactose-free.

Persons with celiac disease should follow a gluten-free diet that eliminates all foods made with wheat, rye, and—to a lesser degree—oats and other cereal grains. Many processed foods also must be avoided because gluten is a very common food filler.

## HOW TO TREAT IT

Treatment varies according to the type of malabsorption. Tropical sprue usually can be cured by taking antibiotics for up to six months, even though there may be no evidence of a bacterial infection. Patients with severe celiac disease may require IV feeding to allow healing.

## HOW TO PREVENT IT

Flare-ups of lactose intolerance and celiac disease are prevented by avoiding the foods that cause them; other malabsorption syndromes may be prevented by early treatment of the underlying diseases that cause them.

### ALTERNATIVE THERAPIES

**Nutraceuticals**

High-dose vitamin and mineral supplements are often needed to counter the deficiencies caused by sprue and other malabsorption syndromes. Dosages should be determined by a doctor or registered dietitian. Persons who suffer from lactose intolerance usually need calcium supplements; adult dosages call for taking two or three 500-mg pills a day. Acidophilus capsules or powder containing live *Lactobacilli* bacteria can help reduce bloating, gas, diarrhea, and other symptoms related to taking antibiotics. Acidophilus works by restoring the beneficial intestinal bacteria that are killed by antibiotics or washed out by diarrhea. Supplements of pancreatic enzymes may be prescribed for malabsorption due to cystic fibrosis.

**WARNING!**

***Celiac disease may not produce obvious symptoms in its early stages, especially when it develops in very young children. It should be suspected if a baby ceases to thrive and grow normally following introduction of solid foods, especially cereals.***

# Anus and Rectum

*These organs, situated at the lowermost end of the digestive tract, collect and expel body waste and intestinal gas. Both are also the sites of common painful disorders—abscesses, inflammation, fissures, tumors, and hemorrhoids, among others.*

## Anal Fissure

### SYMPTOMS

- *Intense pain during or after a bowel movement.*
- *Anal bleeding.*
- *Possible itching, pus discharge, stoolholding (a young child's refusal to defecate), and ineffectual straining.*

### BREAKTHROUGHS!

**Experimental use of topical nitroglycerin—the medication more commonly used to treat angina—indicates that it may also relieve the pain of an anal fissure. It is thought to work by relaxing the anal sphincter. Because the medication is absorbed through the skin, it may cause headaches and other side effects. Researchers also caution that more study is needed to prove the safety and efficacy of nitroglycerin for this purpose.**

### WHO IS AT RISK

*The causes of most anal fissures are unknown, but doctors blame constipation for many. Persons with an inflammatory bowel disorder also may develop anal fissures or ulcers; anal intercourse is also a possible cause.*

### HOW IT DEVELOPS

Acute anal fissures develop suddenly, often while straining during a bowel movement. The intense anal pain is exacerbated by spasms of the anal sphincter muscles, and it often persists for several hours after a bowel movement.

### WHAT YOU CAN DO

Avoiding constipation is the single most important step you can take to ease the pain of an anal fissure. Increase your fiber and fluid intake and, if necessary, use a bulking agent such as powdered psyllium seeds (for example, Metamucil). Taking a warm sitz bath for 10 minutes or so following a bowel movement helps relax the sphincter spasms and ease pain. To avoid infection and an abscess, pay particular attention to cleansing the anal area after each bowel movement. A moistened anal wipe, such as those used to clean a baby's diaper area, is more comfortable to use and does a better job cleaning the skin than toilet paper. This conservative approach prompts most anal fissures to heal on their own in a week or so.

### HOW TO TREAT IT

#### Medications

Doctors sometimes recommend an emollient suppository, such as glycerin, to lubricate the anal canal and promote healing. However, check with your doctor before using any anal medication. Some, such as hydrocortisone suppositories, may ease itching, but they hinder healing.

#### WARNING!

***Chronic anal fissures or ulcers are sometimes manifestations of a serious underlying disease. See a doctor to rule out cancer, syphilis or another infection, and Crohn's disease.***

#### Surgery

In severe cases, an operation may be needed to break the cycle of anal sphincter spasms. This may entail removal of the internal sphincter or the insertion of increasingly large dilators to widen and relax the internal sphincter. Both procedures can be done under local anesthesia.

### HOW TO PREVENT IT

Avoiding constipation is the best preventive.

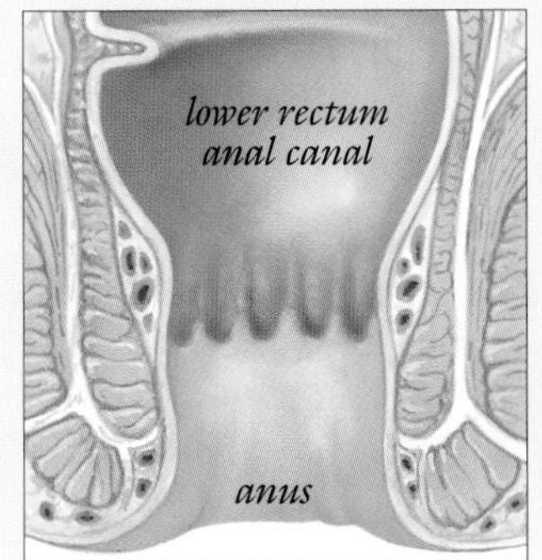


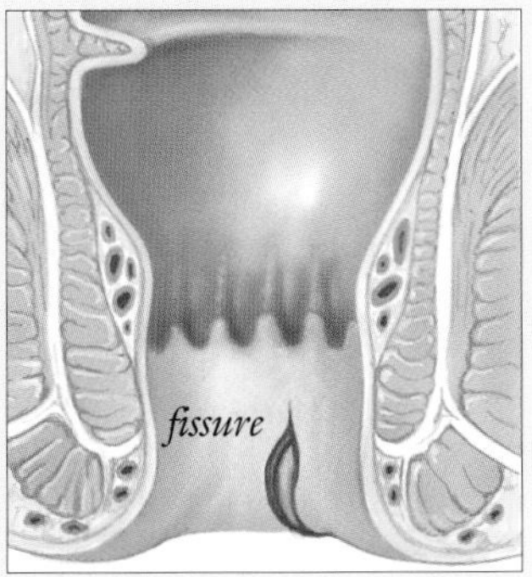


*The rectum—the final five inches or so of the colon—serves as a holding tank for the feces. As the rectum fills, its nerves trigger the urge to defecate, and the stool moves into the anal canal to exit through the anus. Anal fissures are lengthwise tears or ulcers in the lining of the anal canal.*

ALTERNATIVE THERAPIES

**Herbal medicine**

Small amounts of aloe vera gel applied to the anal area are soothing and may also promote healing. Use fresh gel squeezed from an aloe leaf.

# Anorectal Abscess/Fistula

### SYMPTOMS

***Abscess:*** *Acutely painful anal swelling and inflammation.*

***Fistula:*** *Recurrent anorectal abscesses that are very painful; intermittent or constant discharge from the anus or skin.*

### WHO IS AT RISK

***Anorectal abscesses****—painful pockets of pus—sometimes develop at the site of a fissure or ulcer; they are also common in male homosexuals and others who engage in anal intercourse.*

*The abscesses often give rise to* ***anorectal fistulas****—tubelike structures between the rectum or anal canal and adjacent organs, such as the vagina in women, or the skin. Some are due to congenital malformations; predisposing conditions include Crohn's disease, diverticulosis, and tumors.*

## HOW IT DEVELOPS

An **anorectal abscess**, which starts as an encapsulated bacterial infection, becomes increasingly painful as it swells. Superficial abscesses form just under the skin surface and, like a boil, they usually come to a head and rupture. Deep abscesses are less likely to rupture; instead, they cause pain that spreads through the lower abdomen. There may also be a fever. **Anorectal fistulas** often arise from an abscess to provide a drainage route for infectious material.

## WHAT YOU CAN DO

A small abscess can sometimes be healed by applying warm compresses to bring it to a head and allow it to drain. However, do not try to rupture or lance it yourself; this can result in spreading the infection. For larger abscesses or suspected fistulas, see a doctor as soon as possible. In the meantime, a warm (not hot) sitz bath may temporarily ease discomfort, and a stool softener can prevent painful bowel movements.

**WARNING!**

***Anorectal abscesses often promote development of fistulas. After treatment of an abscess, be on the alert for any unusual discharges, including watery fecal matter from the vagina.***

## HOW TO TREAT IT

Abscesses should be lanced and drained; antibiotics may be prescribed to help clear up the infection. Fistulas almost always require surgery to either remove or open the abnormal connection. The operation may be performed under either local or general anesthesia. Antibiotics are usually prescribed.

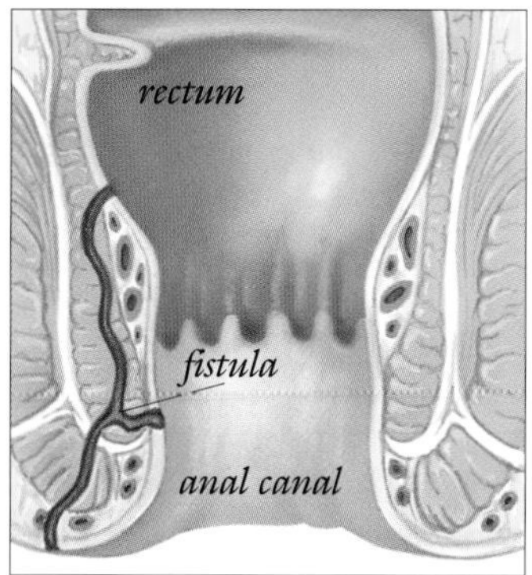


*An anorectal fistula is a tubelike connection that typically links the rectum, anal canal, and skin.*

## HOW TO PREVENT IT

Abscesses due to anal intercourse can be prevented by abstaining from this form of sexual activity or at least always using a well-lubricated condom. Other preventive measures include prompt treatment of Crohn's disease, diverticulosis, and other bowel disorders.

ALTERNATIVE THERAPIES

**Herbal medicine**

Studies show that aloe vera gel inhibits some bacteria and may be useful in healing superficial anorectal abcesses.

# Hemorrhoids

### SYMPTOMS

- *Anal pain, which may be quite severe, especially during bowel movements; anal itching and bleeding.*

### WHO IS AT RISK

*About one-third of Canadian adults have hemorrhoids. They tend to run in families; other predisposing factors include chronic constipation, obesity, and pregnancy.*

## HOW IT DEVELOPS

Repeated straining to pass hard stools or chronic pressure from obesity or a developing fetus can result in permanent swelling of the anal veins and formation of hemorrhoidal tissue. As the mass presses on nearby nerves, it causes pain and itching; the hemorrhoids may also bleed, especially during a bowel movement.

## WHAT YOU CAN DO

Use cold compresses or an ice pack wrapped in a cloth to temporarily ease pain. Apply the cold pack for 15 to 20 minutes, remove it for 10 minutes, and then reapply for another 15 to 20 minutes. A lukewarm sitz bath may also ease pain. For external hemorrhoids that are not thrombosed, look for OTC creams or suppositories to soothe pain as well as astringents such as zinc sulfate. For hemorrhoids inside the anal opening, use a bulk laxative such as psyllium and a stool softener such as docusate. Follow package instructions and use them for only a few days at a time. Try to minimize stool time and, to ease pressure on the veins, sit in a squatting position with your feet resting on a low stool.

**WARNING!**

***Blood in the stool should always be investigated by a doctor. If it's from hemorrhoids, it's harmless. But bloody stools may also be a warning sign of colon or rectal cancer.***

## HOW TO TREAT IT

If pain and bleeding persist, removal of the hemorrhoids may be advisable. To stop bleeding, a doctor may try sclerotherapy, which entails injecting the hemorrhoids with a phenol solution. Internal hemorrhoids that protrude into the anal canal can often be removed by tying them off with a rubber band to cut off their blood supply. Other possible procedures include laser surgery (see *Breakthroughs!*), freezing, burning them off with an electric needle, or conventional surgery. Local anesthesia is used during these procedures; then a topical anesthetic pad or ointment is usually sufficient.

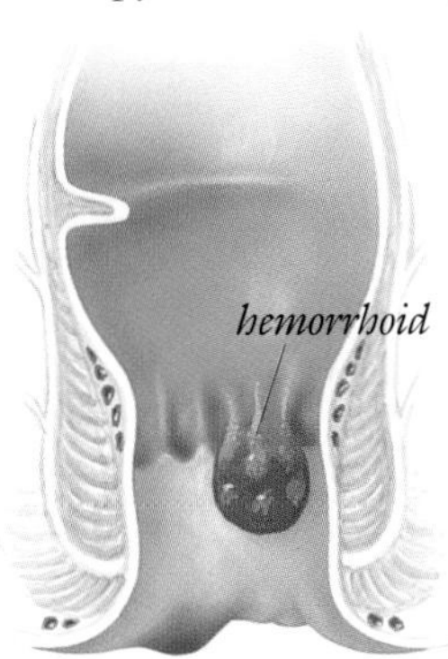


*Hemorrhoids are varicose veins in the anal area.*

## HOW TO PREVENT IT

Strive to avoid constipation (see the strategies outlined in *Constipation,* p 163). Also try to maintain ideal weight.

### ALTERNATIVE THERAPIES

**Herbal medicine**

Astringent herbs may ease itching and pain. Try applying a pad soaked in strong green tea or witch hazel to external hemorrhoids, or add 1/4 to 1/2 cup of witch hazel to a lukewarm sitz bath. Aloe vera gel may also help.

**BREAKTHROUGHS!**

**Laser surgery is fast becoming a preferred method of removing hemorrhoids. This approach, which uses powerful beams of light to vaporize unwanted tissue, causes much less pain and bleeding than conventional surgery.**

# Proctitis

### SYMPTOMS

- *Anorectal pain ranging from mild to very intense.*
- *Inflammation and perhaps ulceration of the mucous membrane lining the anorectal area.*
- *Rectal bleeding and possible mucus discharge.*

### WHO IS AT RISK

*Proctitis may be a component of Crohn's disease or ulcerative colitis; it is also caused by sexually transmitted diseases (STDs), such as gonorrhea, syphilis, chlamydia, and genital herpes, or intestinal parasites, such as pinworms. Anal intercourse can result in proctitis; other possible causes include antibiotics and anorectal radiation therapy.*

## HOW IT DEVELOPS

The rectal pain and other proctitis symptoms are due to inflammation and ulceration of the mucous membranes.

## WHAT YOU CAN DO

See your doctor as soon as possible if you suffer persistent rectal pain and bleeding. In the meantime, avoid anal intercourse and do not insert suppositories or any other object into the anal canal. Cool compresses may ease pain; avoid spicy foods, which can cause further irritation. If diarrhea occurs, take a mild antidiarrheal medication, such as bismuth, to help stop it.

**WARNING!**

***Most sexually transmitted diseases are highly infectious and many are epidemic among young Americans. Anyone who is diagnosed with STD-related proctitis should make sure that all sexual partners are notified.***

## HOW TO TREAT IT

Antibiotics are prescribed to treat bacterial proctitis. Prednisone or another corticosteroid may be used to treat other types of proctitis, including that caused by radiation therapy. The drugs may be administered as an ointment, topical foam, enema, or suppository—forms that reduce the risk of steroid side effects.

## HOW TO PREVENT IT

Proctitis caused by STDs can be prevented by practicing safe sex and using condoms.

### ALTERNATIVE THERAPIES

**Herbal medicine**

Herbal teas that soothe intestinal inflammation and promote healing include slippery elm, marshmallow root, and mullein.

# THE REPRODUCTIVE AND URINARY ORGANS

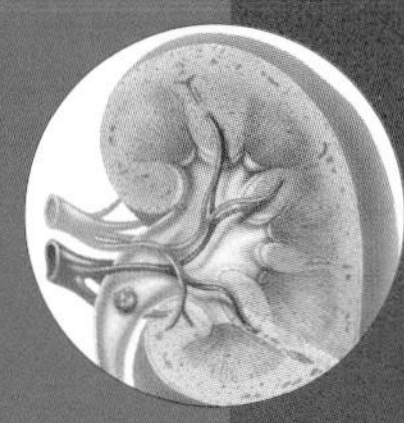

# Kidneys and Urinary Tract

*The kidneys, ureters, bladder, and urethra make up the body's excretory system. All of these organs are common sources of pain, ranging from the excruciating agony of kidney stones to the burning discomfort and urinary urgency of a bladder infection.*

## Cystitis/Urethritis

### SYMPTOMS

*The entire urinary tract is a frequent target of bacterial infections; the bladder (cystitis) and urethra (urethritis) are the most common sites.*

***Cystitis:** Burning pain that starts with the urge to urinate and peaks at the end of voiding; urinary frequency and urgency both day and night; passage of only small amounts of urine, which often contains blood; possible diffuse pubic or low-back pain.*

***Urethritis:** Mild discomfort in the pubic area; urinary frequency; cloudy or pus-streaked urine.*

### WHO IS AT RISK

*Most people develop a lower urinary tract infection (UTI) at some point in their lives. Sexually active women are by far the most common victims of bladder infections, or cystitis; in fact, the incidence of UTIs among women aged 20 to 50 is 50 times greater than in men, and many women suffer several bouts a year. However, the male incidence increases after age 50, often due to an enlarged prostate gland. Other risk factors include diabetes, paralysis from a spinal cord injury or nerve disorder such as multiple sclerosis, the presence of an in-dwelling catheter to drain the bladder, and congenital abnormalities of the urinary tract.*

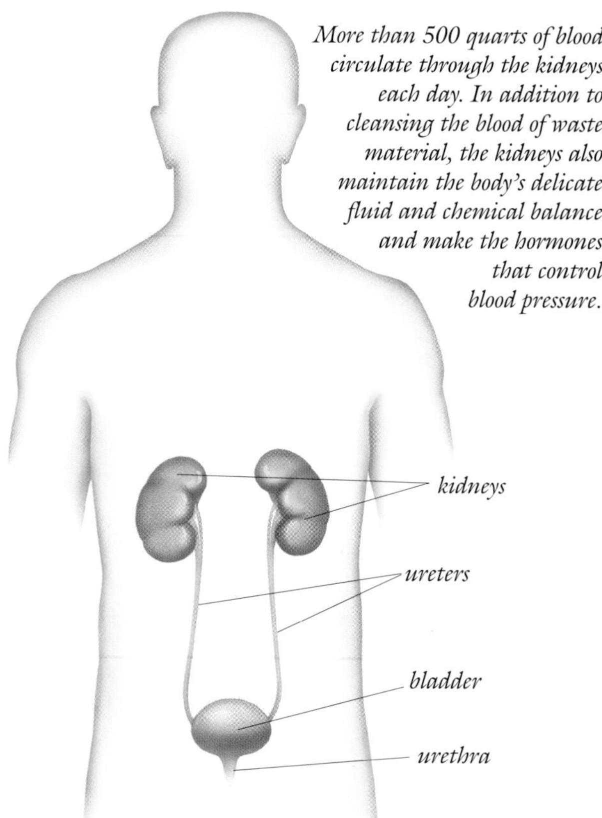


*More than 500 quarts of blood circulate through the kidneys each day. In addition to cleansing the blood of waste material, the kidneys also maintain the body's delicate fluid and chemical balance and make the hormones that control blood pressure.*

## HOW IT DEVELOPS

**Cystitis** usually comes on rapidly with a painful, urgent need to void, difficulty starting the urination, and then passing only a small amount of urine, which may contain blood. Cystitis develops when bacteria—usually *E. coli* that normally live in the intestinal tract—invade the urethra and travel upward to the bladder, where they multiply. Women are so vulnerable because they have a very short urethra—only about two inches compared to eight or more inches in males. Very often, bacteria from the anal area are introduced into the urethral opening during sexual intercourse or when wiping after a bowel movement. Sexually transmitted organisms, especially chlamydia, can also cause cystitis.

**Urethritis** develops more gradually and its symptoms are milder than those of cystitis. In men, the prevailing symptom is often a penile discharge of pus or mucus; the cause is often due to chlamydia, gonorrhea, or another STD. In women, urethritis is often secondary to vaginitis; in addition to itching, inflammation, and other symptoms arising from the vagina, a woman may also experience urinary frequency and mild pain when voiding.

## WHAT YOU CAN DO

See your doctor as soon as possible. In the meantime, a warm sitz bath may relieve the burning discomfort and pain. Drink at least 8 to 10 glasses of water a day to help flush bacteria out of the bladder; abstain from alcohol and caffeine, which irritate the bladder. Cranberry juice may speed healing by creating an acidic bladder environment that is inhospitable to bacteria (see *Nutraceuticals,* p 179).

## HOW TO TREAT IT

Antibiotics quickly clear up most lower urinary tract infections. Although doing a urine culture to identify the infecting bacterium is recommended, in practice many doctors immediately prescribe a broad-spectrum antibiotic, such as sulfamethoxazole with trimethoprim (Bactrim or Septra) or nitrofurantoin (Macrodantin and others), that works against most UTIs. These drugs usually relieve pain and urinary urgency within a few hours; if pain persists, however, phenazopyridine (Pyridium), a bladder analgesic, may be prescribed.

## HOW TO PREVENT IT

Women who have more than three UTIs a year are often advised to take long-term low-dose antibiotics as a preventive measure. Other preventive strategies, especially for women, include:

- Drinking at least 8 to 10 glasses of water a day to increase the flow of urine and wash out bacteria from the bladder. (This is also important for older men who have an enlarged prostate.)
- Emptying the bladder and then drinking a glass of water before sexual intercourse; the water helps the bladder fill so you can urinate again about an hour or so after intercourse and wash out any bacteria that may have invaded the urinary tract.
- Practicing good hygiene; after a bowel movement, always wipe from front to back to reduce the spread of bacteria from the anal area to the urethra.
- Keeping the genital area as dry as possible; wear cotton underwear, avoid very tight jeans and other constrictive clothing, and don't sit around in a wet bathing suit.
- Not using vaginal deodorants, bubble baths, scented soaps, and other potentially irritating substances.
- Practicing safe sex to avoid contracting chlamydia and other STDs that can infect the urinary tract.

### WARNING!

***Home testing kits can detect the presence of bacteria in the urine, but it is still important to see a doctor for a diagnosis and treatment with the most appropriate antibiotics.***

### NEW HOPE FOR SUFFERERS OF INTERSTITIAL CYSTITIS

Interstitial cystitis—chronic, very painful bladder inflammation—afflicts an estimated 30,000 to 50,000 Canadians, mostly women. Until recently, doctors could do little to relieve the condition other than to prescribe aspirin, ibuprofen, and other painkillers. Now a number of new treatments are bringing much-needed relief to thousands of sufferers. These treatments include:

- **Pentosan polysulfate sodium (Elmiron)**, a new oral medication that helps restore the damaged bladder surface, usually works in four to six months.
- **DMSO (Rimso-50)**, a drug derived from an industrial solvent, is instilled directly into the bladder, where it acts as a painkiller and anti-inflammatory agent. Treatments are given every week or two, and it usually takes four to eight treatments to relieve pain and other symptoms.
- **Heparin**, a blood thinner that also has anti-inflammatory and surface protective actions, is instilled into the bladder and held for 20 to 30 minutes. Patients are taught to do this at home, at first daily for three to four months, and then every other day. Improvement is usually seen in 6 to 12 months.
- **Hyaluronic acid (Cystistat)** has effects similar to heparin. It works much faster, however, providing relief after five or six treatments, which are given weekly for four weeks and then monthly.

### ALTERNATIVE THERAPIES

**Herbal medicine**

Goldenseal and echinacea may help prevent urinary infections. They can be blended together and brewed into tea; drink one or two cups a day. For cautions concerning echinacea and goldenseal, see *About the Recommendations*, p 7. During a flare-up, nettle tea or a daily dose of 500 mg of uva ursi extract (standardized to contain 20 percent arbutin) may ease symptoms by increasing urinary flow and making it acidic. Do not take uva ursi with vitamin C or cranberry extract or juice.

**Nutraceuticals**

Cranberry juice (or extract capsules) helps prevent bacteria from adhering to the lining of the bladder and urethra; it also makes the urine more acidic, which may prevent infections. Drink 8 to 16 ounces of cranberry juice (preferably the unsweetened, full-strength kind sold in health food stores) a day or take 400 mg of cranberry extract twice a day. To make full-strength cranberry juice more palatable, mix it with equal parts apple juice. This mixture will also help you increase your fluid intake. High doses of vitamin C

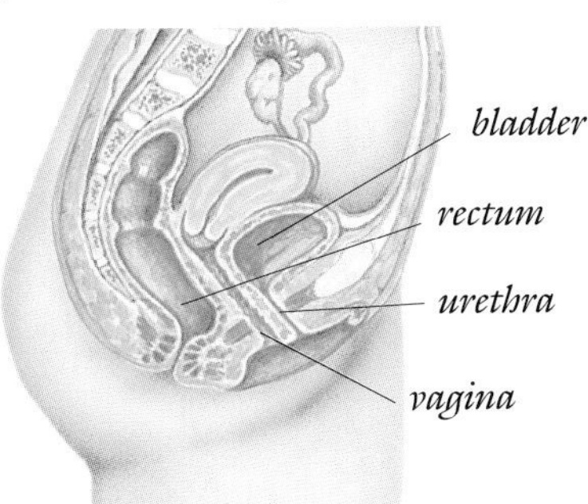


*The shortness of the female urethra and its close proximity to the anal area and vagina account for the increased frequency of cystitis among women.*

(up to 2000 mg spread throughout the day) make the urine acidic and may speed healing. However, high doses of vitamin C can also cause bladder irritation in some people, so use with caution. To prevent yeast infections when taking antibiotics, eat two or three servings of yogurt made with live cultures or take one or two acidophilus pills a day.

# Kidney Cancer

### SYMPTOMS

- *Flank pain or pain on one side of the lower back.*
- *Blood in the urine.*
- *Possible fatigue, frequent gastrointestinal upsets, loss of weight, high blood pressure, and fever.*

### WHO IS AT RISK

*The causes of kidney cancer are unknown, but experts attribute its marked rise in the last five decades to increased exposure to industrial chemicals and pollutants. It is most common in industrialized urban areas; substances linked to an increased risk include cadmium, nitrosamines, lead acetate, and asbestos, as well as aflatoxin, a grain mold, and phenacetin, a nonprescription painkiller that is no longer sold. Age is also a factor; most cases are diagnosed after age 50. Men are twice as likely to develop kidney cancer as women; other possible risk factors include smoking, a high-fat diet, and long-term hemodialysis.*

## HOW IT DEVELOPS

About 85 percent of kidney cancers are renal cell carcinomas, which start in the lining of the nephrons, the kidney's filtering units. Transitional cell cancers start in the lining of the renal pelvis—the central part of the kidney—or the ureters, the tubes that carry urine to the bladder. Wilms' tumor is a relatively rare form of kidney cancer that occurs in children.

At first, only one kidney is usually affected, although in about 20 percent of patients, the second kidney eventually develops cancer. Renal cell cancers typically spread to the nearby lymph nodes and then to the lungs, liver, bones, or brain; transitional cell cancers often invade the bladder, too.

### BREAKTHROUGHS!

**The growth of inoperable kidney cancer may be slowed with a new treatment called arterial embolization. Bits of sponge-like gelatin are injected into the renal artery, where they enter the affected kidney. In effect, this starves the cancer cells by blocking their supply of oxygen and other nutrients.**

## WHAT YOU CAN DO

There is no self-treatment for kidney cancer; see a doctor as soon as possible if you have chronic flank or lower back pain, blood in the urine, or other symptoms that suggest kidney cancer.

## HOW TO TREAT IT

A localized early renal cell cancer may be cured by a partial nephrectomy, in which the tumor and surrounding tissue are removed. More often, a total nephrectomy—removal of the entire kidney and often the surrounding tissue as well—is necessary. If the cancer is in the renal pelvis and/or ureter, the ureter and part or all of the bladder is also removed. The surgery may be followed by radiation treatments.

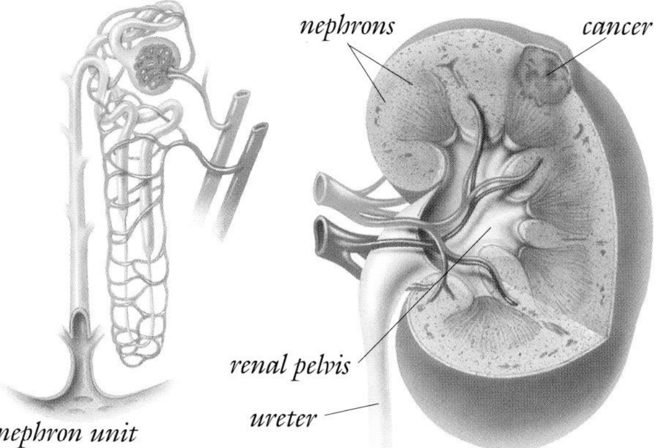


*Most kidney cancers start in the nephrons, the blood-filtering units. Less commonly the tumor starts in the renal pelvis and spreads to the ureter.*

Kidney cancer surgery often requires a large incision, which can cause intense postoperative pain. Patients are often given a morphine pump so they can administer their own pain medication as they need it. After a few days, most patients can be switched to codeine or another milder narcotic painkiller. By the time they leave the hospital, acetaminophen or a nonsteroidal anti-inflammatory drug (NSAID), such as ibuprofen, may be sufficient.

## HOW TO PREVENT IT

Because the cause of kidney cancer is unknown, there are no certain means of prevention. You can, however, reduce risk by not smoking, consuming a diet low in animal fats, and always wearing a protective mask when working with industrial chemicals, asbestos, and heavy metals such as cadmium.

### ALTERNATIVE THERAPIES

**Note:** Alternative therapies should be used only in addition to conventional medical treatments.

**Acupuncture**

Treatments may give temporary pain relief following surgery or from advanced cancer. Guided imagery and meditation may also be helpful in controlling pain.

**Herbal medicine**

Studies in China have found a reduced incidence of kidney cancer among people who drink two or more cups of green tea a day. While this benefit has not been proved, drinking green tea is safe and may help prevent kidney and other types of cancer.

**WARNING!**

***Persons who have been treated for transitional cell cancers of the renal pelvis or ureters should undergo a yearly examination of the bladder with a special viewing instrument (cystoscope). This type of kidney cancer tends to recur in the bladder.***

# Kidney Failure

## SYMPTOMS

*Kidney failure falls into one of two broad categories: acute and chronic.*

***Acute kidney failure:*** *Decreased urine output, nausea, widespread swelling, facial puffiness, and weakness.*

***Chronic kidney failure:*** *Headaches; muscle twitches, cramps, and numbness; leg pain; loss of appetite and weight; nausea and vomiting; uncomfortable dry, flaky skin; unpleasant taste in the mouth.*

## WHO IS AT RISK

***Acute kidney failure*** *is usually a complication of major surgery or a serious illness that causes other organs to fail; it may also be due to a severe kidney infection, dehydration, heatstroke, extensive burns or a major injury that causes shock, or pre-eclampsia (toxemia of pregnancy). Poorly controlled diabetes and glomerulonephritis—inflammation of the kidney's filtering units (the nephrons)—are the most common causes of* ***chronic kidney failure****. Other possible causes include untreated high blood pressure and polycystic kidney disease, a genetic disorder.*

## HOW IT DEVELOPS

Acute kidney failure comes on suddenly and, although it is life-threatening, it is usually reversible as the patient recovers from the underlying cause. Symptoms include sudden, unexplained weight gain, which is due to fluid retention and swelling (edema). The breath may smell of urine; nausea and profound weakness are also common. In contrast, chronic kidney failure develops over time and often produces no early symptoms until it is quite advanced. By the time symptoms appear, the loss of kidney function is usually permanent.

## WHAT YOU CAN DO

There is no effective self-treatment for kidney failure; see a doctor—preferably a specialist in kidney disease (nephrologist)—as soon as possible. You can, however, alleviate some of the uncomfortable symptoms. To relieve dry, flaky skin, bathe or shower in tepid, rather than hot, water and apply a moisturizer while the skin is damp. A heating pad or ice pack can ease leg and muscle pain. To minimize uncomfortable swelling, restrict salt intake and follow the diet prescribed by your doctor or dietitian.

## HOW TO TREAT IT

### Renal dialysis

Acute kidney failure usually requires renal dialysis (also called *hemodialysis*); this involves filtering the blood through an artificial kidney to cleanse it of impurities. Most patients can be weaned off dialysis as they recover from their underlying disease or injury and their kidneys resume normal functioning.

In its early stages, **chronic kidney failure** may be treated with medications to reduce inflammation of the nephrons and boost their ability to function. As the failure progresses, however, dialysis is usually necessary. Sessions last from three to eight hours and are done three or four times a week, depending upon the level of failure and the type of dialysis machine. Dialysis may be performed in an outpatient center or at home with a

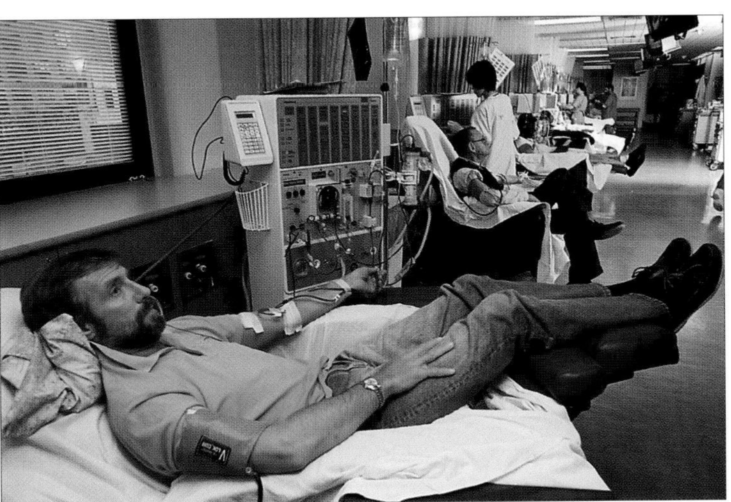

*Kidney failure patients usually obtain their hemodialysis, which must be done three or four times a week, at outpatient clinics.*

portable machine; a technique uses the abdominal lining to filter wastes (see *Breakthroughs!*, below).

### Kidney transplant

A kidney transplant using a donor organ is an alternative to long-term renal dialysis. To prevent the body from rejecting the transplant, the donor kidney must be a close genetic match; the best chances for success rest with receiving an organ from a living relative. If this is not possible, a healthy cadaver kidney taken within minutes of death—usually from an accident—is an option.

A typical kidney transplant operation takes two to three hours, and most patients leave the hospital in two to three weeks to continue recuperating at home. Medications and ice packs are used to reduce postsurgical pain.

> **WARNING!**
>
> ***Some popular weight-loss regimens that are very high in protein and low in carbohydrates are very hard on the kidneys. They should be avoided by anyone with diabetes or another condition that carries a risk of kidney failure.***

## HOW TO PREVENT IT

The best preventive measures involve controlling diabetes, high blood pressure, and other disorders that can lead to kidney failure.

### ALTERNATIVE THERAPIES

**Note:** Any alternative therapy must be checked with the physician specialist overseeing your care.

**Nutraceuticals**

Kidney dialysis patients typically need to take various vitamin and mineral supplements, but these, as well as the overall diet, must be carefully monitored by a nutritionist or dietitian trained in treating kidney failure.

**Physical therapy**

Regular exercise is important to prevent or reverse the weakness and loss of muscle mass that is so common in kidney failure, and physical therapy can help alleviate muscle pain. Exercise helps minimize the bone loss caused by steroids or other drugs that kidney transplant patients need to take. T'ai chi is often ideal for these patients; it helps tone muscles and it also fosters a sense of well-being.

> **BREAKTHROUGHS!**
>
> **Peritoneal dialysis offers many kidney-failure patients an alternative to standard hemodialysis. The peritoneum, the membrane that lines the abdomen, is used to filter wastes from the blood. A small opening is made in the abdominal wall and a soft plastic tube is inserted into it. During dialysis, the peritoneal sac is filled with a fluid to draw off the waste material in one of these techniques:**
>
> - **Intermittent peritoneal dialysis (IPD) takes about 10 hours and is done in an outpatient clinic three times a week.**
> - **Continuous ambulatory peritoneal dialysis (CAPD) is an ongoing process done at home. About two liters of dialysis fluid is always in the peritoneal sac; patients must change the fluid four or five times a day.**
> - **Continuous recycling peritoneal dialysis (CRPD) A machine called an automatic recycler performs exchanges every night while the patient sleeps. About two liters of fluid are left in the peritoneal sac.**

# Kidney Stones

### SYMPTOMS

*Many kidney stones (renal calculi) are passed painlessly or they remain in the kidney. When symptoms occur, they include the following:*

- *Renal colic, excruciating waves of pain arising in the flank or kidney area and spreading through the abdomen, pubic and genital area, and perhaps the thigh.*
- *Unexplained back pain on one side.*
- *Urinary urgency and blood in the urine; possible nausea, vomiting, fever, chills, and abdominal swelling.*

### WHO IS AT RISK

*About one in every thousand Canadian adults is hospitalized each year because of kidney stones, with men outnumbering women three to one. The causes of most kidney stones are unknown. About 80 percent of kidney stones are made of calcium salts (oxalate), leading some experts to theorize that faulty calcium metabolism may be responsible. Faulty metabolism, as well as diet, may be factors in the formation of the other, less-common types of stones. People who have had an attack of kidney stones are likely to suffer a recurrence.*

## HOW IT DEVELOPS

Most kidney stones form in the renal pelvis, the central part of the kidney, where urine pools before it passes into the ureter. Stones may form if the urine contains too much calcium or, less commonly, cystine or uric acid. Small stones usually pass unnoticed, but those that are too large to move easily through the urinary tract can cause renal colic, often described as one of the most excruciating of all pains to afflict humans.

## WHAT YOU CAN DO

Most kidney stones pass on their own; while waiting for this to happen, codeine or other strong painkillers and a heating pad placed on the lower back or abdomen may bring some relief. Drink lots of water to try to dilute the urine and flush the stone through the urinary tract. See your doctor if the pain is especially severe or persists for more than a few hours (see *Warning!*, right).

## HOW TO TREAT IT

Stones that cannot be passed naturally must be removed by one of the following methods:

- **Lithotripsy**, which uses shock waves to break up the stone. The patient sits in a tub of water with a lithotripor machine positioned over the kidneys. The machine beams shock waves into the kidney area to pulverize the stone, which can then be passed. The procedure itself is painless, but there is a small risk that the shock waves can damage the kidneys. Also, bits of stone that remain in the kidney can form new stones.
- **Laser surgery,** which uses an intense beam of light to break up the stone. A thin viewing tube (cystoscope) is equipped with a laser unit and inserted into the urinary tract. When it reaches the stone, the laser beam breaks it up. A local anesthetic is used to allow painless passage of the cystoscope; a mild painkiller may be needed for a day or so.
- **Percutaneous surgery,** an operation in which a viewing tube (endoscope) is inserted into the kidney through a small incision. A small stone can be snared and removed through the endoscope; a larger stone may need to be broken up by sound waves.

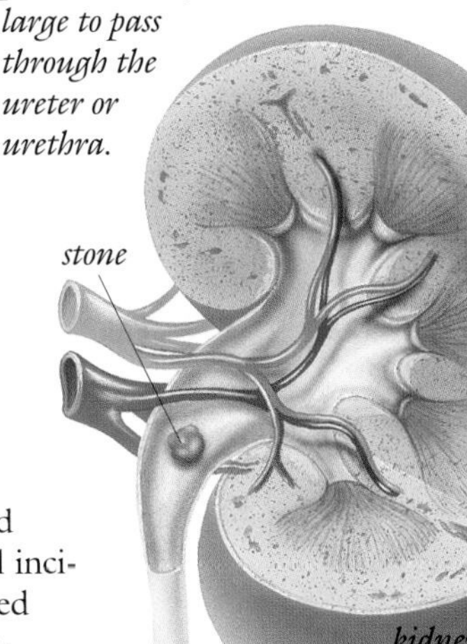

*Kidney stones produce pain when they are too large to pass through the ureter or urethra.*

## HOW TO PREVENT IT

If the stone passes naturally, try to salvage it so that your doctor can have its content analyzed and prescribe medications to prevent new ones from forming. A thiazide diuretic, such as hydrochlorothiazide (HydroDIURIL and others), lowers the amount of calcium in the urine; allopurinol (Zyloprim) prevents uric acid stones.

- Recent studies indicate that dietary changes can help prevent some kidney stones.
- Drink at least 8 to 10 glasses of water a day to dilute the urine and reduce stone formation.
- Cut back on tea and coffee and avoid carbonated drinks that are high in phosphates.
- Foods high in oxalates—salts that bind with calcium ions to form stones—should be limited; examples include spinach, rhubarb, nuts, chocolate, and tea. Similarly, those who are prone to forming stones should cut their intake of animal protein and salt, both of which are linked to an increased risk of kidney stones. (Contrary to popular belief, a high intake of calcium does not cause stones; in fact, it may lower the risk.)
- Increase consumption of fruits and vegetables, foods that are high in potassium, which may lower the tendency to form stones.

**WARNING!**

***A large stone blocking the urinary tract can cause a backup of urine in the kidneys, increasing the risk of infection and organ damage. See a doctor if a kidney stone is not passed in a few hours.***

### ALTERNATIVE THERAPIES

**Note:** Check with your doctor before taking any herbal or nutritional supplement if you have kidney disease.

**Herbal medicine**

Juniper berry tea has a mild diuretic effect that may help flush the kidneys and prevent stone formation.

**Nutraceuticals**

Recent studies indicate that taking 250 mg of calcium citrate with meals may help prevent stone formation because the calcium binds with oxalate in the intestinal tract. Do not take calcium with vitamin D supplements, which encourage it to be absorbed rather than bind with oxalate. People with thyroid disease should check with their doctor before taking calcium. Daily supplements of 250 mg of magnesium and 50 to 100 mg of vitamin $B_6$ may also reduce stone formation by lowering urinary levels of oxalate. Glucosamine sulfate also appears to lower urinary oxalate; the recommended dosage is 250 to 500 mg three times a day. Glucosamine can raise blood sugar levels in people with diabetes.

# Nephritis

### SYMPTOMS

*Symptoms vary according to the type of nephritis—kidney inflammation and infection. Two common types are:*

***Pyelonephritis****: Severe flank pain, usually on both sides; urinary urgency and burning pain when urinating; high fever and chills; nausea and vomiting.*

***Glomerulonephritis****: Headache, general achiness, and vague flank pain; facial puffiness in the morning and swelling (edema) of the lower limbs as the day goes on; amber or rust-colored urine.*

### WHO IS AT RISK

***Acute pyelonephritis*** *is most common among women, especially those who have recurrent urinary tract infections*

*(UTIs) or have undergone cystoscopy, a procedure in which a viewing instrument is inserted into the urethra and bladder. It may also be a complication of kidney stones, especially if they are lodged in the kidneys. Men who have an enlarged prostate or other urinary tract abnormalities are also vulnerable.*

***Chronic pyelonephritis*** *develops mostly in people with structural abnormalities, such as congenital defects that allow a backflow of urine to the kidneys.*

***Acute glomerulonephritis*** *(acute nephritic syndrome) is most common in children and young adults following a streptococcal throat or skin infection.*

***Chronic glomerulonephritis*** *is often a complication of another disease, such as diabetes or lupus.*

## HOW IT DEVELOPS

**Acute pyelonephritis** develops rapidly with a high fever and chills, flank pain, and nausea and vomiting. The kidneys are swollen and tender when pressed. **Chronic pyelonephritis** often does not produce symptoms, even though the urine may contain bacteria.

**Acute glomerulonephritis** often develops two to six weeks after a bout of strep throat or a streptococcal skin infection (impetigo). In about 50 percent of patients, the only obvious symptom is blood in the urine. Others suffer general achiness and other flulike symptoms. Most patients, especially children, recover, but in severe cases, the kidney infection can cause dangerously high blood pressure, possible heart failure, and brain swelling. It can also lead to kidney failure.

## WHAT YOU CAN DO

At any signs or symptoms of a kidney disorder, see a doctor as soon as possible. A heating pad or hot water bottle may ease the flank pain; however, do not take aspirin or acetaminophen, which can worsen nephritis. To reduce the kidneys' workload, restrict salt and protein intake.

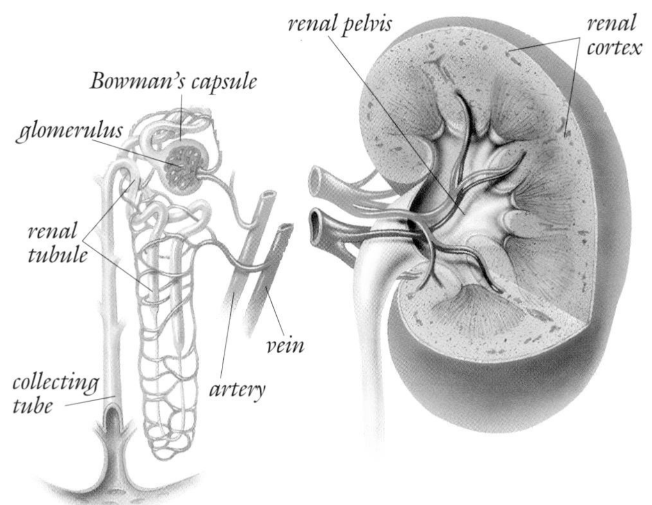


**Nephron** **Normal Kidney**

### BREAKTHROUGHS!

**Recent studies have found that the chronic glomerulonephritis and subsequent kidney failure caused by diabetes may be prevented by taking captopril (Capoten). This drug inhibits the action of angiotensin converting enzyme, a body chemical that regulates blood pressure.**

## HOW TO TREAT IT

Uncomplicated pyelonephritis usually can be cured with 14 days of oral antibiotics. However, hospitalization and more aggressive treatment with intravenous antibiotics and fluids are necessary if there are signs of septicemia (blood infection), dehydration, and other serious complications. **Chronic pyelonephritis** that is not causing symptoms or recurrent urinary infections often does not require treatment. If symptoms develop, however, antibiotics will be prescribed.

Treatment of **glomerulonephritis** varies according to its severity, and may include antibiotics, diuretics and other drugs to treat high blood pressure, and renal dialysis to give the kidneys a chance to heal.

## HOW TO PREVENT IT

Many cases of nephritis can be prevented by prompt antibiotic treatment of strep throat and urinary tract infections. Other possible preventive measures include controlling diabetes and high blood pressure.

### ALTERNATIVE THERAPIES

**Note:** Check with your doctor before taking any medication, herbal product, or nutritional supplement; some may cause additional kidney damage.

**Herbal medicine**

Herbal teas that have a diuretic effect—for example, red clover, juniper berry, and nettle—may reduce the kidneys' workload and promote healing. Drink two or three cups of any of these teas each day. Pregnant and nursing women should avoid red clover and juniper berry.

**Nutraceuticals**

It's a good idea to consult a nutritionist or registered dietitian for specific dietary advice. Supplements that are often needed include vitamins C and $B_6$, folic acid, and calcium; dosages vary according to individual needs.

### WARNING!

***Nephritis sometimes results in a dangerous rise in blood pressure, which can lead to heart failure or life-threatening brain swelling. Have your doctor show you how to monitor your blood pressure, and call him or her if it is consistently above 140/90.***

# Urinary Obstruction/Pain

## SYMPTOMS

- *Pain, which may be constant or occur before, during, or after urination; possible discharge of blood and pus.*
- *Difficulty starting urination and then producing only a scant amount; dribbling after urination stops.*
- *Mild to severe flank or back pain.*
- *Possible urinary urgency or frequency without being able to pass urine normally.*

## WHO IS AT RISK

*Urinary obstruction can occur at any age, but is most common among older men with an enlarged prostate. It may also develop in babies born with a congenital abnormality of the urinary tract. Acute blockages may be a consequence of infection, kidney or bladder stones, or a tumor.*

## HOW IT DEVELOPS

The blockage may develop slowly or come on abruptly, depending upon the underlying cause. Pain, which is often severe, may be centered in the flank and back or spread through the abdominal area. Pain with a discharge usually points to a stone or infection. A tumor or narrowing of a ureter or the urethra can cause hydronephrosis, in which urine backs up into the kidney.

## WHAT YOU CAN DO

Any difficulty in passing urine warrants seeing a doctor as soon as possible. In the meantime, applying a heating pad or soaking in a hot tub and taking a nonsteroidal anti-inflammatory drug (NSAID) may relieve the pain. Avoid acetaminophen; it can worsen a kidney problem.

## HOW TO TREAT IT

A doctor will likely do a bladder catheterization—the insertion of a thin tube through the urethra—to drain the urine and relieve pain due to a distended bladder. At the same time, a doctor may use a special viewing device (a cystoscope) to inspect the bladder and urethra. If this examination fails to find the source of the obstruction, abdominal ultrasound—the painless use of high-frequency sound waves to map internal structures—may be done. It may be combined with Doppler ultrasonography to track blood flow. Other possible tests include CT scans, MRIs, and special X-ray studies of the kidneys and other urinary structures after the injection of a dye or small amounts of a radioactive agent.

**WARNING!**

***A urinary blockage that causes urine to back up in the kidneys can result in serious organ damage and even renal failure. Don't delay seeing a doctor.***

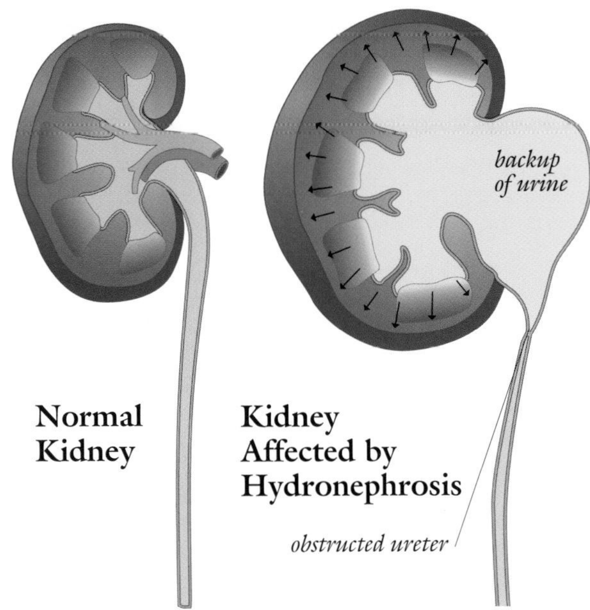


*Hydronephrosis occurs when an obstruction causes a backup of urine in the kidney, resulting in painful swelling and possible permanent damage.*

Treatment varies according to the underlying cause. Codeine or another prescription painkiller may be needed. A urinary drainage catheter is sometimes necessary to relieve or prevent hydronephrosis. Antibiotics and perhaps a bladder analgesic are prescribed for a urinary tract infection (UTI). If a stone is causing the obstruction, it must be removed (see *Kidney Stones,* p 182). An enlarged prostate may be treated with drugs or surgery. If the obstruction has caused acute kidney failure, temporary renal dialysis may be necessary.

## HOW TO PREVENT IT

Prevention entails early detection and treatment of the underlying cause. Men over 50 should have a digital rectal exam as part of their regular physical checkup and should discuss with their doctor the benefits and risks of other tests. Other preventive strategies include early treatment of UTIs and kidney stones.

### ALTERNATIVE THERAPIES

**Herbal medicine**

A number of studies have found that saw palmetto helps prevent benign prostate enlargement. The recommended daily dosage calls for two 160-mg pills, standardized to contain at least 85 percent fatty acids and sterols. Take between meals.

# Female Reproductive Organs

*A woman's reproductive organs and their hormones not only endow her with feminine characteristics but they are also common sources of pain—everything from menstrual cramps and childbirth to various forms of cancer.*

## Cervical/Uterine Cancer

### SYMPTOMS

*Both cervical and uterine cancer rarely cause symptoms in their early stages; when symptoms develop, they may include the following:*

***Cervical cancer:** Bleeding unrelated to menstruation; abnormally heavy periods; painful intercourse; watery, malodorous vaginal discharge. As the cancer advances, pelvic and lower abdominal pain.*

***Uterine cancer:** Abnormal vaginal bleeding; pain centered in the pelvic area, back, and legs; changes in bowel and bladder function. As the cancer advances, increasing pain, weight loss, and fatigue.*

### WHO IS AT RISK

***Cervical cancer** is the eleventh most frequently diagnosed cancer among Canadian women. A recent study from Saskatchewan found that the incidence of cervical cancer in status Indians is 10 times higher than the provincial average. Women at greatest risk, however, are those who have contracted genital warts (human papilloma virus, or HPV), a very common sexually transmitted disease. Other aspects of sexual activity that increase risk include starting sexual intercourse before age 18, having multiple sexual partners, and undergoing more than five pregnancies. Rounding out the list of possible risk factors are infection with genital herpes and HIV, AIDS, the use of medications that suppress the immune system, cigarette smoking, and deficiencies of vitamin C, folic acid, and beta carotene, the precursor of vitamin A.*

***Uterine cancer,** the most common malignancy of the female reproductive organs, usually develops after age 50. Factors that increase risk include obesity, a late (after age 52) menopause, not having children, and taking estrogen replacement or tamoxifen (an estrogen-blocking drug used to treat or prevent breast cancer).*

### HOW IT DEVELOPS

**Cervical cancer** begins with an overgrowth of abnormal cells. In time, the abnormal cells may cover much or all

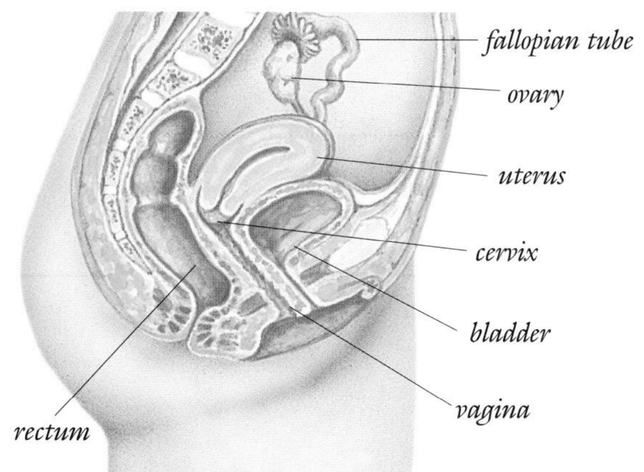


*The female reproductive organs are tucked into the lower pelvic cavity, where they are protected by the pelvic bones and lower abdominal muscle wall.*

of the cervix, a condition called *carcinoma in situ*, and then begin to invade the surrounding tissue. These early stages are painless and asymptomatic. Bleeding and pain develop as untreated cervical cancer spreads to the vagina, pelvic wall and bones, colon, and bladder; cells that invade the pelvic lymph nodes can travel to distant organs.

**Uterine cancer** usually starts with an overgrowth (hyperplasia) of normal cells in the endometrium, the tissue that lines the uterus. A tumor develops when these cells are transformed into cancerous ones, usually in the endometrial glands. Estrogen spurs the process by stimulating growth of endometrial tissue. Before menopause, this is a normal process during the high-estrogen phase of a woman's monthly cycle as the uterus prepares for a possible pregnancy. If conception does not occur, levels of progesterone (another female hormone) rise and cause the endometrial tissue to break down; it is then shed during menstruation.

**BREAKTHROUGHS!**

**A relatively simple blood test can now detect whether endometrial cancer has spread beyond the uterus. Before treatment, cancer experts recommend that the blood be tested for the presence of CA-125, a tumor marker that indicates the cancer may have spread beyond the uterus.**

Untreated uterine cancer usually grows downward to the cervix and vagina, and it may spread through the uterine wall to the fallopian tubes, ovaries, rectum, and bladder. It may also affect the liver, lungs, bones, and brain. As it spreads, pain often develops in the pelvic area, lower back, and legs. A rare form of uterine cancer—called *uterine sarcoma*—develops in the muscle tissue, although some cases—*endometrial stromal sarcomas*—start in the cells surrounding the endometrial glands.

## WHAT YOU CAN DO

In their early stages, both cervical and uterine cancers are highly treatable, so your best chances for a cure rest with undergoing regular screening tests (a Pap smear) to detect abnormal cells. See a doctor as soon as possible if you experience unusual bleeding, pain during or after intercourse, or any other cancer symptoms.

Surgery and other cancer treatments are often painful; talk to your doctor about painkillers and other methods of pain control (see *Alternative Therapies*, p 188). Radiation therapy can cause fatigue, nausea, diarrhea, and other uncomfortable side effects. Plan to get extra rest while undergoing treatments, and ask your doctor about medications to alleviate nausea and other symptoms.

**WARNING!**

***Recurrences are common in uterine cancer. Careful follow-up is necessary during the first two to three years. Most oncologists recommend a physical and pelvic examination, including a Pap smear, every three months for the first two years, then every six months for the next three years.***

It usually takes six weeks to recover from a hysterectomy; avoid lifting heavy objects and straining until healing is complete. Ice packs applied to the incision can numb pain. Before engaging in sexual intercourse, check with your doctor to make sure it is safe. Even then, intercourse may be painful, especially if the vagina has been shortened; in addition, removal of the ovaries—the source of estrogen—causes vaginal dryness. Possible remedies include using a water-based vaginal lubricant and experimenting with different positions to determine which ones are the most comfortable.

## HOW TO TREAT IT

### Surgery

Treatment varies depending upon the site and extent of the cancer. **Cervical carcinoma in situ** often can be treated by cryotherapy, the use of liquid nitrogen to kill the abnormal cells by freezing them. Laser surgery is an alternative that is less painful and heals faster than cryotherapy or conventional surgery.

Early **cervical cancer** often can be treated with conization—the removal of the tumor and a surrounding cone-shaped wedge of tissue. This procedure preserves a woman's ability to have a baby if she so desires. More advanced cervical cancer usually requires a hysterectomy—removal of the uterus and perhaps the vagina, fallopian tubes, and ovaries as well. Pelvic area lymph nodes may also be removed and analyzed for the presence of cancer cells.

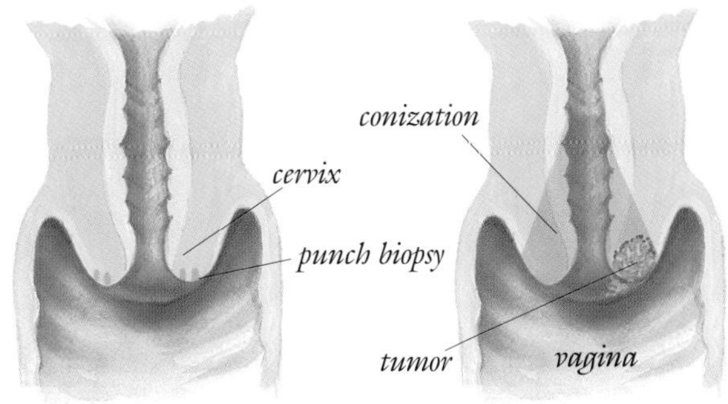


*A punch biopsy (left) is used to remove tiny pieces of cervical tissue to examine for possible cancerous cells. A small tumor can be removed by conization, a procedure in which a wedge-shaped portion of the lower cervix is excised.*

**Endometrial hyperplasia** in a younger woman who still wants to have children can often be treated with dilation and curettage (D&C)—a procedure in which the cervix is widened (dilated) and a spoonlike instrument (curette) is used to scrape away the endometrium. Most often, however, a hysterectomy is necessary to eliminate **uterine cancer**; depending upon the extent of the cancer, other reproductive organs may also be removed.

### Radiation therapy

For most women, cancer surgery is followed by radiation therapy. The radiation may be delivered by an external beam or the temporary insertion of small radioactive seeds in the pelvic cavity. Sometimes if a uterine tumor is very large, external-beam radiation is used to shrink it before surgery to remove it. Uterine cancer that extends into the pelvic wall is inoperable; in such cases, radiation therapy is the primary treatment.

### Chemotherapy

Pain medications range from acetaminophen and aspirin and other nonsteroidal anti-inflammatory drugs (NSAIDs) to codeine, morphine, and other powerful narcotics. Anticancer drugs are administered if the cancer has spread beyond the reproductive organs. They are often given along with antinausea drugs to reduce uncomfortable side effects. Hormones—usually progesterone—may also be used to help prevent a recurrence or to slow the growth of estrogen-stimulated tumors.

## HOW TO PREVENT IT

There are no certain preventive measures, but many cancer experts believe that practicing safer sex can greatly reduce the risk of cervical cancer. This entails delaying sexual intercourse until after the age of 18, limiting the number of sex partners, and using condoms to protect against genital warts, herpes, and other sexually transmitted diseases. To reduce the risk of uterine cancer, strive to maintain ideal weight and consume a diet low in animal fats. If you take postmenopausal estrogen replacement therapy (ERT), add progesterone to the regimen to prevent a buildup of endometrial cancer.

### ALTERNATIVE THERAPIES

**Note:** There are no alternative therapies for the cancers themselves; however, some can alleviate pain and other symptoms.

**Acupuncture**

Treatments may alleviate pain and reduce the need for narcotics or other potent pain medications. Other useful pain-control techniques include self-hypnosis, meditation, music therapy, and guided imagery. T'ai chi and yoga can help preserve muscle tone when recuperating from surgery as well as foster a sense of well-being.

**Herbal medicine**

Ginger tea may ease nausea due to chemotherapy and radiation treatments.

# Childbirth

### SYMPTOMS

*Childbirth pain varies from one woman to another, but it typically evolves from mild to intense during the three stages of labor.*

*New mothers invariably say that the pleasure of holding a newborn baby far outweighs the pain of childbirth.*

***Before labor:*** *Mild, irregular uterine (Braxton Hicks) contractions that are a prelude to birth; they may be mildly uncomfortable but are not painful.*
***Stage I labor:*** *Short (30 to 45 seconds) irregular contractions that may be mildly painful.*
***Stage II labor:*** *Regular, more forceful contractions that cause moderate to intense pain and result in final pushing to move the baby through the birth canal.*
***Stage III labor:*** *Final contractions to expel afterbirth.*
***After birth:*** *Continuing mild contractions to help shrink uterus; pain in perineum (area between the vagina and rectum); breast discomfort as milk "comes in."*

### WHO IS AT RISK

*Labor pains generally start between the thirty-seventh and forty-first weeks of pregnancy.*

## HOW IT DEVELOPS

Hormonal changes during the final weeks of pregnancy prepare the body for childbirth. Braxton Hicks contractions become more forceful and frequent, and may be mildly uncomfortable. The baby turns into a head-down position and moves lower in the uterus, bringing welcome relief from the breathing problems and indigestion that many women experience when the growing fetus compresses the lungs and digestive organs. Ligaments stretch to allow the fetus to pass through the lower pelvis. Early signs of approaching childbirth include the painless passing (show) of bloody mucus and rupture of the amniotic membrane, the bag of water that surrounds the developing fetus.

Short, mildly uncomfortable contractions herald Stage I labor, which goes through three phases: During early labor, the contractions may be up to 30 minutes apart and last less than 45 seconds, and the cervix widens

### APPROACHES TO CHILDBIRTH EDUCATION

Natural childbirth education generally follows one of three main approaches, although many educators draw upon elements of each.

- **The Lamaze method,** which is based on conditioned reflexes. Women are taught how to control pain by using special breathing patterns, massage, and visualization or focusing on specific external objects.
- **The Bradley method**, which uses a childbirth coach. The technique stresses deep abdominal breathing and focusing the mind on relaxing the body.
- **The Read method,** which emphasizes relaxation techniques and understanding the birth process to break the fear-tension-pain cycle.

(dilates) three centimeters, usually over six to eight hours. Phase two is marked by active labor; contractions are stronger, more painful, and come every three to five minutes, and the cervix dilates to eight centimeters. This phase usually lasts three to four hours. Phase three marks a transition; contractions come every minute or two, and the cervix becomes fully dilated.

During Stage II labor, the woman feels an irresistible urge to push or bear down with each contraction—typically the most painful so far. This stage, which may last up to one hour, ends with the baby's birth. In Stage III labor, which lasts only a few minutes, the placenta, or afterbirth, is expelled. By this time, most women are both exhausted and exhilarated, and they hardly notice the passing of the placenta.

## WHAT YOU CAN DO

It's a good idea for both parents (or the mother and her childbirth coach) to attend childbirth preparation classes during the last trimester of pregnancy. These classes teach the parents what to expect and also what they can do to minimize pain during each stage of labor.

When contractions start, notify your doctor but don't be in too big a hurry to get to a hospital or birthing center, especially if this is a first baby. Wait until contractions are occurring every three to five minutes; in the meantime—when contractions are still short and far apart—walk about to allow gravity to help bring the baby down farther into the pelvis. Music, a massage, or taking a warm shower provide distractions and ease discomfort.

Most women do not experience severe pain until the onset of active labor. This is the time to use the relaxation, breathing, and distraction techniques that are taught in childbirth classes (see *Approaches to Childbirth Education*, p 188). Many couples also use self-hypnosis, visualization, massage, and other alternative approaches to control pain (see *Alternative Therapies*, p 190).

### WARNING!

***Any supplement, herbal medication, or tea that is ingested during pregnancy or breast-feeding may affect the baby; always check with your doctor before taking any herb or nutritional supplement.***

## HOW TO TREAT IT

Many women go through labor and childbirth with only moderate pain that they can control themselves, but many others experience severe pain no matter what they do. Many women are reluctant to ask for pain relief, either out of fear that the drugs may harm the baby or that it is a sign of weakness or "failure." These women should know that a pain-relieving medication, such as Demerol, and surgical interventions can bring immediate relief during labor and childbirth. Those most commonly used are:

- **Meperidine (Demerol)**, which is given intravenously or by injection. It relaxes the mother and dulls pain, but doesn't cause a complete loss of sensation.
- **Epidural block**, in which a local anesthetic is injected into the lower back near the spinal cord. An epidural numbs the body from the waist down; it deadens pain sensation, but does not prevent a woman from pushing during labor.
- **A spinal block**, in which the anesthetic is injected directly into the spinal fluid in the lower back. It also numbs the body from the waist down, but is shorter-acting than an epidural and provides more effective pain relief than an epidural. It is usually used during the actual delivery, especially if forceps or a cesarean section is needed.

### GETTING BACK ON YOUR FEET

Most women experience at least some discomfort in the weeks following childbirth. Here are a few tips to help speed recovery:

- **Afterpains**, which are caused by continuing contractions to return the uterus to its normal size. Breast-feeding speeds the process by stimulating the release of oxytocin, a hormone that helps contract the uterus and also increases milk flow.
- **Breast tenderness and engorgement.** Frequent breast-feeding to empty the breasts provides the best relief. For women who do not breast-feed, medication can stop milk production. In the meantime, firmly wrapping the breasts with a long strip of cotton for a few days helps ease discomfort.
- **Perineal pain,** either from an episiotomy or tearing. Warm sitz baths provide temporary relief. Vitamin E oil gently massaged into the area can speed healing and reduce scarring.
- **Painful intercourse.** Sexual intercourse should be avoided for at least two to three weeks after a vaginal delivery and four to six weeks after a cesarean. Breast-feeding mothers often experience vaginal dryness; this can be remedied by using a water-based lubricant. Kegel exercises, which entail tightening and relaxing the pelvic-floor muscles, can help tone the stretched vagina and also overcome bladder-control problems.
- **Postpartum depression,** which doctors attribute to the abrupt hormonal changes following childbirth. This usually passes in a few weeks; consult your doctor or see a mental-health professional if it lasts longer or becomes so severe that you harbor thoughts of suicide or fear that you may harm your baby.

- **Pudendal block**, in which a local anesthetic is injected into the perineum just before an episiotomy (surgical cutting of the perineum) or to repair a perineal tear.
- **Paracervical block**, in which a local anesthetic is injected into the cervical tissue to numb pain from contractions and cervical dilation.
- **General anesthesia**, which is rarely used except for emergency cesareans or other unusual circumstances.

Following birth, a mild painkiller such as acetaminophen may be given. If a stronger medication is needed and the mother is not planning to breast-feed, codeine or meperidine may be used.

## HOW TO PREVENT IT

Childbirth pain cannot be totally prevented, but it can be minimized with breathing exercises and relaxation techniques. These involve deep breathing to relax between contractions and then panting, or taking rapid, short breaths during an actual contraction.

### ALTERNATIVE THERAPIES

**Herbal medicine**

Aloe gel applied to a cesarean incision or episiotomy can speed healing and help reduce formation of scar tissue. Many women experience urinary tract problems, ranging from urinary retention to incontinence, following childbirth. Green tea is a mild diuretic that may help improve urinary function, especially if retention is a problem; it is safe to drink up to two cups a day during pregnancy and breast-feeding. Constipation is another problem; it may be remedied by taking one or two tablespoons of ground psyllium seeds a day. Make sure that you also drink 8 to 10 glasses of water or other fluids, which are necessary for psyllium to work.

**Massage**

Some childbirth classes teach various massage techniques that can be used by a childbirth coach to ease pain. Other techniques, such as visualization, self-hypnosis, and biofeedback, may also help.

## Painful Complications of Pregnancy

| CONDITION | SYMPTOMS | WHAT YOU SHOULD DO |
|---|---|---|
| Constipation | Difficulty moving bowels as pregnancy progresses. | Increase fiber intake and drink at least 8 to 10 glasses of water a day; take a daily 30-minute walk or engage in some other moderate exercise. |
| Edema | Swelling of feet, legs, and hands. | Reduce salt intake; rest several times a day with your feet elevated. |
| Heartburn | Burning sensation in upper chest and throat after meals. | Eat small, frequent meals; avoid lying down for two hours after eating; avoid foods that cause gas or provoke symptoms; ask your doctor about taking a calcium carbonate antacid. |
| Hemorrhoids | Anal burning, itching, and possible bleeding. | Try to avoid becoming constipated; ask your doctor about using an OTC hemorrhoid remedy to ease symptoms; note that pregnancy-related hemorrhoids usually disappear after delivery. |
| Miscarriage | Mild to severe abdominal cramps; heavy vaginal bleeding. | Call your doctor immediately or go to the emergency room; if pregnancy cannot be saved, a D&C may be needed to clear uterus. |
| Morning sickness | Recurring nausea in first trimester. | Eat small, frequent meals. To quell morning nausea, eat dry crackers before getting out of bed. Suck on crushed ice; take daily outdoor walks; drink ginger tea or flat ginger ale. Diclectin may be prescribed to treat moderate to severe nausea and/or vomiting. |
| Pre-eclampsia/eclampsia (toxemia of pregnancy) | Marked swelling, high blood pressure, abdominal pain, fatigue, visual disturbances. | For severe toxemia, treatment is hospitalization, rapid stabilization, and delivery as soon as possible (within hours). Bed rest and medical treatment is reserved for mild "chronic" cases only. |
| Varicose veins | Leg pain and blue, knotted, or bulging veins. | Rest periodically with your legs elevated; exercise regularly to promote good circulation; consider wearing prescription elastic stockings. (Note: Varicose veins often disappear after delivery, but may recur later in life.) |

# Endometriosis

### SYMPTOMS

- *Pelvic pain, ranging from mild to debilitating, before and during a menstrual period.*
- *Chronic pelvic pain; pain during intercourse.*
- *In advanced stages, difficult or painful bowel movements or blood in urine during menstruation.*
- *In rare cases, blood in sputum during menstruation, chest or leg pain, bowel obstruction.*

### WHO IS AT RISK

*Once thought of as "the career woman's disease," endometriosis is now known to affect any woman of child-bearing age. Although it tends to run in families—having a mother or sister with endometriosis increases the risk sevenfold—it also develops when any condition obstructs the outflow of menstrual fluid through the cervix. For example, scar tissue on the cervix following cancer treatment increases the chances of developing endometriosis.*

## HOW IT DEVELOPS

Endometriosis is a chronic disorder, but its symptoms can wax and wane, and may completely disappear when a woman is not ovulating, such as during pregnancy or when taking hormones to suppress ovulation. The disorder develops when tissue that normally lines the uterus—the endometrium—grows in or on other parts of the body, especially the ovaries, fallopian tubes, colon, and other pelvic organs. The misplaced tissue responds to the menstrual cycle's hormonal changes, so when low hormone levels prompt the uterus to shed its lining, this endometrial tissue also breaks apart but, unlike menstrual fluid that flows out through the vagina, it has nowhere to go. The tissue becomes swollen and inflamed, often resulting in severe cramps that become more intense during the latter days of the menstrual period.

When menstruation stops, the endometrial tissue shrinks but, over time, scar tissue and adhesions can form and adhere to other organs. Sometimes blood-filled cysts form on the ovaries and other organs. If the scar tissue, cysts, or adhesions twist other reproductive organs out of their normal alignment, infertility can result.

Because endometriosis does not cause symptoms in about 25 percent of women, it can be difficult to diagnose. A pelvic examination both during and between periods can indicate possible endometriosis, but a definitive diagnosis requires laparoscopy, in which a viewing instrument is inserted into the abdominal cavity through a small incision near the navel. This procedure, usually done under general anesthesia, allows the doctor to examine the pelvic and abdominal organs for signs of endometriosis.

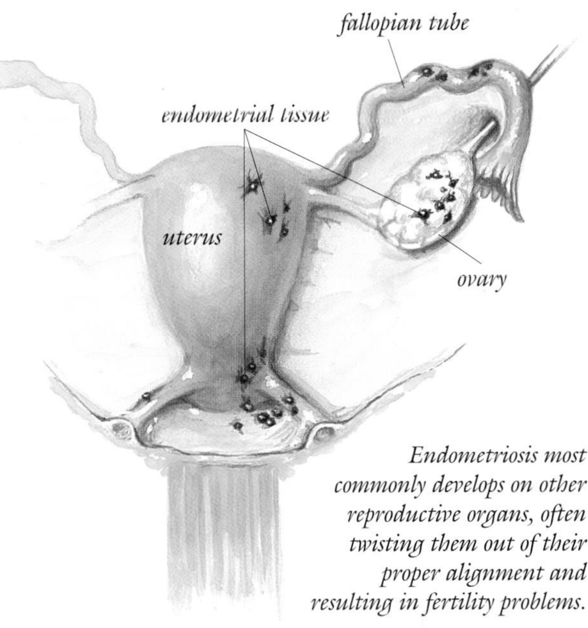


*Endometriosis most commonly develops on other reproductive organs, often twisting them out of their proper alignment and resulting in fertility problems.*

## WHAT YOU CAN DO

If symptoms are mild, aspirin, ibuprofen, or other non-prescription anti-inflammatory drugs (NSAIDs) usually relieve pain. A heating pad applied to the abdominal area may also help. See a doctor if NSAIDs fail to provide adequate pain relief or if you are unable to get pregnant.

## HOW TO TREAT IT

### Medications

Birth control pills that suppress estrogen production are sometimes recommended. If this approach is not feasible, doctors sometimes recommend hormone treatments that mimic pregnancy, thereby slowing the spread of the disease and its resulting pain. Another treatment entails using drugs to induce an artificial menopause that temporarily suspends ovulation. The drugs used most often are danazol (Cyclomen), a synthetic male hormone, and medroxyprogesterone (Provera), a synthetic progesterone. Both these hormones can produce unpleasant side effects (weight gain, bloating, elevated blood cholesterol levels; danazol can also cause abnormal hair growth and other signs of masculinization) and should only be taken for six months. Without the monthly stimulation of the hormones, the endometrial tissue shrinks and can disappear, although sometimes symptoms reappear when drug therapy is stopped. During this therapy, pregnancy is not possible, but if the long-term goal is to restore fertility, this procedure works in some cases.

### Surgery

New microsurgery techniques often can relieve symptoms and are helping some women overcome fertility prob-

**WARNING!**

***In rare cases, endometrial tissue may migrate to the lungs. See a doctor if you start coughing up bloody sputum and have breathing problems during or just after a menstrual period.***

lems. A surgeon uses a laparoscope and magnifying devices to search out even minute clumps of endometrial tissue, which are removed with a laser or tiny surgical instruments that can be manipulated through the viewing tube. At the same time, reproductive organs that have been moved out of their proper alignment can be repositioned. Hormone therapy is usually recommended as a follow-up to surgery to help shrink any remaining tissue. In rare cases, a hysterectomy—removal of the uterus and perhaps the ovaries as well—may be recommended. However, this radical approach should be used only for women with incapacitating menstrual pain who do not want to become pregnant.

## HOW TO PREVENT IT

Endometriosis cannot be prevented, but it can be arrested by becoming pregnant or by going through menopause, either naturally or with drug therapy.

### ALTERNATIVE THERAPIES

**Note:** Alternative therapies cannot cure endometriosis, but some may relieve cramps and other symptoms.

**Acupuncture and acupressure**

The methods that relieve menstrual pain are also helpful in alleviating the pain of endometriosis. Some women report success using a rubber stimulating device that, when strapped around an ankle, presses upon an acupressure point used in treating urinary and genital problems.

**Aromatherapy**

Aromatherapists use juniper, peppermint, or marjoram oils to relieve menstrual pain, and they may also ease the pain of endometriosis. A few drops of one or more of the oils may be added to bathwater or diluted with a neutral oil, such as olive oil, and massaged into the skin.

**Herbal medicine**

Red raspberry leaf tea and valerian extract, tea, or capsules are recommended for menstrual pain and may help endometriosis. The herbal section of many health food stores carries special preparations for menstrual pain.

**Relaxation therapies**

The knee-to-chest yoga position, deep breathing, meditation, visualization, and other relaxation methods may help ease the pain associated with endometriosis.

**BREAKTHROUGHS!**

**A relatively new class of drugs called gonadotropin-releasing hormone (GnRH) agonists (available under the brand names of Lupron and Synarel) have proved effective in relieving pelvic pain and are usually prescribed for up to six months. However, their side effects include the symptoms usually associated with menopause—hot flashes, irregular vaginal bleeding, headaches, weight gain, depression, insomnia, vaginal dryness, hair loss, and possible thinning of the bones—and the endometriosis pain can return after the drugs are discontinued. Still, these drugs may be useful in suppressing the condition enough to allow a woman to get pregnant after the drugs are stopped and before the endometriosis recurs.**

# Menstrual Cramps

### SYMPTOMS

- *Spasms of crampy pain in the lower abdomen, hips, lower back, and thighs during the menstrual period.*
- *Possible nausea, vomiting, and headache.*
- *Frequent diarrhea, constipation, or both, sometimes occurring in the same menstrual period.*
- *In severe cases, vomiting, dizziness, and perhaps fainting at the onset of each menstrual period.*

### WHO IS AT RISK

*All women who menstruate may experience menstrual cramps. In general, cramps occur among women who are ovulating; therefore, they often do not begin until one or two years after the menarche (the first period), or until ovulation is established, and they lessen as a woman approaches menopause and ovulation is more infrequent.*

*In most cases, there is no identifiable cause for the cramps and the condition is referred to as primary dysmenorrhea. When cramps are unusually severe month after month, there may be an underlying disorder, such as uterine fibroids (benign tumors in the uterus) or endometriosis, the migration of tissue that normally lines the uterus to other reproductive organs and more distant parts of the body.*

## HOW IT DEVELOPS

Until the early 1980s, doctors tended to dismiss dysmenorrhea as a psychosomatic condition instead of an organic disorder. We now know that menstrual cramps are most likely caused by prostaglandins, hormone-like chemicals that are produced throughout the body. Those responsible for menstrual cramps are made in the uterine tissue and they help expel the lining that is shed during menstruation. (Prostaglandins are also responsible for the uterine contractions during pregnancy, and have many other functions throughout the body, such as stimulating the intestines and inducing inflammation.)

Menstrual cramps often begin just before the start of a period and are most intense during the first day or so; they may be accompanied by headache, nausea, constipation, diarrhea, frequent urination, and, infrequently, vomiting. Prostaglandin activity is thought to play a role in all of these symptoms. Possible contributing factors include an ill-positioned uterus, lack of exercise, and anxiety about menstruation. Although some women suffer from menstrual cramps throughout their childbearing years, in most cases cramps peak in late adolescence or early adulthood and subside after childbirth or as a woman ages.

## BREAKTHROUGHS!

**The discovery that antiprostaglandin drugs can relieve menstrual cramps for most women has truly revolutionized not only the treatment of menstrual cramps, but also the attitude of many doctors regarding the condition. No longer is dysmenorrhea considered a psychological disorder that can be overcome by adopting a positive attitude toward one's role in life. Instead, it is now known to be a highly treatable medical condition that can be relieved by inexpensive, readily available medications.**

## WHAT YOU CAN DO

Aspirin or stronger nonsteroidal anti-inflammatory drugs (NSAIDs), such as ibuprofen or naproxen, can relieve menstrual cramps for 85 to 90 percent of women with primary dysmenorrhea. These drugs, which all have antiprostaglandin action, help reduce uterine contractions and relieve other symptoms, especially headaches. They can, however, cause intestinal bleeding and ulcers, so they must be used cautiously (see *Warning!*, p 194). Some women get adequate relief from acetaminophen, especially if headaches are their main complaint; even though acetaminophen is not an antiprostaglandin agent, it is an effective painkiller.

Lifestyle changes can also help minimize menstrual cramps and other symptoms: Get adequate rest, reduce stress, and engage in regular aerobic exercise, such as brisk walking, jogging, and bicycling, among others. (Exercise increases the brain's release of endorphins, the body's natural painkillers and mood elevators.) Some women get relief from pain by using a heating pad or hot water bottle applied to the crampy area, or taking a warm bath. In addition, sexual activity that leads to an orgasm can also provide relief. Massage can eliminate backache due to menstruation. Distraction—listening to music, watching an engrossing movie or TV program, even reading a good book—is also a time-honored approach to minimize pain. If self-treatment fails to produce adequate relief, or the cramps are worsening, see a doctor. The problem may have an underlying cause, such as uterine fibroids, a chronic infection, a tumor, or endometriosis.

## HOW TO TREAT IT

If nonprescription painkillers fail to provide relief, a doctor may prescribe a stronger prescription NSAID. Although all NSAIDs have similar antiprostaglandin actions, not everyone responds to any given drug in the same way. So if one NSAID doesn't help, don't assume that others won't work either; several may need to be tried before finding one that is beneficial. For those who cannot use NSAIDs, codeine or a combination of codeine and acetaminophen may be prescribed. However, codeine can cause constipation and drowsiness.

## HOW TO PREVENT IT

Although there is no effective way to prevent cramps, many women take measures to relieve uncomfortable accompanying symptoms, such as bloating, constipation, and breast tenderness around the time of menstruation, by getting regular exercise, eating less salt and more fiber, and drinking lots of water. By avoiding these uncomfortable symptoms, you can minimize menstrual pain.

*Yoga positions that may ease menstrual cramps include pelvic rises, or bridging (far right), which relieves back pain and pelvic congestion, and the spinal twist (right), which relaxes tensed abdominal and pelvic muscles.*

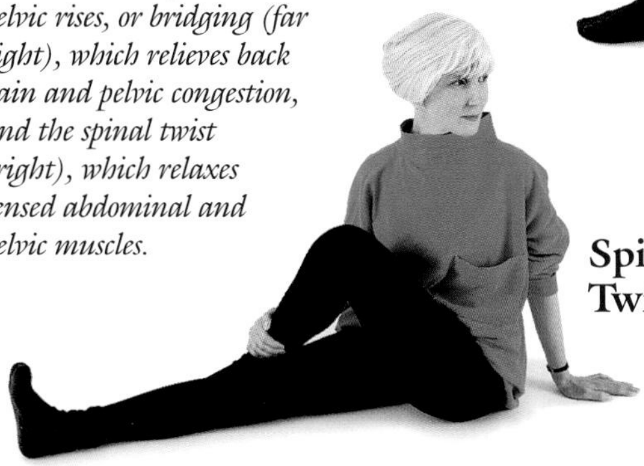

**Pelvic Rises**

**Spinal Twist**

## ALTERNATIVE THERAPIES

**Aromatherapy**

Soaking in a hot bath that contains a few drops of juniper oil in the water may ease cramps. Other aromatic oils that may help include chamomile, tarragon, and marjoram, which may be added to bathwater or diluted in a neutral oil, such as olive oil, and massaged into the skin.

**Herbal medicine**

Teas made from red raspberry leaf, chamomile, or valerian, as well as two or three capsules of evening primrose oil or black currant oil, may help relieve cramps. Ginger tea, extract, or candy can quell the nausea and vomiting that sometimes accompany dysmenorrhea. People taking anticoagulants should use ginger with caution, and avoid evening primrose oil, particularly if they are taking heparin.

> **WARNING!**
>
> ***Women who are taking a blood-thinning medication such as warfarin (Coumadin) or who have a history of ulcers, aspirin allergy, or asthma, should not take aspirin, ibuprofen, or other NSAIDs. Even without such contraindications, anyone using these medications should be alert to possible problems, such as easy bruising, bleeding gums, dark, tarry stools, and shortness of breath—possible signs of anemia caused by chronic intestinal bleeding.***

**Relaxation techniques**

Self-hypnosis, meditation, yoga, and visualization are among the many self-help techniques that help counter stress, which may contribute to symptoms of dysmenorrhea.

**Massage**

This age-old technique is highly effective in reducing menstrual cramps, especially if it is combined with acupressure and aromatherapy. During a massage, which you can do yourself or have someone else administer, apply gentle pressure on the acupoints just below the breastbone, the bottom of the tailbone, the back of the neck, and the pelvic area.

**Yoga**

The most effective positions for relieving cramps are the corpse pose (lying flat on back with legs slightly apart, arms at side with palms facing up), cat stretch (arching the back while on your hands and knees), and pelvic raises and twists (see photos on p 193).

# Ovarian Cancer

### SYMPTOMS

*In its early stages, there usually are no symptoms. As the cancer advances, symptoms may include:*

- *Vague but persistent pelvic pain or pressure, abdominal discomfort, and possible backache and shoulder pain.*
- *Various abdominal or digestive complaints, such as frequent indigestion, gas, nausea, vomiting, constipation, diarrhea, and an uncomfortable feeling of being full.*
- *Unexplained loss of appetite, often accompanied by abdominal swelling, pain, and sudden weight gain.*
- *Frequent urination, nonmenstrual vaginal bleeding, and pain during intercourse.*
- *Unusual abdominal lumps or growths.*

### WHO IS AT RISK

*Ovarian cancer—the second most common female reproductive system cancer—can strike at any age, but it is most common among women just before entering menopause (perimenopause) and then during and after menopause. This disease also tends to run in families, so women with first-degree relatives (a mother or sister) who have had ovarian cancer have a higher-than-average risk. Others at risk include women who have not had children or delayed their first pregnancy until after age 35, and those who have had breast, colon, or endometrial cancer. Other possible risk factors include long-term use of genital deodorants and other products containing talc and treatment with fertility drugs.*

## HOW IT DEVELOPS

Ovarian cancer, the deadliest disorder of the female reproductive system, begins as a malignant growth inside one or both ovaries, where it produces no symptoms. If left untreated, the malignant cells spread quickly to the pelvic organs, the lining of the abdominal cavity (peritoneum), nearby lymph nodes, and the liver.

## WHAT YOU CAN DO

If treatment causes an abrupt surgical menopause and you are unable to take estrogen, you can minimize the discomfort of night sweats by lowering the thermostat in your bedroom, using light covers, abstaining from alcohol in the evening, and taking a tepid shower before bedtime. Taking soy protein or adding tofu, soy milk, and other soy products to your diet may also help (see *Nutraceuticals*, p 195). During the day, wear light, comfortable clothing that can be removed easily if hot flashes occur.

All women over 40 should have a yearly pelvic examination that includes palpating the ovaries, which can detect the presence of abnormalities. If you are at high risk for developing ovarian cancer, you may wish to complete childbearing as early as possible and then take birth control pills, which offer some measure of protection against the disease. Women with a history of other cancers should be vigilant about screening for ovarian cancer. Women who have large uterine fibroid tumors, which are usually benign but may interfere with manual examination of the ovaries, should schedule an annual sonogram to measure any changes in the fibroids and also to check the ovaries.

## HOW TO TREAT IT

Any doctor who suspects ovarian cancer must first rule out other disorders that produce similar symptoms, such as ovarian cysts or endometriosis. If a mass is found, he or she will order an ultrasound examination that can help determine whether the mass is likely to be malignant, and will repeat the procedure a month later to see if any changes have taken place. If there are changes, a biopsy is necessary to make a diagnosis. This can be done by inserting a special viewing tube—a laparoscope—into the pelvic cavity through a small incision near the navel. The patient is given general anesthesia, and while she is still in the operating room, a sample of ovarian tissue is frozen and analyzed for malignant cells. If cancer is found, other tissue samples will be taken from nearby organs and the surgeon will proceed to remove the ovaries, uterus, fallopian tubes, supporting ligaments, and nearby lymph nodes. If the cancer is confined to one ovary and the woman still desires to have children, the surgeon may remove only the affected ovary and leave other reproductive organs intact.

After surgery, almost all women with extensive spread of the disease will receive chemotherapy and radiation treatments. Often, more surgery is required later, since chemotherapy only works for a limited time and may not check the spread of the disease. As the cancer advances, severe pain may develop, requiring a morphine pump or other strong painkillers.

Premenopausal women who have both ovaries removed will immediately enter menopause and experience uncomfortable hot flashes and other menopausal symptoms. If there are no contraindications, hormone replacement therapy may be added to the drug regimen to relieve symptoms. Quite often, however, doctors are reluctant to prescribe estrogen for fear that it will stimulate cancer growth elsewhere. In such cases, some of the new artificial estrogen agents may be prescribed; these do not ease hot flashes, but they help protect against bone loss and heart disease—common postmenopausal problems for all women.

Ovarian cancer often recurs; if it does, experimental treatments such as a bone marrow transplant may be tried.

### BREAKTHROUGHS!

**Researchers recently identified certain genetic mutations, especially one called BRCA1, that increase a woman's risk for ovarian cancer. One option for a woman found to have the gene is removal of the ovaries after childbearing is complete. However, at present there is insufficient evidence to determine if the benefits of such drastic surgery outweigh the risks for all women. If the ovaries are not removed, annual examination that includes ultrasound is highly recommended.**

## HOW TO PREVENT IT

Studies have found that women who take oral contraceptives have a somewhat lower risk of ovarian cancer than women who have not used them. Women who have completed childbearing and are at very high risk for developing ovarian cancer—for example, they carry a recently discovered gene (see *Breakthroughs!*, below) and have a strong family history of the disease combined with their own previous cancer history—may want to consider prophylactic removal of their ovaries and other reproductive organs. A low-fat diet may play some part in preventing all types of cancers, including ovarian (see *Alternative Therapies*, below.) Finally, avoid genital deodorants and other personal hygiene products that contain talc.

### WARNING!

***Unexplained weight gain, abdominal swelling, and vague pelvic discomfort are common warning signs of advancing ovarian cancer. See a doctor as soon as possible if these or other symptoms appear. Early treatment greatly increases the chances of surviving ovarian cancer.***

### ALTERNATIVE THERAPIES

**Note:** Alternative therapies should not be used to treat the cancer itself, but they may be helpful in easing pain and other symptoms.

**Nutraceuticals**

The antioxidant nutrients—vitamins A, C, and E, beta carotene, and the mineral selenium—are believed to help avert the changes in cells that lead to cancer. A diet that provides five or more servings of brightly colored fruits and vegetables a day should provide ample vitamin A and beta carotene. Other antioxidants may need to be taken in amounts higher than can be obtained from diet alone; recommended daily dosages include 1000 to 2000 mg of vitamin C, 400 to 800 IU of vitamin E, and up to 400 micrograms (mcg) of selenium. (Note, however, that long-term high doses of selenium can be toxic.) Soy protein, high in plant (phyto) estrogen, may help ease hot flashes and other menopause symptoms; take 25 to 50 grams a day. To lower the risk of osteoporosis as a consequence of the abrupt loss of estrogen, take at least 1200 mg of calcium (divided into three doses) a day, along with 400 IU of vitamin D, 280 mg of magnesium, and 200 to 300 mcg of vitamin K (a doctor's prescription is required). For further cautions, see *About the Recommendations*, p 7.

**Relaxation therapies**

Many cancer treatment centers now offer music therapy and teach meditation, self-hypnosis, visualization, and other techniques to help control pain. These techniques also help calm anxiety before surgery and ease other discomforts such as nausea while undergoing chemotherapy treatments.

# Ovarian Cysts

## SYMPTOMS

*Sometimes ovarian cysts do not produce symptoms; when they occur, symptoms may include:*

- *Unexplained abdominal discomfort and swelling.*
- *Irregular periods or other changes, such as very heavy bleeding or cessation of menstruation.*
- *Pain during sexual intercourse.*
- *Abnormal growth of facial hair, deepening of the voice, and other signs of masculinization.*
- *If a cyst ruptures, abdominal pain that may travel to the shoulder, nausea, vomiting, and possible shock.*

## WHO IS AT RISK

*Any woman, especially those of childbearing age, can develop ovarian cysts. With the widespread use of ultrasound technology, it is now known that postmenopausal women also develop benign ovarian cysts, sometimes called postmenopausal enlarged ovaries.*

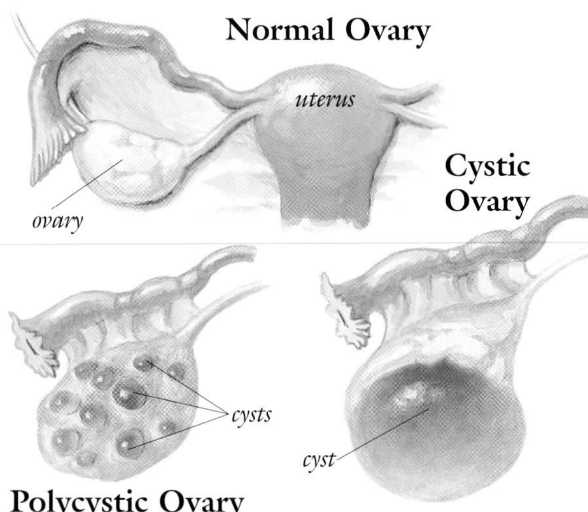


*A single functional cyst (lower right) may enlarge and rupture, causing severe pelvic pain and bleeding. Polycystic ovaries (lower left) are studded with numerous cysts.*

## HOW IT DEVELOPS

There are many different types of ovarian cysts; the most common types include:

- **Functional cysts**, which develop when an egg is not properly released from its follicle sac during ovulation and continues to grow in place. Sometimes the egg releases properly, but the sac (corpus luteum) continues to fill with fluids and blood, thickening on the ovary to form a cyst. Stimulated by estrogen production, the cyst can grow to the size of an orange or larger, can twist or rupture, and can cause severe hemorrhaging and pain. More commonly, however, the cyst produces abdominal pain and menstrual irregularities for a few periods, then disappears.
- **Polycystic ovaries**, in which the ovaries enlarge and may produce high levels of male hormones that lead to increased body hair and other symptoms of masculinization, menstrual disruptions, and infertility.
- **Ovarian chocolate cysts (endometriomas)**, which form when endometrial tissue attaches itself to the ovaries and forms a dark brown growth.
- **Ovarian cystadenomas**, benign growths that contain fluid and other tissue. These cystadenomas occasionally become malignant, although it is not known why.

## WHAT YOU CAN DO

See a doctor as soon as possible if you experience sudden, severe pelvic pain, which may signal a ruptured cyst. Any discomfort from small, functional cysts can usually be controlled with nonprescription painkillers.

Patients with polycystic ovaries may require therapy if pregnancy is desired to prevent abnormal thickening of the lining of the uterus (endometrial hyperplasia) or to minimize the long-term effects of excess androgen on the cardiovascular system. However, one of the common manifestations—unwanted hair growth (hirsutism)—can be treated with electrolysis, depilatories, or waxing.

## HOW TO TREAT IT

No treatment is needed for small benign ovarian cysts in premenopausal women; treatment is indicated, however, if the cysts cause pelvic pain, enlarge, or interfere with fertility. Even if cysts are not treated, a doctor should examine them with ultrasound or an MRI to make sure that they are not enlarging and that they have no internal structure or solid parts. Birth control pills are sometimes prescribed to check the development and growth of functional cysts. If these cysts are suppressing ovulation and a woman wants to conceive, fertility drugs may be used to stimulate ovulation so that conception can occur.

Surgery is indicated if an ovarian cyst enlarges, becomes twisted, or ruptures. A ruptured cyst causes severe pain and internal bleeding, which can be life-threatening. The procedure can usually be done laparoscopically—that is, with small incisions rather than through a large abdominal

> **WARNING!**
>
> ***If surgery is advised to remove a large, benign functional ovarian cyst and you still want to be able to conceive, be sure the surgeon knows of your wishes. Very often the cyst can be removed with little or no damage to the ovary, thereby allowing future pregnancies to take place.***

**BREAKTHROUGHS!**

**Ultrasound screening has been refined so that it can often distinguish between benign and malignant tumors. In postmenopausal women, where the concern is a benign cyst becoming malignant, ultrasound screening combined with a blood test called CA125 may obviate the need for surgery. CA125 detects a specific antigen shed into the bloodstream by malignant cells. If this test detects no antigen and ultrasound screening records no change in the size or shape of the cyst, a doctor may elect to forgo surgery and, instead, schedule periodic ultrasound examinations to monitor for any changes.**

cut, thereby reducing pain and speeding postsurgical recovery. In postmenopausal women, benign cysts are usually surgically removed because of the concern that they may become malignant.

## HOW TO PREVENT IT

Women who use birth control pills do not ovulate and usually do not develop ovarian cysts. Therefore, use of oral contraceptives is one way to prevent cysts from forming. If a woman has a family history of ovarian cysts, or has been treated for them herself, birth control pills are prescribed.

### ALTERNATIVE THERAPIES

Alternative therapies are not effective in treating ovarian cysts, although acupuncture techniques may alleviate any pain associated with them.

# Painful Intercourse

### SYMPTOMS

- *Discomfort or pain during sexual intercourse.*
- *Vaginal dryness, tightness, burning, or stinging.*
- *Avoidance of sexual intercourse.*
- *Feelings of anxiety in intimate situations.*

### WHO IS AT RISK

*Most women experience painful sexual intercourse—known medically as* dyspareunia*—at some point in their lives. The initial sexual experience can cause pain when the membrane covering the vagina, the hymen, tears during initial intercourse. A sexually active woman is at risk for developing local infections, such as yeast vaginitis, that can cause pain during intercourse; friction or deep thrusting can cause small, painful tears in the vagina.*

*Certain forms of birth control, such as condoms, foams, jellies, or creams, may irritate the vagina. Abnormal pelvic growths, such as endometriosis, ovarian cysts, or large uterine fibroid tumors, can cause deep pain. Women who have suffered emotional, physical, or sexual abuse, including rape, often find intercourse painful, as do some women who fear becoming pregnant or the sex act itself.*

*As women age, their estrogen levels decrease. As a result, the vaginal walls get thinner and the vagina itself can become dry and itchy or irritated. In such instances, sexual intercourse becomes painful.*

## HOW IT DEVELOPS

Depending upon its cause, painful intercourse develops in different ways. If the cause is organic in nature—that is, the result of infection, inadequate lubrication, allergic reactions, scarring from an episiotomy (a cut made between the vagina and anus during childbirth) or other surgeries—the pain is likely to intensify if the underlying condition is not treated. When the pain is caused by psychological factors, such as a fear of pregnancy or anxiety about previous physical or sexual abuse, it may manifest itself as avoidance of all intimacy, and thus affect a woman's partner as well.

Conditions known as *vaginismus* (an involuntary tightening of the vaginal muscles) and *vulvodynia* (chronic vaginal burning or stinging that makes penetration impossible) may have both physical and psychological components. Finally, back problems, arthritis, and many other disorders can make sex difficult or painful.

## WHAT YOU CAN DO

Though the condition may be embarrassing, it is important to discuss it with your partner. The problem can often be solved by trying different positions and techniques, or by using a vaginal lubricant. Older women with vaginal dryness may want to consider estrogen replacement therapy to alleviate symptoms. If the pain persists, seek the help of a qualified medical professional. All women over the age of 18 (or as soon as they become sexually active) should have a pelvic examination every year or two. That is a good time to discuss the problem with the doctor, who will either suggest treatment or make a referral to a specialist, such as a sex therapist.

If arthritis or a chronic back problem interferes with sexual pleasure, experiment with different positions that may be more comfortable. For example, lying side by side may be more comfortable for a person who has arthritis in her hip or knee joints. If the problem has psychological roots, you may need to seek out a mental health professional with whom you can

**WARNING!**

***Before beginning sex therapy, check on the therapist's training and qualifications. Many sex therapists have at least one professional degree in a field such as psychology, or marriage and family therapy. Most sex therapists work under a code of ethics prescribed by their professional association. Ask your doctor for a referral.***

discuss your concerns. In such situations, couples therapy involving both partners may also be helpful.

## HOW TO TREAT IT

Infections are treated with antibiotics, antifungal agents, or various other medications, depending upon their nature. Genital warts can be removed chemically or through minor surgery. Scars from an episiotomy or another surgical procedure or an injury may require additional surgery to remove them; this often can be done with a laser (a high-intensity light beam that vaporizes unwanted tissue). Other surgical solutions may be advised for such conditions as endometriosis, a prolapsed uterus, and uterine fibroid tumors.

A doctor may prescribe estrogen replacement therapy, in the form of tablets, transdermal patches, or a vaginal cream, to relieve vaginal dryness. Vaginismus can be treated with vaginal dilators. The woman is given tubes or similar objects that are of progressively larger diameters. She starts by inserting a very small one in the vagina and, over a few weeks' time, working up to a penis-sized dilator. If painful intercourse results from emotional discomfort or anxiety, antidepressant medications—either alone or in combination with psychotherapy—may be in order.

## HOW TO PREVENT IT

Have regular pelvic examinations to detect any physical conditions that might interfere with sexual pleasure. See a doctor as soon as possible if you develop signs of a genital infection; early treatment can prevent the condition from progressing to the point of causing painful intercourse. If discussing the problem with your partner fails to improve the situation, seek the help of a registered sex therapist (see *Warning!*, p 197).

### ALTERNATIVE THERAPIES

**Massage**

Many sex therapists teach couples massage, in which the partners take turns giving each other gentle, pleasurable massages using various aromatic oils. At first, the couple concentrates only on giving each other pleasure through the massage without engaging in intercourse. The couple may also be instructed to share other intimacies, such as showering or bathing together, watching X-rated films, or simply spending more time talking and enjoying each other's company. After the couple learns to relax and give pleasure through touching and other friendly activities, they can proceed to sexual exploration, and finally to intercourse itself.

**Relaxation therapies**

Simple relaxation techniques, such as deep breathing, visualization, and self-hypnosis, promote a sense of well-being and can help alleviate pain.

# Pelvic Inflammatory Disease (PID)

### SYMPTOMS

*In its early stages, PID often has no symptoms, but if it goes untreated, it can cause the following:*

- *Acute pain that can mimic appendicitis.*
- *Pain in lower abdomen and back that varies from mild to severe.*
- *Vaginal discharge with an unpleasant odor.*
- *Irregular menstrual bleeding; bleeding between periods.*
- *Pain during intercourse.*
- *Fever, fatigue, diarrhea, and vomiting.*

### WHO IS AT RISK

*Any sexually active woman may develop PID; however, it is most likely to strike teenagers and women in their twenties. Most PID results from sexually transmitted diseases (STDs); therefore, women who are not in mutually monogamous relationships have a high risk of developing the disease. Women who use intrauterine birth control devices (IUDs) have a slightly higher rate of infection than women using other forms of contraception, particularly right after the device has been inserted. The use of highly absorbent tampons carries a slight risk, and sometimes PID develops after childbirth, a miscarriage, or an abortion, when the cervix is not completely closed.*

## HOW IT DEVELOPS

PID develops when bacteria invades a woman's internal reproductive organs (fallopian tubes, ovaries, uterine lining), resulting in infection and inflammation. Common causes of PID include gonorrhea and chlamydia, STDs that often have no symptoms in their early stages. If left untreated, the smoldering infection can cause pain, fever, fatigue, and nausea; the chronic inflammation can result

### BREAKTHROUGHS!

**PID is the leading cause of female infertility. Researchers at the National Institutes of Allergy and Infectious Diseases in the U.S. are working on several promising approaches to prevent PID-related infertility. These include:**

- **Vaginal suppositories containing lactobacilli, friendly organisms that may prevent the bacteria that cause gonorrhea from invading the reproductive tract.**
- **Easy-to-use and inexpensive kits that allow a woman to test herself for chlamydia and gonorrhea, enabling her to seek early treatment and prevent PID from developing.**

in adhesions and scarring of the pelvic organs, especially the fallopian tubes. These scars can lead to infertility or ectopic (tubal) pregnancy. PID can also produce abscesses (pus-filled sacs) on organs. If these are not drained or removed surgically, they can burst and cause peritonitis, a very painful and life-threatening inflammation of the entire abdomen.

## WHAT YOU CAN DO

See a doctor as soon as possible if you suspect you may have contracted gonorrhea, chlamydia, or any other STD, and make sure that any sexual partner also seeks medical attention. While waiting to see a doctor, an ice pack applied to the lower abdomen may numb the pain; aspirin or ibuprofen can lower a fever. Be sure to take the entire course of antibiotics that the doctor prescribes to prevent the bacteria from developing strains that are resistant to treatment. Refrain from sexual intercourse during the course of treatment. Once you start again, use condoms to prevent reinfection, even if other birth control methods are employed.

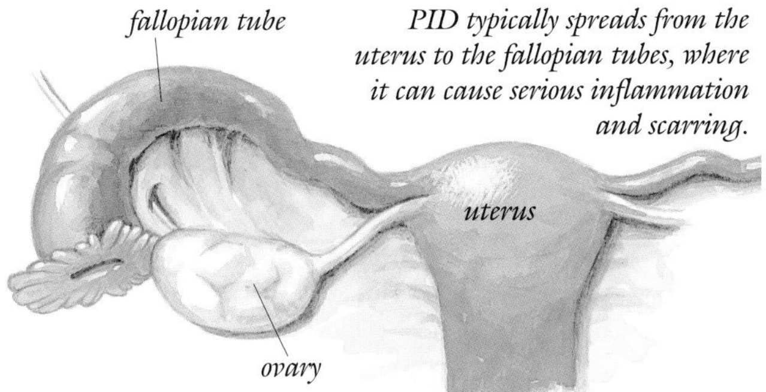


*PID typically spreads from the uterus to the fallopian tubes, where it can cause serious inflammation and scarring.*

## HOW TO TREAT IT

If the doctor suspects PID, he or she will perform a pelvic examination and take blood and urine tests as well as cultures of vaginal mucus and secretions to determine the specific cause of the infection. A pelvic sonogram may be ordered if the doctor feels a pelvic mass that may be an abscess. In mild cases, PID can be treated with antibiotics, which are given either in a single, very large dose or 7 to 10 days of smaller doses.

Hospitalization is necessary in more severe cases in which there is a high fever and acute abdominal pain. Meperidine (Demerol), morphine, or other powerful painkillers will be given, along with intravenous antibiotics and fluids; surgery may be needed to drain any abscesses. After release from the hospital, the woman will be instructed not to resume sexual activity for two weeks, or until the infection is eradicated.

**WARNING!**

***If PID cannot be cured by antibiotics or has caused peritonitis, a hysterectomy may be necessary to remove the diseased organs. This operation ends a woman's ability to have a baby, but may be necessary to prevent further damage to her other pelvic organs.***

## HOW TO PREVENT IT

PID can be prevented the same way STDs are prevented: by using condoms along with spermicides, which not only block sperm and bacteria from entering the female reproductive tract, but also may kill the bacteria that causes STDs. Sexually active women should seek regular gynecological examinations to test vaginal secretions for bacteria, because PID usually does not produce symptoms in its early stages and can cause considerable damage before it is detected. Women with a history of PID or who have multiple sex partners probably should not use an IUD for birth control.

### ALTERNATIVE THERAPIES

**Note:** PID must be treated with antibiotics; therefore, no alternative treatments exist for the disease itself.

**Nutraceuticals**

When taking antibiotics, acidophilus pills can help restore the beneficial bacteria that live in the intestinal tract and prevent yeast overgrowth. Look for products that contain live acidophilus and bifidus; the usual daily dosage is two to six capsules containing one billion live organisms each.

**Relaxation techniques**

Meditation, visualization, yoga, and deep-breathing exercises are among the self-help techniques that help control pain and anxiety during the recovery process.

# Premenstrual Syndrome (PMS)

### SYMPTOMS

*Physical symptoms include:*

- *Breast tenderness.*
- *Abdominal bloating, cramps, constipation.*
- *Migraine headaches.*
- *Backaches.*
- *Acne.*
- *Swelling of the hands, feet, and ankles.*
- *Joint and muscle pain.*
- *Palpitations.*
- *Urinary frequency.*
- *Increased thirst.*

* *Reduced tolerance to alcohol.*

*Psychological symptoms include:*

* *Food cravings, especially for sweets and salt.*
* *Nervousness and anxiety.*
* *Mood swings, which may include crying spells, irritability, lethargy, anger, depression, and panic attacks.*
* *Lethargy, fatigue, insomnia, or increased need for sleep.*
* *Inability to concentrate.*
* *Aggressive or violent behavior.*

### WHO IS AT RISK

*Most women who menstruate experience some symptoms of premenstrual syndrome during the week or so before menstruation, although only 10 percent have severe or incapacitating symptoms.*

*Until recently, PMS was regarded as a psychological problem, but researchers now believe it is an organic disorder, although they are uncertain as to what triggers it. Women who have underlying conditions, such as depression or anxiety, may find their symptoms heightened during the 5 to 10 days before the start of their periods.*

## HOW IT DEVELOPS

The precise cause of PMS is unknown, but researchers theorize that prostaglandins, hormone-like chemicals that are instrumental in menstrual cramps, inflammation, and many other bodily processes, also play some role in PMS. The former theory that PMS might be caused by "hormonal imbalances" has been discounted as new research has shown that women who experience severe symptoms have the same hormonal fluctuations as women who have none.

Regardless of the cause, the syndrome varies greatly from one woman to another. However, PMS usually starts shortly after the onset of menstruation during puberty and continues through the woman's reproductive years. Most women complain of the physical or psychological symptoms listed above, but some find the premenstrual period to be one of increased energy and creativity.

*Depression and mood swings are a common component of premenstrual syndrome.*

## WHAT YOU CAN DO

It is important to understand that you are not alone and that millions of other women also have PMS; joining a support group to share experiences helps many women cope with their symptoms.

Engaging in regular exercise, eating regular meals throughout the day instead of snacking, getting enough sleep, and adopting better stress-coping techniques may help. Some women find that keeping a diary of symptoms for three months helps them recognize predictable physical and emotional patterns. They can then take preventive action—for example, taking a diuretic to reduce swelling—to control symptoms and prevent PMS from disrupting their lives. It should be noted, however, that symptoms can vary from month to month. Ways of reducing discomfort include the following:

* **Breast tenderness**: Wear a slightly larger bra during the premenstrual phase and avoid excessive breast stimulation during sexual activity.
* **Bloating and swelling**: Cut back on salt and caffeine; abstain from alcohol during the premenstrual phase of your cycle.
* **Head, back, and muscle pain**: Take aspirin or another nonprescription nonsteroidal anti-inflammatory drug (NSAID) such as ibuprofen.
* **Migraine headaches**: Take a beta blocker or other preventive medication (see *How to Treat It,* p 201).
* **Abdominal cramps**: Use a heating pad or soak in a hot bath; take aspirin or low-dose ibuprofen.
* **Constipation**: Increase intake of high-fiber foods (whole-grain cereals and breads, fresh fruits and vegetables), drink 8 to 10 glasses of water a day, and exercise for at least 20 to 30 minutes three or four times a week, or even daily.
* **Food cravings**: Avoid sweets and excessive starchy foods; instead, eat 5 to 10 servings of a variety of high-fiber fruits and vegetables a day and increase your intake of high-protein foods.

## HOW TO TREAT IT

See a doctor if PMS symptoms are interfering with your life and you are unable to control them with the self-help measures outlined earlier. Various medications may be tried to relieve specific symptoms. These include:

- **NSAIDs.** If nonprescription analgesics fail to relieve cramps, back pain, and other achiness, a strong NSAID may be prescribed.
- **Diuretics (water pills).** When taken for 10 to 14 days before menstruation, they can help prevent swelling and bloating.
- **Beta-blockers.** These drugs, which are used to treat high blood pressure and angina, are also effective in preventing palpitations and migraine headaches, which afflict many PMS sufferers.
- **Psychotropic drugs.** Antianxiety medications can help calm jittery nerves and calm feelings of irritability; antidepressant drugs can help prevent mood swings.
- **Hormones.** Some doctors prescribe progesterone, one of the female sex hormones, to treat PMS, but this seems to help only a few women.

## HOW TO PREVENT IT

In general, there are no certain preventive measures, but the self-help techniques and medications described above may prevent some symptoms, and the most troublesome symptoms usually can be controlled.

### ALTERNATIVE THERAPIES

**Aromatherapy**

Essential oils that help ease anxiety and nervousness include chamomile, rosemary, lavender, rose, and lemon. They can be added to bathwater or diluted in a neutral oil, such as olive oil, and massaged into the skin. To treat a headache, try sprinkling a few drops of melissa, lavender, or chamomile onto a handkerchief and inhaling the scent. Clary sage is used to improve mood and well-being.

**Herbal medicine**

Numerous studies have found that evening primrose or borage oils, in dosages of 1000 mg three times a day, ease PMS symptoms, especially those associated with inflammation. St. John's wort, standardized to contain 0.3 percent hypericin, may prevent mood swings and depression; take 300 mg three times a day. Other herbs that may be helpful include vitex (chasteberry), 225 mg a day, and dong quai, a Chinese herb, standardized to contain at least 0.8 percent ligustilide. Dong quai may need to be taken in daily doses of 500 to 600 mg for two months before results are noted (see *Warning!,* above). Various herbal teas can be taken for specific symptoms: peppermint to relieve digestive upset, dandelion to help prevent swelling and bloating, and ginger to quell nausea and an upset stomach. For further cautions concerning these herbs, see *About the Recommendations*, p 7.

**Homeopathy**

Homeopaths recommend Sepia, Pulsatilla, and Cimicifuga; use them according to package directions.

**Nutraceuticals**

Supplements that have been shown to relieve PMS symptoms, for at least some women, include: 100 mg of vitamin $B_6$, 1000 to 1200 mg of calcium, 500 mg of magnesium, 8000 IU of vitamin A, and 400 to 800 IU of vitamin D. Glucosamine sulfate may also relieve the back pain and muscle aches associated with PMS. If constipation is a problem, one or two tablespoons of ground psyllium seeds a day may help; be sure to drink at least 8 to 10 glasses of water during the day in order for it to work. For further cautions concerning these supplements, see *About the Recommendations*, p 7.

**WARNING!**

***Caution is needed when self-treating with herbal preparations. For example, dong quai should not be taken by women with uterine fibroid tumors. Dandelion tea should not be taken with prescription diuretics because the combination can upset body chemistry. Also, women who may become pregnant should be careful taking vitamin A supplements; more than 5000 IU a day can cause serious birth defects.***

**Relaxation therapies**

Yoga is effective for calming nerves and preventing muscle cramps. Meditation and self-hypnosis may also be helpful in controlling PMS symptoms. Music and/or dance therapy may also be helpful.

# Sexually Transmitted Diseases (STDs)

### SYMPTOMS

*These vary according to the type of disease; see the table* Common STDs at a Glance, *p 202, for specific symptoms. Among women, symptoms of the most common STDs include the following:*

- *Pelvic or lower back pain, ranging from mild and intermittent to acute and severe; pain may be accompanied by a fever.*
- *Copious or foul-smelling vaginal discharge.*
- *Pain or burning during urination.*
- *Painful intercourse.*
- *Unusually severe menstrual cramps or unusual bleeding between periods.*
- *Blisters, sores, bumps, or warts in the genital area.*
- *Severe itching in the genital area.*
- *Possible sore throat (among those who engage in oral sex).*

# Common STDs at a Glance

| DISEASE | SYMPTOMS | TREATMENT | COMPLICATIONS |
|---|---|---|---|
| Chlamydia | **In women:** Vaginal discharge, burning or painful urination, painful intercourse, pelvic pain.<br>**In men:** Clear, watery urethral discharge; painful or difficult urination. | Antibiotics, often in combination. | **In women:** PID, infertility; reactive arthritis. Pneumonia and eye infection in newborns.<br>**In men:** Urethritis, epididymitis, reactive arthritis. |
| Genital herpes | **Both men and women:** Recurrent, acutely painful genital sores; possible sore throat. | Antiviral drugs to shorten course; long-term antiviral drugs to reduce recurrences. | **Both men and women:** Aseptic meningitis, severe nerve pain; eye infection and nerve damage in newborns if infected during birth. |
| Genital warts | **Both men and women:** Soft, moist warts in genital and anal areas. | Removal with laser surgery, freezing, electric needle, or scalpel; topical treatment with caustic chemicals. | **In women:** Increased risk of cervical cancer. |
| Gonorrhea | **In women:** Urinary frequency and burning; vaginal discharge; pelvic pain.<br>**In men:** Mild penile pain, urinary frequency and burning, pus-filled penile discharge. | Antibiotics, often in combination to overcome drug resistance. | **In women:** PID, infertility; gonococcal arthritis; eye infections in newborns.<br>**In men:** Urethritis, epididymitis, gonococcal arthritis. |
| Hepatitis B & C | **Both men and women:** Flu-like symptoms, loss of appetite, malaise, jaundice. | Rest; otherwise, there is no specific treatment. | **Both men and women:** Chronic hepatitis, liver scarring (cirrhosis), increased risk of liver cancer. |
| HIV/AIDS | **In women:** Chronic vaginitis.<br>**Both men and women:** Increased vulnerability to pneumonia and other infections. | Various antiviral and anti-HIV drugs, often in combination. | **In women:** Cervical cancer.<br>**Both men and women:** Lymphoma, Kaposi's sarcoma, wasting, severe digestive disorders, death. |
| Pubic lice | **Both men and women:** Intense itching in genital area; lice and their nits may be visible. | Anti-lice creams, ointments, shampoos, and lotions. | **Both men and women:** Secondary bacterial infection from scratching. |
| Syphilis | **Both men and women:**<br>**Stage 1**: Painless ulcer, usually in genital area or on hands or mouth (chancre).<br>**Stage 2**: Rash on hands and palms; residual and recurring chancre; swollen lymph nodes; red eyes; diffuse pain in joints, back, and bones; headache, fever, malaise.<br>**Late stage**: see complications. | Antibiotics. | **In pregnant women:** Severe birth defects.<br>**Both men and women:** Late (tertiary) stage—heart disease, dementia, nerve disorders, diffuse pain, death. |
| Trichomonas | **In women:** Frothy, foul-smelling vaginal discharge; itching; urinary pain and burning; soreness of vulva, perineum, and thighs.<br>**In men:** Usually asymptomatic; may have some discharge and urinary frequency and discomfort. | Antibiotics. | **In women:** Chronic or recurrent vaginitis. |

**WHO IS AT RISK**

*Any sexually active woman who is not in a mutually monogamous relationship with an uninfected partner can contract a sexually transmitted disease. Despite continued decreases in Canadian STD rates, STDs remain an important public health problem in this country. While rates are high among young women who have multiple sex partners, they can occur at any age and in all social and economic classes.*

## HOW THEY DEVELOP

More than 100 diseases can be transmitted during sexual activity; these range from such deadly diseases as HIV and AIDS to parasitic disorders, such as pubic lice (crabs) and scabies, that can make life miserable but are not particularly dangerous. Following are the more common STDs affecting Canadian women:

- **Chlamydia**, a bacterial disease, is the most prevalent bacterial STD in Canada. It is asymptomatic in its early stages, but as the infection progresses, it can cause pelvic pain, painful intercourse, burning and painful urination, proctitis (rectal inflammation), vaginal swelling and inflammation, and a foul-smelling vaginal discharge. The smoldering infection can lead to pelvic inflammatory disease (PID) and infertility.
- **Genital herpes** is not a reported STD in Canada; however, international data suggests that it is common. It is caused by a variation of the herpes simplex virus—usually type 2, although type 1, which causes cold sores, can also infect the genital area. It starts as acutely painful blisters or sores, usually in the genital area. Less commonly, it may be transmitted to the mouth and throat during oral sex, causing a very painful sore throat. After 7 to 10 days, the sores clear up, but the virus remains latent in the body. Subsequent outbreaks usually are not as painful as the initial episode, but the virus can be transmitted to others whenever there is an active sore. A baby who contracts the virus from its mother during birth can suffer severe neurological damage and possible blindness.
- **Genital warts**, benign growths in the genital and anal areas, are caused by the human papilloma virus (HPV). Some warts are so small that they are barely visible; others look like miniature cauliflowers that may be three inches across. They are usually painless, but may itch or burn. They are highly contagious and difficult to get rid of; their major danger, however, is an increased risk of cervical cancer.
- **Gonorrhea**, a bacterial STD, is the second most commonly reported bacterial STD in Canada. Between 70 and 80 percent of infected women have no early symptoms; as the infection progresses, however, it can cause PID, chronic pelvic and abdominal pain from adhesions and scarring and infertility. Untreated gonorrhea can also cause septic arthritis, marked by severe swelling and inflammation of the knees or other large joints.
- **Hepatitis B and C**, viral diseases that can cause chronic liver inflammation, can be contracted in many ways, including kissing and sexual intercourse with an infected person. Hepatitis B usually causes mild flu-like symptoms followed by jaundice, a yellowing of the skin and whites of the eyes; most patients recover in a few weeks, but in about 5 percent, it evolves into a chronic liver disease. Symptoms of hepatitis C often go unnoticed at first, but it is even more likely to become a chronic disease. These forms of chronic hepatitis carry a high risk of cirrhosis (liver scarring) and liver cancer.
- **HIV and AIDS**, the most deadly of the STDs, weaken the body's immune system. The HIV virus can be contracted through any exchange of body fluids from an infected person; among women, sexual intercourse is the most common means of transmission. Symptoms vary greatly from one person to another, with increased vulnerability to all types of infections a common hallmark.
- **Pubic lice**, which live in the pubic hair, are most often passed from person to person during sexual activity, although they can also be picked up from contaminated bed linens, clothing, and toilet seats. They cause maddening itching in the infected areas.
- **Syphilis**, a bacterial infection, goes through three distinct stages: It starts as an open sore (chancre) at the site of infection, most often in the genital area. Stage 2 is marked by a rash on the soles and palms, and perhaps eye inflammation or meningitis (inflammation of the lining of the brain and spinal cord) and diffuse pain. Stage 3, or tertiary syphilis, appears years after the initial infection, and may take the form of heart disease, blindness, and dementia; it is often fatal.
- **Trichomonas**, which is caused by a protozoan (a one-celled organism), is one of the most common causes of vaginitis. It starts with a copious frothy vaginal discharge and itching, inflammation, and swelling in the vulvar area. It can also cause urinary frequency and painful, burning urination.

**WARNING!**

***When embarking on a new sexual relationship, doctors advise that the man should use condoms and that the woman also use a barrier contraceptive (a diaphragm or female condom) along with a spermicide. These measures should be continued for at least six months or until both partners test negative for STDs and remain monogamous.***

## WHAT YOU CAN DO

Your best course is to see a doctor as soon as possible if you suspect you may have a sexually transmitted disease.

While waiting to see a doctor, take aspirin, ibuprofen, or another nonsteroidal anti-inflammation drug (NSAID) to ease pelvic pain and lower a fever. A heating pad may also help. A cold compress can numb the pain of genital herpes; a tepid sitz bath may also bring relief. If itching is a symptom, try to avoid scratching, which can spread the primary infection and may also cause a secondary bacterial infection.

Pubic lice and scabies (another skin infestation that can be transmitted by sexual contact) often can be eliminated with nonprescription creams or lotions containing permethrin (Nix, Kwellada-P). These preparations also relieve itching. Repeated treatments may be necessary, and all underclothes, bed linens, towels, and other items that may harbor lice must be washed in very hot water and dried at a high heat.

## HOW TO TREAT THEM

Treatment varies according to the specific disease (see *Common STDs at a Glance*, p 202). Chlamydia, gonorrhea, and syphilis can be cured with antibiotics; however, retesting may be needed after treatment is completed to make sure the bacterium has been eradicated. Antibiotics can also eliminate the trichomonas protozoan. HIV, hepatitis, genital herpes, and other viral STDs cannot be cured, but antiviral drugs can often minimize, delay, or even eliminate symptoms. If pubic lice persist despite initial treatment with permethrin, repeated treatments may be needed.

## HOW TO PREVENT THEM

The best preventive is to limit sexual activity to a mutually monogamous uninfected partner. Although many people find it difficult to discuss such matters with a potential sexual partner, it's important to ask about any infections and previous sexual partners. Even then, practice safer sex by always using condoms and a spermicide until the partner's safety has been established (see *Warning!*, p 203).

If you do develop an STD, do whatever you can to avoid spreading the infection to others. Make sure all sexual partners are tested and, if necessary, treated. Avoid sexual intercourse and other intimate contact until the infection is completely cleared up.

### BREAKTHROUGHS!

**Antiviral drugs, such as acyclovir (Zovirax), famciclovir (Famvir), or valacyclovir (Valtrex), can help reduce the frequency and severity of genital herpes flare-ups. The drugs are taken once or twice a day for an extended period (usually a year or more). In one study, 63 percent of patients who had suffered six or more outbreaks a year were free of recurrences in the third year of treatment.**

### ALTERNATIVE THERAPIES

**Note:** Alternative therapies should not be a substitute for conventional treatment of any STD, but some may ease pain and other symptoms.

**Aromatherapy**

Adding a few drops of geranium oil to bathwater can help soothe itching and heal skin sores.

**Herbal medicine**

Calendula soothes inflammation and may hasten the healing of genital herpes sores. It can be used as an ointment or a compress soaked in strong calendula tea. The tea can also be used as a soothing gargle for a herpes sore throat. Aloe vera gel, squeezed fresh from an aloe leaf, may also ease the pain and hasten healing of herpes sores. Witch hazel, an astringent herb, also relieves skin inflammation and itching.

Creams containing camphor or capsaicin (the active ingredient in hot peppers) may be helpful for the muscle and joint pain associated with some STDs. Capsaicin creams can cause serious burning if it gets in the eyes or on delicate mucous membranes.

**Homeopathy**

Practitioners recommend Rhus toxicodendron to relieve the burning and itching of a herpes outbreak.

**Nutraceuticals**

Acidophilus can help restore a healthy balance of intestinal bacteria that are killed during antibiotic therapy.

# Tubal Pregnancy

### SYMPTOMS

*In addition to signs of early pregnancy—fatigue, nausea, a missed period, and breast tenderness—symptoms include:*

- *Abdominal pressure and unusual, though light, vaginal bleeding 4 to 6 weeks after a missed period. (Heavy bleeding indicates a miscarriage, not a tubal pregnancy.)*
- *Sudden onset of constant, debilitating, sharp pain on one side of abdomen, sometimes with sharp shoulder pain, nausea, or fainting.*

### WHO IS AT RISK

*The risk is greatest among women of reproductive age who have had previous bouts of pelvic inflammatory disease (PID), endometriosis, sexually transmitted diseases (STDs), a ruptured ovarian cyst or appendix, tubal surgery, or a previous tubal pregnancy. Any of these conditions may leave the fallopian tubes scarred, which prevents a fertilized egg from reaching the uterus for proper implantation at the beginning of pregnancy. Also women whose mothers took DES—an artificial estrogen—during their pregnancy have an increased risk of tubal pregnancy.*

## HOW IT DEVELOPS

A tubal pregnancy, also called an ectopic pregnancy, occurs when a fertilized egg implants itself in a fallopian tube, or more rarely, on an ovary or somewhere within the abdominal cavity or cervical canal, instead of inside the uterus. It begins to grow as it would in the uterus, mimicking the symptoms of early pregnancy, although sometimes it produces no symptoms at all. However, during the fourth to sixth week of pregnancy, often before the woman realizes she's pregnant, the tube or organ cannot accommodate the growing embryo and begins to tear. This tearing brings on sudden, sharp pain and severe internal bleeding.

**WARNING!**

***Never ignore sudden, sharp, debilitating abdominal pain; get to the nearest emergency room. This type of pain usually does not go away and, in the case of tubal pregnancy, it can lead to severe internal bleeding and even death.***

## WHAT YOU CAN DO

Call your doctor, or better still, go to the nearest emergency room as soon as possible (see *Warning!*, above).

## HOW TO TREAT IT

In rare instances, a tubal pregnancy dissolves on its own, but to be safe, most doctors intervene to make sure that the embryo does not continue to grow and rupture the fallopian tube or damage other pelvic organs. If the tubal pregnancy is discovered before the tube has ruptured, doctors can administer methotrexate—a drug usually used to treat cancer, severe arthritis, or psoriasis—to immediately stop the embryo from growing and dissolve the tissue, which is reabsorbed by the body. Although you must be monitored carefully during this two-week process, including a hospital stay for a few days to ensure no crisis develops, this method of treatment is the least invasive way to treat a tubal pregnancy. It also preserves the fallopian tubes for future pregnancies.

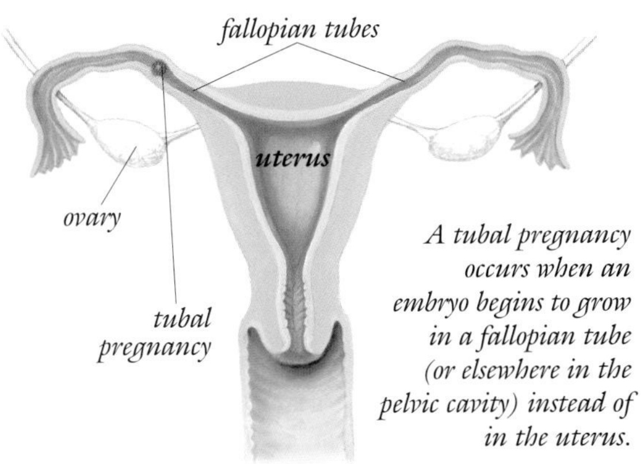


*A tubal pregnancy occurs when an embryo begins to grow in a fallopian tube (or elsewhere in the pelvic cavity) instead of in the uterus.*

More commonly, tubal pregnancies are not discovered until the tube has ruptured and is causing severe internal bleeding. In these cases, emergency surgery is required to remove not only the mass but also the ruptured tube and possibly other affected reproductive organs. The operation can usually be performed by laparoscopic surgery. A general anesthetic is administered, and a viewing tube (laparoscope) equipped with a miniature video camera is inserted into the pelvic cavity through a small incision near the navel; the surgeon then manipulates tiny surgical instruments through the tube while viewing a video monitor. Sometimes the affected tube can be preserved; more often, it is removed (see *Breakthroughs!*, below).

After the operation, meperidine (Demerol) or codeine may be given to relieve post-surgical pain; in a day or two, acetaminophen or a nonsteroidal anti-inflammatory drug (NSAID) should be sufficient.

**BREAKTHROUGHS!**

**Advances in *in vitro fertilization* (IVF) and other methods of assisted pregnancy are enabling increasing numbers of women with a history of tubal pregnancy and damaged or removed fallopian tubes to have a baby. The woman is given fertility drugs to prompt her ovaries to ripen a number of eggs, which are then harvested and fertilized with her partner's sperm in a test tube. After the fertilized eggs have undergone several cell divisions, two or three are placed in the uterus, where, hopefully, at least one will implant itself and establish a pregnancy. Surplus fertilized eggs can be frozen and used to establish future pregnancies.**

## HOW TO PREVENT IT

Practice safe sex to minimize risk of becoming infected with STDs, which in their early stages sometimes produce no symptoms and go untreated. Untreated STDs can lead to pelvic inflammatory disease (PID), which can scar the reproductive organs, including the fallopian tubes. Be sure to inform your doctor if you have been treated for PID or have had a previous tubal pregnancy, which increases the risk of another one.

Women who have a high risk of a tubal pregnancy should use a home pregnancy test as soon as a period is missed, and see a doctor as soon as possible if it is positive. If further tests confirm a pregnancy, a doctor will test for a rise in human chorionic gonadotropin (hCG), a hormone whose production increases after conception. A low hCG level will prompt a doctor to do an ultrasound examination to determine whether the embryo has implanted improperly outside the uterus. Treatment at this early stage can prevent a ruptured tube and other complications of a tubal pregnancy.

### ALTERNATIVE THERAPIES

**Note:** There are none for tubal pregnancy.

# Uterine Fibroids/ Cervical Polyps

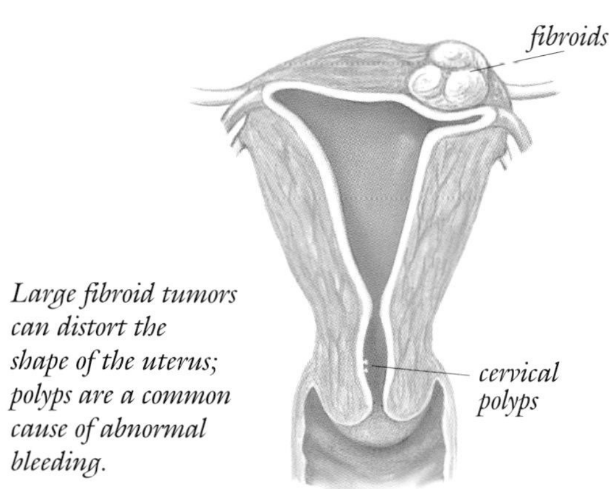


*Large fibroid tumors can distort the shape of the uterus; polyps are a common cause of abnormal bleeding.*

### SYMPTOMS

*These benign growths are often asymptomatic; when symptoms do occur, they may include:*

- *Abdominal or lower-back pain; painful intercourse.*
- *Feeling of abdominal fullness or pressure.*
- *Prolonged menstrual periods with heavy bleeding; possible vaginal discharge.*
- *Anemia due to excessive blood loss.*
- *Difficult or frequent urination; constipation.*
- *Infertility or miscarriage.*

### WHO IS AT RISK

*About one in four women—mostly those of reproductive age—harbors uterine fibroids and/or cervical polyps. They are somewhat more common among women of African descent than Caucasian and Asian women, but the reasons for this are not clearly understood.*

## HOW THEY DEVELOP

Uterine fibroids are benign growths that develop outside or within the uterine wall, or inside the uterus itself. It is not clear how or why fibroids—which are also called myomas, fibromyomas, myofibromas, and leiomyomas—develop, but their growth seems to be stimulated by estrogen, the major female sex hormone. Fibroids are made up of fibrous or muscular tissue and, over time, they can grow to the size of a full-term fetus or even larger. Large fibroids are likely to cause chronic abdominal and lower-back pain, constipation, urinary difficulties, and anemia from excessive blood loss during menstruation. More often, however, they remain small and asymptomatic except for heavy periods and a possible chronic feeling of abdominal fullness. Fibroid tumors tend to shrink after menopause, when the body's estrogen levels drop. Fibroids themselves do not become malignant, but a large growth may mask a cancer. Therefore, any abnormal bleeding or rapidly expanding growth should be checked to rule out cancer.

Uterine polyps are small, smooth growths that resemble grapes. They can grow from mucous membranes anywhere in the body, including parts of the uterus. They, too, can cause heavy menstrual bleeding and a discharge, especially after intercourse.

## WHAT YOU CAN DO

There is no self-treatment for uterine fibroids or polyps. If the growths are causing painful intercourse, experiment with different positions to find those that are the most comfortable. If you plan to become pregnant, check with your doctor to make sure that the growths will not interfere with conception or the pregnancy itself. Shortness of breath and chronic fatigue point to possible anemia; if fibroids are producing heavy bleeding month after month, you should have blood tests to determine whether you should take iron supplements.

## HOW TO TREAT THEM

### Medications

Many uterine fibroids and polyps are discovered during a routine pelvic examination. After cancer has been ruled out, they should be monitored regularly through annual pelvic examination and ultrasound to make sure they are not masking a malignancy or other potentially serious pelvic condition, such as ovarian cysts. This may require a biopsy of the endometrial tissue that lines the uterus or, in the case of polyps or heavy bleeding, a D&C (dilation and curettage), a procedure in which the cervix is dilated and a spoon-shaped curette is used to scrape out the uterine lining.

Sometimes oral contraceptives that reduce estrogen production are prescribed to help control bleeding and halt fibroid growth. (High-estrogen pills, as well as dong quai, a popular herbal remedy, should not be used because they can have the opposite effect and actually spur growth.) If this approach doesn't work, a doctor may prescribe stronger estrogen suppressors, such as leuprolide acetate (Lupron, a GnRH agonist), which causes a temporary menopause and shrinks the fibroids. This drug can be taken for only six months because it can reduce bone density. In addition, the fibroids may regrow after the drug is stopped.

### Surgery

Fibroids that grow larger than a few ounces or the size of a 12-week fetus, or those that are causing chronic pain, anemia and other symptoms, may require surgical removal. (In some cases, fibroid tumors weighing more than 100 pounds have been successfully removed.)

If surgery is needed, there are two possible approaches: Women who still plan to have children may undergo a myomectomy, a procedure to remove the tumor that leaves the uterus intact. If the fibroids are quite large, GnRH agonists may be given first to shrink them and make them easier to remove. Even so, the operation may cause severe bleeding, in which case an emergency hysterectomy may be necessary. If childbearing is no longer an issue, a hysterectomy is the preferred operation. In general, the ovaries are left intact if the woman is under 50, and removed if the woman is older than that.

**WARNING!**

***Don't ignore sudden, sharp abdominal pain. It could be a sign that the fibroid is twisted and is causing tissue death. Emergency surgery may be needed to prevent development of gangrene.***

## HOW TO PREVENT THEM

There is no known way to prevent fibroid tumors from developing, although women with a family history of fibroids may be advised against taking high-estrogen birth control pills because this hormone spurs their growth. After menopause, women with a history of fibroids who are considering hormone replacement therapy may consider taking a selective estrogen receptor modulator (SERM), such as raloxifene (Evista), which—unlike estrogen—does not prompt fibroid growth.

### ALTERNATIVE THERAPIES

**Nutraceuticals**

Iron supplements may be prescribed for women who develop anemia; however, a doctor should determine the dosage after doing blood tests. The time-released forms maybe less likely to cause an upset stomach as regular iron pills. If the iron causes constipation, increase your intake of fruits and vegetables, and drink a glass of prune juice—a natural laxative—before going to bed. Do not take bran or a fiber laxative made from bran, however, because it can interfere with iron absorption.

**BREAKTHROUGHS!**

**Doctors at UCLA and Georgetown University are experimenting with a noninvasive procedure to remove fibroids called uterine artery embolization. This procedure involves injecting a substance into the vessels that supply blood to the growths and, in effect, starving them. Women undergoing the procedure in clinical studies appear to tolerate the procedure well; it can be done using local anesthesia, requires only a short hospital stay, and quickly eliminates symptoms.**

# Vaginitis

### SYMPTOMS

- *Burning, itching, or swelling of the vagina and vulva.*
- *Profuse vaginal discharge that may be gray, greenish, yellow, frothy, cheesy, and/or malodorous.*
- *Pain or burning during urination; painful intercourse.*

### WHO IS AT RISK

*All women—particularly those who are sexually active, are taking antibiotics for other infections, suffering from diabetes, or are going through menopause—are prone to vaginitis, a general term applied to any of several different conditions that cause vaginal inflammation, irritation, abnormal discharges, and other symptoms. Other risk factors include having a condition that lowers immunity and using corticosteroid medications.*

## HOW IT DEVELOPS

All premenopausal women produce vaginal secretions, which are usually clear or milky white and odorless. In its healthy state, the vagina's pH is somewhat acidic to help maintain a proper balance of the yeast and bacteria that normally inhabit it. A change in the normal pH can allow an overgrowth of certain organisms, resulting in itching, inflammation, pain, and an unpleasant, often copious discharge.

One of the most common types of vaginitis is caused by an overgrowth of the intestinal bacterium, *Gardnerella vaginalis*. It is characterized by itching and a white, yellowish, or gray discharge with a fishy odor. An overgrowth of a yeast fungus called *Candida albicans* is also very common; it causes intense itching and a cheesy discharge with a yeasty odor. Vaginitis can also be caused by a number of sexually transmitted diseases, especially chlamydia, a bacterium, and *Trichomonas vaginalis*, a one-celled parasite (protozan). The latter produces a foul-smelling, frothy green, or gray discharge and intense itching.

After menopause, vaginal secretions diminish and the vaginal lining becomes thin and easily irritated, leading to painful intercourse and itching. Vaginitis can also develop when a foreign object, such as a tampon or a diaphragm, is left in the vagina too long, resulting in pain and a profuse, malodorous discharge that may be watery or blood-streaked. Women with diabetes are very vulnerable to vaginitis and other infections (see *Warning!*).

**WARNING!**

***If you suffer from recurrent or chronic vaginal infections, have your blood sugar tested, because recurrent vaginitis is often an early sign of type 2 (adult-onset) diabetes.***

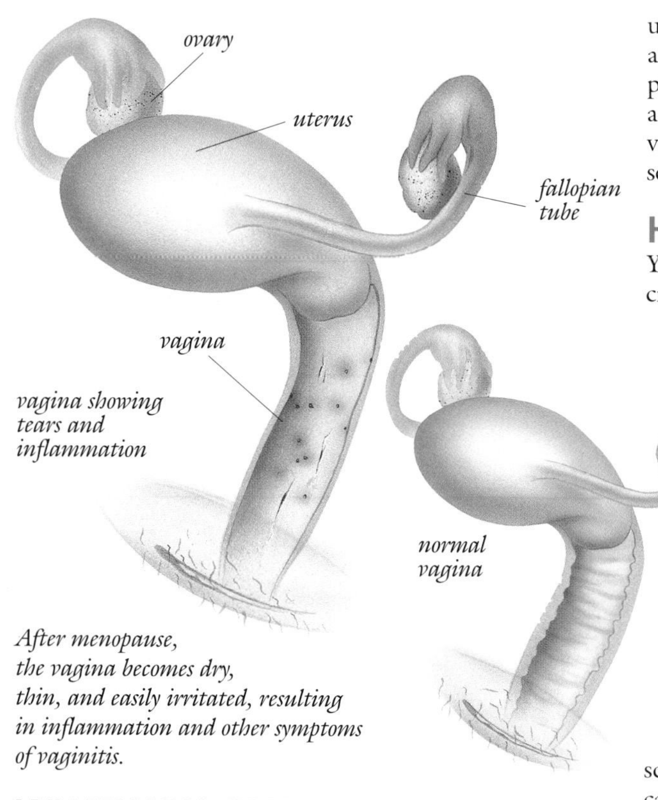


*After menopause, the vagina becomes dry, thin, and easily irritated, resulting in inflammation and other symptoms of vaginitis.*

## WHAT YOU CAN DO

To temporarily ease itching and irritation, add a cup of baking soda to tepid bathwater and sit in it for 15 to 20 minutes. A vinegar or Povidone-iodine (Betadine) douche may also offer immediate relief, but don't douche more than once or twice a week; overdouching can further alter the vagina's pH balance and make matters worse. A nonprescription 0.5 percent corticosteroid cream applied to itchy or painful areas may also help. If symptoms don't improve in two days of self-treatment, however, you should see a doctor, as medical therapy varies according to the type of vaginitis.

If the cause is a yeast infection, your doctor may prescribe one of the antifungal medications that are now available over-the-counter. If the symptoms recur (and you are sure it's a yeast infection), then you can treat it yourself. Plain yogurt made with live cultures inserted into the vagina can help restore the natural balance of vaginal yeast and bacteria. To do this, fill an applicator, such as those used for contraceptive foam, with a tablespoon of yogurt, and then wear a tampon to keep it from leaking out. Reapply the yogurt and change the tampon three or four times a day. Older women who are experiencing dryness (senile vaginitis) may want to try a water-soluble lubricant before sexual intercourse to prevent vaginal pain and irritation.

### BREAKTHROUGHS!

**Fluconazole (Diflucan) is the first of a new class of antifungal drugs to be used orally to treat vaginal yeast infections. A single 150-mg pill brings relief within 24 hours and a cure within two or three days. The most common side effects reported in clinical studies were headaches, mild nausea, and abdominal pain.**

## HOW TO TREAT IT

Yeast infections are treated with antifungal suppositories, creams, or ointments, such as nystatin (Nycostatin), terconazole (Terazol), clotrimazole (Canesten), and miconazole (Monistat). Gardnerella infections may be treated with oral antibiotics, such as metronidazole (Flagyl). Trichomonas is also treated with oral metronidazole. Senile vaginitis is treated with oral, topical, or transdermal estrogens.

## HOW TO PREVENT IT

In general, keep the vaginal area as dry as possible. Wear cotton underwear and loose-fitting clothes. Tight jeans and wet bathing suits restrict air flow and cause the buildup of bacteria that can upset the vagina's naturally acidic balance. Avoid using perfumed soaps, bubble baths, scented tampons, and vaginal deodorants—all of which can cause vaginal irritation. To prevent vaginitis caused by sexually transmitted organisms, practice safe sex to avoid being infected.

### ALTERNATIVE THERAPIES

**Herbal medicine**

Garlic is an age-old remedy for yeast infections, especially candida vaginitis. A number of studies have found that a daily clove of raw or lightly cooked garlic inhibits yeast growth. If you find the odor unacceptable, a 900-mg daily dose of odor-controlled enteric tablets, standardized to provide 5000 micrograms of allicin, can be used as an alternative. Check with your doctor before using garlic if you are taking aspirin or anticoagulants. Other herbal treatments for yeast infections include vaginal suppositories containing 2 percent tea tree oil.

**Nutraceuticals**

If your doctor has prescribed antibiotics to treat an infection, take three acidophilus pills a day to prevent an overgrowth of vaginal yeast. Two or three servings of yogurt made with live cultures may also help, although the beneficial lactobacillus organisms may not survive exposure to digestive juices. It may be more effective to insert the yogurt directly into the vagina (see *What You Can Do*, left). Drinking two or three glasses of unsweetened, full-strength cranberry juice—the kind sold in many health-food stores—may restore the vagina's acidic balance. To make the juice more palatable, dilute it with apple juice.

# Male Reproductive Organs

*The male penis and urethra play key roles in both urinary and reproductive functions, and are sources of pain and other problems stemming from both systems. Tucked between the rectum and bladder is the tiny prostate—a gland that can cause king-size problems.*

## Enlarged Prostate

### SYMPTOMS

- *Frequent urination, with difficulty voiding completely; weak stream, with urine dribbling out after completion.*
- *Pain and burning during urination.*
- *Bladder stones or chronic and severe urethritis as the condition progresses.*
- *Severe blockage causing backup of urine into bladder and kidneys.*

### WHO IS AT RISK

*According to the Canadian Cancer Society, benign enlargement of the prostate, referred to as benign prostatic hypertrophy, or BPH, commonly occurs in men over age 40. By age 50, half of men have BPH. Men who have first-degree relatives (a father or a brother) who have experienced an enlarged prostate run a greater risk of developing the condition themselves.*

### HOW IT DEVELOPS

The prostate is a small, walnut-shaped gland that surrounds the neck of the male bladder and the upper part of the urethra. It produces a milky fluid that is part of the seminal fluid. Why it enlarges with age is not completely understood, but it may be related to hormonal changes, chronic inflammation, or nutritional or metabolic factors.

As the prostate enlarges, it presses against the urethra, preventing the bladder from emptying completely. Typically, a man feels the need to urinate more often, the flow is slow to start, and his stream is weak. He then experiences urine dribbling from his penis after he thought he was finished. He may also experience pain and burning during urination if the prostate is pressing against the urethral canal. Stagnant urine can collect in the bladder, increasing a man's risk of developing urethritis (inflammation of the urethra) and bladder stones. This backup of urine can also damage the kidneys.

### WHAT YOU CAN DO

A warm sitz bath twice a day may temporarily relieve pain and other symptoms. Water temperature should be 40.5° to 46°C (105° to 115°F). Drink at least 8 to 10 glasses of fluid a day to promote urine flow. Cranberry

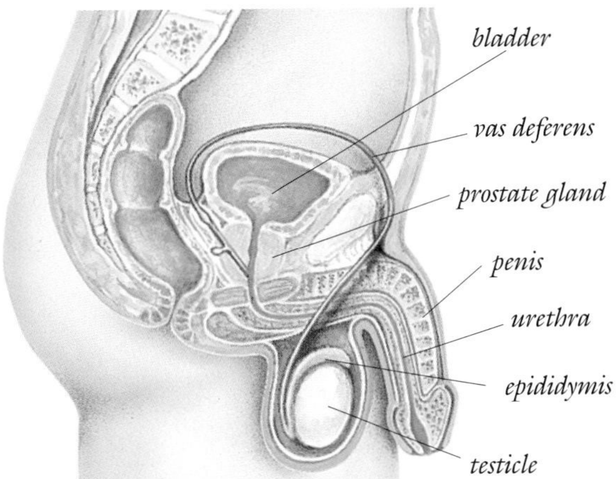


*The male reproductive system manufactures, stores, and releases sperm. The testicles also make testosterone—the hormone that gives a man his masculine characteristics.*

juice—preferably the unsweetened kind—or cranberry extract pills can help prevent urinary tract infections. Abstain from alcohol and use caffeine in moderation; these substances can worsen the symptoms of BPH.

Avoid nonprescription drugs that make the problem worse, especially cold and allergy medicines, as well as certain prescription drugs used to treat ulcers, irritable bowel syndrome, and depression. These drugs cause the retention of urine, which exacerbates BPH symptoms.

Urinate when you first feel the urge, rather than delaying. Avoid sexual stimulation and arousal without ejaculation. Both of these practices can help minimize pressure on the urethra and bladder, reducing symptoms and the risk of inflammation.

### HOW TO TREAT IT

#### Tests

To assist in early detection, physicians recommend that men over age 50 have a regular checkup including the following:

> **BREAKTHROUGHS!**
>
> **A new surgical technique shows promise in relieving the symptoms of BPH without the adverse effects of TURP and other operations. The procedure involves inserting a balloon-tipped catheter into the urethra and then inflating the balloon when it reaches the area narrowed by the enlarged prostate.**

- **A digital rectal exam**, in which a doctor inserts a gloved finger into the rectum and feels (palpates) the prostate to check not only for enlargement, but also for unusual hardness or lumps that could be a sign of cancer. This examination should be done at least annually.
- **Blood tests** to measure levels of prostate specific antigen (PSA). An elevated PSA indicates possible prostate enlargement, and very high levels point to possible prostate cancer.

Suspicious findings indicate a need for additional tests, which may include:

- **Voiding tests**, in which a catheter is inserted into the bladder to measure the amount of urine that remains after voiding.
- **An ultrasound examination**, in which high-frequency sound waves are used to map the prostate and other pelvic organs.
- **Cystoscopy,** in which a viewing tube with magnifying devices is inserted into the bladder to examine it and nearby organs.

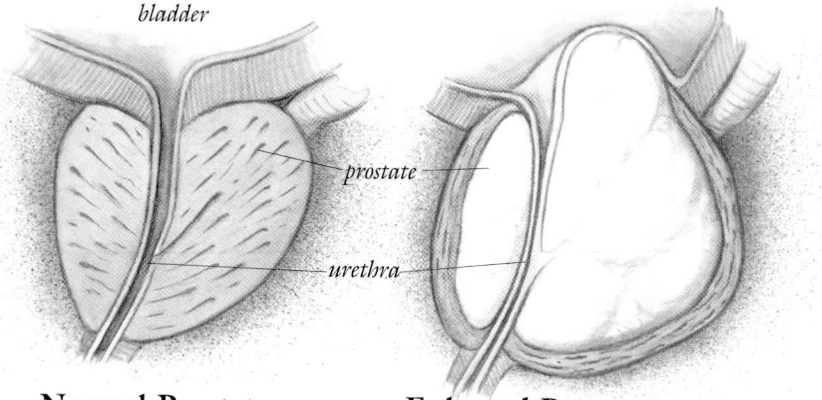


## Medications

Antibiotics or other drugs will be prescribed to treat any urinary infections and kidney problems. New drugs, such as finasteride (Proscar), may be prescribed to help shrink the overgrown prostate. Other medications may help increase urinary flow and reduce urgency.

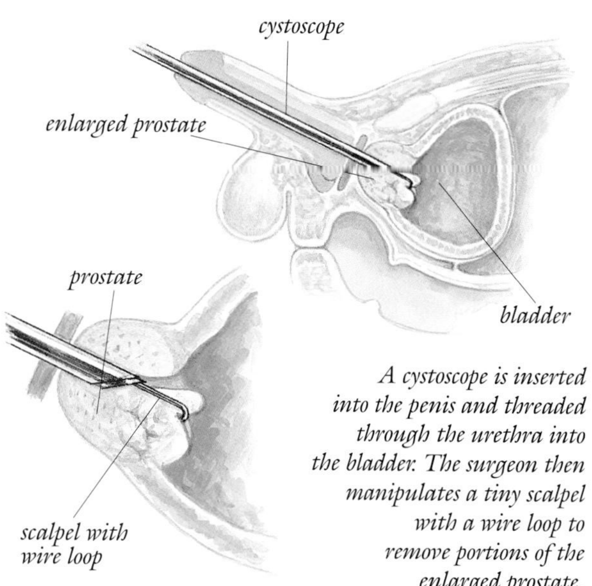


*A cystoscope is inserted into the penis and threaded through the urethra into the bladder. The surgeon then manipulates a tiny scalpel with a wire loop to remove portions of the enlarged prostate.*

## Surgery

If the enlarged prostate is causing urinary retention and other chronic problems, surgery may be necessary to reduce its size. In the most common operation, called TURP (for transurethral resection of the prostate), a surgeon inserts a flexible tube (called a cystoscope) through the urethra to reach the prostate. A tiny scalpel with a wire loop is inserted through the tube to snip away overgrown prostate tissue. This operation, which typically involves a three-day hospital stay, provides long-term relief from the symptoms of enlarged prostate.

Although the operation is generally safe, there is a chance that area nerves may be damaged, resulting in impotence; new nerve-sparing procedures have reduced this risk. Some 60 percent or more of men undergoing TURP experience retrograde ejaculation, which means that they can no longer ejaculate from the penis. Instead, the semen goes backward into the bladder. This does not interfere with sexual pleasure, but it does cause fertility problems. If the man wishes to father a child, his semen can be extracted and used for artificial insemination.

# HOW TO PREVENT IT

BPH cannot be prevented, but the process may be slowed with drug therapy and perhaps herbal preparations (see *Alternative Therapies,* below). Complications can be prevented or at least minimized by undergoing an annual prostate exam after age 50.

### ALTERNATIVE THERAPIES

**Herbal medicine**

A number of studies indicate that saw palmetto extract, which comes from the berries of a dwarf palm that grows wild in Texas and other parts of the southern U.S., can slow prostate enlargement. It contains sterols and fatty acids that inhibit the conversion of testosterone to dihydrotestosterone (DHT), which is thought to spur prostate growth. The usual dosage is 160 mg twice a day.

If saw palmetto alone is not enough, 200 mg of pygeum africanum, standardized to contain 13 percent sterols, can be added to the regimen. Other herbs that may be helpful include nettle, which can be taken as tea or consumed in two 250-mg pills a day. Parsley and corn silk teas may also alleviate mild BPH symptoms. Claims that ginseng can shrink an enlarged prostate have not been proved.

**Nutraceuticals**

Vitamin E, in doses of 400 to 800 IU a day, may reduce inflammation from an enlarged prostate; it may also protect against cancer by preventing the cell damage that occurs when the body burns oxygen. People taking anticoagulants or aspirin should consult their doctor before using vitamin E. One tablespoon of flaxseed oil a day may also reduce inflammation, and some studies indicate that 25 to 30 mg of zinc a day may relieve BPH symptoms. Add 2 mg of copper when using zinc for more than one month.

**WARNING!**

***Symptoms of BPH are often difficult to distinguish from those of prostatitis—an inflamed prostate—and prostate cancer. These more serious disorders must be ruled out before diagnosing BPH.***

# Epididymitis/ Orchitis

### SYMPTOMS

- *Acute pain in one or both of the testicles.*
- *Scrotal pain, reddening, and swelling.*
- *Possible fever and malaise.*

### WHO IS AT RISK

*Men of all ages can develop inflammation and swelling of the epididymis, the coiled tube where immature sperm pass from the testicle to mature, and the testicles themselves. The risk is greatest, however, among sexually active young men. Possible causes include gonorrhea, chlamydia, and other sexually transmitted diseases; a urinary tract infection; prostatitis (inflammation of the prostate gland); and complications after prostate surgery. In the past, orchitis—inflammation and swelling of one or both testicles—was a common complication of mumps.*

## HOW IT DEVELOPS

In epididymitis, the scrotum is painfully swollen and inflamed. The pain usually comes on abruptly and one or both of the testicles may be involved. Other nearby urinary and reproductive organs—especially the urethra, vas deferens (the tube that carries sperm from the epididymis), and prostate gland—may also be infected. A hydrocele—an accumulation of fluid in the sac surrounding the testicles— sometimes forms; a pus-filled sac (an abscess) may also develop. Without prompt treatment, epididymitis and orchitis can result in infertility.

In unusual cases, epididymitis recurs or becomes chronic. This is usually due to an in-dwelling urinary catheter, chronic urethritis, testicular cancer, or a structural abnormality.

**WARNING!**

***Do not attempt to ease the pain by applying a heating pad or warm compresses to the scrotal area. The heat can damage the germ cells that produce sperm.***

## WHAT YOU CAN DO

See a doctor as soon as possible. To relieve pain in the meantime, take aspirin, ibuprofen, or another nonsteroidal anti-inflammatory drug (NSAID) and apply an ice pack to the scrotal area. To ease pressure on the scrotum, place a towel under it and stay in bed until the pain and swelling subside. During recovery, abstain from sexual intercourse and restrict exercise, heavy lifting, and other physical activity. Doctors usually advise patients to wear a scrotal support for six or more weeks.

## HOW TO TREAT IT

To provide immediate pain relief, a doctor may do a temporary nerve block by injecting a local anesthetic into the spermatic cord. An ultrasound examination may be ordered (see *Breakthroughs!*). A culture of the urine or possible penile discharge will be done to determine whether a bacterium is involved; if so, an antibiotic will be prescribed. Hydroceles usually subside on their own, but in some instances, they require drainage with a hollow needle. Abscesses need to be lanced and drained.

Chronic epididymitis may require surgical treatment. Sometimes a vasectomy cures the problem; if pain and other symptoms persist, however, removal of the epididymis may be recommended.

## HOW TO PREVENT IT

Adopt safe sexual practices by limiting the number of sexual partners and always using condoms unless you are in

**BREAKTHROUGHS!**

**Advances in the use of ultrasound—high-frequency sound waves—to examine the male genital organs now make it possible to diagnose more accurately the many causes of scrotal pain. For example, the addition of color Doppler ultrasound to study scrotal blood flow can help a doctor distinguish epididymitis from testicular torsion (twisting)—a condition that sometimes causes similar symptoms—and start the proper treatment more quickly.**

a mutually monogamous relationship with an uninfected partner. Prompt diagnosis and treatment of urinary tract infections and prostatitis help prevent secondary epididymitis and orchitis. Any adult male who is unsure about his childhood mumps immunization should be tested and, if necessary, vaccinated.

### ALTERNATIVE THERAPIES

**Herbal medicine**

Saw palmetto, in dosages of 160 mg twice a day, helps prevent the prostate enlargement and inflammation that can lead to epididymitis. A daily tablespoon of flaxseed oil also reduces inflammation; possible alternatives include borage or evening primrose oils. Borage or evening primrose oil should not be taken by people using anticoagulants such as heparin.

**Nutraceuticals**

High doses (up to 800 IU a day) of vitamin E help quell inflammation. People taking prescription anticoagulants or aspirin should consult their doctor before using vitamin E.

# Priapism

### SYMPTOMS

- *Painful penile engorgement and erection that persists even in the absence of sexual arousal.*
- *Prolonged painful swelling of the penis.*

### WHO IS AT RISK

*Priapism occurs mostly among young and middle-aged men. It sometimes develops as a complication of leukemia, sickle-cell disease, prostatitis, urinary tract infections, bladder stones, and syphilis. Certain drugs may cause priapism; examples include injections and medications such as sildenafil (Viagra) to treat erectile dysfunction, corticosteroids, certain antihypertensives, anticoagulants, and some antidepressant and antipsychotic medications. Prolonged sexual activity sometimes results in priapism; so too can spinal-cord injuries that affect nerves to the penis. In about 75 percent of cases, however, no cause can be found.*

### PEYRONIE'S DISEASE–WHEN THE PENIS GOES ASKEW

Peyronie's disease—a disorder in which the penis deviates to one side—is another cause of painful erections. Fibrous tissue develops in the normally spongy erectile shaft, so that the penis is pulled askew during an erection. Although intercourse may be painful, most men with Peyronie's disease can function normally. Sometimes the abnormality goes away without treatment; if it persists, injections of a corticosteroid or verapamil (Isoptin, a calcium-channel blocker that relaxes smooth muscles and dilates blood vessels) into the penis may help. Surgery to remove the fibrous tissue is another treatment option.

## HOW IT DEVELOPS

The precise mechanism of priapism is unknown, but researchers think that abnormalities in the penile blood vessels and nerves are somehow involved. Without warning, the penis becomes painfully engorged with blood in much the same manner that it does during an erection. In priapism, however, the engorgement occurs without sexual arousal and the erection does not abate. Left untreated, priapism can damage the urinary structures of the penis and cause permanent impotence.

## WHAT YOU CAN DO

There is no self-treatment for priapism; it is a medical emergency that must be treated within three or four hours to prevent irreversible damage. Do not apply an ice pack, which is unlikely to help and can make matters worse. Similarly, doctors advise against using sprays containing ethyl chloride, a priapism self-treatment recommended on some Internet sites.

## HOW TO TREAT IT

Reversing the erection immediately relieves the pain, but this is often difficult to achieve. If an underlying cause can be identified, treating it may relieve the priapism. Norepinephrine or other medications injected into the spongy erectile tissue surrounding the urethra (corpus cavernosum and spongiosum, or corpora) may reverse priapism, especially if it is caused by impotence drugs. Alternatively, a hollow needle may be used to draw off blood pooled in the erectile tissue; unfortunately, this may provide only temporary relief. Creation of a passage (fistula) between the corpora and tip of the penis (glans) is more likely to provide lasting results.

### WARNING!

***Seek immediate medical treatment for any painful erection that lasts more than 20 minutes and is not related to sexual activity. If you can't reach your doctor, go to the emergency room.***

A local anesthetic injected into the spine may relieve priapism related to a spinal-cord injury. Exchange transfusion—replacing part of the patient's blood with healthy red blood cells and saline—may be tried if the patient has leukemia or sickle-cell disease.

If these various treatments fail, surgery may be needed, especially if the erectile tissue is filled with thick, clotted (thrombosed) blood.

## HOW TO PREVENT IT

Because the cause of priapism is usually unknown, there are no certain means of prevention. Priapism caused by injected medications to treat impotence and other drugs may be prevented by stopping the drugs immediately if they produce prolonged or unintended erections. Also exercise caution when using herbal impotence remedies, especially yohimbe, which is derived from the bark of an African tree. High doses have been linked to priapism in some men.

### ALTERNATIVE THERAPIES

There are no alternative therapies for priapism.

# Prostate Cancer

### SYMPTOMS

*There usually are no symptoms in early stages. When symptoms develop, they may include:*

- *Difficulty in starting urination; inability to empty bladder completely.*
- *Frequent urination, particularly at night.*
- *Pain or burning during urination.*
- *Chronic pain in the lower back, pelvis, or upper thighs.*
- *Possible blood in the urine.*

### WHO IS AT RISK

*Prostate cancer is the second most common cancer affecting Canadian men. Skin cancer is the most common cancer, and until recently, lung cancer was the second most common. One in nine men will develop prostate cancer at some point in their lives. In Canada each year about 19,000 men will be diagnosed with prostate cancer.*

*What actually triggers prostate cancer is unknown; experts theorize that a number of factors—including genetic, hormonal, venereal, dietary, and environmental—play a role. A family history of the disease increases risk. For unexplained reasons, men of African descent are 32 percent more likely to develop the disease than Caucasians.*

## HOW IT DEVELOPS

There are at least two general types of prostate cancer. One is relatively benign; it grows very slowly and, although it sometimes becomes aggressive and spreads, it is more likely to remain confined to the prostate for life. The other type is more aggressive and, at the time that it is diagnosed, it may already have spread. In its early stages, it does not produce symptoms other than those associated with a benign enlarged prostate—urinary frequency, burning, an inability to empty the bladder fully, and a slow, weak stream. A prostate examination may reveal hard nodules formed in the enlarged prostate and blood tests will likely, but not always, show an elevated level of prostate specific antigen (PSA).

As the disease spreads beyond the prostate, a man may experience a chronic, dull backache, weight loss, fatigue, and unexplained anemia. Advanced prostate cancer generally spreads to the nearby pelvic lymph nodes and to neighboring organs, especially the bladder, testicles, and seminal vesicles, as well as the pelvis, spine, and ribs.

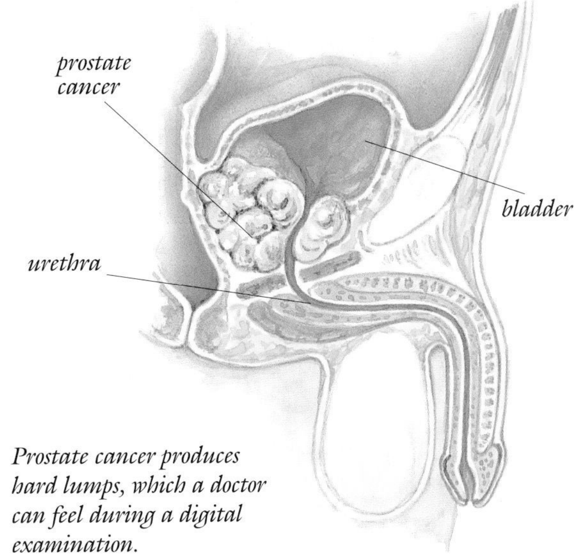


*Prostate cancer produces hard lumps, which a doctor can feel during a digital examination.*

## WHAT YOU CAN DO

To assist in early detection, which is crucial to surviving prostate cancer, physicians recommend that men over age 50 have a regular checkup, including a digital rectal exam, in which the physician inserts a gloved finger into the rectum and examines the prostate for signs of unusual hardness or lumps. In addition, men should discuss with their physicians the benefits and risks of other tests. Men

### BREAKTHROUGHS!

**New high-dose external beam radiation devices have been designed that more accurately pinpoint the target organs. Early studies indicate that these machines are more effective in combating localized prostate cancer while causing less organ damage than older high-dose machines. Treatments are given daily for three to four weeks, and may be followed by several more weeks of lower-dose treatments. After such a course of treatment, patients usually have their PSA levels fall to normal and imaging studies find no evidence of cancer. More study is needed, however, to determine whether the cancer-cure rate from this approach is as high as prostatectomy.**

should also report to their physicians if they have persistent difficulty or discomfort associated with urination.

If you are diagnosed with prostate cancer, treatment options will vary depending on your age and the stage at which the cancer is discovered (see *How to Treat It,* below). Some men whose cancers are slow-growing and of a nonaggressive cell type are advised against invasive treatment and, instead, undergo more frequent testing to monitor its growth. This "watchful waiting" can be emotionally trying for both the patient and his loved ones. Joining a support group of patients in similar circumstances can be reassuring. You can also log on to the Canadian Cancer Society's website (www.cancer.ca) or call their cancer information service at 1-888-939-3333.

**WARNING!**

***Before undergoing either surgical or radiation treatments for prostate cancer, make sure your doctor knows whether you want to father any future children. If so, you may want to preserve sperm for artificial insemination later if you are undergoing surgery for this disease.***

When undergoing treatment, pain control often becomes an important issue. Morphine or another strong narcotic medication is usually needed to control postsurgical pain or relieve the pain of advanced cancer that has spread to the spine and other bones. Talk to your doctor about pain control or ask to be referred to a cancer-pain specialist or center.

## HOW TO TREAT IT

### Tests

The discovery of suspicious lumps during a digital prostate examination and/or elevated PSA levels warrant further diagnostic tests, which usually include:

- **Transrectal ultrasound**, in which the prostate is examined rectally with an ultrasound device.
- **Imaging studies**, such as a CT scan or an MRI, which can help pinpoint small tumors.
- **A biopsy,** in which a hollow needle is used to obtain several tissue samples from suspicious areas.

If cancer is diagnosed, a bone scan and perhaps a full-body CT scan will be ordered to determine whether it has spread beyond the prostate.

### Surgery

When cancer is discovered in men under the age of 65 and there is no evidence of spread, surgical removal of the prostate gland—a *prostatectomy*— produces a cure in 90 percent or more of all cases. The operation, which usually takes two to four hours, is done under general anesthesia, and typically requires a hospital stay of a few days. Prostate surgery usually entails considerable blood loss, so transfusions may be needed to prevent anemia. Many men are asked to have two or three pints of blood removed over a period of a few weeks before the operation; this blood is then transfused back into them in the first day or two after surgery.

Morphine or a similar pain medication is used for the first few days; by the time most men go home, they can get by with codeine or even a nonprescription medication such as acetaminophen. They may still need a urinary catheter when they leave the hospital, but normal bladder function usually resumes in a week or so, especially if a nerve-sparing procedure was used. New nerve-sparing surgical techniques that preserve sexual function and urinary continence have greatly reduced the risk of impotence and urinary incontinence—common problems following prostate surgery a few years ago.

### Radiation therapy

Radiation therapy sometimes follows surgery or it is the sole treatment in some cases, especially for older men or those who are unable to undergo a prostatectomy. The radiation may be administered by external beams of high-voltage X rays aimed directly at the prostate. Because radiation cannot distinguish between tumor and healthy tissue, there is a risk of damage to nearby organs and nerves, which may result in impotence or incontinence. Newer devices are reducing this risk, but they are not yet widely available (see *Breakthroughs!*, p 213). An alternative, called *interstitial radiation therapy*, entails implanting radioactive seeds directly into the tumor, which shrinks and dies as it absorbs the radiation. This approach is less likely to cause extensive tissue damage, although some may occur.

### Drugs and hormones

If the cancer has spread beyond the prostate or the patient is older or a poor candidate for surgery or radiation therapy, drug and hormonal treatments are an option. Since 80 percent of prostate cancer cells respond to the male hormone testosterone, LHRH (luteinizing hormone-releasing hormone) may be given to suppress it. Alternatively, female hormones, such as DES or estrogen, may be used. These hormones have many possible side effects, including reduced sex drive, impotence, breast growth, and fluid retention, but they can slow tumor growth and prolong life. Sometimes surgical removal of the testicles is indicated to stop the body's production of testosterone. Anticancer drugs (chemotherapy) can also control the spread of cells. Such factors as the type of cancer cells involved and how far they have spread throughout the body often determine treatment.

## HOW TO PREVENT IT

Some studies have suggested a link between a high-fat diet—as well as alcohol intake—and the development of prostate cancer, but results are inconclusive. Nevertheless, using alcohol in moderation, eating a diet low in animal fat, and maintaining ideal body weight is the best advice for overall health, and may help prevent prostate cancer. Recent studies indicate that certain food substances may reduce the risk of prostate cancer, but further research is needed to establish this (see *Nutraceuticals*, below).

### ALTERNATIVE THERAPIES

Although prostate cancer is always treated medically, alternative treatments can be helpful in controlling pain, maintaining nutritional requirements, and relieving anxiety.

**Acupuncture and acupressure**

These techniques can be used to control pain from the treatment or the disease itself.

**Herbal medicine**

Studies in China have found that green tea may protect against prostate cancer and other malignancies; drink several cups a day. Your aim is to get 240 to 320 mg of polyphenols.

**Meditation and guided imagery**

Many cancer centers now teach these techniques, as well as self-hypnosis and visualization, to help patients control pain and anxiety.

**Nutraceuticals**

A large-scale study by Harvard Medical School researchers found that men who consumed four or more weekly servings of cooked tomatoes had a significantly reduced incidence of prostate cancer. The protective effects were credited to lycopene, an antioxidant substance found in tomatoes, red grapefruit, and watermelons. Cooking appears to increase the antioxidant effects of lycopene, so foods such as tomato-based spaghetti or pizza sauce and catsup are perhaps more protective than raw tomatoes. Other nutrients—and their daily dosages—that may protect against prostate cancer include: 400 micrograms of selenium; 50 mg of coenzyme $Q_{10}$; and 400 to 800 IU of vitamin E. People on prescription anticoagulants or aspirin should check with their doctor before taking vitamin E.

# Sexually Transmitted Diseases (STDs)

### SYMPTOMS

*These vary according to the type of disease; see* Common STDs at a Glance, *p 202, for specific symptoms. Among men, symptoms of the most common STDs include:*

- *Painful inflammation of the penis glans (balanitis) and foreskin.*
- *Penile discharge, which may be thick or watery.*
- *Pain or burning during urination; urethritis and prostatitis.*
- *Painful intercourse.*
- *Blisters, sores, or warts on the penis or around the anus.*
- *Possible sore throat (among those who engage in oral sex).*
- *Anal inflammation and burning (proctitis), especially among men who engage in anal sex.*

### WHO IS AT RISK

*Although any man who is not in a mutually monogamous relationship with an uninfected partner can contract STDs, men aged 18 to 35 are at highest risk.*

## HOW THEY DEVELOP

More than 100 diseases can be transmitted sexually, ranging from HIV and AIDS—the most deadly—to pubic lice (crabs), which are more annoying than dangerous. Some of the most common STDs affecting Canadian men:

- **Chlamydia**, a bacterial disease that can cause a clear, watery discharge from the penis and painful or difficult urination. Symptoms are usually more pronounced in the morning. Chlamydia can also cause a sore throat and/or proctitis among men who engage in oral and anal sex.
- **Genital herpes**, which is caused by the herpes simplex virus, produces a small cluster of very painful blisters

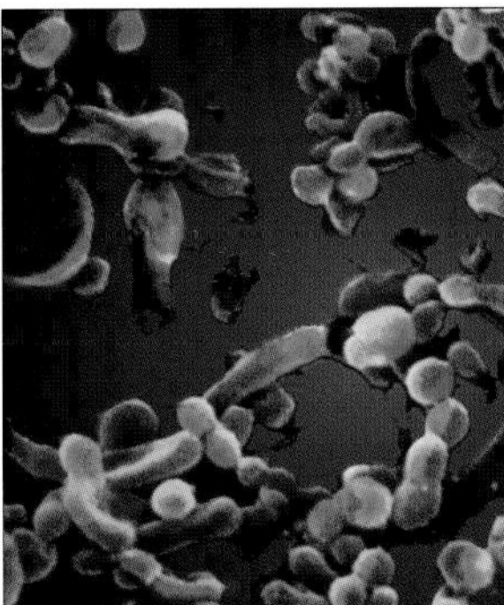

*Chlamydia organism, which can cause urethritis.*

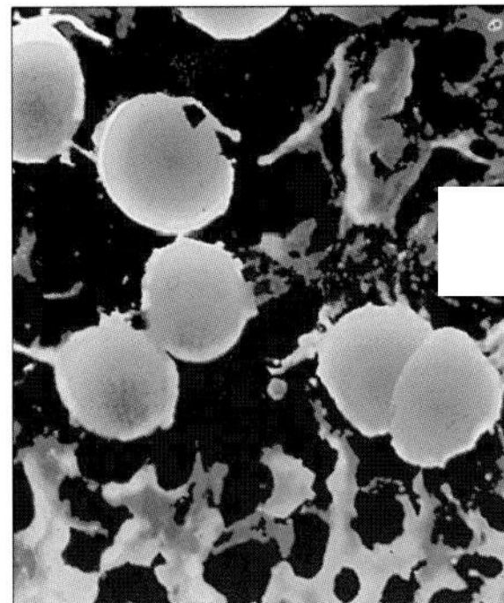

*Gonococcus bacterium, which causes gonorrhea.*

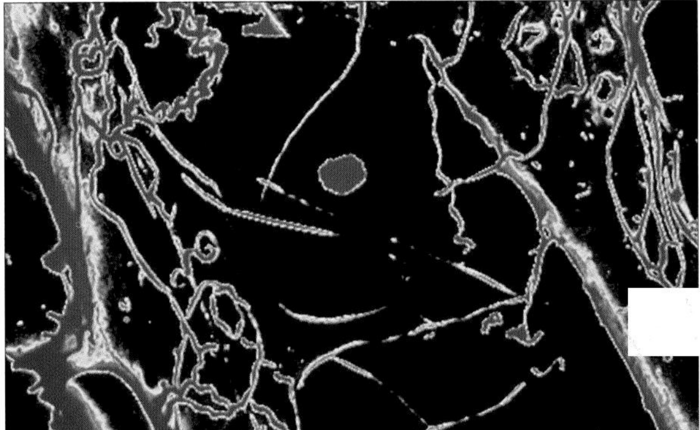

*Syphilis is caused by a rod-shaped bacterium,* T. pallidum.

that crust over in a few days and heal in 7 to 10 days. The virus remains latent in the body and can cause intermittent flare-ups, although subsequent outbreaks usually are not as painful as the first one. Nerve pain sometimes spreads to the hips and legs.

- **Genital warts**, which are caused by the human papilloma virus (HPV), produce soft warts. They are usually painless, but may itch or burn.
- **Gonorrhea**, a bacterial STD, starts with mild discomfort in the urethra, followed by difficulty urinating and a thick, yellow or greenish penile discharge. The tip of the penis may be red and swollen. Untreated gonorrhea can spread to other male reproductive organs, causing pain and inflammation; it may also cause septic arthritis, marked by severe swelling and inflammation of the knees or other large joints.
- **Hepatitis B and C**, viral diseases that can cause chronic liver inflammation, can be contracted in many ways, including kissing and sexual intercourse with an infected person. Hepatitis B usually causes mild flu-like symptoms followed by jaundice, a yellowing of the skin and whites of the eyes; most patients recover in a few weeks, but in about 5 percent, it evolves into a chronic liver disease. Symptoms of hepatitis C often go unnoticed at first, but it is even more likely to become a chronic disease. These forms of chronic hepatitis carry a high risk of cirrhosis (liver scarring) and liver cancer.
- **HIV and AIDS**, the most deadly of the STDs, weaken the body's immune system. The HIV virus can be contracted through any exchange of body fluids from an infected person, including sexual intercourse. Symptoms vary greatly, but the most common is increased vulnerability to all types of infections.
- **Pubic lice**, which live in the pubic hair, cause intense itching. Scabies, another skin parasite, burrow under the skin and also cause intense itching.
- **Syphilis**, a bacterial infection, goes through three distinct stages: It starts as an open sore (chancre) at the site of infection, most often on the penis or the anal area. Stage 2 is marked by a rash on the soles and palms, and perhaps eye inflammation or meningitis (inflammation of the lining of the brain and spinal cord) and diffuse pain. Stage 3, or tertiary syphilis, appears years after the initial infection and is often fatal.
- **Trichomonas**, which is caused by a protozoan (a one-celled organism), is usually asymptomatic in men, but may cause urinary frequency and discomfort.

**BREAKTHROUGHS!**

**FDA-approved home testing for HIV infection allows a person to collect a sample at home, mail it to a testing facility, and get the results over the phone. Health Canada has not received any applications for a license to sell home sample collection or true home tests for HIV.**

## WHAT YOU CAN DO

See a doctor as soon as possible if you suspect you may have contracted an STD, or if a sexual partner is infected. While waiting to see a doctor, a cold compress can numb the pain of genital herpes. Aspirin, ibuprofen, or another nonsteroidal anti-inflammatory drug (NSAID) can ease inflammation, relieve pain, and lower a fever.

Pubic lice and scabies often can be eradicated by using a nonprescription cream or lotion containing permethrin (Nix, Kwellada-P). Repeated treatments may be necessary, and all items that may harbor the parasites must be washed in very hot, soapy water and dried at a high heat.

**WARNING!**

***HIV among young people is again rising, partly because they mistakenly think that new AIDS drugs will cure the disease. While drugs are enabling many AIDS patients to live longer, it remains a deadly disease.***

## HOW TO TREAT THEM

Treatment varies according to the specific disease (see *Common STDs at a Glance*, p 202). Antibiotics are used to treat chlamydia, gonorrhea, syphilis, and other bacterial STDs. Viral STDs cannot be cured, but antiviral drugs can often minimize or eliminate symptoms.

## HOW TO PREVENT THEM

The surest preventive is to limit all sexual activity to a mutually monogamous uninfected partner. Otherwise, practice safer sex by always using condoms until it is firmly established that the partner does not have an STD.

### ALTERNATIVE THERAPIES

See the listings under *Sexually Transmitted Diseases* (in women), p 204.

# Testicular Cancer

### SYMPTOMS

- *Testicular pain; dull aching or heavy sensation in lower abdomen, groin, or scrotum.*
- *Lump in or enlargement of one or both testicles.*
- *Swollen lymph nodes in groin.*

### WHO IS AT RISK

*Testicular cancer is relatively rare, with only 800 new cases and 40 deaths a year. It most often strikes young men; in fact, it is the most common cancer among men aged 15 to 34, and the second most common among men 35 to 39. There is another peak among men in their 70s.*

## HOW TO DO A TESTICULAR SELF-EXAMINATION

Do this examination monthly:

- Take a warm bath or shower to help relax the scrotal tissue.
- While standing, roll one testicle at a time between the thumb and fingers.
- Be alert to any swelling, lumps, or changes in the consistency or "feel" of the testicle. A normal testicle is egg shaped and feels smooth and fairly firm.
- See a doctor promptly if any suspicious signs are found.

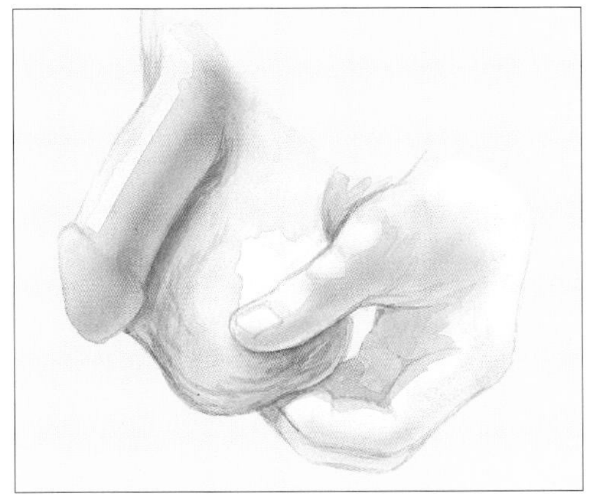

*Caucasian men are about five times more likely to develop this cancer than men of African descent. The cause is unknown, but a family history of the disease increases risk, as does having an undescended testicle at birth. Hormones may also play a role because risk is increased among men whose mothers took birth control pills within a month of conception or used DES, an artificial estrogen, during pregnancy to prevent a miscarriage. Other risk factors include testicular inflammation from mumps, exposure to cadmium and other industrial chemicals or metals, and impaired or low fertility.*

*Certain jobs may also increase risk; miners and oil and gas workers have a 12-fold increased risk of developing nonseminoma-testicular cancer, a fast-growing tumor. Other high-risk occupations may include electrical power workers, bakers, leather workers, janitors, and kitchen workers. These diverse occupations all entail exposure to various chemicals.*

## HOW IT DEVELOPS

Testicular cancer typically appears as a firm, painless lump or swelling in the front part of the testicles. About 95 percent of testicular cancer arises in the sperm-making germ cells. If not caught early, the cancer can spread to surrounding organs, tissues, and bones, resulting in chronic testicular pain and a heavy sensation in the groin and pelvic area.

## WHAT YOU CAN DO

Make sure you know your medical history. Men with undescended testicles are 30 to 40 times more likely to develop testicular cancer than men whose testicles descended normally. All men, especially those at high risk of developing testicular cancer as well as those between ages 15 and 40, should examine their testicles every month for changes that may signal testicular cancer (see *How to Do a Testicular Self-Examination*, left).

## HOW TO TREAT IT

A doctor will order an ultrasound examination of the scrotum, which can help distinguish cancer from benign conditions, such epididymitis, inflammation of the epididymis, a cordlike structure on the back of the testicle. However, a biopsy of cells taken from the suspicious lump is necessary to make a diagnosis. If cancer is confirmed, the other testicle will be examined for possible malignancy, and additional tests will be ordered to determine whether it has spread to other parts of the body.

### WARNING!

***Men who discover lumps in their testicles sometimes delay seeking treatment, for fear that they will somehow lose their masculinity if they lose their testes. Although infertility can result, early treatment is the only chance you have for a cure without a loss of sexual function.***

Treatment usually involves surgical removal of the malignant testicle and nearby lymph nodes. The operation is performed under general anesthesia, and strong painkillers are given afterward to relieve postsurgical pain. Ice packs can numb the incisional pain.

Depending upon the stage of the cancer, surgery may be followed by radiation therapy, chemotherapy, or both. Because treatment is likely to impair fertility, the patient should discuss storing sperm if he thinks he may want to father a child. Potency may also be affected—a possibility that should be discussed with the doctor before undergoing treatment. Some new nerve-sparing surgical procedures are less likely to damage the nerves that control erections.

## HOW TO PREVENT IT

There is no known way to prevent testicular cancer. However, early detection greatly increases the chances of achieving a cure. Any man who has been treated for cancer in one testicle should be especially vigilant about screening examinations of the remaining testicle because there is a high risk that it, too, will develop a malignancy.

### ALTERNATIVE THERAPIES

**Note:** Testicular cancer must be treated medically. But meditation, self-hypnosis, and visualization can help control pain and bring about a sense of well-being.

**Nutraceuticals**

Selenium, in dosages of up to 400 micrograms a day, and 400 to 800 IU of vitamin E may help prevent or slow the growth of testicular cancer. (People on prescription anticoagulants or aspirin should consult their doctor before taking vitamin E.) Some naturopaths recommend zinc supplements for men with testicular tumors, based on research that suggests that zinc injections can shrink these cancers in animals. However, these results have not been repeated in humans and there is some evidence that zinc may actually promote the growth of testicular tumors.

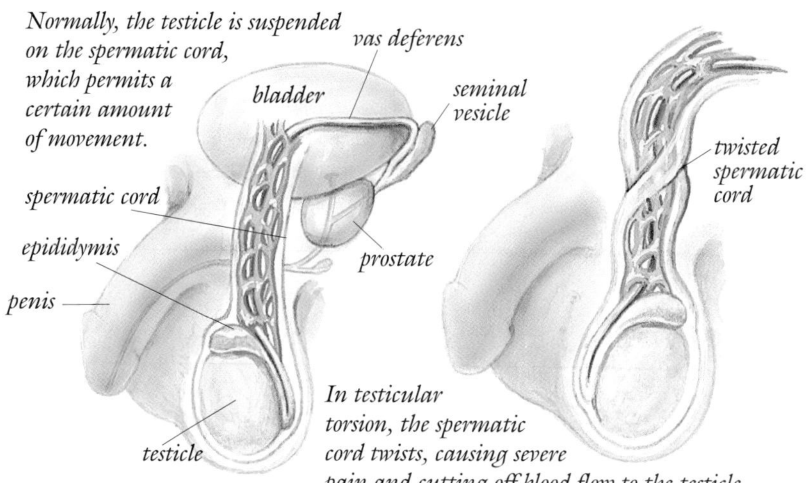


# Testicular Torsion

### SYMPTOMS

- *Sudden, severe pain on one side of the scrotum.*
- *Testicle on painful side is higher than the other.*
- *Scrotal swelling, inflammation, and tenderness.*

### WHO IS AT RISK

*Testicular torsion can occur at any age, but it is most common in adolescent boys; it may also occur in newborns. It is sometimes associated with strenuous lifting or an injury, but most often it develops spontaneously.*

## HOW IT DEVELOPS

Normally, each testicle is held in place by skeins of connective tissue—the spermatic cord—that allow the testicle to move within the scrotum. In testicular torsion, the testicle rotates on the end of the cord, twisting it and constricting the scrotal blood vessels. The twisting causes sudden, severe pain that worsens as the blood supply to the affected testicle is cut off. The pain may recede, but the scrotum will be red and tender, and the testicle will be swollen and higher than normal. Without oxygen, the testicle soon dies (see *Warning!*, above).

**WARNING!**

***Testicular torsion is a medical emergency that demands immediate treatment. A delay can result in tissue death and gangrene, which can threaten the other testicle and cause infertility.***

## WHAT YOU CAN DO

There is little you can do to relieve the pain yourself; instead, go to the emergency room.

## HOW TO TREAT IT

If pain is severe, a doctor will inject a local anesthetic to numb it. Color Doppler ultrasonography—the use of high-frequency sound waves and special sounding equipment to assess scrotal blood flow and reproductive structures—can quickly distinguish testicular torsion from epididymitis (see p 211) and other painful disorders. Treatment usually involves immediate surgery to untwist the cord and restore normal blood flow. If the testicle already has suffered tissue death, it must be removed.

## HOW TO PREVENT IT

Sometimes testicular torsion lasts for only a few minutes and the cord straightens on its own. Future episodes can be prevented by surgery to correct a faulty attachment of the spermatic cord. Otherwise, there are no known means of prevention.

# Varicocele and Hydrocele

### SYMPTOMS

*Both varicoceles and hydroceles can be felt as soft masses in the scrotum. Additional symptoms may include:*

***Varicocele:*** *Scrotal pain or tenderness; feeling of scrotal fullness and warmth; possible fertility problems.*

***Hydrocele:*** *Uncomfortable soft swelling in the scrotum.*

### WHO IS AT RISK

*Ten to 15 percent of adult men develop* ***varicoceles,*** *which are tangles of varicose veins surrounding one or both testi-*

*cles. Small varicoceles usually do not cause pain and other symptoms, but larger ones are often tender or painful, and the scrotum may feel uncomfortably full and warm.*

***Hydroceles**—fluid-filled cysts that develop between the scrotal membranes—are often present at birth or develop shortly thereafter. They may also be a complication of epididymitis (inflammation and infection of the tubes that transport sperm from the testicles), an STD, or an injury.*

## HOW IT DEVELOPS

A **varicocele** develops when the veins around the testicle become swollen and twisted, allowing blood to pool in them. This pooled blood raises the temperature of the affected testicle, which can hinder sperm production. This is why many men with varicoceles have fertility problems.

About 10 percent of baby boys are either born with a **hydrocele** or develop one in the first few weeks of life. These congenital hydroceles are due to pressure on the abdomen during birth, which forces fluid into the scrotum to form a cyst. Most congenital hydroceles are painless and disappear without treatment during the first year or so of life. However, pain and inflammation are signs that the hydrocele is infected and in need of treatment.

Hydroceles in adult men are often secondary to epididymitis or an infection, often gonorrhea or another STD. Unlike hydroceles in infants, these are often tender or painful.

## WHAT YOU CAN DO

See a doctor to make sure that the mass is harmless. An ice pack and nonprescription painkiller such as acetaminophen can ease discomfort.

## Guide to Scrotal Masses

| DISORDER | SYMPTOMS | TREATMENT |
|---|---|---|
| Hematocele | Painful scrotal swelling due to accumulation of blood. | Surgical removal. |
| Inguinal hernia extending into scrotum | Soft mass, usually in the upper part of the scrotum, that often disappears when lying down and pressing gently on it. | Surgical repair to prevent complications. |
| Scrotal abscesses | Painful lump in the scrotum that is warm to the touch. | Surgical drainage, antibiotics. |
| Spermatocele | Soft, usually painless mass above a testicle. | Surgical removal if it causes pain and other problems. |

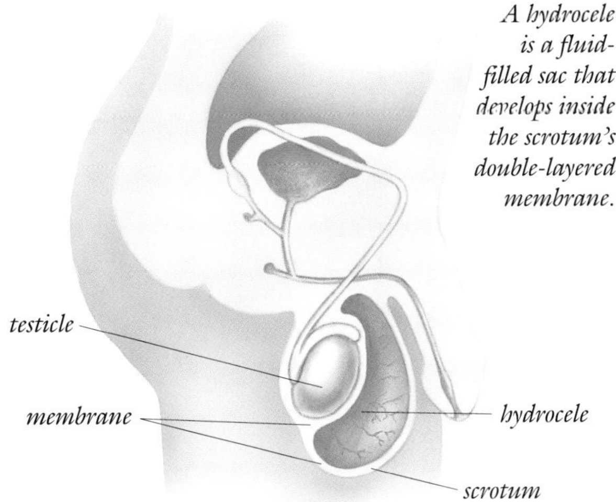


*A hydrocele is a fluid-filled sac that develops inside the scrotum's double-layered membrane.*

## HOW TO TREAT IT

Ultrasound—the use of high-frequency sound waves to examine internal structures—can determine whether the mass is solid or filled with fluid. Transillumination, a test in which a strong light is shone through the swelling, is used to diagnose hydroceles.

Varicoceles usually are not treated unless they are causing infertility or pain. In such cases, the tangles of varicose veins are removed surgically; this usually can be done as an outpatient procedure using local anesthesia. The affected testicle may be tender for a few days afterward; ice packs and acetaminophen or another nonprescription painkiller are usually all that is needed.

**WARNING!**

***Any testicular mass or pain warrants a prompt visit to a doctor to rule out a tumor, infection, and other potentially serious causes.***

Sometimes a doctor may drain a large, painful hydrocele. This is usually a temporary measure, however, as the cyst often recurs; aspiration also increases the risk of infection. Therefore, most doctors advise removal of hydroceles that are causing pain and other symptoms. In infants and young children, the hydrocele is removed through an incision in the groin. The operation is performed under general anesthesia and usually requires a day or so in the hospital. In adults, removal is through an incision in the scrotum; it can be done under local anesthesia as an outpatient procedure. Postsurgical pain is treated with ice packs and acetaminophen or another mild painkiller.

## HOW TO PREVENT IT

There is no way to prevent varicoceles or congenital hydroceles. In adults, hydroceles caused by STDs and other infections can be prevented by safe-sex practices.

# The Skeleton And Muscles

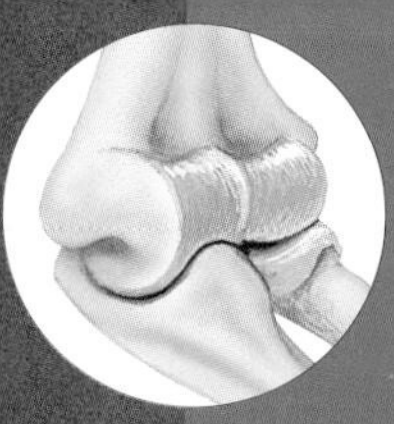

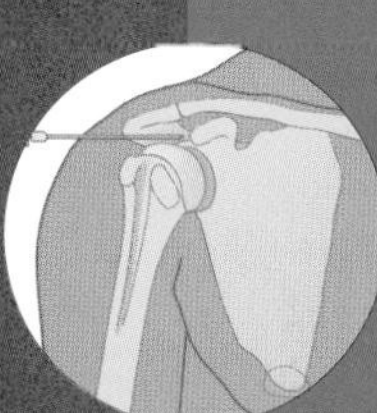

# Joints and Bones

*The skeleton forms the body's protective framework while the joints, which connect one bone to another, allow us to move freely. Arthritis, tendinitis, bursitis, and fractures are among the many sources of pain emanating from our joints and bones.*

## Bursitis

**SYMPTOMS**

- *Joint pain, ranging from minor discomfort to disabling.*
- *Localized joint tenderness and limited range of motion.*
- *Swelling, redness, and sometimes warmth of the affected joint.*

**WHO IS AT RISK**

*Anyone whose occupation or recreational activity involves frequent repetitive movements is susceptible to developing either acute or chronic bursitis. Common examples include housemaid's (or gardener's) knee, tennis elbow, and golfer's shoulder.*

### HOW IT DEVELOPS

Bursas are small fluid-filled sacs or pouches at the ends of bones that act as cushions between the bones and muscles, tendons, or skin. The fluid lubricates the area to eliminate joint friction and maintain smooth movement of tissues over the bones. Bursitis develops when the bursas become inflamed because of sudden, extreme, or constant pressure, causing pain, swelling, tenderness, and limited range of motion at the joint. Joints most commonly affected are the knees, shoulders, elbows, and hips.

### WHAT YOU CAN DO

Bursitis usually clears up in a week or two with prompt self-treatment. Stop the activity that is causing the pain to allow the joint to heal. Depending upon the joint involved, wearing an elastic bandage or a sling for a few days relieves pressure and may ease pain and reduce swelling. Apply an ice pack or cold compress for 15 to 20 minutes every few hours; after a day or two, switching to a heating pad or alternating hot and cold treatments may provide more relief. Aspirin, ibuprofen, or another nonsteroidal anti-inflammatory drug (NSAID) will ease pain and reduce inflammation. If the pain is acute or lingers on, consult your doctor.

As the pain subsides, gradually resume your normal activities and start gentle range-of-motion exercises and strength training. A physical therapist or sports trainer can suggest appropriate exercises that will help prevent recurrences of the bursitis.

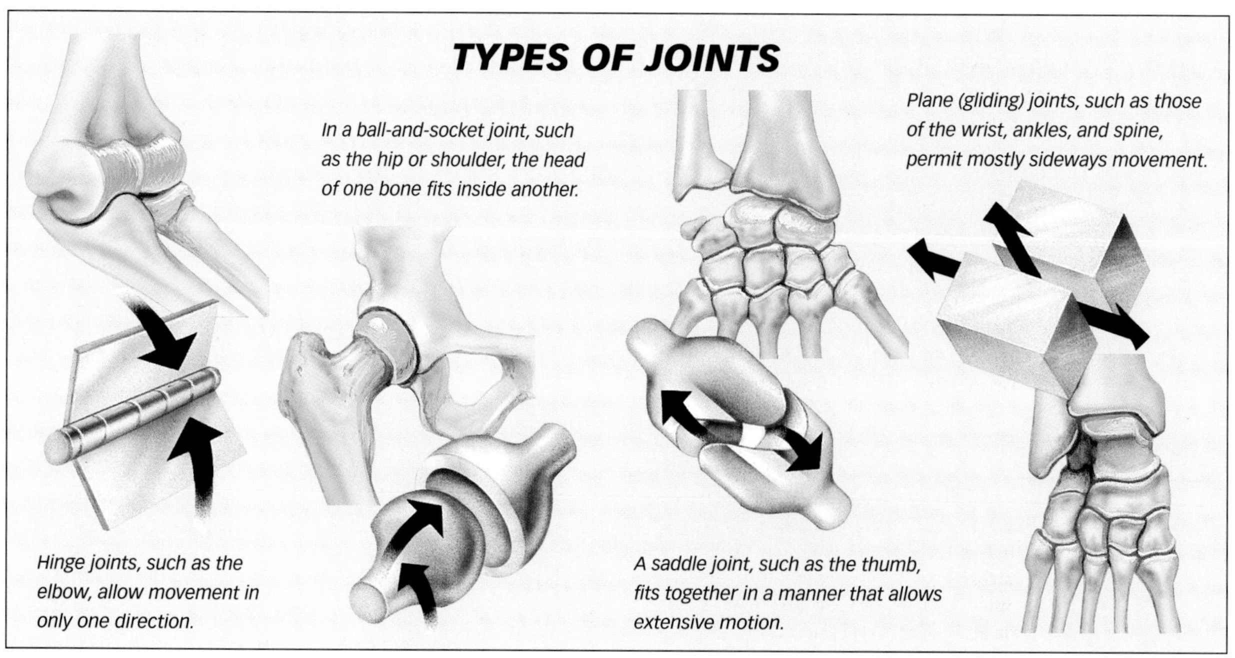

TYPES OF JOINTS
In a ball-and-socket joint, such as the hip or shoulder, the head of one bone fits inside another.
Plane (gliding) joints, such as those of the wrist, ankles, and spine, permit mostly sideways movement.
Hinge joints, such as the elbow, allow movement in only one direction.
A saddle joint, such as the thumb, fits together in a manner that allows extensive motion.

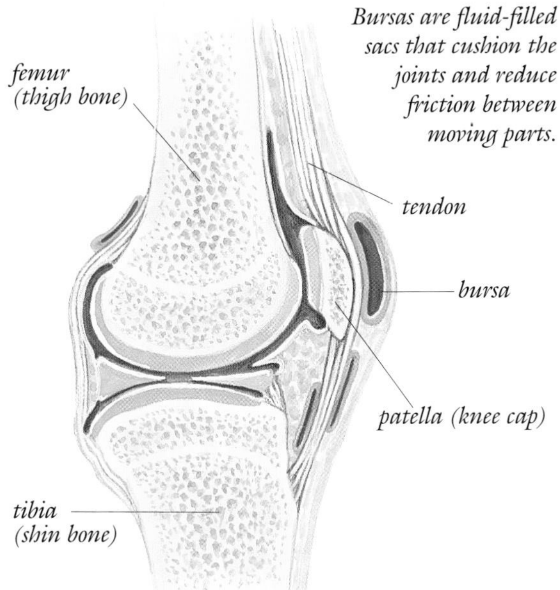


*Bursas are fluid-filled sacs that cushion the joints and reduce friction between moving parts.*

## HOW TO TREAT IT

A doctor may order an X ray, blood tests, and other tests to rule out other conditions that have similar symptoms, such as arthritis, gout, or a torn tendon or ligament. If a nonprescription NSAID does not provide adequate relief, a doctor may prescribe a stronger anti-inflammatory. A corticosteroid injected into the affected joint often gives immediate pain relief and also reduces inflammation and swelling. If the joint is very swollen, the doctor can use a hollow needle and syringe to remove excess fluid.

## HOW TO PREVENT IT

Try to avoid repetitive motions that place extra pressure on a particular joint or part of the body. Use seat cushions or foam padding rather than sitting or kneeling on hard surfaces. If you are a gardener, for example, kneel on a pad to ease pressure on your knees. A faulty golf swing or tennis serve often can be corrected by having a pro analyze your movements and then teaching you less stressful motions. Bursitis often develops in joints that lack flexibility and adequate muscle support; this can be prevented by stretching and strength-training exercises.

Job-related bursitis may be more difficult to prevent. Alert your employer or union representative to the problem. Workman's disability and compensation policies may cover repetitive stress injuries, such as chronic bursitis. Physical therapy and a temporary change in work assignments may be necessary to allow healing, followed by physical therapy and strength training to prevent future episodes.

### BREAKTHROUGHS!

**Diathermy (deep-heat therapy), under the direction of a sports physician, physical therapist, or experienced sports trainer, not only relieves the discomfort and inflammation of bursitis but can also relax tensed muscles, and thus promote healing. Ultrasound can also be used to relax the joint and promote tissue repair.**

### ALTERNATIVE THERAPIES

**Herbal medicine**

Anti-inflammatory herbs may also reduce bursitis pain and inflammation. Boswellia, in dosages of 150 mg of boswellic acids three times a day, is one of the safest and most effective of these herbs, although some people develop diarrhea, a skin rash, or nausea. If you experience such side effects, stop taking it. Other anti-inflammatory herbs include borage and evening primrose oils; look for products that are high in gamma-linolenic acids (GLA) and tailor your dosage to get 240 mg of GLA a day. Do not use borage or evening primrose oil if you are taking anticoagulants. Creams that contain capsaicin (derived from cayenne or hot chilies) are safe and highly effective in easing pain and inflammation. Look for products that provide 0.025 percent capsaicin; apply directly to the painful joint two or three times a day. Be careful not to get the cream near the eyes or delicate mucous membranes, and stop usage if it causes a rash or intense stinging or burning.

### WARNING!

***If pain and inflammation persist for more than a week, see a doctor. Symptoms of bursitis mimic other conditions, such as arthritis or tendinitis, which require different treatments.***

**Magnets**

Small therapeutic magnets applied to the affected joints may ease pain and speed healing for many people suffering from bursitis and other painful joint problems. They are believed to work by increasing circulation to the area.

**Nutraceuticals**

Vitamin E, in daily dosages of 800 IU, has an anti-inflammatory effect, and may provide relief for chronic bursitis. Check with your doctor before taking vitamin E if you are taking aspirin or other blood-thinning medication. SAM-e, a nutritional supplement used to treat arthritis and mild depression, is also an effective anti-inflammatory; the usual daily dosage is 400 mg. SAM-e should not be taken by people suffering from manic depression.

# Dislocations

### SYMPTOMS

- *Severe pain in the affected joint that comes on suddenly.*
- *Swelling and discoloration of the skin overlying the joint.*

- *Possible deformity, with bones at odd angles.*
- *Popping or cracking sound during dislocation.*

### WHO IS AT RISK

*Anyone who suffers a misstep or a fall may dislocate a bone from its joint. Athletes young and old are at particular risk of dislocating shoulders, knees, fingers, and ankles if they suffer trauma or sprains to the area. Repeated sprains, in which ligaments that bind bones together at these joints are torn, can weaken joints and result in subsequent dislocations. A previous dislocation increases the risk of recurrence.*

## HOW IT DEVELOPS

Most dislocations result from some trauma—a fall, a blow, or a movement—that forces the joint beyond its normal range of motion. Ligaments that bind bones together are very strong, but when forced or twisted into an unnatural position, they can tear. Without their normal supportive tissues holding them in place, bones can become dislodged from their sockets or joints, causing pain, swelling, bruising, and a pronounced disfigurement at the site. Finger joints are especially susceptible to dislocation, but other common sites for dislocations are wrists, ankles, toes, jaws, and knees.

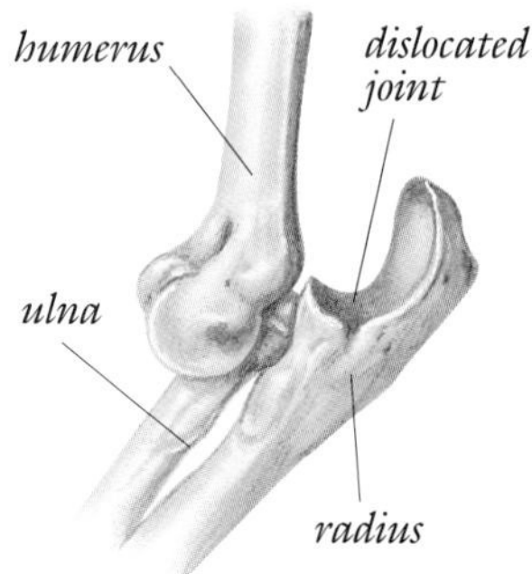


*In a severely dislocated joint, such as the elbow shown here, the bone comes completely out of its socket.*

Some people are very loose-jointed, and can easily pop their fingers—and possibly other joints as well—in and out of their sockets. While many youngsters find this entertaining, it should be discouraged because it can lead to permanent joint damage.

### IMPROVISING A SPLINT AND SLING

1. **Newspapers.** Make a firm roll out of several newspapers (or a blanket) and cradle the dislocated (or fractured) limb in it. Use a sling to prevent movement.

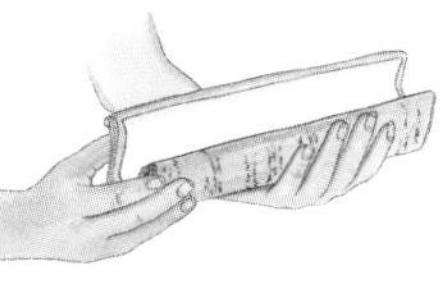

2. **Boards or sticks.** These are best for a leg splint. The object should extend the length of the limb, which is secured against it. The splint is then taped or tied in place and, if possible, the person should be moved on a stretcher or similar object to prevent movement.

3. **Taping.** A dislocated finger or toe can be taped or wrapped firmly between its two adjacent members.
4. **Miscellaneous.** In the case of jaw dislocation, loop an improvised bandage (such as a scarf) under the chin and tie at the top of the head.

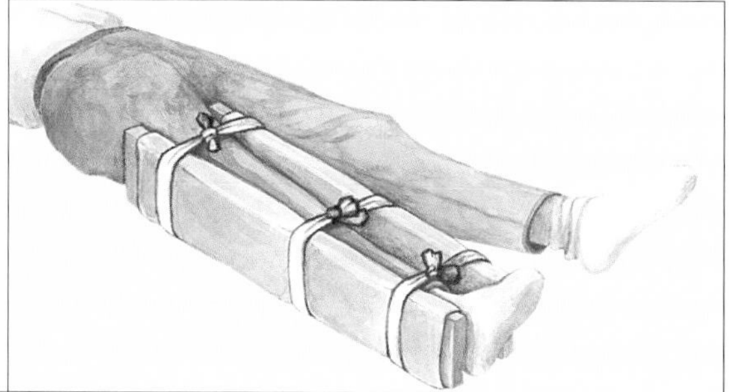

## WHAT YOU CAN DO

Seek emergency medical help. While waiting, immobilize the joint with a splint or sling to prevent movement. Immobilizing the joint provides some pain relief; a cold pack also helps numb the area and reduces swelling and inflammation.

### WARNING!

***When dislocations occur in young people whose skeletons are not fully grown, careful follow-up is advised to make sure the ligaments have healed properly and are keeping bones in place. Any discomfort in the area, limping, impaired motion, or uneven growth indicates a need for further treatment. Young athletes are at particular risk of injury because their joints and ligaments have not fully developed and may give way under the stresses of intense workouts.***

## HOW TO TREAT IT

A doctor will take X rays to rule out a fracture; other imaging studies, such as ultrasound or an MRI, may be ordered to evaluate the extent of joint damage. The dislocated bone can usually be manipulated back into its proper position. A local anesthetic will be given first; general anesthesia is sometimes needed, especially for a child.

Depending upon the degree of pain, morphine, codeine, or a synthetic narcotic may be given. Pain subsides after the bone is returned to its socket, and acetaminophen, aspirin, or another nonprescription painkiller is usually sufficient. The joint may need to be immobilized for a few days; ice, a heating pad, or alternating hot and cold treatments are usually recommended until healing is complete.

Recurring dislocations or badly torn ligaments often require surgical repair. Rehabilitation usually involves physical therapy (see *Alternative Therapies,* below).

## HOW TO PREVENT IT

Walk carefully, particularly on ice and snow, to prevent falls that could lead to dislocations. Athletes should wear the appropriate supportive devices, which, depending upon the sport, may include knee braces, elbow and shoulder pads, and taping. Anyone who has had a dislocated joint should consult a fitness trainer or physical therapist to work out an exercise regimen to strengthen the supporting muscles; strong, well-toned muscles are necessary to help maintain the joints.

### ALTERNATIVE THERAPIES

**Physical therapy**

In addition to helping design an appropriate exercise program, a physical therapist can also provide pain-relieving treatments that may include ultrasound, electrical stimulation, hydrotherapy, hot and cold packs, and massage.

# Osteoarthritis

### SYMPTOMS

- *Persistent and worsening joint pain, especially of the knees, fingers, hips, lower back, neck, and toes.*
- *Stiffness, especially in the morning or after periods of inactivity.*
- *Development of hard nodules or thickening of finger and toe joints.*

### WHO IS AT RISK

*Most people over age 50 have X-ray evidence of some osteoarthritis, but not all experience pain and other symptoms. Other risk factors include being overweight, a family history of osteoarthritis, and repeated stress on affected joints, such as runner's knees and piano player's fingers.*

## HOW IT DEVELOPS

Normally, the joints are protected by a covering of tough cartilage (gristle) and lubricated by a substance called synovial fluid. Osteoarthritis appears to start with an abnormality of the cells that make collagen and other components of cartilage. Eventually, the cartilage thins and develops tiny cracks, weakening the underlying bone, which responds by overgrowing and producing bony spurs (osteophytes). In time, the cartilage becomes so rough and pitted that the joint can no longer move normally. This damages all parts of the joint, and pain, inflammation, and stiffness increase as the cartilage and the synovial membrane, which lines the joint, wear away.

## WHAT YOU CAN DO

Doctors recommend starting pain control with acetaminophen if the joints are not inflamed; aspirin, ibuprofen, or another nonsteroidal anti-inflammatory drug (NSAID) if they are red and warm to the touch. Taking a hot shower or bath upon arising in the morning followed by stretching and range-of-motion exercises helps overcome morning pain and stiffness. Some people find that a heating pad or warm compress helps; others get more relief from an ice pack or alternating hot and cold packs.

A hot paraffin bath is especially helpful in easing painful finger joints. Heat the paraffin to 49°C/120°F, and then immerse the hand in the melted wax for 20 minutes. Knees and other large joints can be treated by coating them with melted paraffin and wrapping the joint with a towel for 20 minutes to retain the heat. The heat increases blood flow and reduces joint inflammation, swelling, stiffness, and pain. As the wax hardens, it is easily peeled from the skin, and can be reused as needed.

Exercise is a critical key to long-term pain control. Find a moderate aerobic exercise—for example, walking, cycling, or swimming—that you enjoy and does not exacerbate the joint pain. A moderate regimen that includes 20 to 30 minutes of aerobic exercise at least three or four times a week, combined with daily stretching and postural exercises and weight training every other day, helps the joints by strengthening the supporting muscles and increasing the flow of lubricating joint fluid. Doctors advise against using a splint because immobilization worsens joint stiffness; however, wearing a knee brace, elastic bandage, or another support during exercise can protect vulnerable joints from excessive stress.

Diet also plays an important role in controlling osteoarthritis; achieving and maintaining ideal weight eases stress on the knees, hips, and other weight-bearing joints (see *Nutraceuticals,* p 226).

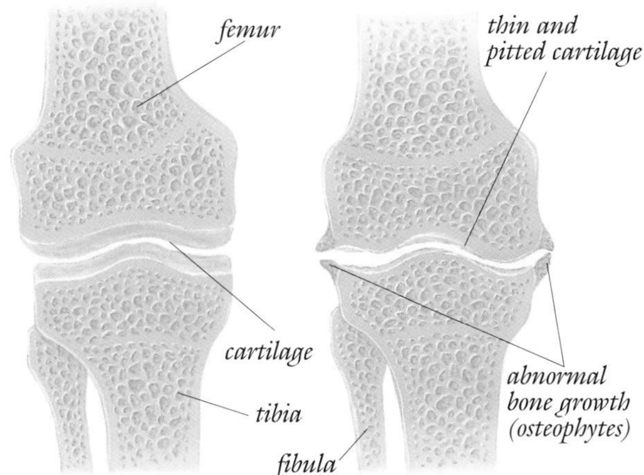


**Normal Knee Joint** **Arthritic Joint**

## HOW TO TREAT IT

### Medications

If nonprescription painkillers do not give enough relief, prescription-strength NSAIDs may be taken. The response to a particular NSAID varies from one person to another, so several may need to be tried. All NSAIDs should be taken with food to reduce the risk of side effects; even so, they may cause stomach upset and bleeding problems. If side effects develop, a doctor may prescribe a $COX_2$ inhibitor (Celebrex or Vioxx), a new class of anti-inflammatory drugs that appear to have fewer side effects than older NSAIDs.

### Creams and ointments

Capsaicin—a substance derived from chili peppers—interferes with substance P, the body chemical that helps relay pain messages to the brain. Capsaicin creams and ointments can reduce joint inflammation and pain. Some people also get arthritis pain relief from creams that contain triethanolamine salicylate or from heat-producing ointments that increase blood flow to the affected area.

**WARNING!**

***Arthritis quackery abounds, ranging from harmless but ineffective baths and copper bracelets to potentially dangerous injections of bee venom or high-dose steroids. Be wary of any treatment that promises a miracle cure or is available only in border towns outside the country.***

### Injections

Sometimes injecting a corticosteroid medication directly into the affected joint eases pain and inflammation. Steroid injections have fewer adverse side effects than oral steroids, but they do carry a risk of causing joint infection. More than two or three steroid injections a year may cause permanent joint damage.

A new approach to treating knee osteoarthritis entails injecting a thick substance similar to the body's synovial fluid directly into the joint. Five or six injections are given at weekly intervals; some studies show that half or more of patients experience knee-pain relief, often for 6 to 12 months.

### Surgery

Surgery is usually the treatment of last resort. Operations include:

- **Arthroscopy,** microsurgery in which a viewing tube (arthroscope) is inserted into the joint to remove damaged cartilage and other diseased tissue.
- **Joint replacement (arthroplasty)**, in which the diseased joint—most often the knee or hip joint—is removed and replaced with an artificial joint.
- **Synovectomy**, in which the synovial membrane—the sac surrounding the joint—is removed, allowing healthy tissue to grow in its place.
- **Osteotomy,** in which bony overgrowth is removed to improve joint alignment.

## HOW TO PREVENT IT

There is no certain way to prevent osteoarthritis, but maintaining ideal weight, practicing good posture, and avoiding excessive stress on the joints can slow its progress.

### ALTERNATIVE THERAPIES

**Acupuncture**

This ancient technique of Chinese medicine is now widely used to ease the pain and inflammation of all types of arthritis.

**Herbal medicine**

Borage and evening primrose oils, which are high in gamma-linolenic acid (GLA), can reduce inflammation. Look for products that supply a minimum of 240 mg of GLA a day. Do not use borage or evening primrose oil if you are taking anticoagulants.

**Magnets**

These are placed over the painful joints in much the same manner as TENS devices. It is not known how they work, but studies show they do increase blood flow, which may explain why they help some arthritis sufferers.

**Massage**

Therapeutic massage helps reduce pain and stiffness by relaxing tensed muscles. However, inflamed areas should not be massaged directly.

**Nutraceuticals**

Studies have found that 400 to 800 IU of vitamin D and up to 1000 mg of vitamin C a day can slow the progress of osteoarthritis. Vitamin C is thought to help repair damaged cartilage, whereas vitamin D appears to work by preventing an overgrowth of bony tissue in the joints. Other supplements that may help ease osteoarthritis pain include 800 IU of vitamin E a day to help reduce inflammation; and a combination of glucosamine (1500 mg a day) and chondroitin (1200 mg a day), natural components of cartilage that may help in its repair and rebuilding.

Another promising nutraceutical, called SAM-e, is a by-product of methionine, a protein that the body uses to maintain cartilage and make dopamine and serotonin,

**BREAKTHROUGHS!**

**New cloning techniques are allowing doctors to replace damaged cartilage. A few healthy cartilage cells are removed from a patient and cloned to grow new cartilage in a laboratory. The new cartilage is then surgically implanted into the diseased joint(s). So far, this appears to work best in patients under age 40 and is especially helpful in treating a knee damaged by running and other sports.**

mood-boosting chemicals. Studies show that SAM-e supplements may reduce arthritis symptoms and counter mild depression. For concerns regarding these nutraceuticals, see *About the Recommendations*, p 7.

**Physical therapy**

Physical therapy is a critical aspect of rehabilitation following joint-replacement surgery; physical therapists also teach proper methods of exercising arthritic joints.

# Sprains and Strains

### SYMPTOMS

- *Pain, which may be severe, and swelling.*
- *Bruising or other discoloration of the affected joint.*

### WHO IS AT RISK

*Sprains and strains are common joint injuries; recreational athletes are particularly vulnerable to ankle, knee, and finger sprains, as well as shoulder strains. Anyone who takes a fall is at risk for a sprain. As might be expected, hospital emergency rooms report that icy weather produces more sprains than at other times of the year.*

## HOW IT DEVELOPS

A strain develops when the ligaments—tough, rather inelastic fibrous bands that bind bones and tissues together—stretch beyond their maximum. Strains are moderately painful, but they usually do not prevent joint movement. If the ligaments actually tear, the injury is referred to as a sprain. These injuries cause an immediate sharp, burning pain. Because the surrounding blood vessels are injured in the process, swelling and bruising quickly develop. Inflammation surrounding the injured tissues causes further swelling and pain.

There are three degrees of strains and sprains:

*Grade 1*

*Grade 2*

- **Grade 1**, in which the ligament has been stretched, but any tears are so minor they can only be detected under a microscope. There is pain and moderate swelling, but the ankle can be used.
- **Grade 2**, in which the ligament is partly torn apart; pain and swelling are more severe, and there is also some bruising.
- **Grade 3**, in which the ligament is completely torn; there is severe pain, swelling, and bruising.

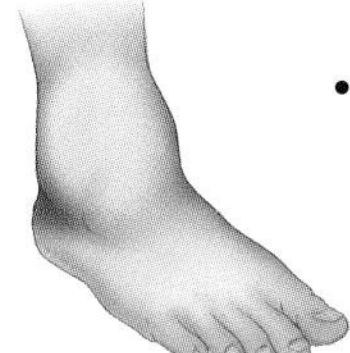

*Grade 3*

Ankles are particularly vulnerable to all kinds of sports injuries, as are knees and fingers.

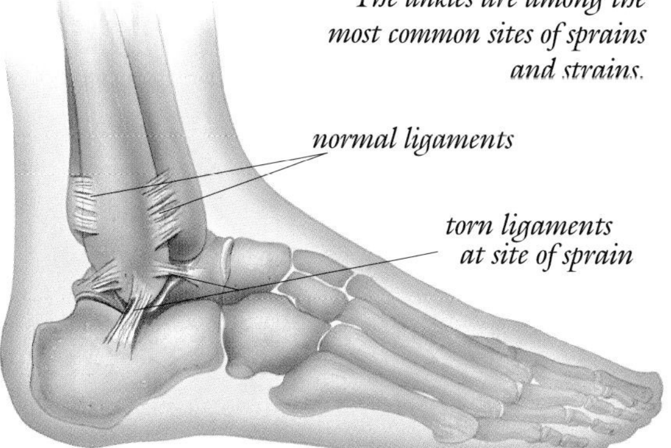


*The ankles are among the most common sites of sprains and strains.*

## WHAT YOU CAN DO

RICE (rest, ice, compression, elevation) is the basic self-treatment for strains and sprains. Rest and elevate the limb immediately and apply ice for 20 minutes each hour to reduce swelling. Compress and immobilize the site by wrapping it in wide cotton gauze or an elastic bandage. In the case of a sprained ankle, take a roll of three-inch gauze or an elastic bandage and make two turns around the foot, then begin wrapping upward using figure-eight turns. Keep bandaging until the foot, ankle, and lower leg are wrapped. For a strained shoulder, immobilize by fashioning a sling to support the painful limb (see *Improvising a Splint and Sling*, p 224). For a finger, tape it to the two adjacent fingers.

> **WARNING!**
>
> ***If the painful area around the sprain has an unusual shape, consider the possibility of a broken bone. Immobilize the area and consult a doctor immediately. If numbness occurs or the site changes color dramatically, swelling may be pressing on area blood vessels and cutting off circulation. Loosen any compression bandage and see a doctor.***

Take aspirin, ibuprofen, or another nonsteroidal anti-inflammatory drug (NSAID) to relieve pain and control the accompanying inflammation. After 48 hours, heat treatments can be substituted for or alternated with ice to increase blood flow to the site and speed healing.

> **BREAKTHROUGHS!**
>
> **Arthroscopic surgery has revolutionized the treatment of badly sprained knees and shoulders. These procedures use viewing tubes (arthroscopes), tiny instruments, and a surgical microscope. The surgeon works on the affected area through a lighted viewing tube without making a large incision, as was necessary until a few years ago. The tiny puncture incisions entail less postsurgical pain and faster recuperation.**

## ANKLE-STRENGTHENING EXERCISES

The following exercises can strengthen supporting muscles of the ankle and help prevent future sprains or development of an unstable ankle. Do each one daily.

1. **Toe raises.** Assume a comfortable stance with your feet 8 to 10 inches apart and the toes pointed straight ahead or slightly inward. If necessary, hold on to the back of a chair to maintain balance. Rise up on your toes as far as you can, hold for a count of two, and lower the heels to the floor. Repeat 10 times and work up to 20.
2. **Heel walks.** Remove your shoes and stand on your heels by raising your toes off the ground. Walk around the room on your heels for two or three minutes. Do this every day or so.
3. **Ankle walks.** First walk about for two or three minutes on the insides of your feet, and then on the outer edges of your feet.

## HOW TO TREAT IT

See a doctor for a bad sprain, especially if you are unable to move the part. X rays are sometimes needed to determine whether any bones have been broken. In addition, an MRI or other imaging techniques may be ordered to assess badly torn ligaments. In some cases, arthroscopy—a procedure in which a lighted viewing instrument is inserted into the joint—may be employed to diagnose the severity of the sprain.

If nonprescription drugs are not strong enough, a prescription-strength NSAID or codeine may be used. In the case of a Grade 3 sprain, especially of the knee and shoulder, surgery may be required to repair the damage (see *Breakthroughs!,* p 227).

## HOW TO PREVENT IT

When walking in icy weather, wear rubber-soled shoes, walk slowly, and be particularly careful where you step. When playing sports, use the correct equipment that fits properly and warm up beforehand. Weight training to strengthen the muscles that support the joints improves stability and helps prevent injuries (see *Ankle-Strengthening Exercises,* above).

### ALTERNATIVE THERAPIES

**Physical therapy**

If you suffer repeated sprains or strains, especially of the ankles, knees, or other weight-bearing joints, physical therapy can help strengthen the supporting muscles as well as relieve pain. Many physical therapists teach exercises that use ankle weights or resistance, for example, with surgical tubing or therapeutic elastic strips. These can relieve pain and help prevent recurrent sprains.

# Tendinitis

### SYMPTOMS

- *Pain, weakness, stiffness, swelling, and tenderness of the shoulder, fingers, elbow, ankle, heel, knees, or other parts of the body.*
- *Pain that increases in intensity, especially when moving the affected joint(s).*

### WHO IS AT RISK

*Middle-aged and older people develop tendinitis as they become less flexible with age, and therefore more likely to strain muscles or joints. Athletes and dancers are also vulnerable if they repeatedly strain the muscles they use in performance activities. Persons who have diabetes, gout, or high cholesterol have an increased risk of tendinitis for unknown reasons. Occupations—for example, those of computer keyboarders, pianists, and assembly-line workers—that involve repetitive motions also increase risk.*

## HOW IT DEVELOPS

Tendons are tough, fibrous bands of tissue that connect muscles to bones. Because they have a limited ability to stretch and contract, they are easily strained or torn when subjected to constant or excessive pressure or trauma. The fibrous sheath that lines or surrounds the tendon may become inflamed, leading to a painful condition called *tenosynovitis.*

Tendinitis begins with weakness, stiffness, swelling, and tenderness in the affected area. If untreated, the tendons become increasingly inflamed and so painful that movement is excruciating. Sometimes bursitis—inflammation of the fluid-filled sacs that cushion the joint—is also present; for example, tennis elbow and housemaid's knee may be a combination of tendinitis and bursitis.

## WHAT YOU CAN DO

Rest and, if necessary, immobilize the affected area by wearing a sling or wrapping it with an elastic bandage. Apply an ice pack to treat acute tendinitis that develops abruptly; the cold numbs pain and reduces inflammation. Long-standing (chronic) tendinitis is better treated with

### BREAKTHROUGHS!

**Sports medicine and rehabilitation specialists are increasingly turning to new diagnostic techniques, especially electromyographic studies and videotapes, to analyze movements of the joints and supporting structures. By pinpointing the specific movements that may induce tendinitis, they can devise a more effective pain treatment and prevention regimen.**

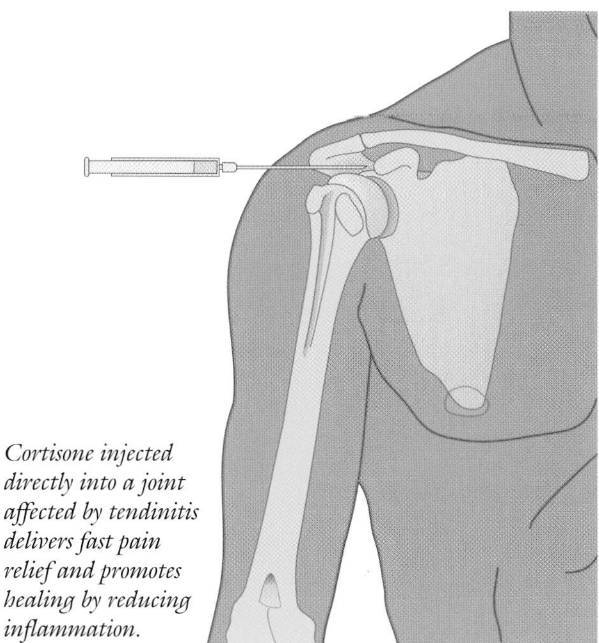

*Cortisone injected directly into a joint affected by tendinitis delivers fast pain relief and promotes healing by reducing inflammation.*

heat, which increases circulation to the area and promotes tissue healing. Take an anti-inflammatory medication, such as aspirin or ibuprofen, which eases pain and reduces inflammation. Once the acute pain is gone, alternate heat treatments and cold packs to the affected site, and begin exercising it slowly, increasing the intensity as the condition improves.

## HOW TO TREAT IT

See a doctor if the pain does not subside in 7 to 10 days. (See *Warning!*, right). A corticosteroid injected into the tender area can relieve pain and reduce inflammation. However, repeated cortisone injections at the affected site can cause the tendon to rupture. If that happens, surgery may be required to repair the tendon.

In severe cases, the doctor may immobilize the affected area with a splint or cast to allow the tendon to heal.

## HOW TO PREVENT IT

Always warm up before exercising and stretch afterward to maintain flexibility. If your job requires repetitive motions, make sure that your work area allows proper posture to reduce undue strain. Take frequent breaks to do range-of-motion exercises and stretching. If possible, vary your activities so that the affected area gets rest during the workday.

To prevent a recurrence of sports-related tendinitis, consult a professional trainer or exercise physiologist to analyze your movements and equipment. Your equipment may be too heavy or in poor working order, or you may be working the affected area too hard, too frequently, or improperly. Weight training to strengthen surrounding muscles can ease pressure on the affected area. For instance, if you suffer from tennis elbow, you may need to strengthen your forearm muscles to support the elbow's tendons.

### ALTERNATIVE THERAPIES

**Alexander technique**

Trained instructors analyze posture to determine if joints and supporting tissues are properly aligned. If they are not, the person is taught how to adopt proper posture for various activities.

**Herbal medicine**

Compresses soaked in comfrey, arnica, or witch hazel can alleviate inflammation and promote healing. Make a strong tincture of the herb, allow it to cool, soak a clean cloth in it, and apply to affected area every three or four hours. Do not ingest. Creams containing capsaicin, the active ingredient in hot chilies, also relieve pain by reducing inflammation and interfering with substance P, a body chemical that transmits pain messages to the brain. Gently rub the cream into the affected joint three or four times a day; be careful to keep the ointment away from your eyes and mucous membranes. Never apply to raw or open skin. Stop using the ointment if it causes severe stinging or a rash.

**Hydrotherapy**

Whirlpool baths, hot and cold soaks, and exercising in water may alleviate pain and restore function to the affected area.

**Magnets**

Studies have found that therapeutic magnets may ease the pain of tendinitis; they are thought to work by increasing blood flow to the area.

**Massage**

Gentle kneading and massaging can ease pain, but avoid directly massaging the inflamed area, as this can worsen inflammation.

**Nutraceuticals**

Supplements that can help heal tendinitis include 800 IU of vitamin E a day, which has an anti-inflammatory effect, and 1000 mg of vitamin C, which promotes healing of inflamed tissues. For cautions concerning vitamins C and E, see *About the Recommendations*, p 7.

**Physical therapy**

Physical therapists can relieve pain through ultrasound, deep heat, electrical nerve stimulation, massage, or hydrotherapy. They can also devise an exercise and rehabilitation program to help prevent a recurrence.

**WARNING!**

***Muscle and joint pain can have other causes, such as arthritis, muscle strain, frozen shoulder, shin splints, stress fractures, runner's knee, and other sports injuries. See a doctor if symptoms do not clear up in 7 to 10 days, as additional treatment may be needed.***

# Shoulder Pain

*The shoulder, a somewhat independent unit attached to the upper skeleton, is instrumental in lifting and most arm movements. Painful shoulder disorders include dislocations, fractures, tendinitis, a "frozen" joint, and rotator-cuff injuries.*

## Dislocated Shoulder

### SYMPTOMS

- *Sharp pain when moving the arm.*
- *Shoulder discoloration, swelling, and deformity.*

### WHO IS AT RISK

*Shoulder dislocations are very common and they frequently recur with little provocation. A fall, blow to the shoulder, or a sudden twisting of the arm can dislocate the joint. Golfers and tennis players often suffer dislocated shoulders; they can also occur in babies and young children who are lifted or swung by their arms.*

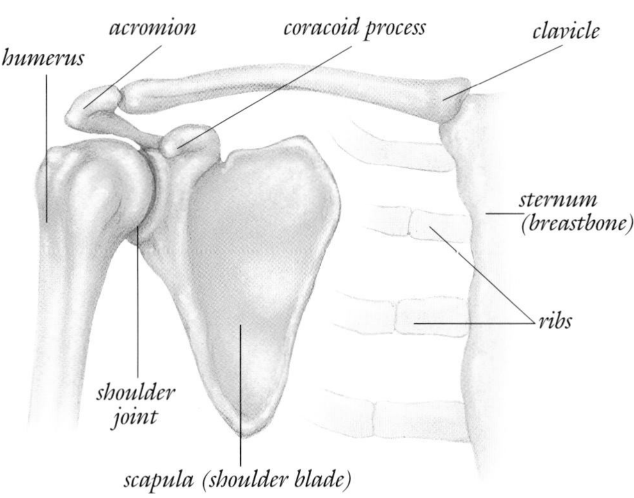


*Each shoulder is made up of a shoulder blade (scapula), which is held in place by a long, curved collarbone (clavicle) and various ligaments, tendons, and muscles. A ball-and-socket joint attaches the upper arm bone (humerus) to the scapula.*

### HOW IT DEVELOPS

In a dislocated shoulder, the head of the humerus—the upper arm bone—slips out of its ball-and-socket joint attachment to the scapula (the shoulder blade). This is a rather shallow joint, and it doesn't take much force to tear its supporting ligaments and allow it to come apart. There may be a loud popping sound, followed immediately by sharp pain and inability to move the arm normally.

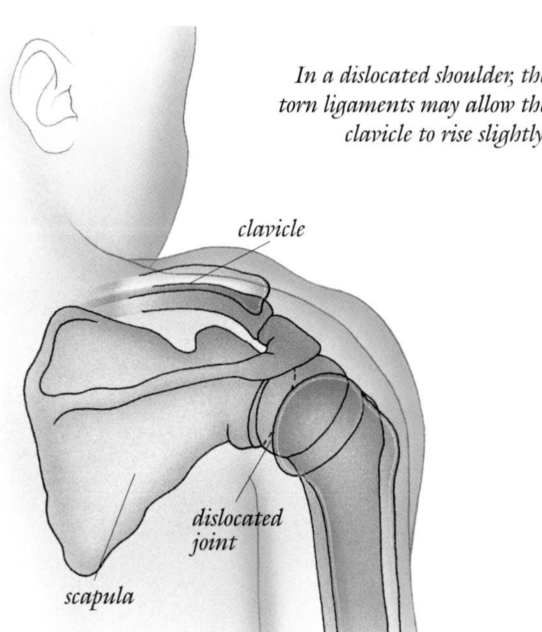


*In a dislocated shoulder, the torn ligaments may allow the clavicle to rise slightly.*

### WHAT YOU CAN DO

See a doctor as soon as possible. Fashion a sling from a long strip of material to help immobilize the dislocated shoulder until you can get to a doctor. To relieve pain and inflammation, apply an ice pack to the area and take aspirin or ibuprofen.

### HOW TO TREAT IT

A doctor will usually inject a local anesthetic to relieve pain and then work the humerus into place. He will firmly wrap the shoulder and the patient will wear a sling

#### BREAKTHROUGHS!

**Arthroscopy and microsurgery techniques have greatly simplified repair of a badly dislocated shoulder. A viewing tube (arthroscope) equipped with a miniature video camera is inserted into the shoulder joint. While viewing a video monitor, the surgeon can then manipulate tiny surgical instruments to make the repairs.**

**WARNING!**

***Resist the temptation to have someone other than a doctor try to "pop" the displaced bone back into its socket. Doing this can cause permanent damage to the ligaments and the joint itself.***

until the ligaments heal, which usually takes two to four weeks.

Shoulder dislocations tend to recur; if this happens more than two or three times, surgery may be needed to tighten the ligaments. The operation requires general anesthesia and a short hospital stay. Codeine or another prescription painkiller may be needed for a few days; full recovery may take four weeks.

## HOW TO PREVENT IT

Never swing a baby or young child by the arms. Sports-related dislocations are often due to improper movements; a few lessons from a trainer not only can help improve your game but may also prevent dislocations.

### ALTERNATIVE THERAPIES

There are no alternative therapies to treat the dislocation itself; physical therapy following treatment can hasten recovery and help prevent recurrences.

# Fractured Collarbone

### SYMPTOMS

- *Severe collarbone pain, swelling, and deformity.*
- *Deformity of the collarbone.*
- *Possible numbness in the affected shoulder and arm.*

### WHO IS AT RISK

*Collarbone (clavicle) fractures are common in children, especially among those who play football or soccer. Falls, such as from a tree or top bunk bed, are also common causes. An adult may also suffer a fractured collarbone as a result of a fall or an auto accident.*

## HOW IT DEVELOPS

Most collarbone fractures occur in the outer third of the bone, and they may be partial (stress) or complete. Most are due to a direct blow to the bone, or to twisting or a violent muscle spasm in people with osteoarthritis or other bone disease.

## WHAT YOU CAN DO

Fashion a sling to immobilize the shoulder and arm and see a doctor as soon as possible. An ice pack will numb pain and reduce swelling. After the bone has been set, ice treatments should continue for 48 hours; then use a heating pad to provide more relief and promote healing.

After the bone has been set, the area will be immobilized for three or four weeks. Ask your doctor or physical therapist to show you how to do the proper strength training. Do not drive or lift anything heavy until healing is complete, which usually takes four weeks.

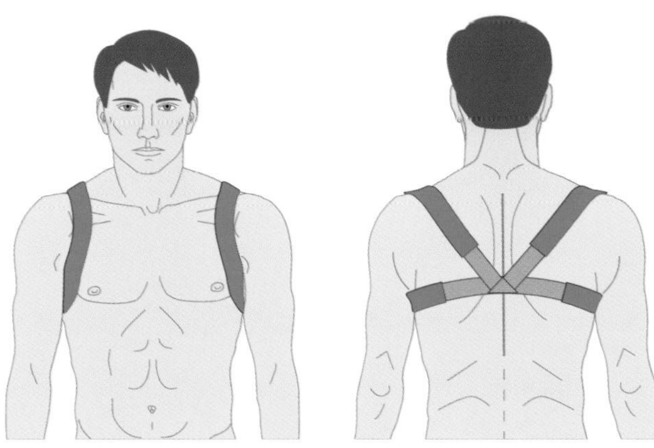

*A special shoulder brace may be fashioned to immobilize a fractured collarbone until it heals.*

## HOW TO TREAT IT

Early treatment is important; the bone should be set within six hours of the injury. A complicated fracture may require general anesthesia and surgery to set. Sometimes, however, a local anesthetic and external manipulation is all that is needed. Severe pain will be treated with morphine or another narcotic medication; after the bone has been set and the area immobilized—usually with a brace but sometimes with a cast—the pain subsides and usually can be controlled with aspirin or acetaminophen.

## HOW TO PREVENT IT

Make sure your child wears protective padding if he or she engages in contact sports. Always wear seat belts, and buckle children into proper car seats.

### ALTERNATIVE THERAPIES

**Nutraceuticals**

To promote healing of a fractured bone, take extra calcium (1200 to 1500 mg a day in 500- to 600-mg doses); 200 to

**BREAKTHROUGHS!**

**A broken collarbone is often slow to heal or the bone may fail to knit together properly because of poor blood circulation in the area. In the U.S., studies have found that low doses of electricity may prompt healing in such cases. The devices, with electrodes that are attached to the skin over the fracture site, are usually worn at night.**

400 IU of vitamin D; and 500 mg of magnesium. Vitamin C, in daily dosages of up to 1000 mg, also promotes bone healing. For cautions concerning these nutraceuticals, see *About the Recommendations*, p 7.

**Physical therapy**

Special exercises and therapy may be necessary to regain shoulder and arm function, especially after a bad break that requires surgical repair.

> **WARNING!**
>
> ***Sometimes scar tissue or swelling impinges on nerves and blood vessels, which can cause tissue death. See a doctor immediately if there is increased pain, swelling, fever, or loss of feeling.***

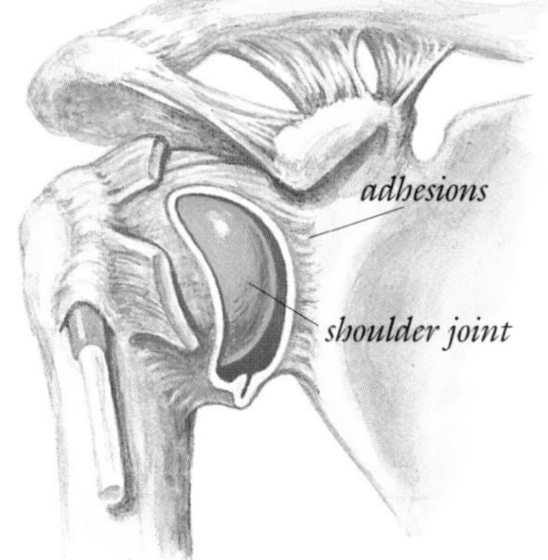


*Inactivity after a shoulder injury can result in scar tissue (adhesions) that causes shrinkage of the shoulder joint capsule and a "frozen" shoulder.*

# Frozen Shoulder

**SYMPTOMS**

- *Mild to moderate shoulder pain that becomes progressively worse and more constant.*
- *Increasing stiffness and difficulty moving the shoulder.*

**WHO IS AT RISK**

*Anyone can develop a frozen shoulder, but the problem is most common among persons in their fifties and sixties, and somewhat more prevalent in women than in men. Diabetes increases the risk about fivefold, but the reason for this is unknown.*

## HOW IT DEVELOPS

The mechanism of frozen shoulder, also called adhesive capsulitis, is unknown and no other joints are similarly affected. Most frozen shoulders appear to start with a minor injury that causes inflammation. The person responds by not moving the affected shoulder, which allows scar tissue, or adhesions, to form. The adhesions cause the joint capsule to shrink, making shoulder movement even more difficult and painful. This results in a vicious cycle of increasing pain with movement and inactivity. Before long, the shoulder is incapable of normal movement.

> **WARNING!**
>
> ***Find the right balance between rest and exercise; wear a sling to restrict unnecessary movements that provoke pain, but remove it two or three times a day and put the joint through its full range of motion.***

## WHAT YOU CAN DO

Treat any shoulder pain or injury early to minimize inflammation and reduce the risk of adhesions. Take aspirin, ibuprofen, or or another nonsteroidal anti-inflammatory drug (NSAID) to reduce pain and inflammation. For added relief, apply an ice pack for 20 minutes, remove it for 20 minutes, and reapply for another 20 minutes; the cold numbs pain and also reduces inflammation and swelling. Repeat this routine every other hour for the first day or two. After 48 hours, a heating pad or alternating heat and cold treatments may provide more relief. Exercise and gentle stretching are essential to help restore movement. At first, the movement may provoke pain, so put the shoulder through gentle range-of-motion exercises after applying ice or taking an NSAID (see *Range-of-Motion Shoulder Exercises*, p 233); apply ice or a heating pad again after exercise. If the pain and stiffness persist for more than a few days, see a doctor.

## HOW TO TREAT IT

Most frozen shoulders eventually get better without special treatment. A doctor or physical therapist can recommend exercises to help restore movement.

In severe cases, manipulation to break the adhesions may be needed. A doctor can often do this by manipulating the shoulder after injecting a local anesthetic; sometimes, however, general anesthesia is needed. A prescription NSAID may be given to control pain and reduce inflammation after the procedure.

In refractory cases, surgery is needed to remove the adhesions. This can usually be done arthroscopically with several small incisions and inserting a viewing tube, rather than making one large incision.

> **BREAKTHROUGHS!**
>
> **A recent study by doctors in the Netherlands compared three standard therapies for shoulder pain and joint dysfunction: physical therapy twice a week, shoulder manipulation weekly, or up to two cortisone injections. At the end of five weeks, the researchers concluded that steroid injections provided the fastest relief from pain originating in the joint itself, while manipulation produced a higher cure rate for pain originating from the shoulder girdle, spine, or rib cage.**

## HOW TO PREVENT IT

Exercises may prevent adhesions from forming, but these should be designed by a physical therapist or doctor. An injection of a corticosteroid directly into the joint may reduce pain and inflammation and also prevent adhesions.

### ALTERNATIVE THERAPIES

**Manipulation**

Chiropractic or osteopathic manipulation of the shoulder may help break up adhesions, especially if it is done before the shoulder joint freezes.

**Massage**

Deep massage techniques, such as Rolfing, may help prevent adhesions. Other massage techniques can relieve pain due to tensed muscles.

**Physical therapy**

A physical therapist will design an exercise program to strengthen the shoulder muscles and improve joint function. Pain-relieving techniques include ultrasound and/or diathermy, both of which deliver deep heat directly into the shoulder joint; electrical nerve stimulation (TENS) to block transmission of pain messages; and hydrotherapy, such as whirlpool baths, needle showers, and hot soaks, to relax tensed muscles.

# Impingement Syndrome

### SYMPTOMS

- *General shoulder ache.*
- *Pain when raising the arm or reaching back.*
- *Pain or "catching" sensation when the arm is lowered.*

### WHO IS AT RISK

*Almost everyone has some degree of shoulder impingement, but most people do not experience pain or other symptoms. The problem is most acute among painters, carpenters, and others who work with their arms raised overhead, people who engage in sports that involve throwing, and those whose jobs require repetitive arm movements.*

## HOW IT DEVELOPS

Raising the arm forces the head of the humerus to push up against the acromion, the tip of the scapula, resulting in impingement or pinching of the rotator-cuff tendons and bursas, fluid-filled pockets that reduce friction when joint parts move. Overuse can cause bursitis—swelling and irritation of bursas—further reducing the space in the joint. The formation of bone spurs—a common response to inflammation—can worsen the impingement.

## WHAT YOU CAN DO

Take aspirin, ibuprofen, or another nonsteroidal anti-inflammatory drug (NSAID) to reduce pain and inflammation. Rest the painful shoulder, but make sure you do range-of-motion exercises several times a day (see *Range-of-Motion Shoulder Exercises*, below). Use an ice pack to numb the area and reduce inflammation. While sleeping, tuck a pillow under the arm to keep it slightly elevated.

## HOW TO TREAT IT

A doctor may inject a corticosteroid into the joint to reduce pain and inflammation. A prescription-strength NSAID also may be tried. If the problem persists despite medication and physical therapy, surgery may be recommended. The operation entails removing any bony spurs that are rubbing on the rotator-cuff tendons and bursa. If necessary, part or all of the acromion and perhaps even the top of the scapula may also be removed.

> **WARNING!**
>
> ***If your job requires frequent overhead lifting or movements, take frequent breaks. Otherwise you run a high risk of shoulder impingement.***

## HOW TO PREVENT IT

Early treatment of shoulder bursitis may prevent impingement syndrome.

### ALTERNATIVE THERAPIES

**Physical therapy**

In addition to designing an exercise program, a physical therapist may treat impingement pain with heat, ice, electrical stimulation, ultrasound, and massage.

### RANGE-OF-MOTION SHOULDER EXERCISES

Any exercise program to treat shoulder pain should be designed by a doctor or physical therapist. For most people, however, the following range-of-motion exercises are safe provided they are done slowly and aren't painful:

- **Elbow:** Slowly bend and straighten the elbow; if this causes pain, try holding the upper arm against the chest.
- **Forearm:** Rotate the forearm up and down and sideways.
- **Wrist:** Move the wrist slowly up and down and then from side to side.
- **Hand:** Open and close the hand; squeezing a soft ball or therapeutic putty strengthens arm muscles.

# Rotator-Cuff Injuries

## *SYMPTOMS*

- *Shoulder and arm pain that worsens when reaching up, bending the arm back, or when lying on the affected shoulder.*
- *Shoulder tenderness, weakness, and impaired shoulder movement.*

## *WHO IS AT RISK*

*Rotator-cuff injuries become increasingly common after age 40. A slouched posture increases risk. They sometimes result from a fall or other injury; more often, they occur in persons who do a lot of overhead lifting or whose jobs entail repetitive arm and shoulder movements. Baseball players have a very high incidence of rotator-cuff injuries.*

## HOW THEY DEVELOP

The onset of symptoms varies according to the cause.

- **Rotator-cuff tendinitis** produces a steady, aching pain that develops when the shoulder becomes inflamed or damaged, usually as a result of repetitive stress or joint impingement from bone spurs or inflammation.
- **Bursitis**—inflammation of the fluid-filled sacs that prevent excessive joint friction—causes similar pain.
- **Muscle strain or tear**, which comes on abruptly, produces sharp, steady pain.

## WHAT YOU CAN DO

See a doctor as soon as possible if you experience severe shoulder pain or are unable to use your arm normally. Pain that persists for more than a week should also be checked by a doctor. Otherwise, mild rotator-cuff injuries usually heal with rest and self-treatment.

- Take a nonprescription anti-inflammatory medication, such as aspirin or low-dose ibuprofen.
- Use an ice pack (a bag of frozen vegetables will do); apply it for 15 to 20 minutes every hour or two. After two or three days, when the inflammation has subsided, switch to a heating pad or hot compresses.
- Give the injured shoulder a few days' rest; don't do any heavy lifting and refrain from painful activities.
- Start with range-of-motion exercises (see p 233) and, as the shoulder heals, rotator-cuff exercises (right).

### WARNING!

***Although shoulder movement may provoke pain, it's important to avoid prolonged inactivity, which can result in a frozen shoulder.***

## HOW TO TREAT IT

A doctor will order a shoulder X ray and perhaps an MRI or an arthrogram, special X rays that are taken after dye is injected into the injured shoulder. A badly torn rotator cuff or a bone spur usually requires surgical repair.

## HOW TO PREVENT IT

Daily shoulder stretches and exercises can help prevent most rotator-cuff injuries.

### ALTERNATIVE THERAPIES

**Physical therapy**

Therapists start with a variety of pain-relieving techniques—heat, cold, exercises, ultrasound, electrical stimulation—and then advance to strengthening exercises.

### ROTATOR-CUFF EXERCISES

**Important:** Check with your doctor or physical therapist to make sure that these exercises, which are commonly recommended following a rotator-cuff injury, are safe for you.

**Cuff strengthening.** This exercise, which uses about six to eight feet of medium-strength rubber tubing or a bungee cord, requires access to a door with a doorknob.

1. Loop the band or tubing securely around the doorknob of a closed door.
2. Stand just over an arm's length (about three feet) away from the door.
3. Face forward so that the arm on your affected side is nearest the door. Grasp both ends of the tubing in that hand and, with your arm bent at a 90-degree angle, slowly pull the band across your midsection and touch your other elbow. Hold for a count of three; repeat 10 times.

**Hints:** It's a good idea to do this exercise on both sides, even if the other shoulder is pain-free. If pulling the cord across your body is painful, lengthen the loop of tubing to decrease tension. As your shoulder recovers, shorten the loop and add an extra set of 10 pulls.

**Upper-arm strengthening.** Start this exercise using a two- or three-pound free weight.

1. Lie on your right side with your right arm tucked under your head and the left arm bent at a 90-degree angle with the hand resting on the mat or floor.
2. Tuck your elbow to your side, grasp the weight in your left hand, and slowly lift it as high as you can.
3. Lower, and repeat 10 times, then switch sides.

**Hints:** As strength improves, use progressively heavier weights. You can also use the free weights to strengthen your other arm muscles.

# The Arms, Wrists, and Hands

*The upper limbs and extremities work almost nonstop during waking hours, performing such varied tasks as eating and writing, working at a computer and driving, playing tennis and golf. Improper or excessive use can bring on many painful conditions.*

## Broken Arm

*An abundance of muscles, tendons, and small bones give the hand and wrist their remarkable dexterity.*

tendons

wrist ligament

forearm muscles

phalanges (finger bones)

metacarpals (the five bones between the fingers and wrist)

**SYMPTOMS**

- *Pain, swelling, and discoloration at the fracture site.*
- *Inability to move arm, with possible deformity.*
- *Possible bleeding, with broken bone protruding through the skin (compound fracture).*

**WHO IS AT RISK**

*A broken arm is one of the most common injuries. It can be caused by a fall or any accident that puts excessive pressure on the long, relatively thin arm bones. Athletes of all ages are at special risk; so too are accident victims who sustain upper-body injuries. Children whose bones have not fully matured often suffer hairline, or greenstick, fractures; the elderly whose bones have thinned from osteoporosis sustain more serious breaks.*

### HOW IT DEVELOPS

Fractures are divided into two main categories: **simple fractures**, in which a bone breaks but the skin remains intact, and **compound**, in which the broken bone protrudes through the skin. Within these two categories are several types of breaks (see *An Illustrated Guide to Fractures,* p 236).

### WHAT YOU CAN DO

Immobilize the arm immediately to prevent further damage and help ease pain somewhat until you can get to a doctor or emergency room. If the skin is not broken, fashion a splint from stiff material (see *Improvising a Splint and Sling*, p 224); make a sling from clean cloth to immobilize the injured arm in a slightly elevated position. A cold compress helps prevent swelling and numbs pain.

If the skin is broken and a bone is protruding through it, cut away or remove any surrounding clothing and press a clean (preferably sterile) cloth on the wound to stop any bleeding. Do not try to reposition the bone. Cover the protruding bone with a large, sterile bandage or other clean cloth and seek medical help at once.

### HOW TO TREAT IT

If the broken bone is causing severe pain, a doctor may first inject a local anesthetic. Broken bones are X-rayed from different angles to determine the exact nature of the fracture. Sometimes the doctor orders a CT scan or an MRI to assess tissue damage. Treatment begins by setting the bone in a process called *fracture reduction*, in which the broken pieces are positioned so they can knit together and heal. With simple fractures, this often can be done using a local anesthetic and manipulation, a treatment called *closed reduction*.

With compound fractures, surgery is often necessary to set the bone and repair damaged tissues, a procedure called *open reduction*. Such surgery requires general anesthesia and an incision that allows the doctor access to the fracture. If the elbow or shoulder is fractured and also dislocated, the displaced bones must be returned to their original positions. If the fracture extends into the joint, the doctor may have to insert a plate, screws, or pins to keep the bones in place.

After the bone has been set, it will be immobilized. A sling may be all that is needed for a greenstick or hairline fracture. Otherwise, a cast is necessary. The doctor will first cover the area with soft bandages to protect the skin.

## AN ILLUSTRATED GUIDE TO FRACTURES

The most common simple fractures are greenstick and transverse; they can cause severe pain and varying degrees of tissue damage, but they do not break the skin. Compound fractures may be either oblique, which involves a diagonal break, or comminuted, in which the bone shatters into several fragments.

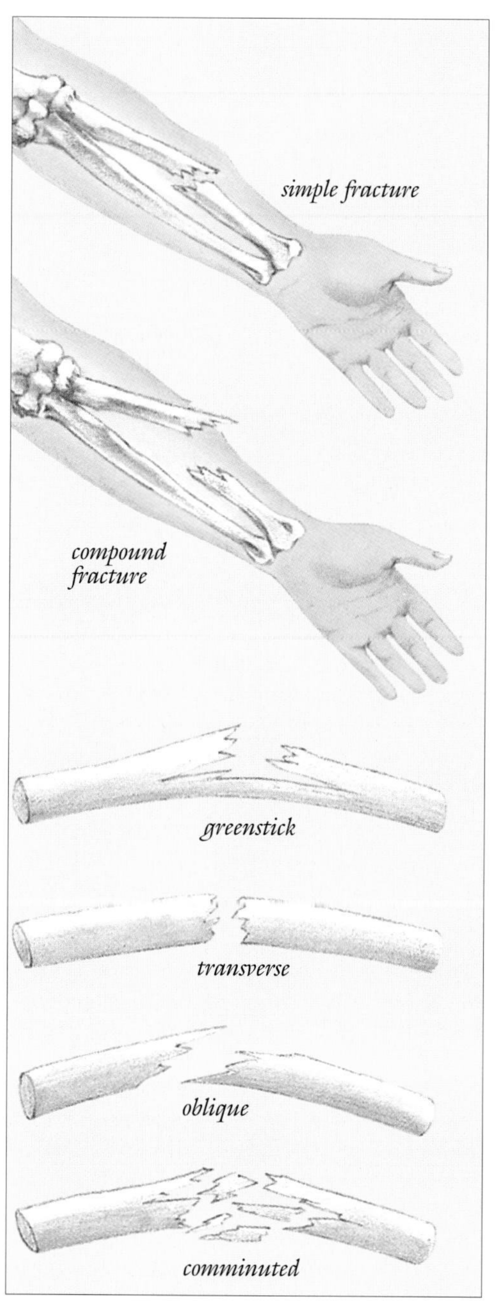


He or she then saturates the wrapping with wet plaster, which hardens almost instantly. The cast often extends beyond the injury site to ensure immobilization of the entire area. For instance, a fractured wrist may need a cast that extends from the base of the fingers to the elbow in order to keep the wrist immobile. The doctor will X-ray the bone every few weeks to ensure that it is healing properly. As healing progresses, the plaster cast may be replaced by a lighter, fiberglass one.

Broken bones can be very painful. A narcotic such as codeine may be prescribed for the first few days. After that, over-the-counter pain relievers such as aspirin (for adults only) are usually sufficient. If the injury involves a compound fracture and tissue damage, medications to prevent blood clots will be prescribed. An antibiotic may be given to prevent infection.

A cast often causes intense itching, especially during hot weather. Resist the temptation to reach into it with a knitting needle or similar device; this can break the skin and cause an infection. Instead, try placing an ice pack on the cast to cool the underlying tissue. If the itching is very bothersome, ask your doctor about an anti-itch medication.

### WARNING!

***A cast that seems fine initially may become too tight if the underlying tissue swells—a common occurrence with bone fractures. This can compress blood vessels and result in serious tissue damage due to lack of circulation. Call your doctor or go to the emergency room if you develop numbness, tingling, finger swelling, or a bluish tinge to the nails.***

## HOW TO PREVENT IT

Take precautions, such as always wearing a seat belt when in a moving car, to prevent accidents. Try to avoid falls; watch your step, particularly on uneven, unfamiliar, or icy terrain. Wear proper sports gear.

### ALTERNATIVE THERAPIES

**Note:** Broken bones are always treated medically, but rehabilitation from the injury may involve a mix of conventional and alternative treatments.

**Nutraceuticals**

Broken bones need extra calcium, vitamin D, and other nutrients to heal. Look for a 600-mg calcium supplement with added vitamin D, magnesium, copper, zinc, boron, and manganese. Take as directed by your doctor. In addition, 1000 mg of vitamin C promotes healing; your diet should have at least 5 to 10 servings of fruits and vegetables a day and two or three servings of high-protein foods, such as lean meat, fish, poultry, eggs, or soy or other legumes. For cautions concerning these nutraceuticals, see *About the Recommendations*, p 7.

**Physical therapy**

During the healing process, movement is necessary to reduce risk of blood clots. A physical therapist can prescribe exercises that preserve muscle tone without interfering with healing. After the cast is removed, prescribed exercise is even more important to restore muscle tone and range of motion. Physical therapists also use a variety of techniques to relieve pain and promote healing and rehabilitation; these include weight training and other exercises, hydrotherapy (water exercise, whirlpool baths), ultrasound or diathermy, electrical stimulation, hot and cold packs, and massage.

# Carpal Tunnel Syndrome

## SYMPTOMS

- *Pain, numbness, burning, and tingling of the hand, which persist and may interfere with sleep.*
- *Stiff, swollen wrist joints.*
- *Loss of hand strength and dexterity.*

## WHO IS AT RISK

*Although reliable estimates of the number of cases are hard to come by, studies of certain occupations show that carpal tunnel syndrome (CTS) is fairly common in Canada. For example, out of 982 supermarket checkers, 614 showed symptoms of CTS. People develop CTS primarily from occupations or hobbies that require repetitive motions. It is most likely to develop if the wrists are continually hyperflexed or hyperextended. Also known as repetitive stress injury, CTS affects keyboard operators, pianists, newspaper reporters, and jackhammer operators, among others. Pregnant women can develop the disorder because of increased fluid volume, causing tissues to swell.*

## HOW IT DEVELOPS

The carpal tunnel is a narrow opening in the wrist, made up of eight bones that form three sides of the tunnel, and the transverse carpal ligament, a tough band of tissue that forms the fourth side. Situated on the palm side of the wrist, the carpal tunnel has nine tendons that pass through it as well as the median nerve, which carries messages between the brain and the hand. When any of these tendons swell or become injured, the space inside the carpal tunnel narrows and presses on the median nerve. The pinched, irritated nerve can lead to pain, tingling, inflammation, additional swelling, and the other characteristic symptoms.

### BREAKTHROUGHS!

**A new, less invasive surgical treatment can help those who suffer from carpal tunnel syndrome. The CTD-Mark 1 machine works by stabilizing the elbow and using pneumatic power to stretch the bones and tissue of the wrist and forearm, relieving the pressure in the carpal tunnel and creating more space for the tendons. Most people feel relief in three to six treatments.**

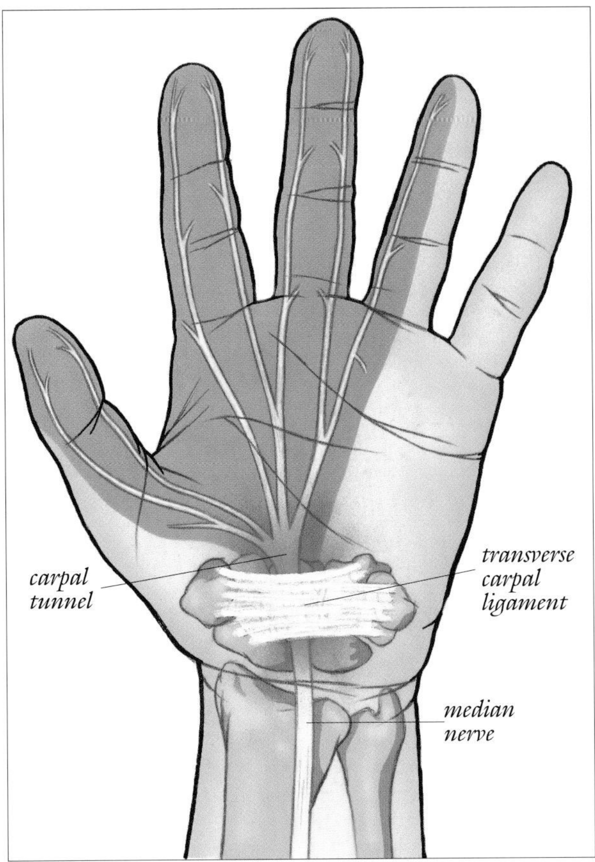


*Compression of the median nerve within the wrist's carpal tunnel causes pain and tingling in the fingers.*

## WHAT YOU CAN DO

It is prudent to avoid developing carpal tunnel syndrome in the first place. (See *How to Prevent It,* p 238.) If you begin to experience symptoms, you should rest and immobilize the affected hand and wrist as much as you can. Take an anti-inflammatory medication such as aspirin and ibuprofen; cold compresses help reduce swelling. See a doctor if symptoms persist.

## HOW TO TREAT IT

A doctor may prescribe stronger anti-inflammatory painkillers as well as muscle relaxants. A corticosteroid injection into the wrist may ease symptoms, although it won't cure the condition. A special splint that holds the wrist in a straight, unflexed position may be recommended; the splint is usually worn at night, but it may be worn continuously if symptoms are severe. Sometimes a cast that is removable while bathing is prescribed.

In severe cases, surgery may be recommended to release the trapped nerve. The surgery cuts the transverse ligament, which relieves pressure on the median nerve. Symptoms are immediately relieved, but may return if the repetitive motions are resumed.

## HOW TO PREVENT IT

Check to make sure that your wrists are properly aligned, neither overflexed nor overextended, if you sit at a computer and type all day (see *Workstation Savvy*, below). If your job involves repetitive motions, take frequent breaks and move about whenever possible; for example, stand up when talking on the phone. Stretch your arm, wrist, shoulder, and neck muscles every hour by crossing your arms over your head and pulling on one elbow, then the other. Rotate your shoulders with hands folded in lap, then reverse the rotation. Massage and stretch your fingers, bend wrists back and forth, clench and unclench fists periodically to prevent tissue swelling.

When working at a computer, your wrists should be straight when you type; if they are not, buy wrist rests at your local computer store and use them. Your posture should be such that you experience minimum stress on all your joints—the back should be straight with feet flat on the floor. If your chair lacks proper support, place a cushion or a rolled-up towel at the small of your back.

### ALTERNATIVE THERAPIES

**Acupuncture**

Meridians affecting the neck, back, and shoulders as well as the hands, wrists, and arms will be stimulated to relieve pain and promote healing.

**Workstation Savvy**

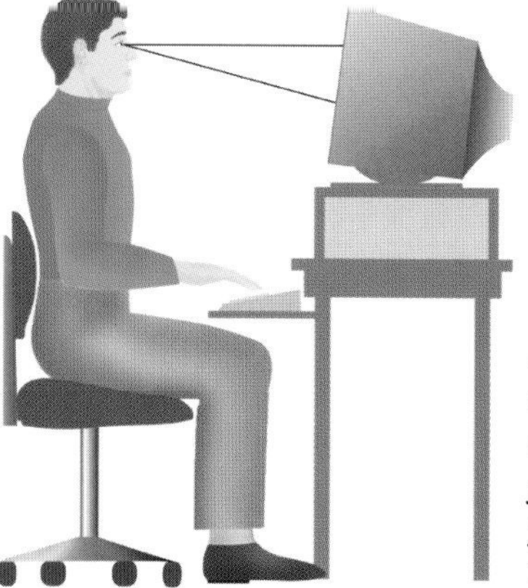

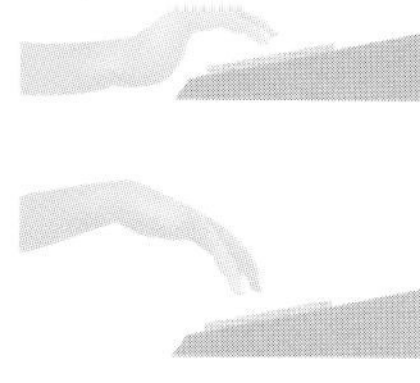

*When working at your computer's keyboard, make sure your back is straight, your feet are flat on the floor, and your lower arms and wrists are straight, not flexed, as shown.*

**Alexander technique**

An instructor will analyze posture, as well as the workstation, and suggest changes to improve posture and prevent work-related stress on the wrists.

**Chiropractic**

Practitioners manipulate misaligned or fixated joints to relieve nerve pressure. Some chiropractors use electrical nerve stimulation to relieve pain by interfering with the transmission of pain impulses.

**Herbal medicine**

Some CTS patients report getting relief from bromelain, an anti-inflammatory enzyme found in pineapple. The usual dosage is 1000 mg taken twice a day between meals. It seems most effective when taken in conjunction with vitamin $B_6$ (see below).

**Nutraceuticals**

Some studies show that vitamin $B_6$, in dosages of 50 mg three times a day, may relieve symptoms. Do not exceed 200 mg a day, however; high dosages can actually worsen the problem by causing nerve damage. Vitamin E, in dosages of 800 to 1000 IU a day, may relieve inflammation and help prevent swelling. For cautions concerning vitamin E, see *About the Recommendations*, p 7.

**WARNING!**

***Don't ignore the early symptoms of carpal tunnel syndrome. A delay in treatment may cause permanent nerve damage and disability of the hand(s).***

**Physical therapy**

Treatments are aimed at not only relieving pain but also correcting the underlying problem. Therapy may include exercises, ultrasound, diathermy, electrical nerve stimulation, hydrotherapy, and alternating hot and cold packs. In addition, physical therapists teach preventive exercises.

# Finger Deformities

### SYMPTOMS

- *Varying degrees of pain that, depending upon the underlying cause, may involve the entire hand and extend to the wrist and arm.*
- *Inability to fully extend the thumb or finger.*
- *Formation of fibrous bands or scar tissue that locks fingers into unnatural positions.*
- *Swelling, numbness, nodules, and finger contractions.*

### WHO IS AT RISK

*In otherwise healthy people, finger deformities often result from hand trauma or sports injuries. Both osteo- and rheumatoid arthritis can attack the finger joints, causing swollen joints and deformity. The so-called "Little*

*Leaguer's Hand" leads to a mallet (claw) finger; it is common among baseball players and other athletes who often suffer broken fingers or torn tendons. People engaged in occupations or hobbies that require repetitive hand movements—keyboard operators, pianists, assembly line workers—may develop deformed fingers as a symptom of repetitive-stress injury or carpal tunnel syndrome.*

## HOW THEY DEVELOP

The manner in which finger deformities develop varies according to the underlying cause.

- **Buttonhole deformity**, a condition in which the first finger joint is flexed and the second is hyperextended, allows the tendons to move out of their normal attachments and form a painful "buttonhole" arrangement that interferes with dexterity. It may be caused by arthritis, dislocations, deep cuts, or fractures.
- **Dupuytren's contracture**, also known as *palmar fibromatosis*, involves progressive contractures or tightening of the fibrous bands in the palm (see *How Dupuytren's Contracture Progresses*, below). Sometimes the foot is similarly affected, and some men with Dupuytren's contracture also have Peyronie's disease, in which the penis extends to one side. Pain tends to subside as the disease progresses, even though the hand becomes more disabled.
- **Heberden's and Bouchard's nodes**—bony nodules on the finger joints—can cause stiffness, pain, and deformity. Arthritis is the most common cause. When the first joint is affected, the deformity is referred to as a Heberden node; it is not as painful as Bouchard's nodes, which involve the knuckle joints.
- **Mallet (or claw) finger**, in which the person is unable to straighten a bent finger, usually results from hand trauma that ruptures a tendon or dislocates a finger.
- **Swan-neck deformity**, in which the first finger joints are hyperextended and the knuckle joints are flexed, makes it impossible to close the hand or pinch the fingers together. It is often caused by severe rheumatoid arthritis; it may also be a consequence of an untreated mallet finger or a fracture that does not heal properly. Spasms of the middle-finger tendons can also lead to this deformity.

Other finger deformities may result from immune system disorders, alcoholism, or epilepsy. There are also numerous congenital finger deformities, in which fingers may be joined, webbed, missing, or misshapen. Most of these are painless, but they often interfere with dexterity.

### BREAKTHROUGHS!

**Artificial finger joints are helping arthritis patients with badly deformed hands regain dexterity. The diseased joints are removed, the fingers are straightened, and the artificial joints are cemented into place.**

## WHAT YOU CAN DO

If the deformity is due to an accident or sports injury, apply ice for 20 minutes every hour or so and immobilize the affected finger by taping it to its adjacent members. Anti-inflammatory medications can ease pain and reduce inflammation; see a doctor as soon as possible to determine whether the injured finger is broken or dislocated, or if the tendons and ligaments are torn.

Heat often eases the pain of arthritic fingers. Many arthritis sufferers use paraffin soaks. Heat paraffin until it melts and is comfortably hot (about 49°C/120°F) but not scalding. Place the painful hands in the paraffin until it

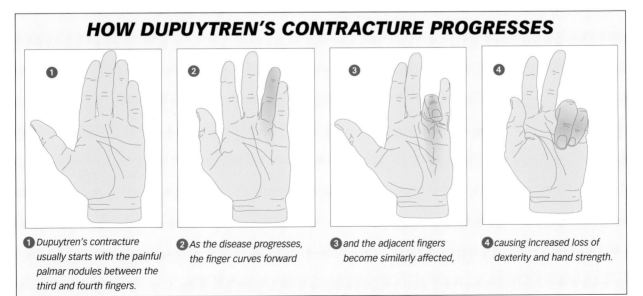

### HOW DUPUYTREN'S CONTRACTURE PROGRESSES

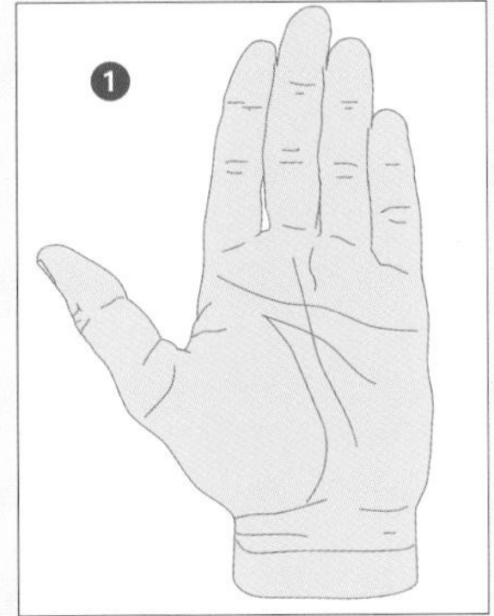

1 *Dupuytren's contracture usually starts with the painful palmar nodules between the third and fourth fingers.*

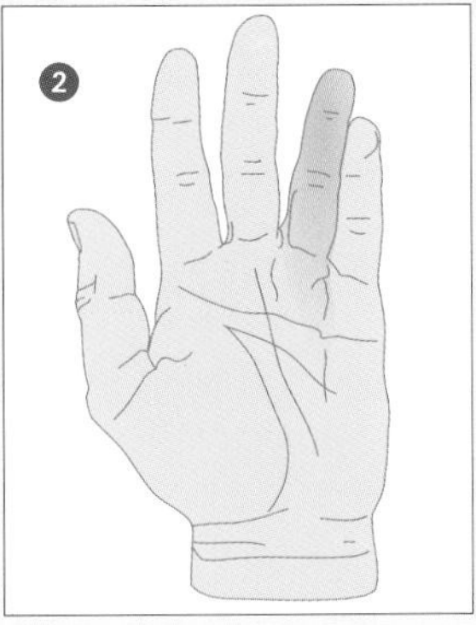

2 *As the disease progresses, the finger curves forward*

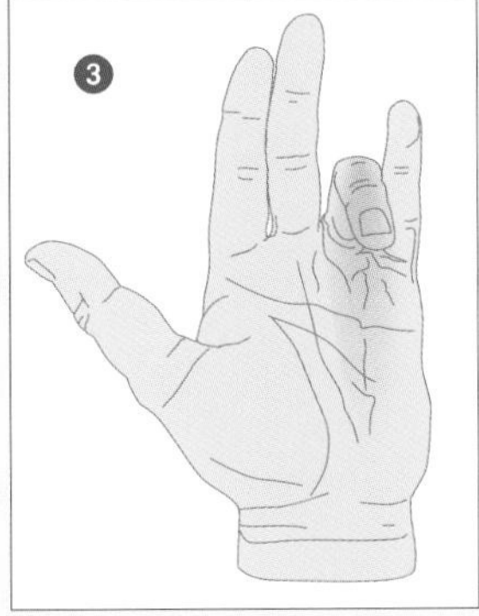

3 *and the adjacent fingers become similarly affected,*

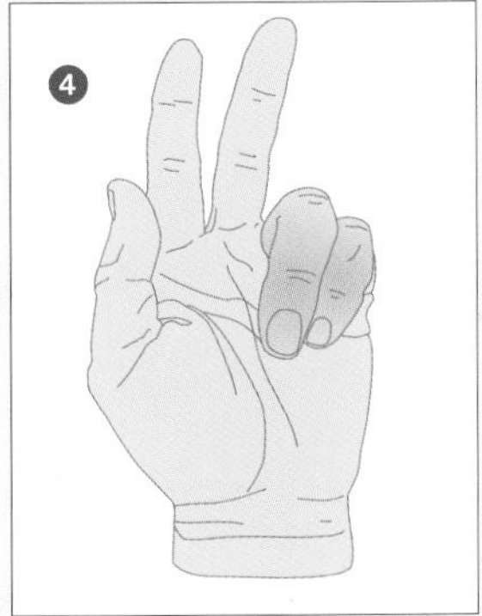

4 *causing increased loss of dexterity and hand strength.*

begins to cool, then peel it off. The paraffin can be rewarmed and the treatment repeated as needed. If only one or two joints are involved, such as in Bouchard's nodes, you can use a very warm tea bag instead (see *Herbal medicine,* right).

**WARNING!**

***Do not delay seeking medical help for a finger injury. Although it may seem trivial at first, a permanent deformity can result from a ruptured tendon or another injury.***

Aspirin, ibuprofen, and other nonsteroidal anti-inflammatory drugs (NSAIDs) can relieve arthritis pain and inflammation. Be sure to take these medications with food; if they still cause stomach upset, use an enteric-coated product, which does not dissolve until it reaches the small intestine.

You can treat finger pain and deformity due to repetitive stress yourself by resting the wrist and hands, immobilizing the affected fingers with a splint, and applying ice to reduce inflammation and swelling (see also *Carpal Tunnel Syndrome,* p 237). See a doctor; early treatment can often prevent permanent damage.

Depending on the underlying cause, exercise may either hurt or help. Arthritic joints should be exercised regularly to help prevent permanent stiffness, but overuse can further injure inflamed joints. Squeezing a soft ball or therapeutic putty may slow the progression of Dupuytren's contracture. Following a finger injury, a few days' rest is advisable to allow healing.

## HOW TO TREAT THEM

A doctor will order X rays and other imaging studies to determine the extent of a hand injury. Treating the underlying cause usually brings lasting pain relief. This often requires surgery to repair a ruptured tendon, remove scar tissue or bands of tissue that are causing painful contractures, and reposition deformed joints.

A fractured bone will be set and immobilized, often with a special splint, until it heals. Arthritis pain that is not controlled with nonprescription NSAIDs may respond to their prescription-strength counterparts. Sometimes a corticosteroid injection into the painful joint provides fast relief by reducing swelling and inflammation. Surgery may be considered to remove nodules or reconstruct badly deformed fingers; in severe cases, the arthritis joints may be removed and replaced with artificial ones (see *Breakthroughs!,* p 239).

## HOW TO PREVENT THEM

Athletes often can prevent finger injuries by wearing the proper gloves and other protective gear. Deformities related to repetitive stress may be prevented by taking frequent breaks, doing arm and hand exercises, and making sure that the arrangement of work space is not adding to the problem. Arthritis cannot be prevented, but its deformities can be minimized by early treatment to control inflammation.

### ALTERNATIVE THERAPIES

**Herbal medicine**

Hot compresses or poultices made from anti-inflammatory herbs can ease pain and reduce inflammation. To make an herbal finger poultice, for example, use ginger tea bags to brew a strong tea. After steeping for three or four minutes, remove the tea bags from the hot tea and apply them directly to the painful joints. Wrapping the fingers with gauze or a strip of clean cloth helps hold in the heat longer; discard the bags after they cool.

Creams containing capsaicin—the active ingredient in hot chilies and cayenne—also reduce pain and inflammation. Gently rub the cream into the painful joints three or four times a day; be careful that it doesn't get in the eyes or touch the lips and other delicate tissue.

**Hydrotherapy**

Warm-water soaks or whirlpool hand baths can ease pain and stiffness.

**Massage**

Massage can ease stiffness in the muscles surrounding the deformed finger; it can also help prevent the hand deformity of Dupuytren's contracture.

**Nutraceuticals**

Vitamin E, in doses of 800 to 1000 IU a day, can reduce inflammation and may slow the progression of thickened tissue in Dupuytren's contracture. Check with your doctor before taking vitamin E if you are taking aspirin or other blood-thinning medication.

**Physical therapy**

This is most useful in regaining hand function following corrective surgery. Occupational therapy can be helpful in teaching new ways to perform everyday tasks, such as buttoning clothes, tying shoes, and eating, with hands deformed by arthritis.

# Hand/Wrist Fractures

### SYMPTOMS

- *Pain, swelling, and bruising of the hand and wrist.*
- *Wrist deformity; inability to move the hand and wrist.*

### WHO IS AT RISK

*Anyone who tries to break a fall with a hand risks fracturing the lower radius bone where it joins the wrist or the scaphoid bone at the base of the thumb. A direct blow, such as having a heavy object fall on the hand, can break one or more of the metacarpal bones. The elderly whose bones are weakened by osteoporosis often break hand and wrist bones in even minor falls. Radiation treatments, long-term use of steroids, and cancer chemotherapy can also weaken bones and result in easy fractures.*

*Among young people, wrist fractures have become one of the most common injuries treated by orthopedists, thanks to the tremendous popularity of in-line skating. Hand and wrist fractures are also very common among football players, boxers, and other athletes who engage in contact sports.*

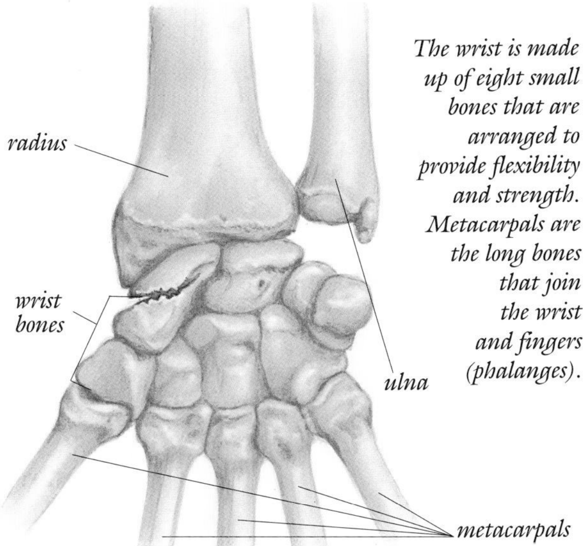


*The wrist is made up of eight small bones that are arranged to provide flexibility and strength. Metacarpals are the long bones that join the wrist and fingers (phalanges).*

## HOW IT DEVELOPS

Often there are no immediate symptoms except for pain and limited range of motion in the hand. The person may think he or she has only a sprain; after a few hours, however, pain, swelling, and bruising usually, but not always, develop.

A fracture in the lower radius produces pain when the wrist is moved in any direction. A fractured scaphoid causes pain in the snuff box, the depression on the outer side of the wrist. Pushing the wrist backward can be especially painful. Pain or difficulty in moving the fingers could mean broken metacarpals.

## WHAT YOU CAN DO

RICE (rest, ice, compression, and elevation) can ease the pain and reduce inflammation due to a hand or wrist fracture. Immobilize the area by fashioning a splint out of any stiff material (see *Improvising a Splint and Sling*, p 224). Aspirin (for adults only) or another anti-inflammatory medication also eases pain and inflammation. Seek medical treatment as quickly as possible.

## HOW TO TREAT IT

X rays are taken to determine the site and extent of the fracture. In the case of wrist fractures, the bone may not need to be set; instead, it will be placed in a plaster cast for several weeks to allow it to heal. Codeine or another prescription painkiller may be needed for a few days.

A more severe fracture will require local anesthesia while the arm and wrist are being manipulated to set the fractured bone. General anesthesia and surgery will be needed to repair a badly fractured wrist or hand. In such cases, a plaster cast is worn for six to eight weeks, although this time may be shortened by using a new injectable cement (see *Breakthroughs!*, below).

A fractured scaphoid does not always show up on an X ray. If a fracture is suspected, the hand will be put in a plaster cast for two weeks, then X-rayed again. If a comparison of the X rays suggests a fracture, the cast will be left on for another six weeks, since these fractures are slow to heal. Pain usually subsides within a few days after the fracture has been set, although there may be a persistent aching sensation. This can be lessened by taking nonprescription ibuprofen, aspirin, or acetaminophen.

### WARNING!

***When wearing a cast for a wrist or hand fracture, make sure you can move your fingers, elbow, and shoulder freely. Swelling of the area encased in the cast can cut circulation and lead to numbness and tissue damage.***

## HOW TO PREVENT IT

Be extra careful when walking on ice or unfamiliar terrain. When engaging in sports, be sure hands are appropriately protected with wrist guards and gloves. If you do fall, try not to use a hand to catch yourself.

### ALTERNATIVE THERAPIES

The alternative therapies recommended for a broken arm usually apply to broken hands and wrists; see p 236 for more details.

### BREAKTHROUGHS!

**Health Canada has approved the use of an injectable cement that can shorten the cast time for a wrist fracture to two weeks from the usual six to eight weeks. The cement, called Norian SRS Cement, is injected between the broken wrist bones. It begins to harden within two minutes, and helps stabilize the fracture. The paste is eventually replaced by bone tissue. Studies in Canada, the United States, and Europe found that the cement was as effective and safe as traditional treatments, but the reduced cast time made it much more convenient.**

# Raynaud's Disease

## SYMPTOMS

- *Uncomfortable coldness, numbness, and tingling sensations in the fingers and, less commonly, the toes.*
- *Changes in skin color—from pale pink or white to blue to deep red—in affected areas.*
- *Smooth, shiny, and tight skin in affected areas.*
- *Spasms in fingers and toes in reaction to the cold or recurring every winter (seasonal Raynaud's).*

## WHO IS AT RISK

*Raynaud's disease is a circulatory disorder that affects about 5 percent of the population. Young women are the most common sufferers; in fact, it is five times more common in women than men. In the most common form, there is no identifiable cause. However, people who have migraine headaches, variant angina (chest pains caused by coronary spasms), and pulmonary hypertension are prone to develop Raynaud's disease, perhaps because they all have similar, as yet unidentified, causes.*

*In Raynaud's phenomenon—the other form of the disease—the symptoms are always a manifestation of another disease (for example, scleroderma, a skin disorder), side effects from a medication, or an anatomical abnormality. Smoking can worsen both types of Raynaud's because nicotine narrows (constricts) blood vessels.*

## HOW IT DEVELOPS

It is not clear how or why Raynaud's disease develops, but the cold hands and other symptoms occur when blood flow is reduced by muscle spasms that constrict the small arteries in the fingers and toes. These spasms are triggered by exposure to cold or, less commonly, emotional stress. There is an uncomfortable sensation of coldness, tingling, and numbness in the fingers (but usually not the thumb) and changes in skin color that go from pale pink or white to blue and then deep red when the spasms cease and blood rushes back to the tissues. Symptoms of this type of primary Raynaud's disease are unlikely to change over time.

Raynaud's phenomenon tends to be more serious, not only because it is associated with an underlying disease but also because the lack of circulation may be more severe and prolonged, leading to skin ulcers and, in rare cases, tissue death.

**BREAKTHROUGHS!**

**Researchers are testing several new drugs that may provide relief from Raynaud's disease. These include:**

- **Thromboxane, a prostaglandin. It is not fully understood how prostaglandins, which are hormonelike chemicals produced by many body tissues, work to prevent artery spasms, but studies using thromboxane appear promising.**
- **Recombinant tissue plasminogen activator (rTPA), a drug that dissolves blood clots. It has been shown to speed healing of finger ulcers related to Raynaud's.**

## WHAT YOU CAN DO

Warming the hands (or feet) usually relieves the discomfort of Raynaud's. Plunging them in warm (not hot) water may reverse the spasms. Exercise—waving your arms, hand rubbing or clapping—also increases blood flow.

## HOW TO TREAT IT

### Medications

Mild primary Raynaud's disease usually can be controlled with self-treatment. If symptoms persist, however, drugs that open (dilate) the small arteries may be prescribed. Medications that may be tried include some of the drugs used to treat high blood pressure, such as calcium channel blockers (verapamil, nifedipine) and alpha blockers (prazosin). Pentoxifylline (Trental), a drug used to treat reduced blood flow to the legs, helps some patients.

Raynaud's phenomenon usually can be alleviated by treating the underlying cause. If the symptoms are due to a medication side effect, finding an alternative drug will usually cure the problem.

**WARNING!**

***Persons who have Raynaud's disease should not take drugs that constrict blood vessels. These include beta-blockers, such as propranolol and clonidine (Catapres)—drugs commonly used to treat high blood pressure and heart disease—and ergot preparations, drugs used to treat migraine headaches.***

### Surgery

For severe cases of Raynaud's disease, an operation called *sympathectomy* may be recommended. In this procedure, which can be done as an outpatient procedure with local anesthesia, the small nerves serving the affected blood vessels are destroyed. The benefits may only be temporary, however, because studies show that symptoms often return within two years. Patients who develop infected skin ulcers may require surgical debridement to remove infected and dead tissue. In such cases, local anesthesia is used and codeine or another painkiller may be prescribed for a few days.

## HOW TO PREVENT IT

Treating the underlying disease helps prevent Raynaud's phenomenon; because the cause of primary Raynaud's is unknown, prevention is more difficult. However, following commonsense preventive measures can reduce the

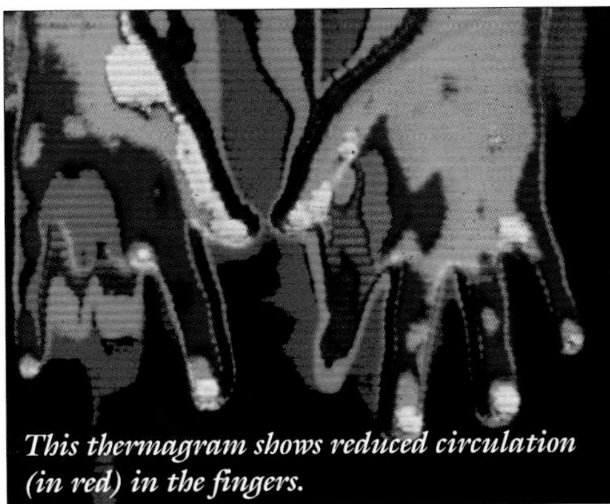
*This thermagram shows reduced circulation (in red) in the fingers.*

number of attacks. If you smoke, make every effort to stop; nicotine reduces peripheral blood flow. Use alcohol in moderation, if at all, and avoid drinking before going out in the cold. Check with your doctor or pharmacist to make sure that none of your medications can provoke Raynaud's symptoms.

Take precautions to protect your hands and feet from exposure to the cold. Wear woolen socks and mittens or wool-lined work gloves when it is chilly outdoors. If you spend a lot of time in the cold, use battery-powered "hot" socks and chemical warmers that can be inserted into gloves and footwear. Make sure your shoes permit free movement of your toes. If you experience symptoms indoors, be extra careful about handling cold items. Wear gloves when you remove food from the refrigerator or freezer; use an insulated glass or a holder for iced drinks. You may also need to wear mittens and socks to bed.

### ALTERNATIVE THERAPIES

**Acupuncture**

Studies have shown that acupuncture can increase blood flow and raise the temperature of hands and feet affected by Raynaud's disease. If symptoms recur, the acupuncture treatments may be repeated.

**Biofeedback training**

Patients with primary Raynaud's disease can be taught to increase circulation and thus warm their hands and feet by using special electronic temperature sensors.

**Herbal medicine**

Numerous studies show that ginkgo biloba—usually 40 mg three times a day—increases circulation, including to the hands and feet. Products should be standardized to provide 24 percent glycosides. One or two capsules of evening primrose oil may also improve Raynaud's symptoms, probably because it is high in gamma-linolenic acid (GLA), which reduces inflammation; borage oil is also high in GLA and may be substituted for evening primrose oil. The typical dosage is 3000 mg (or about 250 mg of GLA) a day. For cautions concerning these nutraceuticals, see *About the Recommendations*, p 7.

**Meditation**

Spasms triggered by stress can be alleviated by meditation, guided imagery, self-hypnosis, yoga, and similar relaxation techniques.

**Nutraceuticals**

Vitamin E improves blood flow; the usual dosage is 400 to 800 IU a day. Check with your doctor before taking vitamin E if you are taking aspirin or other blood-thinning medication. One recent study found that fish oil supplements—in dosages of 2000 to 3000 mg a day—also improved Raynaud's symptoms.

# Tennis Elbow

### SYMPTOMS

- *Pain when bending the wrist upward against a force or when stretching muscles by straightening or bending the elbow or bending the wrist downward.*
- *Pain felt over the bony part on the outside of the elbow.*
- *Swelling of the elbow area.*

### WHO IS AT RISK

*Anyone who overuses his or her forearm muscles can develop tennis elbow, which is by no means limited to tennis*

## ARM-STRENGTHENING EXERCISES

These exercises strengthen the forearm muscles and may help prevent tennis elbow. Start with a small, three- to five-pound weight.

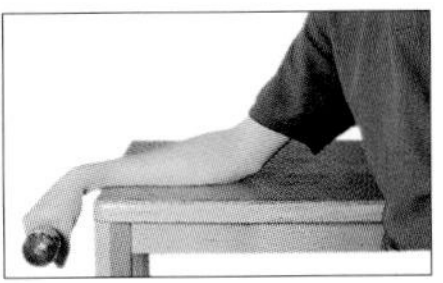
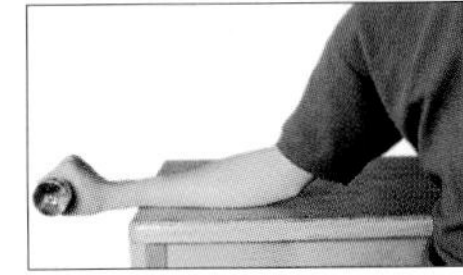

1. Rest your forearm on a firm surface with your hand dangling downward. Grip the weight in your hand and, keeping your elbow on the surface, raise the weight 8 to 10 inches off the table. (If this provokes pain, lower the height of the weight raises.) Repeat 10 times and then switch sides. Work up to three sets with each arm.

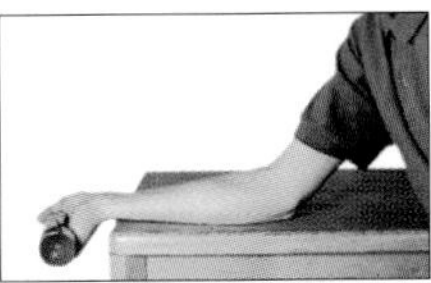

2. Rest your forearm on a firm surface with your palm facing up. Grip the weight and extend and flex your wrist. Repeat at least 10 times, switch hands, and work up to three sets of 10 wrist curls with each hand.

*Tennis elbow can often be traced to faulty movements or a racket with too large or too small a grip.*

***players. In fact, less than 5 percent of all tennis elbow diagnoses are related to playing tennis; it also occurs among people who do a lot of heavy lifting, typists, construction workers, and baggage handlers, among others. Still, tennis players have a high risk of developing this type of tendinitis. Indeed, tennis elbow gets its name from the fact that up to half of all frequent players develop it at some time during their careers. It is especially common among players who swing improperly, use equipment that is not fitted to their grip, or simply overuse their forearm muscles by playing too frequently or too long.***

## HOW IT DEVELOPS

Tennis elbow, also known as *lateral epicondylitis*, is a form of tendinitis caused by continued stress on the forearm muscles used in grasping and extending motions that originate in the elbow. Pain first occurs in the tendons involved in extending the wrist, such as when a tennis player hits a backhand shot. With continued stress, the muscles and tendons begin to hurt when bent or extended, or even at rest due to tiny tears that become inflamed and do not have a chance to heal. Simple tasks, such as lifting a fork, can provoke pain.

## WHAT YOU CAN DO

Rest your elbow for a few days, apply ice to the area, and take an anti-inflammatory medication, such as aspirin or ibuprofen, to relieve pain and reduce inflammation. Place an elastic bandage around the forearm just below the elbow; this often eases pain dramatically. After a day or two of ice treatment—for example, 20 minutes every two or three hours—alternate warm compresses with ice packs to promote healing. See a doctor if the pain persists for more than two weeks.

## HOW TO TREAT IT

In mild cases, self-treatment usually improves the condition. If pain and inflammation persist, a doctor may inject a corticosteroid directly into the painful area. This usually produces quick pain relief and speeds healing, but frequent injections can do more harm than good (see *Warning!,* below).

## HOW TO PREVENT IT

If your problem stems from playing tennis or another sports activity, consult an exercise physiologist or professional trainer to evaluate your movements and equipment. Your doctor or a physical therapist can recommend weight training and other exercises to strengthen the arm muscles and help prevent future episodes (see *Arm-Strengthening Exercises,* p 243). Learn to pace yourself; for example, if playing every day provokes symptoms, cut back to every other day. Overuse of one arm, such as occurs in playing tennis, can stress the muscles and tendons and lead to tendinitis.

### WARNING!

***More than two or three corticosteroid injections a year into the elbow (or any other joint) are inadvisable because this can weaken tendons and prompt them to rupture. If this happens, surgical repair is necessary.***

### ALTERNATIVE THERAPIES

The alternative therapies recommended for tendinitis in general are also helpful in treating tennis elbow; see p 229 for more details.

### BREAKTHROUGHS!

**Graphite tennis rackets have greatly reduced the incidence of tennis elbow among frequent players. Not only are these rackets lighter than older models, but they are also designed to redistribute the impact of the ball on the racket so that less of the force is absorbed by the elbow's tendons, muscles, and bursa. Even so, make sure the racket has the right grip for you, and do not string it too tightly.**

# Neck Pain

*The phrase "He's a pain in the neck" is usually used to describe a rather annoying fellow. Neck pain, however, can range from merely annoying to disabling, and may involve medical conditions that vary from minor to life-threatening.*

## Cervical Disk Disease

### SYMPTOMS

- *Neck pain that can vary from a dull ache to sharp, burning pains that extend down the arm.*
- *Arm weakness and muscle loss.*
- *As disease progresses, increasing neck and arm pain and possible difficulty walking and jerky leg movements.*

### WHO IS AT RISK

*Although cervical neck disease can be congenital or the result of an injury, it is usually a part of the aging process. By age 60, about 90 percent of the population shows deterioration of the spinal disks, although not everyone experiences pain and other symptoms. Poor posture and spinal arthritis can hasten and worsen the problem.*

### HOW IT DEVELOPS

As the spine ages, the disks that cushion the vertebrae begin to dry out and shrink. Sometimes the disks themselves rupture and their spongy centers can push through its outer coating and press on a nerve, resulting in pain that starts in the neck and radiates to the shoulder and perhaps down the arm.

The cervical vertebrae may develop bony spurs, which press on the nerves and may cause constant or intermittent pain. The bony overgrowth can also narrow the cervical canal that houses the spinal cord—a condition called *degenerative cervical stenosis*. Nerve compression in the neck area sometimes affects the legs, resulting in difficulty walking and jerky movements.

### WHAT YOU CAN DO

Any persistent or recurring neck pain warrants seeing a doctor. A heating pad and nonprescription painkillers can provide temporary pain relief. If you frequently wake up with a stiff, painful neck, consider using a cervical pillow. These pillows are designed to cushion the neck while you sleep; they are available in many surgical supply stores and through catalogs. At any rate, avoid sleeping with a plump, firm pillow that holds the neck in a flexed position.

Gentle range-of-motion exercises help maintain flexibility and may ease pain and stiffness (see *Exercises to Overcome Neck Pain,* p 246). However, check with your doctor or physical therapist before undertaking these or other exercises for neck and back pain.

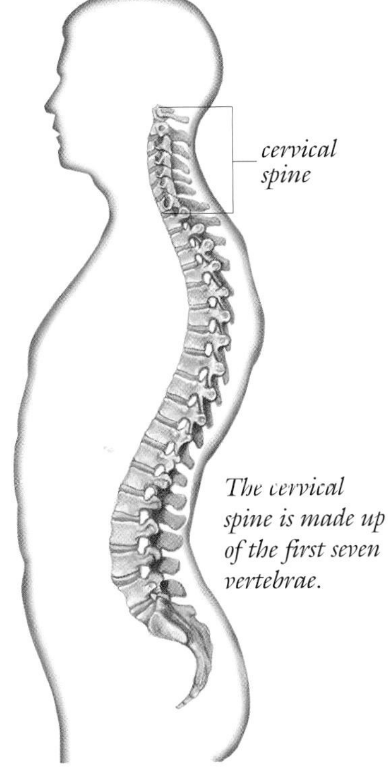


*The cervical spine is made up of the first seven vertebrae.*

### HOW TO TREAT IT

X rays and perhaps other imaging studies, such as a CT scan or an MRI, will be ordered to assess the extent of disk degeneration and bony spurs as well as to determine whether the neural canal is narrowing. Unless there are severe symptoms, such as intractable pain or loss of arm or leg function, doctors generally start with a conservative approach to relieve pain and other symptoms. A local anesthetic may be injected into the neck to provide temporary relief from severe pain; a doctor may also try a corticosteroid injection, prescription-strength nonsteroidal anti-inflammatory drugs (NSAIDs), and a muscle relaxant.

A cervical collar or, in some cases, a neck brace or traction, may be recommended to support the neck and reduce pressure on the nerves. Physical therapy and various complementary therapies may also be tried (see *Alternative Therapies,* p 246).

In severe cases, surgery is needed, especially if the spinal cord or nerves are being compressed. New procedures now allow some operations to be done with local anesthesia on an outpatient basis or with a very brief hospital stay.

**WARNING!**

***Numbness, tingling, or shooting pains in the shoulder and arms point to possible nerve compression. See a doctor as soon as possible; traction or surgery may be necessary to prevent permanent damage.***

## HOW TO PREVENT IT

Avoid slouching. If your work requires long periods of sitting at a computer or work table, take frequent breaks to do neck and shoulder exercises.

### ALTERNATIVE THERAPIES

**Acupuncture**

Many back and pain clinics offer these treatments for persistent neck pain; if six treatments fail to bring improvement, it is unlikely that more will be of any benefit.

**Alexander technique**

Trained instructors analyze posture and movements, and teach new ways of standing, sitting, and moving to reduce pain.

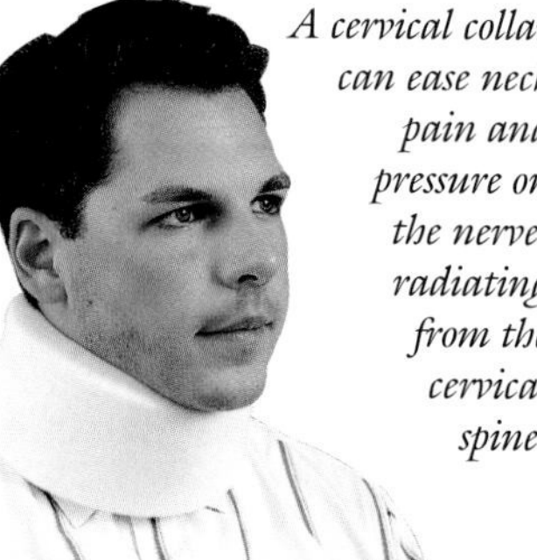

*A cervical collar can ease neck pain and pressure on the nerves radiating from the cervical spine.*

**Chiropractic and osteopathy**

Manipulation can help correct misaligned facet joints in the neck and back. However, in rare cases, neck manipulation has resulted in serious health complications, such as stroke. Some practitioners also offer electrical nerve stimulation, diathermy, and massage. Avoid rigorous manipulation if you have osteoporosis.

**Physical therapy**

These therapists specialize in relieving pain due to structural problems and teaching exercise techniques to prevent a recurrence. Therapies may include whirlpool baths, hot and cold packs, electrical nerve stimulation (TENS), diathermy, ultrasound, and massage.

### BREAKTHROUGHS!

**New techniques in minimally invasive spinal surgery have revolutionized the treatment of severe cervical disk disease. There is very little postsurgical pain, and full recovery takes only a few days. Techniques include:**

- **Endoscopic microsurgery, in which bony spurs or a ruptured disk can be removed through small puncture wounds rather than an open incision.**
- **Laser surgery, in which a viewing tube (endoscope) equipped with a laser is inserted into the area. The laser is then used to vaporize bony spurs and other unwanted tissue. There is little or no bleeding and minimal pain.**

# Neck Strain

### SYMPTOMS

- *Steady, dull, persistent ache in the neck.*
- *Pain, numbness, and tingling in the neck, shoulders, and arms.*
- *Severe spasms of neck pain.*

### WHO IS AT RISK

*Neck pain is caused by a wide range of conditions. Arthritis and degenerative disk disease are common causes of neck pain. Chronic grinding of the teeth can result in severe neck pain radiating from the temporomandibular*

## EXERCISES TO OVERCOME NECK PAIN

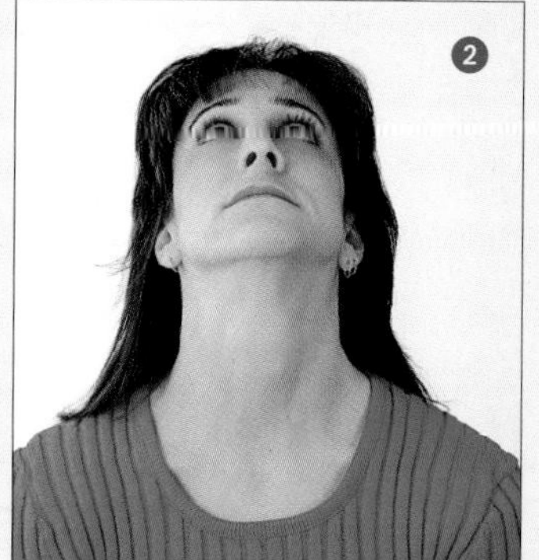

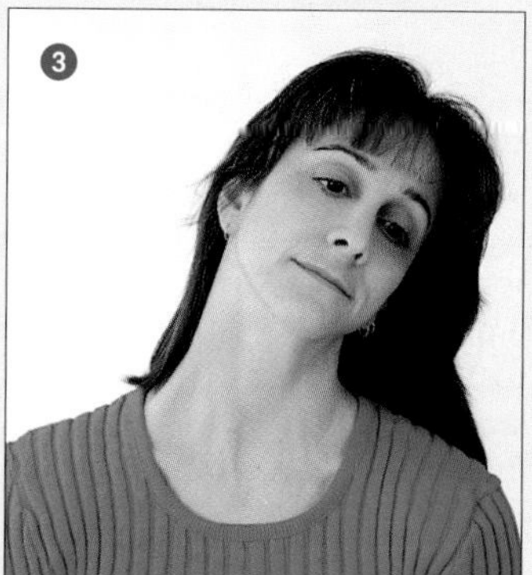

*❶ Start by lowering your head forward and, in a smooth movement, gently roll your head to the right, ❷ and then back slightly, ❸ and finally to the left. Make sure that your shoulders are held still as you move your neck and head. Lower your head forward for a few seconds, and repeat the entire neck roll two or three times. End by rotating your shoulders forward three or four times and then backward.*

*joint of the jaw. Increasingly, chronic neck pain results from job stress caused by repetitive motions of the upper body. Other causes include psychological factors and injuries.*

## HOW IT DEVELOPS

Depending on the underlying cause, the neck pain may develop gradually, come and go, and get progressively worse over time; in other instances, it comes on suddenly, often after an injury. In the case of whiplash, however, neck pain can develop weeks or months after the initial incident. The source may be any of the neck's structures: the muscles, ligaments, tendons, and the disks that cushion the cervical (neck) vertebrae. It can also originate elsewhere—for example, in the shoulders or the jaw—and be felt in the neck because of a common nerve pathway.

## WHAT YOU CAN DO

Neck pain and muscle spasms caused by stress, tension, or repetitive motion respond quite well to self-treatment. A heating pad—preferably one that supplies wet heat—can help relieve pain and muscle spasms. Aspirin or similar medications ease pain and reduce inflammation. Do simple neck exercises several times a day (see *Exercises to Overcome Neck Pain,* p 246).

*Faulty posture is a major cause of neck pain; an Alexander technique instructor shows a model how to position her head and neck properly over the torso to reduce symptoms.*

## HOW TO TREAT IT

To quickly relieve very severe neck pain, doctors sometimes inject a corticosteroid into the area to reduce inflammation. Muscle relaxants, such as baclofen (Lioresal), chlorzoxazone with acetaminophen (Parafon Forte), or diazepam (Valium), may be prescribed to treat spasms. Sometimes an orthopedic collar or neck brace relieves pressure on the neck and resulting pain. Surgery may be recommended for bony overgrowths or herniated disks.

## HOW TO PREVENT IT

If your job requires repetitive motion, such as working at a computer for long periods, make sure your keyboard and monitor are at a comfortable height to avoid neck strain. Use good posture to prevent stress on muscles in the upper body. Avoid sleeping with a very firm, plump pillow that holds the neck in an awkward, flexed position.

### ALTERNATIVE THERAPIES

**Note:** The alternative therapies recommended for cervical disk disease may also relieve neck pain caused by muscle spasms, stress, and overuse injuries; see p 246.

**Aromatherapy**

Lavender or marjoram oils are especially useful in easing minor aches and relaxing tensed muscles. They may be massaged into the neck skin or added to a hot bath.

**Massage**

Simply massaging a painful neck with your fingers often provides prompt relief; Rolfing, shiatsu, or other deep-massage techniques can alleviate deep muscle aches.

**Meditation and yoga**

These relaxation therapies, which may be combined with deep breathing exercises or self-hypnosis, can ease stress-related pain.

**WARNING!**

***A stiff neck that is very painful or difficult to move and is accompanied by a worsening headache and possible fever may be caused by meningitis. This is a potentially fatal disease; go a hospital emergency room right away.***

# Wryneck/Torticollis

### SYMPTOMS

- *Painful spasms of the neck muscles, usually on one side.*
- *Muscle spasms that pull or twist the head to one side.*

### WHO IS AT RISK

*About 1 in 10,000 people in Canada suffer from wryneck or torticollis, neuromuscular disorders that can occur at any age but are most prevalent among people 30 to 50 years of age; women slightly outnumber men. Heredity may play a role; about 5 percent of torticollis patients have a family history of the disease. Congenital torticollis, which occurs mostly in newborns, is quite rare, and is usually due to an injured or malformed neck muscle.*

## HOW IT DEVELOPS

Torticollis is one of several diseases classified as *focal dystonias*, disorders in which specific muscles go into prolonged spasms. Wryneck is a mild form of torticollis, in which the spasms develop suddenly and may come and go. Usually, no cause can be found, although in some cases, the spasms are provoked by inflammation, a pinched nerve, a thyroid disorder, or a dislocated joint. After several years, symptoms often disappear.

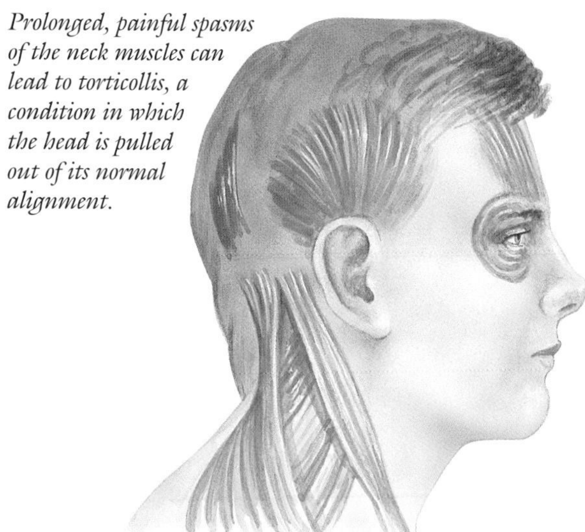

*Prolonged, painful spasms of the neck muscles can lead to torticollis, a condition in which the head is pulled out of its normal alignment.*

Spasmodic torticollis tends to be more severe than wryneck, with the neck muscles remaining painfully contracted on one side, pulling the head toward the shoulder. The person may also suffer facial tics and other muscle spasms.

At one time, torticollis was thought to be caused by hysteria and was treated as a mental disorder. Although it can lead to emotional problems, doctors now know that torticollis is a mysterious organic disorder, rather than a mental illness, that requires medical treatment.

## WHAT YOU CAN DO

Heat treatments sometimes ease the discomfort of simple wryneck. An anti-inflammatory painkiller, such as aspirin or ibuprofen, may help.

Try to sleep on your back, and use a small, rolled neck pillow. Use an inflatable traveler's neck pillow on a long car or plane trip. For home use, consider investing in a special therapeutic pillow that can be cooled in the freezer to provide a cold treatment and then warmed in a microwave or oven set on low for a heat treatment.

If a painful muscle spasm develops, massage it with your fingers or rub it in a circular motion with an ice cube wrapped in a plastic bag. If you don't obtain relief, try taking a hot shower to halt the spasms. Some patients also get relief from a battery-operated vibrating neck massager that can be worn like a scarf.

### BREAKTHROUGHS!

**The discovery that injections of tiny amounts of botulinum toxin type A, commonly known as Botox, can relax spastic neck muscles has revolutionized the treatment of refractory torticollis. Botox—the toxin produced by the organisms that cause botulism—paralyzes the muscles, thereby relaxing the painful spasms and allowing the person to hold his head in a normal position. The effects of Botox last three to six months, after which the injections are repeated.**

## HOW TO TREAT IT

A doctor will order various tests aimed at finding an underlying cause. Often, however, no specific cause can be found, and numerous treatments may be tried, including biofeedback and other unorthodox approaches. Many patients are gaining relief from a new treatment using injections of botulinum toxin (see *Breakthroughs!*, below). In addition to anti-inflammatory painkillers, medications that may help include:

- **Anticholinergic drugs** such as trihexyphenidyl (Apo-Trihex), which work by blocking certain nerve impulses.
- **Muscle relaxants**, such as diazepam (Valium), which help prevent spasms.
- **Antipsychotic drugs**, such as haloperidol (Haldol) or perphenazine (Trilafon), which also relax muscle spasms.

If conservative approaches don't work, neurosurgery to sever some of the neck nerves may help. In time, however, the problem may recur.

### WARNING!

***Babies born with congenital torticollis should be given intensive physical therapy within the first few months of life. The therapy is aimed at stretching the damaged muscle and allowing the baby to hold his or her head in a normal position.***

## HOW TO PREVENT IT

There is little you can do to prevent torticollis, especially if it has no identifiable cause. Lifestyle changes, however, may help prevent wryneck. Maintain good posture at all times, keeping your shoulders down, and try to avoid sudden head movements.

### ALTERNATIVE THERAPIES

**Biofeedback training**

This technique teaches patients how to control and relax neck muscles and is a standard treatment for wryneck.

**Chiropractic**

Many chiropractors specialize in treating wryneck using manipulation and electrical nerve stimulation. In rare cases this may result in serious complications, such as stroke.

**Hydrotherapy**

Whirlpool baths, alternating hot and cold showers, and underwater massage all provide varying degrees of relief for muscle spasms and neck pain.

**Massage therapy**

Combined with other therapies, massage can relax contracted muscles.

# Back Pain

*Backaches are second only to headaches as a source of pain, largely because our backs were designed for walking on all fours, rather than on two hind legs. Even so, there's a lot we can do to keep our backs healthy and free of pain.*

## Herniated Disk

### SYMPTOMS

- *Back pain, usually in the lower back (lumbar spine); less commonly in the neck (cervical spine). The pain can range from a dull ache to severe, burning, or shooting pains.*
- *Back pain that is worsened by movement, especially bending, lifting, straining, coughing, or sneezing.*
- *Numbness or tingling sensations that may run from the back to the buttocks and down the leg, or from the shoulder and down an arm.*
- *Leg weakness and difficulty in lifting a foot when walking.*
- *Loss of nerve reflexes, such as knee or ankle jerk.*
- *In rare cases, loss of bowel or bladder control.*

### WHO IS AT RISK

*Anyone can suffer a herniated disk, but the condition is most common among persons 30 to 50 years of age whose jobs entail a lot of heavy lifting or sitting or standing in one position for long periods. Other risk factors include: a back injury, a narrowing of the spinal canal (spinal stenosis), a sedentary lifestyle, being overweight, and having poor posture.*

### HOW IT DEVELOPS

The spine is made up of 33 vertebrae, which form a bony protective cage for the spinal cord. Arising from the spinal cord are 31 pairs of nerves, each of which pass through an opening between two vertebrae. The vertebrae themselves are separated and cushioned by disks made up of cartilage and fibrous material. Each disk has a tough outer sac, called the annulus fibrosis, that surrounds the soft, spongy nucleus and also holds the disk in its proper place.

A herniated, or ruptured, disk occurs when the nucleus bulges through a weakened or stretched portion of the annulus. Pain and other symptoms develop if the bulging nucleus presses on one of the nerve roots arising from the spinal cord. This is why a herniated disk in the lower back, for example, can cause tingling and pain in the legs.

**Herniated Disk**

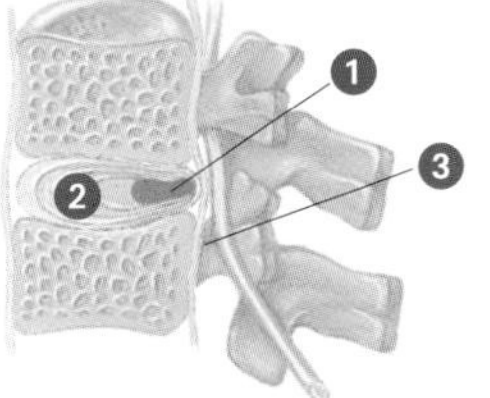


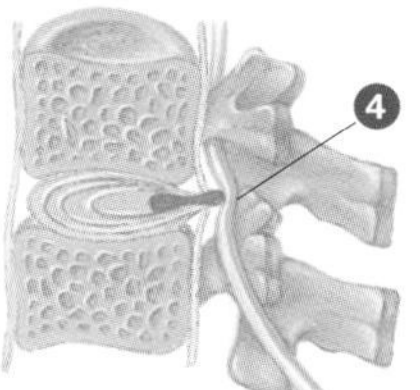


*The nucleus (1) of the disk (2) bulges through the annulus (3). Symptoms occur when the herniated disk presses on a nerve root (4).*

### WHAT YOU CAN DO

A heating pad often provides relief for mild back or neck pain. Soak in a hot tub or warm whirlpool bath, if available. Sleep on a firm but not hard mattress. Properly placed pillows can ease stress on the back; for example, a pillow under the knees for those who sleep on their backs, or one under the waist and another under the shoulder for side sleepers. Until the pain subsides, avoid lifting heavy objects, straining, and bending.

Gentle stretching exercises, such as modified leg lifts (see p 252) and "bridging" (see p 193) often help. However, exercises should not be undertaken without consulting a doctor. Nonprescription painkillers—usually aspirin or a stronger nonsteroidal anti-inflammatory drug (NSAID),

**WARNING!**

***A number of other disorders can mimic a herniated disk. Conditions that should be ruled out include:***

- ***A tumor.***
- ***Spondylosis, a type of spinal arthritis.***
- ***Osteoporosis, a thinning of the bones, especially the spine.***
- ***Fractured vertebrae.***

*The spine is made up of 33 vertebrae: 7 cervical, 12 thoracic, 5 lumbar, 5 that are fused to form the sacrum, and 4 that are fused to form the coccyx.*

such as ibuprofen—can ease pain and reduce inflammation. In severe cases, a few days of bed rest may be necessary. Most experts recommend that this be limited to two or three days; longer periods of total bed rest can make matters worse by causing muscle weakness.

## HOW TO TREAT IT

### Medications

A short course of prednisone or another steroid drug may be prescribed to ease severe inflammation. If even stronger medications are needed, a few days of treatment with a narcotic painkiller such as oxycodone (Oxycontin) or meperidine (Demerol) may be tried; their long-term use should be avoided, however, because they are addictive. Some doctors also prescribe muscle relaxants, such as cyclobenzaprine (Flexeril) or methocarbamol (Robaxin) or tranquilizers—usually diazepam (Valium) or another benzodiazepine—but others doubt that they are very helpful.

### Injections

A local anesthetic drug, such as Novocain, may be injected to give temporary relief of very acute pain. Papain—an enzyme used in meat tenderizers—is sometimes injected into the herniated disk to dissolve the spongy nucleus, but most doctors in Canada shun this treatment as ineffective.

### Traction

A cervical collar may be prescribed to treat a herniated cervical disk. Traction, once a popular treatment, is now rarely used to treat a herniated lumbar disk.

### BREAKTHROUGHS!

**A new operation, called IDET for intradiscal electrothermal annuloplasty, appears promising for patients facing disk surgery. It takes 15 to 20 minutes, is done under local anesthesia, and allows patients to walk out of the operating room. A hollow needle and a tiny tube (catheter) with a heating element is inserted into the ruptured disk. The element is then turned up to 90°C/194°F for about 15 minutes, destroying any blood vessels and nerve fibers that have invaded the disk space, while creating a new seal in the annulus. Of the first 700 patients undergoing IDET in the U.S., more than 80 percent enjoyed reduced pain and increased mobility.**

### Surgery

Surgery is reserved for severe cases in which self-help and medications fail to give relief. It may be done sooner if there is persistent numbness or loss of bowel or bladder control. Microsurgery techniques have simplified most disk surgery. The surgeon removes the herniated disk by using tiny instruments that are manipulated through a tube equipped with a miniature camera and a magnifying device. There is very little bleeding with this type of surgery, and the patient can be up and about in a day or two. Some experimental procedures allow an even faster recovery (see *Breakthroughs!*, above). Traditional surgery through an open incision is still sometimes needed, depending upon the location of the herniated disk.

## HOW TO PREVENT IT

Maintaining physical fitness and good posture is the mainstay of prevention. When sitting—the most stressful position for the lower back—make sure the chair or car

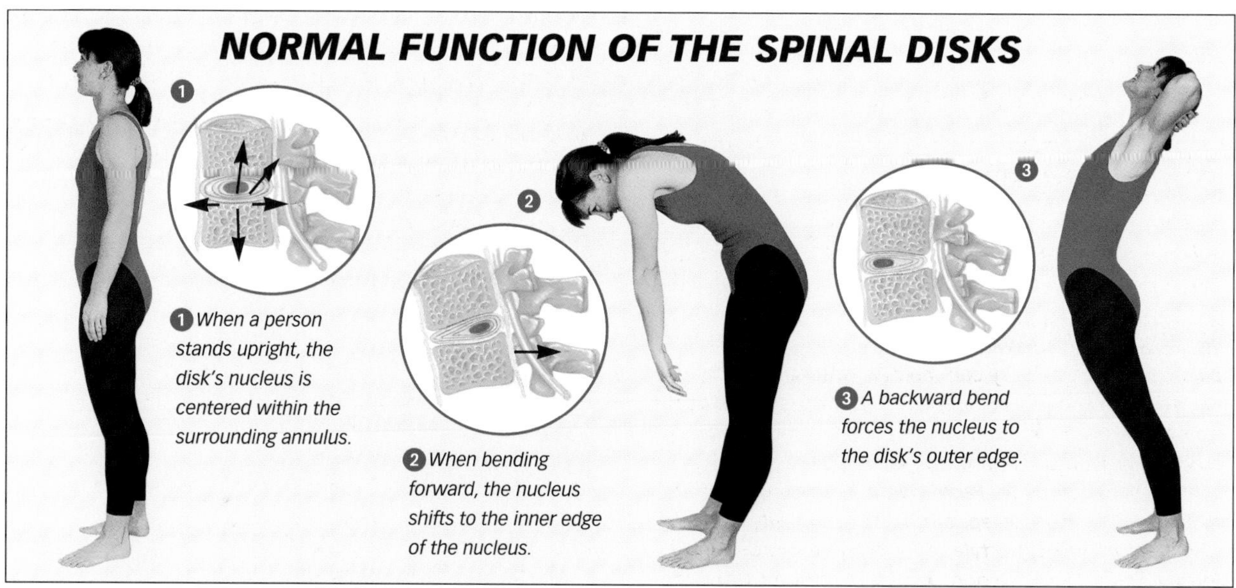
NORMAL FUNCTION OF THE SPINAL DISKS
1
2
3
1 When a person stands upright, the disk's nucleus is centered within the surrounding annulus.
2 When bending forward, the nucleus shifts to the inner edge of the nucleus.
3 A backward bend forces the nucleus to the disk's outer edge.

seat provides good support for the back. Get up frequently to stretch the back and relieve muscle tension. Other preventive measures include:

- Achieving and maintaining ideal weight.
- Wearing properly fitted low-heel shoes.
- Lifting heavy objects by bending at the knees and keeping the back properly aligned.

#### ALTERNATIVE THERAPIES

**Acupuncture**

It may be used alone or as a complementary therapy with other treatments. If six treatments fail to bring improvement, it probably is not going to work.

**Alexander technique**

Trained instructors analyze posture and movements, and then teach corrective measures to maintain proper back alignment.

**Chiropractic or osteopathy**

These manipulative techniques may help by correcting spinal malalignment. In some cases, however, spinal manipulation may worsen a herniated disk, so consult a back specialist or other medical doctor first.

**Massage**

This may be combined with other therapies; it works by relaxing tensed muscles. A doctor should be consulted, however, before undergoing Rolfing and other deep-massage techniques that can worsen a ruptured disk.

**Physical therapy**

Physical therapists treat a variety of painful back problems, including herniated disks, with ultrasound, hot and cold packs, diathermy, massage, and exercise. Physical therapy is an important aspect of rehabilitation after disk surgery; it is also useful in teaching back-strengthening exercises and proper lifting techniques to prevent a recurrence.

# Low-Back Pain

#### SYMPTOMS

- *Acute or chronic pain in the lower back.*
- *Pain may be diffuse or associated with specific tender points.*

#### WHO IS AT RISK

*Low-back pain is a very common condition: 8 out of 10 Canadians will experience an episode of back pain at some point. The problem is likely to become chronic with increasing age; about half of all persons over age 60 have chronic back problems. Factors that increase risk include fatigue, insufficient sleep, bad posture, obesity or pregnancy, a sedentary lifestyle, and certain emotional problems. Arthritis and osteoporosis are common causes of low-back pain. Some lower-back problems are job-related; for example, people whose jobs entail a lot of sitting or lifting of heavy objects are prime candidates.*

## HOW IT DEVELOPS

Most back pain is due to muscle strains and spasms. If you feel serious pain within 24 hours of heavy lifting, you may have ruptured a disk, sprained a ligament, or torn a muscle. Disks are the spongy cushions between each pair of vertebrae that may pinch a nerve when they slip. Ligaments are the tough bands of tissue connecting the vertebrae. The nature of the pain provides clues to its possible cause. For example, back pain stemming from disk, muscular, or other mechanical problems will be worse during periods of inactivity and improve with stretching. In contrast, pain referred from elsewhere and other visceral (nonmechanical) problems are generally not affected by movement or rest and tend to be worse at night.

## WHAT YOU CAN DO

Take aspirin, ibuprofen, or another nonprescription anti-inflammatory medication. If the pain is very severe, try a day or two of bed rest. Lie on your back or side on a firm surface, with your knees bent and supported by a pillow, even if you are more comfortable on your stomach. Use a heating pad, ice pack, or alternating applications of warmth and cold for extra relief.

When the pain subsides, start exercises to strengthen your back (see *Exercises to Ease Low-Back Pain*, p 252). If these exercises hurt, however, stop immediately; pain is a warning that something is wrong.

## HOW TO TREAT IT

If symptoms persist after more than two weeks of self-treatment, or if they recur, see a doctor. Don't delay if the pain is accompanied by other symptoms, such as numbness in your legs or a loss of bowel or bladder control.

Your doctor will examine your back, test your nerve reflexes, and probably order X rays. You may also have imaging studies such as CT scans or an MRI, bone density studies, and nerve and muscle evaluations.

> **WARNING!**
>
> ***At one time, doctors recommended staying in bed for a week or longer to treat low-back pain. We now know that prolonged bed rest can actually worsen the problem because it further weakens the supporting muscles. Bed rest should be limited to one or two days, or three at the most.***

### Medications

A simple backache can usually be controlled with a nonsteroidal anti-inflammatory drug (NSAID); if a nonprescription product does not provide adequate relief, ask your doctor about a prescrip-

## EXERCISES TO EASE LOW-BACK PAIN

**1 Cat and camel.** *Start on all fours. First lower your back while squeezing and lifting your buttocks, (far left) much in the way a cat stretches. Then arch your back to make a camel's hump. Hold each position for a count of 5, and repeat 5 to 10 times.*

**2 Modified leg raises.** *Lie on your back with knees bent and arms comfortably stretched out at your side. Slowly bring your knees toward your chest while keeping your head and upper back flat on the floor (far right).*

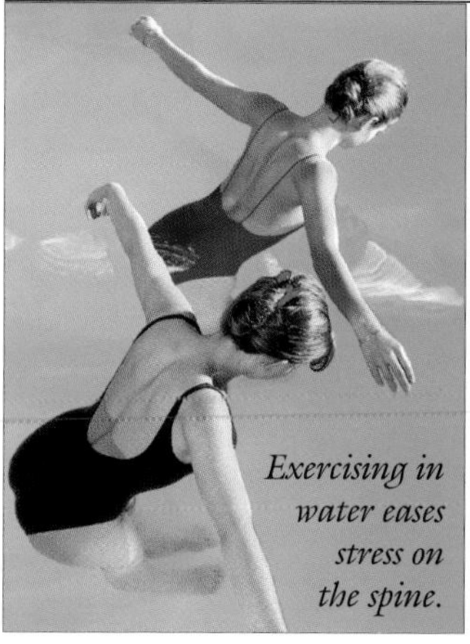

*Exercising in water eases stress on the spine.*

tion-strength one. A muscle relaxant and perhaps a corticosteroid injection may be added if an NSAID alone is not enough. If emotional problems underlie the complaint, an antidepressant may improve sleep and relieve pain.

### Mechanical treatments

Sometimes immobilizing the back with a brace or, on rare occasions, traction may be necessary, especially if the problem stems from a back injury. Manipulation of the affected area is another option. It may be useful when the pain is caused by muscle spasms, but it can aggravate an arthritic joint or further rupture a disk. Physical therapy is often recommended.

### Surgery

Surgery is usually the treatment of last resort unless the pain is due to a badly ruptured disk or an injury. The type of operation depends upon the nature of the problem, but increasingly microsurgery, which requires only small puncture incisions, is used.

#### ALTERNATIVE THERAPIES

The alternative therapies used to treat a herniated disk (see p 251) are also recommended for ordinary low-back pain.

# Osteoporosis

#### SYMPTOMS

- *Mild back pain that worsens as vertebrae become increasingly compressed.*
- *Height loss and development of a dowager's hump.*
- *Painful bone fractures, particularly of the wrist and hip.*
- *Sudden, severe back pain with little or no provocation.*

#### WHO IS AT RISK

*It is estimated that 1.4 million Canadians suffer from osteoporosis, a disease characterized by weak, brittle bones. It is most common among postmenopausal women, especially those who are thin, fine-boned, and of northern European or Asian descent. Younger women who have had their ovaries removed and very thin women who exercise a lot—for example, ballet dancers and gymnasts—may develop premature osteoporosis. Other risk factors include smoking, a sedentary lifestyle, excessive alcohol consumption, long-term use of steroid medications, high blood pressure, and a diet that lacks adequate calcium and vitamin D.*

## HOW IT DEVELOPS

Osteoporosis is a disease in which bones lose calcium and other minerals that give them their density and strength. Bone tissue is constantly "turning over," with calcium and other minerals moving in and out according to the body's needs. We build bone mass until about age 30 to 32; after that, bones slowly lose minerals. Women are protected against excessive bone loss while they are still menstruating and their bodies are producing estrogen, but hormone production drops drastically during menopause (or earlier if the ovaries are surgically removed) and bone loss is accelerated. This process is most pronounced in the first decade after menopause.

In its early stages, osteoporosis does not produce any obvious symptoms. A chronic, mild backache is a common sign that bone loss is progressing. The demineralized vertebrae lead to compression of the spinal column, resulting in a loss of height, development of a dowager's hump in the upper back, and increasingly severe back pain. The vertebrae often develop crush fractures, signaled by sudden, very severe back pain. Other bones, especially the wrists and hips, also break easily; in severe cases, fractures may occur spontaneously or with only a mild blow or sudden movement.

Men are also vulnerable to osteoporosis, although they develop it at least 10 years after women do, because their bones are more dense to begin with and testosterone levels, which protect their bone density, decline at a later age (see *Warning!*, p 254).

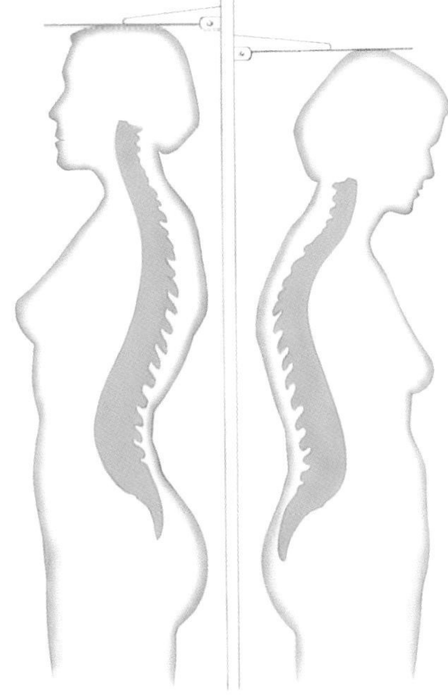

*The spinal compression caused by osteoporosis results in a loss of height and development of a hump in the upper back.*

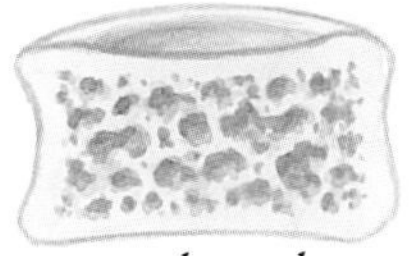

*normal vertebra*

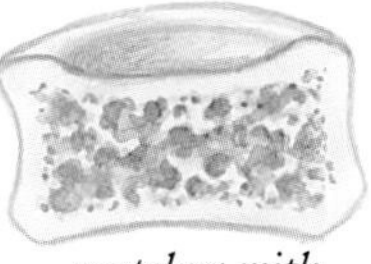

*vertebra with osteoporosis*

## WHAT YOU CAN DO

A heating pad and acetaminophen, aspirin, or another nonprescription painkiller can help ease the mild back pain of osteoporosis. Daily exercise is also important, not only to maintain bone density but also to reduce pain. Bone-building and maintenance require a certain amount of stress in the form of weight-bearing exercise; walking for at least 30 minutes a day is ideal. Jogging, dancing, aerobics, stair-climbing, and racket sports also provide weight-bearing exercise. Remember, too, that the body responds to aerobic exercise by increasing its production of endorphins, natural painkillers and mood enhancers. In addition, strength training—using free weights, rubber tubing, or resistance machines—not only builds muscles but also strengthens bones and improves balance, an important factor in preventing falls.

Make sure that your diet provides adequate calcium and other vitamins and minerals necessary to maintain healthy bones, and strive to maintain ideal weight (see *Nutraceuticals*, p 254). If you are going through menopause or are at risk of developing osteoporosis, talk to your doctor about various preventive and treatment options.

### BREAKTHROUGHS!

**Risedronate (Actonel), a drug now used to treat Paget's disease, a bone disorder, appears to also work against osteoporosis. California researchers found that risedronate reduced the risk of spinal fractures by more than 40 percent and raised bone density by 5 percent among women with osteoporosis. The drug is now awaiting Health Canada approval as an osteoporosis treatment.**

## HOW TO TREAT IT

A number of drugs can slow bone loss and even reverse it; the earlier that treatment begins, the more likely it is to increase bone density. Options include the following:

- **Alendronate (Fosamax)** decreases bone turnover and promotes formation of new bone mass. It must be taken on an empty stomach first thing in the morning, and the person must remain upright for 30 minutes to prevent a backflow into the esophagus.
- **Postmenopausal estrogen replacement therapy** (ERT) helps slow bone loss and reduces the risk of fractures. There are many forms of ERT, but most experts recommend combining estrogen with progesterone, another female sex hormone, to lower the risk of uterine cancer.
- **Raloxifene (Evista)**, the first of the so-called designer estrogens, targets specific organs and helps prevent bone loss.
- **Salmon calcitonin (Miacalcin)**, a synthetic form of a thyroid hormone, increases calcium absorption into the bones. It is available as a nasal spray.

## HOW TO PREVENT IT

Before entering menopause, reserve time to review risk factors with your doctor and decide together whether you are a high-risk candidate. Then create an action plan that could include changes in diet or physical activity, and/or bone mineral density (BMD) testing. Bone densitometers, machines that perform BMD tests to measure the strength of your bones, are available on a limited basis in Canada. People at high risk for osteoporosis are generally given priority for this testing. Other preventive strategies include:

- **Quitting smoking**. Tobacco use not only lowers estrogen production and results in an early menopause, but it also interferes with normal bone metabolism. Studies show that women become more addicted to nicotine than men; new drugs that block nicotine cravings may help.
- **Limiting caffeine intake** to the equivalent of three cups of coffee per day, avoiding soft drinks containing phosphorous, limiting alcohol to no more than two ounces a day, and restricting salt intake—all of these substances increase bone loss.
- **If you use antacids**, taking those that contain calcium carbonate (which the bones can use) rather than aluminum salts, which promote bone loss.
- **Engaging in daily exercise**, which includes both aerobic and strength-building activities (see *What You Can Do* on the previous page).
- **Getting enough calcium** and other nutrients needed to build and maintain bones.

### ALTERNATIVE THERAPIES

**Nutraceuticals**

Calcium and vitamin D are essential to building and maintaining bones. The best dietary sources of calcium are low-fat milk and milk products, canned salmon and sardines with bones, and certain green leafy vegetables, such as broccoli and kale. Experts recommend getting 1200 to 1500 mg of calcium a day, with no more than 500 to 600 mg taken at a time. Calcium carbonate is best taken with meals; calcium citrate can be taken at any time. Vitamin D is necessary to absorb calcium; unless you spend 15 to 20 minutes in bright sun almost daily, take 400 to 800 IU of vitamin D. Magnesium complements calcium; it should be taken in the same daily dosage. Other important bone-building supplements include 1000 to 2000 mg of vitamin C, 20 mg of manganese, 25 to 30 mg of zinc, and 1 to 2 mg of boron. For cautions concerning these nutraceuticals, see *About the Recommendations*, p 7.

**WARNING!**

***Older men also develop osteoporosis, yet doctors often do not warn them about ways to prevent the disease and are less likely to test for it, even when symptoms develop. Men should also take preventive measures, such as exercising regularly and making sure that their diets provide adequate calcium.***

A number of recent studies indicate that isoflavones, plant (phyto) chemicals that are structurally similar to estrogen, may help prevent osteoporosis. Good sources include tofu and other soy products, or take 25 to 50 grams of soy protein a day.

# Posture Defects

### SYMPTOMS

*Posture defects are a common cause of chronic back pain, especially among older people; other symptoms include:*

***Kyphosis:*** *Rounded shoulders, a hunched back, and head thrust forward.*

***Lordosis:*** *Arched lower back; protruding abdomen and buttocks; possible ruptured spinal disks.*

### WHO IS AT RISK

***Kyphosis****—posture characterized by rounded shoulders and a hunched back—is often due to slouching or poor posture habits learned in childhood. It may also be caused by a congenital defect; spinal arthritis; a back injury or infection; scoliosis, an abnormal curvature of the spine; and osteoporosis, a thinning of the bones that results in compression of the spine. Among adolescents, a deformity of several vertebrae can lead to a painful form of kyphosis called* Scheuermann's disease.

***Lordosis****, or swayback, may also stem from poor posture habits; for example, a person who has mild kyphosis may arch the back excessively in trying to correct slouching. Obesity, pregnancy, and arthritis of the hip can also contribute to lordosis.*

## HOW THEY DEVELOP

Posture defects, especially kyphosis, often develop in childhood or during adolescence; they are also common among older persons who have osteoporosis or spinal

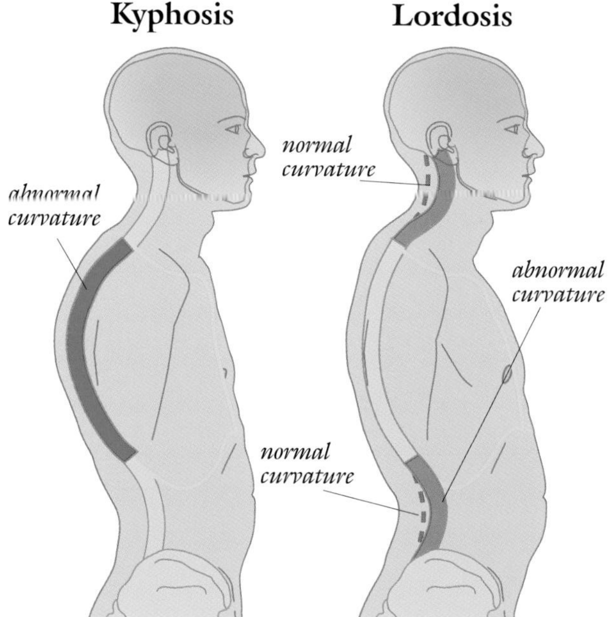

**BREAKTHROUGHS!**

**New surgical procedures now enable doctors to straighten severely curved spines, including those caused by scoliosis and spinal arthritis. Unlike past operations, these procedures do not require wearing casts and heavy braces; instead, the realigned vertebrae are held in place by fine rods, surgical bolts, and wires.**

arthritis. Mild posture defects usually do not cause pain and other uncomfortable symptoms. But as the abnormal posture becomes more pronounced, it can cause a chronic backache, ruptured disks, sciatica, and other nerve problems. Extreme kyphosis can compress the rib cage and cause breathing problems.

## WHAT YOU CAN DO

Aspirin, ibuprofen, or similar anti-inflammatory medications and a heating pad can help ease back pain. Stretching and exercises to strengthen the abdominal muscles, such as pelvic lifts (bridging), straight-leg raises, and modified sit-ups, can improve posture and relieve back pain. Sleep on a firm mattress, preferably on your back or side. If you spend a lot of time sitting, make sure that your chair provides good back support. Wear comfortable, low-heeled shoes and avoid high heels, especially if you have lordosis.

**WARNING!**

***A child who complains of a backache should see a doctor promptly. Backaches in a child or an adolescent are often due to an underlying disease rather than poor posture.***

## HOW THEY ARE TREATED

A doctor will first determine whether the posture defect is caused by spinal arthritis, osteoporosis, or another underlying disease; if so, treating it may not only relieve back pain but also correct the problem. A back brace, physical therapy, and other alternative approaches (see below) may be recommended. In very severe cases, surgery may be necessary to realign the spine (see *Breakthroughs!*, above).

## HOW TO PREVENT THEM

Strive to maintain a natural posture by standing tall with your head straight, abdomen in, and hips tucked under you. An imaginary plumb line should pass from the middle of the skull to the middle of the pelvic cavity. Maintain ideal weight and exercise regularly.

### ALTERNATIVE THERAPIES

**Alexander technique**

An instructor analyzes posture and movements and teaches new ways of sitting, standing, and moving.

**Chiropractic**

Corrective manipulation can realign the facet joints of the spine; this, combined with muscle-strengthening exercises, can correct mild posture defects.

**Physical therapy**

Therapists teach exercises to improve posture by strengthening supporting muscles. They also provide pain-relieving treatments, including hot and cold packs, ultrasound, electrical nerve stimulation, and massage.

**Yoga**

Many yoga exercises emphasize achieving and maintaining good posture. When practiced regularly, these exercises tone and strengthen supporting muscles and make it easier to stand and sit properly.

# Sciatica

### SYMPTOMS

- *Mild to severe pain in the lower back that may extend down a leg.*
- *Burning or shooting leg pain that is worsened by coughing, sneezing, or bending.*
- *Muscle weakness in the buttock, thigh, lower leg, or foot.*
- *Numbness and tingling in the lower leg; loss of knee nerve reflexes.*
- *Possible incontinence and/or sexual dysfunction.*

### WHO IS AT RISK

*Anyone who suffers lower-back pain, a back injury, or a herniated disk can develop sciatica, a type of nerve pain. Also vulnerable are persons who are overweight or sedentary, or whose jobs entail a lot of sitting, standing in one place, or lifting of heavy objects.*

### PIRIFORMIS SYNDROME

This is a painful condition in which part of the sciatic nerve is "pinched" by the piriformis muscle, which lies under the gluteal muscle of the buttock. Normally, the sciatic nerve passes under the piriformis, but in about 15 percent of the population, it travels through the muscle. Muscle swelling or injury can cause nerve impingement, resulting in deep pain in the buttocks or upper thigh. Sitting, squatting, or climbing stairs often worsens the pain, which may also radiate down the leg. Treatment involves exercises to stretch the piriformis muscle; however, any exercise program should be designed by a doctor or physical therapist after the piriformis muscle has been identified as the cause of the pain.

## HOW IT DEVELOPS

The sciatic nerve arises from several points along the lower spinal cord that join to form a single large nerve. This nerve extends through the pelvis, buttock, and down the thigh, where it divides, with a branch running down the side of each leg. Sciatica usually starts with a lower-back strain or pain. At first, the pain may be confined to the back, but if the sciatic nerve is pinched or irritated, shooting or burning pains may develop anywhere along its pathway. Sciatica usually lasts from a few days to several weeks, and then gradually disappears. Sometimes, however, it becomes chronic, and can cause other problems, including numbness, a loss of nerve reflexes, loss of bowel or bladder control, and sexual dysfunction.

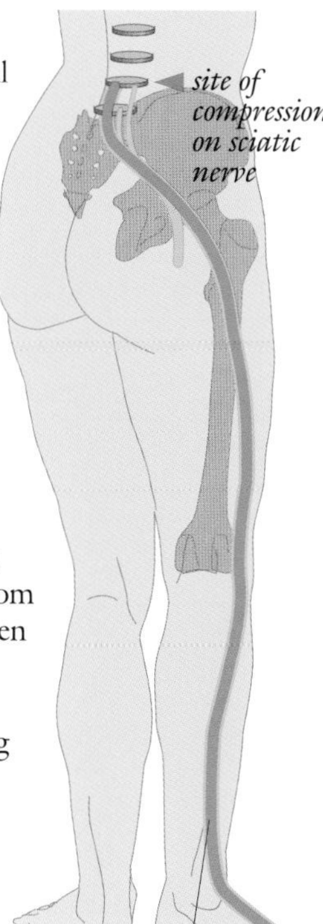


*Irritation or compression of the sciatic nerve near its origin in the back can cause shooting pains down the entire leg and into the foot.*

## WHAT YOU CAN DO

Aspirin, ibuprofen, or another nonsteroidal anti-inflammatory drug (NSAID) can relieve pain and inflammation. A day or two of bed rest may ease pressure on the nerve and promote healing. A heating pad or soaking in a hot bath can also ease pain and relax muscle spasms, which worsen sciatica. Consult a doctor if the pain persists for more than a week (see *Warning!*, above right).

## HOW IT IS TREATED

A doctor will test nerve reflexes in the knee and ankle and order X rays and perhaps CT scans or an MRI to determine the source and extent of the problem. If the nerve is not seriously compressed, conservative treatments will be tried first; these include NSAIDs and physical therapy (see *Alternative Therapies,* above right). Surgery may be necessary if the nerve is compressed or if other therapies fail to relieve the pain.

## HOW TO PREVENT IT

Maintain ideal weight and exercise regularly to maintain muscle strength. When lifting heavy objects, bend from the knees and lift from below while keeping the back straight. If you have a history of back problems, avoid activities that require a lot of twisting, such as bowling or racket sports like tennis or badminton.

### ALTERNATIVE THERAPIES

**Acupuncture**

These treatments are often useful in relieving all types of nerve pain, including sciatica.

**Chiropractic**

Manipulation may help ease pressure on the nerve. Care is needed, however, because chiropractic treatments may worsen pain due to a severely ruptured disk.

**Physical therapy**

Ultrasound, hot and cold packs, electrical nerve stimulation, and hydrotherapy are among the therapies employed by physical therapists to relieve sciatica and lower-back pain.

### WARNING!

***See a doctor as soon as possible if sciatica (or back pain) is accompanied by numbness, paralysis, or loss of bowel or bladder control. Emergency surgery may be needed to prevent permanent nerve damage.***

# Scoliosis

### SYMPTOMS

- *Back looks crooked, especially when bending over; frequent backaches.*
- *Uneven shoulders, legs, or hips; rounded shoulder, swayback, and other postural abnormalities; a shoulder blade (scapula) that sticks out.*
- *Sunken chest and possible breathing or heart problems.*

### WHO IS AT RISK

*Scoliosis usually becomes apparent during puberty, or between the ages of 10 and 16. Two to three percent of children have detectable scoliosis, and 60 to 80 percent are girls. The cause is unknown, but heredity appears to be a factor because it tends to run in families.*

## HOW IT DEVELOPS

Scoliosis is an exaggerated sideways curvature of the spine. Mild scoliosis—defined as a spinal curvature of 10 to 20

### BREAKTHROUGHS!

**New, minimally invasive surgery allows doctors to straighten spines of patients with mild scoliosis by operating through viewing tubes inserted into the back through shorter small punctures, rather than making a long, open incision as in the past. These new procedures cause minimal postsurgical pain, requiring only 48 to 72 hours of morphine, and then oral painkillers for a few more days. Most patients are up and about within a week, and can return to school and normal activities in two to three weeks. No body casts are required, as was the case after scoliosis surgery in the past.**

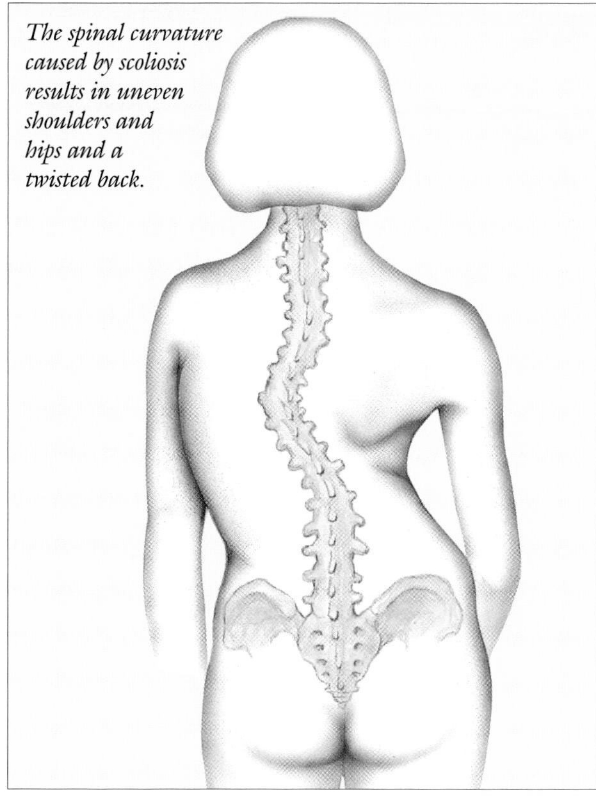

*The spinal curvature caused by scoliosis results in uneven shoulders and hips and a twisted back.*

degrees—usually does not cause problems. A more pronounced curvature of more than 25 degrees may result in uneven shoulders or hips and a visibly crooked back. Moderate to severe scoliosis can cause posture defects and frequent backaches; if the chest cavity is deformed, serious breathing and heart problems may develop.

> **WARNING!**
>
> ***Adolescence is a difficult time to be diagnosed with a chronic disorder such as scoliosis. But it is important that the youngster wear his or her prescribed back brace. Talk to your doctor about the newer braces that can be worn under most clothing.***

## WHAT YOU CAN DO

Swimming, horseback riding, and other exercises that encourage good posture and strengthen muscles can improve posture and help prevent backaches. If a brace is prescribed, it's important to wear it the recommended number of hours each day.

## HOW IT IS TREATED

A doctor—preferably an orthopedist who specializes in back disorders—should be seen regularly to monitor the progress of scoliosis. X rays are taken, and the degree of spinal rotation is measured. Mild to moderate scoliosis is treated with exercise and regular monitoring. If the curvature worsens, a special back brace may be recommended. At first, the brace may be worn 18 or more hours a day; as the curvature stabilizes, it may be needed only at night. In severe cases, surgery may be necessary (see *Breakthroughs!*, p 256).

## HOW TO PREVENT IT

There is no known means of prevention; however, early detection and treatment can prevent severe deformity and other problems.

### ALTERNATIVE THERAPIES

**Physical therapy**

A physical therapist can recommend back-strengthening exercises that help stabilize the spine.

# Spinal Arthritis

### SYMPTOMS

- *Chronic back pain, especially in the lower back.*
- *Morning back stiffness.*
- *As disease progresses, increasing spinal rigidity and a stooped-over posture.*
- *Possible low-grade fever, fatigue, and malaise; eye inflammation and other complications may develop.*

### WHO IS AT RISK

*Spinal arthritis can occur at any age, but it most often begins in young adulthood. Men are afflicted more often than women.*

## HOW IT DEVELOPS

Spinal arthritis, known medically as ankylosing spondylitis, typically begins with pain and inflammation in the sacroiliac joint at the base of the spine. Like rheumatoid arthritis, this disease tends to wax and wane, and its progression varies from one person to another. Typically, however, the joint pain and inflammation tend to spread upward and, in severe cases, eventually affect the entire spine. Over time, new bone tissue gradually replaces the involved joints and fuses the vertebrae, resulting in a rigid, bent-over posture.

In some people, other joints—usually of the shoulders, knees, and hips—are also affected, and iritis—inflammation of the eyes—is a common complication. Some patients experience chest pain that worsens when taking a deep breath, similar to what happens in pleurisy. This is caused by inflammation of the outer lining of the lungs. In addition, spinal arthritis is often associated with psoriasis and inflammatory intestinal disorders, such as ulcerative colitis; the cause for this is unknown.

## WHAT YOU CAN DO

To ease morning stiffness and pain, take a hot shower and then do gentle back stretches. Ibuprofen or other nonsteroidal anti-inflammatory drugs (NSAIDs) can ease pain and reduce inflammation.

To minimize the bent-over posture, do not slouch, and strive to maintain good posture at all times. When sitting, make sure your chair provides good back support. In a car, adjust the head and neck rest to provide maximum support. Tucking a pillow behind the small of your back may help relieve lower-back pain. Try to sleep flat on your back on a firm mattress and without a pillow; if you find this uncomfortable, sleep on your stomach with a thin pillow. In any event, sleep stretched out rather than curled into a fetal position.

*fused (ankylosed) vertebrae*

*In severe spinal arthritis, an overgrowth of the vertebrae causes them to fuse and result in an inability to straighten the back.*

## HOW TO TREAT IT

If nonprescription NSAIDs fail to provide adequate relief, a doctor will prescribe a stronger one, usually indomethacin (Indocid), a potent NSAID that is especially effective against spinal arthritis. Unfortunately, this drug can also cause ulcers and other digestive problems; be sure always to take it with food, and do not exceed the prescribed dosage.

Special orthopedic back and neck braces can help hold the back straight and reduce pain and the risk of spinal deformity. In very severe cases, surgery may be needed to remove some of the bone overgrowth, straighten the spine, and perhaps fuse some of the vertebrae to allow a more normal posture.

### BREAKTHROUGHS!

**Recent discoveries about the causes of spinal arthritis may lead to more effective treatments and a cure. These discoveries include:**

- **A genetic marker—HLA B27—which is a predictor of spinal arthritis.**
- **An apparent link between spinal arthritis and certain intestinal infections, such as salmonella, campylobacter, and klebsiella.**
- **Low blood levels of vitamin E in persons with spinal arthritis, suggesting a possible nutritional link.**

## HOW TO PREVENT IT

There are no known means of prevention because the cause of spinal arthritis is unknown. However, treatment can slow progression of the disease.

### ALTERNATIVE THERAPIES

**Acupuncture**

Treatments reduce pain in many patients; some studies indicate that acupuncture may also reduce inflammation. However, if six treatments fail to bring improvement, it's unlikely that additional ones will help.

**Alexander technique**

An instructor can analyze posture and movements, and teach ways of minimizing slouching, which hastens the bent-over deformity.

**Hydrotherapy**

Whirlpool baths, water massage, and hot showers can reduce pain. Swimming and exercising in warm water help maintain muscle tone and strength without stressing inflamed joints.

**Meditation**

This and other relaxation techniques can help in coping with the pain.

**Nutraceuticals**

Persons with spinal arthritis tend to have low blood levels of vitamin E; supplements of 800 IU a day have been found to reduce inflammation and pain. Because spinal arthritis is often associated with inflammatory bowel disorders, hydrozyme and other digestive enzymes taken with meals may be helpful. Naturopaths also recommend taking one or two capsules of acidophilus a day to help maintain a healthy balance of intestinal organisms. Glucosamine and chondroitin—taken three times a day in dosages of 500 mg each—may help build cartilage, reduce inflammation, and slow progression of the disease. For cautions concerning these nutraceuticals, see *About the Recommendations*, p 7.

### WARNING!

***Inactivity worsens the stiffness of spinal arthritis. Avoid prolonged bed rest and sitting, especially in a slouched position. Get up to stretch and move about every few hours.***

**Physical therapy**

Doctors generally agree that physical therapy is essential in minimizing the effects of spinal arthritis. A physical therapist can design appropriate exercises, which should be done daily to maintain spinal flexibility. In severe cases, an occupational therapist can teach new ways of performing daily activities to maintain independence.

**T'ai chi**

These gentle range-of-motion exercises are ideal for maintaining flexibility.

# Spinal Stenosis

**SYMPTOMS**

- *Chronic dull backache.*
- *Occasional numbness, burning, or sharp pain in the back, buttocks, or legs.*
- *Sensation of leg heaviness or weakness when walking.*
- *In severe cases, loss of bowel or bladder function and possible paralysis.*

**WHO IS AT RISK**

*Anyone can develop spinal stenosis, which involves a narrowing of the canal surrounded by the vertebrae, but the condition is most common among the elderly. Conditions that promote spinal stenosis include a herniated disk, a tumor, infection involving the back, vertebrae fractures, obesity, and inactivity.*

## HOW IT DEVELOPS

The spinal canal, which extends the length of the spine, contains the spinal cord and roots of the nerves that branch off it. A narrowing of the canal can result in compression, irritation, and inflammation of nerves in the area of stenosis. The initial symptoms are usually a constant dull backache and occasional burning or shooting pains that, depending upon the site of the stenosis, extend from the neck down an arm or from the lower back into the hips, buttocks, and down a leg.

## WHAT YOU CAN DO

Aspirin, ibuprofen, or another nonsteroidal anti-inflammatory drug (NSAID) can ease pain and reduce inflammation. Try to lose excess weight and, if you have a tendency to slouch, make an effort to improve your posture. A heating pad or alternating hot and cold packs, gentle stretching, and moderate, low-impact exercise—walking, swimming, cycling—may help, but check with a doctor or physical therapist before embarking on an exercise program if you suffer from chronic back pain.

## HOW TO TREAT IT

Doctors usually need CT scans, an MRI, or a myelogram—X-ray studies taken after injection of a dye—to diagnose spinal stenosis. Treatment varies according to the cause. Surgery is the treatment of choice for stenosis due to a badly herniated disk, tumor, or bone spurs. The goal is to widen the spinal canal and relieve pressure on any compressed and irritated nerves (see *Warning!*, right). Otherwise, doctors are likely to try more conservative treatment first; possible approaches include administration of prescription-strength NSAIDs, injections of a corticosteroid into the affected area, a back brace, and physical therapy (see *Alternative Therapies*, below).

**BREAKTHROUGHS!**

**Many of the new surgical techniques used to treat a herniated disk and certain posture defects also apply to spinal stenosis. See *Surgery,* p 250, and *Breakthroughs!,* p 255, for more details.**

**WARNING!**

***See a doctor immediately if a back problem interferes with bowel or bladder function or causes numbness or paralysis. Immediate surgery may be needed to relieve pressure on a trapped nerve and prevent a permanent loss of function.***

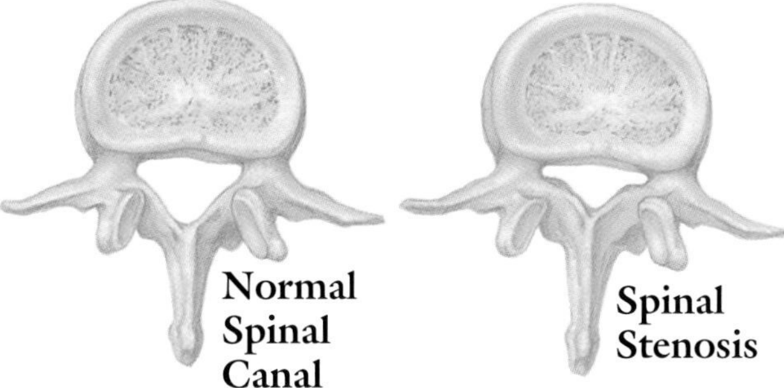


*Spinal stenosis involves a narrowing of the spinal canal, which results in compression of the spinal nerves.*

## HOW TO PREVENT IT

Aside from maintaining ideal weight and engaging in regular exercise, there is not much you can do to prevent spinal stenosis.

### ALTERNATIVE THERAPIES

**Acupuncture**

Treatments have been shown to relieve pain for some patients, but it is unlikely that acupuncture can cure the underlying problem.

**Physical therapy**

Mild to moderate spinal stenosis often can be controlled by physical therapy. Pain may be relieved by ultrasound, diathermy, electrical nerve stimulation, massage, and hot and cold packs. Physical therapists also teach stretching and exercises to improve posture and strengthen supporting muscles. Some also fit patients with various back supports, including special belts that have magnets. It is believed that magnets relieve pain and inflammation by increasing circulation to the area; they may also interfere with the transmission of pain nerve impulses.

# The Pelvis

*The pelvis is structured to provide a strong foundation for the upper body and a protective cavity for the reproductive organs—a common source of pelvic pain. The arrangement of the hip bones also lends itself to special problems, such as dislocations, fractures, and arthritis.*

## Hip Arthritis

### SYMPTOMS

- *Gnawing pain that is most often felt in the groin; may also radiate down the front of the thigh to the knee.*
- *Limping and increasing pain when walking.*
- *Pain and stiffness after prolonged sitting or rest.*

### WHO IS AT RISK

*Osteoarthritis of the hip usually strikes after age 60, and it becomes increasingly common with advancing age. Obesity, congenital hip disorders, and osteoporosis increase the risk. Pain and other symptoms may develop at a younger age in people with rheumatoid arthritis, which often strikes in early adulthood.*

### HOW IT DEVELOPS

Arthritis of the hip, as well as other joints, starts with inflammation and a gradual wearing away of the synovium, the membrane that lines a joint capsule, and cartilage (gristle), the tough, white substance that covers and cushions joints. As the cartilage wears away, the joint bones rub against each other, causing increasing pain. Bony overgrowth adds to the pain and disability. In time, even routine movements—walking, climbing stairs, bending forward, or spreading apart the legs—may be difficult or even impossible.

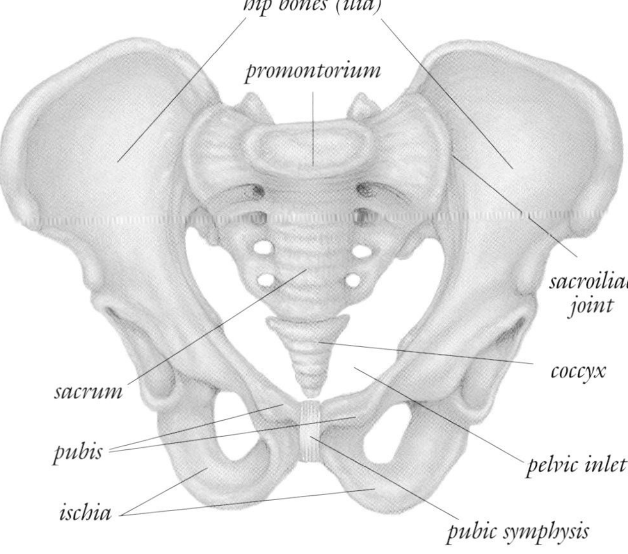


*The pelvis is made up of fused bones that form a protective ring to house the reproductive and lower urinary organs.*

### WHAT YOU CAN DO

Aspirin, ibuprofen, and other nonsteroidal anti-inflammatory drugs (NSAIDs) relieve pain and inflammation; nonaspirin painkillers such as acetaminophen may be sufficient if there is no inflammation. All NSAIDs carry a risk of stomach upset and intestinal bleeding; always take these medications with food (or antacids) and a full glass of water or milk, and abstain from alcohol, which increases the risk of side effects. (Also abstain from alcohol when taking acetaminophen—the combination can cause severe liver damage.) Stop taking NSAIDs and see a doctor promptly if you develop dark, tarry stools, a sign of intestinal bleeding, and/or recurring heartburn.

Strive to balance rest and exercise. If activities like jogging, playing tennis, or aerobic dancing provoke pain, switch to low-impact exercise, such as cycling and swimming. Losing excess weight can help relieve pain; in fact, every pound you lose equals three pounds in stress reduction on the hip joints when walking at a moderate pace.

Consider using a cane. Even our prehistoric ancestors recognized that a walking stick eased the pain of hip arthritis. Today, vanity keeps many people from using a cane; there are, however, many stylish models, including elaborately carved antique ones. Whatever type you choose, be sure to hold it in the opposite hand from the painful side and make sure that it is the right height. If in doubt, have a physical therapist or specialist in a medical supply store check the height.

> **WARNING!**
>
> ***To prevent dislocation of the artificial hip joint, avoid the following movements for at least two months after hip replacement:***
>
> - *Do not lift or flex your leg above the hip (more than 90°).*
> - *When sitting, keep the knees below your hips and do not lean forward.*
> - *When stooping, bend one knee and keep the leg on the affected side behind you. Do not squat.*

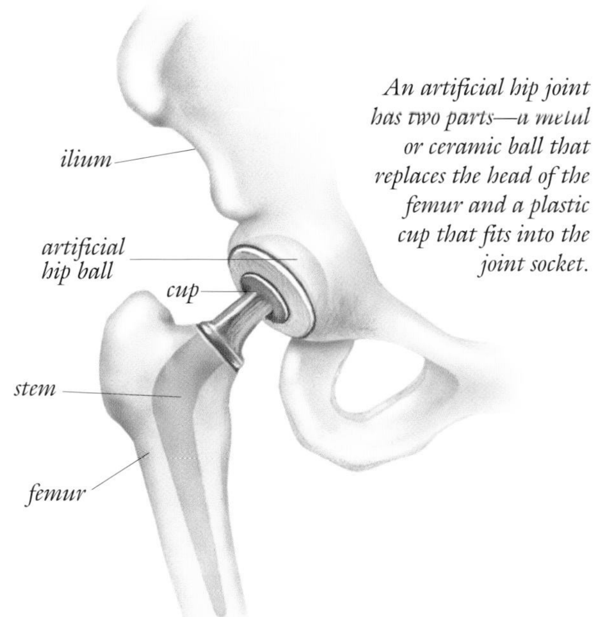


*An artificial hip joint has two parts—a metal or ceramic ball that replaces the head of the femur and a plastic cup that fits into the joint socket.*

## HOW TO TREAT IT

### Medications

If a nonprescription NSAID fails to provide adequate relief, a doctor may recommend a prescription-strength drug. Several NSAIDs may need to be tried before finding one that is effective and does not cause serious side effects. If NSAIDs cannot be tolerated, one of the new $COX_2$ inhibitors (Celebrex or Vioxx) may be tried. These drugs are selective prostaglandin inhibitors; they relieve pain and inflammation, but are less likely to cause bleeding and stomach upset than the older NSAIDs because they do not affect the involved prostaglandins.

### Surgery

The development of total hip replacement surgery in the early 1960s has revolutionized the treatment of severe arthritis of the hip, enabling most patients to again walk without pain. In this operation, which is performed under general anesthesia, the arthritic head of the femur (thigh bone) is removed and replaced with a metal or ceramic ball. This ball is attached to a metal stem that is cemented into the bone's hollow marrow space. The socket part of the hip joint is smoothed out, and a plastic cap is inserted into it. The metal ball fits into this cup.

Although total hip replacement has a 96 percent success rate, there are possible complications. These include:

- Loosening of the implant and loss of bone due to wear and tear on the metal and plastic parts.
- Infection, which is always a danger when a foreign substance is implanted in the body.
- Formation of blood clots, which can result in a pulmonary embolism if a clot lodges in a lung.
- In rare cases, breakage of a ceramic (aluminum or zirconium oxide) component, which requires surgery to replace. (Ceramic is often used in younger patients because it lasts longer than the more traditional cobalt or titanium parts.)

## HOW TO PREVENT IT

Aside from maintaining ideal weight, there is not much you can do to prevent hip arthritis.

### ALTERNATIVE THERAPIES

**Nutraceuticals**

A number of studies show that supplements of 500 mg of glucosamine and 400 to 500 mg of chondroitin—taken three times a day—can ease arthritis symptoms and may slow its progress. Both are substances that the body needs to build and repair cartilage. SAM-e is another natural substance that helps rebuild cartilage—take 200 mg two or three times a day. For cautions concerning glucosamine and SAM-e, see *About the Recommendations*, p 7.

**Physical therapy**

Physical therapy is an essential component of rehabilitation after a total hip replacement. Patients are taught safe ways of moving, especially in the first 8 to 10 weeks after surgery when the artificial joint is "settling in."

### BREAKTHROUGHS!

**Traditional total hip replacement, in which the artificial joint parts are cemented into place, has two major complications: over time, the cement cracks and breaks up, causing the components to loosen and the bone to deteriorate. Newer cementless hip replacement prostheses appear not to have these problems. The surface of the metal parts is porous, resembling coral. Bone tissue grows into the metal pores to hold the implant in place. Because cementless procedures require healthy supporting bone tissue, this procedure usually is not recommended for patients over age 70 and it cannot be done if the patient has osteoporosis.**

# Hip Dislocations/ Dysplasia

### SYMPTOMS

- *Uneven hips, especially when standing with your weight resting on the affected side.*
- *Soft clicking sound as the head of the femur slips out of place.*
- *If uncorrected, a limp and pain in the hip, lower back, and perhaps the knee.*

### WHO IS AT RISK

*About 1 in every 700 babies is born with a dislocated hip, or one in which the head of the femur slips easily out of its ball-and-socket joint. This is referred to as developmental hip dysplasia or dislocation. A breech (feet-first) birth increases the risk of hip dysplasia, and the problem is somewhat more common among girls than boys.*

## HOW IT DEVELOPS

There are three classifications of hip dysplasia:

- **Subluxatable hip**, in which the joint is partially displaced when standing, but goes back into its normal position when lying down.
- **Dislocatable hip**, in which the joint can be fully dislocated but will still slip back into place during rest.
- **Dislocated hip**, in which the joint rests in a dislocated position, and requires manual manipulation to force the femur head into its socket.

At birth, the hip may appear normal, but the joint is easily dislocated. This does not cause obvious problems until the baby starts to stand and walk. At that time, parents may notice that the hips are uneven, with one leg appearing to be longer than the other. Depending upon the severity of the dysplasia, the child may walk with a limp. Pain usually does not develop until the cartilage wears away, which may take 15 to 18 years.

### WARNING!

***All newborn babies should be examined for hip dysplasia. If treatment is delayed until after the child starts to walk, the chances of success are reduced and there is an increased risk of permanent problems, including a limp and joint pain.***

## WHAT YOU CAN DO

If you notice that one or both of your baby's hips seem to slip out of alignment, ask your doctor to refer you to a pediatric orthopedist. In the past, parents often treated congenital hip dysplasia by doubling or tripling the baby's diapers to hold the hips in their proper alignment. Sometimes this works, but doctors now feel that it usually fails to correct the problem, and simply delays more effective treatment.

### BREAKTHROUGHS!

**New lightweight splints and harnesses are more comfortable for the baby than the casts and heavy braces used in the past. If the dysplasia is treated in the first few weeks of life, the problem can often be corrected in six weeks or less, after which the device is worn part-time for a few more weeks, or until X rays show that the joint is normal.**

## HOW TO TREAT IT

If the problem is detected in the first six months of life, the baby will be fitted with a splint or brace that holds the hips in place (see *Breakthroughs!*, below). Surgery to move the joint into its proper alignment is needed if the baby is older than six months. After the operation, a cast is worn for three to six months.

## HOW TO PREVENT IT

Hip dysplasia, which is thought to stem from the baby's position in the womb, cannot be prevented. However, early treatment can prevent later problems, including a limp and joint pain.

### ALTERNATIVE THERAPIES

Physical therapy may be needed after surgical treatment to ensure that the child learns to walk normally.

# Hip Fractures

### SYMPTOMS

- *Sudden, sharp pain in the hip, lower back, or groin.*
- *Pain worsens with leg movement.*
- *Inability to stand or walk.*

### WHO IS AT RISK

*Hip fractures are very common among older women, especially those with severe osteoporosis. There are over 23,000 hip fractures a year in Canada; a recent study estimates the number of hip fractures in the elderly will increase fourfold in the next 45 years. Factors that increase the risk of hip fractures include genetic bone disorders, congenital hip deformities, and bone cancer. Deficiencies of vitamins D and K may increase the risk. People who have an artificial hip joint also have an increased risk of fractures, usually of the upper thigh bone.*

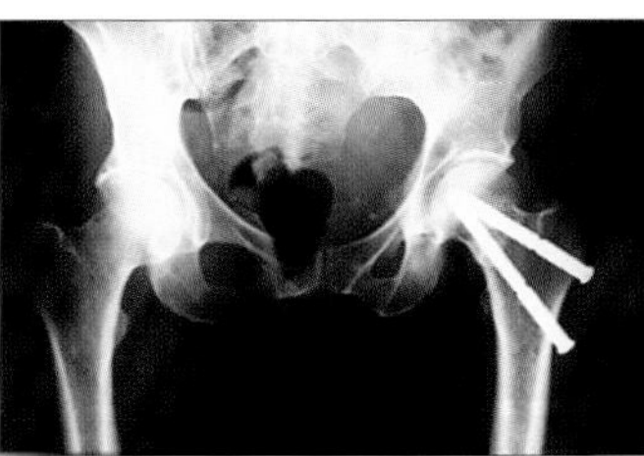

*Hip fractures often require insertion of surgical pins or screws to hold the bones in place while they heal.*

## HOW IT DEVELOPS

Hip fractures most often occur in or near the joint where the head of the femur (thigh bone) fits into the pelvic bone. Most are due to falls, but an older person with weakened bones may suffer a spontaneous hip fracture.

When this happens, a sudden movement or even a sneeze causes the fracture. The person then falls and assumes that it was the fall that caused the break when, in reality, it was the other way around.

Complications of a hip fracture include tissue death (see *Warning!*, below), infection, and formation of blood clots, which can lead to phlebitis, pulmonary embolism, or a stroke. An average of 7 percent of deaths occur during a patient's acute hospitalization for hip surgery.

## WHAT YOU CAN DO

Seek immediate medical help by calling 911 or your local Emergency Medical Service (EMS). If you suspect someone has a fractured hip, do not attempt to move him or her unless it is absolutely necessary. Also, don't try to straighten a leg that is oddly positioned. Instead, keep the person warm and quiet until help arrives.

## HOW TO TREAT IT

A doctor will immediately take X rays to determine the type and extent of the fracture. Morphine or another strong pain medication may be given. A stress fracture of the hip or head of the femur will usually heal with a few weeks of bed rest. But most hip fractures require surgical treatment to set the broken bone and pin or screw it into place so that it can heal properly. If the head of the femur is badly fractured, it will be removed and an artificial hip joint inserted.

Healing requires a few weeks of bed rest. To prevent blood clots from forming in the leg, surgical stockings or a pneumatic leg device may be worn to increase circulation. Broken bones are invariably painful; prescription painkillers may be needed.

### WARNING!

***A hip fracture often interferes with blood flow to the head of the femur, especially if the fracture fails to heal. This can lead to tissue death (avascular necrosis). Symptoms include increasing pain in the groin or buttock, especially when standing. Prompt surgery is needed to prevent permanent tissue damage.***

## HOW TO PREVENT IT

Your best preventive measures, especially if you are a woman over age 50, is to do whatever you can to minimize bone loss due to osteoporosis (see *Osteoporosis*, p 252). Engage in strength-training and weight-bearing exercise, such as walking, which not only strengthens bones but also improves your sense of balance.

Protect yourself against falls. Use extra care when walking on icy or uneven surfaces. Take up slippery throw rugs, and make sure that stairs and walking areas are clear of clutter. Always turn on a light if you get up during the night, and install nonslip mats and grab bars in tubs and showers. Avoid taking long-acting sedatives, which can affect balance, and wear corrective eyeglasses if you have a vision problem. Abstain from alcohol or use it only in moderation; excessive alcohol interferes with balance and also promotes osteoporosis.

### BREAKTHROUGHS!

**Experiments with calcium-phosphate and Norian SRS bone cements show that they may be preferable to surgical pins, wires, and screws in treating some hip fractures. These cements have been used mostly for wrist fractures, but animal studies indicate that they also work well in hip fractures and reduce the risk of infection and other complications.**

### ALTERNATIVE THERAPIES

**Nutraceuticals**

A broken bone requires extra calcium to heal; you should get at least 1200 to 1500 mg a day. You should also take 400 to 800 IU of vitamin D, 300 micrograms of vitamin K, 400 to 500 mg of magnesium, and 1000 mg of vitamin C. Some calcium supplements also contain boron and additional minerals, such as zinc, copper, and manganese, that promote bone health. For cautions concerning these nutraceuticals, see *About the Recommendations*, p 7.

**Physical therapy**

Rehabilitation following a broken hip requires intensive 1physical therapy to regain strength and to learn how to walk again, especially if the hip joint has been replaced.

### DEALING WITH PUBIC PAIN

Pain experienced in the groin and anus often originates in or near the pubic symphysis, the bony area in the front and middle of the hip. The problem is especially common among athletes who engage in strenuous play without adequate training.

- Get in shape before the season for your sport begins. Especially important are exercises to strengthen the abdominal and thigh muscles.
- Warm up and stretch before an event, and stretch at the end of play. Again, pay special attention to the abdominal muscles and the muscles that move the thighs (the adductors).
- Rest for a few days if pubic pain develops. The area is difficult to ice, but a whirlpool bath or soaking in tepid water may help. Anti-inflammatory medications, such as ibuprofen or naproxen, reduce pain and inflammation.

If the pain persists, consult a physical therapist or a doctor who specializes in sports medicine. In severe cases, surgery is needed to tighten the large abdominal muscles and relax the adductors.

# Leg and Knee Pain

*Although our legs are designed to bear the body's weight while carrying out myriad tasks, they are also vulnerable to numerous painful disorders. Among the more common are arthritis, painful knees, shin splints, muscle cramps, and circulatory disorders.*

## Bone Tumors

### SYMPTOMS

- *Localized bone pain, ranging from mild and intermittent to a constant, deep ache.*
- *Increasing pain that is not relieved by painkillers.*
- *Bone pain that is most intense at night.*
- *Painful swelling and possible deformity of a leg bone or joint.*
- *Development of a limp.*
- *Possible fractures, unexplained fatigue, and low-grade fever.*

### WHO IS AT RISK

*Bone tumors—both cancerous and benign—are most common in children and young adults. They usually develop during periods of rapid growth, such as during puberty. The leg bones are most often affected, although some tumors develop in the spine, arms, ribs, and other bones.*

### HOW IT DEVELOPS

There are several types of bone tumors; among the more common are:

- **Osteogenic sarcomas**, which are bone cancers that grow outward. They usually develop in one of the leg bones.
- **Chondrosarcomas**, which are also cancerous, start in the cartilage and form a tender mass, often in the knee and upper thighs, as well as the shoulders and trunk.
- **Osteochondromas**, which are benign tumors made up of bone and cartilage. They usually develop close to the knee or elbow.

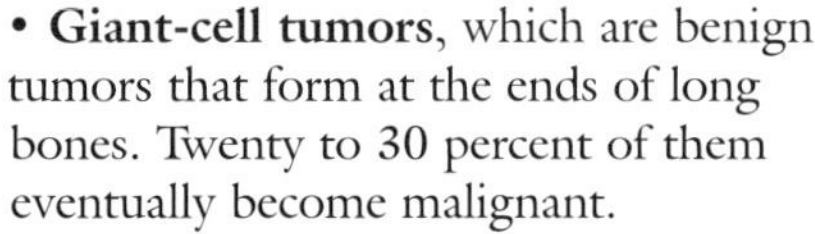

- **Giant-cell tumors**, which are benign tumors that form at the ends of long bones. Twenty to 30 percent of them eventually become malignant.
- **Fibromatous tumors**, which are benign growths of fibrous tissue along the long bones. They often cause fractures.

femur

tibia

fibula

tarsals

metatarsals

phalanges

**Bones of the Legs**

*The legs are made up of the body's longest and strongest bones. In fact, a cubic inch of compact thigh bone can bear 8 to 10 tons of weight, making it four times stronger than reinforced concrete.*

### BREAKTHROUGHS!

**Benign and slow-growing bone tumors often can be cured by new limb-sparing procedures. The tumor and a margin of healthy tissue are removed and replaced with a metal prosthesis or a bone graft from a cadaver. If the patient is a child whose growth is not complete, a special expandable implant is used. These implants can be lengthened later to keep pace with growth of the other leg.**

### WHAT YOU CAN DO

There is no effective self-treatment for bone tumors; see a doctor—preferably an orthopedist—as soon as possible if symptoms suggest one. Because bone tumors can cause severe pain, talk to your doctor about effective pain control, which may call for referral to a cancer-pain specialist and use of a morphine pump or other narcotic medications.

### HOW TO TREAT IT

Most bone tumors are treated with surgical removal of the tumor, which is often followed by radiation treatments and perhaps chemotherapy as well. In the past, the surgery usually entailed amputation of the affected leg, but now this can often be avoided with new limb-sparing operations (see *Breakthroughs!*, left). In some instances, radiation is administered before surgery to shrink the tumor and increase the likelihood of saving the limb. Depending upon the type of bone cancer, chemotherapy may also be administered, either before or after surgery. Advanced bone cancer may be treated with high-dose chemotherapy and a bone-marrow transplant. Strong painkillers are needed until the bone heals.

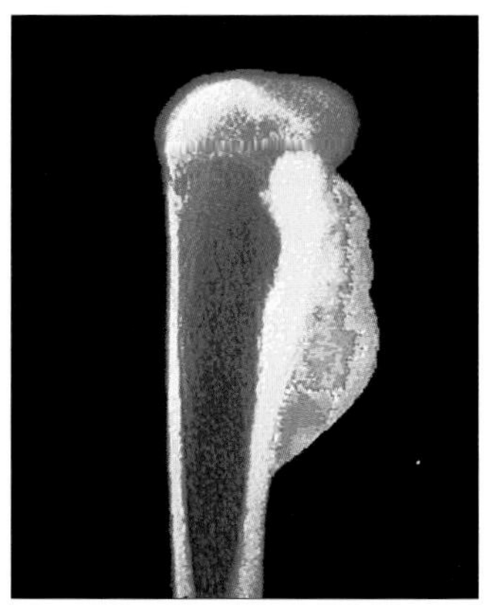

*X rays, such as the one above, can detect a bone tumor, but only a biopsy can determine whether it is cancerous or benign.*

## HOW TO PREVENT IT

There are no known means of preventing bone tumors.

### ALTERNATIVE THERAPIES

**Acupuncture**

Acupuncture, either alone or along with meditation, guided imagery, meditation, or self-hypnosis, is among the pain therapies offered at many cancer centers.

**Physical therapy**

Physical therapy is an important aspect of rehabilitation after removal of a bone tumor. If amputation is necessary, occupational therapy may also be needed to learn new ways of carrying out daily activities.

**WARNING!**

***Nagging bone pain in a child or adolescent is often dismissed as "growing pains." But any recurrent or chronic bone pain should be checked by a doctor to rule out more serious causes, including a tumor.***

# Broken Leg

**SYMPTOMS**

- *Sudden, intense pain at the site of the break.*
- *Bruising, swelling, and possible deformity of the leg.*
- *Inability to bear weight on the affected limb.*

**WHO IS AT RISK**

*Broken legs are among the most common types of fractures, which can happen to anyone who suffers a bad fall or is involved in a car accident. As with other types of fractures, the elderly who have osteoporosis—a thinning of the bones—are the most vulnerable. Other high-risk groups include persons with certain types of bone tumors and other bone disorders, skiers, and in-line skaters.*

## HOW IT DEVELOPS

Although the leg bones are very strong and they can bear many times the body's weight, they will break when they sustain a heavy blow or are twisted during a fall. The person immediately experiences sharp, intense pain, especially when trying to stand or move the affected limb. The skin over the break will be discolored and there may be marked swelling. In a compound fracture, the bone protrudes through the skin; there may be severe bleeding and there is a high risk of infection.

## WHAT YOU CAN DO

If you are called upon to give first aid to a person with a broken leg, call 911 or the local Emergency Medical Service (EMS). Keep the person lying down with the leg extended and flat. If you must move the person, fashion a splint on both sides of the leg; you can use broom handles, boards, rolled newspapers, or other firm objects (see *Improvising a Splint and Sling*, p 224). If the break is in the lower leg, the splint should extend from the knee to the ankle; splint the entire leg if the thigh or knee is fractured. Keep the person warm and quiet until help arrives.

**WARNING!**

***Make sure your crutches are adjusted for your height and length of arms. Never rest your weight on the underarm portion of the crutches, which can damage the nerves in your arms. Instead, use the hand rests to bear your weight.***

An ice pack laid gently over the site of the fracture can numb pain and reduce swelling. If the skin is broken and there is bleeding, cover it with a clean cloth and try to stop the bleeding by applying pressure a few inches above the break. Do not try to reposition the bone; this can increase tissue damage and the risk of infection.

## HOW TO TREAT IT

A doctor will take X rays and perhaps order a CT scan or an MRI to assess the extent of the fracture. An injection of a local anesthetic, morphine, meperidine (Demerol), or another strong painkiller may be given.

Depending upon the type of fracture, the broken bone will be set with either a *closed reduction,* in which the doctor manipulates the broken pieces into a position where they can knit together, or an *open reduction,* which requires general anesthesia and surgery. An incision is made to expose the broken bone, and surgical wires, screws, or pins may be used to hold the pieces together. Sometimes a thin metal rod is inserted in the marrow space to support the broken bone and allow healing.

After the bone is set, the broken bone must be immobilized so it can heal. A fractured thigh may require traction, which uses weights and pulleys to keep the leg elevated and immobile. More often, however, the leg is encased in a plaster cast. Depending upon the site and nature of the break, the cast may extend from the upper thigh to the ankle. At any rate, the toes will be left exposed so the doctor can check to make sure that the cast is not so tight that it is interfering with blood flow. The plaster cast is usually worn for a month or so and,

**BREAKTHROUGHS!**

**Children who suffer a broken leg often end up with limbs of uneven length. A recent study found that this can often be prevented by using special rods to stabilize the broken bone while it heals. There are also new leg-lengthening procedures that can correct uneven legs, which may be preferable to the older approach of shortening the longer leg.**

if X rays show that the bone is healing, it then may be replaced with a lighter, fiberglass cast, and finally a shorter, weight-bearing cast.

Demerol or another narcotic painkiller is often needed for a few days until the intense pain subsides. After that, codeine, acetaminophen, or other milder painkillers will suffice. To prevent blood clots and a possible pulmonary embolism, aspirin or a stronger anticlotting drug, such as warfarin (Coumadin), may be given. The skin under the cast often itches, especially in hot, humid weather. Avoid trying to scratch it; instead, ask your doctor to prescribe an anti-itch medication.

### ALTERNATIVE THERAPIES

**Hydrotherapy**

After the cast is removed, exercising in water may be easier than working out on land. Whirlpool baths and underwater massage can stimulate circulation and ease muscle spasms and soreness, which commonly occur after a long period of inactivity.

**Nutraceuticals**

Doctors typically recommend 1200 to 1800 mg of calcium a day; supplements that provide 600 mg of calcium along with vitamin D, magnesium, copper, zinc, boron, and manganese promote bone healing. Vitamin C, usually 500 to 1000 mg a day, also helps build bone. For cautions concerning these nutraceuticals, see *About the Recommendations*, p 7. The diet should provide at least 5 to 10 servings of fruits and vegetables a day and two or three servings of lean meat, fish, or other high-protein foods.

**Physical therapy**

After the cast is removed, physical therapy may be needed to help rebuild leg muscles. Massage and ultrasound treatments can alleviate muscle spasms and increase circulation.

**Types of Leg Fractures**

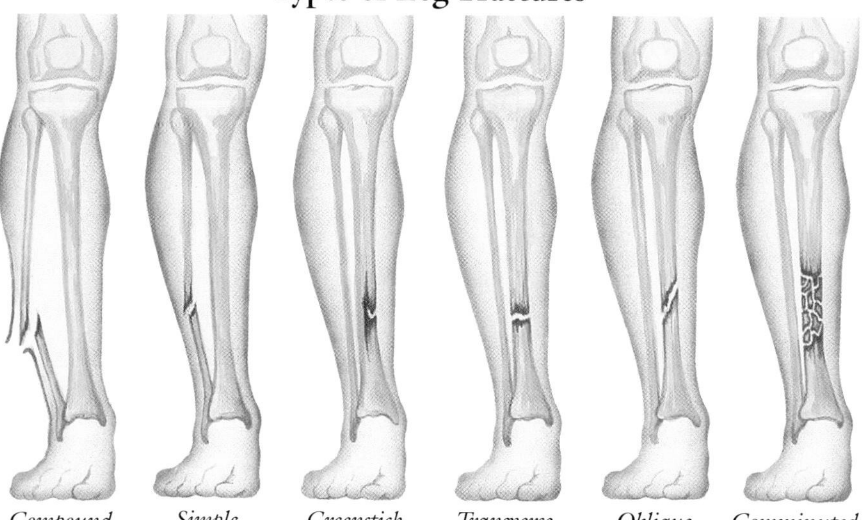

*Compound* *Simple* *Greenstick* *Transverse* *Oblique* *Comminuted*

# Calf Pain/ Shin Splints

### SYMPTOMS

- *Pain, ranging from intermittent discomfort to severe achiness, in the lower leg.*
- *Possible inflammation and a hard swelling in the area that is painful.*

### WHO IS AT RISK

*Runners, hikers, cyclists, dancers, and others who use their legs a lot are the most common victims of the lower leg pain referred to as shin splints. The problem can be worsened by wearing poorly cushioned shoes and running or exercising on hard, unyielding surfaces such as concrete. Conditions that put abnormal stress on the legs—for example, poor posture, flat feet, knock-knees, or bow legs—increase the risk of developing shin splints.*

## HOW IT DEVELOPS

Shin splints are generally caused by an imbalance in the strength and size of the muscles that extend from the knee to the ankle. Overuse of these muscles can result in small tears, scarring, and disabling pain, most often along the shinbone (tibia) at the inside front of the lower leg. Pain may also develop along the inner back of the calf.

Sometimes shin splints are related to a condition called *compartment syndrome,* in which an overtrained muscle grows too large for its outer covering, or fascia sheath. This problem is characterized by tingling pain that often lasts for hours after exercising.

## WHAT YOU CAN DO

Ice packs, applied for 15 to 20 minutes several times a day, can reduce swelling and inflammation. To ease pain, take aspirin (for adults only) or another anti-inflammatory medication. Rest from the activity that precipitated the problem for a few days; then resume it gradually. If the pain recurs, see a doctor.

## HOW TO TREAT IT

A doctor may take X rays to rule out a stress fracture; an MRI or a bone scan may be ordered if a tumor or another

**WARNING!**

*Pain concentrated in a specific area of the shinbone may be due to a stress fracture rather than shin splints. If the leg pain persists and the area is tender to the touch, see a doctor. X rays can determine whether the pain is due to a stress (hairline) fracture.*

bone abnormality is suspected. A corticosteroid injection can quickly relieve inflammation and swelling due to shin splints. A week or two of using crutches or wearing an air cast may be recommended to promote healing.

Surgery may be needed if swelling in the muscle compartment is reducing blood flow. The procedure, which can usually be done under local anesthesia, involves opening the fascia sheath to allow blood to flow freely to the underlying muscle tissue.

## HOW TO PREVENT IT

Make sure that your shoes are properly fitted and appropriate for your chosen exercise. Warm up before exercising and spend at least 10 minutes stretching after each session, paying special attention to the muscles of the lower leg, heels, knees, ankles, and toes. If possible, alternate your exercise activities to give your leg muscles a chance to recover between sessions. Avoid long, uphill runs and exercising on hard, unyielding surfaces. If the pain recurs after rest and treatment, consider switching to an activity, such as swimming or rowing, that doesn't place as much stress on the lower-leg muscles.

### ALTERNATIVE THERAPIES

**Magnets**

Therapeutic magnets may ease the leg pain and reduce inflammation; they are thought to work by increasing blood flow to the area.

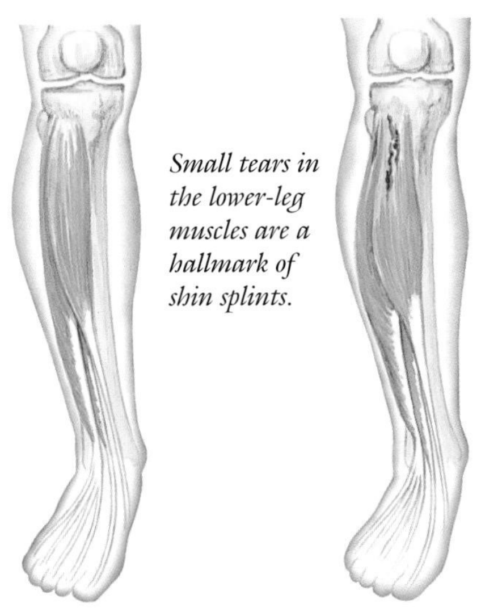

*Small tears in the lower-leg muscles are a hallmark of shin splints.*

*Normal leg muscles* *Shin splints*

**Physical therapy**

Ultrasound or diathermy can relieve pain by producing localized deep heat and increasing circulation. These treatments may be alternated with cold packs. Physical therapists also teach exercises to improve muscle balance and stretch tight, swollen muscles.

**BREAKTHROUGHS!**

**A new diagnostic technique called laser Doppler flowmetry (LDF) is enabling doctors to diagnose chronic compartment syndrome more accurately. The Doppler studies measure changes in muscle blood flow; reduced circulation lasting more than 10 minutes after exercise indicates compartment syndrome rather than ordinary shin splints.**

# Intermittent Claudication

### SYMPTOMS

- *Recurrent aches, cramps, or leg pain, usually in the calf.*
- *Pain worsens when walking or going upstairs or uphill.*
- *Pain may spread to the foot or upward to the thigh, buttocks, or hips.*

### WHO IS AT RISK

*Intermittent claudication, which is caused by reduced circulation in the legs, is a disease of older people, especially those who have arteriosclerosis (hardening of the arteries) and/or diabetes. Smoking, elevated blood cholesterol, high blood pressure, obesity, and inactivity also increase the risk.*

## HOW IT DEVELOPS

Leg cramps and pain when walking or going upstairs are usually the first symptoms. The pain goes away after a few minutes of rest, but recurs when the person resumes the activity that provoked it. The leg cramps and pain are due to a narrowing of the leg blood vessels, which are unable to meet the muscles' demand for more oxygen-rich blood during exercise. The pain is similar to what happens during an attack of angina when the heart muscle becomes starved for oxygen. In time, the person may have to stop every few steps to allow the pain to subside.

The skin in the blood-deprived area may become pale, dry, and scaly; in severe cases, leg ulcers may develop. The foot often feels cold. Sometimes the pain extends to the foot or up the leg to the thigh, hip, or buttock on the affected side.

## BREAKTHROUGHS!

**The Food and Drug Administration in the U.S. has approved cilostazol (Pletal) as a new medication for intermittent claudication. The drug works by inhibiting platelet clumping (clotting) and dilating (widening) small blood vessels, thereby increasing the amount of blood flowing through them. Improvement should be noted in 12 weeks; if not, the drug is unlikely to work.**

**Pletal should not be taken by patients who suffer from congestive heart failure. Similar drugs have been found to increase the risk of death. In Canada, Pletal is currently assigned an "investigational drug" status.**

## WHAT YOU CAN DO

Resting for a few minutes will alleviate the pain and leg cramps; massaging the leg increases blood flow and relaxes tensed muscles. If you smoke, make every effort to quit. Lose excess weight and talk to your doctor about daily low-dose aspirin therapy.

Regular exercise can improve leg circulation and endurance. Walking, swimming, or using a stationary bicycle or rowing machine all provide good leg exercise and help increase blood flow. Exercise for a few minutes each day, and try to force yourself to do a bit more each time. For example, if pain develops after walking two blocks, slow down and try to go a few steps farther before stopping to rest. The next time, extend the distance a few more steps. Keep doing this until you can walk for 10, then 15, or even 20 minutes without pain. This type of exercise conditioning encourages the growth of new vessels (collateral circulation) to bring more blood to the area.

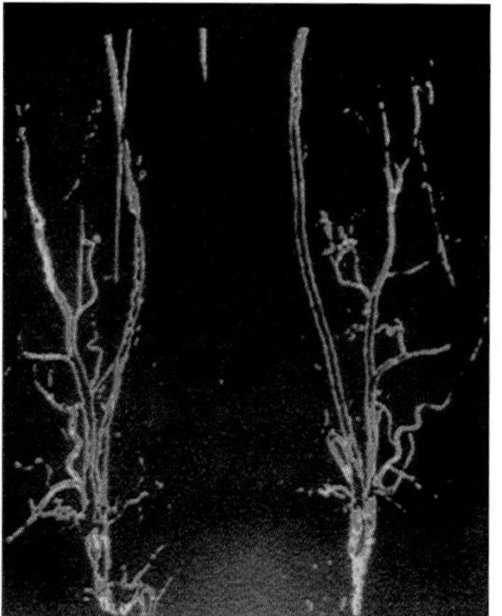

*The arteriogram at the left shows normal leg circulation; the one at the right indicates severely blocked blood vessels.*

## HOW TO TREAT IT

A doctor may order Doppler ultrasound, a test that assesses blood flow, and an angiogram, X rays of the blood vessels taken after injection of a dye, to determine the severity of the blocked arteries. Blood-thinning (antiplatelet) drugs are often prescribed; patients who cannot tolerate aspirin may be given clopidogrel (Plavix), a drug that also helps prevent stroke and heart attacks. Pentoxifylline (Trental), a drug that increases blood flow, helps some patients. Other disorders, such as diabetes, high blood pressure, or elevated cholesterol levels, will be treated.

If these conservative measures do not work, the next step is usually balloon angioplasty. A balloon-tipped catheter is inserted into the diseased artery and the balloon is inflated at the site of the blockage(s) to expand the vessel and allow more blood to flow through it. Expandable stents—devices that keep a blood vessel open—may be implanted to increase blood flow. Other procedures may include endartectomy, in which a surgeon opens the artery and removes fatty deposits, or bypass surgery, in which a graft of a healthy blood vessel from elsewhere in the body or a plastic tube is used to carry blood around the blocked area.

## WARNING!

***Severely reduced leg circulation can lead to tissue death and require an amputation. Be especially alert for such warning signs as very cold feet, skin ulcers that do not heal, numbness, tingling, and a bluish tinge to the toenails.***

## HOW TO PREVENT IT

The preventive measures are the same as those that lower the risk of a stroke or heart attack: Do not smoke, maintain ideal weight, exercise regularly, and consume a low-fat diet built around fruits, vegetables, and starches. If you have high blood cholesterol, diabetes, and/or high blood pressure, work with your doctor to bring them under control.

### ALTERNATIVE THERAPIES

**Herbal medicine**

Standardized ginkgo biloba extract (GBE), up to 240 mg a day, increases peripheral blood flow and has been shown to improve intermittent claudication. Do not take GBE if you are also taking warfarin (Coumadin) or other anticoagulant drugs; the combination can cause bleeding. For cautions, see *About the Recommendations*, p 7.

**Nutraceuticals**

Vitamin E, in dosages of 400 to 800 IU a day, has been shown to reduce leg pain and other symptoms; it works by inhibiting platelet clumping and increasing blood flow to the peripheral arteries. Vitamin C strengthens blood vessel walls and may help promote collateral circulation; the usual dosage is 1000 mg a day; reduce the amount if it provokes diarrhea. For other cautions, see *About the Recommendations*, p 7.

# Knee Pain

### SYMPTOMS

- *Pain, swelling, and inflammation of the knee joint and/or kneecap (patella).*
- *Morning knee stiffness and increasing inability to move the knee.*

- *Clicking sensation when the knee is straightened.*
- *Locking, weakness, or instability of the knee.*

### WHO IS AT RISK

*At some point, almost everyone experiences knee pain. Athletes often develop so-called runner's knee, a condition marked by inflammation and pain from overworked tendons and a tendency to overpronate (rolling the foot inward when walking or running). Torn knee ligaments are very common injuries among skiers and other persons who may twist a knee when falling. Among persons over the age of 50 or so, chronic knee pain is usually due to osteoarthritis, a wearing away of the cartilage that cushions the knee. Obesity increases the risk of knee problems; so do structural abnormalities, such as flat feet or uneven leg lengths. (For a more detailed listing, see the table* Common Knee Problems at a Glance, *p 270.)*

## HOW IT DEVELOPS

The knee is a complicated joint that must bear the entire body's weight and is instrumental in almost all leg movements. It forms at the juncture of the femur (thigh bone), fibula (the thinner bone of the lower leg), and the tibia (the shinbone); the patella (kneecap) sits over the joint, providing extra leverage to the leg muscles and added protection to the underlying bones and tissue. Cartilage and pads of connective tissue called the *menisci* separate and cushion the ends of the bones forming the knee; ligaments—strong elastic bands of tissues that connect the bones and muscles—also give the knee strength and stability.

Pain as a result of injury, excessive wear and tear, the aging process, or a variety of disorders, can develop in any or all of these knee structures. Depending upon the cause, the pain can come on abruptly with acute inflammation, swelling, and difficulty moving the joint. In other cases, it develops slowly over a period of many years. Some of the more common causes and their manifestations include:

- **Arthritis**, which is marked by gradually worsening pain and difficulty using the knee. Inflammation often develops, which accelerates the joint destruction.
- **Infection**, in which bacteria or other organisms invade the joint and cause severe inflammation, swelling, pain, and often fever and chills. Examples include Lyme disease, rheumatic fever, and gonococcal arthritis.
- **Kneecap injuries and disorders**, which range from a fractured patella to softening and wearing away of the knee cartilage (chondromalacia patellae), usually due to an injury or poor alignment of the kneecap.
- **Tendinitis and bursitis**—so-called housemaid's knee—which are especially common among runners and persons who kneel a lot or engage in other activities that stress the knee tendons, ligaments, and bursas.
- **Torn ligaments**, in which there is sudden, severe pain, swelling, and joint instability.

## WHAT YOU CAN DO

See a doctor as soon as possible if the knee pain develops abruptly and is accompanied by other symptoms, such as marked swelling, inflammation, and a high fever (see *Warning!*, p 271). An injury in which the kneecap may be broken or the ligaments torn also demands prompt medical attention. Knee tendinitis or bursitis usually can be self-treated with rest, ice packs, and perhaps an elastic bandage; an anti-inflammatory medication such as aspirin or ibuprofen can ease pain and reduce inflammation.

Nonprescription painkillers can also help control mild to moderate arthritis of the knee. Doctors recommend acetaminophen as the first-choice drug for osteoarthritis in which there is no inflammation. However, if the joint is swollen and warm to the touch—signs of inflammation—aspirin, ibuprofen, or another nonsteroidal anti-inflammatory drug (NSAID) should be used. Regular low-impact exercise—for example, walking, swimming, or cycling—is an important component in controlling arthritis pain and maintaining joint flexibility. Exercise is also important in controlling chondromalacia, in which the goal is to strengthen the leg muscles to help hold the kneecap in its proper alignment.

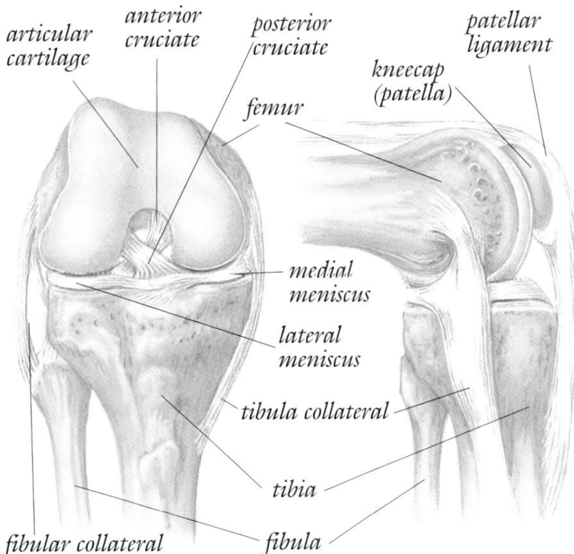


**Structures of the Knee**

*The knee is a hinge joint made up of the three major leg bones and numerous ligaments. The kneecap (patella) overrides the joint and is protected by a sheath of ligaments. The illustration at the left is a frontal view of the knee when it's bent at a 90-degree angle; the illustration at the right is a profile view of a bent knee.*

# Common Knee Problems at a Glance

| DISORDER | SYMPTOMS | CAUSES | TREATMENTS |
|---|---|---|---|
| Arthritis | Increasing pain and disability; possible swelling, inflammation, and deformity. | Inborn defect in the knee cartilage coupled with wear and tear of normal use; sometimes due to repeated knee stress or trauma. | NSAIDs to reduce pain and inflammation; combination of rest and exercise, physical therapy, and nutritional supplements; possible corticosteroid injections into the knee. In severe cases, knee-replacement surgery. |
| Chondromalacia patellae | Increasing knee pain, especially when going up and down stairs; a feeling of grittiness under the kneecap. | Trauma, overuse, muscle weakness, malalignment of the kneecap. | Avoid high-impact activities and bending the knee more than 90 degrees; muscle-strengthening exercises; possible arthroscopic surgery to remove cartilage fragments and correct kneecap alignment. |
| Knee tendinitis | Pain, inflammation, and swelling. | Overuse, falls, muscle injuries; repeated stress from kneeling or jumping. | Rest, ice packs, NSAIDs to ease pain and reduce inflammation; torn patellar tendon requires surgical repair; partial tear may heal with immobilization of the knee in a cast. |
| Osgood-Schlatter disease | Pain, usually just below the knee joint; possible painful, bony lump on the upper tibia. | Repeated stress or injury to growth area of the upper tibia; usually affects adolescent boys who do a lot of running and jumping. | Apply ice to relieve pain; limit running, jumping, and other activities that cause pain. The disorder usually heals itself and disappears when growth is complete. |
| Osteochondritis dissecans | Sharp knee pain; weakness and locking of knee joint. | May be hereditary or due to an injury that cuts blood flow to bone (avascular necrosis). | Usually heals itself; in severe cases, surgery may be needed to repair damaged cartilage and stimulate blood flow. |
| Plica syndrome | Pain, swelling, clicking sensation in the knee; joint weakness or locking. | Remnants of synovial tissue (plicae) are irritated by overuse or injury, resulting in pain and inflammation. | NSAIDs to reduce pain and inflammation; application of an ice pack, then wrapping the knee with an elastic bandage; physical therapy to strengthen muscles. If problem persists, a corticosteroid may be injected into the knee. |
| Popliteal cysts | Knee pain, swelling, and tenderness; joint instability; weakness of quadriceps. | Cyst forms near the popliteal artery at the back of the knee. | Needle is inserted into cyst to drain it. |
| Runner's knee | Knee pain that worsens with movement. | Overuse and tendency to overpronate, resulting in a twisting of the lower leg that pulls kneecap inward as quadriceps pull it outward. | Stop running until pain disappears; do exercises to stretch the hamstrings and quadriceps; use orthotic inserts in shoes to correct overpronation. |
| Torn cruciate ligament (ACL or PCL) | Popping sound when injury occurs; leg may buckle when attempting to stand; pain and swelling may develop in a day or so. | A twisting fall; a torn ACL is very common among skiers and soccer players. | An incomplete tear is treated with physical therapy to strengthen muscles and promote healing; a complete tear usually requires surgery to graft the ligament, using either a nearby tendon from the patient's own leg, or if this is not feasible, a cadaver graft. |

## Common Knee Problems at a Glance (con't.)

| DISORDER | SYMPTOMS | CAUSES | TREATMENTS |
|---|---|---|---|
| Torn medial or lateral collateral ligaments. | Sudden popping sound and sideways buckling of the knee, followed by pain and swelling. | A blow, usually to the outer side of the knee; common injury among hockey and football players. | Collateral sprains are treated with ice, NSAIDs, and a brace to stabilize knee; severe tear or sprain requires surgical repair. |
| Torn meniscus | Pain, especially when knee is straightened or during exercise; severe pain and swelling if part of meniscus is lodged between the femur and tibia; knee may lock, click or buckle. | Trauma due to twisting, such as falling while skiing. | Minor tears heal with rest and physical therapy; NSAIDs relieve pain and reduce inflammation; larger tears require surgical repair. |

## HOW TO TREAT IT

### Medications

Again, treatment varies depending upon the underlying cause. If the painful knee is badly swollen and inflamed and the doctor suspects **infectious arthritis**, he or she may insert a hollow needle to drain off (aspirate) some of the fluid. This immediately relieves some of the pain; the doctor will also have the fluid analyzed to identify the infecting organism (and rule out gout and other disorders) and then prescribe an appropriate antibiotic.

If nonprescription painkillers fail to adequately relieve knee **osteoarthritis**, a prescription-strength NSAID may be tried. NSAIDs often cause stomach and bleeding problems, in which case one of the newer $COX_2$ inhibitors (Celebrex or Vioxx) may be prescribed. A corticosteroid injection into the knee can also give prompt pain relief and reduce inflammation. However, these injections should be limited to two or three a year; otherwise, there is a risk of increased knee damage. A newer approach entails injecting a thick, gel-like substance into the knee to bolster its natural joint (synovial) fluid (see *Breakthroughs!*, p 272).

**WARNING!**

***Infectious arthritis often attacks knees that are already weakened by arthritis. See a doctor as soon as possible if the knee pain suddenly worsens, the joint is red, swollen, and warm to the touch, and you develop a fever. Prompt treatment is needed to prevent the infection from causing permanent joint damage and spreading to other parts of the body.***

### Surgery

Knee surgery has changed markedly in recent years with the advent of arthroscopy, a procedure in which surgery is performed using an arthroscope (a viewing tube that is equipped with a miniature video camera and tiny instruments) and a video monitor. **Torn ligaments** and **menisci** can now be repaired without having to make a large incision; there is also less pain, a reduced risk of infection and other complications, and faster healing of wounds than with traditional surgery.

A badly **broken kneecap** is usually removed and any damaged ligaments are repaired. The knee may lose some of its stability, but the person will still be able to walk normally. Severe **chondromalacia** may require surgical repositioning of the kneecap to relieve friction that is being caused by malalignment.

If severe **arthritis** has destroyed most or all of the knee cartilage, knee-replacement surgery can restore function and provide dramatic pain relief. The operation, which may be done under either general anesthesia or a spinal block, takes about two hours and involves replacing the diseased knee with an artificial one made of plastic and metal. Patients stay in the hospital for five or six days, or until they can walk with a cane or walker.

Morphine or another narcotic painkiller is used for the first few days after surgery, but by the time most patients go home, they need only acetaminophen or an NSAID. After two months of rehabilitation and physical therapy, most patients can walk normally with little or no pain and, eventually, many can again play tennis, ski, and engage in other activities that were impossible before the operation. Unless both knees are equally disabled, doctors prefer to operate on them one at a time, replacing the most diseased one first and, if necessary, the second one a few months later.

## HOW TO PREVENT IT

Some knee problems, such as arthritis and unpredictable accidents, cannot be prevented. But commonsense measures can minimize the risk and slow the progress of degenerative disorders like osteoarthritis. These include:

## Breakthroughs!

**A new approach to treating severe arthritis of the knee is helping many patients avoid or delay knee-replacement surgery. The treatment involves injecting the knee with hyaluronic acid (e.g., Synvisc), a substance obtained from chicken combs that thickens and increases the joint's natural synovial fluid. Five or six injections are given at weekly intervals; in one large clinical study, 77 percent of patients had reduced pain and improved knee function that lasted for an average of eight months, after which the injections can be repeated.**

- Wearing shoes that fit properly, are in good condition, and designed for the particular activity. Wear orthotic inserts if you have flat feet or you overpronate; these shoe inserts help reduce stress on the knee and lower the risk of injury.
- Losing excess weight and then trying to maintain a weight that is ideal for you.
- Warming up before exercising by walking or riding a stationary bicycle for 5 to 10 minutes and then stretching for a few minutes. Be sure to cool down and then stretch again at the end of the workout.
- Working to strengthen the leg muscles if you have arthritis of the knees, chondromalacia, or another chronic problem that causes pain and joint instability. Good exercises for this include walking upstairs, riding a stationary bicycle, or doing leg lifts, with or without weights.
- Avoiding sudden changes in the intensity of exercise. For example, engage in a conditioning program before ski season or other activities that are hard on the knees.

### ALTERNATIVE THERAPIES

**Nutraceuticals**

See *Osteoarthritis,* p 225, for a list of recommended supplements.

**Physical therapy**

This is an essential aspect of rehabilitation after knee surgery. At first, the knee will be exercised passively by placing the leg in a perpetual motion machine that automatically flexes and relaxes it. At first, the machine bends the knee only slightly and is used for 15 to 20 minutes every hour or two. As the joint regains flexibility, the degree of bending and time are increased.

Within a day or so after the operation, most patients are able to walk with the aid of crutches or a walker. leaving the hospital, a physical therapist will teach the patient how to go up and down stairs using a cane, get in and out of a chair or car, and perform other routine tasks. As the joint heals, physical therapy is directed to strengthening the leg (and perhaps upper body) muscles and improving balance, as well as walking, bending, and lifting normally.

# Leg Cramps/ Restless Legs

### SYMPTOMS

*These problems are often related; some people, however, suffer from one and not the other.*

***Leg cramps:*** *Sudden, intense leg pain, usually in the calf muscle but sometimes also in the feet.*

***Restless legs:*** *Aching, crawling, or jittery sensation deep in the legs; irresistible urge to move the legs to relieve the uncomfortable sensations.*

### WHO IS AT RISK

***Leg cramps*** *occur in people of all ages, but they are most common among middle-aged and older people. In most cases, there is no obvious cause, but overexertion, pregnancy, high blood pressure, and the use of diuretics (water pills) appear to increase their frequency. Dehydration and nutritional deficiencies, especially a lack of potassium, play a role. Patients on long-term kidney dialysis are also susceptible to leg cramps.*

***Restless leg syndrome****, a puzzling neurological disorder that afflicts more than 12 million North Americans, usually develops after age 30 and becomes increasingly common with advancing age. Smoking, a high intake of caffeine (for example, more than five cups of coffee a day), and alcohol abuse increase the risk; the syndrome has also been linked to iron and folic acid deficiencies.*

*To ease a foot cramp, extend the feet and wiggle the toes. To relieve a leg cramp, slowly straighten and lift the leg with the toes pointed toward your head.*

**BREAKTHROUGHS!**

**A recent controlled study conducted by Taiwan researchers found that a B-complex pill helped 75 percent of elderly patients who suffered from leg cramps. The dosage called for 7.5 mg of vitamin $B_{12}$, 90 mg of $B_6$, and 15 mg of riboflavin. Although these amounts greatly exceed the recommended nutrient intake (RNI), they do not appear to cause adverse side effects.**

## HOW THEY DEVELOP

Both conditions typically occur at night, often making it difficult to fall or stay asleep. **Restless leg syndrome** begins with a distinctive aching or tingling sensation that is relieved by moving the legs. It most often disturbs sleep, although some sufferers also experience symptoms during the day, preventing them from sitting or standing still. This can make it difficult to concentrate, drive, or carry out other routine activities.

**Leg cramps** usually strike without warning, often when a person shifts position while sleeping. Most last for only a minute or so, but they tend to recur and may also interfere with sleep. Most occur in the calf muscles, but some people also suffer cramps in their feet.

## WHAT YOU CAN DO

To relax a **leg cramp**, slowly lift and straighten the leg and point the toes upward. Foot cramps can be relaxed by extending the foot and wriggling the toes. Massaging the cramped muscles can also relax them and may help prevent a recurrence.

**Restless legs** can be relieved by getting up and walking about for a few minutes. Relaxing in a hot tub or taking a hot shower may also help.

## HOW TO TREAT THEM

Clonazepam (Rivotril), a benzodiazepine anticonvulsant, is often prescribed to calm **restless legs**. Researchers think that it works by stabilizing conduction of nerve impulses, but its exact mechanism of action is unknown. Clonazepam should never be taken with alcohol, sleeping pills, and other drugs that cause drowsiness; the combination may interfere with breathing. Other drugs that may be tried for restless legs include carbidopa and levodopa, medications more often used to treat Parkinson's disease. Again, how they calm restless legs is unknown, but researchers think they work by altering brain chemistry.

**WARNING!**

***Persons who suffer from restless legs and frequent leg cramps should see a doctor to rule out serious disorders that may cause these symptoms. These include kidney disease, diabetes, phlebitis, and Parkinson's disease.***

The antimalarial drug quinine is sometimes prescribed for severe **leg cramps**. However, its use is limited by such side effects as ringing in the ears (tinnitus), irregular heartbeats, and vertigo.

## HOW TO PREVENT THEM

Correcting nutritional deficiencies may prevent some leg cramps (see *Breakthroughs!*, left, and *Nutraceuticals*, below). Stretching and massaging the leg and feet muscles before going to bed may also help.

Although taking a hot bath before going to bed does not always prevent restless legs, it may reduce the number of episodes. Not smoking, restricting caffeine intake, and abstaining from alcohol may also help.

### ALTERNATIVE THERAPIES

**Herbal medicine**

Valerian extract promotes sleep and may also help prevent restless legs. Start with 250 mg of standardized extract at bedtime and if the problem persists, work up to 500 mg. Do not use valerian if you are pregnant or breast-feeding.

**Nutraceuticals**

Studies have found that 1000 to 1500 mg of calcium a day helps prevent the leg cramps that often occur during pregnancy. Other supplements that may prevent leg cramps include 400 to 800 IU of vitamin E and 500 to 1000 mg of magnesium; B-complex may also help. Iron supplements may benefit persons with iron deficiency anemia, but a doctor should determine the dosage. A diet that includes at least 5 to 10 daily servings of fruits and vegetables plus several servings of whole-grain products will provide ample potassium. For cautions concerning these nutraceuticals, see *About the Recommendations*, p 7.

# Thrombophlebitis

## SYMPTOMS

*Thrombophlebitis is generally classified as superficial or deep; symptoms of each include:*

***Superficial thrombophlebitis:*** *Pain, tenderness, inflammation, warmth, and a lump that can be felt in a vein just under the skin surface.*

***Deep-vein thrombosis:*** *Often asymptomatic in the early stages. When symptoms occur, they may include leg pain or soreness, often when standing or walking, and, depending upon the site, swelling, warmth, skin discoloration, and a bulging of nearby superficial veins.*

## WHO IS AT RISK

***Superficial thrombophlebitis****—often referred to simply as phlebitis—is a common problem among older people,* *especially those who are sedentary or bedridden.* ***Deep-vein thrombosis*** *is a serious complication of surgery, a broken hip or leg, paralysis, or other circumstances that may require prolonged bed rest. Smoking increases the risk; other precipitating causes include the use of high-estrogen birth control pills or replacement estrogen following menopause, recent childbirth or miscarriage, and clotting disorders. Passengers on long plane flights also have an increased risk of deep-vein thrombosis because of inactivity and a change in air pressure.*

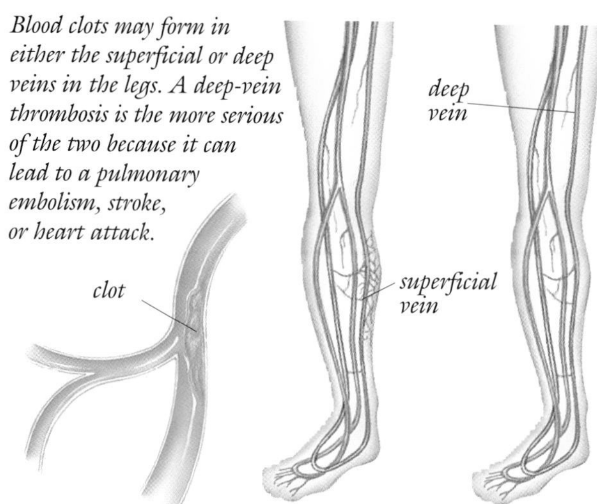


*Blood clots may form in either the superficial or deep veins in the legs. A deep-vein thrombosis is the more serious of the two because it can lead to a pulmonary embolism, stroke, or heart attack.*

## HOW IT DEVELOPS

Both types of thrombophlebitis develop when one or more clots (thrombi) form in a vein, most often in the calf. **Superficial phlebitis** typically develops over one or two days, with increasing tenderness and pain. The affected vein becomes swollen and inflamed; with a warm, hard knot just under the skin. The pain and other symptoms gradually subside and usually disappear in one to two weeks.

> **WARNING!**
>
> ***Many patients ignore the pain of deep-vein thrombosis because they mistakenly think it's minor muscle soreness. However, any leg pain that is provoked by walking and improves during rest warrants seeing a doctor to rule out deep thrombophlebitis or another circulatory problem.***

In **deep-vein thrombophlebitis**, the clot forms in one of the inner veins, usually in the calf or thigh. It is often asymptomatic until a piece of the clot breaks free and lodges in a lung, the heart, or brain, resulting in a pulmonary embolism, heart attack, or stroke. In other instances, the person may complain of leg pain or soreness that develops when standing or walking and disappears during rest or when the leg is elevated. If untreated, there may be marked swelling in the affected leg due to a pooling of blood; skin ulcers that are difficult to heal and easily infected may also develop.

## WHAT YOU CAN DO

**Superficial phlebitis** usually can be self-treated; keep the leg elevated as much as possible. To relieve pain, apply warm compresses to the affected area several times a day. Aspirin, ibuprofen, or another nonsteroidal anti-inflammatory drug (NSAID) can ease pain and reduce inflammation. See a doctor if the phlebitis persists for more than 10 to 14 days. In contrast, seek immediate medical attention if **deep-vein thrombophlebitis** is suspected; hospitalization and intensive treatment may be needed to prevent life-threatening complications, such as pulmonary embolism.

> **BREAKTHROUGHS!**
>
> **The development of various stents—umbrella-like devices that can be implanted in blood vessels—is helping prevent pulmonary emboli and other serious complications in high-risk patients. For example, a stent implanted in the lower vena cava—the large vein that carries blood from the legs to the heart—can catch even tiny clots before they do major damage.**

## HOW TO TREAT IT

Treating deep-vein thrombosis centers on preventing a pulmonary embolism, stroke, or heart attack. The patient is usually hospitalized and given intravenous heparin, a drug that discourages new blood clots from forming. Depending upon the site of the thrombosis, drugs that dissolve blood clots—for example, tissue plasminogen activator (TPA) or urokinase (Abbokinase)—may be used. These drugs, which can dissolve clots in 24 to 48 hours, work best if they are administered in the first 72 hours after they form and the clots are in the popliteal or other proximal veins.

The affected leg is kept elevated by raising the foot of the bed six to eight inches; warm compresses may be applied to ease leg pain.

After the immediate danger is past, the patient is weaned off the heparin and switched to warfarin (Coumadin), an oral anticlotting drug. If the patient is young, healthy, and has no prior history of a clotting disorder, the warfarin may be stopped after a week or so. But those with a high risk of recurrence or evidence of a pulmonary embolism may be kept on the drug for six months and often longer.

After the patient is allowed to get out of bed, he or she will probably be fitted with a surgical elastic stocking to increase flow through the leg veins and prevent swelling (edema), skin ulcers, and other complications. If skin ulcers do develop, treatment usually requires bed rest with the leg elevated and application of a compression bandage.

## HOW TO PREVENT IT

Avoid prolonged inactivity. If you must stay in bed, move your legs as much as possible; if you can't do this yourself, have a caregiver administer passive leg exercises (see *Physical therapy,* below). Elevate the foot of the bed to help prevent blood from pooling in the lower legs; wearing surgical elastic stockings may also help. When you are on a long plane trip, get up and move about every hour or so. Even when you are seated, stretch and flex your legs and feet frequently. If you smoke, make every effort to stop. Women who smoke or who have a history of clotting problems should not take birth control pills or other products containing estrogen.

### ALTERNATIVE THERAPIES

**Nutraceuticals**

Vitamin E, in doses of 400 to 800 IU a day, reduces blood clotting. However, if you are taking warfarin (Coumadin) or another blood-thinning medication, check with your doctor before taking high doses of vitamin E; the combination may cause bleeding problems.

**Physical therapy**

Passive leg exercises for bedridden or paralyzed patients can help prevent deep-vein thrombosis. A physical therapist can teach bedridden patients safe leg exercises. Whirlpool baths and other forms of hydrotherapy may be needed to promote healing of refractory skin ulcers.

# Varicose Veins

### SYMPTOMS

- *Aches, itching, and sensation of warmth, burning, heaviness, or throbbing in the legs.*
- *Leg discomfort and cramps, which often disrupt sleep.*
- *Discolored veins, ranging from red "spider" veins to thick, bulging blue ridges that are most prominent in the lower legs.*
- *In severe cases, painful skin ulcers may occur and surrounding skin may develop brownish-gray splotches.*

### WHO IS AT RISK

*Varicose veins are very common; according to some estimates, about 25 percent of adult women and 10 percent of men have them. They tend to run in families, so doctors assume that there is an inherited tendency to develop them. Many women develop varicose veins during pregnancy due to hormonal changes and increased abdominal pressure from the developing fetus. These varicose veins often disappear after childbirth, but may recur years later. Obesity, chronic constipation, and abdominal tumors increase the risk of varicose veins. A history of phlebitis—the formation of clots in the superficial leg veins—is also linked to increased risk of varicose veins.*

*Persons whose occupations involve a lot of standing can experience a worsening of symptoms if they already have varicose veins but, contrary to popular belief, long hours of standing do not cause the condition.*

## HOW THEY DEVELOP

Varicose veins usually start during early middle age and worsen as the person gets older. At first, the discolored veins may be small, resembling red or blue spider legs. Some never progress beyond this stage, but multiple failures of the tiny one-way valves within the vessels allow blood to seep backward. The blue bulges develop in sections where the blood collects, or pools. The legs are most commonly affected because the force of gravity counters the efforts of the veins to push blood upward to the heart. However, varicose veins can also develop in the anus (hemorrhoids), the esophagus (esophageal varices), and the testicles (varicoceles).

## WHAT YOU CAN DO

Cold compresses can ease discomfort. Try to rest several times a day with your legs elevated above your heart. Night cramps linked to varicose veins may be eased by elevating the foot of your bed six inches or so. Also avoid crossing your legs, which further hinders blood flow in the legs. Try not to sit or stand in one place for long periods; moving about frequently promotes blood flow. During a long car trip, stop every hour to stretch and walk. On a plane trip, get up and move about every hour or so and, when sitting, rotate your ankles and flex your feet and toes periodically. At other times, daily exercise—for example, walking, cycling, swimming, or low-impact aerobics—is crucial to maintain good muscle tone and improve circulation in your legs. Exercise also increases the body's production of endorphins, natural painkillers that can help ease the leg discomfort.

Elastic support stockings compress the veins and promote blood flow. Prescription stockings are more effective than ordinary support stockings. They should be put on first thing in the morning, even before getting out of bed.

If you smoke, try to stop; smoking interferes with circulation and can worsen varicose veins. Other self-help measures include losing excess weight and increasing fiber and water intake to prevent constipation. Consult a doctor—preferably a vascular specialist—if self-treatment fails to provide adequate relief.

## HOW TO TREAT THEM

Most varicose veins are a cosmetic, rather than a medical, problem and treatment is usually directed at improving appearance. However, doctors generally recommend removal of severe varicose veins that are causing pain, skin ulcers, or reduced circulation to the lower legs and feet.

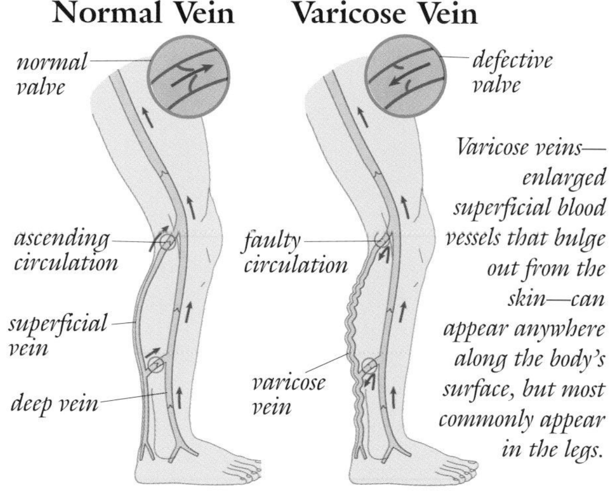


Approaches to treatment include the following:

- **Sclerotherapy**, which is used for small varicosities and spider veins. An irritating solution such as sodium tetradecyl sulfate (Trombovar) is injected into the varicose veins. The solution collapses the diseased vein and, when pressure is applied, blood is diverted to nearby healthy veins. Cotton balls and tape are used to cover and compress the injection sites to prevent bleeding. The leg is then wrapped with a compression bandage for a few days, after which an elastic surgical stocking is worn until healing is complete. The injection site may be uncomfortable and itchy for a day or two; the injections themselves are moderately painful, which can usually be controlled with acetaminophen. Several treatments may be needed.
- **Laser therapy**, which uses powerful light beams to destroy the small varicosities and spider veins, is an alternative to sclerotherapy. A gel is applied to the skin, and the area is then exposed to the laser beam. There is little or no pain and bleeding. Several sessions may be needed, but usually fewer than in sclerotherapy. In time, the treated veins fade, although some discoloration may persist. The blood flow is diverted to nearby veins.
- **Phlebectomy**, or surgical stripping, in which the diseased veins are removed through small incisions in the skin. Phlebectomy is recommended for large varicose veins, especially those affecting much or all of the saphenous vein, the large blood vessel that runs from the ankle to the groin. The procedure is usually done on an outpatient basis and requires only local anesthesia. Tiny incisions are made along the vein and its branches are tied off; the surgeon then passes a plastic stripper up the length of the vein and removes it through an incision in the groin. If deeper veins are contributing to the problem, they too may be removed. The procedure usually takes about 30 minutes and when stitches are removed a week later, moderate activity can be resumed. A nonprescription painkiller usually eases any discomfort; cool compresses may also help. Vigorous exercise should be avoided until healing is complete, which usually takes two weeks. Complications are uncommon, although a few patients may develop ankle numbness if nerves are damaged.

**WARNING!**

***Anyone with varicose veins should avoid saunas, hot tubs, heating pads, and hot compresses, which can worsen the problem by increasing blood pooling in the distorted veins. Cold compresses or ice packs are safe and provide relief.***

## HOW TO PREVENT THEM

Most varicose veins are hereditary and cannot be prevented. However, maintaining ideal weight and other self-help measures can slow their progression.

### ALTERNATIVE THERAPIES

**Herbal medicine**

Herbalists recommend covering the affected veins with compresses soaked in a solution of horse chestnut extract and witch hazel, astringent substances that soothe the discomfort and itchiness of varicose veins. Gotu kola extract enhances blood flow and also helps keep veins supple; the usual dosage is 200 mg of extract taken three times a day. Pregnant women or those trying to conceive should not use gotu kola. Leg ulcers, often difficult to heal, may be treated with compresses soaked in comfrey. Do not ingest. Aloe vera gel from a fresh-cut leaf also promotes healing.

**Homeopathy**

Homeopaths recommend Pulsatilla, Arnica, and Aconitum to ease discomfort, itchiness, and other symptoms related to varicose veins. Carbo vegetabilis is said to improve circulation and reduce symptoms that interfere with sleep; Hamamelis is taken to help heal skin ulcers or sores.

**Nutraceuticals**

If constipation is a chronic problem, take two tablespoons of ground psyllium seeds with 8 to 10 glasses of water a day. Nutritional supplements that help build healthy blood vessels include 1000 mg of vitamin C, 400 to 800 IU of vitamin E, and 500 mg of flavonoids, substances that enhance vitamin C. See *About the Recommendations*, p 7.

**BREAKTHROUGHS!**

**A new treatment in the U.S., PhotoDerm, is similar to laser therapy but gives doctors additional options in treating varicose veins. Although it is most widely used to treat small superficial varicosities and spider veins, the settings can be adjusted to destroy deeper veins as well. Several treatments may be required, especially if the vessels are large and bulging.**

# The Ankle and Foot

*Almost everyone now and then has an occasion to moan, "Oh, my aching feet!" Despite their amazing strength and resilience, our feet and ankles are highly vulnerable to strains, sprains, fractures, bunions, and many other painful disorders.*

## Achilles Tendon Pain

### SYMPTOMS

***Achilles tendinitis:*** *Burning pain in the heel that lessens with exercise but recurs during rest; tenderness in the heel cord at the back of the ankle; heel pain that may disrupt sleep.*

***Torn Achilles tendon:*** *Snapping or popping sound followed by sharp pain in the back of the ankle; swelling and bruising in the heel that may extend to the calf; buckling or instability of the foot and difficulty walking normally.*

### WHO IS AT RISK

***Achilles tendinitis*** *is very common among people who undertake a new physical activity, such as jogging or playing tennis, after a period of inactivity; weekend athletes are especially vulnerable. An abnormal gait, especially excessive tilting of the heel inward (overpronation) or outward (hypersupination), increases the risk of Achilles tendinitis; other risk factors include obesity and metabolic or inflammatory disorders such as diabetes, arthritis, and gout. Women who frequently wear high-heeled shoes may develop a shortening of the Achilles tendon and experience heel pain and inflammation when they switch to low-heeled or athletic shoes.*

*A* ***torn Achilles*** *occurs when sudden force or a twist ruptures the tendon at the back of the ankle. These ruptures are most common among people whose Achilles tendons have been weakened by chronic inflammation, but they can also occur in anyone who suddenly twists a foot or the lower leg.*

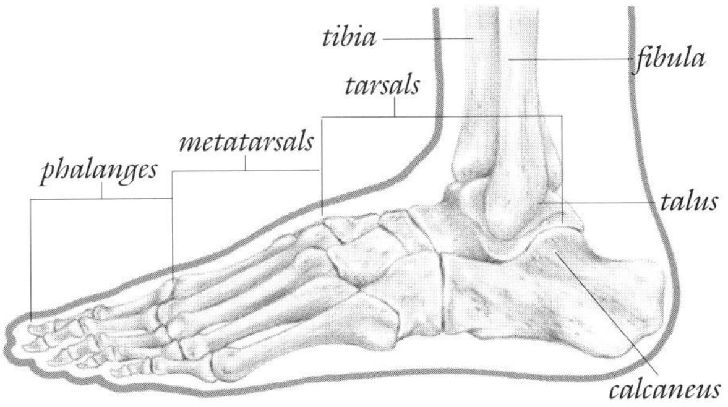


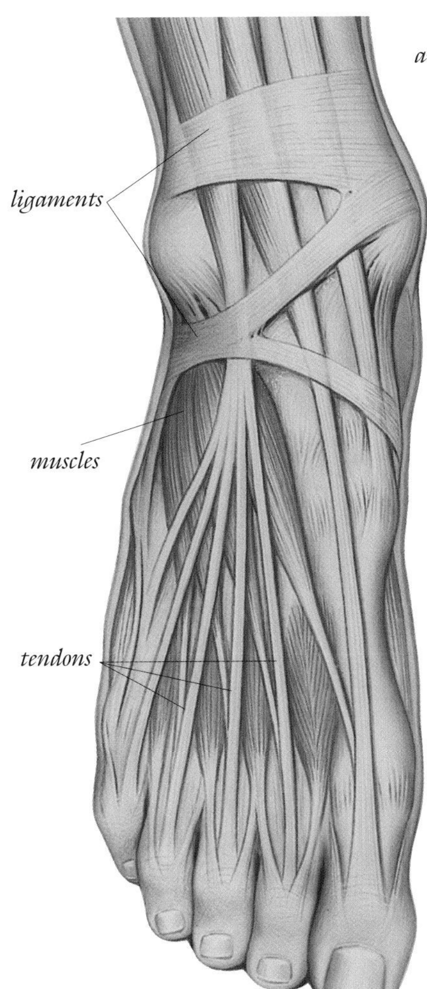


*The ankle and foot are made up of some 26 small, flexible bones that are held together by a web of sinewy muscles and strong ligaments. On their own, any of these bones can be easily broken, but the manner in which they are bound together enables the foot and ankle to bear a force equal to many times the body's weight.*

### HOW IT DEVELOPS

Tendons, or sinews, are tough, rather inelastic cords of connective tissue that grow out of bundles of muscles and bind them to the bones. The Achilles tendon, which attaches the calf muscles to the heel bone, gets its name from the fact that, like the mythical Greek warrior's heel, it is very vulnerable to injury. Even minor stretching of the Achilles tendon can result in pain, swelling, and inflammation. **Achilles tendinitis** often becomes chronic, resulting in heel and lower calf pain that is typically worse during rest and improves with exercise.

Almost any excessive force at the back of the ankle can result in a **torn Achilles tendon**. The person usually remembers hearing a popping sound, followed immediately by a sharp pain. Because the calf muscle is no longer attached to the heel, moving the foot and walking normally are difficult or impossible. The person may be able to feel a gap between the calf muscle and heel, or the calf on the injured side may be higher than on the other leg.

## WHAT YOU CAN DO

Acute **Achilles tendinitis** is treated with anti-inflammatory medications, such as aspirin or ibuprofen, and a day or two of RICE—rest, ice, compression with an elastic bandage, and elevation. A topical anti-inflammatory cream can also ease pain and reduce inflammation (see *Herbal medicine,* p 279). As the inflammation subsides, begin a program of gentle calf-stretching exercises (see *How to Prevent It,* p 279). Gradually resume walking and other leg exercises, but make sure that your shoes are appropriate for the activity and properly fitted. You may need orthotic shoe inserts to help correct an abnormal gait. If pain persists, consult a doctor—preferably an orthopedist or sports medicine specialist—or a physical therapist.

If you suspect a **torn Achilles tendon**, see a doctor as soon as possible. Do not attempt to walk on the injured limb; instead, immobilize it with an elastic bandage or splint and use crutches.

## HOW TO TREAT IT

To treat **Achilles tendinitis**, a doctor may prescribe a stronger anti-inflammatory drug. Injections of a corticosteroid, which are often used to treat acute tendinitis in other parts of the body, are not recommended for an inflamed Achilles because they increase the risk of a rupture. In severe cases, the ankle may be immobilized with a lightweight cast and the person will need to use crutches for six to eight weeks. Physical therapy will likely be recommended.

Although a **torn Achilles tendon** can sometimes be treated by immobilizing the ankle in a cast until it heals, it usually requires surgical repair. The severed ends of a ruptured tendon are sewn together and the ankle is put in a cast. If the tendon is intact but has pulled away from the heel bone (or a part of the bone is broken off and attached to the tendon), it will be reattached with surgical pins or screws and a cast will be applied. After two or three weeks, a lighter walking

**WARNING!**

***Without treatment, a torn Achilles tendon can result in a permanent limp and disability. See a doctor as soon as possible, and avoid putting any weight on the injured leg until the doctor says it is safe to do so. Physical therapy is also essential for proper rehabilitation following Achilles tendon surgery.***

### ACHILLES-STRETCHING EXERCISES

Do the exercise pictured here two or three times a day, and especially before and after exercising.

1. Stand about a foot away from a wall and extend one leg behind you. Keep both feet on the floor with the toes pointed straight ahead and the back knee straight but not locked.
2. Move your hips forward and lean into the wall until you feel a pulling sensation in the calf muscle of the extended leg. Hold for a count of 10, then stretch the other leg. Repeat three times on each leg.

Here's another good calf stretch, which can be alternated with the one shown here:

1. Stand at least 18 inches from a wall, with your hands on the wall and feet a few inches apart. Keep your back and legs straight.
2. Bend your arms and lean forward, trying to touch your shoulders and chest to the wall. You should feel a stretch in your calf muscles. Hold for 30 seconds and repeat three times.

*A torn Achilles tendon—commonly referred to as the heel cord—is a common injury among baseball and tennis players, runners, and other athletes who often twist their ankles. But it also occurs among older people who twist an ankle when stepping off a curb or when falling.*

cast may be put on. Healing time varies depending upon the extent of the injury and the patient's age and general health; some heal in a few weeks, while others take six months or longer. In any event, physical therapy is needed afterward to regain function.

## HOW TO PREVENT IT

Simple exercises to stretch the lower calf muscles can help prevent Achilles tendinitis (see illustrated box, *Achilles-Stretching Exercises*, p 278). Other preventive measures include wearing an Achilles tendon strap when jogging, playing tennis, or engaging in other activities that may stretch the tendon and result in tendinitis; these are sold in many sports shops. Orthotic devices that cushion the heel may also prevent Achilles tendinitis; start by trying the shoe inserts available at most pharmacies. If these don't help, consult a podiatrist, who can fit you with custom-made orthotics.

Women should avoid wearing high-heeled shoes every day. Instead, wear comfortable shoes with one-inch heels, and reserve high heels for special occasions that do not demand a lot of walking.

### ALTERNATIVE THERAPIES

**Herbal medicine**

Boswellia cream has anti-inflammatory properties that may ease the pain of Achilles tendinitis; gently massage the cream into the painful area two or three times a day. Creams or ointments that contain 0.025 percent capsaicin—the active ingredient in hot chilies—also ease pain and reduce inflammation. Avoid contact with the eyes, other mucous membranes, and raw or open skin.

**Magnets**

Therapeutic magnets applied to the back of the ankle may be effective against chronic Achilles tendinitis. Magnets are thought to reduce inflammation and promote healing by increasing blood flow to the inflamed area.

**Physical therapy**

Physical therapists treat Achilles tendinitis pain with ultrasound, diathermy, and hot and cold packs. They also teach proper stretching techniques and exercises to strengthen the calf and ankle muscles.

# Ankle Sprains/Strains

### SYMPTOMS

- *Ankle pain or tenderness that develops soon after an injury.*
- *Swelling and inflammation.*
- *Discoloration and bruising.*

### WHO IS AT RISK

*Most people experience a strained or sprained ankle at some point in their lives. They are especially common among runners, joggers, hikers, tennis players, skiers, and other recreational athletes, as well as people who are obese or prone to falls, such as habitual drinkers.*

## HOW THEY DEVELOP

An ankle strain occurs when one or more of the ligaments—the bands of tough, fibrous tissue that are attached to the muscles and bound to the joints—are overly stretched but not torn. This often occurs when twisting an ankle during a fall or when stepping off a

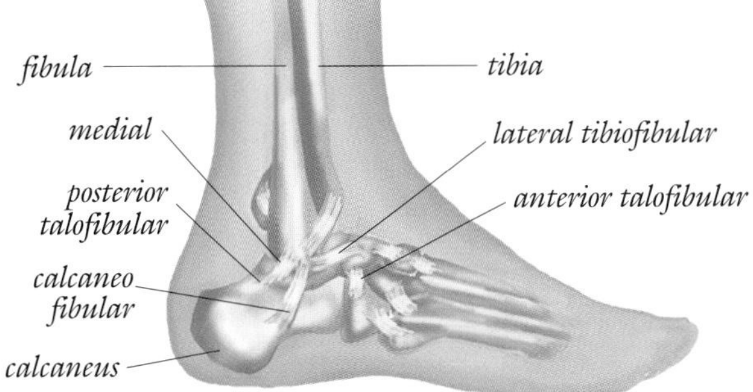

> **WARNING!**
>
> *Although a badly sprained ankle can be very painful, the joint should still function and the foot should be able to move normally. If you are unable to move the ankle or foot, a bone may be broken; see a doctor as soon as possible.*

curb or stumbling. A strained ankle is painful and moderately swollen, but there usually is no discoloration or bruising and it heals quickly, usually in three or four days.

In a moderate sprain, the ligament is partially torn; if the ligament is completely torn, the injury is classified as a severe sprain. Sprains cause more severe swelling, pain, and extensive bruising from bleeding under the skin. They usually take one to two weeks to heal, and the ankle may be tender and vulnerable to reinjury for several months.

## WHAT YOU CAN DO

Rest, ice, compression, and elevation (RICE) is the standard treatment for any strain or sprain. Do not apply ice directly to the skin, which can cause tissue damage. Instead, wrap an ice pack (a bag of frozen peas or other small vegetables will also work) in a thin towel and apply it to the elevated ankle. Leave the pack on for 20 minutes, and reapply for 20 minutes every hour or two. After 36 to 48 hours—or when the swelling subsides—you can switch to a heating pad and alternate hot and cold treatments. The heat is soothing and it also promotes healing by increasing blood flow to the area. An anti-inflammatory medication such as aspirin (for adults only) or ibuprofen relieves pain and reduces inflammation.

Wrap the injured ankle with an elastic bandage (see below), and limit walking on it for a few days. See a doctor if the pain worsens, the swelling and bruising increase, or improvement is not noticed after 24 hours.

## HOW TO TREAT IT

A doctor will examine the foot and ankle and order X rays to rule out a fracture. If the pain is intolerable, a doctor may inject a local anesthetic, and then prescribe codeine or a strong nonsteroidal anti-inflammatory drug (NSAID). Some very severe sprains require immobilization in a cast; more often, however, wearing an elastic bandage and using crutches for a few days will allow the ankle to heal.

Recurrent sprains or one in which the ligaments are badly torn may require surgical repair.

## HOW TO PREVENT IT

Commonsense measures can prevent many ankle injuries; these include the following:

- Wearing low-heeled (preferably one and a half inches or lower) shoes, especially if you have weak ankles. When exercising, wear athletic shoes that are fitted and designed for the activity.
- Stretching and doing ankle exercises before and after workouts.
- Wrapping your ankles with support bandages before engaging in sports that carry a high risk of falls or twisting your ankle.
- Losing excess weight and abstaining from alcohol or using it only in moderation.

### ALTERNATIVE THERAPIES

**Physical therapy**

Consult a physical therapist after a bad sprain or if you suffer recurrent ankle strains or sprains. Your various movements will be analyzed, and you will be taught special exercises to correct any gait problems and others to strengthen the muscles that support the foot and ankle.

### *HOW TO APPLY AN ELASTIC BANDAGE*

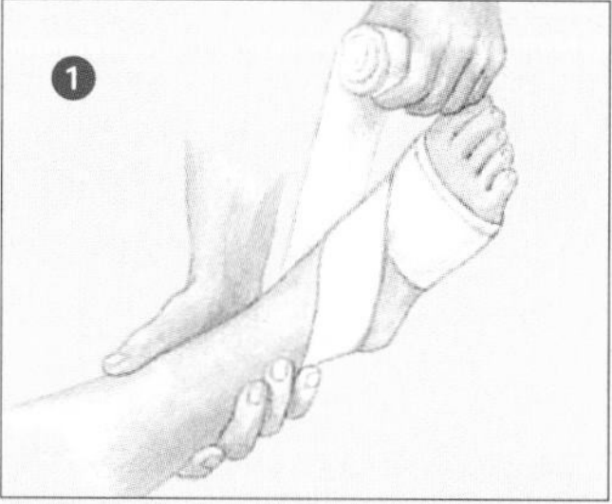


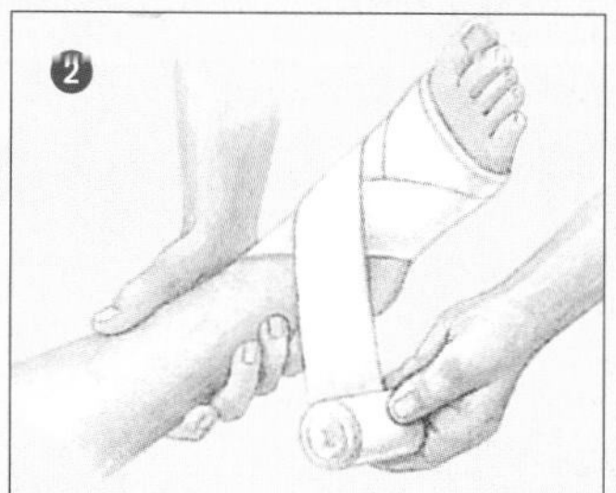


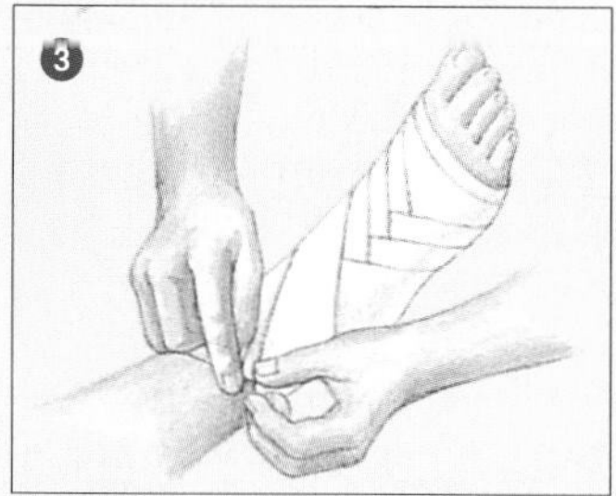


*1 Using a three-inch-wide bandage, start by making two turns around the foot. 2 Support the lower leg with one hand and use the other to begin wrapping upward, using figure-eight turns. 3 Continue bandaging until the foot, ankle, and lower leg are wrapped, and then anchor with a safety pin or a clip that comes with the bandage. Be careful not to wrap the bandage too tightly. It should be comfortable and loose enough for you to work your finger under the edge. If the toes become numb or the nails turn bluish, the bandage is too tight; remove it immediately and rewrap it more loosely.*

# Athlete's Foot

### SYMPTOMS

- *Persistent itching on soles and between toes.*
- *Increasing inflammation and tenderness.*
- *Skin thickening and peeling.*
- *Painful cracks (fissures).*
- *Possible itchy rash on the palms (tinea manuum).*

### WHO IS AT RISK

*Anyone can develop athlete's foot, or tinea pedis, a very common fungal skin infection. It is most common, however, among males 16 to 50 years of age.*

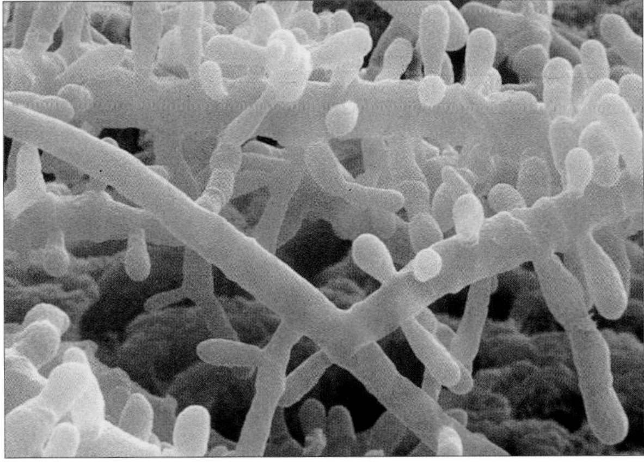

*An enlarged view of the tinea pedis organism.*

## HOW IT DEVELOPS

Athlete's foot has nothing to do with athletics; instead, it is a fungal skin infection. These fungi thrive in the moist, warm environment of the feet in enclosed shoes, especially those made of materials that hold in moisture. The microscopic fungal spores are easily spread by walking barefoot around public pools and shower rooms or by sharing towels with an infected person. There are four general types of athlete's foot, each with somewhat different symptoms.

- **Common athlete's foot**, which starts with uncomfortable itchiness, usually develops on the soles or between the fourth and fifth toes. In time, it may spread to other parts of the foot, and the infected areas become inflamed, tender, and ooze a watery discharge; eventually, the skin thickens and peels.
- **Ulcerative tinea pedis**, in which skin cracks (fissures) develop, is more painful than typical athlete's foot. The infection often spreads to other parts of the body, and bacteria may invade the fissures, leading to more serious infections.
- **Moccasin foot**, so named because of its pattern of spread, starts as a red, itchy rash that covers the lower part of the foot. The skin eventually becomes thick and scaly.
- **Inflammatory tinea pedis**, which usually starts around the ball of the foot and spreads to the toes, has an intensely itchy, raised red rash. Scratching increases the risk of a secondary bacterial infection.

Any of these may be accompanied by a similar itchy rash on the palms; this is an immune reaction to the antibodies that are formed against the primary infection on the foot.

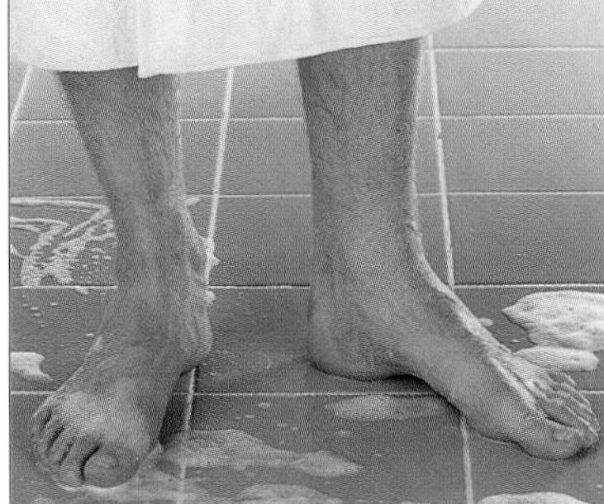

*Athlete's foot is commonly contracted by going barefoot in public showers or locker rooms.*

## WHAT YOU CAN DO

First, make sure that the problem is, indeed, athlete's foot and not another skin problem, such as contact dermatitis (an allergic reaction). Nonprescription antifungal foot sprays, powders, and creams will often relieve the itching and other uncomfortable symptoms of athlete's foot. Topical antifungal medications speed up shedding of the top layer of skin, thereby interfering with the fungi's food supply.

> **WARNING!**
>
> ***Persons who have diabetes or a weakened immune system must be especially careful about any foot infection, including athlete's foot. If you have diabetes or reduced immunity and develop an itchy foot rash, see your doctor as soon as possible.***

Wash your feet at least once a day with warm, soapy water, and dry them meticulously, paying special attention to the areas between the toes. Wear white, cotton socks, and alternate shoes daily to give them a chance to dry out between wearings. Dust the inside of shoes with an antifungal powder before putting them on. Wear sandals or open-toed shoes in hot, humid weather, when the feet tend to sweat.

## HOW TO TREAT IT

Persistent athlete's foot is notoriously difficult to treat because it tends to recur. Until recently, systemic antifungal drugs, such as griseofulvin (Fulvicin U/F), have been used only as a last resort because they often cause headaches, nausea, and other side effects. Newer antifungal drugs are more effective against athlete's foot; they also work faster and cause fewer side effects.

## Breakthroughs!

**Prescription-strength terbinafine (Lamisil) tablets have fewer side effects than griseofulvin and older systemic antifungal drugs. Terbinafine produces a gradual buildup of compounds that are toxic to fungi, and usually clears up most cases of athlete's foot in four to six weeks.**

## HOW TO PREVENT IT

Always wear protective footwear around pools, public showers, or other areas where the feet may come in contact with fungi. Use the antifungal footbaths that are available in many locker rooms and pool areas. Avoid sharing towels and other personal items. If you have a history of athlete's foot, sprinkle an antifungal powder in your exercise shoes before each workout.

If you have athlete's foot, be careful not to spread it to other areas of the body. For example, a woman who has athlete's foot should be extra careful not to nick the skin if she shaves her legs; even a tiny cut or scrape can provide an entry point for fungi.

### ALTERNATIVE THERAPIES

**Herbal medicine**

Garlic has potent antifungal properties. Apply a paste of crushed garlic and olive oil to the infected areas and cover with a clean cloth for 15 to 20 minutes. Remove the paste, wash the foot with warm, soapy water, and dry thoroughly. Repeat daily until the infection clears up, usually two to three weeks. Other herbal remedies include compresses dipped in pau d'arco tea and applied to the area. Tea tree oil, rubbed directly into the infected skin, is another popular herbal treatment for fungal infections of the skin.

# Bunions

### SYMPTOMS

- *Protrusion of the joint at the base of the big toe.*
- *Pain, inflammation, and swelling of the joint.*
- *Big toe turns inward to overlap with second toe.*

### WHO IS AT RISK

*Women tend to develop bunions—known medically as* hallux valgus*—more often than men for several reasons. Women are more likely than men to have lax ligaments and unstable feet, which allow the toe joint to slip out of its normal alignment. The problem is exacerbated by wearing pointy-toed and/or high-heeled shoes or shoes that are too narrow and crowd the toes. Other contributing factors include flatfeet and overpronation, a tendency to roll the foot abnormally when walking or running.*

## HOW IT DEVELOPS

Individuals who have an inborn weakness of the joint at the base of the big toe (the metatarsophalangeal joint) develop bunions over time from the pressure of the body's weight on the foot when walking or exercising. Women's penchant to wear trendy shoes with high heels and narrow toe boxes adds to the pressure the joint sustains every day. When toes are crowded in an ill-fitting shoe, they are forced together in an abnormal position, which eventually leads to a permanently deformed joint.

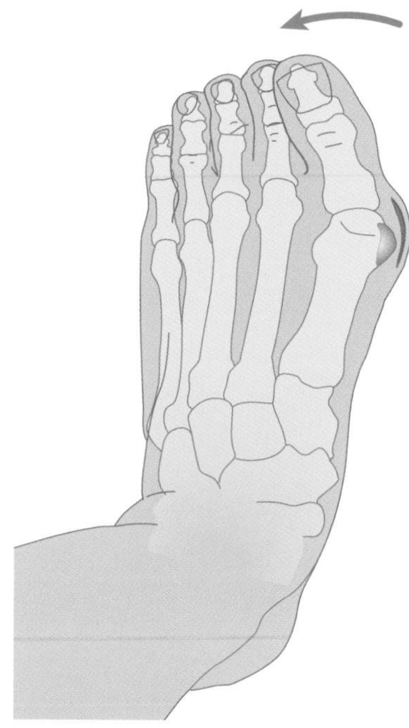

*A bunion develops when the joint at the base of the big toe becomes deformed and protrudes outward, possibly causing the toe to overlap the second toe.*

As the bunion develops, the nearby bursa—a fluid-filled sac that cushions bony prominences—becomes inflamed and painful. As the big toe bends inward, it may overlap the second toe and push it out of alignment, too. Often a bunionette—an enlargement and deformity at the base of the little toe—also develops.

## WHAT YOU CAN DO

If the bunion is inflamed and painful, applying a cold compress or ice pack for 15 to 20 minutes several times a day may help. Aspirin or ibuprofen can also relieve pain and reduce inflammation. Wear low-heeled shoes that fit properly so that toes are not crowded—you should be able to wiggle them freely. The toe box should also be wide enough to accommodate the deformed joint, with heels no higher than one inch. Avoid pointy-toed shoes or shoes that are too narrow. When buying shoes, be sure that the style you select can accommodate the bunion. If the deformity is severe, you may need a larger shoe size or a cut-out style, such as a sandal. Athletic shoes are a good choice for comfort.

Also pay attention to sock size; avoid those that are too tight or too big to prevent having them bunch up inside the toe box.

Shoe repair shops and pharmacies sell products designed to adapt the shoe to relieve pressure on the bunion. Arch supports and ring-shaped adhesive pads may help. Make sure these items fit properly; otherwise, they may do more harm than good. To keep the big toe properly aligned, try placing a small foam pad or piece of moleskin between it and your second toe.

## HOW TO TREAT IT

If you reach a point when walking becomes painful, no matter what kind of shoes you are wearing, consult a doctor or podiatrist. X rays will be taken to determine the extent of the joint deformity. To relieve pain, a doctor may also prescribe stronger anti-inflammatory medications. However, if the pain interferes with walking and other activities, surgery is usually recommended to remove the bunion and realign the toe joint.

The operation—called a *bunionectomy*—usually can be done under local anesthesia and on an outpatient basis. If the bunion is relatively mild, an incision is made on the side of the bunion and the joint capsule is opened. The protruding bone is then shaved and the bursa(s) and other soft tissue around the toe are repaired. The tendons attached to the base of the metatarsal and toe bone may be also be adjusted to hold the toe in its proper alignment. After the operation, the foot is firmly bandaged and the person wears a rigid plastic shoe for a few days; at first, a cane or crutches may be needed for walking because the foot should not bear the full body weight until the stitches are removed.

Full recovery from bunion surgery takes about six weeks; until healing is complete, it's advisable to keep the foot bandaged and to wear sandals or athletic shoes that do not put pressure on the toe. Most people are able to return to normal activities within a few days of the operation, but vigorous exercise is not recommended until the incision is completely healed.

If more correction is needed, the bones of the big toe may have to be surgically fractured and then realigned. Alternatively, a wedge-shape piece of the metatarsal bone is removed, and the toe is brought into proper alignment. The repositioned bones are then stabilized with surgical screws, wires, or plates. A painful bunionette may also be corrected. These more extensive operations may require a walking cast and crutches for six to eight weeks, or until healing is complete.

After any bunion surgery, the foot will be quite painful, so a strong painkiller such as meperidine (Demerol) or ketorolac (Toradol) may be given for a few days. After that, codeine or a nonprescription painkiller, such as acetaminophen or ibuprofen, usually provides sufficient pain control.

### BREAKTHROUGHS!

**Bunions have an unfortunate tendency to recur, even after extensive surgery. Increasingly, recurrences are being prevented or at least minimized by advances in the design of orthotics, custom-made devices that are inserted into shoes. A mold is made of the patient's foot, and the inserts are custom-made to increase the foot's stability. Orthotics are especially beneficial for people who have flatfeet or a tendency to overpronate.**

## HOW TO PREVENT IT

Because bunions involve a hereditary weakness of the foot, they are often impossible to prevent. However, wearing properly fitted shoes can slow their progression, and may help avoid surgery.

### ALTERNATIVE THERAPIES

**Hydrotherapy**

Soaking the painful foot in a whirlpool bath or basin of warm water can ease pain. For extra relief, try adding a few drops of peppermint oil or a cup of white vinegar to the footbath. Or soak a cold compress in a solution of a half cup vinegar diluted with a cup of cold or tepid water and apply it to the painful joint.

**Massage**

An inflamed joint should not be massaged directly because the increased blood flow can worsen inflammation. Instead, gently massage the surrounding area. Some massage therapists press a point on the side of the foot just below the second toe and parallel to the bunion. Other pain points are located just below the ankle bone, near the tip of the thumb, and in the space adjacent to the first joint of the thumb.

**Physical therapy**

Special foot exercises can sometime stave off the effects of bunions by strengthening surrounding muscles. Picking up a marble or cotton balls with your toes, rolling your foot over a round bottle on the floor, and foot and toe stretches are ways to strengthen foot muscles. To stretch foot and toe muscles, sit and lift one bare foot six inches off the floor. Make six small circles in both directions with the entire foot. Next, stretch your toes down, outward, and upward as far as you can. Repeat with the other foot.

### WARNING!

***After bunion surgery, check the incision every day or so for inflammation, pus, and other signs of infection. Some pain and bleeding are normal, but a foot infection can have very serious complications, so call your doctor if you think one seems to be developing.***

# Corns and Calluses

## SYMPTOMS

***Corns:*** *Small, round, firm yellow mounds of dead skin on top of and between toes that turn reddish and are painful under pressure.*

***Calluses:*** *Thickened areas of skin on balls and heels of feet (as well as the hands, elbows, and knees) that can develop painful cracks.*

## WHO IS AT RISK

*Corns and calluses are quite common among adults who do a lot of walking and wear improperly fitted shoes; having flatfeet increases the risk of developing calluses. Calluses can develop on the hands of people who do manual labor or whose jobs or hobbies involve repetitive motions. For example, violinists and guitarists often develop calluses on the tips of their fingers from pressing the strings against the neck of their instruments.*

## HOW THEY DEVELOP

Both corns and calluses develop when skin constantly rubs against the shoes or anything else. Sometimes arthritis or bone deformities cause bones to protrude and the skin to rub, become irritated, and then thicken. Hard corns form over bony protuberances; soft corns develop between toes. They are usually yellowish in appearance, but turn red when they get irritated and become inflamed. They have a hard, waxy core that can bore into the underlying tissue and nerves of the dermis, causing extreme pain when pressure is applied.

Calluses develop as thickened areas of skin on the balls and heels of feet in response to pressure, protecting tissue structures underneath. People in undeveloped countries who habitually walk barefooted develop thick calluses over the entire soles. Calluses are generally painless, but thick ones can develop painful cracks, which often become infected, especially among people with diabetes and circulatory disorders. Wearing narrow, high-heeled shoes that put extra pressure on the balls of the feet can also provoke callus pain.

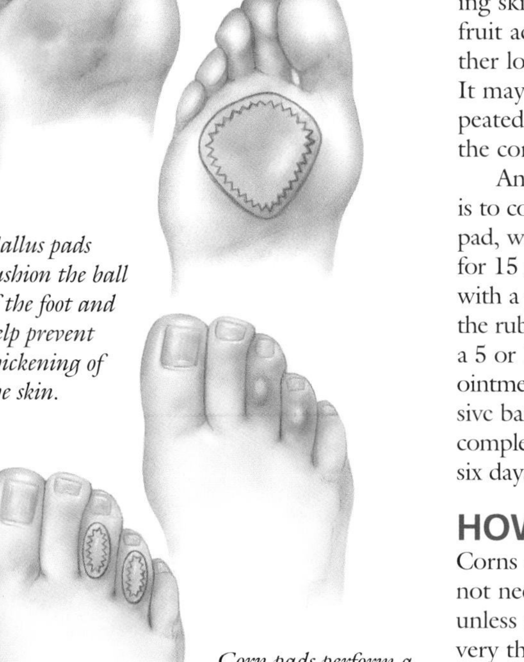

*Callus pads cushion the ball of the foot and help prevent thickening of the skin.*

*Corn pads perform a similar function, and reduce pain from the pressure of shoes.*

## WHAT YOU CAN DO

To ease the pain of corns and calluses, try soaking your feet in oatmeal water. Boil two cups of finely ground oatmeal in five quarts of water until the mixture cooks down to about four quarts. Strain it, put the liquid into a large basin, let it cool until comfortably warm, and then soak your feet in it for at least 20 minutes.

Nonprescription corn and callus pads relieve pain by reducing pressure. Some are medicated with salicylic acid or other chemicals that soften the clumps and dead skin to make the corns easier to remove. You can also remove corns and calluses by soaking the foot in Epsom salts and warm water for 15 minutes, then gently rubbing them with a pumice stone and applying a moisturizing skin cream containing mild fruit acids, which encourage further loosening of the dead skin. It may take a week or so of repeated treatments to get rid of the corns or calluses.

Another way to soften a corn is to cover it with a moist gauze pad, wrap the foot in plastic wrap for 15 minutes, and then rub it with a pumice stone; stop when the rubbing produces pain. Apply a 5 or 10 percent salicylic acid ointment and cover with an adhesive bandage. The corn should completely disappear after five or six days of repeated treatments.

## HOW TO TREAT IT

Corns and calluses generally do not need medical treatment unless they protrude or become very thick, are causing unusual pain, or if an infection develops under a callus, which is quite common. A doctor or podiatrist will cleanse the area with an antiseptic solution and inject a local anesthetic before paring away the thickened, dead skin. The area will be covered with an antibiotic ointment and bandaged; an oral antibiotic may also be prescribed.

### BREAKTHROUGHS!

**A number of soothing foot creams rich in various fruit acids have been developed to help soften calluses and make it easier to rub away the layers of dead skin. Look for topical products such as Neostrata body lotion that contain at least 8 percent alpha hydroxy acid.**

## HOW TO PREVENT THEM

Check the fit of your shoes and discard any that rub the toes and callused areas. Make sure that your socks also fit properly; they should not be so tight that they cause pressure on the toes, nor should they be so loose that they wrinkle and cause rubbing. Use moisturizing creams and lotions generously to keep the skin supple.

### ALTERNATIVE THERAPIES

**Folk remedies**

Rub castor oil into the corn twice a day; after a week or so, it should be soft enough to peel off easily. Alternatively, tape a thin slice of pineapple or a strip of fresh lemon peel (with the inside of the peel against the corn) over the corn. The lemon acids or pineapple enzymes help loosen the corn for easy removal. You can also soften a corn or callus with a poultice made by soaking a piece of bread in vinegar and applying it to the thickened skin. Cover the poultice with gauze and leave it on for at least an hour (or overnight if possible). Most corns will peel off after one or two applications. If you're treating a callus, rub the softened area with a pumice stone and then apply a moisturizing cream.

**WARNING!**

***Don't try to pare corns or calluses with a razor blade or other sharp object, especially if you have poor eyesight, an unsteady hand, or diabetes or poor circulation. Even a small cut can result in a serious foot infection.***

**Herbal medicine**

Green tea softens corns and calluses to ease their removal. Immerse a green tea bag in hot water for a minute or so, let cool slightly, and apply it directly to the corn or callus for 15 minutes. Repeat daily until the corn lifts off; rub a callus with a pumice stone after each treatment.

# Diabetic Foot

**SYMPTOMS**

- *Numbness, tingling, shooting pains, and weakness in the feet or lower legs.*
- *Tendency for any small cut or other wound to become a slow-healing infection or chronic foot ulcer.*
- *Feet often feel cold and numb.*
- *Increasing difficulty walking.*
- *Skin on the feet becomes thick, dry, scaly, and cracked.*

**WHO IS AT RISK**

*More than 1.5 million Canadians have diabetes, and about 25 percent of these will develop chronic foot problems. The risk is greatest among overweight persons whose diabetes is poorly controlled, resulting in chronically high levels of blood sugar (glucose).*

*The prevalence of diabetes among Canada's aboriginal peoples is at least three times that of the general population. The Sandy Lake First Nations community in northeastern Ontario has a diabetes rate of 26 percent—the third highest in the world.*

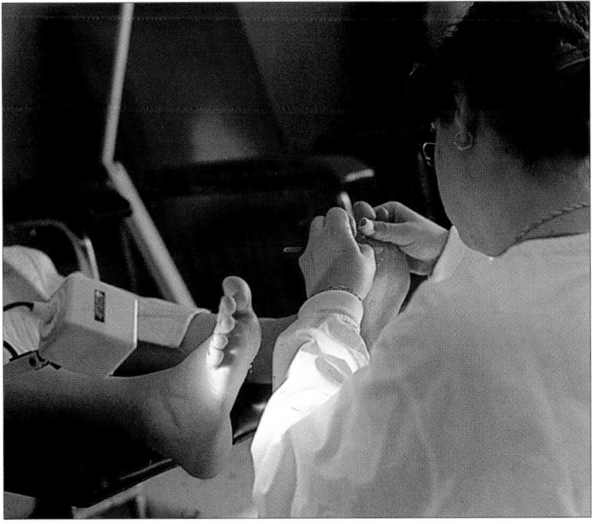

*All diabetic patients should undergo a careful foot examination at least twice a year, and more often if the person has chronic foot ulcers or other problems.*

## HOW IT DEVELOPS

The first symptoms are usually shooting pains, numbness, tingling sensations, and coldness in the lower legs and feet—signs of reduced circulation and nerve damage (diabetic neuropathy). The skin on the feet becomes thick and dry, and the soles develop deep calluses. Even a minor cut or scrape can evolve into a severe, slow-healing infection. At first the sore or infection may go unnoticed, especially if it develops under a callus, because of a lack of feeling in the feet. If untreated, however, tissue death (gangrene) may develop, requiring amputation of the affected part. In fact, 50 percent or more of nontraumatic limb amputations in Canada are due to diabetes. Often, one or more toes need to be removed, but a large number of diabetics also lose an entire foot and perhaps the lower leg as well.

**WARNING!**

***If you are diabetic, see your doctor or podiatrist as soon as possible if you develop a blister, ingrown toenail, corn, or similar lesion. These seemingly minor problems can quickly escalate into an infection that may require amputation.***

**BREAKTHROUGHS!**

**The healing problems of diabetic foot ulcers are often complicated by the fact that in diabetes, the body often fails to produce the growth factors needed for proper healing. Now there is a topical gel, becaplermin (Regranex), that stimulates natural healing. Regranex contains an artificially engineered growth factor that prompts the body to grow new tissue to heal the open wound and allow it to heal.**

## WHAT YOU CAN DO

Daily exercise, such as walking or using a stationary bicycle, helps maintain circulation to the lower limbs and may reduce the shooting pains, tingling, numbness, and other uncomfortable symptoms.

## HOW TO TREAT IT

Treatment varies according to the nature of the problem. If the arteries in the lower legs are clogged with fatty deposits—a common problem in diabetes—bypass surgery or angioplasty may be considered. Antibiotics are prescribed to treat infections, but their effectiveness is hampered by poor circulation. Hospitalization is often needed; infected skin ulcers are debrided and large ones may need to be covered with a skin graft in order to heal. The person may need to use crutches or a wheelchair until the ulcer is completely healed. If gangrene develops, surgery is necessary to remove the dead tissue and prevent further deterioration.

## HOW TO PREVENT IT

Numerous studies show that the risk of amputations and other serious complications can be lowered by keeping blood glucose levels under control. In addition, meticulous self-care is the key to avoiding amputations and other diabetic-foot complications.

- Wash your feet daily in lukewarm (not hot) water, inspect them carefully, and apply a moisturizing lotion to prevent the skin from cracking. Do not apply lotion to the soles or between the toes, where the moisture may promote fungal growth.
- Keep toenails trimmed and smooth; if you have poor eyesight or difficulty cutting your nails, consult a podiatrist who specializes in treating diabetic feet.
- Wear cotton socks that do not have tight, binding tops, which can further hinder blood flow.
- Never go barefooted, which increases the risk of a stubbed toe, splinter, or cut.
- Always check your shoes carefully for objects before putting them on—e.g., small pebbles or a paper clip—or for rough spots that can cut or rub against the foot.
- Avoid sitting with your legs crossed, which further hinders blood flow to the feet.
- Wear shoes that are properly fitted and break in new ones slowly to avoid blisters. Shoes should have cushioned soles and uppers made of soft leather, canvas, or other material that allows air to circulate.

### ALTERNATIVE THERAPIES

Note: Check with your doctor before trying any alternative therapy to make sure that it is safe and will not interact with your prescribed medications and treatments.

**Herbal medicine**

Ginkgo biloba extract helps maintain circulation in the lower limbs and may also prevent diabetes-related nerve and eye damage. The typical dosage is 120 mg a day divided into two or three doses. Aloe vera gel, gently massaged into the skin, keeps it soft and supple; it also has mild antibiotic properties that help prevent skin infections and promote healing.

**Magnets**

A recent study at New York Medical College found that magnet therapy reduced diabetic foot pain and also lowered the risk of skin ulcers and other complications. The researchers do not know exactly how or why magnet therapy works, but they theorize that improved circulation may be a factor.

**Nutraceuticals**

Daily supplements that have been shown to improve glucose control and reduce nerve damage and other complications of diabetes include: 1000 to 2000 mg of vitamin C, 800 IU of vitamin E, 1000 to 1500 micrograms (mcg) of vitamin $B_{12}$, 800 mcg of folic acid, 250 mg of niacin, 9 to 16 mg of biotin, and 120 mg of coenzyme $Q_{10}$.

# Flatfeet

### SYMPTOMS

- *Possible persistent foot and ankle pain, especially when walking, running, and engaging in other activities that put extra stress on the feet.*
- *Awkward gait; increased risk of foot fractures, Achilles tendon injuries, and other types of leg, knee, and hip pain.*

### WHO IS AT RISK

*Flatfeet may result from a congenital weakness of the foot ligaments. Obesity can cause flatfeet; risk is also increased by diabetes and diseases that cause muscle weakness.*

## HOW IT DEVELOPS

The foot has two arches—a high, longitudinal one in the midfoot and a shorter one in the forefoot. Babies are born with flatfeet, but the condition normally disappears as the foot ligaments strengthen and arches develop to form bony bridges that support the foot and act as shock absorbers. Flatfeet may persist, however, if a child has a congenital malformation of the foot bones or a neuromuscular abnormality that prevents arch development. Among adults, flatfeet—or fallen arches—can be caused by obesity, diabetes, and arthritis.

Symptoms related to flatfeet vary greatly—for some people, they pose no special problems; others experience pain when they overwork their feet; and still others are unable to walk without pain.

## WHAT YOU CAN DO

Arch supports can usually ease the discomfort of flatfeet. Sometimes, wearing shoes that have high arch supports, such as those in athletic walking shoes, is all that is needed. If these do not provide adequate relief, corrective orthopedic shoes or orthotic inserts may be needed.

**WARNING!**

***People with flatfeet have an increased risk of Achilles tendon injuries and foot fractures. Pay special attention to wearing appropriate shoes and, if necessary, orthotic devices to reduce stress on the Achilles tendon and small foot bones.***

Walking, especially going barefoot, is one of the best foot exercises. Doing toe raises also strengthens the arch: Stand with your feet about five or six inches apart with the toes pointed slightly inward. With your hands resting on the back of a sturdy chair for support, slowly rise to your toes, hold for a count of two, and lower the heel to the floor. Do three sets of 10 toe raises daily and before taking a long walk or jogging.

To soothe aching feet, try using a foot whirlpool bath or soaking them in a basin of warm water that contains a half cup of Epsom salts or a few drops of lavender oil.

## HOW TO TREAT IT

Flatfeet that cause pain, difficulty walking, and other problems may be treated with custom-made orthotic devices. A plaster mold is made of the feet and then used to fashion rigid plastic and metal orthotic devices. Surgical correction of malaligned bones may be considered, especially if the abnormality interferes with walking and other activities.

### WHEN THE ARCH IS TOO HIGH

Although not as common as flatfeet, the opposite problem of an overly high arch can be more painful. During early childhood, the foot appears to be normal, but this changes during adolescence. Examination of the foot will show a very high arch, the result of muscle imbalances in the sole that pull the overlying bones upward. Pain is concentrated in the ball of the foot and the toes, which are usually drawn upward into a deformity called hammertoes. Sometimes physical therapy helps, but surgical correction is usually needed for long-term relief.

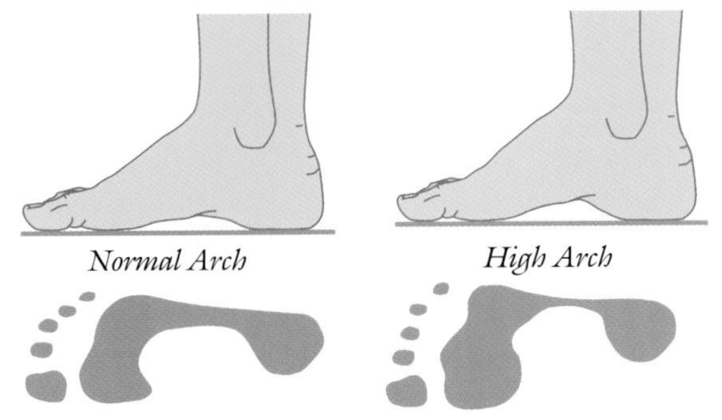


## HOW TO PREVENT IT

Congenital flatfeet cannot be prevented. Maintaining ideal weight can prevent flatfeet related to obesity.

#### ALTERNATIVE THERAPIES

**Foot massage**

Simply rubbing and massaging a foot can ease pain; massage therapy, which may be combined with acupressure

**Normal Foot**

*Normally, the foot's arch prevents the inner edge from resting flat on the ground when a person stands.*

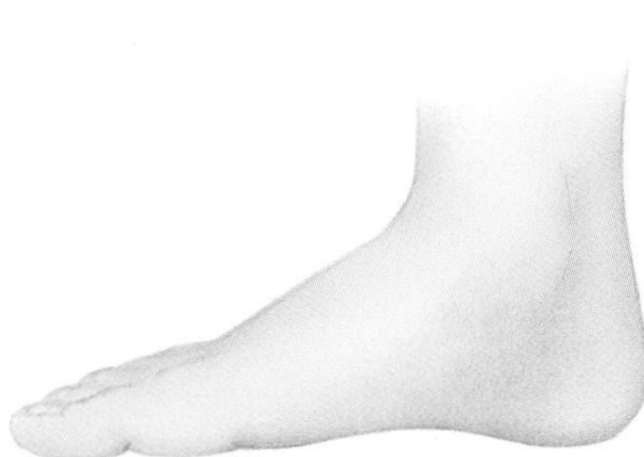

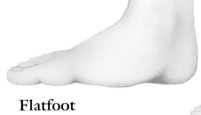

**Flatfoot**

*A flatfoot lacks an arch, allowing it to rest flat on the floor.*

**Corrective Orthotics**

*An orthotic device acts as an artificial arch, supporting and cushioning the foot structures.*

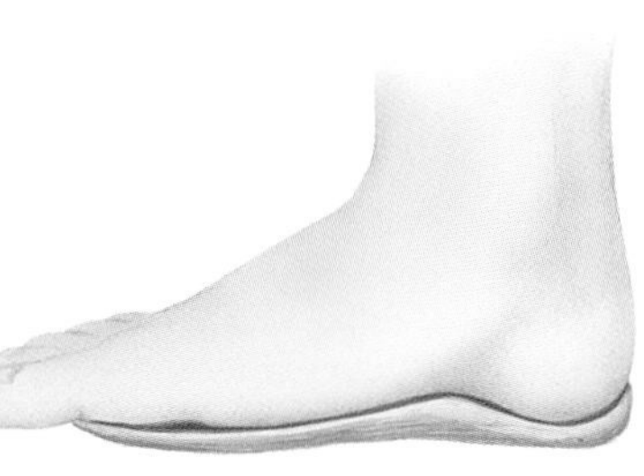

and reflexology, may be even more beneficial. Diluted aromatic oils, such as lavender or peppermint, may also be massaged into the foot.

**Physical therapy**

Physical therapists can teach special foot exercises and help correct a faulty gait.

# Gout

### SYMPTOMS

- *Sudden pain and swelling in a joint, most often joints of the big toe.*
- *Skin around the joint is shiny, and red or purple; the joint itself is extremely sensitive, painful, and hot to the touch.*
- *Possible fever.*

### WHO IS AT RISK

*Gout, a metabolic disorder that allows a buildup of uric acid in the blood, affects about 5 out of every 1,000 Canadians from all walks of life. It is predominantly an affliction of men between the ages of 40 and 50, although some women develop it following menopause. Obesity increases the risk, especially in people who have the inherited susceptibility; attacks can be precipitated by overconsumption of alcohol and foods high in purines, such as organ meats, sardines, anchovies, and dried beans and other legumes.*

*Other possible risk factors include exposure to lead in the environment and the use of certain medications, such as diuretics, niacin, cyclosporin (used to prevent organ transplant rejection), and the Parkinson's disease drug Levodopa. Stress may also bring on an attack of gout.*

**WARNING!**

***If you think that a medication you are taking for another condition, such as high blood pressure, is causing your gout, consult your doctor as soon as possible. Switching to an alternative medication may prevent future attacks.***

## HOW IT DEVELOPS

Uric acid, a metabolic waste product, is generally excreted from the body in the urine. When the body fails to properly eliminate uric acid or overproduces it (a condition known as hyperuricemia), tiny needle-like uric acid crystals collect in the joints, causing the extreme pain associated with gout.

Overconsumption of foods rich in purines can increase the levels of uric acid and bring on an attack of gout, since the breakdown of purines creates uric acid. Similarly, excessive alcohol consumption causes uric acid levels to rise. Obesity hinders the body's ability to eliminate uric acid, as can certain medications. In some cases, high levels of uric acid are caused by an inherited metabolic disorder.

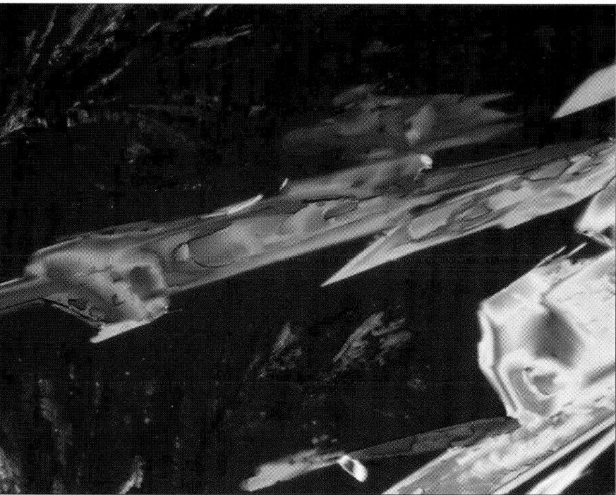

*The sharp, pointed projections of uric acid crystals cause the intense joint pain during an attack.*

Gout attacks usually occur in the joint of the big toe, but may also affect other foot joints, the ankles, knees, elbows, and wrists. Attacks often start during the night, and as the pain worsens, even the slightest pressure, such as a sheet touching the toe, is excruciating.

If left untreated, the attacks become more frequent, increase in duration, and may cause permanent damage to the affected joints. In addition, uric acid crystal deposits, called tophi, may collect in the joints or the ear, break through the skin, and cause infection. Kidney stones are another danger associated with gout.

## WHAT YOU CAN DO

Take ibuprofen or another nonsteroidal anti-inflammatory drug (NSAID) and, if you have a history of gout, start antigout medication as soon as you sense an impending attack (see *How to Treat It,* below). Drink a glass of water every hour or so to increase urine output to rid the body of the excessive uric acid. Elevate the foot and, if you can tolerate the pressure, apply a cold compress to help reduce inflammation. Rest as much as possible until the acute attack subsides.

## HOW TO TREAT IT

To immediately relieve some of the pain during an acute attack, a doctor may withdraw (aspirate) the fluid from a badly swollen joint. Treatment is then centered on reducing inflammation and stopping the attack. For some sufferers, prescription-strength NSAIDs may provide adequate relief. One of the most-used treatments, however, is an ancient remedy using colchicine, a drug derived from the autumn crocus. This drug is taken in frequent, small oral doses, until the pain subsides or signs of toxicity—nausea, vomiting, diarrhea, abdominal cramps—develop; the drug must then be stopped.

Doctors generally advise the older patient with hyperuricemia to treat acute attacks as they come and avoid using long-term medications, since there are associated side effects. If the frequency of attacks increases, however, patients may take a daily medication that curtails uric acid production and helps dissolve tophi; these drugs include probenecid (Benemid), sulfinpyrazone (Anturan), and allopurinol (Zyloprim).

Large tophi that interfere with movement or are causing frequent infections may be surgically removed.

## HOW TO PREVENT IT

Patients who suffer frequent attacks may reduce their number by taking preventive medications, such as allopurinol or a small, daily dose of colchicine. Drink at least 8 to 10 glasses of water a day to help eliminate uric acid from the body, and avoid foods containing purines. Keeping fit and slim will also aid in uric acid removal; it is important to lose weight gradually, however, since sudden weight loss may actually raise uric acid levels. Abstain from alcohol or use it only in moderation.

### ALTERNATIVE THERAPIES

**Acupuncture**

Acupuncture can help ease pain during an acute gout attack, as can acupressure.

**Herbal medicine**

Herbalists recommend putting fire weed or balm of Gilead ointment on painful joints. A mixture of burdock root, celery seed, yarrow, and thuja can be taken in capsule or infusion form, or as a tincture, to treat gout.

**Homeopathy**

Homeopaths recommend Guaiacum, Benzinum acidum, belladonna, or Pulsatilla begricans to reduce symptoms.

**Meditation**

Since stress may cause gout attacks, yoga, meditation, and other relaxation techniques may be helpful.

# Hammertoes/ Clawtoes

### SYMPTOMS

- *Painful foot deformity that draws one or more toes into a bent, clawlike position.*
- *Formation of painful corns on the top of the toe and calluses or ulcers on the side of the toe or, more often, on the sole of the foot.*

### WHO IS AT RISK

*A genetic abnormality in the alignment of the foot's metatarsal bones often leads to development of hammertoes, especially if the person wears high heels or poorly fitted shoes that crowd and press on the toes. Diabetes, stroke and other neuromuscular disorders, and arthritis can lead to hammertoes; obesity also increases the risk. People who have Morton's toes—an inherited anomaly in which the second toe is longer than the big toe—are also susceptible to developing hammertoes, especially if they wear shoes that are too short.*

## HOW IT DEVELOPS

The clawlike deformity, which most often affects the second toe, is due to an imbalance of the foot's muscles and tendons, but the underlying cause is not always clear. Each toe is controlled by six sets of muscles, which—along with a complex arrangement of tendons and ligaments—help stabilize the foot and provide the balance needed to walk normally. If muscles and tendons on the sole of the foot are stronger than those on the top, the affected toe can be pulled out of its proper alignment. Shortened tendons can also result in hammertoes.

**WARNING!**

***Hammertoes can cause increasing pain and disability. If left untreated, they can harden into fixed deformities that make it impossible to walk normally without pain.***

Painful corns form when the hammertoes rub against shoes. Rubbing can also cause calluses or ulcers on the sole of the foot or sides of the affected toes.

## WHAT YOU CAN DO

Wear low-heeled, wide-toed shoes to ease friction and pressure on the bent or raised toe. To relieve pain and protect the skin on the deformed toe, cover it with an unmedicated corn pad or piece of moleskin. Painful corns can be removed after soaking the feet (see *Corns and Calluses,* p 284). See a doctor or podiatrist for more definitive treatment.

## HOW TO TREAT IT

A doctor or podiatrist will carefully examine your feet, gait, and the pattern of wear on your shoes. X rays may be ordered. An injection of a local anesthetic, such as lidocaine (Xylocaine), provides temporary pain relief; it may be combined with a corticosteroid, especially if the hammertoes are inflamed and swollen.

Sometimes wearing custom-fitted shoe inserts (orthotics) can relieve pressure and ease the pain of mild hammertoes. Quite often, however, surgical correction is necessary. If the problem is due to a shortened tendon, the toe is straightened by cutting the tendon and allow-

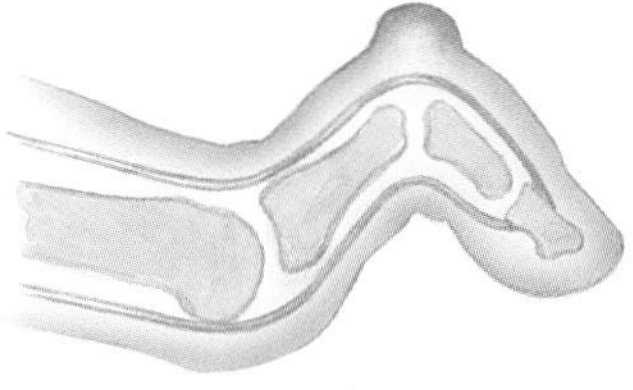

*A tight, shortened tendon can draw the toe into a clawlike position to form a hammertoe with a painful corn on top.*

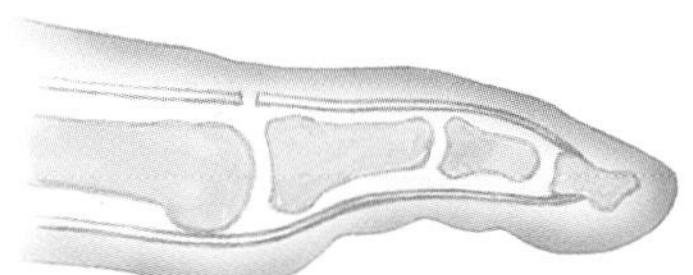

*Surgical correction entails cutting the tendon to allow the toe to straighten itself.*

ing the toe to flatten itself. This is done on an outpatient basis using a local anesthetic. As the tendon heals, which usually takes 7 to 10 days, the severed ends reattach and lengthen to straighten the toe. In severe cases, part of the metatarsal bone may be removed. Alternatively, two of the toe bones may be fused together and some of the cartilage removed.

Codeine or a prescription-strength anti-inflammatory drug will be given for pain while healing takes place, usually three to four weeks. For the first week or so, patients must wear surgical shoes and use a cane to minimize pressure on the foot. As the pain eases, sandals or athletic shoes that do not press on the toes can be worn. When healing is complete, orthotic devices should be worn to maintain the correction.

## HOW TO PREVENT IT

Hammertoes due to congenital defects and certain neuromuscular disorders cannot be prevented. However, those due to wearing poorly fitted or inappropriate shoes can be prevented by the following measures:

- Shop for shoes in the late afternoon, when your feet are their largest. Be sure shoes fit comfortably when you try them on; "breaking in" will not make a poorly fitted shoe comfortable.
- Make sure the toes have enough room to wiggle comfortably, and that the toe box is high enough to accommodate them without squeezing or rubbing. If you have hammertoes, sandals or other cutout styles are more comfortable than enclosed shoes.
- If your feet are different sizes (and many people do have feet that are not the same size), fit the larger foot and use an insert or heavier sock to improve the fit for the other foot. If the size difference is pronounced (more than a half size), you may need to buy two pairs in different sizes and discard the odd ones that do not fit.
- Go through your shoe closet periodically and discard those that no longer fit. Feet enlarge with age, so shoes that are a few years old may no longer fit.

### ALTERNATIVE THERAPIES

**Alexander technique**

An instructor will analyze your gait and teach you new ways of walking and moving to make sure that weight is properly distributed to ease pressure on the feet.

**Massage**

Foot massage using reflexology techniques may temporarily relieve the pain associated with hammertoes. A massage therapist may use soothing aromatic oils, such as peppermint, lavender, or tea tree. These oils can also be added to a footbath.

# Heel Spurs/ Plantar Fasciitis

### SYMPTOMS

***Heel spurs:*** *Pain, tenderness, and swelling in the ball of the heel, especially after standing or walking; increasing difficulty walking.*

***Plantar fasciitis:*** *Heel pain that is most intense when walking or running; pain also occurs when standing after a period of rest.*

### WHO IS AT RISK

***Bony spurs****—one of the most common causes of heel pain—most often develop in people who are overweight, runners, tennis players, and others whose feet are subjected to unusual stress. Obesity and overuse also increase the risk of* ***plantar fasciitis****—inflammation of tissue between the ball of the foot and the heel—but it is also common among women who wear high-heeled shoes (or men who wear cowboy boots) and runners whose shoes fail to properly cushion the heel. Having flatfeet, abnormally high arches, or arthritis and other inflammatory conditions can increase the risk of plantar fasciitis and heel spurs.*

## HOW THEY DEVELOP

The heel bone (calcaneus)—the largest foot bone—must withstand enormous force whenever we use our feet. The plantar fascia—the layer of tough, tendonlike connective tissue at the bottom of the foot—attaches to the heel bone and is cushioned by fatty tissue. The excessive stress of obesity or overuse can break down this fat pad and, without a protective cushion, the fascia becomes irritated and painfully inflamed. Chronic or untreated plantar fasciitis may then stimulate growth of heel spurs where the fascia attaches to the calcaneus.

Wearing high-heeled shoes a lot can result in a shortening of the plantar fascia, which causes pain when it is stretched, such as when walking barefoot after getting up in the morning. Walking or running in shoes that do not cushion the heel properly can also cause tissue injury, inflammation, and pain. A walking or running gait that places excessive stress on the heels may also be a factor.

## WHAT YOU CAN DO

Aspirin, ibuprofen, or similar anti-inflammatory medications can temporarily relieve pain and reduce inflammation; massaging a topical anti-inflammatory cream or one that contains 0.025 percent capsaicin (the active ingredient in hot chili peppers) into the painful area may also help. If the heels are red and swollen, apply an ice pack for 15 to 20 minutes every two or three hours; this eases pain and reduces inflammation. After two days, you can switch to a heating pad or alternate hot and cold treatments. Stay off your feet as much as possible for a few days to allow the fascia to heal. If the pain persists, consult a doctor.

## HOW TO TREAT THEM

A doctor will X-ray the feet to determine whether heel spurs have developed; he or she will also study your gait and examine the pattern of wear on an old pair of shoes. A corticosteroid injection provides quick pain relief and also reduces inflammation; a prescription-strength anti-inflammatory drug may be recommended. The doctor may also advise wearing an orthotic shoe insert to cushion the heel and refer you to a physical therapist.

If these conservative measures do not work, and heel spurs are contributing to the pain, arthroscopic surgery to remove them may help. A viewing tube equipped with a miniature video camera and tiny surgical instruments is inserted through a small incision in the heel area. The surgeon then manipulates the instruments to shave away the bony spur while viewing the site on a video screen. The procedure can be done under local anesthesia and on an outpatient basis. Codeine or a similar painkiller is prescribed for a few days, after which acetaminophen or ibuprofen is usually sufficient. The patient must use crutches until the bone has healed.

**WARNING!**

***Surgery should be considered a treatment of last resort for heel pain. Unless the underlying causes are corrected, the pain is likely to recur. This is what forced the retirement of Joe DiMaggio, whose heel never properly healed after removal of a bony spur.***

## HOW TO PREVENT THEM

If you are overweight, consult a nutritionist or your doctor for an eating and exercise program that will help you achieve and maintain ideal weight. Wear low-heeled (one to one and a half inches) shoes that provide proper heel support and cushioning; save high heels for occasions that do not entail a lot of walking. If you jog or run, make sure that your shoes are properly fitted; if you have a history of heel pain, avoid running on hard surfaces or hilly terrain and alternate running with cycling and other aerobic activities. Always do foot and ankle stretches before and after workouts.

### ALTERNATIVE THERAPIES

**Physical therapy**

A physical therapist (or specialist in sports medicine) can analyze your gait and teach you corrective exercises. Physical therapists also treat chronic heel pain with ultrasound, diathermy, electrical nerve stimulation, hot and cold packs, and whirlpool baths. They may also fit patients with a splint to keep the foot stretched during sleep.

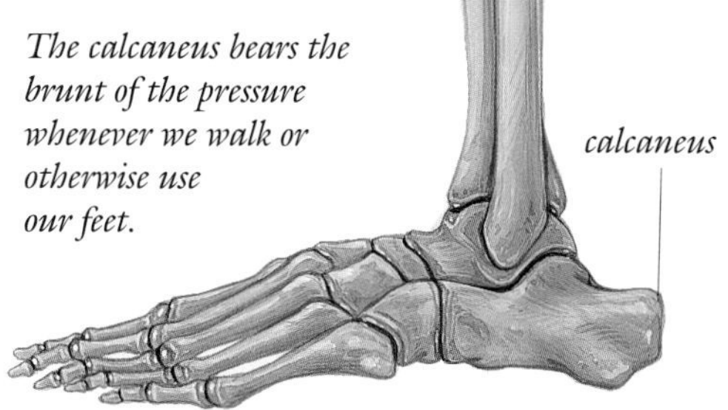


*The calcaneus bears the brunt of the pressure whenever we walk or otherwise use our feet.*

# Ingrown Toenails

### SYMPTOMS

- *Toe or foot pain that occurs when skin on the side of a toenail (usually on the big toe) grows over the edge of the nail, or when the nail curves and grows into the skin.*
- *Possible increasing pain, inflammation, swelling, and pus discharge from ingrown nail.*

### WHO IS AT RISK

*Ingrown toenails, known medically as* onychocryptosis, *are very common, especially among people who favor pointy-toed shoes or stockings that are too tight. Overmanicuring or cutting the nails too short or on a curve can prompt them to grow improperly. Repeated foot trauma, such as frequent stubbing of the big toe or undue pressure from long-distance running, can result in ingrown nails. People with flatfeet have an increased risk of developing ingrown nails. Other risk factors include chronic fungal nail infections and having nails that grow at an abnormal angle.*

## HOW IT DEVELOPS

This common but painful condition develops when skin on the side of the nail grows over the edge of the nail, or when the nail itself grows into the skin. Repeated pressure on the site can lead to pain and inflammation and, if left untreated, an infection may develop. Sometimes small corns grow in the groove just under the nail, creating even more foot pain.

## WHAT YOU CAN DO

If the nail is only mildly ingrown, with no obvious infection, try making a V-shaped notch in the center of the nail. This notch will redirect the growth of the nail toward the center and away from the painful sides. For more painful ingrown nails, you can try removing the ingrown portion (see *How to Remove an Ingrown Nail,* right). However, if there are signs of infection, or if the problem recurs, consult a doctor or podiatrist.

## HOW TO TREAT IT

A doctor will inject a local anesthetic to relieve pain, and then remove the ingrown portion of nail. In severe cases, a larger portion or perhaps all of the toenail will be removed. If the nail is deeply embedded in the skin, some of the soft tissue will also be cut away, and stitches may be needed to close the wound.

If the nail is infected or grows in a distorted way, the entire nail and the nail bed (matrix), from which it grows, may have to be removed. After injecting a local anesthetic, the doctor makes a small incision in the skin on three sides of the nail, the flap of skin is pulled back, and the matrix and the entire nail are removed. The matrix is then cauterized with an electric needle to prevent further nail growth. The doctor then reattaches the skin flap with small stitches, which are removed in four or five days.

After the operation, the toe is wrapped in a soft dressing and the patient must wear a soft surgical shoe and perhaps use crutches until full weight can be put on the foot. Codeine or a similar painkiller may be prescribed, along with an oral antibiotic to treat or prevent infection. The toe will be periodically checked to make sure it is healing properly; stitches are removed after a few days. While the toe heals, the foot should be kept elevated as much as possible. Healing may take a few weeks.

### WARNING!

***Some ingrown toenails are caused by fungal infections, which must also be treated in order to cure the condition. If the infection persists, the ingrown nail is likely to recur.***

### BREAKTHROUGHS!

**Laser surgery to remove infected or badly ingrown toenails is quicker and less painful than conventional methods. However, the doctor must be sure that all the matrix cells are removed; if any are left behind, the toenail will grow back.**

### HOW TO REMOVE AN INGROWN NAIL

Start by soaking the affected foot for 10 minutes in warm soapy water to soften the skin. Have clean gauze and a sterilized nail clipper and tweezers close at hand.

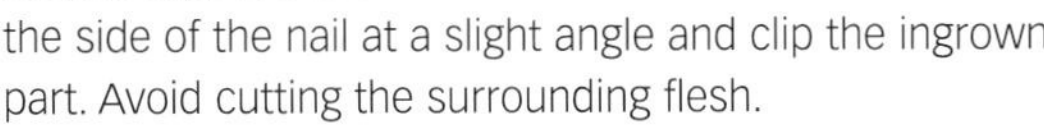

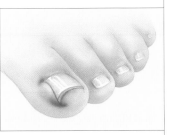

1. Dry the foot, then place an ice cube at the site for about three minutes to numb the surface.
2. Insert the sterilized toenail clipper under the side of the nail at a slight angle and clip the ingrown part. Avoid cutting the surrounding flesh.
3. With sterilized tweezers, gently remove the loose portion of the nail. If the toe bleeds, elevate the foot and apply an ice pack.
4. Dry the foot, swab with an antiseptic solution (for example, povidone-iodine [Betadine] or rubbing alcohol) and cover with sterile gauze. When the bleeding stops, cover the toe with an adhesive bandage.

While the toe is healing, soak it twice a day in warm soapy water, apply an antiseptic solution, and put on a new adhesive bandage. Wear only low-heeled shoes with a wide toe box until the toe is completely healed.

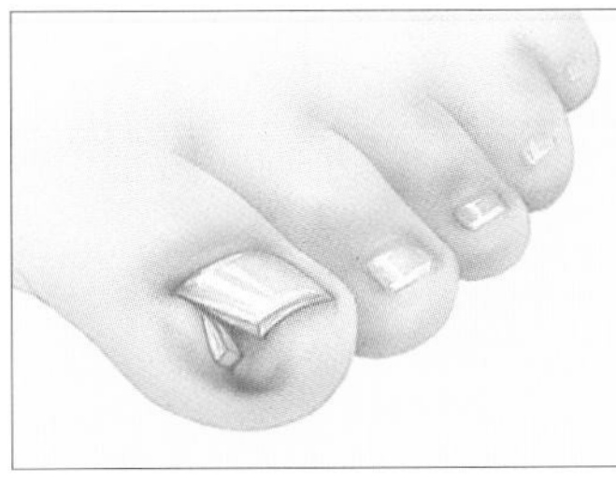

## HOW TO PREVENT IT

Unlike fingernails, toenails should be cut straight across, not rounded, to prevent ingrown toenails. Avoid cutting the nails too short, which encourages them to start growing into the flesh. Protect your feet from repeated trauma by wearing shoes with adequate room for your toes. Do not wear socks that are so tight that they cramp your toes. To reduce the risk of stubbed toes, avoid walking barefoot in the dark.

### ALTERNATIVE THERAPIES

There are no alternative therapies to prevent or treat ingrown toenails.

# Morton's Neuroma

### SYMPTOMS

- *Sharp or dull pain between the third and fourth toes, usually on only one foot, that worsens when walking.*
- *Pain that radiates from ball of the foot to the toes.*

### WHO IS AT RISK

*Morton's neuroma, a benign tumor on the plantar nerve that runs along the sole, is more common in women than in men, presumably because the tighter shoes that women wear exert excessive pressure on the affected nerve. These neuromas may also be due to congenital malformations, such as flatfeet, abnormally high arches, a shortening of the first metatarsal (the bone leading to the big toe), or webs of skin between the toes. Foot injuries may also promote growth of Morton's neuroma.*

## HOW IT DEVELOPS

Morton's neuroma usually develops between the third and fourth toes where the lateral plantar nerve enlarges and combines with the medial plantar nerve. It can be distinguished from other painful foot conditions by pressing between the third and fourth toe on the sole of the foot; sharp, intense pain indicates a probable nerve tumor and inflammation.

The neuroma starts with a thickening and inflammation of the nerve, which evolves into a benign growth. Walking compresses the neuroma and produces mild to severe pain. Anything that adds to the pressure, especially wearing shoes that are too narrow, increases the pain and burning or tingling sensations. Patients often liken the discomfort to having a marble or pebble lodged in the shoe just under the ball of the foot. As the neuroma grows, the nerve becomes more inflamed and the person may experience a constant burning that radiates to the tips of the toes.

## WHAT YOU CAN DO

To minimize the foot pain, wear low-heeled shoes with soft, supple soles and uppers and ample cushioning under the ball of the foot. Many people with Morton's neuromas prefer to walk barefooted, when possible, or to wear soft moccasins and other slipperlike shoes. See a doctor if the pain persists or worsens.

### BREAKTHROUGHS!

**Laser surgery is lowering the incidence of recurrence of Morton's neuroma pain. This procedure, which uses intense light beams to vaporize unwanted tissue, is less likely to produce scar tissue than traditional surgical procedures.**

## HOW TO TREAT IT

Sometimes a doctor will inject a local painkiller, such as lidocaine (Xylocaine), to relieve symptoms temporarily. Injection of a long-acting corticosteroid may also be tried. The injections may be given once or twice a week for a month or so in an attempt to achieve long-term reduction of the inflammation and lasting pain relief.

### WARNING!

***Morton's neuroma tends to be a progressive disorder. Early detection and corrective action can often prevent this; consult a doctor for any burning foot pain that recurs frequently or lasts for more than a few days.***

Long-term treatment is aimed at trying to disperse the weight away from the neuroma. Shoe inserts to provide soft padding under the ball of the foot may help. If the patient is flat-footed, arch supports will be tried.

If all else fails, surgery to remove the growth and resection the nerve often brings relief. Sometimes, however, the pain recurs, especially if the neuroma regrows or scar tissue forms and presses on the adjacent nerves.

## HOW TO PREVENT IT

Morton's neuromas due to congenital malformations often cannot be prevented. Wearing low-heeled, properly fitted shoes with adequate sole cushioning may prevent some neuromas.

### ALTERNATIVE THERAPIES

**Acupuncture and acupressure**

These treatments are effective against many types of nerve pain and inflammation, including Morton's neuroma. Typically, six or more treatments are needed to achieve lasting relief.

# Plantar Warts

### SYMPTOMS

- *Pain in the soles of the feet when standing or walking.*
- *Small, bumpy growths on the bottom of the feet that bleed slightly when they are scraped or scratched.*
- *Clusters of warts on the soles that elicit pain when pressure is applied to them.*

### WHO IS AT RISK

*Plantar warts—like some 50 other varieties of warts that occur on the hands and other parts of the body—are caused by the human papilloma virus (HPV). They are most common in children and young adults, and become less common with age as the immune system develops defenses against the HPV. The HPV virus is highly contagious, how-*

*ever, so epidemics can occur among people who share gym or athletic facilities where they walk about with bare feet.*

## HOW IT DEVELOPS

Plantar warts grow on the soles of the feet when the HPV virus invades the skin and stimulates an overgrowth of epithelial cells. The wart starts as a tiny bump no larger than a pinhead, and may grow to two inches across. Very often, tiny plantar warts form clusters; these are referred to as mosaic warts. Sometimes plantar warts are difficult to distinguish from calluses; to tell one from the other, rub the thickened skin with a pumice stone or piece of fine sandpaper. In plantar warts, the underlayer is studded with small black dots and scraping produces pinpoint bleeding.

**WARNING!**

***If you have diabetes, poor circulation in your legs and feet, or lowered immunity, do not try to remove a plantar wart yourself. This can result in a serious infection that may require amputation. If you fall into any of these groups, see a doctor as soon as possible for any foot problem.***

Plantar warts are benign and generally harmless, but they make walking painful because the growth presses on underlying tissue and nerves. They can be dangerous in persons with diabetes, poor circulation, or lowered immunity (see *Warning!,* above).

## WHAT YOU CAN DO

To reduce the pain when walking or standing, wear a soft pad over the warts; moleskin or callus pads often work well. Because plantar warts embed themselves in the sole of the foot, they are often difficult to remove, but self-treatment is worth a try, especially if the warts are small and not causing a lot of discomfort. Sometimes the removal techniques (applications of salicylic acid followed by debridement) used on calluses work (see *Corns and Calluses,* p 284).

Remember, too, that like all warts, these foot growths are highly unpredictable. They often disappear on their own, only to recur months or years later. Consult a doctor, preferably a dermatologist, if the warts are painful and self-treatment fails to get rid of them.

## HOW TO TREAT IT

Doctors use various techniques to remove plantar warts. One of the most common involves applying a tape impregnated with 40 percent salicylic acid over the warts for a few days. After removing the tape, the doctor will pare (debride) the area to remove any remaining wart tissue. A local anesthetic may be injected to prevent pain during the debridement. Deep warts may require several applications of the salicylic acid followed by debridement. If this approach does not work, a stronger caustic, such as 30 to 70 percent trichloroacetic acid, may be used.

**BREAKTHROUGHS!**

**Oral isotretinoin (Accutane) or topical tretinoin (Retin-A), powerful antiacne drugs derived from vitamin A, have proven effective in clearing stubborn cases of extensive warts. Studies have also found that injecting bleomycin (Blenoxane), an anticancer drug, or interferon, a drug that interferes with the ability of a virus to reproduce, can clear up persistent or recurring warts.**

Very large or hard-to-remove warts often require even more aggressive treatment, such as burning them off with an electric needle, freezing with liquid nitrogen, or laser surgery. Very stubborn warts may require surgical removal; the procedure is done under local anesthesia on an outpatient basis. The foot will be bandaged, and the person will need to walk with a cane and wear a surgical shoe until it heals.

## HOW TO PREVENT IT

Because plantar warts are caused by a very common, highly contagious virus, prevention is often impossible. You can, however, reduce your risk by always wearing protective footware in public shower rooms, around pools, and other places where people often go barefoot. If this is impractical, at least wash your feet thoroughly with an antibiotic soap after any possible exposure.

### ALTERNATIVE THERAPIES

**Note:** The following wart-removal techniques work for some people, and may be worth a try. All are painless and harmless, so nothing is lost if they fail.

**Herbal medicine**

Daily applications of aloe vera gel, taken from a fresh-cut leaf, may make a wart disappear in a few weeks. Apply the gel directly to the wart and cover with an adhesive bandage. Rubbing the wart once or twice a day with a cut garlic clove is another popular remedy that many herbalists swear by, although there is no scientific proof that garlic has any antiviral actions.

**Naturopathy**

Many naturopaths recommend vitamin A oil to remove plantar warts. Break open a vitamin A capsule, apply the oil to the warts, and cover with an adhesive bandage. Repeat daily until it disappears, which may take several months. A similar approach uses castor oil.

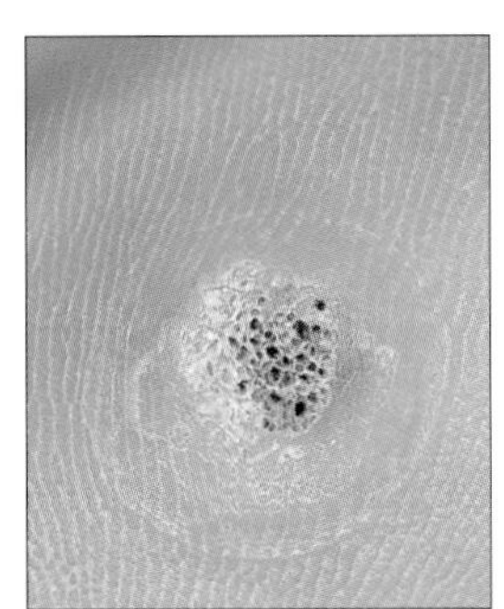

*Clusters of tiny plantar warts are distinguished by small, black dots that bleed when scraped.*

# Stress Fractures

**SYMPTOMS**

- *Sudden, sharp foot or ankle pain.*
- *Pain that intensifies when standing or walking.*

**WHO IS AT RISK**

*Stress fractures—incomplete breaks in the small bones of the foot, ankle, or lower leg—are common injuries among runners, dancers, and others whose repetitive activity stresses a bone. They were originally discovered among soldiers who complained of foot pain after long marches; at that time, they were called march, or fatigue, fractures.*

*Today, stress fractures are usually considered overuse injuries, and they are most common among adolescents and young adults. Older people, especially women with osteoporosis, also develop unexplained stress fractures.*

## HOW IT DEVELOPS

Stress fractures occur when repeated pressure cracks a bone, causing a sudden, sharp pain. At first, the person may suspect a sprain; rest, ice, compression, and elevation (RICE) may provide temporary relief, but the pain is more persistent than in ligament injuries.

Sometimes an X ray will show a tiny crack, or hairline fracture. More often, however, early X rays do not detect the injury. However, a bone scan taken after injection of a radioactive material will reveal the fracture.

## WHAT YOU CAN DO

Stop the activity that precipitated the injury and see if RICE provides lasting relief. If so, you have probably suffered a sprain rather than a stress fracture. Pain that persists or worsens when the foot bears weight indicates a possible stress fracture and you should consult a doctor. In the meantime, a nonprescription painkiller such as aspirin or acetaminophen should ease pain. Either hot or cold packs will also provide relief.

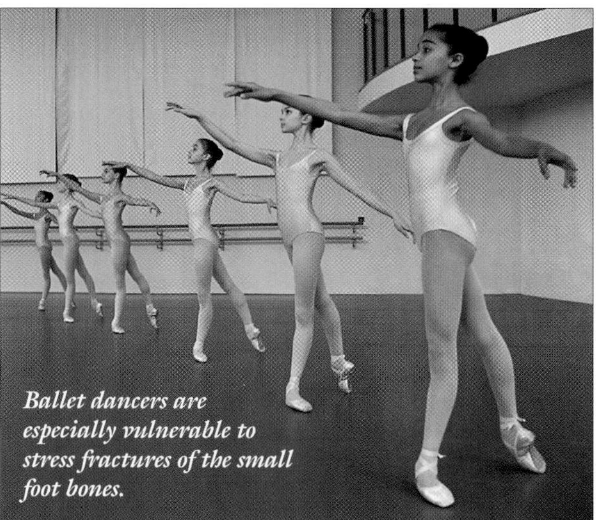

*Ballet dancers are especially vulnerable to stress fractures of the small foot bones.*

## HOW TO TREAT IT

Continue taking nonprescription painkillers as needed. Most stress fractures heal themselves in 6 to 12 weeks of reduced pressure on the injured bone. Use of the foot can be resumed gradually as the pain subsides.

In some instances, immobilization may be necessary. If taping or an elastic bandage do not provide sufficient immobility, crutches and a brace or air cast may be needed. In unusual cases, the injured foot may be put in a cast, usually a light, fiberglass one.

## HOW TO PREVENT IT

When embarking on an intensive activity, such as training for a marathon or starting ballet or gymnastic lessons, begin gradually to build endurance. Foot and ankle exercises using weights can help strengthen the bones' supporting muscles and help prevent stress fractures. Make sure that your shoes provide good support and are designed for the activity. If you have a tendency to overpronate (rolling the foot too far inward when walking or running), look into orthotic shoe inserts that are designed to correct such gait problems.

### ALTERNATIVE THERAPIES

**Magnets**

Therapeutic magnets can relieve pain and may speed healing by increasing circulation at the site of injury.

**Nutraceuticals**

Doctors recommend 1200 to 1800 mg of calcium a day to foster bone healing; look for supplements that provide 500 to 600 mg of calcium along with 200 IU of vitamin D, and other minerals, such as magnesium, copper, zinc, manganese, and boron. Vitamin C, in dosages of 500 to 1000 mg, also helps build bone tissue. For cautions concerning these nutraceuticals, see *About the Recommendations*, p 7.

**Physical therapy**

A physical therapist can teach stretching and strengthening exercises to help prevent stress fractures. Ultrasound, diathermy, and other treatments that provide deep heat and increased blood flow to the injured area relieve pain.

**WARNING!**

***After a fractured bone heals, it is usually somewhat thicker than before. This can lead to inflammation and pain in the attached tendons. Stretching exercises and a gradual resumption of activity will resolve the tendinitis.***

# The Skin

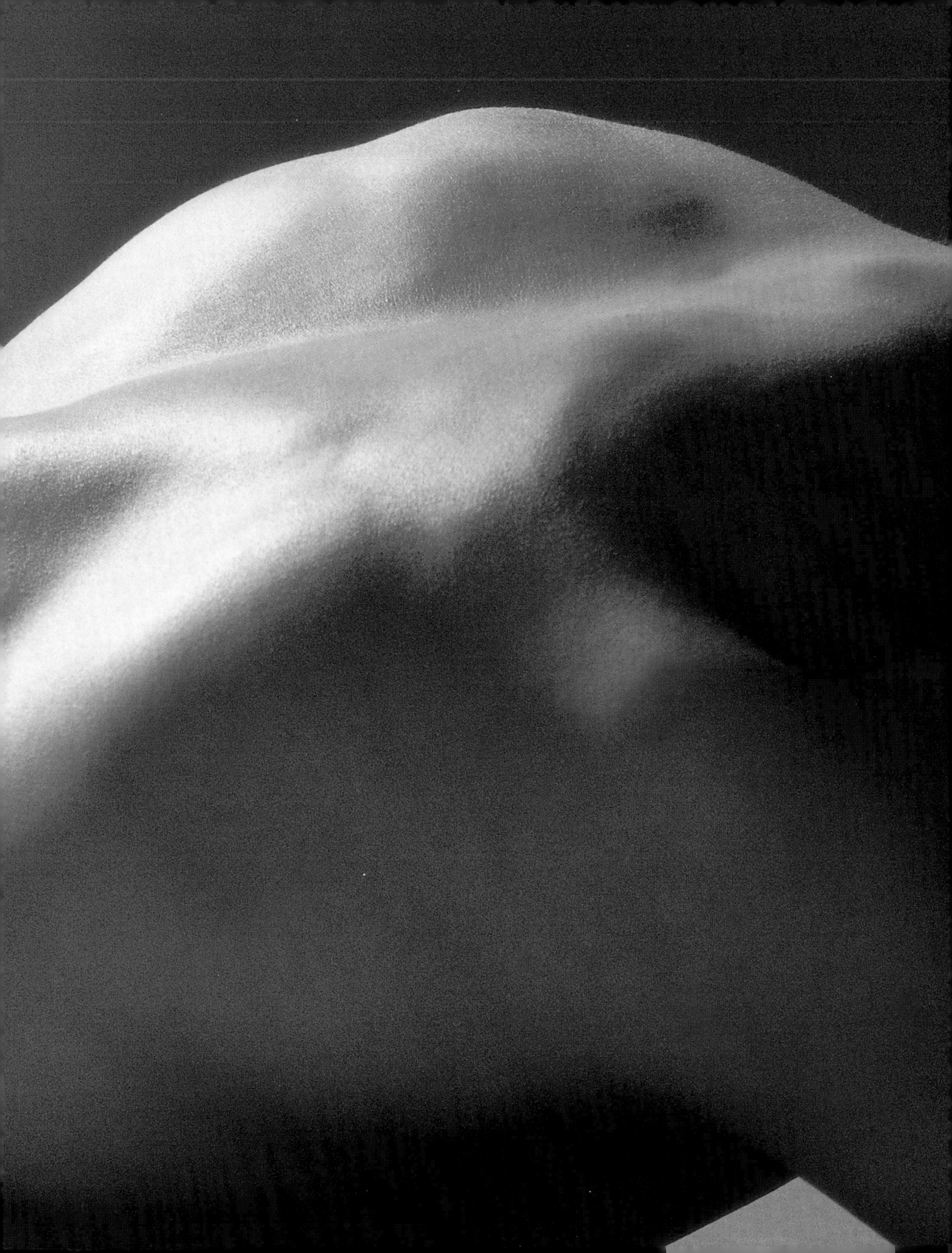

# The Skin

*The skin does much more than just cover the body—it also holds in vital fluids, protects us from the sun, regulates body temperature, and is instrumental in touch and the manufacture of vitamin D. It is also the source of many painful disorders.*

## Abscesses/Boils

### SYMPTOMS

***Abscesses:*** *Collections of pus and other infectious material that cause the surrounding skin to become red, swollen, warm, and very painful to the touch.*

***Boils:*** *Skin nodules that become inflamed, tender, and acutely painful.*

### WHO IS AT RISK

*Abscesses can form after any skin injury—for example, a minor cut, bruise, or surgical incision. They can also develop on infected internal organs, such as the tonsils, or in the breasts. Persons with compromised immune systems, diabetes, mastitis (breast inflammation), or cellulitis (a skin infection) are especially vulnerable to developing abscesses.*

*Although most people occasionally have boils, they are most prevalent among those who live in crowded, unsanitary conditions. They are somewhat more common in men than women; persons with diabetes or severe acne and other inflammatory skin disorders also have an increased risk of boils.*

### HOW THEY DEVELOP

Abscesses can develop on any part of the skin when it is invaded by bacteria as a result of a cut or a bruise. The body's natural defense mechanisms fight the bacteria by increasing blood flow to the area and sending in white blood cells to kill the invading organisms. These cells also wall off the infected area to confine the infection. An abscess forms when the walled-off cavity fills with pus, which is made up of dead bacteria and white blood cells. The increased blood flow results in inflammation; the infected site becomes red, warm to the touch, and increasingly painful. If left untreated, abscesses sometimes clear up by themselves, but the infection may spread to surrounding tissue and invade the bloodstream, which can lead to life-threatening blood poisoning (sepsis).

Boils (furuncles) form when bacteria invade a hair follicle; thus, they are most common on hairy parts of the body, such as the face, scalp, nape of the neck, chest, armpits, and buttocks. They can be acutely painful until they come to a head and rupture. Although this eases the pain, it increases the risk of spreading the infection. The infecting bacteria can also be carried to other parts of the body on towels, washcloths, tissues, unwashed hands, shaving implements, and similar objects. When a number of boils appear simultaneously in different parts of the body, the infection is referred to as *furunculosis*. Sometimes several boils develop in the same area and merge to form a carbuncle. These are also very painful and can be disfiguring, especially if they form on the face.

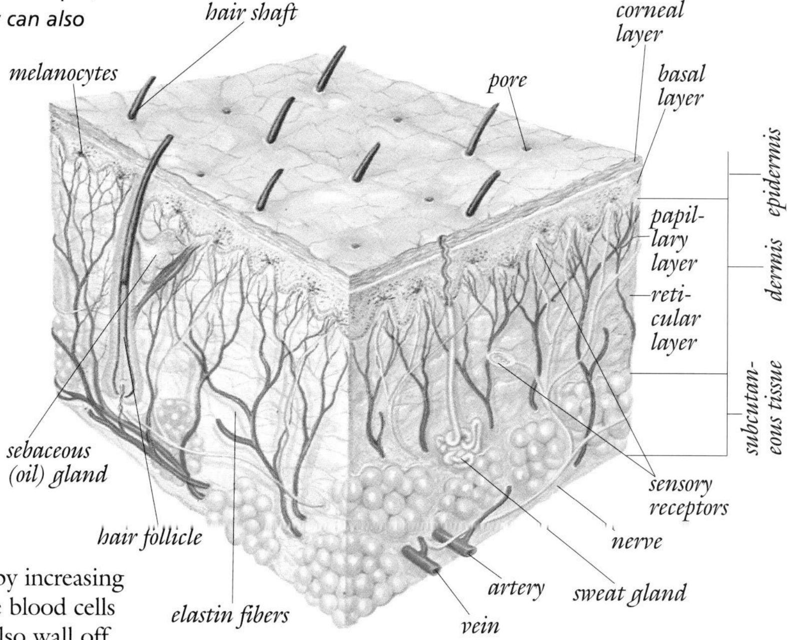


*The skin's visible part—the horny or corneal layer of the epidermis—is composed of dead cells that are constantly being shed. The basal layer contains living cells that are pushing their way to the surface. The melanocytes (pigment cells) mingle with basal cells and give the skin its color. The dermis, which houses millions of tiny blood vessels, nerves, sweat and oil glands, and hair follicles, is composed mostly of collagen—a tough, fibrous protein—and elastin, another protein that gives skin its elastic suppleness. The subcutaneous layer of fat and connective tissue helps protect internal organs and regulate body temperature.*

## WHAT YOU CAN DO

Apply warm compresses to the abscess or boil; this helps bring it to a head, which immediately relieves the pain. However, do not try to hasten the process by squeezing or puncturing the infected site. When the abscess or boil ruptures, wash the area with warm, soapy water, blot with a clean towel, and apply an antibiotic ointment or cream. Covering the area with sterile gauze reduces the risk of spreading the infection. However, do not apply an air-tight bandage; exposure to oxygen helps kill some bacteria and also speeds healing.

Aspirin, ibuprofen, or other anti-inflammatory medications can ease pain and reduce inflammation. Continue to apply warm compresses and, if possible, keep the area elevated. See a doctor if the abscess does not come to a head, is very painful, or appears to be spreading.

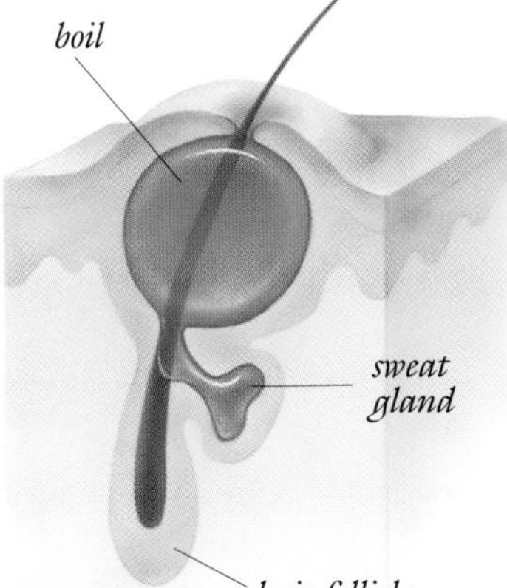


*A boil forms in a hair follicle and its infectious material may spread to the surrounding tissue.*

## HOW TO TREAT IT

A doctor will lance a large abscess or carbuncle by making a small incision in it and allowing the pus to drain. A local anesthetic is used to reduce pain. After the abscess has drained, the area will be washed with an antiseptic solution; a large cavity may be packed with sterile gauze and covered with a bandage for 24 to 48 hours. A deep one may be left uncovered, but a gauze wick impregnated with antibiotics may be inserted into it. The wick is then gradually removed to allow the cavity to close and heal.

Antibiotics may be prescribed if the person has multiple boils or an abscess in the facial area. In severe cases of furunculosis, intravenous antibiotics may be needed.

> **WARNING!**
>
> ***Most boils are caused by the Staphylococcus aureus bacterium, which normally lives on the skin. These superficial staph infections usually are not dangerous, but some strains can cause a life-threatening infection if they invade the bloodstream. Seek immediate medical attention if you develop a rapidly spreading skin infection or a fever, malaise, and other signs of a systemic illness.***

## HOW TO PREVENT THEM

Practicing good hygiene reduces the risk that a minor skin wound will become abscessed. Wash your hands frequently, and do not squeeze or pick at a sore, abscess, or boil. Even a minor cut should be washed promptly with soap and swabbed with alcohol, hydrogen peroxide, or another antiseptic solution. A topical antibiotic can speed healing and prevent infection. Even so, the cut may become infected. Keep it clean and loosely covered.

Avoid sharing towels, shaving utensils, and other personal items. If you get frequent boils, see a doctor. You may have a nutritional deficiency or an undiagnosed illness, such as diabetes, that increases the risk of boils.

### ALTERNATIVE THERAPIES

**Nutraceuticals**

People who suffer from recurring boils may benefit from taking 10,000 IU of vitamin A for a few weeks. Vitamin A helps control overproduction of sebum, the fatty substance that nourishes skin bacteria. Excessive vitamin A is highly toxic; women planning a pregnancy should not take more than 8000 IU a day. Higher doses can cause birth defects. Stop supplements at least three months before becoming pregnant. Do not give vitamin A pills to children unless prescribed by a doctor. Vitamin C, in dosages up to 1000 mg a day, also may reduce recurrence of boils. Do not exceed 500 mg a day if you have kidney stones, kidney disease, or hemochromatosis.

# Burns

### SYMPTOMS

***First-degree burns:*** *Sharp, burning pain and redness at the site, but no blisters.*

***Second-degree burns:*** *Pain, redness, and blisters.*

***Third-degree burns:*** *Skin that looks charred, white, or blackened and extends to tissue well below the skin; pain may not be noticed at first, because the nerve endings have been damaged.*

### WHO IS AT RISK

*Fire is an essential part of our lives; consequently, everyone faces a risk of being burned. In fact, 200,000 Canadians are burned severely enough each year to require medical attention. Roughly 11 people per day die in home fires in Canada. Most people associate burns with fire and flames, but painful burns to the skin can result from chemicals, steam, electricity, even too much sun.*

*As might be expected, the most common burns happen in the kitchen around hot stoves or grills, but burns can—and do—occur in any room in the house as well as outdoors. Some professions carry a high risk of burns, especially those that involve working with chemicals, welding units, electricity, heating elements, and similar substances. For firemen, the risk of being burned on the job is a daily threat. Smokers (and their families) are at risk of serious or even fatal burns, especially if they smoke in bed or when watching TV late at night, when they are likely to fall asleep with a lighted cigarette.*

*Among Canadian children and youths, fires are the fifth leading cause of injury-related deaths. Radiators, portable heaters, woodstoves, and open fireplaces all pose a danger of fire and burns; scalds can occur if tap water is set at a high (over 54°C/130°F) temperature. Even overexposure to the sun can inflict serious burns* *(see* Common Sense in the Sun, *p 301).*

## HOW IT DEVELOPS

Injuries from burns can range from mild to fatal, but severe pain is associated with almost all burns. The severity of a burn is determined by two factors: the percentage of the body's total skin that has been burned and the extent of damage to the underlying tissue.

- Mild, or **first-degree burns**, are confined to the outer layer of skin; they produce pain and redness, but the skin is intact with no blistering. They usually heal on their own in a few days.
- Moderate, **or second-degree burns**, produce painful blisters and damage both the epidermis and the dermis layers of skin. Though painful, these burns are not serious unless they cover a large percentage of the body or the resulting blisters become infected.
- Severe, or **third-degree burns**, char or blacken the skin and are considered a medical emergency. They penetrate deep into the skin and underlying tissue and can damage nerves, blood vessels, glands, muscles, and bones. They can be fatal if they cover more than 30 percent of the body's surface or if they affect the functioning of vital organs.

### WARNING!

***When administering first aid for a burn, never put butter, cooking oil, ointments, or other substances on it. These increase the risk of infection, and a doctor will need to remove them before starting treatment—a process that will add to the pain. Instead, cover the area with a cool, wet compress and seek prompt medical help.***

## WHAT YOU CAN DO

First- and second-degree burns respond well to self-treatment. Run the affected skin surface under cool water, then apply a cool compress to the area and elevate it. To reduce pain and swelling, apply cold packs for 20 minutes, remove for 10 minutes, and reapply. Do not apply ice directly to burned skin. Take acetaminophen, aspirin (for adults only), or ibuprofen for pain. An anesthetic skin spray can also relieve the pain of minor burns; however, do not use it or any other home or nonprescription remedy on deep or extensive burns (see *Warning!,* left).

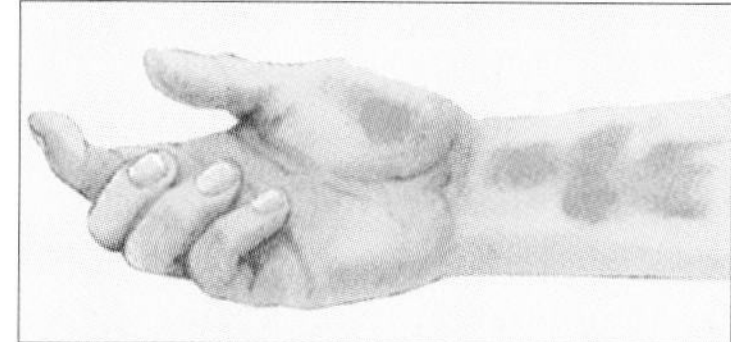

*First-degree burns, like a sunburn, damage only the epidermis, the outermost layers of skin.*

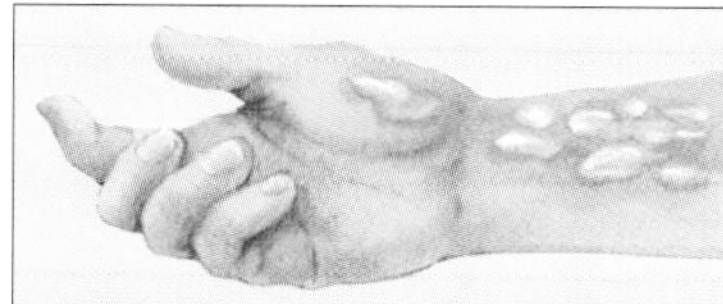

*Second-degree burns extend to the dermis layers and can cause blistering.*

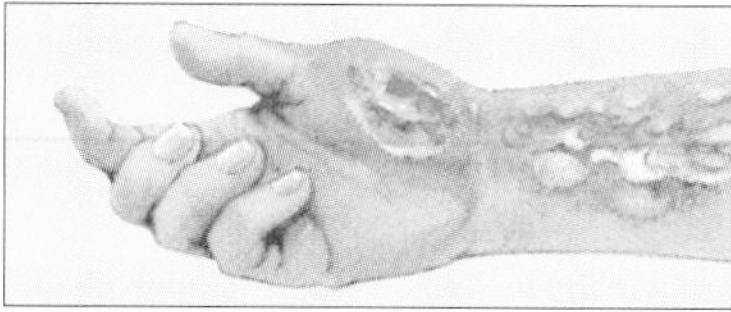

*Third-degree burns go through the epidermis and dermis, and damage the subcutaneous and other underlying tissues.*

If blisters develop, do not puncture them because of the risk of infection. They will eventually subside or open on their own; when this happens, wash the area gently with soap and water, apply an antibiotic ointment, and cover with a sterile bandage. Change the bandage once a day and call your doctor if you see any signs of infection or spreading inflammation.

If the burn has been caused by a corrosive chemical, such as lye or drain cleaners, remove all contaminated clothing and jewelry, immediately flush the burned area with cool water for 15 to 30 minutes, and then see a doctor. If the substance has splashed into an eye, flush with water for several minutes, but be careful not to contaminate the other eye. Cover the affected eye with a cool compress and go immediately to the nearest hospital emergency room. If you receive an electrical burn, call your doctor right away; these burns are often more severe than they appear because they often cause more damage within the body than on its surface.

If a burn produces blisters more than one inch across, or if you develop blisters on your hands, feet, face, or genitals, see a doctor for treatment. Third-degree burns always require medical treatment; to get help, call 911 or the Emergency Medical Service (EMS) and ask to be taken to the nearest hospital emergency room.

## HOW TO TREAT IT

Treatment depends upon the severity and extent of the burn. Extensive third-degree burns require hospitalization and intensive care. A tetanus shot and antibiotics are given to prevent infection, and intravenous fluids are administered to reduce the risk of dehydration from fluid lost through the damaged skin. Morphine or other narcotic drugs are used to control pain. If the burn involves a joint, manipulation and perhaps splinting will be needed to prevent skin and scar tissue from shortening as it heals. Physical therapy may also be prescribed.

Extensive or third-degree burns should be treated in a hospital's critical care unit or, preferably, at a burn center where specialists are available. A person suffering third-degree burns will probably be in shock, so blood or plasma will be administered to combat it. Burn victims often need oxygen, which will be given through a breathing tube if lungs have been damaged.

Deep burn wounds need special care. The damaged tissue must be removed and the remaining tissue covered with a sterile tissue or artificial skin. Skin does not regenerate itself after third-degree burns because of the damage to underlying tissue. Instead, thick scar tissue replaces it unless skin from elsewhere in the body or artificial skin is grafted over the area (see *Breakthroughs!*, below).

## HOW TO PREVENT IT

Any fire or source of heat can burn, so always be diligent about fire safety. Install smoke detectors and inspect them periodically to make sure they are working. Conduct fire drills every few months, and make sure that every member of the household knows what to do in a fire emergency and the fastest way to get out of each room.

Keep matches out of the reach of children, and teach them the dangers of fire at an early age. When cooking, keep all flammable objects (curtains, sleeves, pot holders) away from open flames and turn pot handles inward and out of the reach of a young child. Set the hot water thermostat at 54°C/130°F (or 49°C/120°F if there are young children in the household). Cover radiators and use portable space heaters only with great caution.

Use a fireplace screen to keep sparks and live embers from falling out. Make sure the fire is out before going to bed. These are only a few of the dozens of fire-safety precautions that should be second nature to everyone.

### ALTERNATIVE THERAPIES

**Note:** Herbal medicine and home remedies should be used only to treat minor burns.

**Herbal medicine**

Aloe vera's natural anesthetic and healing properties make it a good choice to treat first-degree burns that produce no blisters. It is best used as a gel squeezed from a freshly cut leaf; most commercial aloe products contain only minimal amounts of the herb. Other herbs used to treat minor burns include witch hazel, comfrey, and calendula, typically applied as compresses soaked in tea.

**Homeopathy**

Homeopaths often prescribe Urtica urens or Causticum to promote healing of minor burns and scalds.

**Nutrition therapy**

Proper nutrition is essential in ensuring the recovery of persons who sustain extensive burns. Extra calories and protein will be needed for tissue repair. Supplements usually include: vitamin C to promote wound healing; B-complex vitamins to ensure proper metabolism; vitamin A to help rebuild skin; and potassium and other salts to maintain a proper fluid and chemical balance. A registered dietitian or burn specialist should determine the needed dosages. As healing progresses, vitamin E applied directly to the skin may speed the process and reduce scarring; discontinue use if it causes an allergic reaction.

### COMMON SENSE IN THE SUN

Both UVB and UVA rays damage the skin, but of the two, UVA penetrates deeper and can cause more extensive burns. Even a few minutes in the midday sun can cause serious skin damage. Always wear a sunblock with an SPF of 15 or higher to screen out both ultraviolet A and B rays, and limit sun exposure between 10 A.M. and 3 P.M. Reapply frequently after swimming or sweating. Wear a wide-brimmed hat and sunglasses.

### BREAKTHROUGHS!

**Advances in artificial skin have greatly increased survival and reduced disability and disfigurement from extensive third-degree burns. In many instances, these substances are preferable to natural skin grafts because there is less risk of rejection and infection.**

**Physical therapy**

Recovery from extensive third-degree burns usually involves intensive physical therapy. At first, damaged joints may be splinted or exercised passively to prevent them from becoming permanently "frozen" or fixed. A program of daily stretching, weight training, and exercise will be designed to regain strength and function. Exercising in water and other forms of hydrotherapy are especially beneficial for patients with extensive burns.

# Cellulitis

## SYMPTOMS

- *Localized, often very painful skin inflammation that increases in size as the infection spreads.*
- *Thin red lines extending from the infected area toward the heart (lymphangitis).*
- *Fever, chills, muscle aches, and general malaise.*
- *Possible nausea and vomiting, joint stiffness, swollen lymph nodes, and hair loss at the site of infection.*
- *Local abscesses and pus discharge.*

## WHO IS AT RISK

*Anyone who has a break in the skin can develop cellulitis, a potentially serious bacterial infection of the skin and underlying fatty tissue. The most common victims, however, are people with diabetes, poor circulation in or paralysis of the legs, and compromised immunity. Cellulitis is sometimes a complication of chronic athlete's foot (tinea pedis).*

## HOW IT DEVELOPS

Cellulitis develops when staphylococcus or streptococcus bacteria, which normally live harmlessly on the skin, gain entry through a cut, burn, insect bite, or another break in the skin. Normally, the body's immune system can fight off these common bacterial invasions, but among people whose immunity is lowered by a chronic disease or who have poor circulation, the infection can spread rapidly.

The initial symptoms are sudden tenderness, swelling, and redness in an area of skin, often on the lower legs. A thin red line may extend from the middle of the infected area upward toward the heart. Other symptoms include fever, chills, increasing pain, muscle aches, and malaise.

**BREAKTHROUGHS!**

**People with chronic or recurrent athlete's foot often suffer repeated bouts of cellulitis. Studies show that these infections can be prevented by a monthly injection of high-dose penicillin or taking erythromycin pills for a week each month. The antibiotics can be stopped after the athlete's foot is completely eradicated.**

Staph cellulitis tends to remain relatively localized, but if a strep organism is involved, the infection may spread rapidly and, within a day or so, cover a large area. Without treatment, the bacteria may enter the bloodstream, leading to life-threatening blood poisoning (sepsis). Tissue death (gangrene) is also a danger.

Cellulitis usually develops on the legs, but in rare cases, it occurs on the face, which can be life-threatening (see *Warning!*, below).

## WHAT YOU CAN DO

See a doctor as soon as possible; intensive medical treatment is needed to clear up cellulitis. To relieve pain, apply warm, wet compresses and, if the infection is on a leg, keep it elevated. Aspirin, ibuprofen, or other nonsteroidal anti-inflammatory drugs (NSAIDs) also ease pain and help reduce inflammation.

Stay in bed as much as possible until the fever, pain, and other symptoms subside; continue the warm compresses and keep the leg elevated until healing is complete.

## HOW TO TREAT IT

Antibiotics will usually eradicate cellulitis in 7 to 10 days. If a large area is involved, intravenous antibiotics may be given. Unless there are other medical problems, they can usually be administered on an outpatient basis once or twice a day for two or three days; the patient is then switched to an oral drug. Pain and inflammation usually subside soon after starting the antibiotics, but it is very important to take the entire course to fully eradicate the infection. Stopping too early can result in a relapse that requires even more intensive drug therapy.

**WARNING!**

***Facial cellulitis, known medically as erysipelas, can be disfiguring and lead to life-threatening meningitis without prompt treatment. Early symptoms include a painful red lesion or rash on the cheeks or nose, facial swelling, fever and chills, headache, and muscle pain.***

Staph cellulitis is often difficult to cure, especially among elderly patients who have poor circulation. Sometimes surgery is needed to remove damaged tissue, followed by a skin graft to close the wound.

## HOW TO PREVENT IT

Keep the skin clean, especially if you have diabetes or a circulatory problem, and strive to avoid any skin damage. Treat any cut or scrape, however minor, by washing the area with soap, swabbing it with an antiseptic such as alcohol or povidone-iodine (Betadine), and watching it for any signs of infection. Avoid swimming if you have any skin sore. Minimize the risk of insect bites and stings by wearing protective clothing and using insect repellent.

# Common Skin Infections at a Glance

| TYPES OF INFECTIONS | PAIN RELIEF | TREATMENTS |
|---|---|---|
| **Bacterial Infections**<br>Abscesses<br>Boils/Carbuncles<br>Cellulitis<br>Erythrasma<br>Folliculitis<br>Furuncles<br>Lymphangitis | Acetaminophen, aspirin, ibuprofen, other OTC painkillers; warm compresses. (See also *Abscesses/Boils,* p 298, *Cellulitis,* p 302.) | Antibiotics to eradicate the bacteria; depending upon the infection, drugs may be given orally or by injection, intravenous drip, topical creams or ointments. |
| **Fungal/Tinea Infections**<br>Athlete's foot (tinea pedis)<br>Barber's itch (tinea barbae)<br>Jock itch (tinea cruris)<br>Nail fungus (tinea unguium)<br>Ringworm of the body (tinea corporis)<br>Ringworm of the scalp (tinea capitis) | Anesthetic sprays to relieve itching; cool compresses; tepid baths with baking soda added to bathwater. (See also *Athlete's Foot,* p 281.) | Topical antifungal creams or ointments; systemic (oral) antifungal drugs. |
| **Parasitic Skin Infections**<br>Body lice (pediculosis corporis)<br>Head lice (pediculosis capitis)<br>Pubic lice (pediculosis pubis)<br>Creeping eruption (larva migrans)<br>Scabies | OTC antihistamines or hydrocortisone creams to ease itching; cool compresses and showers for itching; aloe vera gel and/or witch hazel to relieve itching and promote healing. | Topical creams, lotions, or shampoos containing permethrin to kill parasites; prescription anti-itch drug or corticosteroid ointment for itchiness; antibiotics to treat secondary bacterial infections from scratching. |
| **Viral Skin Infections**<br>Cold sores/fever blisters (herpes simplex type 1)<br>Genital herpes (herpes simplex type 2)<br>Molluscum (molluscum contagiosum)<br>Warts (human papilloma virus) | Cool compresses; OTC painkillers such as aspirin or ibuprofen. (See also *Cold Sores,* p 97; *Sexually Transmitted Diseases,* p 201; *Plantar Warts,* p 293.) | Antiviral drugs (e.g., acyclovir, valacyclovir, famciclovir) to speed healing and reduce recurrences; caustic acids to help remove warts; possible laser surgery and/or debridement. |
| **Yeast Infections**<br>Candida nail infections (candidal paronychia)<br>Genital candidiasis<br>Oral thrush | Vinegar compresses or plain water douches to ease itchiness, OTC anti-yeast creams and ointments. | Prescription-strength anti-yeast creams, ointments, or tablets. |

## ALTERNATIVE THERAPIES

**Physical therapy**

Whirlpool baths and leg exercises can increase blood flow in the legs and promote healing of stubborn leg cellulitis.

# Dermatitis/Eczema

### SYMPTOMS

- *Itchy, uncomfortable patches of reddened skin that have small, oozing blisters.*
- *Skin may become thickened, scaly, and discolored.*
- *Possible pain, inflammation, and infection, especially if the patches are rubbed or scratched.*

### WHO IS AT RISK

***Dermatitis**—a general term for any inflammation of the skin—is very common, affecting large numbers of people whose skin is sensitive to certain environmental substances, everything from poison ivy and household cleaners to chemicals in synthetic dyes or clothing and nickel and other metals. People taking certain medications may develop allergic skin reactions to them. The elderly, whose skin has lost some of its fat and elasticity, can become more sensitive to irritants that cause dermatitis. Women often develop dermatitis from chemicals in cosmetics or hair dyes. Dermatitis may also be associated with a person's occupation or hobbies; artists, hairdressers, chemical workers, and farmers and gardeners are among the many examples of people who often develop job-related dermatitis.*

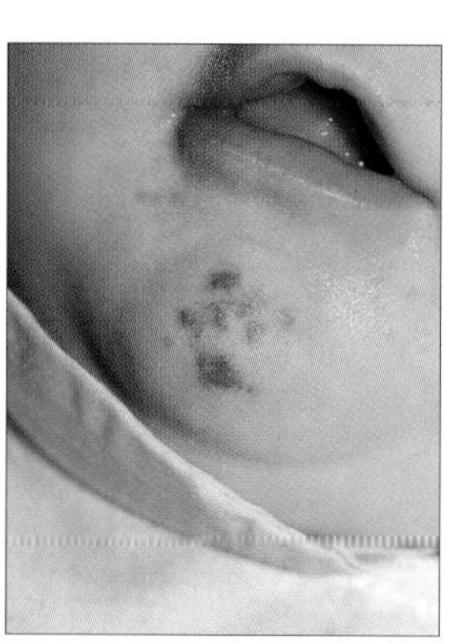

*Itchy blisters are a hallmark of infantile, or atopic, eczema.*

***Eczema**, which produces the same symptoms and is often closely related to dermatitis, seems to be an inherited skin condition that is often associated with allergies. It can affect people of all ages, but certain forms of eczema occur at specific life stages. **Atopic**, or infantile, **eczema** is very common among babies and young children; it often persists into adulthood. People with eczema are also susceptible to developing asthma. Older adults may develop **nummular**, or discoid, **eczema**, which is characterized by swollen, blistered, or crusty coin-shaped patches. Elderly people sometimes develop **steatotic eczema**, in which the skin becomes dry and scaly. Allergies and stress can trigger eczema, which tends to run in families.*

## HOW THEY DEVELOP

Dermatitis and eczema have many of the same symptoms, but they develop in different ways. Dermatitis occurs when the skin comes in contact with a specific irritant, whereas eczema often develops as the result of stress or an allergic reaction. In either case, the affected skin becomes itchy and very uncomfortable; it may be swollen and inflamed, or the person may have patches of oozing blisters. In time, the skin thickens and becomes scaly and dark or discolored.

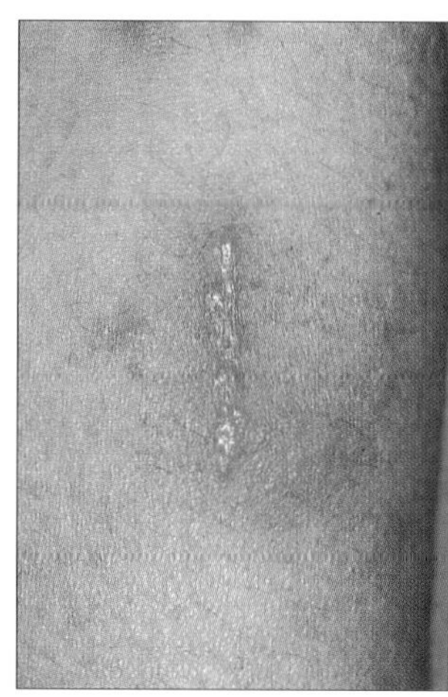

*When a patch of dermatitis has distinct borders and is confined to a specific area, it suggests an allergic reaction to a specific substance.*

Both dermatitis and eczema tend to be localized to specific areas of the body, such as on the elbows, hands, wrists, and feet. In extreme cases, the entire body is affected. The major danger is development of a secondary bacterial skin infection from scratching. These can be serious in young babies, the elderly, or persons with diabetes or lowered immunity.

## WHAT YOU CAN DO

Dermatitis usually can be treated with over-the-counter anti-itch creams, an application of a nonprescription hydrocortisone ointment, or home remedies. The most effective approach, however, involves determining the cause of the dermatitis and then avoiding it. Keeping a food diary can help identify suspect foods. The pattern of the dermatitis often gives important clues to the cause; for example, a circle of dermatitis around a wrist may be from a leather or metal watchband. Dermatitis confined to the hands may be from a dish detergent or household cleaner; suspect hair products or cosmetics for dermatitis of the scalp or face. Other common culprits include jewelry that contains nickel, clothing fibers, and chemicals, such as those used in dry cleaning or swimming pools.

Switch to hypoallergenic skin products formulated for dry skin to prevent outbreaks. Brief exposure to sunlight can relieve eczema's symptoms; be careful not to burn the skin, as sunburn can make the disorder worse, damage the skin, and promote later skin cancers. Avoid rapid changes of temperature, which can worsen symptoms, and consider installing a humidifier to keep the air moist.

Try to stay cool; excessive sweating aggravates both eczema and dermatitis. Although the itchiness of dermatitis and eczema can be maddening, try not to scratch. To ease itchiness, try adding one cup of Aveeno powder or another colloidal oatmeal product, or a half cup of baking soda, to a tepid bath. If itching interferes with sleep, taking a nonprescription antihistamine before going to bed may help; these not only ease itchiness but they also make you drowsy. If the problem does not improve with self-treatment, or it gets worse, consult a dermatologist.

## HOW TO TREAT THEM

A doctor may order a prescription-strength hydrocortisone ointment or a short course of corticosteroids to control severe itching. Antibiotics are prescribed if an area has become infected. Eczema is treated with anti-inflammatory medications taken orally or applied topically. For maximum effectiveness, apply topical medications, such as a corticosteroid cream or coal tar ointments, liberally before going to bed, and cover with a plastic wrap.

Oral antihistamines are often used to reduce itching in order to break the itch-scratch-itch cycle that can spread the inflammation. Sedatives or tranquilizers can also help severe itching.

## HOW TO PREVENT THEM

To prevent dermatitis, protect your skin as much as possible from irritating substances. Use a mild, nonmedicated soap and warm water to maintain enough surface oil to prevent the skin from getting too dry. Bathe or shower only every other day, especially during the winter, using tepid rather than hot water. Apply a nonirritating moisturizer while the skin is still damp. Protect your skin from the sun, especially if you are taking medications that make your skin sun-sensitive. Sunscreens can be effective, but try out a few to make sure your skin is not sensitive to any of their particular ingredients, such as PABA.

When doing housework, coat your hands often with a moisturizer containing lanolin and wear gloves to protect them from dish detergents and household cleaners. Some forms of dermatitis may be triggered by clothing fibers or chemical finishes sprayed in them; if possible, wash new clothes, bedding, and towels before using them to prevent possible skin irritations.

Eczema can be more difficult to prevent than dermatitis, because eczema is often linked to stress or allergic reactions. Avoid foods and other substances to which you might be allergic and try to keep stress under control.

### BREAKTHROUGHS!

**A number of prescription-strength topical corticosteroid products, such as mometasone furoate (Elocom), have been developed that are safe and effective in relieving the itchiness of dermatitis and eczema. They can also improve the skin's absorption of moisturizers to prevent recurrences.**

### ALTERNATIVE THERAPIES

**Aromatherapy**

Massages with aromatic oils such as rose, clary sage, or peppermint may reduce stress and relieve itching.

**Herbal medicine**

Creams or ointments containing witch hazel, calendula, chickweed, stinging nettle, or heartsease (tricolored violets) can reduce the itchiness and oozing lesions of eczema. Aloe vera gel applied directly to the skin also soothes symptoms of dermatitis and eczema. Teas made from burdock or stinging nettles may relieve eczema.

**Hydrotherapy**

Baking soda or colloidal oatmeal added to bathwater can help alleviate itching. Compresses dipped in a mixture of one quart cool water and one cup Burow's solution (a nonprescription skin product) helps soothe itchy skin. Apply to the affected areas for 10 to 15 minutes two or three times daily.

**Nutraceuticals**

Evening primrose oil, which is high in gamma linolenic acid (GLA), has been shown to relieve eczema; other studies have found that fish oil capsules that provide 1800 mg of eicosapentaenoic acid (EPA) also improve eczema. Consult a doctor before using either if you have a blood disorder or if you are taking anticoagulants. Other supplements that may be beneficial include 800 IU of vitamin E, which has anti-inflammatory properties, and up to 10,000 IU of vitamin A, which helps maintain healthy skin. (Women who are or may become pregnant should not take more than 8000 IU of vitamin A. Stop any Vitamin A supplements three months before becoming pregnant. Supplements should never be given to children unless they are prescribed by a doctor.)

### WARNING!

***Other skin conditions, such as impetigo (bacterial) or ringworm (fungal), can produce similar symptoms, but must be treated differently. See a doctor for any skin infection that worsens rapidly or persists for more than a few days.***

**Relaxation therapies**

Meditation, yoga, self-hypnosis, and biofeedback are among the relaxation techniques used to treat stress; they may be helpful in reducing or preventing eczema.

# Hives

### SYMPTOMS

- *Uncomfortable, very itchy skin bumps ranging in size from one-fourth inch to two inches.*
- *Possible widespread swelling and difficulty breathing (signs of anaphylaxis).*

## WHO IS AT RISK

*Children are especially vulnerable, but anyone who has allergies can develop hives—itchy, highly unpredictable skin rashes. Hives are most often triggered by food allergies; the most common culprits are peanuts, tree nuts, shellfish, strawberries, and eggs. Penicillin, aspirin, and certain other medications can cause hives in persons allergic to them. Other allergens that often produce hives include bee venom, animal dander, and chemicals such as those used in dry cleaning. In unusual cases, hives reflect sensitivity to exposure to the sun or extreme temperatures. Stress can aggravate hives, but it is uncertain whether it can actually cause them.*

## HOW IT DEVELOPS

Hives start as itchy red or pink bumps on the skin. They usually appear shortly after exposure to the triggering substances, but sometimes the reaction is delayed for hours. The itchy rash may disappear after a few hours or days, only to crop up elsewhere on the body. This can go on for a week or more, but eventually, the itchiness disappears. The hives can recur if the person is again exposed to the offending substance. Future attacks may be more severe, with the bumps running together and causing widespread swelling (angioedema). Hives and swelling of the mouth and throat can be life-threatening if they block the airway.

> **WARNING!**
>
> ***Widespread hives may be a warning of impending anaphylaxis, a life-threatening allergic reaction. Call 911 or your local Emergency Medical Service if the person develops facial swelling or has difficulty breathing.***

## WHAT YOU CAN DO

Mild hives can be self-treated with applications of hydrocortisone cream, calamine lotion, or other nonprescription anti-itch preparations. The itchiness can also be eased by adding a cup of baking soda to a tub of lukewarm water and soaking in it for 15 or 20 minutes. If the itchiness interferes with sleeping, try taking a nonprescription antihistamine, such as diphenhydramine (Benadryl), before going to bed; these ease itchiness and also cause drowsiness. Hives that cause widespread swelling warrant seeing a doctor as soon as possible (see *Warning!*, left).

*Foods that often cause hives include shellfish and strawberries.*

## HOW TO TREAT IT

Mild hives may be treated with prescription-strength antihistamines and anti-itch medications. A short course of a corticosteroid such as prednisone may be prescribed for more widespread hives. An immediate injection of epinephrine (Adrenalin) can stop an anaphylactic reaction (see *Warning!*, left); antihistamines may also be given.

## HOW TO PREVENT IT

The best approach to prevention involves identifying and then avoiding allergens that can cause hives. Keeping a food diary can pinpoint sources of food allergies. Skin tests and blood studies can identify other allergens. Persons allergic to penicillin and other medications should wear a MedicAlert bracelet so that emergency medical workers will not unwittingly administer the drug. If the allergens cannot be avoided, allergy shots (desensitization) may be recommended. This treatment involves injecting minute amounts of the allergens to help the body build resistance against them. It may take several years to achieve this.

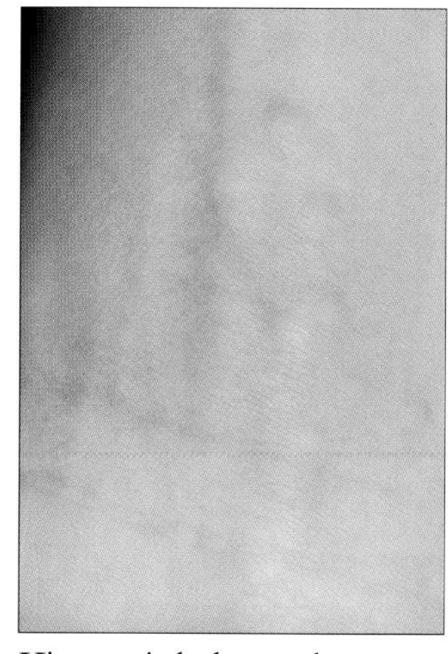

*Hives are itchy bumps that typically move from one part of the body to another until they disappear entirely, usually in a week.*

Anyone who has had widespread hives or other signs of hypersensitivity should also wear a MedicAlert bracelet and carry an adrenaline autoinjection device that a person can use to stop a severe allergic reaction. Allergy shots may be recommended for people who have difficulty in avoiding allergens that can cause anaphylaxis.

### ALTERNATIVE THERAPIES

**Herbal medicine**

Stinging nettle (*Urtica dioica*) tea or extract may relieve the itching and other symptoms of hives related to allergies. Witch hazel, which contains astringent tannins, applied to the skin also eases itchiness.

# Insect Bites/Stings

## SYMPTOMS

***Bee stings:*** *Sharp, burning pain that is followed immediately by swelling and continued pain.*

***Biting insects (mosquitoes, spiders):*** *Mild to moderate pain, development of itchy, red welt; possible swelling and an expanding ulcer resulting from a spider bite.*

***Ticks:*** *Possible fever, rash, muscle aches, joint pains, and other systemic symptoms.*

## WHO IS AT RISK

*Anyone who ventures outdoors in warm weather can sustain an insect bite or sting. Insects—especially mosquitoes and spiders—often come indoors and bite their hosts.*

## HOW IT DEVELOPS

**Bee stings** produce immediate pain followed quickly by swelling. Most people will experience a day or two of discomfort, which eventually disappears, at the site of the sting. But people who are hypersensitive to bee venom can quickly develop an anaphylactic reaction, marked by widespread swelling, difficulty breathing, and possible collapse and even death.

### WARNING!

***Some spider bites can be serious, causing severe pain, swelling, breathing problems, and—in the case of the brown recluse spider found in the U.S.—skin ulcers and possible tissue death. Go to the emergency room if you are bitten by a brown recluse or another highly venomous spider.***

The bites of **mosquitoes** or **spiders** may not be felt immediately, but itching, pain, and swelling usually develop within minutes, and some spider bites are life-threatening (see *Warning!*, left). Although mosquito bites can cause a maddening itchiness (see *Why Mosquito Bites Itch*, right), most are relatively harmless. However, some mosquitoes can transmit serious diseases, such as malaria and encephalitis, so bites should be avoided, especially in areas where these diseases occur.

**Scorpion stings** are immediately painful, and some are potentially fatal. The stings of scorpion species in North America are quite painful, but they are not especially dangerous.

**Tick bites** are painless, but some types can transmit serious diseases, including Lyme disease, Rocky Mountain spotted fever, and ehrlichiosis, a serious infection that is often misdiagnosed as Lyme disease. These diseases, which usually become apparent 3 to 14 days after the bite, are characterized by fever, chills, muscle and joint pain, and a possible rash.

## WHAT YOU CAN DO

First aid for bites and stings varies according to the insect and the type of reaction.

- **Bee stings:** Gently remove the stinger by scraping the skin with a fingernail, knife blade, or similar object. Wash the wound with soap and water and immediately apply ice or a cold compress to ease pain and slow the spread of the venom. A topical anesthetic ointment or spray can relieve pain. Get immediate medical help if widespread swelling or breathing problems develop.
- **Mosquitoes:** Apply ice to the bite and try to avoid itching; nonprescription hydrocortisone cream and/or nonprescription antihistamines can ease itchiness.
- **Spiders and scorpions:** Try to identify the type of spider; see a doctor immediately if it is one of the very venomous types (e.g., brown recluse—see *Warning!*, left). Ordinary spider bites and scorpion stings can be treated like bee stings.

### Why Mosquito Bites Itch

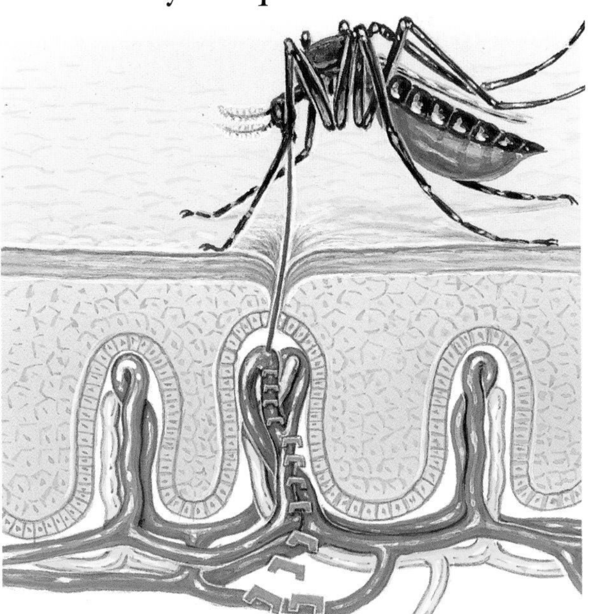

*When a mosquito bites, it injects small amounts of saliva as it draws out the blood. The immune system recognizes it as a foreign substance and dispatches white blood cells to the site to destroy it. Histamines are also released, resulting in swelling and itchiness.*

*Honeybees leave their stinger embedded in the skin; be careful not to squeeze it, which can release even more venom.*

- **Ticks:** Remove the tick with tweezers (use your fingers if tweezers are not available) and immediately wash the site with warm, soapy water. See a doctor right away if fever, a rash, and other symptoms develop.

## HOW TO TREAT IT

An injection of epinephrine (Adrenalin), and perhaps an antihistamine, will stop an anaphylactic reaction following a bee sting. Injection of a local anesthetic eases the pain of a scorpion or severe spider bite. The venom of the brown recluse spider causes almost immediate tissue death and severe pain. Debridement and intensive antibiotic therapy are necessary to prevent gangrene. Narcotic painkillers may also be given.

## HOW TO PREVENT IT

Insect repellents can help prevent mosquito and tick bites. Wear protective clothing when outdoors, and be on the watch for spiders, bees, and other biting or stinging insects. Remember, bees are attracted to brightly colored clothes, flower prints, and perfumes.

Keep window screens in good repair and inspect bedding (especially sleeping bags when camping) and other favorite hiding places of spiders. Pets often bring ticks indoors; during tick season, take measures to protect pets from picking up ticks.

### ALTERNATIVE THERAPIES

**Herbal medicine**

Citronella and peppermint can repel mosquitoes. Aloe vera is soothing and helps prevent an insect bite from becoming infected. Witch hazel and other astringent herbs can also ease itchiness. A comfrey poultice may speed healing of scorpion and spider-bite wounds. Dip the comfrey leaves in boiling water, drain and place them between two layers of gauze, and apply the poultice to the wound. Change it twice a day until the wound heals.

**BREAKTHROUGHS!**

**A vaccine (LymeRix) is now available for Lyme disease, a condition spread by deer ticks. Two shots are administered a month apart and the third a year later. Immunization should take place in the late winter or early spring, before ticks emerge.**

# Pressure (Bed) Sores

### SYMPTOMS

- *Painful skin ulcers at a point of chronic pressure; sores can deepen and infect underlying bone.*

### WHO IS AT RISK

*Pressure sores—also called bedsores or decubitus ulcers—are most common among people who are bedridden. Paraplegics who spend a lot of time sitting in one position can also develop pressure sores.*

## HOW IT DEVELOPS

A pressure sore starts as redness of the skin over a pressure point, usually where the bone lies close to the skin, such as the base of the spine, heels, hips, and elbows. The skin gradually swells and thickens; blisters and finally an open sore develop. If allowed to progress, the ulcer moves deeper into the underlying tissue until the bone is exposed.

## WHAT YOU CAN DO

Do whatever you can to ease pressure on vulnerable areas (see *How to Prevent It*, below), which not only relieves the pain but also promotes healing of the bedsore. Wash the skin at least once a day, pat it dry, and apply a moisturizing lotion to prevent dryness. A dusting of cornstarch or talcum powder helps to reduce friction on the skin.

**WARNING!**

***Deep pressure sores that invade the underlying bone can lead to osteomyelitis, a serious bone inflammation and infection. Any skin ulcer that exposes the bone requires aggressive treatment.***

## HOW TO TREAT IT

An anesthetic cream or spray may be used to relieve pain. Topical antibiotics and healing ointments are applied to small, shallow sores. Deeper sores are treated by debridement to remove dead tissue. Special gels or a 1.5 percent hydrogen peroxide solution may be applied to make the dead tissue easier to lift off. Very deep sores require surgery to remove the damaged tissue and bone; a skin graft may be necessary to close the wound.

## HOW TO PREVENT IT

Bedsores are prevented by relieving pressure on vulnerable sites. Persons who are bedridden and unable to move themselves must be turned every few hours. Those who can move should do so every hour or so.

A water bed cradles and distributes the body's weight more effectively than a regular mattress. Some hospitals

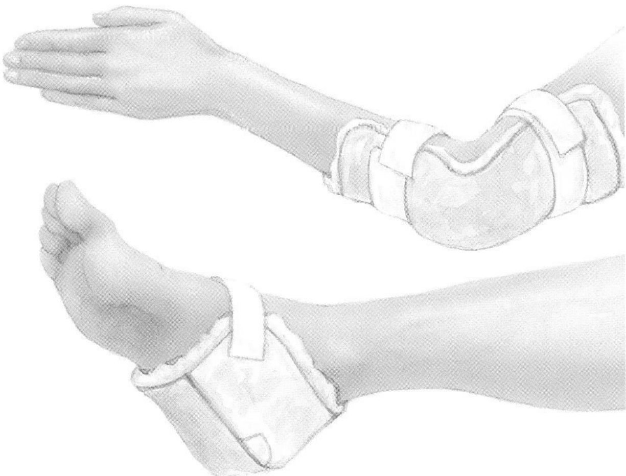

*Sheepskin pads, with the fleece side placed next to the skin, can help prevent pressure sores in vulnerable areas where the bone is near the body's surface.*

and nursing homes have special beds for patients who are vulnerable to developing bedsores. At home, place a foam rubber pad under the sheet; sheepskin pads also protect vulnerable areas. Change the sheets at least daily, or whenever they are damp or soiled, and make sure they are pulled tight. Persons who are confined to a wheelchair should sit on a foam-rubber cushion that is covered with a sheepskin pad. Inspect the skin daily for any signs of reddening, swelling, or blisters.

### ALTERNATIVE THERAPIES

**Herbal medicine**

Dr. Andrew Weil, the University of Arizona expert on herbal medicine, has found that comfrey speeds the healing of pressure sores. He prescribes a comfrey paste, which is made by blending fresh comfrey leaves with a little olive oil. The paste is applied directly to the sore and changed once or twice a day until the sore heals.

### BREAKTHROUGHS!

**Maggots have been found to be useful in healing deep pressure sores. The maggots are placed on the sore, which is covered with an occlusive wrap. The maggots clean the sore by feeding on the dead tissue. Several applications may be needed to completely debride the ulcer.**

# Psoriasis

### SYMPTOMS

- *Dry, silvery patches of skin that are scaly and may be painful and itchy.*
- *Well-defined skin lesions of varying sizes.*
- *In severe cases, joint pain and stiffness.*

### WHO IS AT RISK

*Psoriasis affects between 2 and 4 percent of Canadians, or about 1 million people. The disease can occur at any age, but it is most common among adults; men and women are affected equally. About one-third of patients have a family history of the disease, leading researchers to suspect a possible genetic cause for the disorder.*

## HOW IT DEVELOPS

Psoriasis is a chronic skin disease characterized by the overproduction of skin cells, which results in scaling, inflammation, itching, discomfort, and its other symptoms. In its most typical form, psoriasis is characterized by patches of thick, red skin covered with silvery scales. These patches, known as *plaques*, usually itch and burn, and can develop painful cracks. They most commonly appear on the elbows, knees, scalp, lower back, face, palms, and soles of the feet, and can also affect the nails and soft tissues in the mouth and genital area. In very severe cases, much of the body may be covered with psoriasis lesions. About 15 percent of psoriasis sufferers also develop joint pain and inflammation, a condition called *psoriatic arthritis*.

Psoriasis usually develops gradually and, initially, it tends to come and go. Flare-ups may be triggered by changes in climate, infection, stress, dry skin, trauma, irritation, sunburn, drug reactions (especially to lithium and beta-blockers), and withdrawal of a systemic corticosteroid, such as prednisone.

## WHAT YOU CAN DO

In mild cases, discomfort, scaling, and other symptoms can be reduced by applying lubricants such as white petroleum ointment or vegetable shortening to the affected site(s). Psoriasis of the scalp may be self-treated with coal tar shampoos; check with a dermatologist first. A typical regimen calls for applying the solution to the plaques and covering the scalp with a plastic shower cap to increase effectiveness and protect bedding.

A nonprescription hydrocortisone cream can reduce itchiness. Using an oatmeal soap and adding a cup of sea salt to bathwater may also ease itching. A little exposure to the sun can improve mild psoriasis, but be careful, as overexposure can worsen psoriasis (see *Warning!*, p 310). If symptoms persist or worsen, consult a dermatologist.

## HOW TO TREAT IT

Doctors usually try a three-step approach in treating psoriasis: topical medications, light treatments (phototherapy), and—if these measures don't work—oral (systemic) drugs. Patients respond to these treatments differently, so doctors generally use a trial-and-error approach.

- **Topical preparations:** These may include prescription-strength corticosteroid creams or ointments (e.g., Diprolene Glycol or Ultravate), which are usually applied twice a day; calcipotriol (Dovonex), a synthetic form of vitamin $D_3$ that is applied twice a day to control excessive production of skin cells; anthralin (Micanol), which slows turnover of skin cells; and topical retinoids such as tazarotene (Tazorac), substances derived from vitamin A that may also slow production of skin cells. Older topical drugs that are still used include coal tar, which is applied directly to the skin, added to bathwater, or used as a shampoo; for increased effectiveness, light treatments may be added. Lotions containing salicylic acid help remove skin scales; they may be combined with corticosteroid creams, anthralin, or coal tar.

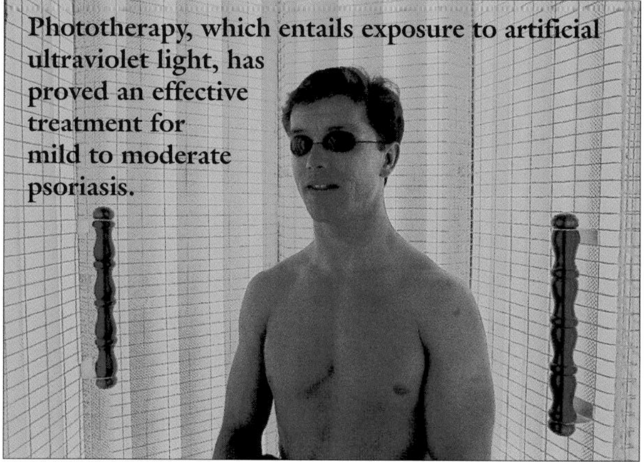

**Phototherapy, which entails exposure to artificial ultraviolet light, has proved an effective treatment for mild to moderate psoriasis.**

- **Phototherapy:** The sun's ultraviolet (UV) rays reduce skin inflammation and slow the overproduction of skin cells that causes the scaling of psoriasis; phototherapy employs artificial UVA or UVB light. UVB may be used alone or, for increased effectiveness, after an application of either coal tar ointment or a paste containing anthralin and salicylic acid. These are applied to the skin 6 to 24 hours before the UVB exposure. PUVA treatment combines oral or topical application of methoxsalen, a psoralen drug that increases the body's sensitivity to light, and exposure to ultraviolet A light.
- **Systemic treatments:** Severe cases of psoriasis may be treated with powerful drugs that suppress the immune system. Methotrexate, which is more commonly used to treat severe arthritis and cancer, is taken orally or by injection; it works against psoriasis by slowing production of skin cells. Cyclosporine (Neoral), which also slows skin-cell turnover, is more often used to prevent rejection of a transplanted organ. These drugs carry a high risk of serious side effects, including liver and kidney damage, so their use must be monitored closely by a doctor. Oral retinoids, such as acitretin (Soriatane), may also be prescribed; they are not as toxic as methotrexate and cyclosporine, but they can cause serious birth defects, so they should not be taken by women who are or may become pregnant. The psoriasis often recurs after acitretin is stopped.

**BREAKTHROUGHS!**

**Although the cause of psoriasis remains unknown, recent research points to a defect in the immune system as a possible culprit. Studies have found that overactive T-cells, a type of white blood cell that normally protects the body against infection and disease, can trigger the inflammation and excessive skin cell production characteristic of psoriasis.**

## HOW TO PREVENT IT

There is no known way to prevent psoriasis. However, some flare-ups may be prevented by reducing stress, protecting the skin from trauma, and avoiding sunburns.

### ALTERNATIVE THERAPIES

**Herbal medicine**

To reduce scaling and itchiness, herbalists recommend lavender, bergamot, yarrow, or comfrey oils, which are diluted with olive oil and applied directly to the plaques, or a few drops can be added to bathwater. Capsaicin, the active ingredient in hot chilies, may relieve itchiness and pain. Look for creams or ointments that contain 0.025 percent capsaicin. The first few applications will cause temporary burning or stinging; discontinue use if burning is prolonged or a blistering rash develops. Be careful not to get the capsaicin near the eyes or on delicate mucous membranes. Do not apply to raw or open skin.

**Nutraceuticals**

Fish oils, which are high in eicosapentaenoic acid (EPA), have been shown to improve psoriasis symptoms. In one study, patients receiving 3.6 grams of EPA a day for five months showed a 50 percent reduction in symptoms. To get this much EPA, take 20 grams of fish oil. Consult a doctor before using fish oils if you have a blood disorder or are taking anticoagulants.

**WARNING!**

***A little sun goes a long way in the treatment of psoriasis. While brief sunlight exposure—15 to 30 minutes, depending upon the season and time of day—can improve psoriasis symptoms, even a mild sunburn can make them much worse.***

**Spa therapy**

Many spas offer special mineral baths for psoriasis. Some of the most popular are in the Dead Sea area in Israel. Because it is 1,300 feet below sea level, this area offers the world's highest concentration of natural UVA rays. Dead Sea water is very salty and rich in other minerals, which appear to reduce scaling and other psoriasis symptoms.

# Scleroderma

## SYMPTOMS

- *Finger or hand swelling and coldness (Raynaud's phenomenon) followed by painful tightening and thickening of the skin of the hands, forearms, and face.*
- *Joint pain, swelling, and stiffness, especially of the fingers and knees.*
- *Muscle pain and weakness.*
- *Depending upon the organs involved, possible chest pain, shortness of breath, high blood pressure, dry eyes and mouth, episodes of severe facial pain (trigeminal neuralgia), and impotence.*

## WHO IS AT RISK

*Scleroderma is a relatively rare rheumatic disorder in which the immune systems attacks the body's connective tissue (collagen) and blood vessels. It is most likely to strike women between the ages of 35 and 55.*

*The cause of scleroderma is unknown, but recent studies found some evidence that leftover fetal cells that circulate in a woman's blood for years after pregnancy may somehow trigger the immune system to attack the body's collagen. Other studies have linked scleroderma to exposure to certain industrial chemicals, such as vinyl chloride and epoxy resins.*

## HOW IT DEVELOPS

Scleroderma typically starts with Raynaud's phenomenon, in which blood-vessel spasms cut circulation to the fingers and toes, resulting in tingling, numbness, and coldness. This is followed by swelling of the fingers, hands, and other affected parts. The skin becomes painfully tight, thick, and dry. Calcium deposits may collect in the skin, causing further stiffness and tightening. There may also be small red spots (telangiectasias) caused by swollen blood vessels. Fingers, knees, and other joints can become painful, swollen, and stiff; a thickening of tendons leads to muscle weakness and pain. Facial scleroderma causes dry eyes and mouth and nerve pain (trigeminal neuralgia).

Scleroderma can also attack many internal organs, a condition referred to as *systemic sclerosis*. Intestinal problems—severe heartburn, bloating, abdominal pain—are common. Shortness of breath, a chronic dry cough, chest pain, abnormal heart rhythms, and swelling of the lower limbs indicate lung and heart involvement. A spread to the kidneys can result in high blood pressure, headaches, reduced urine flow, and seizures.

The course of scleroderma is unpredictable. The initial skin swelling may last for several months, followed by thickening and other symptoms, which may peak in two or three years and then gradually improve. In mild cases, the disease remains confined to the skin; in others, internal organs are also involved.

### BREAKTHROUGHS!

**Bone marrow (stem cell) transplantation shows promise in treating some types of scleroderma. Stem cells, which stimulate regeneration of other cells, are harvested from a patient's blood. High doses of chemotherapy are then administered to destroy the patient's bone marrow, after which the stem cells are injected back into the patient. The cells quickly generate new bone marrow and immune cells. A recent study at the University of Washington found marked improvement in at least some scleroderma patients who underwent this procedure.**

### WARNING!

***Several studies have found that scleroderma patients who undergo radiation treatments for cancer and other conditions have an increased risk of adverse reactions, which may not show up for several years. The reasons for this are unknown, but many oncologists now warn that persons with scleroderma should avoid radiation therapy.***

## WHAT YOU CAN DO

See a doctor as soon as possible. Aspirin, ibuprofen, and other anti-inflammatory drugs can ease pain and may also improve circulation by thinning the blood. Avoid exposure to the cold to minimize the effects of Raynaud's phenomenon. If you smoke, it's imperative to stop; smoking further reduces peripheral blood flow and can worsen symptoms. Put all joints through gentle range-of-motion exercises every day to maintain flexibility.

If heartburn is a problem, eat small amounts of food throughout the day, and avoid lying down for at least two hours after meals. Take antacids to prevent or relieve symptoms. If a dry mouth causes swallowing problems, chew your food well and sip water while eating. To reduce the kidney's workload, drink at least 8 to 10 glasses of water a day, cut back on salt, and limit high-protein foods to two or three small servings a day. Artificial tears and saliva substitutes can ease the discomfort of dry eyes and a dry mouth; these are sold at most pharmacies.

## HOW TO TREAT IT

Scleroderma cannot be cured at present, so treatment is aimed at reducing symptoms. Nonsteroidal anti-inflammatory drugs (NSAIDs)—aspirin, ibuprofen, naproxen, and similar products—are used to ease pain and improve blood flow. Aggressive treatment with drugs that suppress the immune system (for example, D-penicillamine [Caprimine] or azathioprine [Imuran]) can sometimes keep scleroderma in check. Steroids may be given to reduce scleroderma-related inflammation of the muscles and other tissues. Diuretics are prescribed to treat swelling; Raynaud's symptoms are treated with calcium channel blockers (nifedipine or diltiazem) and other medications that expand (dilate) the blood vessels.

## HOW TO PREVENT IT

There are no known ways to prevent scleroderma.

### ALTERNATIVE THERAPIES

**Herbal medicine**

Evening primrose oil, borage oil, and other herbal products high in gamma linolenic acid (GLA) reduce inflammation and thin the blood; dosages that provide 250 to 500 mg of GLA a day have been shown to ease symptoms for some scleroderma patients. People taking anticoagulants should not use products containing GLA. Echinacea and other herbal remedies that stimulate various immune system cells should be avoided because they may worsen scleroderma and other autoimmune diseases. Aloe vera gel or lotion can help reduce skin dryness.

**Massage therapy**

Therapeutic massage can ease discomfort and also help maintain skin suppleness.

**Nutraceuticals**

Vitamin E, in dosages of 800 to 1000 IU a day, may reduce pain from inflammation and improve blood flow. Other potentially helpful supplements include 1000 mg of vitamin C, which is needed to maintain blood vessels, and up to 10,000 IU of vitamin A, which fosters healthy skin. For cautions concerning vitamins A, C, and E, see *About the Recommendations*, p 7.

**Physical therapy**

Intensive physical therapy is needed to minimize contracture of the affected joints and maintain muscle strength. Therapists will do passive range-of-motion exercises for patients who have difficulty moving, and design an exercise regimen for those who have more mobility.

# Shingles

### SYMPTOMS

- *Painful skin rash, usually on one side of the body.*
- *Possible fever, chills, upset stomach, and malaise.*
- *Lingering nerve pain.*

### WHO IS AT RISK

*Anyone who has had chickenpox can develop shingles as an adult. It usually strikes after age 50; it also occurs in younger people with lowered immunity.*

## HOW IT DEVELOPS

After chickenpox clears up, the herpes zoster virus that causes it goes dormant along the pathway of a root nerve. Shingles develops when the virus is reactivated, often when the body's immune defenses are weakened by aging, disease, or stress. The attack starts with flulike symptoms and tingling, burning, or shooting pains on one side of the body—usually the upper torso or face. A few days later, a rash of raised, red bumps appears, followed by formation of painful, water-filled blisters. After a week or so, the blisters dry up and form crusts.

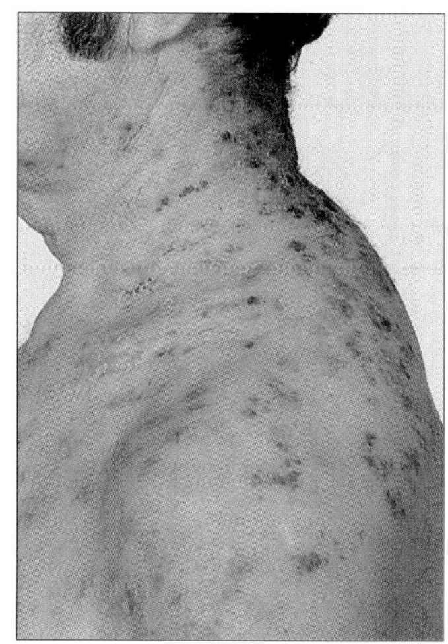

*The shingles rash follows the pathway of a root nerve, almost always on one side of the body and usually on the upper torso.*

Most people recover fully in two weeks, but there are exceptions. For example, the virus can spread to other parts of the skin and even internal organs in people with lowered immunity. Shingles involving the facial nerve can infect the eye and threaten sight (see *Warning!*, p 313).

Following an attack of shingles, many people, especially the elderly, develop lingering nerve pain, a condition called *postherpetic neuropathy*. This can last for months or even years, and it can be very debilitating. An attack of shingles usually confers lifelong immunity, but about 4 percent of patients do suffer a recurrence.

## WHAT YOU CAN DO

Cool compresses or soaking in a tepid bath provides some relief from the pain and tingling. To ease itchiness, try adding a cup of baking soda or colloidal oatmeal to the bathwater. Mild to moderate pain can be treated with aspirin, acetaminophen, ibuprofen, or other OTC medications. Rest as much as possible.

### BREAKTHROUGHS!

**The growing practice of childhood immunization against chickenpox promises to reduce the incidence of shingles during adulthood. The vaccines are given during the first two years of life. They may also be given to adolescents or young adults who never had chickenpox during childhood.**

## HOW TO TREAT IT

Shingles usually clears up without treatment in two weeks. Antiviral drugs such as acyclovir (Zovirax) or famciclovir (Famvir) can speed recovery. AIDS patients and others with lowered immunity may be hospitalized and given intravenous acyclovir. Shingles in or near the eye is treated with antiviral drugs and a corticosteroid eye ointment.

> **WARNING!**
>
> ***See your doctor immediately if you develop blisters on the nose or upper part of the face; in such cases, aggressive treatment is needed to prevent blindness.***

The nerve pain that often follows shingles can be very difficult to treat. Codeine sometimes helps, but more effective drugs include carbamazepine (Tegretol), an antiseizure medication, and amitriptyline (Elavil), an antidepressant. These drugs are thought to work by reducing the number of pain impulses that the brain processes. Electrical nerve stimulation using a TENS (transcutaneous electrical nerve stimulation) machine sometimes eases the nerve pain by interfering with the transmission of nerve impulses.

## HOW TO PREVENT IT

There is no way to prevent shingles once a person has contracted chickenpox.

### ALTERNATIVE THERAPIES

**Acupuncture**

This has helped many patients with postherpetic nerve pain; improvement may require six treatments.

**Herbal medicine**

Aloe vera gel is soothing and speeds healing of the skin blisters. Compresses soaked in goldenseal or peppermint tea are also soothing. Goldenseal should not be used by pregnant women or people with heart disease. Postherpetic nerve pain may be eased by applications of capsaicin—the active ingredient in hot chilies. Capsaicin should never be used near the eyes or applied to unhealed blisters.

**Nutraceuticals**

Some studies have found that high doses of vitamin E—1000 to 1800 IU a day—may reduce the risk of postherpetic nerve pain. Vitamin C, in doses of 1000 mg a day, may speed healing. For cautions concerning vitamins C and E, see *About the Recommendations,* p 7.

# Skin Cancer

### SYMPTOMS

- *A sore, mole, or other skin lesion that does not heal and changes in shape, color, size, or thickness.*
- *A persistent skin lesion or sore that is painful or itchy; it may form an ulcer, bleed, scab over, heal, and then recur.*
- *An unhealing skin ulcer that develops in a site exposed to earlier radiation therapy.*

### WHO IS AT RISK

*Skin cancers are the most common form of cancer in Canada, with an estimated 69,500 cases diagnosed in 1999. Although most common among older people, no one is immune to skin cancer. According to the Canadian Cancer Society, people who have had prolonged exposure to the sun's ultraviolet (UV) rays over many years have a higher-than-average incidence of skin cancer. Prolonged exposure during childhood, combined with a history of blistering sunburns, also increases the risk.*

*Red-haired, blue-eyed persons who have fair skin that freckles and burns easily are the most vulnerable. Bald men who go hatless in the sun often develop scalp cancer; others who are at risk include persons who are heavily freckled or have large moles, patients who have undergone radiation therapy, people who regularly work outdoors such as farmers or construction workers, burn victims, and those with lowered immunity or inflammatory disorders, such as lupus, that weaken the skin's resistance to cancer.*

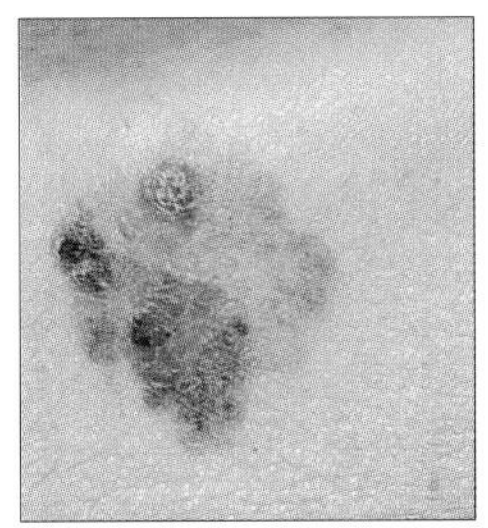

*Squamous cell cancers can be very painful if they hit a nerve.*

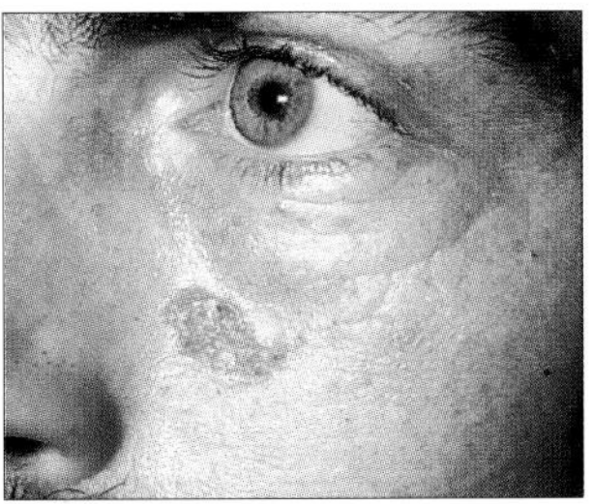

*Basal cell cancers—the most common form of skin cancer—often develop on the face.*

## HOW IT DEVELOPS

Basal cell and squamous cell carcinomas are the two most common—and most curable—skin cancers. Other forms include malignant melanoma, Paget's disease of the nipple or anus, and Kaposi's sarcoma, which is associated with AIDS and other conditions that reduce immunity. Development varies according to the type of cancer.

Basal cell carcinomas start in cells in the lower layers of the epidermis (the outer skin); more than 80 percent are on the head and neck. They form superficial skin ulcers that are irregularly shaped and may take on many different appearances—firm, shiny, almost translucent ulcerated nodules; flat, scarlike plaques; or red, thin areas with distinct borders. If left untreated, basal cell cancers develop a shiny or pearly border with prominent,

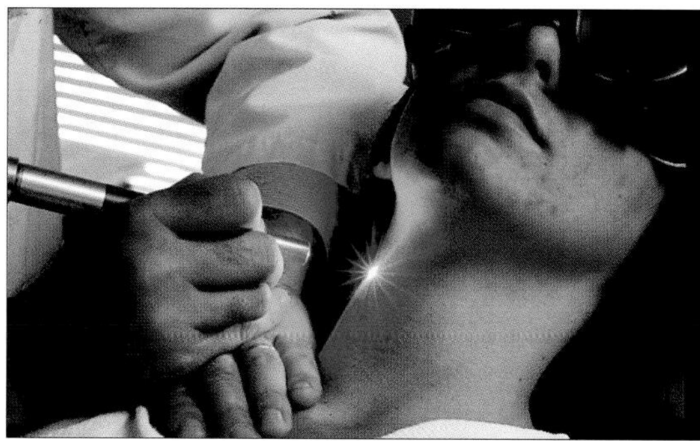

*Many small skin cancers can be removed with laser surgery, which uses intense light beams to vaporize the cancerous tissue.*

engorged vessels on the surface and a central ulcer that bleeds, forms a crust, appears to heal, and then recurs. Basal cell carcinomas can be disfiguring, especially on the face. But they are easy to remove, highly curable, and they rarely spread (metastasize) to other parts of the body.

Squamous cell carcinomas develop in the cells just under the skin's protective outer (horny) layer of dead cells; about 75 percent are on the head and face, 15 percent are on the hands, and the remaining 10 percent are on other parts of the body. These cancers may first appear as a red papule or plaque with a scaly or crusted surface and then become nodular, with a warty surface. Sometimes the bulk of the tumor lies below the skin's surface. It eventually develops ulcers and invades the underlying tissues; if left untreated, 3 to 10 percent spread to nearby tissues, such as regional lymph nodes, underlying nerves, or distant organs, including the liver, lungs, and brain. This type of skin cancer can be very painful if it engulfs an underlying nerve, especially the facial trigeminal nerve.

## WHAT YOU CAN DO

Learn the warning signs of skin cancer and examine your skin thoroughly and regularly in a brightly lit room (see *How to Examine Your Own Skin,* p 315). See a doctor promptly if you note any suspicious signs, such as:

- Any new skin growth that does not disappear in four to six weeks.
- Sores or lesions that grow and turn translucent, brown, black, or multicolored.
- Moles, birthmarks, or beauty marks that grow, change color or texture, or develop irregular borders.
- Any skin spot or growth that itches, hurts, crusts over, erodes, or bleeds for more than three or four weeks.

### BREAKTHROUGHS!

**A new approach that appears to work against skin cancer is biological therapy, in which treatments are aimed at improving the body's natural ability to fight cancer. Substances being used in biological therapy include interferon, which stimulates the body's immune system to fight cancer, and tumor necrosis factor, substances secreted by certain cells to kill tumor cells. In Canada, biological therapy is used for advanced skin cancers that have spread (metastatic melanoma).**

## HOW TO TREAT IT

Skin cancers are usually removed surgically, although radiation may be the treatment of choice when surgery is not possible. Topical chemotherapy may also be used. Surgical procedures include:

- **Curettage,** in which a surgeon uses a sharp surgical instrument to scrape away a small, superficial cancer. A local anesthetic is injected to control pain; cauterization stops any bleeding.
- **Cryosurgery,** in which liquid nitrogen spray or a device called a cryoprobe is used to freeze the cancerous tissue and destroy malignant cells; local anesthesia controls pain.
- **Laser surgery,** in which powerful light beams are used to vaporize small skin cancers. This procedure produces little pain and virtually no bleeding.
- **Surgical excision**, which involves removing the growth along with a margin of healthy tissue; plastic surgery may be needed later.

### MELANOMA: THE KILLER SKIN CANCER

The incidence of melanoma, the most deadly form of skin cancer, has doubled over the past 20 years. According to Health Canada's Cancer Bureau statistics, the estimated number of new cases of melanoma for the year 2000 is 3,700. Melanoma arises in the pigment-producing cells (melanocytes) in the skin and, less commonly, the colored portion of the eyes. Its risk factors are the same as those of other skin cancers; in addition, persons born with large brown moles or who develop large, atypical moles called *dysplastic nevi* are also at risk.

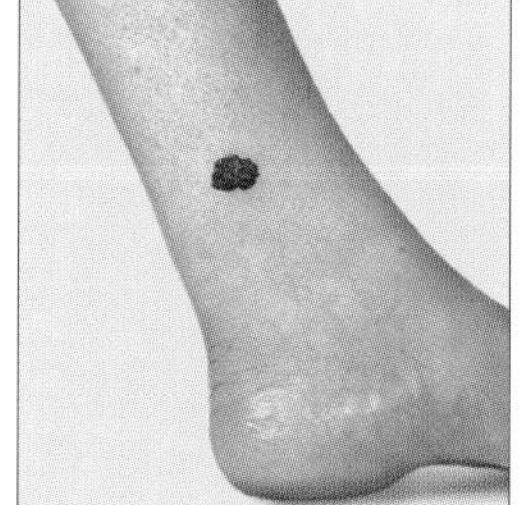

*At first, a melanoma may resemble a mole, but it has irregular margins and continues to grow.*

Melanoma is highly curable if it is treated early with surgical removal. Chemotherapy is used to treat some melanomas, especially those that are very large or considered inoperable. Advanced melanoma can cause severe pain; a narcotic drug or other strong prescription painkillers may be needed.

- **Mohs procedure,** in which layers of tissue are cut away in an expanding circle around the cancer. Each layer is examined under a microscope to determine the extent of the malignancy. The procedure ends when only normal tissue is excised. It, too, is usually done with local anesthesia. Codeine or similar painkillers may be taken for a few days afterward.

**WARNING!**

***Use special care in protecting children from overexposure to the sun. Even a mild childhood sunburn greatly increases the risk of skin cancer, including melanoma, later in life.***

## HOW TO PREVENT IT

Minimize exposure to the sun's ultraviolet rays, which are most intense between 10 AM and 2 PM. If you must be outdoors at that time, wear a hat with a wide brim and sunscreen with a sun protection factor (SPF) of at least 15. Dermatologists recommend that everyone always apply sunscreen to any exposed skin before going outdoors. Do not patronize tanning booths and don't use sun lamps.

### ALTERNATIVE THERAPIES

**Nutraceuticals**

Antioxidant supplements of vitamins C and E, beta carotene, and selenium may help prevent skin cancer by reducing the cellular damage caused by free radicals, unstable molecules released when the body burns oxygen. Recommended dosages include 1000 mg of vitamin C, 400 to 800 IU of vitamin E, 25 to 50 mg of beta carotene (in the form of mixed carotenoids), and 100 to 400 micrograms (mcg) of selenium. For cautions concerning these nutraceuticals, see *About the Recommendations*, p 7. The diet should provide 5 to 10 servings of fruits and vegetables a day. In addition, recent studies indicate that a diet low in animal fats also reduces the risk of skin cancer.

# Skin Injuries

### SYMPTOMS

***Abrasion:*** *Painful scraping or wearing away of a portion of skin; possible oozing of blood.*

***Bruise:*** *Painful area of discolored—usually black, blue, or purple—skin; possible swelling and inflammation.*

***Cut:*** *Break in the skin that results in pain and bleeding; possible inflammation and infection.*

### WHO IS AT RISK

*Everyone now and then suffers a minor skin injury. Children are especially vulnerable to skinned knees and other abrasions. Any blow or fall that injures the tiny surface*

## HOW TO EXAMINE YOUR OWN SKIN

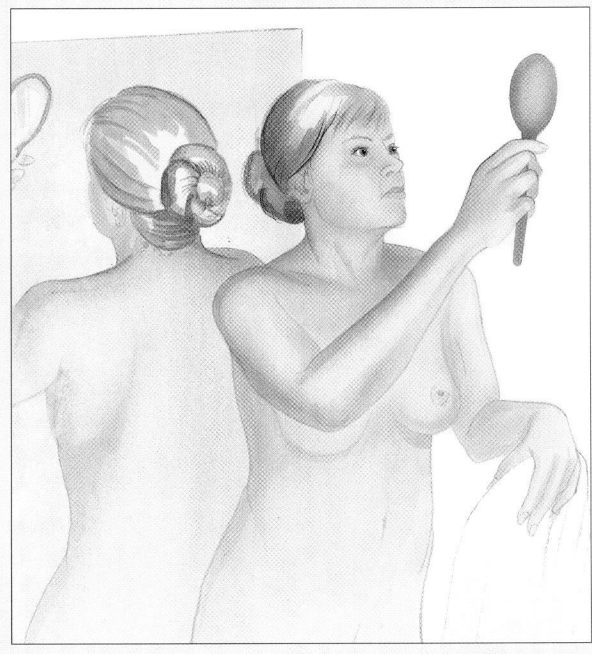

- *Use a full-length mirror and a hand mirror that allow you to inspect every part of your skin once a month. If you can't see an area yourself, enlist the help of your spouse, a family member, or someone else who is close to you.*
- *Examine your body front and back, right and left sides with arms raised, then check your forearms, upper underarms, and palms carefully. Don't forget to examine your feet, including the soles and the spaces between your toes.*
- *Check the nails for changes or discolored spots in the underlying flesh. Also check the scalp, especially if you are bald or have thin spots, the lower back, and the buttocks.*
- *Create a body map on which you note the size and placement of moles, skin tags, and other anomalies. Then during monthly skin self-examination, check this map for any new moles and growths and inspect old ones for any changes.*
- *Have a doctor investigate any suspicious findings.*

*blood vessels without actually breaking the skin can develop the characteristic black or blue mark of a bruise.*

*Some people, especially elderly women and people who take a lot of aspirin and other blood-thinning medications, develop bruises from only slight pressure. Various blood disorders, such as anemia, leukemia, or hemophilia, also cause the skin to bruise very easily. Although the skin is tough, almost any sharp object can cut it.*

## HOW THEY DEVELOP

A **bruise** develops when a blow to the skin allows blood to escape from a damaged blood vessel into surrounding tissue. Although the skin remains intact, the affected area almost immediately changes color, initially to a bright red, then to "black and blue" or purple; a few days later, it turns yellow, pale green, or brownish as the bruise fades. Sometimes the area also swells or becomes hard. The discoloration occurs as the escaped blood cells die and become reabsorbed in the bloodstream. In the case of a black eye, the injury may actually be to the temple or forehead, with the escaped blood cells draining downward into tissue underneath the eye. Most bruises heal themselves in 7 to 10 days; exceptions are the large, flat, mostly painless bruises that are often sustained by older persons, which may last for weeks or even months.

In **cuts** and **abrasions**, the skin is actually broken; this not only causes bleeding and immediate pain, but such injuries also provide a point of entry for potentially harmful bacteria and other organisms. The body responds by forming a clot to seal off the wound and stop bleeding, and by then sending disease-fighting white blood cells to destroy any foreign organisms (see *How a Cut Heals*, below).

## WHAT YOU CAN DO

Prompt treatment eases pain and reduces the risk of infection and other complications. Many doctors advise against taking aspirin or similar painkillers because they hinder clotting and may increase bleeding. Instead, take acetaminophen, which does not affect clotting.

If the skin is not broken, application of an ice pack or cold compress can reduce the size and severity of a bruise by reducing blood flow to the area. Also apply gentle pressure to reduce the bleeding under the skin. If the injury involves a limb (arm or leg), elevating it will mini mize painful swelling. After the first 24 to 36 hours, you can switch to a heating pad or warm compresses. By this time, the broken blood vessels have been sealed off, and the heat will increase blood flow to the area and promote healing by speeding reabsorption of the errant blood cells.

Any blow to the head and upper face can result in a black eye; again, apply an ice pack or cold compress as soon as possible to reduce swelling. There is no truth to the old wives' tale that covering the eye with a raw steak will prevent a black eye. Any benefit comes from the cold temperature of the meat; a cold compress is more conve-

### HOW A CUT HEALS

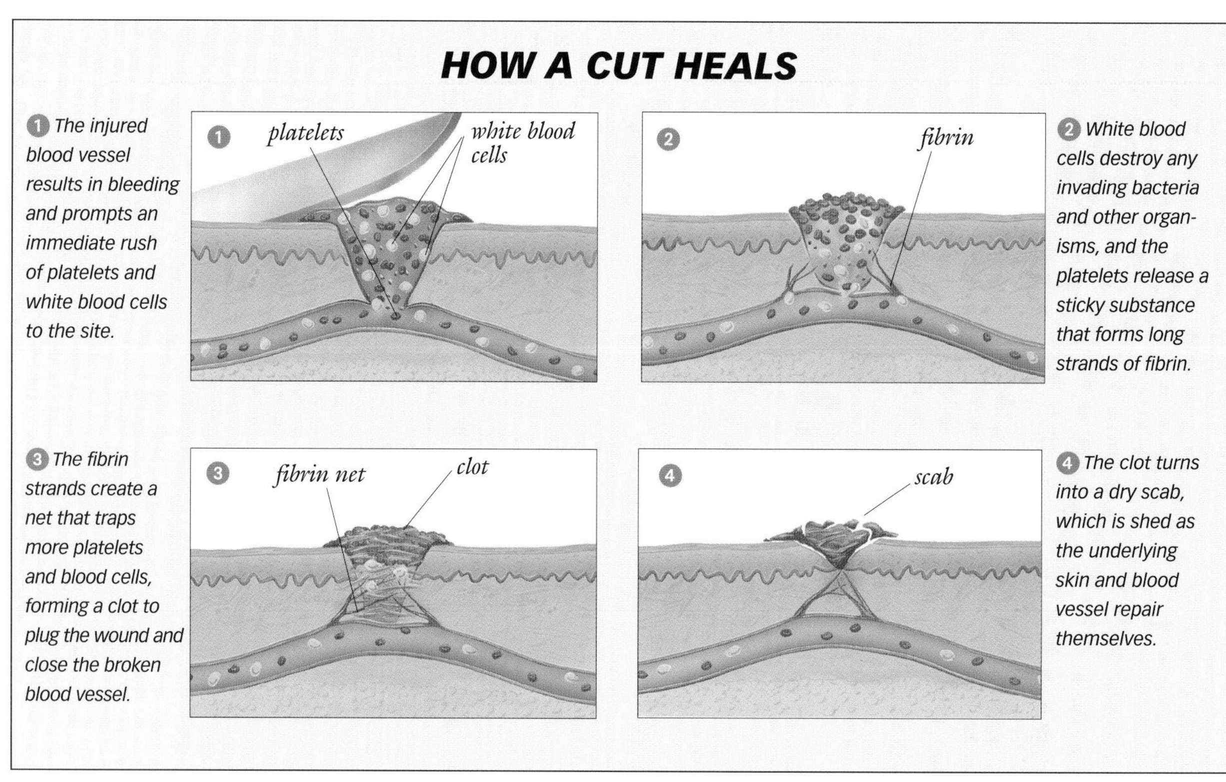


1 The injured blood vessel results in bleeding and prompts an immediate rush of platelets and white blood cells to the site.

2 White blood cells destroy any invading bacteria and other organisms, and the platelets release a sticky substance that forms long strands of fibrin.

3 The fibrin strands create a net that traps more platelets and blood cells, forming a clot to plug the wound and close the broken blood vessel.

4 The clot turns into a dry scab, which is shed as the underlying skin and blood vessel repair themselves.

nient and sanitary than a steak. Minor cuts and scrapes usually can be self-treated. Hold a clean pad over the injured area and apply gentle pressure until bleeding stops, and then bandage (see *How to Stop Bleeding*, below). Wash a skinned knee, elbow, or other minor scrape with lukewarm water and soap. Gently remove any visible dirt or other debris, and swab the injury with an antiseptic solution, such as alcohol or povidone-iodine (Betadine).

An antibiotic cream or ointment further reduces the risk of infection. Cover the wound with sterile gauze or an adhesive bandage. See a doctor or go to the emergency room if you are unable to stop the bleeding or the cut is large enough to require stitches; deep puncture wounds and animal or human bites almost always require medical attention.

**WARNING!**

***Bruises that appear spontaneously without a precipitating blow may indicate a serious medical condition that should be diagnosed and treated. Such blood disorders as hemophilia, leukemia, and anemia can trigger spontaneous bruises, as can long-term use of corticosteroid medications.***

## HOW TO TREAT THEM

Most bruises heal in a week or so of self-treatment. However, a doctor should be consulted if bruises develop on many parts of the body and with little or no provocation (see *Warning!*, above). Also consult a doctor if a black eye is very painful, swollen, or interfering with vision.

When treating extensive cuts or abrasions, a doctor will first do whatever is necessary to stop the bleeding. A local anesthetic may be injected to provide quick pain relief. Severe hemorrhaging may require emergency surgery to repair torn blood vessels and damaged tissue. After the wound is thoroughly cleansed, it will be closed with stitches or surgical staples. A booster tetanus shot may also be given, especially if immunization against this deadly disease is more than five years old. Antibiotics may be prescribed to prevent infection.

## HOW TO PREVENT THEM

Many skin injuries can be prevented by following commonsense safety precautions. Always keep knives and other sharp objects out of the reach of young children. While a certain number of falls, cuts, and scrapes are a normal part of childhood, guard against serious injuries. Make sure that children of all ages are securely strapped into car seats. Install safety gates at the top and bottom of stairs until a toddler can safely negotiate them.

Playgrounds should have padded surfaces under swings, slides, climbing structures, and other equipment. Inspect play areas for bits of broken glass and other objects that can cause injuries.

### ALTERNATIVE THERAPIES

**Herbal medicine**

A comfrey poultice can speed healing of all types of skin wounds; comfrey is high in allantoin, a substance that promotes rebuilding of damaged skin tissue. Steep one or two tablespoons of comfrey leaves (fresh or dried) in a cup of boiling water. Drain off the water, place the leaves between two layers of gauze or clean cotton, and apply directly to the bruise or skin wound. Leave the poultice on for 20 minutes; repeat two or three times a day until healing is complete. If comfrey is not available, a compress soaked in diluted tincture of arnica is an alternative. (**Note:** Do not ingest comfrey; it has been linked to liver damage.)

**Nutraceuticals**

Vitamin C is instrumental in building and maintaining healthy skin and blood vessels. Take 500 mg a day to promote healing. If you bruise easily and are not suffering from anemia or another underlying disease that requires treatment, try increasing the dosage to 1000 mg a day. Do not take more than 500 mg if you have kidney stones, kidney disease, or hemochromatosis.

### HOW TO STOP BLEEDING

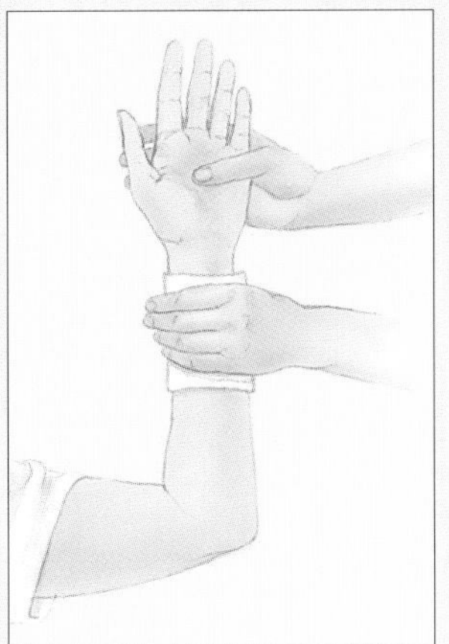

*Stop bleeding by placing a clean cloth over the wound, applying gentle pressure, and elevating an injured limb to reduce blood flow to the injury.*

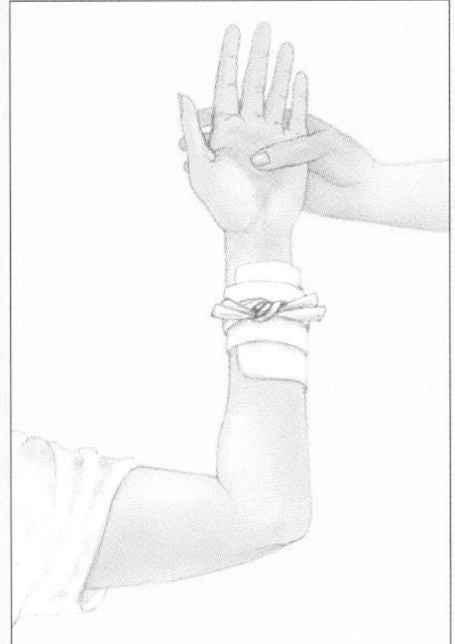

*After the bleeding stops, don't remove the compress, which may cause the wound to bleed again. Instead, cover it with additional gauze and tie it securely.*

# Systemic Pain

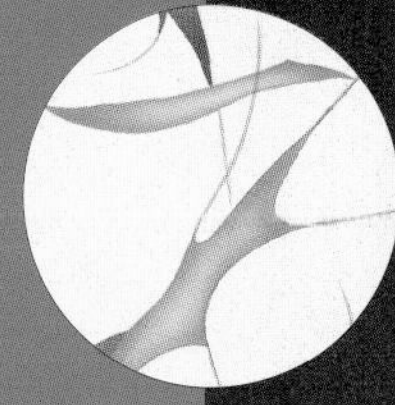

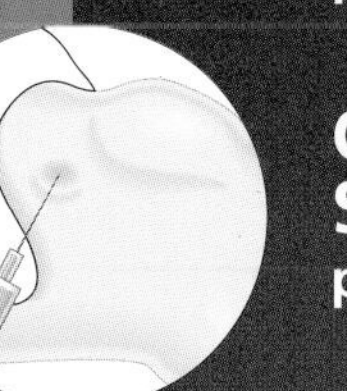

# Systemic Pain

*Systemic pain doesn't necessarily affect the entire body, although it can. Instead, it refers to pain caused by any disorder that affects multiple sites or produces pain that travels from one place to another. Examples include infections, certain cancers, and nerve diseases.*

## Anemia

### SYMPTOMS

Many types of anemia are painless; those that generally produce pain are discussed below.

**All anemias:** Unexplained fatigue, weakness, shortness of breath, pallor or yellowish skin (jaundice).

**Immune hemolytic anemia:** Joint stiffness, swelling, and pain; dark urine; enlarged spleen.

**Iron-deficiency anemia:** Headache, sore tongue, dizziness or fainting due to sudden drop in blood pressure when shifting position, appetite loss or unusual cravings.

**Megaloblastic anemia:** Headache, sore mouth and tongue, diarrhea, appetite loss.

**Sickle-cell anemia:** Mild-to-severe pain in the joints, back, chest, legs, arms, abdomen, and penis; headache; swollen hands and feet; rapid pulse; fever; vomiting; recurrent infections, especially pneumonia and meningitis; kidney problems and bloody urine; possible prolonged, painful erection (priapism); leg ulcers.

### WHO IS AT RISK

Although there are many types of anemia with different causes, most are characterized by an abnormality of the red blood cells (erythrocytes), which carry oxygen to all the body's cells. This shortage of oxygen explains why anemia invariably causes fatigue, weakness, and shortness of breath; the other symptoms vary according to the type of disorder.

**Immune hemolytic anemia** is an autoimmune disease in which the immune system attacks the body's red blood cells as if they were foreign invaders. More than half of all cases are idiopathic, meaning that doctors can't pinpoint their cause. The rest may be triggered by an adverse drug reaction or occur as a complication of blood transfusions, pregnancy (if the mother and baby have different blood types), and certain cancers, such as leukemia.

As its name suggests, **iron-deficiency anemia** is due to an abnormally low level of iron, which the body needs to make hemoglobin—the pigment that gives red blood cells their color and, more important, carries oxygen. Iron-deficiency anemia is the most prevalent form of anemia in Canada. A diet lacking in iron-rich foods is a possible cause, but more likely factors include an inability to absorb iron, pregnancy, and any condition that entails significant blood loss, such as heavy menstrual flow, stomach ulcers, intestinal cancers, and chronic bleeding due to long-term use of aspirin and similar drugs. This type of anemia is also common in fast-growing children and adolescents whose diet may not provide enough iron.

**Megaloblastic anemia**, in which the bone marrow produces abnormally large (megalo), underdeveloped (blasts) red blood cells, usually results from deficiencies of vitamin $B_{12}$ (known as pernicious anemia) or folic acid. A lack of intrinsic factor—a protein produced in the stomach that is necessary to absorb vitamin $B_{12}$—is the leading cause of the pernicious form of megaloblastic anemia. A strict vegetarian diet that eliminates all animal products can also result in vitamin $B_{12}$ deficiency. Other causes of megaloblastic anemia include an adverse drug reaction or myelofibrosis, a bone-marrow disease; it may also be secondary to certain cancers, such as leukemia.

**Sickle-cell anemia** takes its name from the abnormal, crescent shape of the red blood cells. It is a hereditary disease that occurs in most racial and ethnic groups, but that afflicts mostly persons of African descent. In fact, 1 in 10 people of African descent carry the aberrant gene, known as hemoglobin S. If both parents carry the gene, there is a one-in-four chance that each child they conceive will develop sickle-cell anemia, even though both parents may be symptom-free.

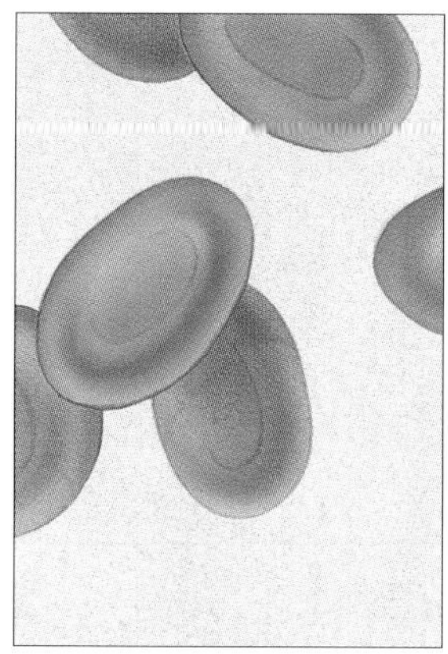

*Normal red blood cells, which carry oxygen to all body cells.*

*Misshapen red blood cells in sickle-cell anemia, which carry minimal oxygen.*

## HOW IT DEVELOPS

Mild anemia, especially that due to iron deficiency, is often asymptomatic; when symptoms develop, one of the first is usually chronic, unexplained fatigue that is often accompanied by weakness and shortness of breath. Any exertion is likely to result in a racing pulse, as the heart speeds up its beating in an effort to pump out more blood. Headaches, joint and muscle pain, dizziness, and pallor (or sometimes jaundice) are common.

Sickle-cell anemia is by far the most painful type of anemia. The fragile, odd-shaped red blood cells die off prematurely, and their debris clogs the blood vessels. Physicians call this a *hemolytic* or *aplastic crisis.* Over time, these episodes damage most body organs, especially the central nervous system, kidneys, lungs, liver, and spleen. The joints become swollen and very painful; deep, aching bone pain is also common.

Patients with megaloblastic anemia also have diminished levels of white blood cells and platelets. Thus, in addition to their anemia symptoms, patients must contend with a low resistance to infection and a tendency to bleed and bruise easily.

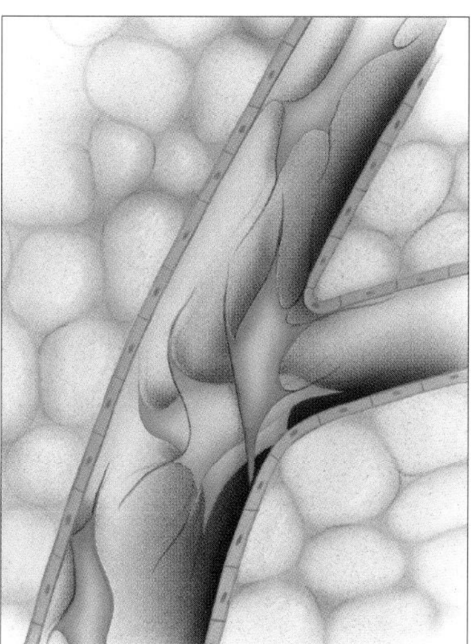

*The sickle cells cause pain when they clog small blood vessels.*

## WHAT YOU CAN DO

Work with your doctor to bring the anemia under control. If pain is a problem, talk to your doctor about safe medications to relieve it. In iron-deficiency anemia, for example, aspirin and similar medications may be harmful because they increase the risk of bleeding.

Listen to your body—it's important to stay active without overdoing it. Time your more strenuous activities for when you have the most energy. For example, some anemia patients feel sluggish in the morning, but find they have more energy in the afternoon. Even so, take frequent rests and don't push yourself to the point that you're short of breath and have a racing pulse.

Learn as much as you can about your particular type of anemia and its potential complications. For example, the accelerated breakdown of red blood cells increases the risk of developing blood clots, which may trigger a heart attack, stroke, or pulmonary embolism. Be aware of the warning signs of such complications, and seek immediate medical attention if any develop.

Dehydration can worsen anemia symptoms. Drink at least 8 to 10 glasses of water, juice, and other nonalcoholic fluids a day. Infections are especially hazardous for anyone with megaloblastic anemia; see a doctor as soon as possible if you develop a fever, upset stomach, or other signs of possible infection. Anyone who has sickle-cell disease should call his or her doctor immediately if joint pain and other symptoms of an impending crisis develop.

### BREAKTHROUGHS!

**The use of erythropoietin (Eprex), a hormone secreted by the kidneys, has revolutionized the treatment of many types of anemia. Erythropoietin stimulates the bone marrow to increase production of red blood cells. It is given by injection, and it is especially useful in treating patients with anemia resulting from chronic kidney failure, cancer therapy, or HIV infections.**

## HOW TO TREAT IT

The goal of therapy for most anemias is twofold: to treat the underlying disease and to manage pain and other symptoms. Nutritional deficiencies will be corrected; in severe cases, blood transfusions may be necessary. In recent years, the need for transfusions to treat anemia has declined, thanks to the use of erythropoietin (Eprex), which stimulates increased production of red blood cells (see *Breakthroughs!,* below).

Immune hemolytic anemia can often be controlled by administering drugs such as prednisone (e.g., Winpred) or other corticosteroids to alleviate symptoms and suppress the immune system. The spleen may be removed to reduce its abnormal storage of red blood cells.

Treatment of sickle-cell anemia usually centers on relieving the various symptoms and consequences. During a hemolytic crisis, which can be intensely painful, morphine or another narcotic medication may be needed. Adults with sickle-cell disease may be given individual morphine pumps so they can control their own pain medication as needed. At other times, acetaminophen, ibuprofen, and other nonprescription painkillers are usually sufficient; if not, prescription-strength drugs may be necessary. Kidney failure, stroke, and other possible complications are treated as they develop.

## HOW TO PREVENT IT

Some anemias cannot be prevented, but complications can usually be avoided by seeking early diagnosis and treatment if symptoms develop. Consuming a diet that includes a variety of foods high in vitamin $B_{12}$, folic acid, and iron helps anemias caused by deficiencies of these nutrients (see *Alternative Therapies,* p 322). People of

African descent can have their blood tested for hemoglobin S, the gene that carries the sickle-cell trait. If both partners carry the trait, genetic counseling may be helpful in assessing the risk of having a child with sickle-cell disease. During pregnancy, amniocentesis—a test in which a small amount of the amniotic fluid surrounding the developing baby is withdrawn and analyzed for various genetic abnormalities—can determine whether the fetus has inherited the sickle-cell genes.

### ALTERNATIVE THERAPIES

**Nutraceuticals and nutrition therapy**

People diagnosed with anemia due to nutritional deficiencies should consult a registered dietitian or a doctor with a background in nutrition. Persons who lack intrinsic factor will need vitamin $B_{12}$ shots because they cannot absorb the vitamin when it is taken orally. The diet should emphasize foods high in the deficient nutrients—lean red meats, liver and other organ means, sardines, sunflower and other seeds, fortified breads and cereals for iron; meat, poultry, seafood, milk, eggs, and other animal products for vitamin $B_{12}$; and green leafy vegetables, legumes, orange juice, nuts, wheat germ, and whole-grain cereals for folic acid. Iron supplements are usually necessary to treat iron-deficiency anemia, but the dosage and type should be determined by a dietitian or doctor. Be sure to keep iron pills and all supplements containing iron out of the reach of young children; just five high-potency iron pills can kill a small child.

**WARNING!**

***Whenever a person receives a blood transfusion, there's a 1 in 25 chance of a transfusion reaction. The risk can be cut by insisting that donated blood also be tested for ABO compatibility, a screening test to make sure that the donor blood does not contain antibodies incompatible with yours.***

# Cancer

### SYMPTOMS

*In its early stages, cancer usually is not painful. As the disease progresses, however, it can cause mild to intense pain. Cancer's early warning signs include:*

- *A thickening or lump in the breast or other part of the body.*
- *A sore that will not heal.*
- *Unusual bleeding or discharge.*
- *Persistent coughing or hoarseness.*
- *A change in bowel or bladder habits.*
- *Indigestion or difficulty swallowing.*
- *A noticeable change in a mole or wart.*

### TYPES AND CAUSES OF CANCER-RELATED PAIN

Following are some of the more common types and sources of cancer pain.

- Pain caused by a tumor growing within or pressing against an organ or obstructing a vessel or passageway. For example, cancer of the esophagus can block the gullet and make swallowing painful. The severe headaches of a brain tumor are usually caused by tissue swelling within the skull.
- Pain caused by cancer treatment, including surgery and the effects of chemotherapy and radiation. For example, anticancer drugs can cause stomach, joint, and muscle pain; headaches; and pain while urinating.
- Pain from indigestion, constipation, and other digestive problems caused by an expanding tumor.
- Pain and weakness from prolonged bed rest.
- Phantom-limb pain following amputation of a limb.
- Pain associated with infection.
- Nerve pain, due to a tumor infringing on a nerve, or as a side effect of radiation therapy.

### WHO IS AT RISK

*An estimated 129,200 Canadians were diagnosed with cancer in 1998—a 30 percent increase in the number of new cases in the last decade. Although cancer can occur at any age, it usually takes decades of exposure to carcinogens—cancer-causing agents such as tobacco or certain chemicals—for many forms of the disease to develop. Among Canadians, 70 percent of new cancer cases occur in people 60 years and older.*

*Despite the widespread fears of carcinogens in the environment, the majority of cancers are actually attributed to lifestyle factors, such as smoking and a high-fat diet. Heredity is also a factor. According to the B.C. Cancer Centre, 5 to 10 percent of cancer patients have a genetic predisposition to one or more forms of the disease. However, a genetic predisposition does not necessarily mean that the person is predestined to develop the disease; instead, the abnormal gene merely indicates an increased risk that can be modified or eliminated by lifestyle changes.*

**BREAKTHROUGHS!**

**A number of recent studies have uncovered widespread patterns of undertreating cancer pain, especially among children. These results have focused new attention on the need for adequate pain control at all stages of cancer care, especially when death seems certain. Increased efforts to control pain are greatly improving the quality of life for many cancer patients.**

## HOW IT DEVELOPS

Cancer begins when a single cell bearing a defective gene proliferates out of control. Eventually, the rapidly dividing cells form a mass, which begins to crowd out normal cells, and when it infiltrates healthy tissue, it is classified as an invasive cancer. Without treatment, the malignancy will continue to enlarge, and it may encroach upon a neighboring organ, in what is called local extension. Or a cluster of cells from the original (primary) tumor may break away and seed a new (secondary) cancer elsewhere in the body; the medical term for this is *metastasize*. A common example is metastatic breast cancer that spreads to one or more bones.

Localized cancer rarely induces pain in its early stages. But as the cancer invades nearby tissue and spreads to other organs, it can be very painful (see *Types and Causes of Cancer-Related Pain,* p 322). Cancer treatments can also be quite painful. In fact, many cancer patients must contend with pain from two or three sources at the same time, and each may call for a different approach to treatment.

*Studies have found that pet therapy can lessen the nausea that often occurs during chemotherapy.*

## WHAT YOU CAN DO

Nine in 10 cases of cancer-related pain can be controlled, but this may require working with a pain specialist. Don't wait until pain becomes unbearable to seek help; the earlier it is treated, the greater the likelihood of achieving successful pain control. Very often, nonprescription painkillers such as acetaminophen or ibuprofen provide adequate relief; if not, don't hesitate to ask for stronger prescription drugs. From the outset, make it clear to your cancer-treatment team that you expect pain to be managed aggressively. If a narcotic is prescribed, use it as needed. Don't be afraid of becoming addicted; numerous studies have found that cancer patients rarely if ever become addicted to narcotics taken for pain relief (see *Narcotic Painkillers,* p 33).

## HOW IT IS TREATED

### Medications

In treating cancer pain medically, doctors generally follow the three-step "ladder" to prescribing pain relievers that has been developed by the World Health Organization:

- **Step 1:** For mild pain, a non-narcotic (nonopioid) pain reliever such as acetaminophen or one of the nonsteroidal anti-inflammatory drugs (NSAIDs), like aspirin, ibuprofen, or naproxen, is given. An antidepressant or other medications may be added to the regimen as needed.
- **Step 2:** For moderate pain, a mild opioid (synthetic narcotic) analgesic is given, with or without a non-opioid painkiller and other medications. Mild opioids include oxycodone (Oxycontin) and propoxyphene hapsylate (Darvon-N). About 80 percent of cancer patients derive adequate relief from oral analgesics.
- **Step 3:** For severe pain, a strong narcotic or opioid analgesic is prescribed, with or without other painkillers. Examples of strong opioids include meperidine (Demerol), hydromorphone (Dilaudid), and morphine.

Recent discoveries about the intricate connections between mind and body have altered the way many physicians approach pain control. The anxiety and depres-

## Other Drugs to Ease Pain

*In addition to painkillers, medications that may relieve symptoms associated with cancer and its treatment include the following:*

| TYPE OF MEDICATION | SYMPTOMS TREATED | EXAMPLES |
|---|---|---|
| Antianxiety drugs | Anxiety and muscle spasms. | alprazolam (Xanax), lorazepam (Ativan). |
| Anticonvulsants | Nerve pain. | clonazepam (Rivotril), carbamazepine (Tegretol), phenytoin (Dilantin). |
| Antidepressants | Depression, nerve pain. | amitriptyline (Elavil), doxepin (Sinequan), imipramine (Tofranil). |
| Antihistamines | Pain, anxiety, nausea, itching, insomnia. | hydroxyzine (Atarax, Vistaril). |
| Corticosteroids | Bone pain, inflammation, swelling (edema), especially of the brain. | prednisone (Winpred), dexamethasone (Decadron). |
| Neuroleptics | Chronic pain, anxiety, nausea. | methotrimeprazine (Nozinan). |
| Stimulants | Drowsiness from narcotic medications. | dextroamphetamine (Dexedrine), methylphenidate (Ritalin). |

sion that are so common among cancer patients may not be painful themselves, but they do exacerbate physical pain and the ability to cope with it. Adjuvant therapy combines a painkiller with another medication that either enhances the pain control or relieves one or several cancer related symptoms (see *Other Drugs to Ease Pain,* p 323).

## Surgery

Surgery to remove the tumor or eradicate it through other means often alleviates or eliminates cancer pain. In fact, surgery remains the principal treatment for most cancers, and it provides the best chance for a cure. Increasingly, however, combining surgery with radiation and/or chemotherapy further increases the chances of a cure. Sometimes, one or both therapies may be given prior to cancer surgery, perhaps to shrink a tumor to make it easier to remove.

Following cancer surgery, morphine or another narcotic painkiller is often used. Many patients are given a morphine pump so they can control their own medication dosage and schedule. It's important to stay ahead of the pain; that is, to administer small amounts of the painkiller at the first twinge rather than waiting until the pain is intolerable.

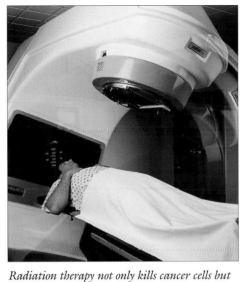

*Radiation therapy not only kills cancer cells but can also reduce pain by shrinking a tumor.*

## Palliative treatment

When cancer is beyond a cure, therapy focuses on making patients more comfortable and perhaps prolonging their lives. Examples of this include surgery, chemotherapy, and/or radiation to reduce the size of an inoperable tumor that is causing pain. At other times, a surgeon may perform surgery to restore an organ's ability to function, even though it is unlikely to change the course of the cancer itself. For example, an advanced pancreatic cancer may block the bile duct and result in jaundice and unbearable itching. Surgery to bypass the obstructing tumor can restore bile flow freely and alleviate the itching.

**WARNING!**

***Never skip a doctor-ordered dose of pain medication, even if you don't feel the need for it. Ultimately, you may end up taking more of the medication if you wait until severe pain occurs.***

## Radiation therapy

Aiming high-energy X rays at localized tumors, such as bone cancers, can relieve pain for up to a year. However, radiation is used only for isolated, small tumors; irradiating a large area can cause too much tissue damage and may worsen pain.

## Blocking pain nerves

Pain that cannot be controlled by other means may be treated by the following methods:

- **Nerve blocks**, which entail injecting local anesthetics into specific areas to prevent pain impulses from reaching the brain.
- **Nerve ablation**, which involves destroying a nerve, either chemically or by severing it.
- **Electrical nerve stimulation**, in which a small wire electrode is implanted near the spinal cord (spinal-cord stimulation, or SCS) or in the brain (deep-brain stimulation, or DBS). Running an electrical current through the electrode prevents pain signals from reaching the brain.

## HOW TO PREVENT IT

Fortunately, cancer pain often can be prevented by giving analgesic medications before it gains a foothold. Pain medications should be scheduled in such a way to maintain a consistent amount of drug in the body at all times.

### ALTERNATIVE THERAPIES

Alternative pain treatments definitely have a place in cancer medicine, so much so that many renowned cancer centers now have departments devoted solely to alternative and complementary therapies. These may include meditation, guided imagery, visualization, hypnosis, biofeedback, skin stimulation, transcutaneous electrical nerve stimulation (TENS), and acupuncture. Physical therapy may also help relieve pain and regain function following surgery and other cancer treatments.

# Chronic Fatigue Syndrome

### SYMPTOMS

- *Debilitating fatigue lasting six months or more.*
- *Swollen lymph nodes, especially in the armpit.*
- *Joint and muscle pain, weakness, numbness, tingling, and/or stiffness.*
- *Exacerbation of existing allergies or the sudden appearance of new ones.*
- *Numerous other unexplained pain syndromes, which may*

*include headache, abdominal and chest pain, earache, and recurrent sore throat.*

- *Psychological symptoms such as depression, anxiety, difficulty sleeping, impaired memory, poor concentration.*
- *Possible fever, nausea, diarrhea, weight loss.*

### WHO IS AT RISK

*Experts estimate that between 20,000 and 35,000 Canadians have chronic fatigue syndrome (CFS) or a comparable disorder. It affects mostly young professional adults, with women outnumbering men. It has been given various names—neurasthenia, chronic mononucleosis, and Yuppie flu, among others. In 1988, the Centers for Disease Control and Prevention (CDC) in the U.S. gave the disorder its present name. However, in Canada and elsewhere, it is often referred to as myalgic encephalomyelitis (ME). Regardless of what it's called, CFS remains a controversial diagnosis that is difficult to define, much less treat. Its symptoms resemble those of fibromyalgia and many other disorders, but its cause remains unknown.*

## HOW IT DEVELOPS

Chronic fatigue syndrome tends to come on abruptly, often in the wake of another illness that produces flulike symptoms. Mononucleosis is a frequent offender; so are viral respiratory and intestinal infections. Interestingly, the symptoms sometimes emerge shortly after an emotional crisis or physical trauma, such as the death of a loved one, a serious accident, or surgery.

Patients report a wide range of symptoms, including various aches and pains. The predominant feature, however, is incapacitating fatigue that lingers for six months or more. The effects are typically most severe during the first year or two; they then plateau and, after that, the course is unpredictable. Roughly half of those afflicted with CFS make a full recovery within five years. For others, the symptoms come and go indefinitely.

## WHAT YOU CAN DO

Strive for moderation in all aspects of your life. Get enough (but not too much) sleep; eat regular meals, but don't overindulge or go for long periods without eating; engage in regular, moderate exercise, but don't overdo it (see *Breakthroughs!*, p 326). Listen to your body and set realistic goals for yourself. Consult an occupational therapist to learn new ways to conserve your energy.

Strive for emotional equilibrium. That is no simple task, of course, since living with a chronic illness can be stressful in itself. Depression and anxiety are widespread among people with chronic fatigue syndrome. If you find yourself feeling depressed or on edge, don't suffer in silence. There are numerous self-help support groups for people with CFS; psychotherapy, such as cognitive behavioral therapy, is often helpful.

Try to educate family members, friends, and coworkers about the disease, or have your physician explain it to them. Because people with chronic fatigue syndrome often look perfectly healthy, those around them may not be as patient or as sympathetic as they are when confronting many other chronic disorders. It's important to understand that CFS is a real illness, and should not be regarded as malingering or hypochondria.

## HOW TO TREAT IT

Mild muscle and joint pain, headaches, and fever may be brought under control with over-the-counter nonsteroidal anti-inflammatory drugs (NSAIDs), such as aspirin, ibuprofen, or naproxen. More intense pain may warrant stronger, prescription NSAIDs. Joint pain that resists oral medication may be alleviated with injections of a local anesthetic, such as lidocaine (Xylocaine), to help break the cycle of chronic pain.

Low doses of tricyclic antidepressants, such as doxepin (Sinequan) or nortriptyline (Aventyl), relieve depression, ease mild, generalized pain, and induce drowsiness, which may help overcome sleep problems.

Alternatively, selective serotonin reuptake inhibitors (SSRIs)—a newer family of antidepressants—may be prescribed. These include fluoxetine (Prozac), paroxetine (Paxil), and sertraline (Zoloft). Antianxiety agents such

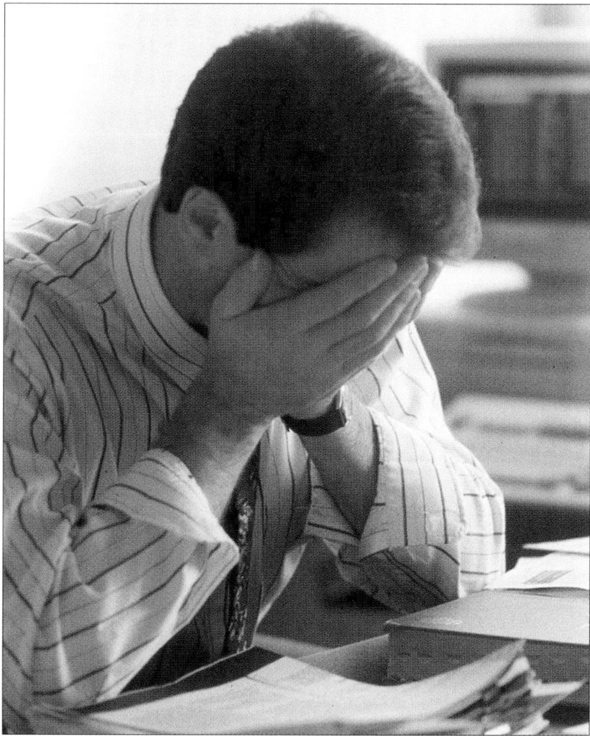

*In addition to debilitating fatigue and vague aches and pains, persons with CFS often suffer depression and difficulty in concentrating.*

## BREAKTHROUGHS!

**A large-scale study in England found that regular, moderate exercise can improve symptoms in more than half of CFS patients. In the 12-week study, the exercise group engaged in moderate exercise—walking, cycling, or swimming—5 to 30 minutes a day. At the end of the study, 55 percent reported feeling much or very much better.**

as alprazolam (Xanax) may be prescribed if anxiety or feelings of panic are present.

## HOW TO PREVENT IT

Since chronic fatigue syndrome has no known cause, there is no way to prevent it.

### ALTERNATIVE THERAPIES

**Hands-on therapies**

Some patients have found pain relief through acupuncture, massage, chiropractic treatments, and therapeutic touch.

**Herbal medicine**

Capsaicin cream, which is derived from the active ingredient in hot chilies (cayenne), may relieve joint and muscle pain. Apply the cream to the painful areas two or three times a day; avoid your eyes, lips, or other delicate tissue. Herbalists also recommend general tonic herbs, such as 100 to 300 mg of Siberian ginseng twice a day; look for products standardized to provide 0.8 percent eleutherosides. Do not take Siberian ginseng if you are taking digoxin or other heart medications. CFS patients who suffer recurrent sore throats and other infections may benefit from a two- or three-week course of echinacea (200 mg twice a day). For cautions concerning echinacea, see *About the Recommendations,* p 7.

**Nutraceuticals**

SAM-e may be helpful in relieving joint and muscle pain and also fighting mild depression; the typical dosage is two or three 200-mg pills a day. Do not take SAM-e if you suffer from manic depression. Several studies have found marked improvement in CFS symptoms after vitamin $B_{12}$ injections. In one clinical trial, 50 to 80 percent of the participants reported improvement after several weeks of $B_{12}$ shots every two or three days. Another B vitamin, carnitine, also shows promise for easing CFS symptoms.

## WARNING!

***Chronic fatigue, with or without various aches and pains, is a symptom of many serious diseases, including anemia, rheumatoid arthritis, lupus, certain cancers, and a smoldering infection. If fatigue persists for more than a few weeks, see a doctor for tests to rule out these or other causes.***

**Relaxation therapies**

Meditation, yoga, self-hypnosis, and other relaxation therapies are often helpful in overcoming CFS symptoms. T'ai chi not only provides gentle exercise but also fosters an enhanced sense of well-being that can be beneficial in treating chronic fatigue.

# Fibromyalgia

### SYMPTOMS

- *Chronic muscle pain, stiffness, and twitching; impaired coordination.*
- *Chronic fatigue lasting more than three months.*
- *Sleep problems, anxiety, depression, memory and concentration difficulties.*
- *Numbness or tingling in the extremities or the face; heightened sensitivity of the skin.*
- *Possible headaches, dizziness, intestinal problems, overactive bladder, and other symptoms that mimic various diseases.*

### WHO IS AT RISK

*Fibromyalgia, a chronic musculoskeletal disorder that affects the muscles, tendons, and ligaments, afflicts 2 to 5 percent of Canadians, mostly women between the ages of 20 and 50. It has baffled scientists for decades because it has no known cause or cure. At one time, it was mistakenly considered a psychological problem. Some researchers now theorize that it may be due to low levels of serotonin, a brain chemical that transmits messages to the nerves and receptors throughout the body. Until the 1980s, this constellation of symptoms went by the name fibrositis, which denotes an inflammation of the fibrous tissue. But research has found that it is not an inflammatory process. Nor is it a form of arthritis, even though patients often experience painfully aching joints.*

## HOW IT DEVELOPS

Fibromyalgia produces widespread muscle aches; victims describe the pains as searing, throbbing, gnawing, shooting, or stabbing. Others say they ache all over as if stricken with the flu or they feel like they've pulled every muscle in their body. The intensity waxes and wanes throughout the day, depending on the weather, sleep patterns, stress, and other variables, but most sufferers say they're rarely pain-free.

The onset of fibromyalgia frequently follows a triggering event, such as an automobile accident, an infection, or onset of another disorder, such as lupus, rheumatoid arthritis, or thyroid disease. However, these other conditions do not cause the fibromyalgia; rather, the precipitating event seems to awaken a dormant vulnerability to the disorder. At first, the pain may be confined to a single area (trigger point), such as the neck. Over time, however, the pain radiates to other "trigger points," such as the shoulders, chest, elbows, outer side of the hips, and the knees. The pain is usually bilateral—that is, on both sides. These trigger points are a defining trait of fibromyalgia; they are not seen in other conditions associated with persistent muscle and bone pain.

## WHAT YOU CAN DO

First, seek out a physician who is experienced in treating fibromyalgia and therefore more likely to be attuned to any new therapies, including experimental ones. Rheumatologists are generally the medical specialists who are the most qualified to diagnose and treat the syndrome.

A hot shower helps ease morning muscle pain. Aspirin, acetaminophen, and other nonprescription painkillers may ease mild pain. Symptoms and flare-ups often can be minimized through regular exercise, stress-reduction techniques, and some of the alternative therapies outlined below.

## HOW TO TREAT IT

Fibromyalgia is not a progressive disorder, meaning that its symptoms eventually stabilize. With therapy, approximately two in five patients show a marked improvement. Few patients, however, are ever fully free of the disease.

Relief of severe fibromyalgia pain is often difficult to achieve. Even powerful narcotic analgesics, so effective at managing many types of pain, are of little or no value. Nonsteroidal anti-inflammatory drugs (NSAIDs) such as ibuprofen and aspirin can help reduce muscle stiffness. One controversial approach to managing fibromyalgia pain entails injections of the local anesthetic lidocaine (Xylocaine) directly into the tender points—it can provide temporary relief, but does not break the pain cycle.

The sleep problems of fibromyalgia are caused by alpha-EEG anomaly, in which patients have no trouble falling asleep, but fail to achieve the uninterrupted deep (REM) levels necessary for true rest. These patients often wake up more exhausted than when they went to bed. This sleep deprivation exacerbates their pain, as well as other symptoms, for it is during REM sleep that the body recuperates from the day, repairing damaged tissue and shoring up its reserves of infection-fighting antibodies. Patients are typically prescribed low doses of antidepressants and muscle relaxants to help them sleep more soundly.

Depression and anxiety, common among fibromyalgia sufferers, contribute to flare-ups and should be treated. Tricyclic antidepressants and benzodiazepine antianxiety agents can cause daytime drowsiness, and therefore may not be suitable to treat fibromyalgia patients. Doctors generally prescribe one of the selective serotonin reuptake inhibitor (SSRI) antidepressants (e.g., Paxil, Prozac, and Zoloft), which may cause less drowsiness.

### BREAKTHROUGHS!

**A recent study found that a combination of 150 mg of magnesium and 600 mg of malic acid—an extract from apples, pears, and certain other fruits—brought pain relief for a significant number of fibromyalgia patients. The combination is available at many health foods stores as magnesium malate. Allow two months to note improvement.**

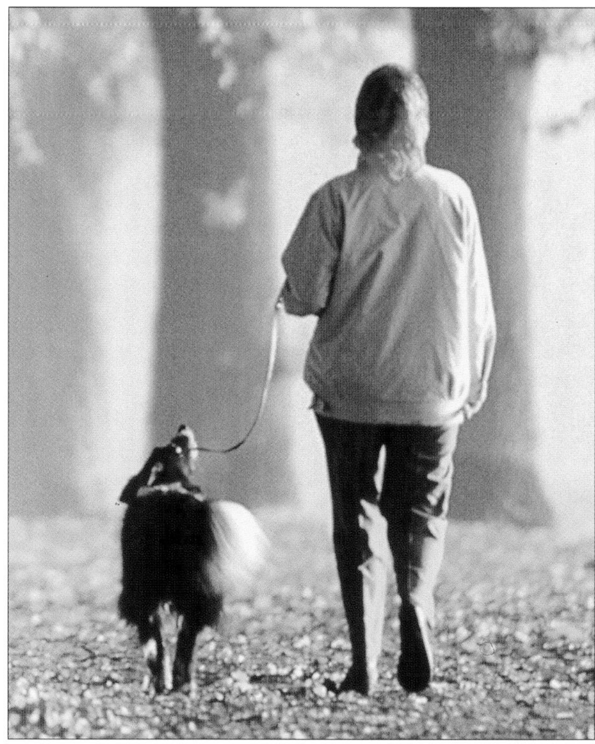

*A daily walk or similar exercise often eases the discomfort and other symptoms of fibromyalgia.*

## HOW TO PREVENT IT

Since the cause of fibromyalgia is unknown, there is no way to prevent it.

### ALTERNATIVE THERAPIES

**Acupuncture**

Several studies have found that this ancient technique of Chinese medicine can relieve fibromyalgia pain for at least some patients; six treatments should be tried before concluding that acupuncture will not help.

**Biofeedback**

This technique uses a special machine and sensors attached to the body to teach patients to self-regulate certain involuntary responses, such as muscle tension, heart rate, blood pressure, and breathing. Some fibromyalgia patients find it helps relieve their pain.

**Herbal medicine**

St. John's wort, in a dosage of 300 mg three times a day, helps increase serotonin levels. It interacts with antidepressants and certain other drugs, so check with your pharmacist or doctor before taking it to make sure that it is safe for you. Valerian, in dosages of 250 to 500 mg taken 30 to 45 minutes before going to bed, may improve the quality of sleep. Do not take valerian if pregnant or breast-feeding.

**Manipulative techniques**

Chiropractic and osteopathic treatments may provide some relief. Massage therapy may also help.

**Nutraceuticals**

People with fibromyalgia often have low levels of the brain chemical serotonin, which plays a crucial role in mood, sleep, and pain perception. Five-hydroxytryptophan (5-HTP) is a compound derived from seeds of the plant *Griffonia simplicifolia*. The body converts 5-HTP to serotonin. Patient studies testing the supplement report benefits comparable to those of SSRI antidepressants, but with fewer and milder side effects. The usual dosage is 50 to 100 mg taken three times a day. While 5-HTP has not been approved for sale in Canada, Canadians may import it for personal use (defined as a three-month supply).

**WARNING!**

***Although daily exercise has been shown to relieve fibromyalgia symptoms, start slowly if you have been sedentary. Overdoing it when embarking on a new exercise regimen can actually worsen symptoms.***

# HIV/AIDS

## SYMPTOMS

*People who are HIV-positive or have full-blown AIDS suffer from a wide variety of illnesses related to their lowered immunity. The most prevalent sources of pain include the following:*

- *Abdominal pain (from intestinal infections).*
- *Chest pain (from AIDS-related lymphoma, Kaposi's sarcoma, pneumonia, and tuberculosis).*
- *Headaches (from AIDS-related lymphomas, toxoplasmosis, and other infections).*
- *Difficult, painful swallowing (from thrush and other infections).*
- *Painful skin blisters (from vaginal candidiasis and herpes infections).*
- *Confusion or delirium (from brain infections).*
- *Itchy rashes and skin lesions (from AIDS-related lymphomas, Kaposi's sarcoma, and various infections).*

*In addition, generalized symptoms of AIDS include fever, night sweats, fatigue and weakness, weight loss (wasting syndrome), chronic diarrhea, nausea and vomiting, swollen lymph nodes.*

## WHO IS AT RISK

*AIDS is a viral disease that is spread by direct contact with infected body fluids—for example, blood, semen, vaginal secretions, and breast milk. Worldwide, heterosexual intercourse is the most common route of transmission, followed by use of contaminated hypodermic needles and, in some countries, HIV-contaminated blood transfusions. In Africa and Asia, where the disease is spread mostly by hetero sexual intercourse, women have a somewhat higher infection rate than men.*

*The picture is quite different in Canada and many other developed countries. Since the first case of AIDS in Canada was reported in 1982 until December 1999, 16,913 AIDS cases have been reported to the Laboratory Centre for Disease Control at Health Canada. Of these, about 74 percent have been males, more than half of whom contracted HIV, the virus that causes AIDS, through homosexual intercourse. Intravenous drug users, who often share needles, make up 5 percent of cases. While there has been a decline in the number of AIDS cases reported in Canada, an increasing number of women, youth, and aboriginal people in Canada are contracting AIDS, especially among IV drug users. Also, women are twice as susceptible as men to heterosexual transmission of the virus. Children born to women with HIV have a 35 percent chance of contracting the disease.*

## HOW IT DEVELOPS

After the human immunodeficiency virus (HIV) enters the body, it takes over one of the immune system's most essential defenders against disease: a type of white blood cell known as T-lymphocyte helpers, commonly referred to as helper T-cells or simply T-cells. Ordinarily, the helper T-cells mobilize other T-cells and instruct B-lymphocytes to produce antibodies. But T-cells that have been abducted by HIV are forced to churn out copies of the

## Drugs Used to Treat AIDS

| NUCLEOSIDE REVERSE TRANSCRIPTASE INHIBITORS | PROTEASE INHIBITORS | NON-NUCLEOSIDE REVERSE TRANSCRIPTASE INHIBITORS |
|---|---|---|
| abacavir (Ziagen) | indinavir (Crixivan) | delavirdine (Rescriptor) |
| didanosine (Videx) | nelfinavir (Viracept) | efavirenz (Sustiva) |
| lamivudine (3TC) | ritonavir (Norvir) | nevirapine (Viramune) |
| stavudine (Zerit) | saquinavir (Invirase, Fortovase) | |
| zalcitabine (Hivid) | | |
| zidovudine (Retrovir) | | |

virus. After a few weeks, the body's immune system counterattacks, and the battle is on. For how long, no one can say. Many years can pass before HIV progresses to full-fledged AIDS. But eventually the virus wears down the ranks of healthy T-cells. In a healthy person, the T-cell count is about 1,000 per cubic microliter of blood. Below 500 is considered abnormally low, and the person becomes increasingly susceptible to opportunistic infections, in which normally harmless organisms proliferate and cause an illness.

**WARNING!**

***Any unprotected sexual activity carries a risk of HIV infection. Unfortunately, recent studies find that a growing number of young people think they no longer need to worry about AIDS, and that they can revert to the sexual practices that have made the disease a worldwide epidemic. Although AIDS can be treated, it remains a fatal disease.***

Each infection can bring a precipitous drop in T-cells; once the level falls below 200, the person has full-blown AIDS. The disease may also be diagnosed if the person develops any of some 25 opportunistic infections or cancers. Many of these opportunistic diseases can be very painful; up to 60 percent of AIDS patients experience moderate to severe pain, either from the disease itself or its treatment. Types of pain experienced by AIDS patients include recurrent or worsening headaches, peripheral nerve pain (neuropathies), and joint, muscle, abdominal, throat, and chest pains.

There may be multiple origins for each pain syndrome. For instance, headaches may be caused by fever, a parasitic infection such as toxoplasmosis, cryptococcal meningitis, lymphoma of the central nervous system, or the antiviral agent zidovudine (Retrovir).

AIDS-related disorders also produce many other symptoms—chronic diarrhea, severe weight loss (wasting syndrome), itchy rashes, skin sores, brain swelling and dementia, debilitating fatigue, and muscle weakness—that can be additional sources of pain; they also make life miserable. The HIV virus itself does not kill its victims; instead, death results from the complications of repeated infections or AIDS-related cancers.

## WHAT YOU CAN DO

Living with AIDS can be especially difficult, not only because of its many symptoms, but also because of the lingering stigma, fear, and widespread misinformation that surrounds the disease. Fortunately, there are many AIDS support groups that can help patients and their loved ones deal with the emotional burden of the disease.

Day-to-day self-care can help control AIDS symptoms and slow its progression. Medications must be taken as prescribed, and often according to a complicated schedule. People who have difficulty remembering what to take when should use a pill organizer, in which each day's medications are arranged according to when they should be taken. Because powerful AIDS drugs can interact with some pain medications, ask your doctor to recommend or prescribe a safe drug (see *Pain Control in AIDS,* p 330). Other important aspects of self-care include maintaining good nutrition, engaging in regular, moderate exercise, reducing stress, and practicing safe sex to prevent infecting others.

## HOW IT IS TREATED

There have been great advances in the treatment of AIDS since it first came to the public's attention. Doctors now have an armamentarium of drugs that are enabling AIDS patients to live longer and enjoy a higher quality of life than just a few years ago (see *Breakthroughs!,* p 330, and *Drugs Used to Treat AIDS,* p 328).

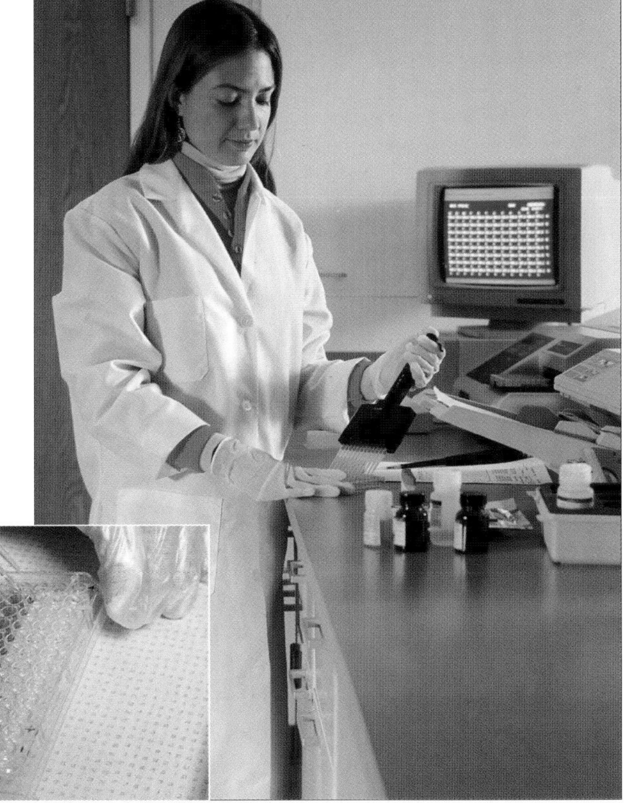

*Blood tests to detect HIV antibodies are recommended for anyone who is at risk of possible infection, because early diagnosis and treatment are critical in slowing the progression of the disease.*

## HOW TO PREVENT IT

The single most important preventive measure is to always practice safer sex. Unless you are in a mutually monogamous relationship with an uninfected partner, always use latex condoms, along with a spermicidal foam or gel (the latter offers some added protection against HIV and other sexually transmitted diseases). Use only water-based lubricants with a condom; oil-based petroleum products like petroleum jelly, skin lotions, or vegetable oil can damage the latex.

All used hypodermic needles should be discarded or carefully sterilized before reuse. If your job brings you in contact with blood products or other body fluids, always wear latex gloves and protect yourself from needle pricks or other direct contact that might expose you to HIV. Any woman who is unsure of her HIV status should be tested before becoming pregnant; anti-AIDS drugs taken during pregnancy can reduce the risk of infecting the baby. HIV-positive women should not breast-feed because the virus can be passed to the baby in the breast milk.

### ALTERNATIVE THERAPIES

**Acupuncture**

Treatments may be helpful in relieving nerve and many other pain syndromes.

**Herbal medicine**

Ginger can help quell nausea, a frequent problem for many AIDS patients. It can be taken as tea or pills or capsules. Otherwise, self-treatment with various herbal products can be dangerous for HIV or AIDS patients. Some herbs, especially St. John's wort, contain substances that interact with anti-AIDS medications. Others have actions that increase the body's vulnerability to infection and other problems. For cautions concerning these herbs, see *About the Recommendations,* p 7.

**Mind-body therapies**

Meditation, guided imagery, self-hypnosis, and biofeedback are among the various relaxation techniques that reduce stress and also help a person cope with pain.

### BREAKTHROUGHS!

**There have been many significant breakthroughs in treating AIDS. Since 1987, several new classes of anti-AIDS drugs have been developed—various antiviral medications, protease inhibitors, and a new class of drugs known as non-nucleoside reverse transcriptase inhibitors. These drugs work together in different ways to slow the proliferation of the HIV organism. So instead of prescribing a single drug to treat AIDS, as was the case in the early days of treating the disease, doctors now give the so-called AIDS cocktail, a regimen consisting of several drugs. Occasional "drug holidays" from this regimen may increase its effectiveness. As a result, the AIDS death toll has fallen dramatically.**

### PAIN CONTROL IN AIDS

In AIDS, pain control takes place on three fronts:

1. Slowing the progression of the virus.
2. Treating any AIDS-related condition that is contributing to the pain.
3. Managing the pain itself.

Following is an overview of specific pain syndromes and their treatment:

- **Headache:** About 40 percent of AIDS patients experience headaches. Treating the underlying cause, such as AIDS-related cerebral toxoplasmosis, cryptococcal meningitis, and central nervous system lymphoma, usually relieves the pain.
- **Peripheral neuropathy:** About 30 percent of AIDS patients develop nerve problems in their extremities, either from the disease itself or as a side effect of the drugs used to treat it. Neuropathy may take the form of shooting pains, tingling, or numbness. Discontinuing the offending medication usually brings relief; otherwise, codeine or a stronger narcotic medication may be prescribed. Some antidepressants may also help by altering brain chemistry and reducing the number of pain messages that are processed. Talk to your doctor before discontinuing any drug.
- **Joint and muscle pain:** About half of AIDS patients suffer from joint and/or muscle pain, often as a side effect of drugs such as zidovudine (Retrovir). Stopping the drug usually solves the problem; if pain persists, a nonsteroidal anti-inflammatory drug such as ibuprofen or naproxen may help. A short course of corticosteroids may be needed to quell muscle or joint inflammation; unrelenting pain may require stronger narcotic painkillers.
- **Abdominal pain:** Treating the underlying intestinal problem usually relieves the pain. Mild to moderate pain from abdominal cramps may be managed with an antispasmodic agent; otherwise, intravenous opioid therapy is usually the treatment of choice.
- **Throat pain:** A throat spray or mouthwash containing lidocaine (Xylocaine) can temporarily numb the throat. If the pain persists, the doctor will follow the three-step analgesic ladder, starting with acetaminophen or an NSAID in combination with a mild opioid, and progressing to a strong opioid if necessary. Patients who find it too painful to swallow tablets or even liquids can be given the pain medication by injection.
- **Chest pain:** Treating the underlying cause—usually pneumonia, tuberculosis, or inflammation of the esophagus—can relieve the pain.

**Nutraceuticals**

People who are HIV-positive or who have full-blown AIDS often suffer numerous nutritional deficiencies, especially if they have chronic diarrhea or other conditions that interfere with proper digestion and absorption. However, patients should not try to treat themselves with high-dose supplements; some may interact with medications. A registered dietitian experienced in treating AIDS can analyze a patient's diet and recommend changes as well as specific supplements and their dosages.

# Infectious Arthritis

## SYMPTOMS

- *Joint pain, inflammation, and tenderness.*
- *Weakness and general malaise.*
- *Fever and chills; possible rash and other symptoms of a systemic infection.*

## WHO IS AT RISK

*Infectious arthritis develops when a virus, fungus, or bacterium invades the body and settles in a joint. It can occur at any age, but more than half of patients are over 50. The risk is highest among persons who have a lowered resistance to infection, most often because of certain cancers, AIDS, kidney disease, diabetes, sickle-cell anemia, hemophilia, or long-term use of corticosteroids or other drugs that suppress the immune system. IV drug users are also at a high risk, not only because of their lowered immunity, but also because unsterile needles allow organisms an easy point of entry into the body. People whose jobs expose them to animals, marine life, or plants that may harbor infectious organisms have a higher-than-average risk of developing this type of arthritis.*

*A history of other joint diseases, especially rheumatoid arthritis, predisposes a person to infectious arthritis because damaged joints are more vulnerable to infection. An infected skin wound or an animal or human bite can result in infectious arthritis; the risk is also increased by the presence of an artificial joint.*

*In many cases, the arthritis is a consequence of an infection elsewhere in the body; examples include strep throat, hepatitis, bacterial endocarditis (a heart infection), infectious mononucleosis, and tuberculosis. Among adults, however, gonorrhea is the most common cause of bacterial arthritis; chlamydia—another sexually transmitted organism—is a major cause of a type of infectious arthritis that occurs mostly among men (see* Reiter's Syndrome—A Special Type of Arthritis, *above).*

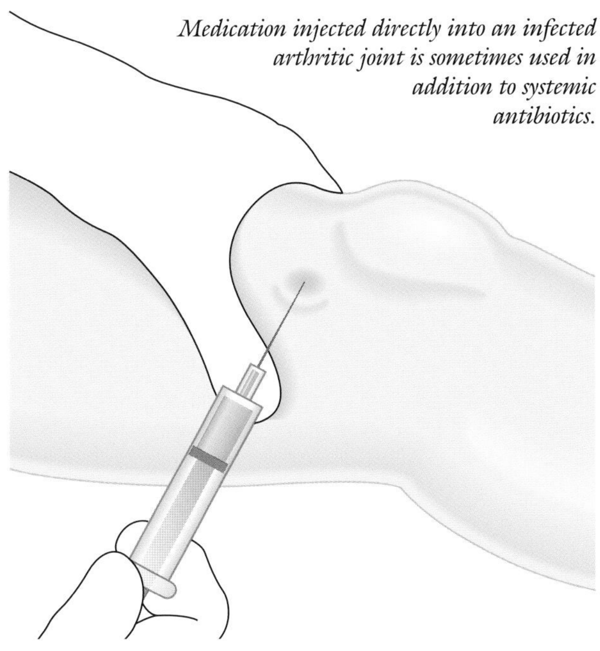

*Medication injected directly into an infected arthritic joint is sometimes used in addition to systemic antibiotics.*

## REITER'S SYNDROME—A SPECIAL TYPE OF ARTHRITIS

This is a mysterious type of arthritis that is triggered by chlamydia, a very common sexually transmitted organism, or, less often, by shigellia, salmonella, or another intestinal bacterium. It generally strikes men between the ages of 20 and 45, and is characterized by joint pain and inflammation of the back, knees, and feet. The person may also have an unusual skin rash or blisters in the mouth or on the penis, tendinitis, urinary pain, and red, crusty eyes (conjunctivitis). Tetracycline, which may be given for three months or longer, sometimes shortens the course of Reiter's syndrome, but the disease is very difficult to clear up. Symptoms sometimes keep recurring for several years. Aspirin, ibuprofen, or other NSAIDs ease pain and inflammation; local corticosteroid injections may relieve tendinitis pain. Physical therapy is also prescribed to reduce pain and restore joint function.

## HOW IT DEVELOPS

The pattern of symptoms varies, depending on the infecting organism. Bacterial joint infections—the most common kind—generally come on abruptly. They may appear following recovery from a sore throat or another infection, or develop after an animal or human bite. The affected joint(s) will be very painful, markedly swollen, red, and warm to the touch; these symptoms may be accompanied by a high fever and shaking chills. Typically, only one joint—usually a knee, shoulder, or hip—is infected. An exception is gonococcal arthritis, in which several joints may be affected at the same time or the arthritis may go from joint to joint—a condition referred to as *migratory arthralgias*. Gonococcal arthritis can also cause tendinitis; other symptoms may include a rash or skin sores, a high fever, and shaking chills.

Patients with viral infectious arthritis frequently complain that they ache all over; they may also have a mild fever, upset stomach, and other flulike symptoms. The affected joints are achy, but not necessary swollen or warm to the touch. This type of infectious arthritis usually clears up on its own as soon as the body overcomes the viral infection.

Fungal arthritis—the rarest type—usually takes weeks or months to progress. Eventually, the joints become swollen and painful, but fever is rare. Without treatment, the colonies of fungi can slowly destroy the joint.

**WARNING!**

***Infectious arthritis can cause permanent joint damage and disability. It also carries a high mortality rate (25 percent) among patients who have rheumatoid arthritis or an artificial joint implant. See a doctor as soon as possible if you suddenly develop a painful, inflamed joint, especially if you also have a fever and other symptoms.***

## WHAT YOU CAN DO

See a doctor as soon as possible if you suspect infectious arthritis (see *Warning!*, above). In the meantime, aspirin or acetaminophen will lower a fever and help ease pain. A heating pad, ice pack, or alternating hot and cold treatments can provide temporary relief. Rest the affected joints, as overuse can exacerbate cartilage damage. However, gentle range-of-motion exercises should be done daily to relieve stiffness and maintain joint flexibility.

After the infection is under control, self-treatment centers on regaining joint function and preventing further damage. This may entail losing excess weight, engaging in regular exercise to keep joints flexible and well-lubricated, and undertaking weight training to tone and strengthen supporting muscles. Take aspirin, ibuprofen, or another nonsteroidal anti-inflammatory drug (NSAID) to reduce any lingering joint inflammation and pain.

## HOW TO TREAT IT

Viral infectious arthritis usually clears up on its own. However, if the joint is very swollen and painful, a doctor may use a hollow needle to aspirate excessive fluid and pus. This brings almost immediate pain relief. Most other types of infectious arthritis are treated with drugs. Acute infectious arthritis often requires hospitalization and treatment with an intravenous antibiotic or antifungal drug. After the immediate crisis is past, treatment may continue on an outpatient basis with home intravenous or oral antibiotics. Some types of bacterial arthritis clear up in a few days; others may require weeks or even months of treatment to cure.

If a nonprescription NSAID fails to provide adequate pain relief, stronger prescription drugs may be tried. If standard NSAIDs cause gastrointestinal disturbance, a $COX_2$ inhibitor (e.g., Celebrex or Vioxx) may be tried. This is a new class of NSAIDs that are less likely to cause bleeding and stomach upset than older drugs.

Surgery is sometimes necessary, especially if the infection involves an artificial joint; the prosthesis may need to be removed and then replaced after the infection heals. Even so, there is a one-in-three risk of reinfection when the artificial joint is replaced, so long-term antibiotic therapy is usually needed. Joint replacement surgery also may be considered if the infection leaves a natural joint—usually the knees—so badly damaged that it no longer functions normally.

Arthroscopic surgery is often used to treat gonococcal arthritis or infections in joints already affected by rheumatoid arthritis; it is also an option in fungal infections that cannot be cleared up with antifungal drugs. In this procedure, a viewing tube (arthroscope) is inserted into the infected joint through a small incision, and miniature instruments are used to remove pus and infected tissue. The joint is splinted for a few days to relieve pain, followed by physical therapy to regain joint function (see *Alternative Therapies*, below).

## HOW TO PREVENT IT

People who have a high risk of infectious arthritis should be especially careful to avoid skin and other infections. Even a minor nick should be cleansed with an antiseptic and treated with an antibiotic cream or ointment. Wash your hands frequently with soap and warm water and see a doctor promptly if you develop skin ulcers, a bad sore throat, or other symptoms of infection.

Gonococcal and other sexually transmitted forms of arthritis can be prevented by adopting safe sex practices (See *Sexually Transmitted Diseases,* pp 201 and 215; also *HIV/AIDS*, p 328). Some types of infectious arthritis, such as Lyme disease, can be prevented with vaccines (see *Lyme Disease,* p 335).

### ALTERNATIVE THERAPIES

**Note:** During recovery, the alternative therapies recommended for osteoarthritis may be helpful; see p 225.

**Physical therapy**

Passive range-of-motion exercises—designed to restore joint flexibility—are started as soon as pain and the acute arthritis begin to abate. Weight training and perhaps exercising in water will also be started with a goal of strengthening the supporting muscles. Ultrasound, diathermy, and heat treatments reduce joint pain and increase circulation to the painful area, which speeds healing.

# Leukemia/ Lymphoma

## SYMPTOMS

***Leukemia:*** *Pain in the bones and joints; increasingly severe anemia and bleeding problems; enlarged lymph nodes, spleen, and liver; weight loss; night sweats; generally ill feeling; possible headache, vomiting, confusion, loss of muscle control, and seizures.*

***Lymphomas:*** *Enlarged spleen and lymph nodes in the neck, underarm, or groin; chronic fatigue; fever and night sweats; weight loss; itchy, reddened skin; nausea and vomiting.*

## WHO IS AT RISK

*Each year, about 3,000 new cases of leukemia and 7,000 of lymphoma are diagnosed in Canada. Both cancers can occur at any age, but leukemia is more common during childhood and old age, whereas lymphomas are more prevalent among young to middle-aged adults. Their causes are largely unknown, although a small percentage have been attributed to several viruses. The Epstein-Barr virus (EBV) is estimated to be at the root of 35 to 50 percent of all Hodgkin's lymphomas and 10 percent of non-Hodgkin's lymphomas; HIV, the virus that causes AIDS, can also lead to non-Hodgkin's lymphoma; and the human lymphotropic virus type I (HLVT-1) accounts for about 5 percent of leukemia and lymphoma.*

*Environmental risk factors include prolonged exposure to certain industrial chemicals, such as those used in rubber and petroleum refining. Leukemia sometimes arises as a late side effect of radiation treatments or cancer chemotherapy.*

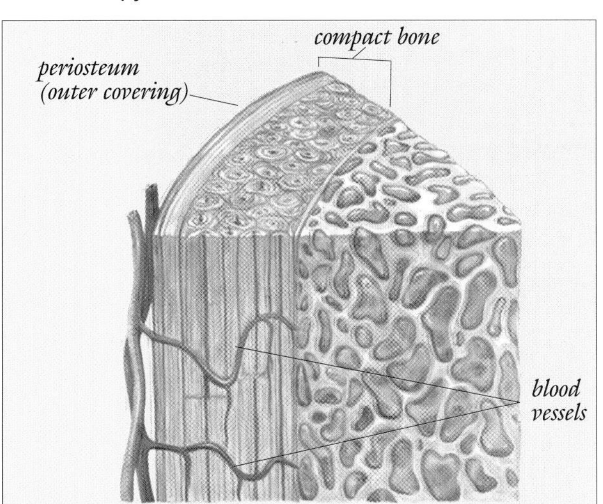


*The spongy marrow inside certain bones acts as a factory to manufacture red blood cells, at the rate of about 3 million per second, as well as white blood cells and mature lymphocytes.*

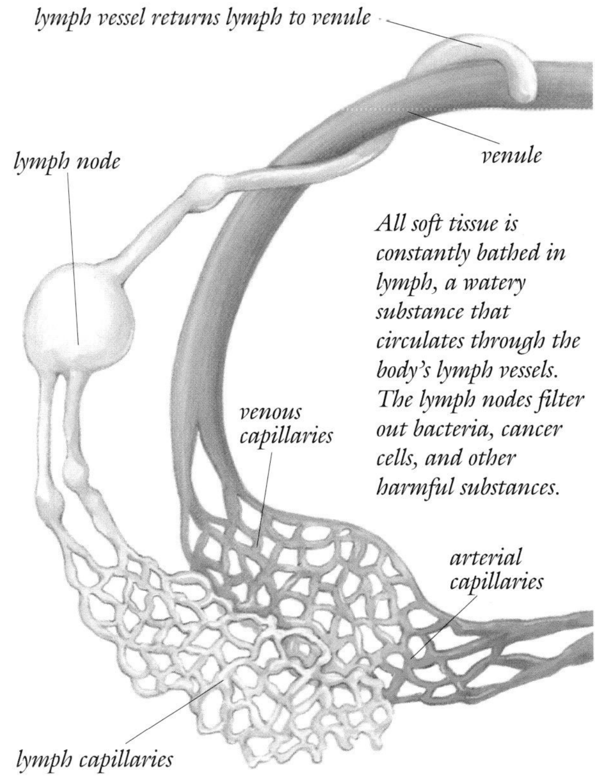


*All soft tissue is constantly bathed in lymph, a watery substance that circulates through the body's lymph vessels. The lymph nodes filter out bacteria, cancer cells, and other harmful substances.*

## HOW THEY DEVELOP

Leukemia, a cancer of the blood cells, arises mainly in the bone marrow, the production center of all blood cells; the marrow floods the circulation with abnormal white cells that cannot defend the body from infection. Production of red blood cells and platelets is also disrupted. Consequently, patients typically experience the fatigue and weakness of severe anemia. They also bruise and bleed easily, because their blood doesn't clot properly; bleeding into the joints causes severe arthritislike pain.

The acute forms of leukemia trigger severe symptoms from the outset. In contrast, chronic leukemia often mimics lingering flu until it advances to an acute stage. About 25 percent of patients with a chronic form of leukemia can go for years without experiencing obvious symptoms. In these people, the cancer is frequently discovered by accident when a routine blood test reveals a suspiciously elevated white count.

Lymphomas are cancers of the lymphatic system, the network of lymph vessels and the spleen, lymph nodes, and other tissues that filter the fluid (plasma) portion of the blood. Most white blood cells (lymphocytes) mature in the bone marrow, but the bean-shaped nodes and other lymphatic tissues serve as their incubators. In lymphoma, cancer cells crowd out healthy lymphocytes, leaving patients with little resistance to infection. Like chronic leukemia, low-grade lymphomas may not cause symptoms, even after the cancer has spread, or metastasized, to other organs.

Of these cancers, the acute leukemias are the most painful. The rapidly proliferating white blood cells accumulate in lymph nodes, the spleen, and sometimes the liver and men's testicles, causing painful swelling. Bone and joint pain may mimic severe arthritis. Patients whose disease has formed a secondary tumor in the brain often experience severe headaches. Pain from non-Hodgkin's lymphoma occurs primarily if the disease spreads to the bones, although tumors and swelling in the intestinal tract are also painful.

## WHAT YOU CAN DO

If possible, seek treatment from a hematologist-oncologist; these specialists are the doctors most likely to try new or experimental treatments. Aggressive treatment of these cancers is usually debilitating and may cause appetite loss, nausea, and other uncomfortable side effects. Eat frequent, small meals that emphasize nutritious, high-calorie foods to keep from losing too much weight.

### THE EMOTIONAL PAIN OF HAIR LOSS

Patients who have gone through chemotherapy invariably call hair loss one of the most emotionally difficult aspects of cancer treatment. Here are tips for coping with the loss.

- If you are thinking of buying a wig, it's a good idea to select it before your hair falls out. That way it's easier to match it to your own hair color and style.
- Compare different types of wigs before buying. Wigs made of real hair look more natural, but synthetic ones are easier to care for, lighter, and less expensive.
- Start wearing the wig before hair loss occurs. Adjusting to wearing a wig is easier if it's part of your lifestyle before it is actually needed.
- You may be able to claim a tax credit for your wig or toupee, or it may be covered by your private health insurance from work. Along with your sales receipt, you will need to submit a doctor's letter that states you have experienced hair loss due to medical treatment.
- If you don't want to wear a wig, invest in several stylish scarves that can be tied in attractive turbans.
- Even if you don't mind being seen bald, be sure to cover the scalp when going outdoors to protect it from a sunburn in the summer and to prevent excessive loss of body heat in the winter.
- Remember, too, that the hair almost always regrows after chemotherapy stops, and it is often thicker than before. It may also be a different color.

### BREAKTHROUGHS!

**Recent advances in stem-cell transplantation hold new hope for lymphoma patients. Stem cells—often referred to as immortal cells—give rise to new tissue. Autologous stem cell transplantation entails collecting a few stem cells from the patient's blood, and then administering a very high dose of chemotherapy to destroy his or her bone marrow. The stem cells are then infused back into the patient, where they migrate to the bones and begin making healthy new marrow. So far this procedure is experimental, but researchers hope that it will be widely available in the next few years.**

## HOW TO TREAT THEM

Chemotherapy remains the principal treatment of leukemia; depending upon its type, lymphoma may be treated with a combination of chemotherapy, radiation, surgery, and perhaps a bone-marrow transplant.

Treating the underlying malignancy will usually relieve pain symptoms, but the side effects of treatment are sometimes more painful than the disease itself. Fortunately, they can usually be controlled. For example, antinausea drugs can quell the nausea and vomiting brought on by chemotherapy and radiation treatments. Antidepressants can lift mood, and other medications can stimulate a poor appetite.

A bone marrow transplant represents the best hope for a cure for recurrent leukemia and prolonged survival against lymphoma. In the weeks after a transplant, a patient is very vulnerable to infection (see *Warning!*, right). But after a few weeks, the transplanted marrow begins producing new blood cells, and eventually the recipient's immunity is restored.

Non-Hodgkin's lymphoma that spreads to the bones usually responds well to either of two radioactive substances—strontium-89 (Metastron) and samarium-153 (Quadramet). The radioactive substances are injected into the bloodstream, just like chemotherapy, and they then make their way directly into the bone tumors. A single injection can alleviate bone pain for several months.

### WARNING!

***The treatments for leukemia and lymphoma can further weaken an already compromised immune system. During treatment, great care is needed to avoid exposure to various disease-causing organisms. Avoid crowded indoor places, especially during the cold and flu season. Be sure to get an annual flu shot, and talk to your doctor about other preventive measures.***

## HOW TO PREVENT THEM

There is no known way to prevent either leukemia or lymphomas.

## BREAKTHROUGHS!

**A group of Italian researchers have discovered a possible remedy for people who suffer from frequent muscle cramps. In a three-month study, the researchers gave low doses of gabapentin (Neurontin), an anticonvulsant drug, to 20 women and 10 men.**

**At the end of the study, the participants, who had averaged 18 muscle cramps a day, reported that their cramps had disappeared. Even after the drug was stopped, the patients had fewer cramps than before they started treatment.**

***Myalgia:*** *Persistent muscle achiness that can be localized or widespread.*

***Polymyalgia rheumatica:*** *Persistent body aches and painful stiffness (especially of the shoulders and hips), fatigue, low-grade fever, appetite and weight loss, anemia.*

### WHO IS AT RISK

*Almost everyone suffers* ***muscle pain****, or myalgia, from time to time. The many precipitating causes include overuse, injuries, tension, flu and numerous other diseases, infection, and certain medications.* ***Muscle cramps*** *are also very common, and may be caused by dehydration, restless leg syndrome, nutritional deficiencies, overuse or extended rest, and other diseases, such as multiple sclerosis.*

***Inflammatory myopathies.*** *Although their cause is unknown, researchers think they are autoimmune disorders in which the immune system attacks body tissue—in this instance, the muscles and perhaps the skin. These disorders are most common among women aged 40 to 60.*

***Polymyalgia rheumatica****, or PMR, is a disease that combines many of the symptoms of myalgia and inflammatory arthritis. It generally occurs after age 50 and is most common among persons over 70. Women are affected twice as often as men. There is a high incidence among people of northern European descent; it also tends to run in families, suggesting it may have an inherited susceptibility.*

## HOW IT DEVELOPS

Simple **muscle aches** are often precipitated by overuse, especially engaging in strenuous or prolonged exercise after a period of inactivity. The achiness indicates some degree of muscle damage, such as small tears, bleeding, and inflammation in the muscle fibers. Generalized muscle aches are also a symptom of many diseases, often infectious disorders such as flu, Lyme disease, malaria, or polio. Excessive stress that results in constant muscle tension can also cause pain. Most muscle aches disappear as healing takes place.

**Muscle cramps** come on suddenly and usually last for only a few seconds. But they can seem to last much longer because they are acutely painful and the affected muscle cannot be used until the contraction stops. Frequent muscle cramps may be due to an electrolyte imbalance, such as a deficiency of potassium or excessive calcium circulating in the blood; dehydration can also cause cramps.

**Inflammatory myopathies** usually develop gradually and cause symmetrical (affecting both sides of the body) muscle weakness and pain. In one type—known as *dermatomyositis*—the pain is preceded by a patch of red or purplish rash on the cheeks, eyelids, nose, chest, or back, as well as around the joints.

Hardened nodules, caused by calcium deposits, also form under the skin. The muscles of the shoulders, neck, upper arms, and hips are most often affected. At first, patients may notice increasing difficulty reaching overhead; as the disease progresses, walking or climbing stairs may become more difficult. Swallowing may also be affected, increasing the danger of choking. Thus, patients often need to switch to a liquid diet or one of puréed foods.

**Polymyalgia rheumatica** may come on gradually, with various muscle aches, or it may begin suddenly, with flu-like symptoms. The stiffness and muscle pain range from moderate to severe. As its name suggests, the disease attacks multiple areas, most often the neck, shoulders, and hips. Symptoms are most severe in the early morning and, as the disease progresses, the pain is constant.

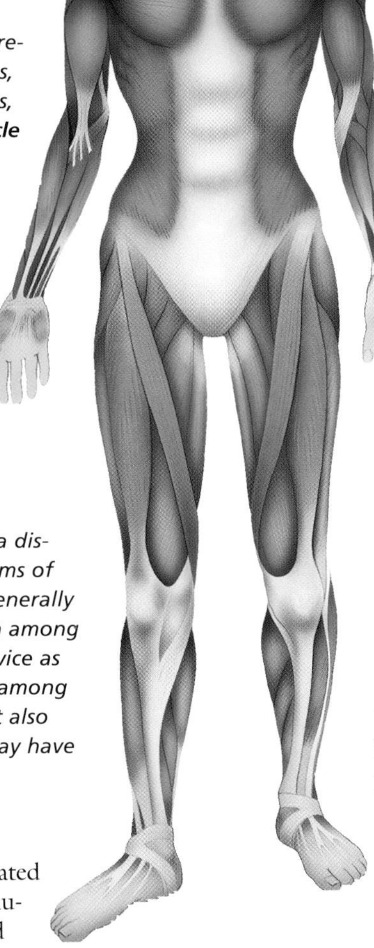

*Any of the body's hundreds of muscles can become inflamed and painful.*

## WHAT YOU CAN DO

Nonprescription painkillers, such as aspirin, acetaminophen, or ibuprofen, can relieve most simple muscle aches. Soaking in a hot tub or applying cold or hot compresses, or alternating heat and cold, may help. Gently massaging the aching muscles may also bring relief; don't, however, massage muscles or joints that are inflamed. This increases blood flow to the area and can worsen inflammation.

Slowly stretching and gently massaging a cramped muscle prompts it to relax and immediately relieves the sharp pain. A cold compress or heating pad can prevent it from cramping again. Also drink plenty of water, especially if the cramp occurs after exercising.

> **WARNING!**
>
> ***Refrain from massaging a muscle ache or cramp if you have diabetes or a circulatory problem. The pain may indicate a blood clot (thrombosis), and massage may break off a part that can travel to the lungs, heart, or brain, causing a pulmonary embolism, heart attack, or stroke.***

The pain of inflammatory myopathies can usually be controlled with an OTC nonsteroidal anti-inflammatory drug (NSAID), such as ibuprofen (Advil). Hot baths and alternating hot and cold packs can also ease mild pain. It's important to maintain as much muscle strength and joint flexibility as possible. Range-of-motion exercises should be done daily; regular aerobic exercise and mild weight-training are also important. However, check with a doctor before embarking on an exercise program to make sure your chosen activities will not cause further harm.

Self-treatment of polymyalgia rheumatica is similar to that of inflammatory myopathies. But both of these conditions also demand careful medical treatment, so if symptoms suggest either, see a doctor promptly.

## HOW TO TREAT IT

Simple muscle aches and cramps usually do not require medical treatment. In contrast, inflammatory myopathy and polymyalgia rheumatica often demand intensive medical treatment to control pain and prevent disability. If nonprescription NSAIDs are inadequate, ask your doctor for a prescription-strength NSAID or perhaps codeine.

Both inflammatory myopathies and PMR are treated with prednisone (Winpred) or another corticosteroid drug. Steroids reduce inflammation and usually relieve pain and other symptoms within a few weeks. PMR usually requires 6 to 24 months of steroid treatment to bring the disease under control and reduce the risk of a recurrence.

About half of patients suffering from inflammatory myopathy fail to get adequate relief from steroids alone; they may also be given drugs to further suppress the immune system. They include azathioprine (Imuran), methotrexate (Rheumatrex), cyclosporine (Neoral), and cyclophosphamide (Cytoxan). These drugs increase the risk of infection, so care is needed to guard against exposure to infectious diseases.

A persistent rash may be treated with a prescription-strength hydrocortisone cream or oral hydroxychloroquine (Plaquenil). Painful calcium nodules are sometimes relieved by taking colchicine, a drug used to treat gout. In severe cases, they are removed surgically.

If walking is difficult or very painful, a cane, walker, braces, or even a wheelchair may be necessary. Patients who develop severe swallowing problems may require a gastrostomy, a procedure in which a feeding tube is inserted directly into the stomach through a small incision in the abdomen.

## HOW TO PREVENT IT

Muscle aches caused by overuse can be prevented by stretching and doing warm-up exercises before working out and by cooling down and stretching again after each session. When embarking on an exercise program, begin slowly and gradually increase your endurance. These same measures can help prevent muscle cramps (see also *Leg Cramps/Restless Legs*, p 272).

There are no known means of preventing inflammatory myopathies and polymyalgia rheumatica.

### ALTERNATIVE THERAPIES

**Nutraceuticals**

Calcium, in dosages of 1000 to 1500 mg a day, may help prevent muscle cramps. High doses of B-complex vitamins may also help (see *Breakthroughs!*, p 273). Up to 1000 mg of vitamin E a day may reduce the inflammation and pain of PMR and inflammatory myopathies. For cautions concerning these nutraceuticals, see *About the Recommendations*, p 7.

**Physical therapy**

Therapists can ease muscle pain with a variety of techniques, including ultrasound, diathermy, hot and cold packs, and whirlpool baths. They can also devise an appropriate exercise program to help maintain muscle strength and flexibility in PRM and inflammatory myopathies.

# Neuropathy/ Neuralgia

### SYMPTOMS

- *Numbness of the hands and feet, with an uncomfortable pins-and-needles sensation (paresthesia).*
- *Burning skin pain or skin that is painful to the touch.*
- *Loss of sensation.*
- *Muscle cramping and shrinking (atrophy).*

### WHO IS AT RISK

*Neuropathy, neuralgia, and neuritis are general terms for nerve disorders or pain and inflammation; peripheral neu-*

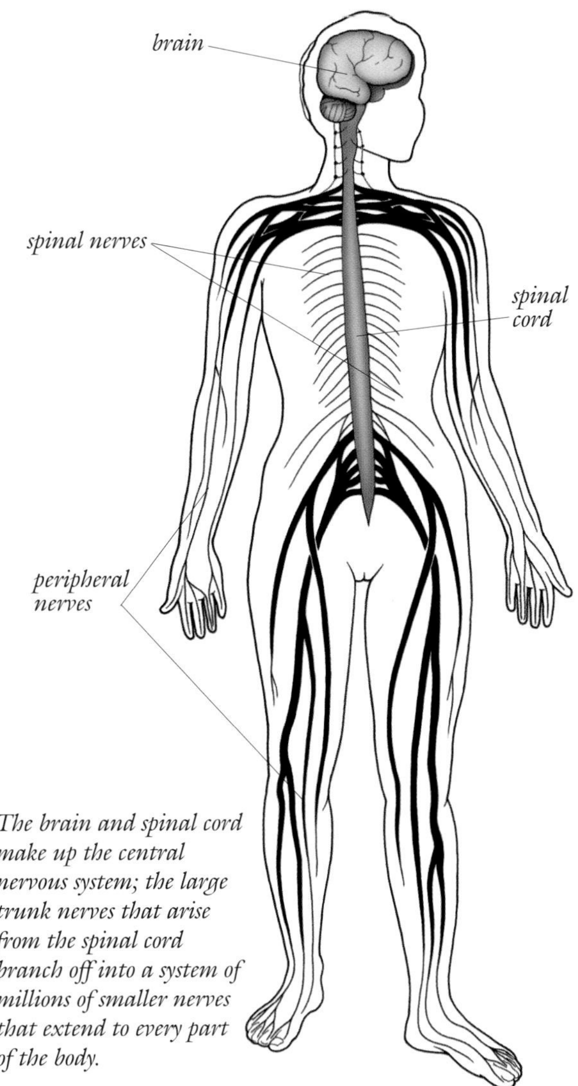


*The brain and spinal cord make up the central nervous system; the large trunk nerves that arise from the spinal cord branch off into a system of millions of smaller nerves that extend to every part of the body.*

*ropathy refers to pain arising in the network of motor nerves and sensory nerves outside the central nervous system (the brain and spinal cord). Diabetes is a common cause of peripheral neuropathy; other possible causes include alcoholism, infection, lead poisoning, and exposure to toxic chemicals. Poor posture and chronic back problems can contribute to neuropathy; it may also be associated with hardening of the arteries (arteriosclerosis), shingles, rheumatoid arthritis, Lyme disease, scleroderma (thickening and hardening of the skin), AIDS, and lupus.*

*Certain drugs can cause neuritis, especially those used in cancer chemotherapy; isoniazid (Isotamine), which is used to treat tuberculosis; and phenytoin (Dilantin), an anticonvulsant medication. Chronic overdoses of vitamin $B_6$ can cause neuropathy as can nutritional deficiencies, especially of vitamin $B_{12}$ and thiamin, which often occur among alcoholics. Smoking, which reduces blood flow, can contribute to neuropathy and neuralgia. A history of frostbite or chilblains can contribute to tingling sensations from exposure to cold temperatures.*

## HOW IT DEVELOPS

Peripheral neuropathy develops slowly, typically beginning with numbness, tingling, and an uncomfortable pins-and-needles sensation in the hands and feet. As the disorder progresses, the loss of sensation eventually spreads to the arms and legs. The lack of sensory input can make it difficult to use the affected limbs; imagine trying to pick up an object that you cannot feel, or walking without feeling your feet touch the ground. As a result, the muscles in the hands and feet grow progressively weaker; there may also be muscle cramps. In some instances, the skin becomes so hypersensitive that the slightest touch is painful.

> **WARNING!**
>
> ***Prolonged neuropathy can lead to a loss of sensation in the affected area. If this happens, extra care is needed to avoid burns and other injuries that may occur because the person does not feel any warning pain.***

Sometimes only the localized nerves are affected. For example, inflammation of the trigeminal nerve of the face produces episodes of trigeminal neuralgia, severe shooting pains around the eye and other parts of the face on the affected side (see *Trigeminal Neuralgia,* p 77). Shingles, a reactivation of the herpes zoster virus that causes chickenpox, often causes neuralgia in the area of the rash.

Nerve pain caused by an infection or shingles usually disappears as the underlying cause clears up. Sometimes, however, the pain can linger for months or even years (see *Shingles,* p 312).

## WHAT YOU CAN DO

Nonsteroidal anti-inflammatory drugs (NSAIDs), such as aspirin, ibuprofen, and naproxen, may relieve pain caused by nerve inflammation. If your neuropathy is related to diabetes, do everything you can to maintain normal blood sugar (glucose) levels and if you have high cholesterol, strive to lower it. Regular exercise helps maintain circulation and reduce the risk of neuropathy.

Examine lifestyle factors that may be contributing to the nerve pain. Abstain from alcohol and if you smoke, make every effort to stop. If poor posture is a factor, consult a physical therapist or Alexander technique instructor for help in improving it (see *Alternative Therapies,* p 342). Don't take megadoses of vitamin $B_6$, which can cause nerve damage, and if you suspect a medication is causing the problem, talk to your doctor about an alternative drug. If exposure to the cold provokes the tingling sensations, dress warmly and, if possible, avoid going out when it is very cold.

*Messages to and from the central nervous system travel as electrical impulses along chains of nerve cells (neurons). Chemicals called neurotransmitters help the electrical impulses go from the axon of one neuron to the dendrites of the next one, forming a chain reaction along an entire nerve pathway.*

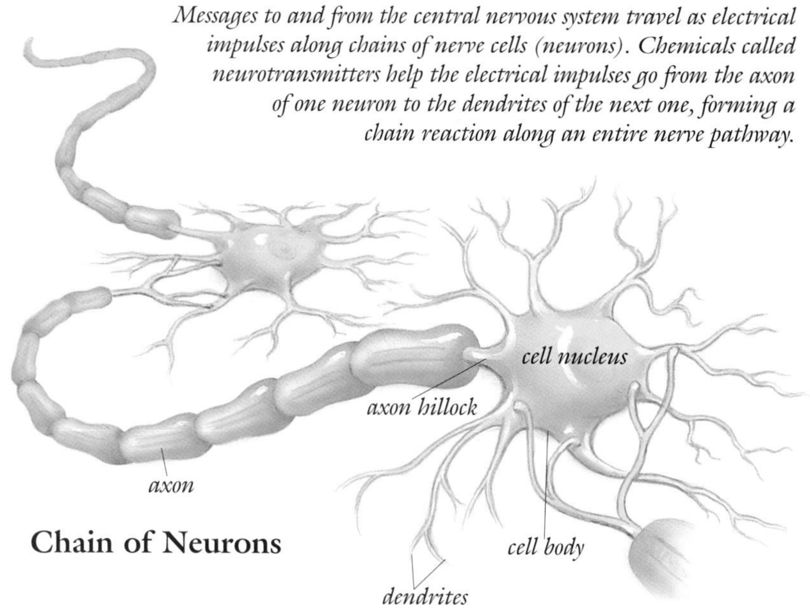


**Chain of Neurons**

**Alexander technique**

An instructor can detect and help correct posture problems that contribute to nerve pain.

**Aromatherapy**

Massaging the painful area with diluted peppermint oil may provide temporary relief.

**Herbal medicine**

The fatty acids in certain herbal oils have been shown to reduce nerve inflammation and pain. Good sources include flaxseed, evening primrose, and borage oils, which are high in gamma linolenic acid (GLA). They should be taken in amounts that provide about 250 mg of GLA. Products with GLA should not be used by people taking anticoagulants. Capsaicin cream may relieve nerve pain. Avoid contact with the eyes, mucous membranes, and raw or open skin.

## HOW TO TREAT IT

Treatment of peripheral neuropathy centers on controlling or, if possible, eliminating the underlying cause. Sometimes prednisone or another corticosteroid relieves nerve pain related to rheumatoid arthritis, lupus, scleroderma, and other systemic inflammatory disorders. In some cases of localized nerve pain, surgery to sever the nerve may help. Another procedure, called thermocoagulation, uses an electric needle to selectively eradicate pain fibers within nerve cells.

## HOW TO PREVENT IT

Neuropathy cannot always be prevented, but it often can be minimized by early treatment of its underlying cause. This is especially important in preventing or reducing diabetic neuropathy; numerous studies show that keeping blood sugar within normal limits markedly reduces the incidence of diabetes-related nerve problems. Other possible preventive measures include exercising regularly, maintaining good posture, abstaining from alcohol and tobacco use, and consuming a low-fat diet that emphasizes fruits, vegetables, and whole grains to keep blood cholesterol in check.

### ALTERNATIVE THERAPIES

**Acupuncture**

This form of ancient Chinese medicine is one of the most effective alternative approaches for relieving nerve pain. Western researchers still do not understand how or why acupuncture works, but many theorize that the insertion and twirling of the fine needles somehow elicit a response along the stimulated nerve pathways. However, it may take six treatments to bring improvement.

**Magnet therapy**

A study by neurologists found that therapeutic magnets applied to the legs of patients with diabetic neuropathy reduced pain and helped prevent leg ulcers and other complications. The magnets are thought to work by increasing circulation in the area and perhaps interfering with the transmission of pain impulses.

**Massage and manipulation**

Gentle massage can sometimes relieve numbness and tingling by increasing blood flow to the affected area. Chiropractic or osteopathic manipulation may be helpful against pain caused by compressed or pinched nerves.

**Nutraceuticals**

Alpha-lipoic acid, a powerful antioxidant supplement, has been found to improve the pain of diabetic neuropathy when taken in high dosages (see *Breakthroughs!*, below). Inositol, a substance found in nuts, legumes, whole wheat, and wheat bran, plays a role in proper nerve function; some studies have found that 1000 mg of inositol a day can reduce diabetic neuropathy. Other supplements that

### BREAKTHROUGHS!

**German researchers have found that alpha-lipoic acid (ALC) may reverse some of the neuropathy suffered by diabetic patients. In one study, 73 patients who had serious nerve damage were given either 800 mg of ALC a day or a placebo. After four months, the patients receiving ALC showed improved nerve function and reduced symptoms, while those in the placebo group had a worsening of symptoms. Researchers do not know exactly how ALC works, but they theorize that the benefits derive from its antioxidant action, which protects cells against the harmful effects of oxygen metabolism.**

may be helpful include 400 to 800 IU of vitamin E (check with your doctor first if you are taking blood-thinning medication), 1000 to 1500 micrograms (mcg) of vitamin $B_{12}$, 400 to 800 mcg of folic acid, and 50 mg of thiamin; all have important antioxidant properties or promote proper nerve function.

# Phantom Limb Pain

### SYMPTOMS

- *Pain and other sensations that are felt as emanating from an amputated limb or body part.*
- *Stump pain from the slightest pressure or touch.*

### WHO IS AT RISK

*Almost everyone who has undergone an amputation experiences sensations of warmth, mild squeezing, pressure, and itching, as if the amputated limb or other body part were still intact. For about 50 to 80 percent of patients, the sensations are painful, which is often intense. The intensity of phantom limb pain appears to correlate with the degree of preoperative pain. Women who have had a mastectomy may perceive phantom breast pain.*

*Diabetes, which often leads to peripheral vascular disease, is the leading cause of amputations during peacetime. Other reasons for amputations include accidents, bone tumors, and osteomyelitis, a serious bone infection.*

## HOW I[illegible]

Pain messa[illegible] the body are processed
by the ho[illegible] cortex
of the br[illegible]
the body [illegible]
you wer[illegible] of
the pai[illegible] ec-
tion. [illegible] ne
brain [illegible] d
conti[illegible] -
whe[illegible] and
the [illegible]

[illegible] ed sen-
sa[illegible] sation
in[illegible] w pro-
[illegible]

[illegible]

[illegible] b pain is
[illegible] pular belief,
[illegible] a change in
[illegible] n exacerbate
[illegible] the pain inter-
[illegible] cialist.

## HOW TO TREAT IT

Complete relief of phantom limb pain is not always possible, but there are a number of strategies that can provide at least some relief. Some are complementary therapies, such as biofeedback and transcutaneous electrical nerve stimulation (TENS) (see *Alternative Therapies*, below). Medical treatments may include:

- Medications, which may include non-narcotic and narcotic painkillers and amitriptyline (Elavil) and other antidepressants.
- Surgery to remove scar tissue or keloids that may be pressing on stump nerves. Sometimes painful pressure ulcers form in the area, which may require surgery.
- Nerve blocks or spinal cord stimulation, which are aimed at blocking transmission of pain messages.

> **WARNING!**
>
> ***Exposure to the cold often exacerbates phantom limb pain. Make sure that the stump is warmly wrapped whenever venturing outdoors during cold weather.***

## HOW TO PREVENT IT

Preliminary studies indicate that aggressive treatment of limb pain may reduce the incidence of severe postoperative phantom limb pain (see *Breakthroughs!*, below).

### ALTERNATIVE THERAPIES

**Acupuncture**

This form of Chinese medicine is sometimes successful in treating phantom limb pain.

**Biofeedback training**

This technique, which uses sensors and monitors to teach patients to control normally involuntary bodily processes, is one of the most effective treatments for phantom limb pain. Patients are taught to raise the temperature and reduce muscle tension in the stump area.

**Herbal medicine**

Ointments or creams containing capsaicin, the active ingredient in cayenne (hot chilies), sometimes reduces phantom limb pain. It should not be applied until the wound is fully healed, and it should not be used if there is a pressure ulcer, such as a bedsore, or another open sore. Care is also needed to keep it away from the eyes and delicate mucous membranes.

> **BREAKTHROUGHS!**
>
> **The observation that intense preoperative limb pain often predicts severe phantom limb pain has led some doctors to try to prevent it through preemptive pain control. This strategy involves starting a spinal (epidural) block 72 hours before the amputation. More study is needed to determine whether preemptive pain control helps prevent phantom limb pain.**

# Postoperative Pain

## SYMPTOMS

- *Localized pain at the incision site.*
- *Mild to severe pain involving internal organs, either at the site of the operation or elsewhere in the body.*
- *Pain due to postsurgical complications, such as an infection or a blood clot.*
- *Possible breathing problems, sore throat, constipation, and abdominal discomfort.*

## WHO IS AT RISK

*Anyone who undergoes a surgical procedure, no matter how minor, can expect at least some pain. Understandably, an operation that requires a large, open incision, such as a coronary bypass or removal of an abdominal tumor, causes more pain than those that use small puncture openings, such as a biopsy or arthroscopy.*

## HOW IT DEVELOPS

Surgery constitutes an assault on the human body. Making an incision obviously damages the skin, nerves, muscle, and other tissue. Suturing it after the operation creates another source of pain. But in addition to the tightness and achiness of the incision itself, any operation can have repercussions that are felt throughout the body. General anesthesia stops the normal muscular contractions that propel food through the gastrointestinal tract, and the opioid painkillers that are given to control postoperative pain have a similar effect, which can result in nausea, bloating, and constipation. Operations that entail manipulating or cutting the intestines and other internal organs also can cause severe abdominal cramps and pain; stress ulcers may also develop after any operation.

The insertion of a breathing (endotrachial) tube can result in a sore throat. After open-heart surgery, patients experience pain not only from the chest incision but also from lungs that become clogged with mucus while the patient is on a heart-lung machine and respirator. Coughing, essential to clear the lungs, can be very painful.

The stress from surgery and pain also sets in motion a number of hormonal and biochemical changes that increase the risk of developing blood clots. In addition, stress-related hormonal changes prompt the body's blood vessels to narrow, or constrict, which increases the risk of venous thrombosis, in which a clot blocks a leg vein and may eventually lodge in a lung.

Optimal healing takes place only when you are well rested, well nourished, and as physically active as your condition allows. Pain interferes with all these essentials—it disrupts sleep, suppresses appetite, and prevents patients from moving about. Prolonged inactivity further increases the risk of blood clots, bedsores (pressure ulcers), and pneumonia (when patients are unable to clear their lungs by breathing deeply and coughing).

### BREAKTHROUGHS!

**One of the most significant advances in controlling postsurgical pain has been the advent of patient-controlled analgesia (PCA), in which patients are fitted with a computerized pump that dispenses intravenous drugs as they are needed. The pumps, which usually administer morphine or a similar narcotic drug, are programmed to prevent an overdose. But studies show that patients using PCA actually take less medication and have more pain relief than those who are on a strict medication schedule or are given the drugs only when pain becomes severe.**

## WHAT YOU CAN DO

Talk to your doctor before the operation about pain control, and make sure that you both agree on how it should be administered. Don't hesitate to demand adequate pain medication (see *Warning!*, p 345). Let your doctor know of any previous experiences with various pain medications—what worked and what did not—as well as your history of side effects, allergies, and a list of other medications you are taking. It's important to understand that modern medicine has the means to control almost all postoperative pain. Yet study after study shows that many, if not most, surgery patients continue to suffer needlessly. Why? Experts agree that both doctors and patients are to blame, often because they adhere to lingering social attitudes about pain—for example, that it is somehow noble to be stoic about pain or that temporary reliance on narcotic painkillers will lead to addiction.

As soon as your doctor approves, get up and move about as much as you can. When coughing, hug a pillow to your chest—this eases pain and allows you to cough harder. Good nutrition is essential to proper healing; if the hospital food doesn't appeal to you, ask your doctor or dietitian if you can have food brought to you.

## HOW TO TREAT IT

A local anesthetic or spinal block is usually all that is needed during minor surgery; postoperative pain often can be controlled with acetaminophen or nonsteroidal anti-inflammatory drugs (NSAIDs). These include ibuprofen, naproxen, and a number of prescription-strength drugs. One of the most potent—ketorolac (Toradol)—can be given orally or intravenously.

More severe postoperative pain warrants codeine or stronger narcotic (opioid) medications, which are given alone or in combination with milder, non-narcotic painkillers. Studies have found that adding an NSAID to the regimen allows a lower dose of the opioid and reduces the risk of such adverse side effects as depressed breathing, constipation, drowsiness, and nausea.

Patients who cannot tolerate powerful pain medicine, or those whose pain cannot be controlled by drugs alone, may benefit from a nerve block. In this procedure, a doctor injects an anesthetic into a specific area to prevent pain impulses from reaching the brain. For example, a local anesthetic may be injected directly into the incision site; more extensive regional pain can be controlled by blocking nerves in the chest (intercostal block) or the abdomen (celiac plexus block), to cite two examples.

Severe pain that persists despite these approaches may be controlled with electrical stimulation, which prevents pain impulses from reaching the brain. One procedure—spinal-cord stimulation (SCS)—involves implanting a small wire electrode in the spinal canal, near the spinal cord. In a more involved procedure—deep-brain stimulation (DBS)—the surgeon places the wire within the brain itself. The electrode connects to a small electrical generator, similar to a cardiac pacemaker, that delivers a low-energy current that short-circuits the pain impulses.

**WARNING!**

***Don't wait until you're suffering severe pain to ask for medication. Analgesics are less effective against pain once it has taken hold. Tell your nurse or doctor that you're experiencing what is called "breakthrough pain"—a change in medication, dosage, schedule, or method of delivery can make a big difference. If you're told that nothing more can be done for your pain, insist on a second opinion.***

Another treatment for unrelenting pain is neuroablation, in which a nerve is destroyed (ablated) by cutting it or injecting a toxic chemical. Examples include a rhizotomy, which entails cutting a nerve close to the spinal cord, or a cordotomy, in which a surgeon severs a cluster of nerves in the lower end of the spinal cord. These procedures, however, are used as a last resort to treat unrelenting pain because they carry a risk of numbness and other complications; however, they can provide pain relief for months or even years.

## HOW TO PREVENT IT

Preemptive analgesia, which involves giving patients opioid analgesics, local anesthetic blocks, and other forms of pain control for up to 72 hours before surgery, is being offered at a growing number of medical centers. A study conducted at the University of Pennsylvania Medical Center compared two groups of patients undergoing removal of their prostate glands. Nine and a half weeks after the operations, 81 percent of the patients who were given preoperative pain medication reported no pain, compared with only 44 percent of the men who did not receive preemptive analgesia.

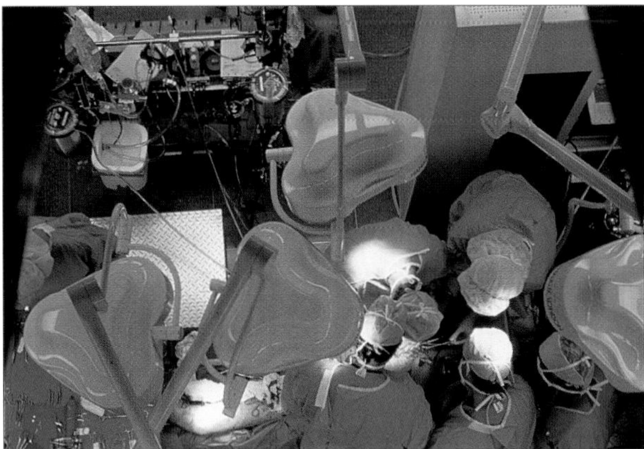

*Surgery, whether minor or major, invariably results in pain.*

### ALTERNATIVE THERAPIES

Postoperative pain is one area in which various alternative therapies have proven their worth. Acupuncture, therapeutic massage, guided imagery, visualization, meditation, self-hypnosis, biofeedback training, touch therapy, and transcutaneous electrical nerve stimulation (TENS) are among the many complementary therapies now offered.

# Rheumatoid Arthritis

### SYMPTOMS

- *Painful, red, warm, and swollen joints.*
- *Fatigue, possible fever, and malaise.*
- *Possible anemia and weight loss.*
- *Periods when symptoms disappear and then recur.*

### WHO IS AT RISK

*About 300,000 Canadians suffer from rheumatoid arthritis (RA), one of the most severe of the 100 or more forms of arthritis. The disease is more than twice as common in women as in men. It can strike at any age, but it usually develops between the ages of 35 and 55.*

*The cause of rheumatoid arthritis is unknown, but researchers have identified a class of genes that appear to increase susceptibility. The disease is then triggered by a viral or bacterial infection, prolonged stress, hormonal changes, or other environmental factors that stimulate the immune system to attack normal tissue.*

## HOW IT DEVELOPS

Rheumatoid arthritis is a systemic disease in which the immune system goes awry and attacks the joints and other normal body tissue. White blood cells—especially

T-helper cells—that normally protect against infection rush to the joints and attack their lining, the synovial tissue, as if it were a foreign invader. The lining becomes thick and inflamed, resulting in painful swelling and progressive destruction of the cartilage—the thick, rubbery substance covering the ends of the joints. As the cartilage breaks down, the destructive process extends into the underlying bone, and the supporting muscles, ligaments, and tendons weaken.

The joints become increasingly painful, stiff, and deformed, and hard nodules often form over them. By definition, RA affects three or more joints, usually symmetrically. Thus, if joints on one side are affected, those on the opposite side will also be attacked. Symptoms are usually most severe in the morning.

Rheumatoid arthritis tends to wax and wane—an acute flare-up may last weeks or months, and then symptoms abate. Then, without warning, the symptoms recur, and the destructive process continues. During a flare-up, there may be a low-grade fever; other possible complications include eye inflammation, vasculitis (inflamed blood vessels), anemia, and pleurisy and/or pericarditis (inflammation of the membranes covering the lungs and heart).

cartilage

**Normal Joint**

*Cartilage cushions the ends of the bones and allows a joint to move freely and without pain.*

**Early Arthritis**

*The inflammation of rheumatoid arthritis erodes the cartilage, resulting in joint pain and stiffness.*

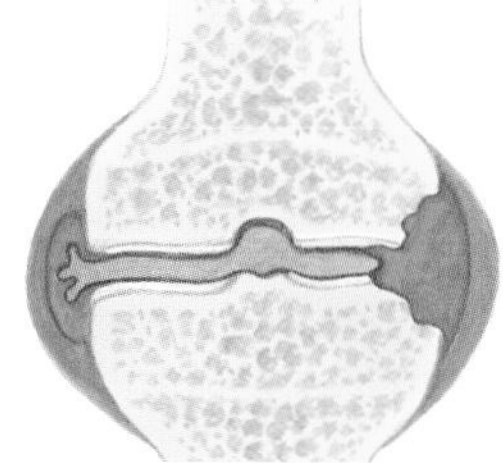

**Advanced Arthritis**

*As the arthritis worsens, the joint becomes more painful, swollen, and deformed; complete destruction of the cartilage results in immobility.*

## WHAT YOU CAN DO

See a doctor—preferably a rheumatologist—if you experience symptoms suggesting rheumatoid arthritis; although the disease is incurable, early, aggressive treatment minimizes its effects. It's very important to pay attention to your body. During a flare-up, avoid becoming overly tired, but balance increased rest with exercises designed to keep the joints limber without causing further damage.

### BREAKTHROUGHS!

**Health Canada is expected to approve several new drugs for rheumatoid arthritis by the end of 2000:**

- **Etanercept (Enbrel), which blocks tumor necrosis factor, a substance that causes joint inflammation; it is taken by injection twice a week.**
- **Infliximab (Remicade), which also blocks tumor necrosis factor; it is given by intravenous infusion every two to eight weeks.**
- **Leflumomide (Arava), which blocks overproduction of immune cells; it is taken by pill twice a day.**

Aspirin is one of the most effective drugs for rheumatoid arthritis because it eases pain and reduces inflammation. But to work, it must be taken in very high doses—often 16 or more 325-mg tablets a day—which many people cannot tolerate. Other nonsteroidal anti-inflammatory drugs (NSAIDs), such as ibuprofen, generally cause fewer side effects than high-dose aspirin. But all NSAIDs can cause ulcers and intestinal bleeding, so take them with food and a full glass of water or milk.

Taking a hot shower or soaking in a hot tub first thing in the morning can relieve stiffness and reduce pain. A heating pad or warm compresses can ease aching joints; some patients, however, get more relief from ice packs or alternating hot and cold compresses.

There are many devices that make day-to-day tasks easier; these include special eating utensils, toothbrushes, combs, button hooks, as well as shoes with elastic laces, shower stools, and other gadgets that enable disabled patients to care for themselves (see *Physical and occupational therapy*, p 347). During a flare-up, splints to support an inflamed joint help prevent deformity. However, these should be worn for only short periods; prolonged immobility increases the risk of a joint becoming frozen.

As with any chronic, progressive disease, rheumatoid arthritis can be emotionally devastating. Joining a self-help group of other arthritis sufferers often helps in coping with emotional and day-to-day problems.

## HOW TO TREAT IT

### Medications

If aspirin or other nonprescription NSAIDs fail to control pain and inflammation, a doctor may try a prescription-strength drug. Patients who cannot tolerate high doses of NSAIDs may be able to take one of the newer $COX_2$ inhibitors (Celebrex or Vioxx)—these drugs are also NSAIDs, but are less likely to cause bleeding and stomach upset. However, some people also experience problems with them, so caution is needed.

Sometimes a corticosteroid is injected into a severely swollen and inflamed joint, but more than two or three treatments a year can cause joint damage. A short course of prednisone (Winpred) or another oral corticosteroid can quell an acute flare-up or control other inflammatory complications, such as pericarditis or vasculitis. Although these drugs can bring fast, dramatic relief, their benefits lessen over time, and they have many adverse side effects—bone loss, weight gain, bleeding problems, and a thinning of the skin, among others.

**WARNING!**

***Avoid any treatment that involves injections or medications that are available only offshore or from clinics or practitioners outside the country. Any improvement is usually due to dangerously high doses of steroids. The same is true of some Chinese arthritis remedies, which are sold as herbal products but actually contain steroids and other drugs. Bee stings—a popular folk remedy—can provoke life-threatening anaphylaxis in people who are hypersensitive to bee venom.***

Disease-modifying antirheumatic drugs (DMARDs), also referred to as slow-acting antirheumatic drugs (SAARDs), slow the progression of rheumatoid arthritis, induce remissions, and help preserve joint function and structures. They can produce serious side effects, so they are reserved for severe cases. These drugs, which may be used alone or in combination with NSAIDs or each other, include:

- **Antimalarial drugs**, such as hydroxychloroquine (Plaquenil), which are thought to reduce the autoimmune response and lessen mild to moderate symptoms.
- **Gold compounds** (aurothioglucose or sodium aurothiomalate), which often induce a remission of symptoms; they are usually given as weekly injections until symptoms improve or adverse reactions develop.
- **Immunosuppressive drugs** (methotrexate, azathioprine, or cyclosporine), which suppress the overactive immune system.
- **Penicillamine** (Cuprimine), which appear to rid the body of rheumatoid factor—antibodies that contribute to the inflammatory process.
- **Sulfasalazine** (Salazopyrin EN-tabs), which also reduces the inflammation of RA.

## Surgery

Severely diseased joints—especially the hips and knees, but also the fingers, elbows, and shoulders—may be removed and replaced with artificial ones. Removal of inflamed synovial tissue—a synovectomy—helps preserve joint function; however, the tissue usually regrows and becomes inflamed. Severely deformed hands and feet may be treated by surgical repair of tendons and ligaments.

## HOW TO PREVENT IT

There is no known way to prevent rheumatoid arthritis.

### ALTERNATIVE THERAPIES

**Note:** Each year, North Americans spend more than $1 billion on alternative arthritis remedies. Many, if not most, of these are worthless, and some are dangerous (see *Warning!*, left). Alternative or complementary approaches that are generally safe include the following:

**Herbal medicine**

Recent studies found that boswellia, an herb often used in Ayurvedic medicine, has an anti-inflammatory effect that may benefit RA patients. Look for products containing 37.5 percent boswellic acids; the usual dosage is 400 mg three times a day. Ginger is also an anti-inflammatory herb; it can be taken as a tea or pills; the fresh herb can be used to flavor various dishes. Capsaicin cream—which is derived from hot chilies (cayenne)—can reduce pain and inflammation when gently massaged over an affected joint. Other herbal products that reduce inflammation include evening primrose and borage oils; they should be taken in dosages that supply about 250 mg of gamma linolenic acid. For cautions concerning these herbs, see *About the Recommendations,* p 7.

**Nutraceuticals**

Omega-3 fatty acids, which are found in cold-water fish such as salmon and mackerel, have been shown to reduce RA symptoms. Because omega-3 fatty acids inhibit blood clotting, consult a doctor before using fish oil supplements if you have a blood disorder or if you are taking anticoagulants. Studies have also found that high doses (1000 IU a day or more) of vitamin E also reduce RA-related inflammation. People on prescription anticoagulants or aspirin should consult their doctor before using vitamin E. Supplements of glucosamine and chondroitin—natural components of cartilage—do not appear to be as effective against RA as they are in treating osteoarthritis. SAM-e, another substance the body uses to make cartilage, helps some patients; it is also a mild antidepressant (see *Osteoarthritis, Alternative Therapies,* p 226). SAM-e should not be taken by people with manic depression.

**Physical and occupational therapy**

Many of the treatments—whirlpool baths, hot and cold packs, diathermy, and ultrasound—offered by physical therapists can help reduce RA pain. These therapists can also teach gentle range-of-motion exercises to retain joint mobility and function. Occupational therapists teach disabled patients new ways to perform day-to-day tasks, such as dressing, bathing, and other aspects of self-care.